Psychology Revivals

Handbook of Behavioural Family Therapy

First published in 1988, behavioural family therapists worked in an area that had greatly changed since its inception over 20 years before. Growing out of the pioneering work of Gerald Patterson, Robert Paul Liberman, and Richard Stuart, whose backgrounds vary from psychology to psychiatry to social work, behavioural family therapy (BFT) had evolved to encompass systems theory, considerations of the therapeutic alliance, as well as approaches to accounting for and restructuring family members' subjective experiences through cognitive strategies.

As BFT had not been the 'brain child' of any one charismatic innovator, but rather of a wide array of clinicians and researchers developing and rigorously testing hypotheses, it is fitting that this much-needed summation of the field was a collaborative product of an array of well-established practitioners of the time. They discuss in Part 1 of the book the theoretical parameters of BFT, focusing on modular behavioural strategies, the indications for therapy, assessment of family problems, pertinent issues arising in clinical practice, and approaches to the problem of resistance to change. Contributors to Part 2 then apply theory to such clinical situations as 'parent training' and helping families cope with patients suffering from developmental disabilities, alcoholism, schizophrenia, senile dementia, as well as anxiety, obsessive-compulsive, and depressive disorders. Specific attention is also given to acute inpatient and primary health-care settings.

While BFT had already proved quite effective in treating a great number of family problems, it was only in its infancy at the time of writing. As Falloon says in his overview 'all exponents of the method are constantly involved with the process of refinement, each clinician is a researcher, each family member is a research subject, and each researcher is contributing to clinical advancement.'

This openness, in combination with a willingness to modify 'sacred' tenets of behaviourism while adapting proven techniques from other family therapies, made this title a landmark in its field. As such, it was not only of interest to all clinicians and researchers with a behavioural slant, but also to all family therapists who wished to challenge themselves to develop an integrative approach.

Handbook of Behavioural Family Therapy

Edited by
Ian R.H. Falloon

Routledge
Taylor & Francis Group
LONDON AND NEW YORK

First published in Great Britain 1988
by Hutchinson Education

This edition first published in 2015 by Routledge
27 Church Road, Hove BN3 2FA

and by Routledge
711 Third Avenue, New York, NY 10017

Routledge is an imprint of the Taylor & Francis Group, an informa business

Publisher's Note
The publisher has gone to great lengths to ensure the quality of this reprint but points out that some imperfections in the original copies may be apparent.

Disclaimer
The publisher has made every effort to trace copyright holders and welcomes correspondence from those they have been unable to contact.

A Library of Congress record exists under ISBN: 0898627095

ISBN: 978-1-138-92306-5 (hbk)
ISBN: 978-1-315-68529-8 (ebk)
ISBN: 978-1-138-92312-6 (pbk)

HANDBOOK OF BEHAVIOURAL FAMILY THERAPY

Edited by
IAN R. H. FALLOON

HUTCHINSON

London Melbourne Auckland Johannesburg

Hutchinson Education

An imprint of Century Hutchinson Ltd

62—65 Chandos Place, London WC2N 4NW

Century Hutchinson Australia Pty Ltd
P O Box 496, 16—22 Church Street, Hawthorn,
Victoria 3122, Australia

Century Hutchinson New Zealand Ltd
P O Box 40-086, Glenfield, Auckland 10
New Zealand

Century Hutchinson South Africa (Pty) Ltd
P O Box 337, Bergvlei 2012, South Africa

First published in the United States of America by Guilford Publications, Inc. 1988
First published in Great Britain 1988

A Division of Guilford Publications, Inc.
72 Spring Street, New York, New York, 10012

Printed and bound in the United States of America

British Library Cataloguing in Publication Data

Handbook of behavioural family therapy.
1. Medicine. Family therapy
I. Falloon, Ian R. H.
616.89'156

ISBN 0-09-182262-9

Contributors

ALEXANDER, JAMES F., PhD, Department of Psychology, University of Utah, Salt Lake City, Utah

ARRINGTON, ANGELA, PhD, Department of Psychology, University of California, Los Angeles, California

BAUCOM, DONALD H., PhD, Department of Psychology, University of North Carolina, Chapel Hill, North Carolina

BIRCHLER, GARY R., PhD, VA Medical Center; and University of California School of Medicine, San Diego, California

BRUEY, CAROLYN THORWARTH, PsyD, Private Practice, Marlton, New Jersey

CHRISTENSEN, ANDREW, PhD, Department of Psychology, University of California, Los Angeles, California

CROWE, MICHAEL, MD, Maudsley Hospital, London, England

CURRAN, JAMES P., PhD, Brown University Medical School; and the Veterans Administration Medical Center, Davis Park, Providence, Rhode Island

FALLOON, IAN R. H., MD, Buckingham Mental Health Service, Buckingham, England

FARAONE, STEPHEN V., PhD, Brown University Medical School, Providence, Rhode Island (Current affiliation: Brockton VA Hospital, Brockton; and Harvard Medical School, Boston, Massachusetts)

FICHTER, MANFRED M., MD, Department of Psychiatry, University of Munich, Munich, West Germany

FOLLETTE, WILLIAM C., PhD, Department of Psychology, Memphis State University, Memphis, Tennessee

GLYNN, SHIRLEY, PhD, Camarillo State Hospital, Camarillo, California

GRAVES, DEBORAH J., MA, University of South Florida, Tampa, Florida

HAFNER, R. JULIAN, MD, Dibden Research Unit, Glenside Hospital, Flinders Medical Centre, Bedford Park, South Australia

HAHLWEG, KURT, PhD, Max Planck Institute of Psychiatry, Munich, West Germany

HAND, IVER, MD, Psychiatric University Clinic, Hamburg, West Germany

HARPIN, R. EDWARD, PhD, Private Practice, San Diego, California

HARRIS, SANDRA L., PhD, Department of Clinical Psychology, Graduate School of Applied and Professional Psychology, Rutgers, The State University of New Jersey, Piscataway, New Jersey

JACOBSON, NEIL S., PhD, Department of Psychology, University of Washington, Seattle, Washington

LIBERMAN, ROBERT PAUL, MD, Brentwood Division—West Los Angeles VA Medical Center; Camarillo State Hospital; and Department of Psychiatry, University of California School of Medicine, Los Angeles, California

LILLIE, FRANCIS J., MA, Department of Psychology, Central Clinic, Colchester, England

MARKMAN, HOWARD, PhD, Department of Psychology, University of Denver, Denver, Colorado

MCAULEY, ROGER, MD, Department of Child Psychiatry, The Royal Belfast Hospital for Sick Children, Belfast, Ireland

MORRIS, STEPHEN B., PhD, Comprehensive Psychological Services, Salt Lake City, Utah

MUESER, KIM, PhD, Camarillo State Hospital, Camarillo, California (Current affiliation: Department of Psychiatry, Medical College of Pennsylvania, Philadelphia, Pennsylvania)

PEMBLETON, TERENCE, SRN, RNN, Buckingham Mental Health Service, Buckingham, England

POSTPISCHIL, FELICITAS, PhD, Department of Psychiatry, University of Munich, Munich, West Germany

SULLAWAY, MEGAN, PhD, Department of Psychology, University of California, Los Angeles, California

TODD, THOMAS C., PhD, Forest Hospital; Illinois School of Professional Psychology; and The Family Institute of Chicago/Center for Family Studies, Chicago, Illinois

WALDRON, HOLLY, PhD, Rivendell of Utah, Salt Lake City, Utah

ZARIT, STEVEN H., PhD, Department of Individual and Family Studies, College of Human Development, The Pennsylvania State University, University Park, Pennsylvania

Foreword

The present volume constitutes a statement about an ending and a beginning. It marks the end of almost a quarter century's effort to develop behavioral techniques appropriate to intervention with distressed families. A range of applications that now includes almost the whole spectrum of psychiatric problems suggests that we are beginning a whole new enterprise.

The early years were characterized by a strange mix of characters working together to develop a technology that could be applied to the task of helping families change themselves. The group was comprised of turncoat traditional clinicians (e.g., the present writer), academics who knew much about pigeons and laboratories but nothing about the inside of outpatient clinics, and rogue entrepreneurs who knew a parade when they saw one. National conferences were held on an almost monthly basis, all of them characterized by a high level of emotional fervor and irreverence for traditions. Those of us studying families sat on panels with investigators who claimed to be changing institutions, removing forever a fear of spiders and snakes, remediating autism, controlling pain, and redesigning not only classrooms but society as well. For each of us, the rite of passage included a box of slides with single-subject data showing the past and a new, magical present.

That revolution ended, though some tenets may survive. The following section chronicles my perceptions about which of them might be useful. The present volume shows that the next phase is already in motion.

THINGS PAST

Behavior modification was a social movement having a cumulative impact on the field of family treatment. There were two characteristics embedded within its foundations that produced that impact. They actually came from two rather disparate regions of psychological research ordinarily not present in clinical research. The first was a direct outgrowth of publications such as Skinner's *Science and human behavior* (Skinner, 1953). Changing contingencies of reinforcement were a powerful basis for changing human behavior. Applying it seemed relatively straightforward. One went directly to the social environment, the home, or the classroom, and altered the contingencies being provided for prosocial and deviant behavior. It was a whole new idea, and it worked. This simple premise led to the development of technologies for changing behavior in families, in institutions, classrooms, and so forth.

The second characteristic combined two different ideas. The first was that one should go into the real world and observe what contingencies were being applied before, during, and after intervention. This naturally followed from the Skinnerian position, but it also dovetailed beautifully with the emerging ecological movement of the Roger Barker group (Barker, 1963). It is hard to imagine now what it was like for a therapist trained to work in the playroom and office to find him- or herself in the real world of the home and the classroom, where one could see from watching the ebb and flow of behavior that most previous notions about child aggression were fundamentally erroneous.

The idea of observing in natural settings led to the development of observation code systems that more precisely described baseline, intervention, and follow-up changes. The development of an observation technology to measure behavioral change contained the seeds for a new idea. It was now possible to precisely describe sequences of family interaction, and that lay the groundwork for the gradual accumulation of a solid body of information about family change.

This highly reliable and relatively nonreactive observation data allowed us to continually modify, and we hoped improve, the treatment procedures we used. For example, those of us working with conduct problem children and their families soon learned that Skinner had been wrong about one of his key assumptions. Contrary to his position, punishment *did* have long-term effects. The data also showed that reinforcement of competing child behaviors, such as cooperation and compliance, did *not* lead to reductions in antisocial behavior. The data showed that introducing punishment contingencies (e.g., time out, point loss) produced long-term reductions in antisocial behavior.

Earlier therapeutic studies of problem children relied primarily on parental reports as feedback to the therapist. However, several studies showed that parental reports tended to be positively biased such that improvement is reported even though *no* changes were observed in children's behavior. What this meant was that no matter what the well-intentioned therapist did, the feedback he or she received was that he or she was effective: A beautifully crafted trap for those of us who wish to believe we help people. Even today the most frequent treatment provided for conduct disordered children is play therapy, although it has been used in at least two studies of intervention for conduct disorders as a placebo comparison condition. Doubtless it will be used for decades to come because it is fun for the therapist and parents report it as being successful for at least two in three cases.

The first step in moving a therapeutic field forward is to solve the problem of this trap. This means developing a relatively *nonreactive* outcome measure that is also reliable and valid. Programmatic studies of families of depressed and schizophrenic individuals described in this volume are beautiful exemplars of a possible solution. The use of "return to the hospital" as one of the criterion measures in evaluating treatment is a major innovation.

YET TO COME

There are currently three areas of research in family intervention that seem to be ready to move on to a more advanced stage of development. These areas include work on conduct-disordered children, marital conflict, and schizophrenic adults. Each has a well-articulated technology available in manuals; each has developed tailor-made assessment procedures to evaluate outcome; and each has produced at least a small number of replicated random assignment designs that were successful.

This type of progress implies that there is obviously something here; the problem is that we do not as yet know what it is. For example, only about half the well-controlled studies applying parent training to conduct-disordered children have been successful. Why is this? According to Jacobson and Follette (Chapter 11) only about 55% of the couples in marital therapy could be termed *clinical* successes. Why is this? It is too early to say what the analogous problems might be in the studies of schizophrenic adults and their families, but they, too, will presumably require improvements.

About five years ago, a number of us decided that successful intervention required not just the one component, a parent training technology, but two. As my colleague John Reid notes, part of the cohesion of the previous revolution lay in the fact that none of us clearly recorded our procedures. Aside from the parent training technology itself, none of us really knew what the others were doing. The missing second component would have traced the skills of therapists as they worked with their clients.

Jim Alexander and his colleagues (see Chapter 5) were some of the first to work on this problem in the area of conduct disordered children. They were soon followed by Jacobson and Follette (Chapter 11) in the area of marital therapy, and by my own studies on client resistance during parent training (Chamberlain, Patterson, Reid, Forgatch, & Kavanagh, 1984; Patterson & Forgatch, 1985), but, even taken together, these studies hardly constitute a beginning. If this enterprise is to progress, the next generation of investigators must continue to build a solid empirical base for our understanding of what clinical skill and resistance are all about. If these data are not forthcoming, then advances in the behavioral approach to family treatment will stall, as have other approaches with equally promising beginnings, and will join the great collection of calliope wagons mired alongside the road: Immersed in giant clouds of steam, whistling and tooting and going nowhere.

As noted earlier, the collection of data describing social interactions in natural settings provided a means for breaking out of the therapist trap. Recent analyses of family interactional sequences have taught us a great deal about the nature of the process that leads to marital dissatisfaction. These new studies by Hahlweg, Baucom, & Markman (Chapter 17) and Gottman and Levenson (1984) employ sophisticated statistical techniques borrowed from fields outside psychology. The application of structural equation modeling to understanding family processes in conduct disordered children (Patterson, 1986) is a means of studying families that uses data from both micro- and macrosocial levels.

To improve our therapy techniques, we must make changes in therapist and client behavior during treatment a focus for systematic empirical studies. We must also build a better understanding of what brings about such pathological outcomes as conduct disorders, marital conflict, and schizophrenic reactions. Both kinds of understanding are going to require a higher quality of data collected at multiple levels and more complex statistical tools. It will be this marriage of technologies that will define the next chapter.

Gerald R. Patterson

REFERENCES

Barker, R. G. (1963). The stream of behavior as an empirical problem. In R. G. Barker (Ed.), *The stream of behavior* (pp. 1–22). New York: Appleton-Century-Crofts.

Chamberlain, P., Patterson, G. R., Reid, J. B., Forgatch, M. S., & Kavanagh, K. (1984). Observation of client resistance. *Behavior Therapy*, *15*, 144–155.

Gottman, J. M., & Levenson, R. W. (1984). Why marriages fail: Affective and physiological patterns in marital interaction. In J. C. Masters & K. Yarkin-Levin (Eds.), *Boundary areas in social and developmental psychology* (pp. 67–106).

Patterson, G. R. (1986). The contribution of siblings to training for fighting: A microsocial analysis. In D. Olweus, J. Block, & M. Radke-Yarrow (Eds.), *Development of antisocial and prosocial behavior: Research, theories, and issues* (pp. 235–261). Orlando, FL: Academic Press.

Patterson, G. R., & Forgatch, M. S. (1985). Therapist behavior as a determinant for client resistance: A paradox for the behavior modifier. *Journal of Consulting and Clinical Psychology*, *53*, 846–851.

Skinner, B. F. (1953). *Science and human behavior*. New York: Free Press.

Contents

HANDBOOK OF BEHAVIOURAL FAMILY THERAPY

PART ONE

GENERAL ISSUES

1

Behavioral Family Therapy: An Overview

IAN R. H. FALLOON
Buckingham Mental Health Service, England
FRANCIS J. LILLIE
Central Clinic, Colchester, England

BACKGROUND

Historical Perspectives

Behavioral family therapy has developed from the application of learning theory principles in several different clinical settings and client groups. No one charismatic innovator can be attributed with its discovery. However, it is evident that the earliest reports of family-oriented interventions tended to be associated with the involvement of parents in the modification of the disturbed behavior of their children. These initial programs were extremely simple single case studies.

Williams (1959) reported a successful intervention to reduce the bedtime tantrums of a young child. The parents were instructed to put the child to bed in an affectionate manner, to close his bedroom door, and ignore his subsequent protestations. The use of this extinction paradigm typified efforts to transfer the principles of social learning theory, which were based on studies in the psychology laboratory, including animal research, to clinical intervention in the natural environment.

An approach that has continued application today is the use of classical conditioning in the control of enuresis. Lovibond (1963) developed a bed and pad apparatus that parents employed to assist them with their bedwetting children. Boardman (1962) trained parents in the effective use of a punishment paradigm to deal with the aggressive, antisocial behavior of a 5 year old. Wolpe (1958) described involving spouses as cotherapists in anxiety management interventions. Risley and Wolf (1967) trained parents in the operant reinforcement of speech in their autistic children. In all of these approaches, the family was involved in the application of the specific modification of a target behavior in a family member.

One of the earliest reports that reflected a shift from a patient-focused analysis of behavioral deviance was that of Wahler, Winkel, Peterson, and Morrison (1965). Their views were postulated in the following paragraph:

> Most psychotherapists assume that a child's parents compose the most influential part of his natural environment. It is likely, from a learning theory viewpoint, that their behaviors serve a large variety of stimulus functions, controlling both the respondent and operant behaviors of their children. It then follows that if some of the child's behavior is considered to be deviant at a particular time in his early years, his parents are probably the source of eliciting stimuli and reinforcers which have produced, and are curently maintaining this behavior. A logical procedure for the modification of the child's deviant behavior would involve changing the parents' behavior. These changes would be aimed at training them both to eliminate the contingencies which currently support their child's deviant behavior, and to provide new contingencies to produce and maintain more normal behavior which would compete with the deviant behavior. (p. 114)

Despite extensive observations of the reciprocal nature of child and parent interactions associated with deviant behaviors, however, the interventions employed tended to resemble the methods employed with laboratory subjects. Parents were instructed to respond to their child's behavior in a highly specific way *by the therapist*, and success was determined by a reduction in deviant behavior during the treatment sessions.

This role of the behavior therapist as the expert adviser to the family was clearly established at the time Gerald Patterson and his colleagues from Eugene, Oregon, wrote their landmark paper entitled "Reprogramming the Social Environment" (Patterson, McNeal, Hawkins, & Phelps, 1967). Patterson *et al.* realized that observation of family interaction in a laboratory or clinical environment was far removed from the behavior displayed in the natural environment of the home. As a result, they developed methods of sampling periods of family interaction in the home. Observers were trained to spend time collecting data in the home at times when all the family members were together. This often required constraints on family behavior to achieve the goal of having all family members together in one or two rooms. Observers were instructed to avoid interacting with family members and to adopt a "fly-on-the-wall" role. It can be argued that such "unnatural" conditions must inevitably have changed family interaction patterns and may have produced no more naturalistic behavior than that obtained in clinical settings.

The empirical basis for behavioral family interventions was clearly demonstrated by these extensive efforts to obtain observations of family behavior. Family interactions were coded in a standardized manner. The antecedents and the responses associated with a targeted behavioral episode (e.g., tantrum or violent outburst) were analyzed. Repetitive patterns of behavior that were contingent on each specified episode were hypothesized as contributing to the origin and/or maintenance of the undesirable behavior. The undesirable behavior was defined by the family, not the therapist, and its frequency was assessed during the series of observations prior to planning any intervention strategies. This provided a baseline measure with which therapeutic progress could be compared.

The interventions attempted to train parents in the principles of social learning theory, with the assistance of programmed workbooks (e.g., Patterson, 1971), and in the application of specific strategies designed to eliminate the contingencies that appeared "programmed" to induce the undesired behavior. In the case example in the 1967 article cited earlier, Patterson and his colleagues acknowledged that to produce change in the case of a 5-year-old boy with isolated, withdrawn, and bizarre behavior, merely training the parents to respond to his deviant behavior was insufficient.

> To produce a change it seemed necessary to change several aspects of this social system, simultaneously. Therefore, the initial programmes were designed to fulfil four functions: (1) train the mother to use positive reinforcers, (2) train her to initiate more social contacts, *and* (3) *at the same time* train Earl to function as a more effective social reinforcer for the behavior of the parent, and (4) initiate more social contacts to his parents. (p. 187)

Such an approach, which attempted to alter behavior in a reciprocal manner, even when disturbed young children were involved, distinguished behavioral family therapy from the parent-training approaches that were employed widely during the 1970s.

Patterson's pioneering work extended into the realms of parental behavior patterns, where his brilliant exposition of the manner in which reciprocity in coercive exchanges between couples tends to lead to increasingly ineffective problem solving contributed to the development of behavioral marital therapy. This is demonstrated in the following excerpt from a case study (Patterson & Hops, 1972):

> "Wife: You still haven't fixed that screen door.
>
> "Husband: (Makes no observable response, but sits surrounded by his newspaper.)
>
> "Wife: (There is a decided rise in the decibel level of her voice.) A lot of thanks I get for all I do. You said three weeks ago. . . .
>
> "Husband: Damn it, stop nagging at me. As soon as I walk in here and try to read the paper I get yelling and bitching.
>
> "Wife: (Shouting now) You're so damn lazy that's all I can do to get things done!
>
> "Husband: All right, damn it, I'll fix it later! Now leave me alone!"

In this situation, the husband has trained the wife to increase the volume in order to get him to comply. She is more likely to resort to shouting next time she needs some change in his behavior. He, on the other hand, has learned that a vague promise will "turn off the pain."

The second major figure in the development of behavioral family therapy was Robert Liberman. In his 1970 paper, "Behavioral Approaches to Family and Couple Therapy," he outlined the application of an operant learning framework to the family problems of four adult index patients with depression, intractable headaches, social inadequacy, and marital discord. In addition to employing contingency management of mutual reinforcers of deviant behavior, Liberman introduced the use of the imitative learning concepts of Bandura and Walters (1963) to family therapy. He also emphasized the importance of basic therapeutic skills, such as the development of a therapeutic alliance with the family. In contrast to Patterson's focus on observable interaction patterns between parents and children, Liberman conducted a behavioral analysis largely through interviews with each family member. Family members were invited to suggest changes they desired in the behavior of themselves and others in the family, both in relation to identified problem behaviors as well as constructive life goals. The ultimate choice of specific behavioral goals remained the prerogative of the therapist as did the formulation of the therapeutic strategy. However, it was made clear that behavioral analysis would continue throughout therapy and that the therapy would be modified according to changes in the problem behaviors. Throughout, the therapist adopted the role of an expert educator. An example of this appoach was described in Liberman's Case 2 (1970):

> My behavioral analysis pointed to a lack of reinforcement from Mrs. S's husband for her adapative strivings. Consequently her depressions, with their large hypochondriacal components, represented her desperate attempt to elicit her husband's attention and concern. Although her somatic complaints and self-depreciating accusations were aversive for her husband, the only way he knew how to "turn them off" was to offer sympathy, reassure her of his devotion to her, and occasionally stay home from work. Naturally, his nurturing her in this manner had the effect of reinforcing the very behavior he was trying to terminate.
>
> During five half-hour sessions I focused primarily on Mr. S, who was the mediating agent of reinforcement for his wife and hence the person who could potentially modify her behavior. I actively redirected his attention from his wife "the unhappy, depressed woman" to his wife "the coping woman." I forthrightly recommended to him that he drop his extra job, at least for the time being, in order to be at home in the evening to converse with his wife about the day's events, especially her approximations at successful homemaking. I showed by my own example (modeling) how to support his wife in her effort to assert herself reasonably with her intrusive mother-in-law and an obnoxious neighbor. (p. 113)

Liberman's approach, based on self-report data alone, is in stark contrast to the detailed observations employed by Patterson; this may reflect the differing backgrounds of the psychodynamic training of the psychiatrist and the psychology laboratory training of the psychologist, as was prevalent in the United States at that time. However, the crux of both approaches was the restructuring of the reciprocal exchange of rewards in family relationships, so that mutually desirable transactions replaced interactive patterns hypothesized as contributing to the development and maintenance of problem behaviors.

The behavioral approach was contrasted with other developing family therapy methods in two major ways. First, the behavior therapist specified family problems in concrete, observable terms. Second, therapeutic strategies were planned in a highly specific manner based on an empirical theory of behavior change. Strategies were subjected to empirical analyses of their effects in achieving specific behavioral goals. Although brief case reports did not convey the significance attached to the therapeutic alliance, this was regarded as important as in any other approach. Liberman (1970) emphasized that

> [T]he behavioral approach does not simplistically reduce the family system and family interaction to individualistic or dyadic mechanisms of reinforcement. The richness and complexity of family interaction is appreciated by the family therapist working within a behavioral framework. (p. 116)

Liberman went on to describe the family dynamics of one of his case reports in family systems terms. The behavioral family therapist and the clients do not need to understand these dynamics in order to change the system, *if* a careful behavioral analysis is conducted. Treatment failures are viewed as failures of the behavioral hypotheses and in need of further assessment and different strategies. Liberman (1970) offered one final comment:

> Hopefully, further clinical and research progress made by behavioral oriented therapists will challenge all family therapists, regardless of theoretical learnings, to specify more clearly their interventions, their goals, and their empirical results. If these challenges are accepted seriously, the field of family therapy will likely improve and gain status as a scientifically grounded modality. (p. 117)

It is a sad comment that this challenge has not been adequately answered by family therapists of all persuasions, including behavior therapists! There remains a dearth of well-designed empirical studies to match the enthusiastic clinical applications of these methods.

The third major influence on the early development of behavioral family therapy was the contingency contracting approach of Richard Stuart (1969). Stuart, a social worker, focused on the interpersonal environment in which family members responded to one another. Rather than considering how undesired responses of a "deviant" family member could be modified, the therapist focused on how the exchange of positive behavior could be maximized. The principle of reciprocity was introduced. Stuart cited Thibaut and Kelley (1959) when postulating that

> [T]he exact pattern of interaction which takes place between spouses is never accidental; it represents the most rewarding of all the available alternatives. This implies that the interaction between spouses is never accidental; it represents the best balance which each can achieve between individual and mutual rewards and costs.

These concepts of balance and behavior exchange had been developed earlier in the work of Don Jackson (1965), using the medical and social analogies of "homeostasis" and "*quid pro quo*." Stuart suggested that in order to influence the behavior of another person, a family member must build up his or her status as a mediator of reinforcement and that this was best achieved by providing noncontingent rewarding behavior to the target person. In other words, a family member is more likely to change his or her behavior in order to please somebody who pleases him or her and will be less motivated to change behavior to please a person who is not seen as unconditionally rewarding. The frequently repeated phrases "I'd do anything to please him" and "Why should I please him?" reflect these basic tenets on the social context of behavior change.

Stuart's formulation suggested a strategy for enhancing the mutual attractiveness of family members, even in situations where long-standing acrimonious, coercive interaction existed. This approach involved taking the initial focus of intervention away from the presenting problems of the family to constructing a setting in which the frequency and intensity of mutual positive reinforcement are maximized. Family members are required to search for the positive qualities of one another rather than to dwell on their weaknesses. This is carried out in four steps:

1. There must be a rationale for mutual change.
2. Each partner of a dyad must initiate changes in his or her behavior first.
3. The frequency of targeted behavior must be recorded on a chart.
4. There must be a contract for a series of exchanges of desired behaviors.

In his initial efforts, Stuart (1969) employed the operant method of exchanging tokens as rewards for targeted desired behaviors. In this way, one person could build up a "credit" balance by performing a high frequency of behaviors desired by other family members, which could later be exchanged when he or she was the recipient of rewarding behavior from others. Refinements of this approach dispensed with tokens. Mutual exchanges were based on written contracts. Although much of Stuart's work has been devoted to marital discord, his contingency contracting and principles of enhancing the mutual positive reinforcement potential of family members has been used widely by behavioral family therapists (e.g., Patterson, 1971).

It may be concluded that behavioral family therapy developed from the careful application of learning theory principles to the problems of family discord and distress. This approach owed less to the charismatic leadership of its early protagonists and more to evidence of its effectiveness in clinical practice. Although I have focused on three pioneers who played major roles in the initial developments of this approach, many others contributed to this body of work. The early efforts depended almost entirely on applications of operant conditioning technology and appeared most successful where behavioral problems could be defined in terms of relatively straightforward stimulus–response exchanges. The focus of these methods was on interpersonal transactions, the methods were highly dependent on the therapist as the prime mediator of change, patients were expected to follow the therapist's instructions, and conflict resolution was not considered. Such methods were clearly limited in their application, yet they were surprisingly effective.

Further Developments

During the 1970s, behavioral family therapy underwent a transformation. The developing method, with its core of carefully considered yet roughhewn strategies, spawned a wide variety of purpose-made packages. The three major packages were parent training for deviant children, behavioral marital therapy (BMT) for marital discord (with divorce mediation for the failures, marital enrichment for secondary prevention, and premarital counseling for primary prevention), and sexual therapy for those whose primary concern was the technical side of marriage. These approaches were derived chiefly from the influence of Gerald Patterson and Robert Weiss in Oregon. Weiss took over the development of marital therapy from Patterson and was particularly influential in establishing a substantial body of research into the assessment and treatment of marital discord. The continued interest of Stuart and Liberman provided further support for BMT, but both of these pioneers had diversified into other areas of behavior therapy. Most of these offshoots of behavioral family therapy tended to simplify the approach in an attempt to broaden its application.

Parent Training

The early work of Patterson, Risley, Wolf, and others working with disturbed children was developed into a diverse range of educationally oriented programs that aimed to train parents in the application of specific behavioral skills. With the aid of programmed workbooks, parents were taught the application of social learning principles to temper tantrums, bed-wetting, autistic behavior, doing homework, hyperactivity, toilet-training, disobedience, phobias, and aggressive behavior. Parent training was applied to the problems of child abuse, where the parents displayed the identified problem behavior. Many of these training programs were conducted in workshops attended by large numbers of parents and presented by professionals with limited therapeutic skills and understanding of behavior therapy principles (Falloon & Liberman, 1983). As a result, the cornerstone of behavior therapy, the behavioral analysis and evaluation of specific goals, was frequently overlooked. The virtues of behavioral family therapy in being straightforward and using readily defined strategies almost became its downfall as attempts to popularize the methods neglected to preserve these vital components. Fortunately, well-trained practitioners continued to work in a painstaking manner, employing increasingly sophisticated interventions with carefully designed single-case assessment procedures.

Behavioral Marital Therapy

During the 1970s, marital therapy developed into a major intervention strategy. The behavioral approach was repeatedly shown to be highly effective in reducing marital distress (Baucom & Hoffman, 1986). Coupled with the rising rates of family breakup and divorce, this efficient approach became the therapy of choice.

The methods employed tended to differ very little from those described by Stuart (1969) and Liberman (1970). The contingency contract remained the mainstay of BMT, both in enhancing the quality and quantity of mutually pleasing transactions and in diminishing the frequency of negative communication sequences and arguments. An additional strategy directed toward enhancing intimacy within the marital relationship involved teaching couples more effective interpersonal communication skills. Research studies of brief observation of family interaction indicated that the major difference between "distressed" and "nondistressed" couples was their communication patterns. Distressed couples tended to direct more negative emotional comments to each other than positive statements, whereas the ratio favored positive statements in nondistressed relationships (Vincent, Weiss, & Birchler, 1975). These data helped therapists to modify their approaches; whereas earlier efforts had attempted to minimize all forms of negative emotion, developments in communication training tended to acknowledge the value of expressing negative feelings in a clear, direct manner that would foster effective conflict resolution. Communication of positive emotion was similarly enhanced through improving its specificity, nonverbal features, and immediacy of response. Empathic listening skills were similarly taught. These methods were derived largely from assertiveness and social skills training research conducted during the early 1970s. Greater use was made of imitative learning techniques, such as modeling and repeated rehearsal of communication skills, in the sessions and in homework assignments.

Although these efforts achieved the goal of changing couples' behaviors so that they resembled their nondistressed neighbors, BMT was in danger of forgetting to address the highly significant issues that brought the couples to the therapist in the first place (Gurman, Knudson, & Kniskern, 1978). These issues were more frequently related to difficulties in conflict resolution. As a result, many couples completed a course of BMT having satisfied the therapist's goal of achieving competent communication skills, but they left with the same set of unresolved problems that they had at the beginning of therapy. Consequently, separation, divorce, and dissatisfaction with the marriage remained high (Jacobson, Follette, & Elwood, 1984).

Offshoots at the basic BMT technology extended the concepts of behavioral exchange and communication skills training into the realm of prevention of marital deterioration. L'Abate (1977) reviewed the broad range of applications, including family, marital, and premarital enrichment programs. Like the encounter groups of the previous decade, these approaches stressed the improvement of intimacy through clear emotional communication. They were often conducted in brief weekend workshops with little individualized assessment or coaching of specific couples' problems.

Sexual Therapy

The place of sexual therapy in this overview of behavioral family therapy is somewhat unclear. Although many couples seek marital therapy with sexual difficulties as a major problem, this topic is generally avoided in discussions of clinical research in this area. One exception is the work of Michael Crowe (1978). In his controlled comparison of BMT with a systems approach, he found the greatest advantage for the behavioral approach was in the management of marital discord where sexual difficulties were a targeted problem. However, most marital therapists would appear to view sexual dysfunction as a somewhat independent problem. Contingency contracting around the issue of increasing the frequency of sexual behavior is often described, but this would imply that the only problems with sexual behavior concerned issues of quantity not quality.

An explosion in the development of sex therapy rivaling that of BMT occurred in the 1970s. The work of Masters and Johnson (1970) suggested that relatively straightforward behavioral strategies could alleviate the vast majority of problems of sexual dysfunction. This work cannot be linked to specific learning theory applications, but it was readily adopted by behavior therapists, who favored the direct, educational training that was employed. The relationships between marital and family stress factors and sexual behavior have not been adequately explored. In Chapter 3, Crowe offers one of the first attempts to provide a rational basis for the decision to apply either sexual or marital therapies, at least as the initial therapeutic intervention.

RECENT DEVELOPMENTS

Neil Jacobson (1985) wrote that the current phase in the development of behavioral family therapy is one of greater maturity characterized by self-critical reflection on the relative strengths and weaknesses of the approach. This contrasts with the initial period of pioneering enthusiasm and with the second phase when the approach was applied in an uncritical fashion to almost every condition.

This book reflects this more sober view of behavioral family therapy. While not attempting to underplay the value of this approach, we have attempted to describe some of the important recent developments in the application of behavioral family therapy, behavioral assessment methods, and efforts of leaders in the field to address limiting features. It will be clear to the reader that the approach remains immature, that a clear overall conceptual framework is lacking, that notions of what constitutes a well-functioning family are primitive, and that our understanding of the key therapeutic ingredients is far from complete.

Assessment of Family Functioning

Perhaps the greatest strength of behavior therapy remains its rigid adherence to an empirical basis that enables new developments to be criticized not merely in terms of their elegance or the charismatic promotion of their advocates, but also in terms of their effectiveness in achieving the specific changes desired by the consumers. However, this empirical base is limited by the measurement tools currently available. The complexity of family functioning is such that the traditional measures employed in psychology do not adequately address the key issues. People do not always do what they say they do, nor do the things they do always reflect the way they think or feel. Communication patterns among family members develop over many years, so overt verbal expressions may carry messages at many different levels. Of course, many of these levels are nonverbal, and they are also often habitual or involuntary. Simple analysis of stimulus–response sequences of reinforcement and reciprocity are unlikely to discriminate at a level useful for the clinician. However, moving to more complex assessments, while preserving empirical rigor, increases the time and cost of the assessment process and again mediates against clinical utility. A compromise must be found that allows reliable and valid assessment of family functioning that is highly relevant to the clinician and a sensitive reflection of the state of the family and yet is readily applied by the average clinician in everyday practice.

Arrington, Sullaway, and Christensen (Chapter 4) describe a process of assessment that extends far beyond the classic behavioral analysis. Many of the issues they address in describing their contextual assessment model are reiterated in specific applications of behavioral family therapy with different disorders in the latter section of this book. No longer does the behavioral family therapist view the family from a psychological laboratory perspective and a pure learning theory framework. The family is seen within the context of a dynamic unit. However, before abandoning the empirical basis of this field, it should be pointed out that the field has evolved to the point where the same analysis of the antecedents and consequences of behavior that were so clearly defined in the early work of Patterson, Liberman, and Stuart are applied in an identical manner in this broader context.

Hahlweg and his colleagues (Chapter 17) illustrate this increasingly sophisticated behavioral assessment. Rather than simply counting the frequency of positive and negative statements, they examine longer sequences of interaction, which demonstrate that the differences between effective and ineffective crisis resolution may lie in the systematic buildup of positive and negative chains. This supports the intuitive view that an argument does not usually develop from one specific comment made by one person but rather results from a series of coercive statements by both people that gradually escalates. In the same manner, constructive problem resolution on the same topic may include many similarly negative comments, but it does not escalate into a destructive conclusion. Simply encouraging more positive and less negative communication may achieve little change in the effectiveness of problem-solving sequences.

The task of devising standardized instruments for measuring change that are suitable for both clinical and research purposes is an outstanding problem. A fascinating volume entitled *Marriage and Family Assessment*, edited by Erik Filsinger (1983), describes recent efforts in this area. While many family therapists argue that measurement of a family system is illogical (Dell, 1982), behavioral family therapy is founded on the need for continued progress through the systematic use of the scientific method. As a result, all exponents of the method are constantly involved with the process of refinement, each clinician is a researcher, each family member is a research subject, and each researcher is contributing to clinical advancement.

BEYOND THE FAMILY SYSTEM

Behavioral analysis, as conducted by sophisticated behavioral psychotherapists, has always examined the family system in a microanalytic fashion. Kanfer and Saslow (1968), in their landmark paper entitled "Behavioral Analysis: An Alternative to Diagnostic Classification," highlighted the need to explore hypotheses associated with socioenvironmental contingencies that might contribute to symptom formation, maintenance, and resolution. Unlike many family theorists, however, behavioral therapists are encouraged to adopt an open-systems approach that examines the multiplicity of systems that may operate on the psychopathology expressed by the index patient at any time. For this reason, the behavioral family therapist may be interested in the physiological status of the patient and the patient's behavioral, cognitive, and emotional responses, as well as the interpersonal transactions that occur within family, social, work, and cultural–political networks. No single system is the focus of attention to the exclusion of all others. The multimodel assessment approach outlined by Arnold Lazarus (1976) is probably the clearest expression of this method. While it is seldom feasible to provide an extensive assessment of every system operating at one time, efforts are made to screen for significant factors in a multidimensional way.

It is evident that the nature of the presenting problem will usually provide clues to the most relevant systems involved. For example, a person presenting with panic attacks, characterized by a palpitating heartbeat occurring mainly at work, will be examined from the physiological and work relationship aspects—at least at first. On the other hand, a person presenting with depression that started at the retirement of her husband will be examined for the status of her marital relationship. However, it is recognized that in many cases more complex interactions may be contributing to the presenting problems; these may be uncovered only after painstaking detective work aiming to pinpoint key issues. Such an extensive assessment, however, may not prove feasible prior to initiating therapeutic intervention. Behavioral analysis is an ongoing procedure that allows the testing of specific hypotheses in a stepwise fashion. The most straightforward treatment strategies are applied first, followed by methods of increasing complexity when the more basic efforts have shown limited efficacy. A theory of the factors that may contribute to a problem is less important than methods that are successful in resolving the problem as quickly as possible. Although many persons suffering agoraphobic disorders may have spouses who appear excessively tolerant, *in vivo* desensitization strategies usually result in permanent improvement and this is usually associated with parallel improvement in marital adjustment. However, this does not always occur, and as Julian Hafner and Iver Hand point out in Chapters 9 and 10, respectively, it is sometimes necessary to examine the family system and to devise strategies for resolving factors that contribute to the continuing problem.

Behavioral analysis of the family system has progressed beyond the simple *quid pro quo* hypotheses of the pioneering behavioral family therapists. Indeed, interactional research has offered scant support for the *quid pro quo* transactions. However, many behavioral studies have provided validation for the systemic theories. For example, Christensen, Phillips, Glasgow, and Johnson (1983) have observed that "scapegoating" of a child depends on the parental perceptions of that child rather than the child's manifest behavior, which may be indistinguishable from that of his or her siblings. Further, this scapegoating tends to be enhanced by parental discord. Depression of one spouse tends to increase parental discord as well as strengthening the perception of deviance in the index child's behavior. Similar studies by Griest, Forehand, Wells, and McMahon (1980) and Lobitz and Johnson (1975) have shown similar links between parental cognitions and scapegoating.

Thus, intervention strategies may differ according to whether a family member does indeed exhibit a persistent pattern of deviant behavior, the deviancy is merely a misperception based on stress and distress experienced by other family members, or a combination of both factors. In the case of persons with mental illness, there may be clear examples of disturbed behavior. However, the manner in which family members cope with behavioral disturbances (behaviorally, affectively, and cognitively) will largely determine its severity. The "expressed emotion" research has shown that hostile and critical or highly overinvolved responses to symptomatic behavior tends to contribute to a more chronic or relapsing course of schizophrenia and depressive disorders (Vaughn & Leff, 1976).

Curran, Faraone, and Graves (Chapter 12) and Falloon (Chapter 13) describe behavioral family therapy methods that look beyond the family system in the management of schizophrenia. Optimal drug therapy and dealing with stress factors outside the family are important ingredients of the family management approaches that have resulted in dramatic improvements in the outlook for schizophrenia.

These methods differ from earlier efforts to resolve schizophrenia through family interventions. Clear distinctions are made between symptoms of schizophrenia (e.g., hallucinations, delusions, thought interference) and behavioral disturbances. The latter may be controlled by the patient, even when provoked by symptoms that are not usually under voluntary control. Patients and their families are taught to view schizophrenia as a stress-related disorder affecting brain biochemistry that is best treated by combining drug therapy with psychosocial stress management.

The biological system is responsive to drugs, while psychosocial factors are modified by a family-based approach, which aims to maximize the efficiency of the family as a problem-solving unit that may counter the myriad of intra- and extrafamilial stressors that affect the vulnerable individual. It is recognized that major stress affecting any one person in a family is likely to have repercussions for every other household member and that the overall reduction in family stress may assist the person at risk for schizophrenic episodes.

Family systems approaches have focused almost exclusively on interfamilial stress factors and have tended to view extrafamilial stresses as somewhat irrelevant issues. A behavioral analysis of the family explores all systems operating on each family member that might contribute to the development and maintenance as well as the resolution of the presenting problems.

A further crucial issue that is raised by behavior therapists is that beneficial changes in the family system do not automatically generalize to other systems including school, peer groups, work, and friendships. It is important that generalization of behavioral patterns is planned to ensure that changes are observed in all settings in which such change is likely to prove beneficial. The temper tantrums of a child may be controlled by the parents in the home but may continue unchanged at school until the teacher learns to adopt the same skills that have proven successful at home. Of course the contingencies surrounding tantrums in each setting may differ, so that a somewhat different approach may be considered.

The importance of assessment and intervention occurring in different settings was recognized by the pioneers of behavioral family therapy. Patterson (1974) described this approach with behaviorally disturbed children. Liberman (1970) pointed out that "much of the effort involves collaboration and involvement with adjunctive agencies such as schools, rehabilitation services, medication and work settings. Family therapists are moving toward this total systems approach" (p. 117). Tharp and Wetzel (1969) considered the broader social context in their description of the principles of reinforcement:

> Reinforcers lie within the environment of the individual, and are embedded within this social nexus: whether the reinforcer is a smile or a candy, a bicycle or a slap, reinforcement is frequently dispensed by people articulated into the individuals' social environment. If the environment is the hospital, these people are the nurses, doctors, or other patients; if the environment is the school, they are the principal, teachers, or other pupils; if it is the family, they are siblings, the spouse, or the parents. (p. 3)

They go on to make the further point that, "the potent reinforcers for an individual ordinarily lie within his natural environment, and these reinforcers are controlled by those people to whom he is naturally related." (p. 3) They argue that the family and intimate social contacts are the most potent sources of behavior change and that it makes little sense to attempt to displace this resource with an "artificial relationship" with a psychotherapist, who inevitably pushes natural relationships into second place and devalues their potency on account of their "unpredictability, lack of professional knowledge, or previous deleterious effects on the patient."

Behavioral family therapists attempt to validate family efforts to assist each family member but remain open to the possibility that there are dangers in overvaluing the potency of the family as well as in dismissing this valuable resource.

RESISTANCE TO CHANGE OR INCOMPLETE BEHAVIORAL ANALYSIS?

Behavioral family therapists have been reluctant to adopt the psychodynamic jargon frequently employed by other systems therapists. A lack of theoretical framework provides greater freedom in describing the observed behavior of family members without the necessity of labeling and classifying specific patterns. Concepts such as transference, countertransference, and resistance to change were all observed by behavior therapists in the course of their practice but were considered in a matter-of-fact way as important general therapeutic issues. Focus on the specific intervention strategies and efforts to measure their benefits tended to distract behavior therapists from the less specific, but no less crucial, aspects of the therapeutic alliance. Indeed, many behavior therapists claimed that the nonspecific aspects of therapy were of little consequence and that behavior therapy could be applied equally well by having patients read therapy manuals or engage in computer-based therapy (Ghosh, Marks, & Carr, 1987).

Much of this downplaying of the significance of the therapeutic alliance derived from the work of researchers who considered groups of patients rather than individual cases. The "average" patient was considered in these group studies. The more difficult case was seldom discussed. However, it is the latter case that is of major interest to the clinician, who is aware that most forms of psychotherapy tend to produce at least some significant benefits for "average" people, many of whom tend to improve spontaneously without formal intervention. Significant improvement in two thirds of cases treated with specific intervention may appear impressive to the researcher, but the clinician will be left trying to seek solutions for the remaining one third.

One of the major developments in behavioral family therapy in recent years has been the consideration of the family that does not improve quickly and readily. The behavioral family therapist is not content merely to observe and label such lack of progress as a resistance to change or to postulate homeostatic mechanisms to account for such a phenomenon. Rather, the therapist attempts to pinpoint the specific mechanisms that may underlie the ineffectiveness of the therapeutic strategy. These mechanisms may include a wide variety of factors, some simple, others complex, some therapy-related, some client-based. Once the specific mechanisms hypothesized as underlying lack of progress toward the therapy goals of a family have been pinpointed, the behavioral family therapist devises a specific strategy to counter each specific mechanism.

This problem solving is reminiscent of the initial behavioral analysis and is indeed merely an extension of this process, which is an integral part of every behavioral treatment session. It has been argued by the eminent behavior therapist Joseph Wolpe (1977) that lack of therapeutic progress reflects an inadequate initial behavioral analysis. It is true that a thorough initial behavioral analysis may target areas of potential resistance and that the therapist may plan strategies to deal with such anticipated difficulties in the initial management plan. In reality, many resistance factors in families may not be readily recognized until the therapist has begun to intervene, for example, the family that fails to carry out homework assignments or family members who miss sessions.

In Chapter 6, Gary Birchler provides a superb review of the behavioral approaches to resistance to interventions. A much earlier account of this problem was provided by Tharp and Wetzel (1969). Although many of the therapist and client factors were similar to those described by Birchler, Tharp, and Wetzel also discuss one area that has received only limited attention from family therapists: the manner in which change is impeded by community organization. Among the problems cited were a lack of coordination of community agencies, such as the police, legal system, schools, social services, and the cultural conflicts of ethnic minorities. Behavioral family therapists, like other therapists, have frequently failed to assess the impact of such problems on the families of mentally disordered persons.

A more sinister form of community resistance is that that arises from other mental health professionals. This resistance often results in the failure of advances in therapeutic methods being deployed in mental health clinics and hospitals. Ideological, organizational, and economic barriers are placed before the innovator. Seldom is the new approach challenged on valid scientific grounds.

Remarkably few controlled research studies have been conducted that demonstrate the cost-effectiveness of family therapies. Without adequate support for the benefits and economic feasibility of a new approach, the innovator is at the mercy of colleagues who argue for preservation of the *status quo*. With research data, there can be little resistance to establishing new approaches, except perhaps ethical issues. However, one ethical issue that can be addressed readily is why an agency prevents (either actively or passively) its clients from receiving the most effective methods for managing their disorders.

Most, but not all, of the approaches described in this book have demonstrated their effectiveness under controlled research conditions. More research studies are urgently needed before family therapies can be established as valid components of the management plans of many mental disorders.

A final form of community resistance highlighted by Tharp and Wetzel is the manner in which the community supports the deviance of certain of its members. Common examples of this are gambling, inappropriate sexual activity, drug taking in the forms of alcohol and tobacco, eating problems, and the models of violence provided by certain contact sports, particularly boxing and wrestling. The line between acceptable social behavior and that defining deviance is seldom clear in these instances. Furthermore, a greater tolerance for deviance is expected among family members than among other community members. For example, sexual abuse and violence is considered less of a problem when contained within the confines of the family. Confused community guidelines and double standards provide a major ingredient impeding change for many persons.

The use of mental disorders as labels of social deviance are a well-known source of community resistance. However, there are more subtle forms than the usual negative discrimination directed toward individuals so labeled. These include the discrimination that allows persons labeled as having suffered a mental illness, being admitted to a mental hospital, or even merely being assessed by a psychiatrist to be "permitted" to engage in violent, illegal, or other antisocial behavior and to have criminal charges against them dropped or to be acquitted on the grounds of insanity. Such a widespread double standard, in which there is one set of community rules for the mentally disordered and another for the remainder of the community, would appear to provide a powerful reinforcement for the mentally disordered to behave irresponsibly in the community or, alternatively, for antisocial individuals to seek the immunity against prosecution that a mental disorder label provides.

All of these issues may limit the effective changes that can be sustained as the result of highly effective family intervention. They further highlight the need for assessment and intervention strategies to extend beyond the confines of the family boundary to the broader content of the social environment. A comprehensive behavioral analysis of the family is the cornerstone of this effort. Attempts to abbreviate this often lengthy assessment process should not be made at the expense of neglecting to consider all major areas of potential resistance to long-term beneficial change. Although behavioral strategies may appear deceptively straightforward, their ultimate success depends on the context in which they are applied. The assessment of this context remains an often complex and painstaking procedure that continues throughout the course of therapy. I have read no better account of this process than that of Arrington, Sullaway, and Christensen in Chapter 4 of this book.

INDICATIONS FOR BEHAVIORAL FAMILY THERAPY

Behavioral interventions with families cover a range of approaches. Behavioral marital therapy (BMT) is the best-known approach and has been subjected to the most extensive research. Specialized extensions of BMT are the behavioral methods of sexual therapy, divorce mediation, and premarital counseling. Behavioral family therapy can be further subdivided into (1) the more typical family therapy approach that addresses stress within the family unit, (2) parent training, and (3) the approach in which a family member becomes involved in the behavioral treatment program of another family member. The latter is sometimes termed spouse-aided therapy. With such a range of variations, it may be difficult for the therapist to choose the most appropriate approach for each case. Crowe (Chapter 3) attempts to shed light on this dilemma and offers some guidelines to assist in selecting the most appropriate approach for different presenting problems. He advocates a flexible approach guided by the initial and ongoing behavioral analysis.

A more difficult question, as yet unanswered by empirical data, is, What are the contraindications for behavioral family approaches? Evidence that behavioral family therapy has contributed to distress or deterioration is lacking. Such harmful effects are probably the only absolute contraindication for a therapeutic approach. In practical terms, the only contraindications are an inability of one or more key family members to be able to process information during a major part of each therapy session. This may occur when a member is severely mentally handicapped, severely psychotic, or affected by the toxicity of alcohol, drugs, or other toxins. As well as persisting deficits in information processing, persistent lack of attendance of key family members at therapy sessions may prove a contraindication to therapy. However, it is sometimes possible to intervene effectively in a family through training no more than one family member in skills that can then be applied to change the remainder of the family system. Behavioral family therapists show little reticence about moving the location of treatment sessions into the family home itself. Home-based family therapy minimizes poor attendance at sessions and is more likely to engage reluctant family members in the therapy.

Undoubtedly, there are cases in which behavioral family approaches have contributed to a negative outcome. The positive focus and lack of coercive strategies would seem to minimize this risk. It is important that all cases of harmful effects attributable to family interventions are reported. It is recognized that these methods are powerful psychological strategies that require responsible handling by their practitioners. A lack of adequate training in these methods may lead to abuse of the approaches.

THERAPIST TRAINING

Behavioral family therapy has been disseminated without the institutional training programs associated with most other forms of family therapy. The lack of charismatic leadership, while detracting from the promotional aspects encouraged by such leaders, has enabled developments to be pursued along scientific empirical lines rather than along rigid ideological channels. However, training in these methods has not been systematized or widely available, even to therapists enamored by behavior therapy methods. Training courses have tended to be organized through the association of behavior therapists and have usually been limited to workshops of no more than two days' duration. In such a setting, skilled behavior therapists may be able to learn the rudiments of the approach but no more. It will be apparent to the reader of this book that the refinements of this approach cannot be competently assimilated in an hour or two of basic training. Although the specificity of the approach and the manner in which procedures can be operationally defined may enhance the efficiency of training, there is no substitute for employing case-supervised training as a crucial part of any training course.

Behavioral family therapists have been slow to evaluate therapist training strategies. Such evaluation is urgently needed. In its absence, haphazard brief workshop training is likely to create large numbers of incompetent exponents of the methods with subsequent increased likelihood that the method will be inadequately disseminated and considered ill-conceived by its consumers as well as the administrators of mental health services. Falloon (Chapter 13) describes efforts to train and maintain competent application of behavioral family therapy with a cohort of therapists in a major study that employed these methods. It is hoped that this will be the first of many such training efforts and that research into the efficiency of therapist training will become a field of endeavor in its own right.

COGNITIVE STRATEGIES IN BEHAVIORAL FAMILY THERAPY

The early behavioral interventions with families tended to focus on the measurement and modification of readily observable, easily operationalized behaviors. It was assumed that the frequency of behaviors such as arguments, sexual intercourse, positive statements, or a child's temper tantrums served as markers of the quality of family relationships. In a gross sense this is probably true. However, very few normative data were available to ascertain whether the frequency of such behaviors was any different in those families presenting for treatment than those who were satisfied with their condition. Thus, the goal of therapists was to achieve some mythical state of family, marital, or sexual bliss where cross words were never spoken, positive behaviors were always praised and reciprocated, and sex was always ecstatic. It was clear that such goals were unrealistic.

One unfortunate consequence of this early approach was that some simplistic exponents took the "marker" behaviors as the only goals of treatment and developed interventions that sought merely to eliminate or potentiate these behaviors, without pinpointing any of the conflictual attitudes or feelings that contributed to the overt behavioral problems. A mother who had never felt positive about her child from birth was trained to award stars and to praise her enuretic child when he had a "dry" night. Although she was able to perform this behavior in a competent fashion, it was not associated with any change in the frequency of her child's bedwetting. Change in the child's behavior occurred once the mother's negative attitude had been modified by cognitive restructuring, which helped her to recognize that her negative thoughts about her child were irrational and that he had many positive attributes and many negative attributes, not unlike her two other children.

The benefits of cognitive strategies are difficult to measure in a reliable fashion; for this reason, they have tended to be regarded with disdain by many behavior therapists. However, there is an increasing interest in utilizing these methods in behavioral family therapy. Impetus to this change has been provided by empirical findings from marital therapy research, which have shown that a substantial proportion of couples who were considered to have achieved a satisfactory level of communication and problem-solving behavior, as measured in problem-solving discussions, had not experienced any significant changes in their attitudes toward their partners and their overall satisfaction with their marriages (Jacobson, 1984). Another study has shown that happy couples, while exchanging positive behavior frequently, do not tend to do this in a contingent fashion. In other words, their positive regard seems unconditional, and they do not expect a positive response in exchange for their positive behavior. Jacobson (1984) has suggested that a successful behavioral outcome can only be achieved when such a state exists and that this state cannot be achieved without specific therapeutic strategies that address the mutual cognitions of family members directly. He proposed strategies such as relabeling negative attributions, debunking unrealistic expectations of family members and the concept of marriage, and creating realistic, yet positive, expectancies for therapeutic change. Further examples of the systematic use of cognitive strategies in marital therapy are provided by Follette and Jacobson (Chapter 11) and Hahlweg *et al.* (Chapter 17). The latter describes a four-stage training in self-control for couples that aims to teach family members to recognize the precipitants of an argument and to restructure their behavior along lines that would be more likely to achieve successful conflict resolution.

Although marital therapy has been a focus of the perceived need for cognitive restructuring, cognitive methods have been employed to enhance the efficacy of behavioral family therapy methods (Crowe, Chapter 3; McAuley, Chapter 7), as well as to assist families to cope with serious disorders such as mental handicaps (Harris and Thorwarth, Chapter 8, agoraphobia (Hafner, Chapter 9), obsessive-compulsive disorders (Hand, Chapter 10), schizophrenia (Falloon, Chapter 13), alcoholism (Fichter and Postpischil, Chapter 14), and dementia (Zarit, Chapter 15).

The most straightforward of these methods has been the education of patients and their families about the nature of their mental disorders and the optimal management of these conditions. The patient and family members are encouraged to integrate their informal self-help efforts within the medical and psychosocial management plan of the professional caregivers. Such efforts range from the spouse-assisted exposure therapy for agoraphobia (Hafner, Chapter 9) to family stress management for schizophrenia (Falloon, Chapter 13; Curran, Faraone, and Graves, Chapter 12).

The realistic appraisal of the disabilities of the mentally disordered as well as the mentally handicapped forms the basis for family-based interventions that aim to teach index patients and their families to target problems that can be resolved. This can lead to significant improvements in the quality of family life (Harris and Thorwarth, Chapter 8; Zarit, Chapter 15). Hand (Chapter 10) describes several fascinating examples of cognitive restructuring of obsessional patients. In particular, he describes cases in which obsessional behavior appears to be a family trait, yet the behavior of one member is viewed in a positive light while almost identical behavior in another is viewed as a deviant illness. To date, behavioral family therapy has not embraced the three-generational perspectives of many systems-oriented therapists. However, the use of genealogical data in family education is a valuable cognitive strategy, especially where the effective coping behavior of a disturbed member of a past generation can be used as a model for the current sufferer. For example, the manner in which grandmother coped with her phobic symptoms that enabled her to lead a full, active life may assist her granddaughter who experiences similar disability but appears to be extremely handicapped in her functioning.

It is evident that behavioral family therapy is moving cautiously toward cognitive strategies. Empirical support for these methods is lacking in family settings. Until studies have shown that the addition of such strategies enhances the outcome of behavioral family therapy, they will not be embraced in a widespread fashion.

CONCLUDING COMMENTS

This overview of behavioral family therapy explores some of the developments in this field over the past two decades. The earliest methods were brilliantly straightforward in their conception and highly effective in many, but not all, target areas. Subsequent developments have sought to find specific, cost-efficient ways of treating the failures of the basic methods. Whether such methods have become part of the standard repertoire of behavior family therapy has depended more on the results of careful empirical studies than on the enthusiasm shown by exponents of these methods or their charismatic promotion. Progress is slow in such a system, but one can argue that the foundations are firmly laid and likely to endure.

It is not clear whether behavioral family therapy can be considered to have come of age. By its very nature, behavioral family therapy is a field that continues to grow. This book attests to that growth, both in refinement of the technical methods employed and the extension of target populations who have enjoyed the benefits of the approach. In addition to disseminating some aspects of these methods, it is hoped that this book will stimulate discussion throughout the field of family therapy and lead to further empirically based creative interventions.

REFERENCES

Bandura, A., & Walters, R. (1963). *Social learning and personality development.* New York: Holt, Rinehart & Winston.

Baucom, D. H., & Hoffman, J. A. (1986). The effectiveness of marital therapy: Current status and application to the clinical setting. In N. S. Jacobson & A. S. Gurman (Eds.), *Clinical handbook of marital therapy* (pp. 597–620). New York: Guilford Press.

Boardman, W. K. (1962). Rusty: A brief behaviour disorder. *Journal of Consulting Psychology, 26*, 293–297.

Christensen, A., Phillips, S., Glasgow, R. E., & Johnson, S. M. (1983). Parental characteristics and interactional dysfunction in families with child behavior problems: A preliminary investigation. *Journal of Abnormal Child Psychology, 11*, 153–166.

Crowe, M. J. (1978). Conjoint marital therapy: A controlled outcome study. *Psychological Medicine, 8*, 623–636.

Dell, P. F. (1982). Beyond homeostasis: Toward a concept of coherence. *Family Process, 21*, 21–41.

Falloon, I. R. H., & Liberman, R. P. (1983). Behavioral therapy for families with child management problems. In M. R. Textor (Ed.), *Helping families with special problems* (pp. 121–147). New York: Jason Aronson.

Filsinger, E. E. (1983). Assessment: What it is and why it is important. In E. E. Filsinger (Ed.), *Marriage and family assessment.* Beverly Hills, CA: Sage Publications.

Ghosh, A., Marks, I. M., & Carr, A. C. (1987). Self-exposure for phobias. *British Journal of Psychiatry*, *152*, 234–238.

Griest, D. L., Forehand, R., Wells, K. C., & McMahon, R. J. (1980). An examination of differences between non-clinic and behavior-problem clinic-referred children and their mothers. *Journal of Abnormal Psychology*, *89*, 497–500.

Gurman, A. S., Knudson, R. M., & Kniskern, D. P. (1978). Behavioral marriage therapy: IV. Take two aspirin and call us in the morning. *Family Process*, *17*, 165–180.

Jackson, D. D. (1965). Family rules. *Archives of General Psychiatry*, *12*, 589–594.

Jacobson, N. S. (1984). The modification of cognitive processes in behavioral marital therapy: Integrating cognitive and behavioral intervention strategies. In K. Hahlweg & N. Jacobson (Eds.), *Marital interaction: Analysis and modification*. New York: Guilford Press.

Jacobson, N. S. (1985). Toward a nonsectarian blueprint for the empirical study of family therapies. *Journal of Marital and Family Therapy*, *11*, 163–165.

Jacobson, N. S., Follette, W. C., & Elwood, R. W. (1984). Outcome research on behavioral marital therapy: A methodological and conceptual reappraisal. In K. Hahlweg & N. S. Jacobson (Eds.), *Marital interaction: Analysis and modification*. New York: Guilford Press.

Kanfer, F. H., & Saslow, G. (1965). Behavioral analysis: An alternative to diagnostic classification. *Archives of General Psychiatry*, *12*, 529–538.

L'Abate, L. (1977). *Enrichment: Structured interventions with couples, families and groups*. Washington, DC: University Press of America.

Lazarus, A. A. (1976). *Multimodal behavior therapy*. New York: Springer.

Liberman, R. P. (1970). Behavioral approaches to family and couple therapy. *American Journal of Orthopsychiatry*, *40*, 106–118.

Lobitz, G. K., & Johnson, S. M. (1975). Normal versus deviant children: A multimethod comparison. *Journal of Abnormal Child Psychology*, *3*, 353–374.

Lovibond, S. H. (1963). The mechanism of conditioning treatment of enuresis. *Behaviour Research and Therapy*, *1*, 17–21.

Masters, W. H., & Johnson, V. E. (1970). *Human sexual inadequacy*. London: Churchill.

Patterson, G. R. (1971). *Families: Applications of social learning to family life*. Champaign, IL: Research Press.

Patterson, G. R. (1974). Interventions for boys with conduct problems: Multiple settings, treatments and criteria. *Journal of Consulting and Clinical Psychology*, *42*, 471–481.

Patterson, G. R., & Hops, H. (1972). Coercion, a game for two: Intervention techniques for marital conflict. In R. E. Ulrich & P. Mountjoy (Eds.), *The experimental analysis of social behavior*. New York: Appleton-Century-Crofts.

Patterson, G. R., McNeal, S., Hawkins, N., & Phelps, R. (1967). Reprogramming the social environment. *Journal of Child Psychology and Psychiatry*, *8*, 181–195.

Risley, T. R., & Wolf, M. M. (1967). Experimental manipulation of autistic behaviors and generalization into the home. In S. W. Bijou & D. M. Baer (Eds.), *Child development: Readings in experimental analysis* (pp. 184–194). New York: Appleton.

Stuart, R. B. (1969). Operant-interpersonal treatment for marital discord. *Journal of Consulting and Clinical Psychology*, *33*, 675–682.

Tharp, R. G., & Wetzel, R. J. (1969). *Behavior modification in the natural environment*. New York: Academic Press.

Thibaut, J. W., & Kelley, H. H. (1959). *The social psychology of groups*. New York: Wiley.

Vaughn, C. E., & Leff, J. P. (1976). The influence of family and social factors on the course of psychiatric illness: A comparison of schizophrenic and depressed neurotic patients. *British Journal of Psychiatry*, *129*, 125–137.

Vincent, J. P., Weiss, R. L., & Birchler, G. R. (1975). A behavior analysis of problem solving in distressed and non-distressed married and stranger dyads. *Behavior Therapy*, *6*, 475–487.

Wahler, R. G., Winkel, G. H., Peterson, R. F., & Morrison, D. C. (1965). Mothers as behavior therapists for their own children. *Behaviour Research and Therapy*, *4*, 169–177.

Williams, C. D. (1959). The elimination of tantrum behaviour by extinction procedures. *Journal of Abnormal and Social Psychology*, *59*, 269.

Wolpe, J. (1958). *Psychotherapy by reciprocal inhibition*. Palo Alto, CA: Stanford University Press.

Wolpe, J. (1977). Inadequate behavior analysis: The Achilles' heel of outcome research in behavior therapy. *Journal of Behavior Therapy and Experimental Psychiatry*, *8*, 1–4.

2

Modular Behavioral Strategies

ROBERT PAUL LIBERMAN
UCLA Department of Psychiatry, Brentwood Division–West Los Angeles VA Medical Center, Camarillo State Hospital

KIM MUESER

SHIRLEY GLYNN
Camarillo State Hospital

With the broad and sophisticated approaches extant in behavioral family therapy, it is hard to believe that the first fledgling efforts to apply learning principles to families in distress occurred less than 20 years ago. At that time, the pioneering interventions resembled the tools utilized by laboratory experimentalists. Behaviors of deviant children or adults were pinpointed, counted, and differential consequences were applied to achieve reductions in tantrums, aggression, noncompliance, and symptoms, along with increases in cooperation, social conversation, household chores, and shared recreational activities. The handful of hardy stalwarts who explored behavioral family therapy, braced against the criticisms that they were dehumanizing patients and modifying behavior feebly and transiently, were buoyed by their early successes and remained afloat to see their efforts endorsed as part of the mainstream of clinical psychiatry and psychology (Liberman, 1978).

While behaviorists continue to specify and measure behaviors of members in family systems, behavioral family therapy has extended to a wider and more complex array of problems and phenomena. Behavior therapists are now targeting the social insularity of parents as an obstacle to parent training; the communication and problem-solving skills of family members coping with major mental disorders or marital distress; the tension and stress experienced by families containing a schizophrenic member, indexed by "expressed emotion"; and the cognitions and attributions of family members who show "resistance" to change. What has been most encouraging has been the expansion of the identities of workers in this field to "scientist-practitioners" from "behaviorists," embracing a biopsychosocial concept of psychological disorders.

Behavior therapists working with phobics, obsessives, and depressives continue to use individual behavioral techniques and behavioral strategies with the family system, but they are also making judicious use of psychoactive medications that can block panic attacks, reduce ruminations, and remit depression. Once the intrusive and distracting symptoms of a disorder are under medication control, behavior therapy can more readily proceed toward helping a patient to acquire and generalize better cognitive functioning and behavioral repertoires. The synergistic effect of combining behavioral with pharmacological interventions is no better highlighted than in the treatment of schizophrenia (Falloon & Liberman, 1983; Liberman, Falloon, & Wallace, 1984). Without the effective symptom control exerted by neuroleptic drugs, behavior therapy would be of little value for the majority of patients suffering from schizophrenic disorders (Wallace & Liberman, 1985).

The two great empirical traditions in modern clinical psychiatry—behavior therapy and psychopharmacotherapy—have found congruence in their common adherence to measurement and the scientific method. Other domains of psychobiological research also are contributing to new developments in behavioral assessment and therapy: developmental, social, and cognitive psychology; psychoimmunology and neuroendocrinology; brain imaging; and social systems theory. Once a "bad word" in behaviorism, theory-driven research can now be seen as a productive path to new and more efficient and effective interventions. One conceptual framework that can inform us in our efforts to design more efficacious therapies for psychiatric disorders encompasses "vulnerability-stress-competence-coping" factors in a longitudinal perspective.

COPING AND COMPETENCE AS GOALS FOR FAMILY THERAPY

Major mental disorders are now understood as emerging from the interplay of (1) psychobiological vulnerability (e.g., genetic factors, autonomic and cognitive dysfunctions, neuroendocrine abnormalities); (2) socioenvironmental stressors and potentiators (e.g., family conflict and tension, major life events); and (3) personal protective factors (e.g., social support, self-efficacy, interpersonal competence, antidepressant and antipsychotic medications). These factors, as depicted in Figure 2-1 for schizophrenia, interact in a multivariate fashion to determine the development, recurrence, and outcome of major mental disorders. Family factors—both stressful or potentiating on the one hand and protective on the other—play an important role in this conceptual scheme. When specific protective, stressful, or potentiating family factors in mental disorders can be identified, then intervention strategies can be designed with maximal impact.

In this scheme, stressors are defined as time-limited events with noxious effects on individuals or families (e.g., change in residence, loss of a job, termination from therapy, discharge from hospital). In contrast, po-

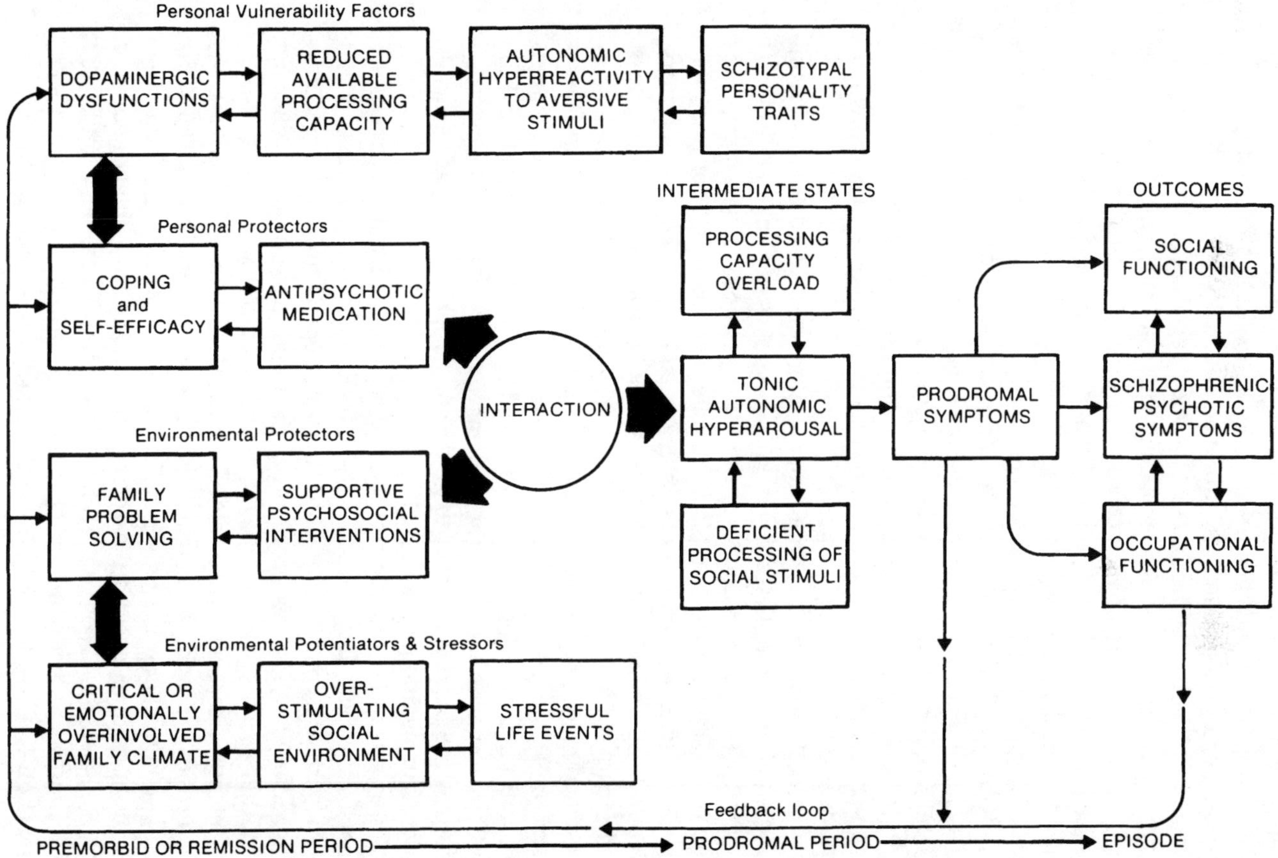

Figure 2-1. Interactional and multifactorial conceptual framework for understanding the onset, course, and outcome of schizophrenic disorders. Schizophrenia disorders are viewed as influenced by environmental, psychobiological, and personal–behavioral factors that interact in a dynamic fashion, permitting change to be instigated by a variety of treatment strategies.

tentiating factors are more enduring aspects of individual or family life that create chronic stress and high ambient levels of tension or conflict (e.g., "expressed emotion" in families, sustained poverty, overstimulating treatment milieu). Protective factors include biomedical interventions such as psychotropic medications used for treatment and prophylaxis as well as psychosocial attributes of the patient and his or her environment. Low expressed emotion in the emotional climates of some families, whether acquired naturally or through behavioral family therapy, would be an example of a protective factor in the course of schizophrenia or depression (Leff, Knipers, Berkowitz, Eberlein-Vries, & Sturgeon, 1982; Vaughn, Snyder, Jones, Falloon, & Liberman, 1982; Vaughn & Leff, 1976). Through the interaction among vulnerability and stressful, potentiating, and protective factors, intermediate states of hyperarousal and symptomatic prodomata arise and, unless prevented by early intervention, inexorably lead to episodes of illness.

It is likely that the sociobehavioral factors discovered to be stressful or potentiating in families are generic to most major mental disorders associated with psychotic, affective, and anxiety symptoms. The nonspecific nature of these factors will amplify the generality and utility of treatment methods designed to buffer or eliminate stressful and potentiating factors. With our inchoate understanding of psychobiological vulnerability factors, it is too early to have confidence that biopsychosocial interventions may be designed to actually reduce underlying vulnerability in the central nervous system. However, it is plausible that well-designed family interventions may protect against relapse not only through effects on the person and the family environment but also through changes in neuronal substrates. What road maps are available, then, to guide our design and testing of family therapies for mental disorders?

Three sets of factors relevant to the design of family interventions are the personal coping and competencies of family members; the tension and stress experienced by a family; and the level of social support for adaptive coping. Many studies have highlighted the importance of premorbid and postmorbid social competence as a predictor of course and outcome in major mental disorders (Hirschfeld, Klerman, & Clayton, 1983; Liberman, 1982; Presley, Grubb, & Semple, 1982). They suggest that social skills training, conducted in the family context, might improve long-term prognosis by upgrading postmorbid social competence of patients and their relatives. Certain types of family interaction patterns have been implicated in the course of schizophrenia, depression, anorexia, obesity, and alcoholism (Leff & Vaughn, 1985). Studies conducted in several different countries and over a 15-year span have shown that criticism and emotional overinvolvement by relatives significantly increase the probability of relapse. If improving the problem-solving and communication skills of family members, as well as the social and independent living skills of patients, could reduce or remove the stressful and risk factors implicated in relapse, then a preventive intervention would be available that might lift family burden and improve social adjustment as well.

Family therapies can also be designed to strengthen members' social networks, attributes of which have been found to be correlated with degree of psychiatric illness. For example, in schizophrenic disorders, those individuals with the most chronic and severe illnesses have significantly smaller networks, characterized by few friends, diminished contact with network members, relative overreliance on a small cohort of family members, and higher levels of negative emotionality associated with network members (Liberman, 1982). Even when the size of a social network is held constant, it has been found that more severely ill patients perceive less support being available and have fewer network members available for support. The proportionately greater use of a few family members for support produces family burden, the stress from which further diminishes coping and self-efficacy of the entire family system. These findings have been replicated in the families of conduct-disordered and oppositional children, where the insularity of the parents reduces the family's capacity for social support and effective coping (Patterson, 1982; Wahler, Leske, & Rogers, 1979). Similar trends have been noted to play a major role in the course of depressive disorders. Thus, it would appear that interventions that connect a family containing an individual deemed vulnerable for mental disorder with constructive outside support—both professional and informal—may reduce morbidity and improve outcome.

ADVANCES IN BEHAVIORAL FAMILY THERAPY

The past ten years have witnessed a profusion of new and creatively designed behavioral family interventions to meet the illness-inducing vulnerability, stress, and potentiating factors noted above. For example, in conducting family therapy with a member who suffers from schizophrenic symptoms and attentional deficits, provision has been made for overlearning, visual as well as auditory instructional input, and titration of the training "dose" (Falloon, Boyd, & McGill, 1984; Liberman, Falloon, & Aitchison, 1984; Liberman, Nuechterlein, & Wallace, 1982). Behavioral family therapy in schizophrenia has demonstrated how criticism and other communication dysfunctions producing tension and stress can be reduced through training members in making positive requests and expressing negative feelings directly (Falloon, 1985). Behavioral marital therapy has moved from reinforcing discrete instrumental and affectional behaviors to the teaching of general problem-solving, cognitive, and communication skills (Jacobson, 1984). Family treatment with deviant children and adolescents has yielded greater efficacy as innovations have been made in improving the social support available to stressed parents (Patterson, 1985; O'Leary & Carr, 1982). Thus, behavioral therapies have expanded their scope, goals, and methods as they have entered their third decade of maturity. Added complexity in treatment strategies mirrors the realization by behavioral family therapists that the patient's resistances, noncooperativeness, and illness factors, as well as the clinician's skills, all influence treatment outcomes.

Three major advances made in behavioral family therapies augur well for the continued vigorous growth of this field. Perhaps of greatest importance is the wealth of reliable and valid assessment methods that have been applied to the tasks of initial evaluation for treatment planning as well as ongoing monitoring of progress and outcome. Measurement and assessment are the strengths of behavior therapy and of the scientific method—it is not surprising that they are serving as beacons for refinement and improvement of intervention strategies. Since many chapters in this book emphasize the general and particular measurement approaches now being used and those on the horizon, further discussion of this topic will not be made here.

A second important advance has been the movement toward longer term therapeutic programs. Given the growing awareness of the chronicity and enduring vulnerability of individuals at risk for psychopathology, it is only reasonable that behavior therapists—once proud of their brief therapy doctrine—have adopted longer term treatment approaches. Behavioral marital therapy now takes up to 20 sessions on the average, except in the halls of academia where research grants and dissertations constrain the therapist from providing what is truly needed by a couple in distress. The most effective version of family therapy yet produced for schizophrenics and their relatives is delivered in weekly sessions for 3 months, biweekly for 6 months, and then monthly for up to 2 years or even longer (Falloon, 1985).

Scanning the conceptual schema shown in Figure 2-1 reveals another rationale for extended treatment of families. Most mental disorders are recurrent, with relapses and remissions affected by vulnerability and stressful, potentiating, and protective factors that vary greatly both within and across families. In addition, these determinants of course and outcome vary over time. Since it is hard to predict when the confluence of factors will create the intermediate states that are associated with prodromal or incipient symptoms, a continuing, albeit intermittant, treatment "contract" with a family may be the most effective form of secondary prevention of illness. Longer term family treatment can also produce the strengthening of self-help and problem-solving skills that require repeated practice and trial-and-error learning over many months and years. Long-term therapy is not necessarily synonymous with intensive treatment since fading and dispersion of sessions are desirable. It is very likely, therefore, that longer term family may turn out to be less costly in the end.

Linked to the need for flexible and long-term provision of services is the third major advance of current behavioral family therapy: modular treatment interventions organized to meet the specific and changing needs of the individual and his or her relatives. A modular strategy for behavioral interventions builds on the multidimensional conceptual framework for understanding the nature and course of mental disorders shown in Figure 2-1 and offers the clinician rules or guidelines for treatment decision-making.

MODULAR STRATEGY FOR INTERVENTIONS IN PSYCHIATRIC DISORDERS

Rather than pine for the day when we will have the optimal treatment for each patient, a modular approach assumes that needs change and that the therapist must be flexibly responsive with interventions that fit the priorities of the moment and are cost-effective as well. Most of medical practice follows this inductive and highly individualized approach. Understandably, the medical practitioner recognizes the overarching importance of individual differences in pathology, host factors of susceptibility and resistance, physiological impairments, functional disabilities, and handicaps. Individual differences, even within a particular mental disorder, override commonalities and require tailored and unique combinations of interventions for each patient.

Adherence to the special needs and responses of the individual patient is appreciated in medical therapeutics, as even a cursory review of medical records and charts will reveal. While a common disorder such as congestive heart failure has a similar endpoint in terms of symptoms and signs, there are as many different treatment regimens for this disorder as there are individual differences in pathophysiology, lifestyle, compliance to treatment, allergies and responsiveness to drugs, and chronicity. Various types and doses of digitalis and diuretic preparations, a variety of diets, different levels and rates of ambulation and exercise, and different antihypertensive, antiarrhythmia, and coronary vasodilator drugs will be prescribed. Furthermore, even in patients who have similar regimens, the patterns by which the discrete components of the regimen are introduced over time will vary immensely across individuals. Another medical analogy is in the use of antibiotics in the treatment of infectious disease. While we know from studies in vitro that penicillin is bacteriocidal for pneumococci, variations in bacterial sensitivities and resistances, host factors, immune responses, and allergic reactions require the clinician to determine empirically the best antibiotic and the proper dose level and route of administration, along with needed ancillary treatments, for each patient.

There are a number of advantages of a modular approach to therapeutics that permit the clinician considerable latitude in designing a program to fit the specific needs of a given patient and family. The compleat clinician can draw from a wide variety of interventions—somatic as well as cognitive and behavioral— to maximize eclectic clout. The multimodal approach to treatment has been recognized and developed for some time by astute clinicians (Lazarus, 1974; Taylor, Liberman, & Agras, 1982). One advantage of a modular approach is its adaptability to the special conditions and constraints of local settings; for example, a particular mental health center might not have the personnel qualified to conduct communication skills training in family groups containing schizophrenic members, but it could provide an educational program about schizophrenia and its treatments. In this case, one of three modules from behavioral family therapy (Falloon *et al.*, 1984) could find application. Even large and comprehensive programs can be disassembled and refabricated into small modules for export to other settings where the treatment goals, patient population, and personnel are different. Modularization of treatment simplifies operational use and eases the learning and adoption of the methods by other professionals.

The modular approach to treatment also facilitates cost-effectiveness through the application of a minimum–maximum provision of flexible levels of intervention. The clinician provides only that module of treatment consistent with the realistic goals decided mutually by patient, relatives, and clinician. Additional modules can be delivered, if necessary, at later times when the needs of the patient (e.g., increased symptoms or prodromata to relapse), family (e.g., increased burden or loss of social support), or clinician (e.g., increased experience or training) dictate. This emphasis on efficiency in the provision of mental health services is consistent with the adherence of behavior therapy to realistic, feasible goal-setting and integration of treatment with assessment as an important point of departure.

A modular strategy for sex therapy has worked well in the framework of minimum—maximum services rendered (Annon, 1975). In behaviorally oriented therapy for sexual dysfunctions, a certain proportion of couples only need a small amount of information to correct their misbeliefs; for example, a single session with some reassurance and information can produce improvement in about 10% of cases. Depending on their assets and deficits, more severely disordered couples require more extensive counseling, advice, and reassurance; still others need more systematic behavioral interventions such as training in sensate focus or in the "squeeze technique" for premature ejaculation. A residual number of couples need the full, maximum array of services, including shaping of sexual behaviors plus communication skills and problem-solving training.

Similarly, behavioral family therapy of schizophrenia can also become more efficient by providing only as much as is needed and desired. Some families will do very well with just a few sessions of educational counseling or even a single anamnestic Camberwell Family Interview (Leff & Vaughn,

1985), which often yields an emotionally satisfying catharsis. Such families are likely to have good coping and communication skills to start with and an ill member with an excellent premorbid level of adjustment and a good and durable remission of symptoms. Many more families will have to go through a survival skills workshop or an extended educational program, perhaps sponsored by self-help or advocacy groups. It is possible that well-designed and professionally produced videocassettes could help to fill the need for family education, some of which could be carried out in the privacy of the home (Backer, Liberman, & Kuehnel, 1985). Families with fewer coping skills will have to go through intensive training in problem-solving and communication to obtain favorable outcomes. Some families will require a combination of modules, including individual therapy for some members and group social skills training for other, poorly functioning, members (Liberman, Falloon, & Wallace, 1984).

The remainder of this chapter describes the modular approach as it contributes to clinical decision trees. Examples are given for behavioral marital therapy, depressive disorders, and schizophrenia. A final section describes the adaptation of the modules comprising behavioral family therapy for the special subgroup of schizophrenics and their relatives who face chronicity and unremitting symptoms and disabilities.

A Modular Approach to Behavioral Marital Therapy

A decision tree, organized from initial assessment to termination, is shown in Figure 2-2 for treatment modules associated with behavioral marital therapy. If a couple needed only some abreaction and goal-setting and demonstrated no problems in recreational activities, reinforcement patterns, communication skills, problem-solving skills, child management, or sex, it is conceivable that the partners could quickly move to termination. On the other hand, the modules shown for use if one or more problem areas surfaced would take varying amounts of time, depending on resistance, clinician skill, and rate of progress. Perhaps a year or longer of weekly sessions might be required if the couple evidenced a large number of deficits and were not readily engaged in a therapeutic alliance. Moreover, the decision tree allows for a detour into treatment for a major mental disorder should one or both of the partners have depressive, anxiety, or psychotic symptoms.

At any point in the process of treatment, the couple and the responsible clinician can review progress to date and determine whether to continue or to terminate. If it is decided to continue working on additional goals, a treatment contract should be renegotiated to ensure that the couple and the therapist have a consensus on what is to be achieved and at what cost in time and effort. Once a satisfactory endpoint has been reached, the

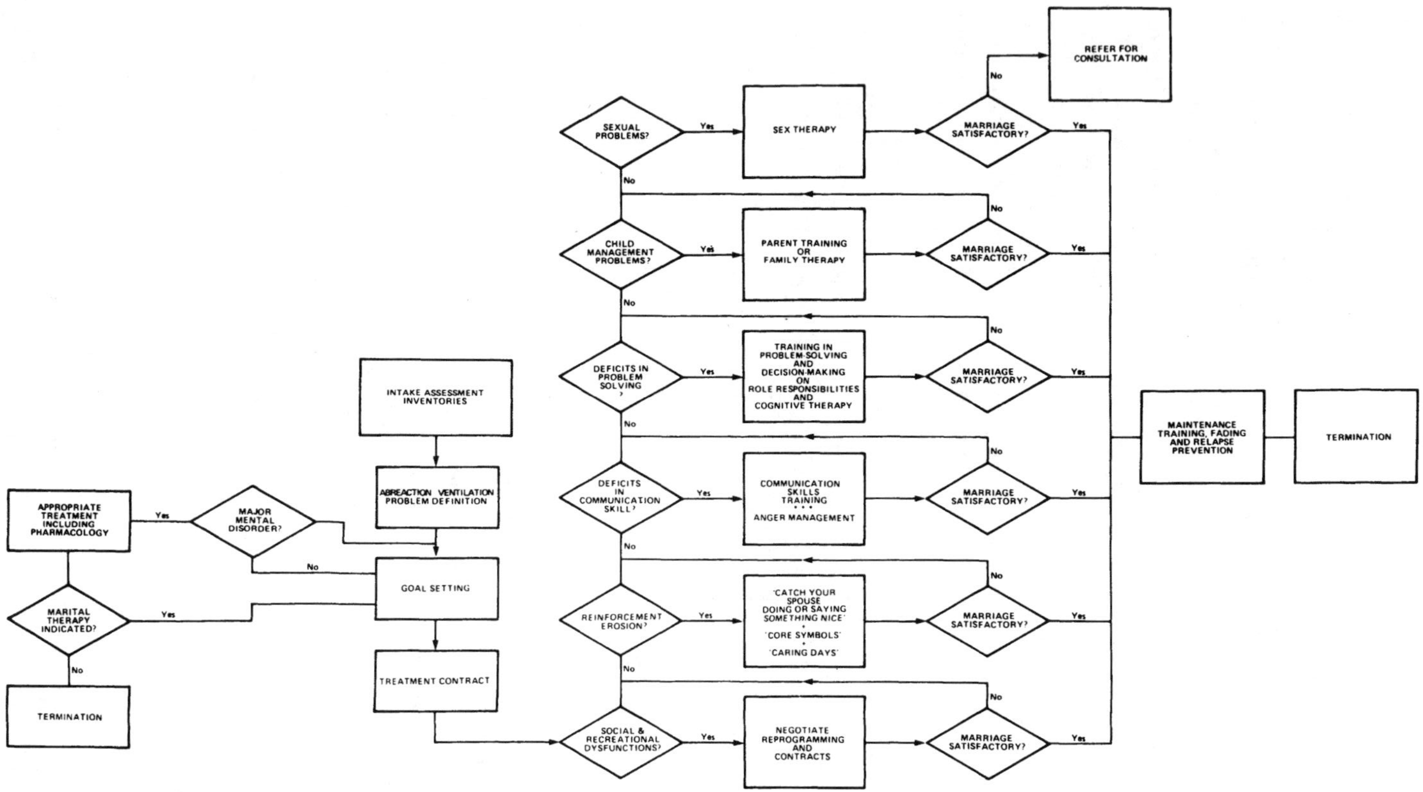

Figure 2-2. Clinical decision tree for behavioral marital therapy. The couple and clinician negotiate the desired amount of treatment modules through specific and recurrent goal-setting.

couple and clinician embark on a program of gradually less frequent contacts that are widely spaced and directed toward maintenance of improvement and generalization. In most cases, it is wise to terminate with the "door left ajar," encouraging a couple to return for booster sessions, annual checkups, or reevaluation and additional treatment at a later time.

A Modular Approach to Behavior Therapy of Depression

A flowchart depicting the decision points of a stepwise, minimum–maximum use of behavioral modules in the treatment of depression is shown in Figure 2-3. The discussion that follows would be equally applicable to patients who are being treated with behavior therapy alone or in combination with drugs. At each choice point in the progress of the patient through the behavior therapy modules, the therapist and patient should review the amount of improvement gained and decide whether additional therapy is needed. The informational resources the therapist can use in making treatment decisions include (1) the changes occurring in the patient's symptoms and other behavioral and social measures, and (2) the available techniques that have been reported to be helpful to depressed patients.

Behavioral Analysis Module

Before introducing more complex and time-consuming treatment modules, the therapist should begin with one to three sessions using a problem-solving focus. The patient is helped to view his or her problems, including symptoms, not as hopeless burdens but rather as challenges to cope with and overcome. The first step in this process is to identify the problems—the symptoms, functional impairments, and their antecedents and consequences. It is important for the therapist to help the patient to describe the problems in the patient's terms and then, afterward, to translate feelings and concerns into behavioral terms. The focus is on pinpointing what the patient is doing and saying and the environmental context. In a collaborative fashion and a spirit of inquiry, the patient and therapist together conduct a behavioral analysis by asking the following questions:

- Which problems are interfering most with the patient's functioning? (E.g., if the person is self-destructive, the immediate priority may be hospitalization and close supervision; if the person is about to lose a cherished job, then the immediate intervention may be intercession with employer or behavioral rehearsal of a scene with job supervisor aimed at obtaining sick leave.)
- Which problems are most responsible for the patient's being main-

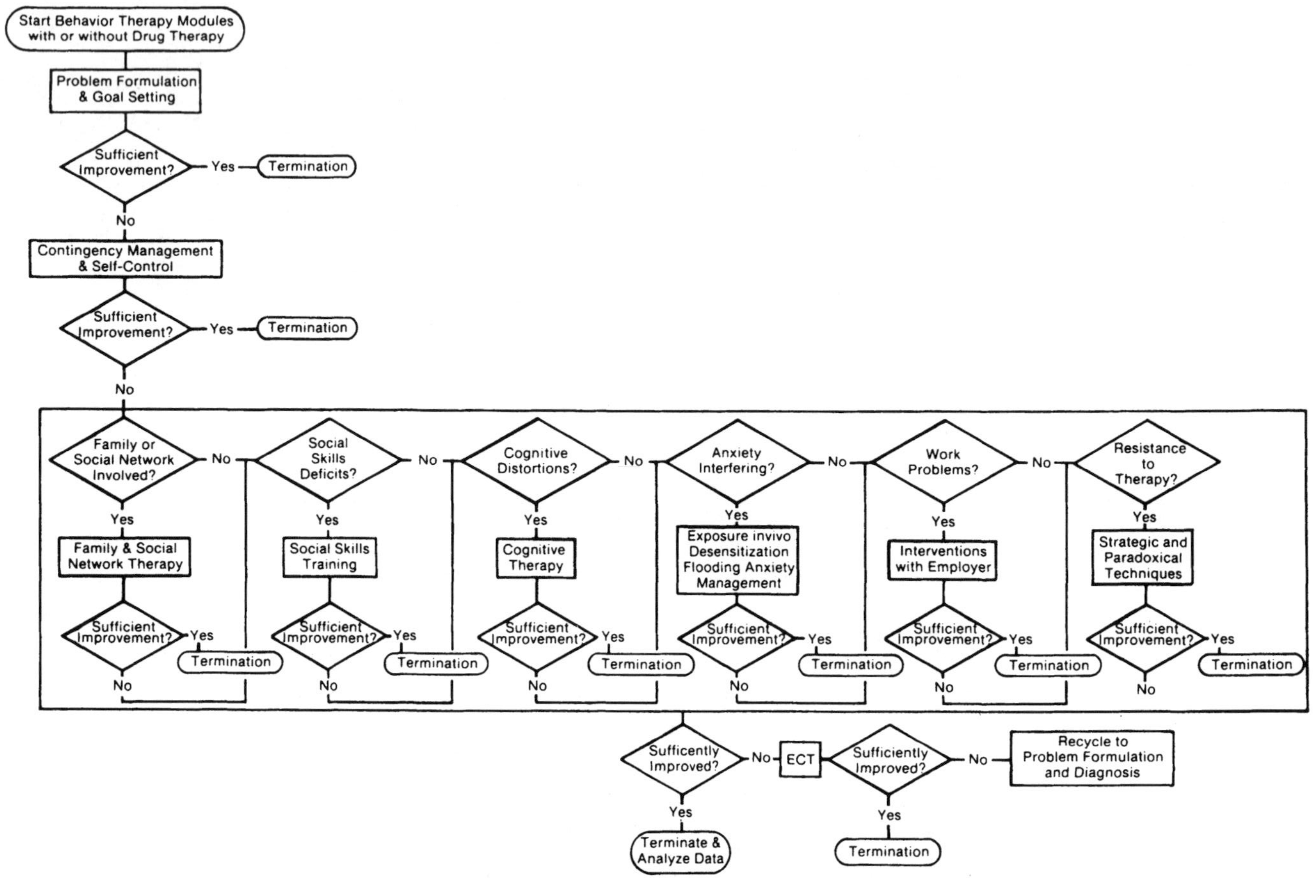

Figure 2-3. Clinical decision tree for treatment of depressive disorders. Modules of treatment are provided depending on the ongoing assessment of deficits, needs, and motivation. The sequence of modules in the diagram does not necessarily reflect priorities or any standardized temporal ordering of treatment. Improvement sufficient for termination can be based on multiple methods and sources of assessment, including the judgment of the patient and family.

tained in a state of depression? (E.g., a patient with chronic depression whose symptoms are being reinforced by a sympathetic relative may have immediate need for intervention with the relative to change the reinforcement contingencies.)

• Which assets, if strengthened, can serve as a wedge toward breaking the depressive cycle? (E.g., if a person has had good social relationships that have been recently dormant, the therapist may initially aim at social skills training that reconstitutes these relationships.)

• What are the most practical means that can produce the desired changes in this individual? (E.g., changing the environment or the self-attitudes of the client may be most helpful.)

Once some problem definition has occurred, the therapist helps the patient set goals for the therapy. The therapist asks the patient for possible alternative behaviors to those currently producing an impasse. The therapist also suggests alternatives for the patient's evaluation. Questions are asked such as, "What would you like to do that you're not now doing?" "How would you like your everyday life to be different from the way it is now?" "What changes would you like to make in your routines and relationships?" "How might you cope with the problems confronting you?"

Problem formulation and goal-setting alone can provide the necessary impetus for some patients to cope better and get symptomatic improvement sufficient for termination. This evaluation module can be carried out in a total of three to seven sessions, including the initial visit. It should be noted that the median number of visits made by outpatients to community mental health centers around the country is six; thus, it is important for efficiency of service delivery to begin with a module that provides a modicum of intervention capable of being utilized by most patients. A brief module, such as the one just described, is obviously cost-effective and will often be sufficient with patients who come to therapy with many assets and good premorbid adjustment.

Since depressive symptoms are almost always influenced by the patient's interpersonal relationships, this evaluation and goal-setting module should include at least some presence and participation by family members or close friends. With this approach, these relationships can be more readily assessed for their actual and potential impact on the designated patient; also, the therapist can solicit the collaboration of friends and family as mediators in the therapeutic process.

Contingency Management and Self-Control Modules

For those patients who need additional therapy beyond the problem-identification and goal-setting phase, the therapist can use attention and praise as contingent reinforcers for adaptive verbalizations during the therapy session and for reports of attempting homework assignments between therapy sessions. The therapist will be able to use the already established positive therapeutic alliance in a contingent manner to strengthen assets and to help the patient accomplish goals that were selected during the earlier problem-formulating module. Family members' contingent attention and responsiveness can also be interlocked in a natural way. If the patient is hospitalized because of functional incapacity or suicidal risk, contingencies can be used that stem from hospital privileges and from social reinforcement by the entire interdisciplinary staff. By using graded assignments for adaptive behavior coupled with positive feedback, the therapist ensures that instructions are given clearly, specifically, affirmatively, and with the structuring of positive expectations for success. At times, this must be accomplished in subtle ways, including the use of paradoxical instructions. Shaping is also kept in mind as this module progresses.

While the therapist is using the therapeutic relationship as a contingent reinforcer for the reestablishment of positive conversations and activities as alternatives to depressive behaviors, the patient can also be taught to use self-control methods to increase desired behaviors and interactions. One such method is to make the patient's performance of highly probable behavior (e.g., withdrawal to bed, smoking, being alone) contingent on the patient's first engaging in positive, desirable, but less likely self-statements or activities. Another method is self-monitoring, self-evaluation, and self-reinforcement with an emphasis on monitoring positive events and setting realistic, attainable behavioral goals that would be expected to reduce depressive affect. This module might continue as long as good progress is being made, with termination for satisfactory improvement occurring after perhaps two to ten sessions.

Behavioral Family Therapy Modules

Family therapy would be appropriate for patients who have not made progress after a few sessions of contingency management and self-control and whose family interactions might conceivably be maintaining the depressive behaviors. Relatives who are critical or emotionally overinvolved with the patient can be ascertained through careful interviewing (Vaughn & Leff, 1976) and would be predicted to place the patient at high risk for relapse. Identification of high expressed emotion in a family member can point to the need for family therapy.

The family or marital therapy itself can proceed along several flexible levels of intervention, ranging from simple instructions to relatives to provide differential attention for adaptive and depressive behaviors to such instructions plus social and recreational activities, communication skills training, problem-solving training, and contingency contracting. Thus, the implementation of family therapy with a depressed person might involve one or more of the submodules inherent in this form of treatment. The use of minimum–maximum levels of intervention in behavioral family therapy was illustrated by Liberman and Roberts (1976), who detailed a case study with a depressed woman.

Other Modules for Depressive Disorders

A variety of other behavioral methods (e.g., cognitive therapy, anxiety management techniques, social skills training, and paradoxical or strategic methods) have been well-described in the literature, and varying amounts of evidence support their efficacy. The decision to utilize any one of these techniques would be made on the basis of cost, intrusiveness, acceptability to the patient, insufficient progress from previous modules, and information regarding specific deficits of the patient that could be remediated by the technique.

The decision points for these modules are shown in Figure 2-3 as having equal significance; however, only the accumulation of empirical experience with large numbers of depressed patients can indicate how often and how valuable any one of these techniques might be. For example, while it appears that a sizable majority of depressed patients demonstrate cognitive distortions, it does not necessarily follow that all such patients would require a full course of specific cognitive therapy for relieving their depression. Some of these patients might improve sufficiently with five sessions of ventilation, catharsis, and problem-formulating and goal-setting. Others might improve sufficiently with the addition of a few sessions of contingency management. When a patient continues to show cognitive distortions and depressive symptoms, even after initial treatment modules, then the use of cognitive therapy would be more strongly indicated. Similarly, the use of the other techniques currently in vogue for depression might not be required unless the patient does not respond well to initial treatment. It should be clear that a modular approach to behavior therapy for depression offers a more stringent test of the efficacy of any one technique than does the use of a variety of these techniques from the very start of a patient's professional contact. As time passes and experience with a modular strategy accumulates, both individual clinicians and the research community can "shake down" the various modules and adapt and evolve new techniques that can be expected to have greater impact on depressive behaviors.

Strategic or paradoxical therapy techniques deserve a special note because they can be employed together with other more straightforward behavior therapies to enhance cooperation and commitment and increase compliance with instructions and assignments. As we develop a wider body of techniques for depression, we learn that the discovery of what people need to do to overcome their problems is not the most difficult clinical task: *getting* people to do what they need to do is the most difficult task.

We now possess a group of prescriptive methods that, if followed properly by the patients, can yield meaningful improvement. But, as any experienced behavior therapist will admit, motivating patients usually provides the greatest challenge to therapeutic acumen.

A Modular Approach to Treatment of Schizophrenia

Schizophrenia, the most complex and poorly understood of the major mental disorders, poses the largest challenge to the behaviorally oriented clinician. Only recently have behavioral therapists designed treatment interventions that have had more than limited and temporary effects on the core psychotic symptoms and associated disabilities of schizophrenia (Falloon, 1985; Paul & Lentz, 1977; Wallace & Liberman, 1985). To offer a rational treatment strategy for schizophrenic disorders, interactions between drug and psychosocial interventions must be considered. Optimal targets for therapeutic leverage, as delineated by the conceptual framework shown in Figure 2-1 above, will vary according to the characteristics of the patient, family emotional climate, and stage of illness. The complexity and comprehensiveness of treatments for schizophrenia—including behavioral family interventions—can be systematically and sequentially organized by a modular approach to service delivery.

In Figure 2-4 is outlined a clinical decision tree for determining how much of what treatment module to consider for any given patient at various points in time in the course of illness. For convenience, the decision-making process begins with an acute episode, which could be a patient's first episode or one of many in a pattern of recurrence. The key to effective use of this flowchart is to match flexible levels of intervention with a comprehensive and iterative process of assessment. Much as a diabetic repeatedly measures urine for traces of sugar, the behavioral clinician must fabricate measurement technology that can be used in an ongoing fashion.

Once the acute episode is successfully treated, the choice of treatment modules is determined by assessing the patient's work and social skills deficits and the family environment. If the family is high on expressed emotion, some form of family intervention is indicated. Family intervention comprises a set of submodules that are each targeted at different needs of the patient and his or her support network.

The multifaceted behavioral family therapy for the management of schizophrenia encompasses a wide array of therapeutic modules or components. These include case management, antipsychotic drug therapy, emergency services, vocational rehabilitation, social skills training, and advocacy services. Depending on the individual's severity of illness and the coping capacities of the family, the actual number of modules provided

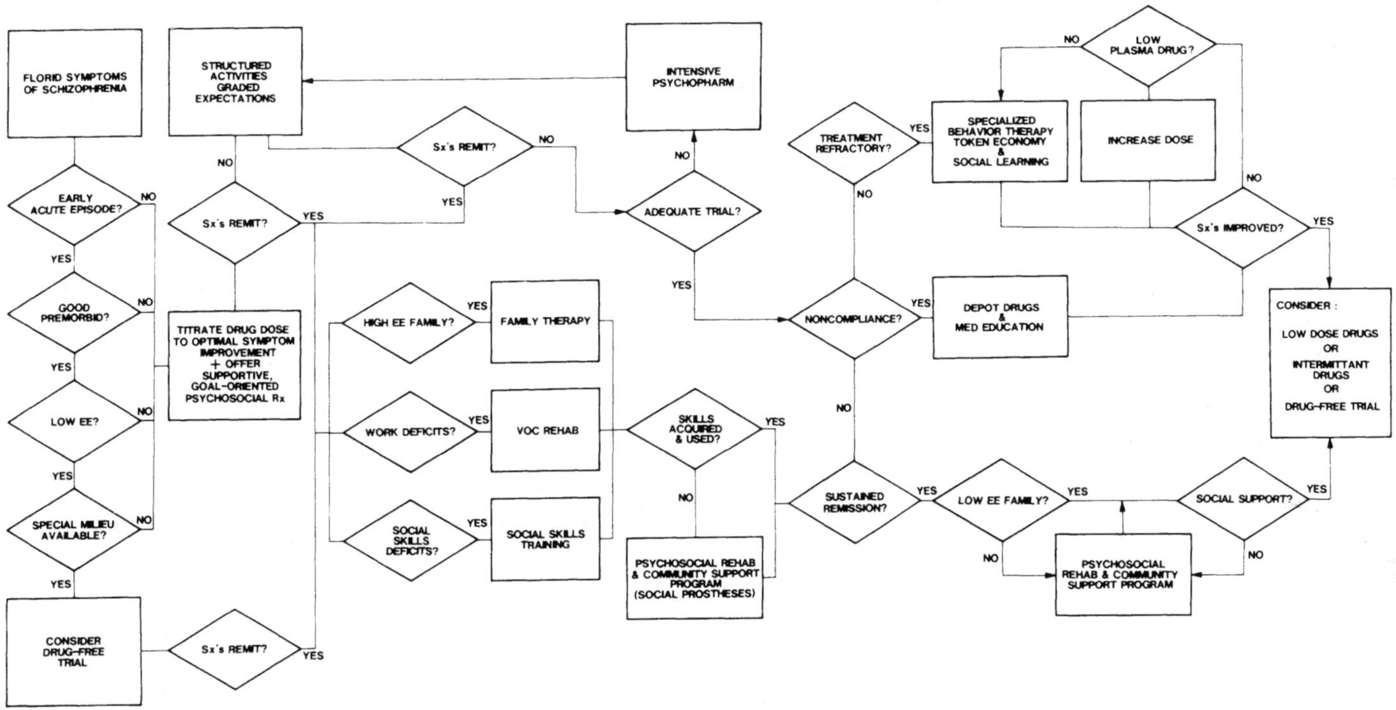

Figure 2-4. Clinical decision tree for treatment of schizophrenic disorders. The types and timing of drug and psychosocial treatments are modularized for delivery to patients based on initial and ongoing assessment over the course of the disorder.

may vary. Even with a single patient and family, the extensiveness and intensity of treatment via modules may change from one point in the course of illness to another. But what type of adaptation of the overall program of family intervention is necessary for situations in which a patient is continously hospitalized for lengthy periods because of unremitting symptoms and serious behavioral deficits and excesses?

Adapting Family Interventions for the Chronically Disabled

Behavioral family therapy with psychiatric patients who periodically experience acute exacerbations of their symptoms emphasizes modifying the family environment to reduce ambient stress and likelihood of relapse. However, when working with families containing a chronically and severely ill member, who has either been continuously hospitalized for a long time or is floridly symptomatic, the goals of family therapy must be modified, with intervention modules tailored to the needs of each specific family.

Conducting behavioral family therapy with chronic rather than acute patients may involve several practical considerations. Family sessions must frequently be conducted in the hospital and not at home. Conducting therapy in the hospital can present severe logistical problems, since families often live a great distance from their hospitalized ill relative. For example, one family with five members traveled three hours every other week to participate in family sessions at the hospital. All the members of this family commented on the strain of the commuting, particularly the mother who was in poor health.

Since chronic patients are often refractory to neuroleptic therapy and spend proportionally more time in the hospital and less time with their families, any favorable impact of family therapy on the patient's clinical condition will be less than with patients who achieve remissions. Even when a patient lives at home but is continuously symptomatic, the therapist cannot expect a significant improvement in psychopathology following family therapy, unless modules are provided to increase social and living skills. Severe and chronic symptomatology that is refractory to psychotropic medications and customary psychosocial interventions will usually not be dramatically affected by family therapy, although the patient and relatives may experience other benefits from the therapy. This is illustrated by a couple who recently completed a half year of behavioral family management. The husband had a 15-year history of chronic schizophrenia characterized by intermittent hospitalizations and persistent auditory and visual hallucinations, but he was able to live with his wife and child in the community. At the end of the therapy, the husband's symptomatology had not changed, although he was now able to manage a regular volunteer community job. The family felt that the therapy had helped them cope more effectively with his illness and the accompanying stress. He also no longer denied that he had a disease, stating instead "I need all the help I can get."

Family therapy with highly symptomatic patients often requires the therapist to deal effectively with socially disturbing behaviors in the immediacy of the treatment session. This provides a good opportunity for the therapist to model methods for interacting successfully with an ill person. For example, the schizophrenic son in one family had severe attentional deficits, to the point of asking irrelevant questions, drifting off while others were speaking, and forgetting to do his homework. The therapists gave the parents instructions and modeled how to establish and maintain the son's attention. These instructions included asking the patient to repeat back what he had just heard, establishing eye contact when speaking, cutting off irrelevant statements by either verbal statement or nonverbal means (e.g., tapping him on the shoulder), and giving positive reinforcement for attending well. Attention-focusing techniques, if learned by relatives, can alleviate some of the frustration felt by family members, who may blame the patient for his inattention or withdraw from future interactions because of the patient's unresponsiveness.

Conducting family therapy with a symptomatic patient may also require the therapist to actively demonstrate strategies for dealing with "crazy talk" in the family session. This involves managing the fine line between being responsive to the patient and reinforcing his or her bizarre verbalizations. In one family, the son had an elaborate delusional system including numerous delusions of reference, person, and persecution. When he shifted the conversation to an unrelated topic containing delusional material, the therapist interrupted him by asking him to "hold on to (his) thought for a minute." The conversation was then redirected to the original topic. Family members were also taught how to acknowledge the patient's feelings of fear arising from his paranoid thoughts, without endorsing his belief system. The analogy of phobias, a relatively common problem, was used to convey to one unsympathetic family member the importance of accepting a person's feelings when one does not fully agree with the basis for those feelings.

The attentional dysfunctions present in many floridly symptomatic patients may necessitate briefer therapy sessions, and the amount of material learned may be limited for the ill relative. In addition, the possibility that the therapy is stressful for the patient and may even worsen his or her symptoms must be considered. At times, a temporary or permanent cessation of therapy sessions with the patient may be required. In such cases, family members may continue in therapy without their ill relative, in order to improve their interactional skills for the time they do spend with the patient.

The reduced level of interaction between chronic, institutionalized psychiatric patients and their families necessitates a shift in the goals of family therapy. When working with families of an episodically ill member, the basic goal of therapy involves lessening tension and conflict via improved communication and problem-solving skills. However, families with a chronic patient usually need less problem-solving training since the patient and family spend so little time together. On the other hand, the harsh reality of the patient's unremitting illness poses a challenge to the therapist who must deal with some families' unwillingness to accept the prognosis and their unrealistic expectations that the patient engage in more normal behaviors. Increasing the family's acceptance of a patient's chronic illness becomes a major therapeutic goal. This helps family members to establish reasonable performance expectations on their ill relative, to be aware of and reinforce tiny improvements, and to gain hope from longer term prospects for change.

One fruitful avenue for working with chronic disability is to place an increased emphasis on the educational module in the family therapy. In addition to the initial presentation of information and handouts, this requires continuously recycling the educational material throughout all stages of the therapy. One useful way the therapist can assess whether family members have accepted the chronicity of their relative's illness is by observing the incidence of unrealistic expectations on the patient. Such demands can be intercepted by the therapist, who may inquire of the family member whether any of the patient's core symptoms (e.g., memory deficits, distractibility) might prevent him or her from complying adequately with their expectations. When working with chronically ill patients who live at home, one must guard against the possibility that family acceptance of the illness may reinforce the patient's "sick role" when the patient is faced with tasks he or she is capable of doing. The therapist can help the family arrive at a suitable compromise that structures some of the patient's time but is minimally demanding and stressful.

While families with chronically ill patients may need less training in problem-solving skills since they spend less time together, the need for some problem-solving typically still exists. When a patient has difficulty participating fully in the problem-solving process, the therapist can teach family members other techniques for managing a stressful situation. For example, one hospitalized patient repeatedly telephoned home every day, sometimes as frequently as 15 or 20 times. His parents were upset about the number of calls and conflicted with each other about how often they should respond to them. With the patient's acquiescence, the family was helped to establish a contingency contract in which the parents would respond to only the first of the patient's calls within a specified time period. The patient continued to telephone but not as often as before; more importantly, the parents no longer felt ambivalent about whether they should respond to a call, and their emotional burden was relieved.

Families who have a chronically ill member, with dim chances of recovery, can experience despair leading to therapeutic nihilism. Relatives may question the utility of engaging in therapy that is unlikely to improve the condition of the most disturbed member. The therapist can employ several strategies to add meaning to the therapy for the family members. Despite the minimal effect of the family therapy on the patient's psychopathology, the quality and pleasantness of patient–family interactions can substantially improve through the development of effective communication skills. By enhancing the relationship between patients and their relatives, the role of family members as advocates for the patients is maximized. In the event that the patient subsequently experiences a partial or full remission, the relatives are galvanized to take suitable action for rehabilitative services.

Sometimes a patient's illness is so disturbing to a relative that the latter is unable to enjoy any interaction with the patient, dwelling instead on the misfortunes. In such cases, it is often helpful to encourage an existential–humanistic attitude, wherein the tragedy of the illness is acknowledged, but at the same time the patient's own humanity—his or her capacity for love, curiosity, sadness, and anger—is recognized and appreciated. Helping families to see beyond their relative's illness to the actual person, and to enjoy whatever limited relationship they can have, will enable them to overcome their sense of futility and to make the most of the limited time they can spend together. Families may need to be reminded that their relative *has*, rather than *is*, an illness, and has sensitive feelings as we all do.

Moreover, recent studies have revealed a more hopeful and optimistic long-term prognosis for even chronic and disabled schizophrenics, albeit requiring 15 or more years. Restrained optimism can propel family therapy past the obstacles of despair and temporary impasses. The long-term view can also nurture the therapist, preventing burnout and disillusionment and maintaining a measured but persistent engagement with the patient and relatives.

Families with a chronic patient who are engaged in family therapy need to be informed that the therapy is for the whole family and that members who are not ill may expect to learn more effective ways of coping with the stresses they experience in having an ill relative. Thus, the therapy is not strictly "patient-oriented"; instead, it focuses on the entire family and seeks to improve the daily functioning of all members who participate.

SUMMARY

Behavioral family therapy has made remarkable strides since the 1960s when pioneers such as Patterson, Stuart, and Liberman first demonstrated the value of applying behavioral learning principles to the assessment and treatment of psychiatric problems in the family context. It is a testimony to the reinforcement received by these pioneering clinical researchers that they are still actively involved in clinical and research work in the same areas almost 20 years later. The vitality of behavioral family therapy is no better documented than by the content and thrust the present volume, which spans most of the major psychiatric disorders and several areas in which psychological distress causes impediments to social functioning.

Advances have been made in behavioral assessment and in the clarification of the specific benefits and limitations of behavioral family therapy. New methods have been introduced that utilize a wider range of modalities and draw inspiration from multidimensional concepts for understanding psychiatric disorders. It is recognized that the interventions inherent in behavioral approaches must be designed to improve the coping, self-efficacy, and competencies of all members of the family group to provide protection against the stress and vulnerability that produce symptoms and disability. The affective and attitudinal atmosphere of a family, its communication patterns and problem-solving skills, and the size and quality of its social network may moderate the impact of stressors or potentiators on the individual who has the psychobiological vulnerability for a mental disorder. Because of the complex influences bearing on the course and outcome of major mental disorders, it is likely that no single treatment approach will prevent relapse or remediate disability; rather, a modular approach to treating specific problems may provide a more cost-effective and rational therapy for our patients and their relatives.

ACKNOWLEDGMENT

This chapter was prepared with the partial support of NIMH Grant No. 30911 to the Mental Health Clinical Research Center for the Study of Schizophrenia.

REFERENCES

Annon, J. L. (1975). *The behavioral treatment of sexual problems*. Honolulu: Enabling Systems.

Backer, T., Liberman, R. P., & Kuehnel, T. G. (1985). *Living on the edge: An educational video for families coping with schizophrenia*. Available from Clinical Research Center for Schizophrenia and Psychiatric Rehabilitation, Box A, Camarillo, CA 93011.

Falloon, I. R. H. (1985). *Family management of schizophrenia: A study of clinical, social, family and economic benefits*. Baltimore: Johns Hopkin University Press.

Falloon, I. R. H., Boyd, J., & McGill, C. (1984). *Family care of schizophrenia*. New York: Guilford Press.

Falloon, I. R. H., & Liberman, R. P. (1983). Interactions between drug and psychosocial therapy in schizophrenia. *Schizophrenia Bulletin, 9*, 543–554.

Hirschfeld, R. M. A., Klerman, G. L., & Clayton, P. J. (1983). Assessing personality: Effects of the depressive state on train measurement. *American Journal of Psychiatry, 140*, 695–699.

Jacobson, N. S. (1984). The modification of cognitive processes in behavioral marital therapy: Integrating cognitive and behavioral intervention strategies. In K. Halweg & N. S. Jacobson (Eds.), *Marital interaction: Analysis and modification* (pp. 220–241). New York: Guilford Press.

Lazarus, A. A. (1974). Multimodal behavior therapy. In C. M. Franks & G. T. Wilson (Eds.), *Annual review of behavior therapy* (pp. 151–224). Washington, DC: American Psychiatric Press.

Leff, J. P., Knipers, L., Berkowitz, R., Eberlein-Vries, R., & Sturgeon, D. (1982). A controlled trial of social intervention in the families of schizophrenic patients. *British Journal of Psychiatry, 141*, 121–134.

Leff, J. P., & Vaughn, C. E. (1985). *Expressed emotion in families*. New York: Guilford Press.

Liberman, R. P. (1978). Behavior therapy in psychiatry. In J. P. Brady & H. K. Brodie (Eds.), *Controversy in psychiatry* (pp. 429–467). Philadelphia: Saunders.

Liberman, R. P. (1982). Social factors in schizophrenia. In L. Grinspoon (Ed.), *Psychiatry 1982 annual review* (pp. 97–111). Washington, DC: American Psychiatric Press.

Liberman, R. P., Falloon, I. R. H., & Aitchison, R. A. (1984). Multiple family therapy for schizophrenics: A behavioral approach. *Psychosocial Rehabilitation Journal, 4*, 60–77.

Liberman, R. P., Falloon, I. R. H., & Wallace, C. J. (1984). Drug-psychosocial interactions in the treatment of schizophrenia. In M. Mirabi (Ed.), *The chronically mentally ill: Research and services* (pp. 175–212). New York: SP Medical & Scientific Books.

Liberman, R. P., Nuechterlein, K. H., & Wallace, C. J. (1982). Social skills training and the nature of schizophrenia. In J. P. Curran & P. M. Monti (Eds.), *Social skills training: A practical handbook for assessment and treatment* (pp. 5–56). New York: Guilford Press.

Liberman, R. P., & Roberts, J. (1976). Contingency management of neurotic depression and marital disharmony. In H. Eysenck (Ed.), *Case studies in behavior therapy* (pp. 207–226). London: Routledge & Kegan Paul.

O'Leary, K. D., & Carr, E. G. (1982). Behavior therapy for children: Outcome and evaluation. In G. T. Wilson & C. M. Franks (Eds.) *Contemporary behavior therapy: Conceptual and empirical foundations* (pp. 425–477). New York: Guilford Press.

Patterson, G. R. (1982). *Coercive family process* Eugene, OR: Castalia.

Patterson, G. R. (1985). Beyond technology: The next stage in the development of parent training. In L. L'Abate (Ed.) *Handbook of family psychology and psychotherapy* (pp. 431–457) Chicago: Dow Jones-Irwin.

Paul, G. L., & Lentz, R. (1977). *Psychosocial treatment of the chronic mental patient*. Cambridge, MA: Harvard University Press.

Presley, A. S., Grubb, A. B., & Semple, D. (1982). Predictors of successful rehabilitation in long-stay patients. *Acta Psychiatrica Scandinavica, 66*, 83–88.

Taylor, C. B., Liberman, R. P., & Agras, W. S. (1982). Treatment evaluation and behavior therapy. In J. Lewis & G. Usdin (Eds.), *Treatment planning in psychiatry* (pp. 151–224). Washington, DC: American Psychiatric Press.

Vaughn, C. E., & Leff, J. P. (1976). The influence of family and social factors on the course of psychiatric illness: A comparison of schizophrenic and depressed neurotic patients. *British Journal of Psychiatry, 129*, 125–137.

Vaughn, C. E., Snyder, K. S., Jones, S., Falloon, I. R. H., & Liberman, R. P. (1982). Family factors in schizophrenic relapse: A replication. *Schizophrenia Bulletin, 8*, 425–426.

Wahler, R. G., Leske, G., & Rogers, E. S. (1979). The insular family: A deviance support mechanism for oppositional children. In L. A. Hamerlynck (Ed.), *Behavioral systems for the developmentally disabled* (pp. 72–123). New York: Brunner/Mazel.

Wallace, C. J., & Liberman, R. P. (1985). Social skills training for patients with schizophrenia: A controlled clinical trial. *Psychiatry Research, 15*, 239–247.

3

Indications for Family, Marital, and Sexual Therapy

MICHAEL CROWE
Maudsley Hospital, London

Except among single-minded practitioners for whom the only solution for all problems is their own chosen therapeutic approach, the question must sometimes arise as to which form of therapy is appropriate for a given problem. In my own work setting, in which my units provide inpatient and outpatient psychiatric treatment as well as specialized family, marital, and sexual therapy, the question is constantly arising. Although sometimes one may make a wrong choice, the cases in this setting appear by and large to be appropriately assigned to the different clinics. This chapter is an attempt to provide a rational basis for making such decisions; it draws on the literature and on the observed outcome of therapy in the different modalities.

RADICAL OR CONSERVATIVE FAMILY APPROACHES

In carrying out family and marital therapy, one may take a radical or a conservative approach (Crowe, 1983). In the radical approach, the position is taken that all problems and symptoms must be seen as arising from the systemic interaction among family members and that such symptoms or problems usually fulfill a purpose for the family: for example, stabilizing it or keeping it together. In the conservative approach, on the other hand, the symptom or problem is seen as an entity in its own right, caused by individual and environmental factors; the family may indeed be an important part of that environment, and, where an interpersonal dimension can be clearly seen, family therapy may be used to help solve the problem. A particular illustration of the radical–conservative dichotomy is given by family approaches to schizophrenia. In the volume edited by McFarlane (1983), this contrast is highlighted by the approaches of Whittaker and Madanes on the one hand and Falloon on the other. The first two authors work from the assumption that schizophrenia arises from faulty family communication and should be resolved by family therapy. Falloon, on the other hand, assumes the presence of an illness of unknown and probably multifactorial etiology for which improving family problem-solving and providing information to relatives can improve the prognosis and reduce the relapse rate.

The approach advocated in the present chapter is essentially a conservative one, although at times pure family therapy techniques will be described. The family therapy approaches are used not as part of an indivisible systems philosophy in which individual factors are ignored, but as a useful adjunct to a therapeutic plan that may involve individual counseling sessions, conjoint marital sessions, and family sessions for different cases at different stages of therapy. Allied to this mixed and conservative approach to family, marital, and sexual therapy is a belief that most therapeutic interventions should be seen as helping individuals and families to adjust to problems rather than as providing a radical cure. Thus, a couple with a sexual problem that responded to therapy would be informed at the end of treatment that the problem might well recur, and they might be given specific instructions to follow in such a case. For example, in the actual case of a couple who had experienced an almost complete resolution of secondary impotence in four sessions of Masters and Johnson therapy, the problem recurred during the three-month follow-up period. Without consulting the therapist, they used once again the ban on intercourse and the progression from sensate focus to genital sensate focus; by the time of follow-up, intercourse was again satisfactory in frequency and quality.

Thus, we are not expecting "cure" from marital, sexual, or family therapy, just as we should probably not expect individual behavioral, psychoanalytic, or drug-orientated approaches to cure the individuals in treatment; however, we should see therapy as a means of improving adjustment and making the best of one's abilities, taking into account both personal and environmental limitations.

THE ECLECTIC APPROACH

It will become clear in the course of this chapter that the approach being put forward is not only conservative in treating systems theory and family hypotheses as only one of many ways of understanding the origin of symptoms and problems: it is also eclectic in two senses. First, it is eclectic in using various combinations of persons as the therapeutic system: for example, a problem of jealousy might be dealt with by seeing the individual who is jealous, the marital couple, or the couple together with other family members. Second, within the family or marital therapy itself, the approach is eclectic in choice of technique: one might give a couple behavioral training in sexual or communication technique and, in the same session, a paradoxical injunction to maintain the problem in order to stabilize the relationship. It may well be that the choice of which system to work on (individual, couple, or family) is not as important as it seems. There is some evidence that improvement in one subsystem can have important therapeutic effects in the rest of the family. For example, in one family, the improvement achieved in the parents' marital interaction was followed by a great improvement in their daughter's school work. In a study by Bennun (1985), it was shown, surprisingly, that one could achieve equally good results in improved marital adjustment by marital therapy with the couple together or by similar therapy with only one spouse, who was instructed to take home the therapist's suggestions and discuss them with the spouse who had not attended.

Thus, the choice of family, marital, or individual therapy may to some extent be arbitrary. Much will then depend on the preferences of the therapist or the therapeutic team involved. There are those who are intimidated by the idea of a family therapy format, while others are uncomfortable with individual therapy. Still others would be willing to carry out either type of therapy. However, in spite of the above considerations, it does seem that in the majority of cases a particular suitability for family, marital, sexual, or individual therapy exists and that an appropriate choice of therapeutic format may make problems soluble that would otherwise remain intractable.

EARLIER ACCOUNTS OF THE INDICATIONS FOR FAMILY AND MARITAL THERAPY

It is a curious fact that very few articles and books have been published in recent years on the indications for marital and family therapy. A scan through copies of the *Journal of Family Therapy* and *Family Process* between 1980 and 1985 showed no papers on the subject, and there are no contributions to the *Handbook of Family Therapy* (Gurman & Kniskern, 1981a) on the indications for family therapy. One may speculate on explanations for this state of affairs. It is possible that all the contributors to these publications are convinced "radical" family therapists (see above) who feel that all problems should be dealt with in conjoint family therapy whenever possible. However, if this is the case, it would be unfortunate for the future of family therapy, since therapies that depend on radical enthusiasm in the absence of evidence for efficacy are vulnerable to the swings of fashion and may become historical curiosities like animal magnetism and phrenology.

A more plausible explanation for the lack of recent articles on the subject is the daunting nature of the task itself. In order to research the indications and contraindications for a form of therapy, one needs (1) an agreed-upon method of discriminating among presenting problems so as to distinguish those that will respond from those that will not and (2) an agreed-upon measure of outcome to use as the dependent variable. Neither of these criteria is present except to a very small degree in the case of family therapy.

The problem of family "diagnosis" or taxonomy has been recognized since the early days of family therapy. Many attempts have been made to formulate an effective typology of families, perhaps the most successful being the Circumplex model (Olson, Russell, & Sprenkle, 1983) and the Beavers systems model (Beavers & Voeller, 1983). The two models have in common two important variables in family functioning, namely adaptability (with its opposite, rigidity) and enmeshment (with its opposite, disengagement). Most family therapists would agree that the aim of therapy in most cases is to shift the family toward greater adaptability and toward limited disengagement. However, there is very little in the writings of either group to indicate which types of family are most or least suitable for family therapy.

Skynner (1974), in a valiant attempt at linking family typology, Kleinian theory, and indications for treatment, suggested that family therapy was suitable for (1) families with severe deprivation, disadvantage, and disorganization who use "paranoid–schizoid" defense mechanisms and are somewhat similar to Minuchin's *Families of the Slums* (Minuchin, Montalvo, Guerney, Rosman, & Shumer, 1967); and (2) families with fairly good communication and "ego strength." He felt that families with an intermediate level of functioning, for instance, those with quite rigid family structure and unresolved "depressive" defence mechanisms, were less suitable for family work and should be treated instead by various forms of individual intervention. The notion of a "sandwich" of suitability is an interesting one, but as with the work of Olson and Beavers, the difficulty is in finding a reliable way of distinguishing families from each other by the rather vague and subjective criteria that Skynner suggests.

Most authorities use a simpler but less satisfactory classification of families, not by the type of family interaction observed, but by the type of problem presented by the symptomatic member. Thus, Selvini Palazzoli and her team refer to "families in schizophrenic transaction" (Selvini Palazzoli, Boscolo, Cecchin, & Prata, 1978). Other workers talk about families of delinquents, families of anorexics, families of alcoholics, etc. Although this is unsatisfactory from a family therapy point of view, because families whose members display specific problems are not necessarily similar in other ways, at least such a classification has the advantage of simplicity in assigning families to different prognostic groups. A number of authors have used a "symptomatic" classification to distinguish between families suitable or unsuitable for family therapy (see below).

The second difficulty in determining indications and contraindications for family therapy is that of measuring the outcome of therapy. Outcome studies have been reviewed by Gurman and Kniskern (1981b), and the problem, as with family typology, is that the outcome measures themselves are unsatisfactory. Symptom removal, the most common criterion used, is quite helpful, especially as it allows easy comparison between family therapy and other modes of treatment. However, most family therapists would postulate that the aim of therapy is not simply symptom removal but also the more nebulous concept of system change. There are very few suitable measures of system change. The Olson and Beavers measures of family interaction mentioned above may be adaptable to produce measures sensitive to the changes induced by family therapy. There are other measures of family interaction that can be used; some are based on self-report, others on more indirect methods such as repertory grids, others on analysis of recorded observation of family interaction (Loader, 1985), and still others on global and subjective impressions of clinical progress. None has so far achieved adequate reliability and validity, and, in a recent study on family therapy in anorexia nervosa (Russell, 1985), it was decided to use weight gain in the identified patient as the main outcome criterion in preference to any measure of family functioning.

In spite of the difficulties in discriminating among presenting problems in family therapy and in measuring the outcome of therapy, some authors have presented their own views on indications and contraindications for family therapy. Ackerman (1966) was probably the first to do this, and in some ways his recommendations have stood the test of time. They are mostly of a practical nature. For instance, he suggested that family therapy is indicated where problems in one individual seem to reflect problems in the family as a whole and where the identified patient spends individual sessions talking about a family member. His contraindications included situations in which a family is breaking up; some family members are unavailable geographically; the behavior of the identified patient would prevent effective communication in therapy; there is lying in the family as a regular event; there is an organic cause for the symptoms; or there is no obvious family involvement in the symptoms.

Glick and Kessler (1974) have adapted and extended Ackerman's indications. Further indications for therapy include situations in which the identified patient shows no improvement with individual therapy, when stress in other family members follows improvement in the patient, and where a discharge from hospital of the identified patient is imminent. Contraindications include situations in which the consequences of treatment are worse than its benefits; the patient has a fixed drug or alcohol dependency; there is a secret that cannot be discussed; there are religious or cultural objections to open family discussion; or there is a necessity for other forms of psychiatric treatment as an emergency.

Wynne (1965) who is more all-embracing in his indications for family therapy, suggested that it is suitable wherever there are relationship difficulties, that is, problems in transactional patterns to which each person is contributing, either collusively or openly. Wynne certainly thought that intensive, prolonged family therapy was indicated for families of schizophrenics, a view that would not be shared by Ackerman or many family therapists today.

Walrond-Skinner (1976), in a chapter dealing with indications and contraindications, made the points that have been stated above on the lack of suitable taxonomy of families and the lack of a body of outcome research, both of which are essential if one is to deal definitively with indications for therapy. She then suggested that family therapy is clearly indicated when a relationship is the focus of complaint. If this is a marital relationship and the couple are socially isolated, Walrond-Skinner suggests a couples' group. She considers family therapy when one or more members are seeking to become independent of the others (in this she seems to be in opposition to Ackerman, although the differences may relate to the way in which the family is attempting to split). Third, she considers family therapy where individual members who need help are hard to engage but would be willing to attend with the family. Contraindications, as in Ackerman's formulation, include unavailability (either physically or psychologically), the presence of individuals who cannot share therapy with their families, and the presence of sociocultural blocks to therapy. Walrond-Skinner also included an interesting contraindication in the case of families whose problem resists therapy and seems to represent a kind of entrenched sadomasochistic gratification for the members.

In spite of the fairly extensive lists of indications and contraindications mentioned so far, there appears to be very little in the way of hard data on which to base such guidelines. As Walrond-Skinner put it (1976, p. 132) "lists of contraindications often say more about the therapist's own areas of defensiveness, rather than offering an overall generalization about the probable outcome of family therapy." In attempting to consolidate and elucidate indications and contraindications, I have found that I myself have little more to fall back on than the fairly small area of literature quoted above, an acute awareness of the behavioral outcome of therapy, and a good deal of experience in the eclectic application of family and marital therapy as part of a range of therapeutic techniques.

THE INDICATIONS FOR FAMILY THERAPY

The Age of the Presenting Patient

When presented with a preschool or school child with a psychiatric or behavior problem, almost all child and family psychiatric units would insist on seeing both parents, and the majority of units would have at least some conjoint family sessions. By and large, the child's dependence on the family lessens as he or she grows up, and a mother obviously needs to be supervising a 2 year old much more closely than a 10 year old. Thus, the behavior of a young child is much more bound up with the behavior of other family members (especially the parent most involved in caretaking) than is the behavior of an older child or teenager. A mother who comes to the clinic with an "impossible" 3 year old will certainly be involved in any management program, whether this is of behavioral or family therapy. With a 10 year old, parental involvement in therapy is still very likely, but with a teenager there may be a case for peer-group or individual treatment as well as, or instead of, family therapy. With adult offspring living at home with their parents, there is again a choice of family therapy or a whole range of other approaches, depending on the problem presented.

The Way the Problem Is Presented

Some general practitioners are very aware of family tensions and pressures and may refer patients, particularly younger patients, with their families for treatment. They are usually right, and for many such patients family therapy seems the treatment of choice.

In other cases, one or both parents may attend the initial appointment and insist on being involved at all stages of the consultation. This is almost an invitation to family therapy and should certainly lead to family sessions as part of the management. There may be a tricky stage to be negotiated in the course of the early involvement with the family in which the focus begins to shift from the patient to interaction among various family members and even "pathology" in another member. However, if this can be overcome there is every possibility of a productive series of family interviews.

In other cases, there may be a situation in which one family member (e.g., the mother) appears to be the most worried but spends almost all the available time complaining about another (e.g., the teenage son). Here too family therapy is indicated, and again the problem will arise of moving from focusing on the son's behavior to focusing on mother–son interaction, on mother herself, and later perhaps on problems in the parents' marriage.

This change of focus does not necessarily have to be accompanied by insight on the family's side; it is quite possible to achieve far-reaching changes in both the problem and the system without the family members realizing that there is a "family" problem at all.

The Nature of the Presenting Problem

Some presenting problems in children lend themselves more to family therapy than others. On the whole, within each type of condition, the younger the presenting patient the more strongly is family therapy indicated (see above).

Families presenting with an interactional problem are suited most clearly to a family therapy approach. For instance, in some families, sibling rivalry, which is of course very common in normal families, reaches such a pitch of intensity that family consultations are needed. Similarly, the behavior of one child may be interferring with brothers or sisters: a so-called overactive child, for instance, may monopolize the attention of one or both parents to the detriment of siblings.

Related to these interactional problems are problems of behavior disorder in one child. Usually, such children are behavior-disordered in one setting and not another; if the problem occurs more frequently at home than at school, family therapy is clearly indicated. One can often find a related difficulty, for instance, that the parents are undermining each other's authority and thus effectively encouraging the disturbed behavior in one child.

Problems such as incest and child abuse clearly involve interaction among family members; in both situations, family therapy has been advocated as a mode of intervention. In the case of child abuse, there is now much evidence that many abusing parents have themselves been abused as children (Kempe & Helfer, 1972). The parent very often expresses immature and unrealistic attitudes, such as expecting a baby of 9 months to be doing his or her best to please the parent and believing that persistent crying is being done deliberately to annoy or punish. Much can be done by a family therapist in reducing these expectations and improving the self-image of the parent. However, any therapy must be done in the context of firm control by social services and other agencies to ensure the safety of the child—if necessary, by separation of child and parent on a temporary basis.

Incest presents a similar problem, with an abnormally intimate relationship usually between father (or stepfather) and daughter and psychological barriers between mother and father and between mother and daughter (Furniss, 1983). The very fact that in most cases the mother does not know about the incest for some time indicates a lack of joint parental responsibility for the family. Faced with this family constellation, the family therapist has the task of attempting to restore something like normal family structure while ensuring that the sexual abuse does not recur. The best way of ensuring this appears to be to underpin the family structure with outside individuals with statutory responsibilities for each member: a social worker to look after the daughter and siblings, a probation officer to relate to the father, and a family therapist/psychiatrist to oversee the interests of the mother and the family.

Most neurotic problems in children—anxiety, phobias, depression, suicidal attempts, and obsessional symptoms—are well dealt with by family therapy. If the presenting child is over 12, however, there may be a case for combining individual and family sessions, according to the nature of the problem.

Problems of delinquency, with the frequently associated problems of lying and truancy, are often highly suitable for family therapy, which would aim at encouraging better communication within the family and better parental limit-setting for the delinquent child.

Anorexia nervosa has been highlighted by the work of Selvini Palazzoli (1974) and Minuchin (1978) as an indication for family therapy. Indeed, Minuchin claimed a success rate of 86% for family therapy in this condition. Recent work by Russell (1985), however, has shown that while family therapy was significantly better than individual therapy in anorexic patients whose illness had begun before the age of 18, and had lasted less than 3 years, there was no superiority in older patients or in those with a longer history. Those with bulimia did badly with both kinds of treatment. This is a highly important study, as it is one of the few controlled trials of family therapy to date.

Alcoholism and drug abuse occupy an ambiguous position in the indications for family therapy. In some cases, especially where the addiction is not fully established or is recent in origin, some family therapy approaches may be relevant; however, fixed dependency may render the affected patient impervious to normal communication and thus vitiate any attempts at family therapy. This is unfortunate, as in many cases family stress can be seen as an important factor in promoting and perpetuating the substance abuse.

Schizophrenia is a condition about which there are several opinions of the relevance of family therapy. Some authorities would hold that family therapy is not an effective way of coping with schizophrenia, and it is very clear that family therapy alone is unlikely to effect a radical cure of the condition. This is a disappointing state of affairs as one of the pioneering movements within family therapy was aimed at showing that schizophrenia was a disorder of family communication to be cured by family therapy (Wynne, 1965). However, it has been shown (Falloon & Liberman, 1983) that if one accepts that schizophrenia is an illness that needs treatment by neuroleptic drugs, the prognosis for the individual patient can be significantly improved by also helping the family of the patient to improve communication patterns. One could perhaps characterize this type of family approach as palliative rather than radical, as it aims at helping the family to adjust to the symptomatic patient rather than at curing the symptoms by family system change.

The Family Life Stage and Transitions

Many families encounter problems at points of transition within the life cycle: for instance, at times of birth, of first school attendance, of adolescent rebellion, of children leaving home (the "empty nest"), of divorce, of death, and of remarriage. It is unusual for families to seek therapy simply on these grounds, but many problems such as behavior disorder in children or adolescents and depression in parents arise at these times of transition. It can be useful to point out the "normality" of the experiences the family is having so as to reduce anxiety about the disturbed behavior or other symptoms. This may in itself reduce the disturbed behavior, and most family therapists of whatever school take considerable note of the stage the family has reached in the family life cycle.

Availability and Other Practical Limitations

As mentioned by Glick and Kessler (1974, p. 110), the unavailability of key family members may make family therapy impossible. However, the therapist's attitude to this may be more or less flexible according to his or her theoretical bias. Some hard-line family therapists who had asked to see the whole family would refuse to see three out of four family members even if they arrived expecting to be seen. This approach may lead to an improved motivation on the part of the family to ensure full attendance at sessions, but it may also lead to defaulting because of the perceived unreasonableness of the therapist. Other therapists would see the family members who are present and perhaps send a message to the absent members to encourage attendance or, alternatively, would give a written intervention to the family (including the missing member) to be discussed at home.

The policy on my own unit is more in line with this latter, flexible approach, and it may be that we would in any case choose to work with the parents or with a subsystem, such as the mother and identified patient, at some stages of therapy. We feel that the nuclear family (or at least the family members who live under the same roof) is to some extent an arbitrary unit and that the problem in the identified patient may impinge very little on an elder brother who is away from home most of the time, while it may be of great moment to a grandmother who visits frequently.

We may also opt to see an individual family member either before or after family therapy. It is quite possible that a case that begins with the family seen together for a problem in a teenager may continue with couple therapy for the parents' communication problems and end with one parent being seen for individual counseling.

THE INDICATIONS FOR MARITAL THERAPY

What Constitutes a Marital Couple?

Marital therapy is primarily concerned with couples, but there is every gradation in the couples referred to us from those who have been married for 30 years to those who are both still married to other partners but have been cohabiting for some months and are having communication problems. In some ways, the latter are more "married" than married couples where one partner is working abroad or at sea and the couple only meet twice a year for a fortnight's holiday or shore leave. We also see younger couples who are living together in an informal way and occasionally also gay couples, both male and female, who are in stable relationships. Couples with very young babies are often seen, and the question may arise whether to label a session including the baby a marital or a family session. Couples on the brink of divorce are sometimes referred, and the question then arises whether to work on helping communication in the marriage or to work on practical aspects of the divorce in the conciliation approach (see Robinson, 1982).

Another dilemma often arises during treatment: whether to treat one individual or to insist on seeing the couple. This is particularly acute when one partner (often the wife) is complaining of no problems in herself but spends the whole session in describing her husband's unsupportable behavior. The most appropriate solution would almost certainly be marital therapy, but often the wife says that her husband would not come to therapy. The therapist can then either insist on conjoint therapy (and run the risk of neither partner attending) or go along with the wife and her individual sessions in the hope of including the husband later in the series. Couples who are of two minds about separation also pose a dilemma: whether to see both together exclusively or (as I usually do) to have some individual sessions with each partner in addition to the conjoint sessions.

The Way the Problem Is Presented

As with family referrals above, there is a wide variety in the presentation of marital problems. Some general practitioners referring cases have done a good deal of preparation with the couple and have pinpointed the problem as one of communication (a slightly problematic term because of its current usage as a cliché) or more precisely in terms of arguments, tensions, resentment, etc. Others see the problems in more traditional medical terms and may emphasize the depression in one partner or the excessive drinking in the other—both of which may be present but do not detract from the relevance of marital therapy as a valid way of helping the couple. General practitioners are not the only source of referrals in my unit, although they refer probably 60% of the cases seen. Hospital psychiatrists probably refer another 25% of cases, and others, including social workers and probation officers, refer the remainder. In one study of a series of marital problems (Crowe, 1978), it was found that cases referred by general practitioners had a significantly better outcome than those referred by hospital psychiatrists. The reasons for this were not altogether clear but may have related to the chronicity and severity of problems in the hospital referrals or to their long habituation to the "illness model" compared with the general practitioners' referrals. It is more likely that a marital referral letter will refer to a "marital problem" than that a family referral letter will refer to a "family problem." This is because of the tendency of problems between parents and children to be labeled as behavior problems in the children, whereas problems between husband and wife cannot be so easily labeled as depression or irresponsibility in one partner.

Problems can arise in the early stages of marital therapy when one partner believes the problem to be marital in nature while the other is convinced that the problem lies in the personality of the first. The marital therapist is naturally in favor of the problem being labeled marital but cannot be seen to be totally one-sided in dealing with the couple: a compromise, with the therapist apparently siding with the "personality problem" explanation, may bring the couple round to working on their relationship.

One of the more important aspects of referral is that both partners must be at least willing to discuss marital problems. I have had particular difficulties with couples who are referred after family therapy sessions, with a child as the original presenting patient, for "further marital work." The problem seems to be that these couples are not really convinced that there is a marital problem even though the previous treatment team have discerned it. The pattern has been that these couples rapidly default from treatment: a better outcome would probably have been obtained by the original team working indirectly on the marital problem by getting the couple to cooperate over parenting issues.

Different Presenting Problems and Different Therapy Techniques

I have argued elsewhere (Crowe, 1985) that marital therapy is most appropriately carried out in a combined behavioral–systems approach. This approach makes use of the behavioral methods of reciprocity negotiation and communication training, which have been shown in numerous controlled trials to be effective (Jacobson, 1978). It also makes use of some techniques derived from structural and strategic family therapy.

By and large, the behavioral approaches seem to be best suited to couples who present with an acknowledged marital problem. Such problems as intractable arguments, resentment, power struggles, and sexual motivation issues respond quite well to *reciprocity negotiation*, in which the therapist takes the role of an intermediary or negotiator and tries to encourage the couple to be positive, forward-looking, specific, and practical in their negoiations for an improved day-to-day relationship.

Communication training, a behavioral technique that aims to train the couple to communicate positively, constructively, and efficiently, is useful for couples with arguments, power struggles, and resentment and for those whose natural communication is characterized by overinclusive discussions, misunderstandings, repetition, and monologues.

Not all couples with marital difficulties present with these on the first visit. Some couples have a problem that is affecting both of them equally although both attribute the blame for it to one partner: for instance, a husband who responds to marital stress by spending large amounts of money on drink. These "saint-and-sinner" couples may need some preliminary work on analyzing and redefining the problem before they are willing to negotiate on how to improve communication or interaction in the relationship. The same considerations apply, but more strongly, to couples where the main presenting problem appears to be psychiatric symptoms in one partner. Such symptoms might be depression, anxiety, panic attacks, headaches, unspoken resentment, or unexplained refusal of sex. In such cases, especially where the power in the relationship appears unevenly distributed and the couple will not engage in arguments, it is quite useful to apply a *structural approach*. This approach, based on the work of Minuchin (1974), aims to escalate conflict in the couple in order to overcome the inhibitions that are thought to be perpetuating the symptoms. The therapist has to "decenter" himself or herself and help the couple to communicate directly with each other; where conflict arises, the therapist attempts to intensify it to the extent that the couple find a new solution to their problem. A depressed or anxious wife may in this approach assert herself and criticize her husband, making him abandon his bland helpfulness; eventually, the couple discover that arguments can replace the vicious circle of depression and overprotection.

There are some couples who are unable to respond even to structural interventions. They often appear to have intractable symptoms in one partner, such as morbid jealousy, hypochondriasis, some phobias and obsessions, some forms of anorexia, resistant sexual dysfunctions, and even severe depression. However, in these couples too, one can discern a marital element to the problem, for instance, a spouse who appears more concerned about the problem than does the actual patient or a wife whose depression develops soon after her husband retires from work. Reciprocity negotiation is not indicated in such cases, in that there is no difference of opinion to be negotiated, and communication training and structural techniques fail because a dialogue cannot be stimulated between the partners. In such couples, a *strategic approach* may be used in which, at the end of a probing series of questions, the therapist (often with the help of an observation group) gives an instruction for the couple to carry out between sessions. This may take the form of a paradoxical injunction for the couple to continue the behavior complained of (e.g., the wife to remain depressed and the husband to remain bland and helpful) because this is preventing them from looking at the dangerous disagreements that would otherwise threaten the marriage.

As in family therapy, I do not consider that schizophrenic patients and their spouses are suitable for marital therapy in the usual sense, but it is very reasonable to hold joint sessions with the couple to try to reduce "expressed emotion" in the relationship and to suggest that they aim for less than 35 hours of week face-to-face contact (Leff, Kuipers, & Berkowitz, 1983). The problem-solving approach of Falloon and Liberman (1983) is also quite appropriate for this group.

When Not to Offer Marital Therapy

It should not be concluded from the preceding section that all psychiatric problems in patients who are married should be dealt with by conjoint marital therapy. There are many problems that are more expeditiously dealt with in other ways; many cases of depression, for example, are quite adequately treated with antidepressants or cognitive therapy, and cases of phobic or obsessional disorder are probably more effectively dealt with by behavioral therapy than marital therapy (Cobb, McDonald, Marks, & Stern, 1980). Some psychiatric problems, of course, are so severe that inpatient treatment is the only safe course. There are also some clearly marital problems where marital therapy is not possible: for instance, when one partner is unwilling to attend, where the relationship is about to break up, or when all the approaches mentioned in the preceding section have failed. It is in these circumstances that it is an advantage to have other approaches available, including pharmacological treatments, behavioral and cognitive therapy, bereavement counseling, dynamic psychotherapy, and supportive counseling.

THE INDICATIONS FOR SEXUAL THERAPY

Although sexual dysfunctions are a more circumscribed group of conditions than marital or family problems, they are nevertheless varied in the ways they present, in the degree to which the relationship contributes, and in the predisposing and causative factors. Sexual dysfunctions range from "technical" problems such as impotence and anorgasmia to motivational problems such as inability to compromise between partners with high and low sex drives. They also often present in individuals who have no partner, such as the male with primary impotence who is afraid to approach a woman because of the fear of failure.

The setting in which sexual problems are treated in my own unit is in a psychiatric outpatient department, and this probably slants the clinic population more toward psychiatric symptoms (in one or both partners) than in most other clinics. We also find that many of the couples who attend have marital problems in addition to their technical sexual difficulties. While agreeing with Sager (1974) that it is difficult to mix sexual and marital therapy, we would still in most couples find it useful at times to digress from the direct path of sexual therapy while marital power struggles, etc., are dealt with, and then to return to the sexual issues in a subsequent session.

The sequence of events in the typical couple case is as follows. The partners are seen separately for history taking, but thereafter they are seen together with sessions spaced at 2-week intervals, with homework exercises between. The sessions comprise work on communication and negotiation (sexual and nonsexual), with some structural or strategic marital interventions included if necessary, and a good deal of discussion of the preceding and projected homework tasks. These tasks will be, in the early stages, relaxation, sensate focus, and a ban on intercourse. Later, according to the problem, specific techniques such as the stop–start technique for premature ejaculation and the use of dilators in vaginismus are taught. In some couples, self-assertion is encouraged, while in others a timetable of sexual encounters is imposed in order to overcome power struggles over timing and frequency (Crowe & Ridley, 1986).

In the case of the single patients (more frequently male patients, although some single women are referred) we use an anxiety-reduction, educational, and social skills approach, either individually or in groups. While the individuals remain unattached, such improvement as they experience is somewhat theoretical and disconnected from reality, but it is not uncommon for them to form outside relationships while attending the clinic; in these cases, homework tasks can be suggested as with couples.

Previous Work on Indications for Sexual Therapy

Approaches to sexual dysfunction in couples began with the now classic publication of *Human Sexual Inadequacy* by Masters and Johnson (1970). Their findings are of limited relevance to most current sexual therapy because their approach was quite unusual in its use of a 2-week residential program, which must have excluded a large number of poorly motivated couples from the series by purely social and financial factors. Masters and Johnson did not list indications or contraindications as such, but they did list some factors that carried a poor prognosis, including personality difficulties, marital problems, and religious orthodoxy.

Kaplan (1974) was more explicit in her contraindications, which she listed as "exclusion criteria" (p. 464). She ruled out couples in whom there was a serious medical illness that precluded sexual function and also those with drug addiction, alcoholism, schizophrenia, paranoia, acute depression, or a highly destructive or imminently collapsing marriage.

More recent authorities such as Jehu (1979) and Bancroft (1983) do not mention indications for therapy as such, although good motivation for behavioral work in this rather sensitive area of cooperation is generally accepted as a prerequisite for sexual therapy.

Annon (1975) is prepared, as is Kaplan, to take on quite disturbed neurotic individuals for sexual therapy, but both authors distinguish between the more superficial (usually couple) therapy and more intensive (usually individual) work along psychodynamic lines. Annon calls the first type of work "permission, limited information, and specific suggestions" and the second "intensive therapy."

Thus, as in family and marital work, there is a fairly general lack of data on indications for sexual therapy, even though the much clearer definitions of the problem and the more obvious differences between success and failure in therapy make the task of researching the area considerably easier than in family and marital therapy.

The Nature of the Presenting Problem

Most sexual therapists would agree that all the specific problems described by Masters and Johnson in the sexual dysfunction field are indications for sex therapy. Thus, couples complaining of erectile impotence, premature ejaculation, or retarded ejaculation in the male partner or anorgasmia, vaginismus, or dyspareunia (painful intercourse) in the female partner are normally accepted for therapy. A further series of problems combined by Kaplan under the title of "general sex dysfunction" are also highly suitable: these include low sex drive, reduced sex drive, incompatible sex drives between partners, and fear or dislike of sex.

There are other factors associated with sexual dysfunctions, which carry their own prognostic implications. Thus, the presence of sexual performance anxiety is usually taken to be a good indication for sexual therapy. Certainly Ansari (1976) found that anxiety was a positive prognostic factor in the treatment of impotence. At the other end of the spectrum are cases that appear to have a more organic or constitutional basis. Here the scope for altering sexual function appears to be somewhat limited, for instance in impotence associated with diabetes or in dyspareunia associated with endometriosis. However, there is in most "organic" cases both an anxiety component and a relationship component, and many of these couples can be helped to a better sexual interaction regardless of the unalterable organic factor.

Relationship aspects of sexual dysfunction are in some ways a positive indicator and in other ways a negative indicator for therapy. Some of the most gratifying results are obtained in couples who have no technical problem with sexual intercourse but are hampered by poor motivation, resentment, or inhibition from having a good and frequent sexual interaction (Crowe and Ridley, 1986). Such couples are quite easy to treat if the therapist moves away from Masters and Johnson behavioral techniques and uses instead approaches based on assertive therapy or marital therapy as a way of bypassing sexual power struggles. Sometimes, however, the relationship problems are so severe, whether they involve total war, silent lack of cooperation, undermining of each other, or unalterable inequality, that sex therapy becomes impossible. The couple may come to the clinic with an overt sexual dysfunction, but it will become clear within very few therapeutic sessions that their aims are ambiguous at the very least and that at worst their hidden agenda may be to prove that the therapist is just as impotent as they are themselves.

Some particular presenting problems seem to have a poor prognosis. This was recognized by Masters and Johnson in the problems of retarded ejaculation and primary impotence, both of which they regarded as difficult to treat. In fact, these two conditions are only relative contraindications. Retarded ejaculation has a much better prognosis if the patient can ejaculate in masturbation than if he cannot. The presence of the tonic glandipudendal reflex (Brindley & Gillan, 1982) is also a good prognostic indicator. Primary impotence, too, can sometimes respond quite well to a very patient and lengthy series of sessions in well-motivated couples. Another problem that seems to do badly is dissatisfaction with the quality of pleasure experienced. This can occur in both men and women and relates to an orgasm or ejaculation that is perceived as unpleasant, painful, or less exciting than before. I cannot recall success with any of several couples presenting with this problem.

Loss of sex drive associated with physical illnesses such as rheumatoid arthritis or leukemia presents problems in sex therapy; indeed, it might be doubted in some cases whether sex therapy is appropriate. In general, sexual activity springs from a sense of health and well-being, and the reproductive urge can be seen as an expression of that well-being. There are some situations in which sexual activity may have to be curtailed simply because it doesn't seem right to either partner. Some physical illnesses, however, do not carry the same antisexual connotations. Men who have had cardiac infarcts may be physically quite well after the acute phase and may abstain from sex only because they or their wives are frightened of precipitating another attack during strenuous activity. However, sexual relations without excessive expenditure of energy may be quite harmless for such men and may well protect from frustration, which itself could contribute to further cardiac infarction.

A related problem is that of "widower's impotence." Here a man whose wife has died some years before, and who has had no sexual contact in the intervening period, meets a new partner and finds, to his surprise, that he is impotent. Given cooperation by both partners, and an acceptance that sex may not be as frequent or as exciting as when he was first married, it is quite easy to help such couples to a fairly satisfactory relationship.

Associated Psychiatric Factors

There seems no doubt, even though there is little research data on the subject, that psychiatric symptoms in one or both partners make sex therapy more difficult and less successful. This was found in a survey by Crowe, Czechowicz, and Gillan (1977) in an unselected series of 75 cases. Some psychiatric conditions seem to undermine therapy by causing disruption of the relationship, others by reducing the motivation for sex.

Conditions that lead to unpredictable changes of mood or behavior, such as manic–depressive psychosis, some forms of schizophrenia, sociopathic personality disorder, and binge drinking, can totally disrupt the kind of cooperation necessary for sexual therapy to be successful.

Other psychiatric conditions reduce sex drive. Depression is the best recognized of these, and it may be unwise to embark on therapy for sexual dysfunction until the depressed partner is adequately treated. Antidepressant drugs, both tricyclics and MAOI preparations, may of course exacerbate such problems as impotence or anorgasmia, so their effect in a depressed patient with sexual dysfunction is double-edged. Dependence on drugs and alcohol will generally reduce sex drive, although there are other factors here, including negative attitudes in the nondependent partner, that reduce sexual activity in the couple. It is probably better not to initiate sexual therapy while substance abuse in one partner remains a major problem.

Other conditions may impair sexual enjoyment but do not contraindicate therapy. For example, obsessional cleanliness in one partner will be a block to progress, but it may be overcome simultaneously with sexual therapy by behavioral or marital interventions. Phobias often coexist with sexual dysfunctions but may similarly be treated in parallel. Thus, like most other negative factors, psychiatric conditions are to be seen as relative rather than absolute contraindications to sexual therapy.

Social Factors and Living Arrangements

Limitations on the applicability of sexual therapy are provided to different degrees by various associated factors of a social nature. The stability of the relationship is, of course, a major factor here, and it is usually going to be fruitless to embark on therapy with a couple who are in the process of splitting up. Something may be done for the dysfunctional individual in such a case, but this will be somewhat limited both by the greater difficulty of helping individuals in general and by the fact that someone going through the painful process of breaking an intimate relationship is likely to be preoccupied with that process and thus less able to concentrate on sexual therapy. The problem is obviously greater when divorce is occurring after a long-lasting marriage with children involved, but it is still present even after the break-up of a steady but brief relationship. In both circumstances, we would usually advise the couple or individual to seek sexual therapy later, when either a new relationship has formed or the dysfunctional individual has recovered from the upset brought on by separation.

The age of the partners or presenting patients is not a major factor as an indication for therapy or the reverse. We have had considerable success with couples in their 60s as well as those in their teens. In general, the teenagers have the advantage of a strong sexual drive, at least in one partner, while the older couples have the advantage of stability in their relationship and conscientiousness in carrying out tasks. Some of the natural changes with age, such as reduced frequency of sex urges, delay in establishing erection and lubrication, and delayed ejaculation, have to be taken into account; also, as mentioned in an earlier section, there has to be a less ambitious series of goals in older couples.

The presence of sexual deviation in one partner limits one's options in sex therapy, and the usual way of dealing with the problem is to treat the deviation as a competing urge that will decrease if the heterosexual relationship can be improved. I have often noticed that deviant urges can be stronger when the deviant partner feels resentful and weak in relation to the other partner, so that at times assertive therapy can be used with the deviant partner within the relationship in order to improve the sexual side. One may, in some cases, also use aversive techniques to counteract the deviant urges directly. These considerations apply to most of the common deviations, including bisexuality in both male and female partners, transvestism, exhibitionism, and fetishism. It even applies to some extent to sadomasochism, although here the deviation is intimately involved in the heterosexual relationship itself, and elaborate compromises may have to be worked out on how much deviant activity the partner will tolerate in order to make the sexual act rewarding for the deviant partner. In almost all cases where deviation is present, the prognosis for the sexual dysfunction itself is poorer than in the absence of deviation.

A similar handicap in sexual dysfunction work is provided by the presence of an outside heterosexual relationship in either partner. As with deviations, the aim should be to improve the marital relationship in competition with the outside relationship; often, a good deal of work on communication and priorities within the couple is necessary both as a preliminary to sexual therapy and during the course of therapy. It is difficult, for instance, for a wife whose husband is having an ongoing affair to feel motivated to have sexual relations with him and perhaps more difficult still for her to help him with a sexual problem or to cooperate in solving her own sexual problem in the marriage. Work is often uphill in such cases but can sometimes be rewarding if the couple can reach a better adjustment in nonsexual ways and thereby perhaps lessen the need for the outside relationship.

Social and living conditions may also provide an added handicap to giving help with sexual problems. The young couple who do not have their own place, but have to meet in parental homes, are one example of this. Similarly, couples living in cramped or unsuitable accommodations have great difficulties in overcoming sexual problems. For example, a man with secondary impotence was married to a divorcee who had children: they all lived in a basement flat through which the landlord had open access in order to get to the backyard. The couple were only able to solve their difficulties after moving to a suburban council house.

Social problems can impinge in other ways, such as the unpredictable and damaging effect of crises in "multiproblem" families. Worries over such events as court appearances or drug addiction in teenage children, nonpayment of rent or electricity bills, reception of children into care, arguments, and harassment by neighbors all contribute to difficulties experienced in the sexual relationship and make therapy more difficult to carry out. Again, one should not despair of helping these couples, but goals should be kept at a realistic level.

Motivation

In all cases, no matter what the psychiatric, social, organic, or marital factors altering the likely outcome, one of the most important prognostic indicators is motivation for change. In the initial history-taking, this is sometimes difficult to assess, as patients or couples will often present a hopeful picture at this stage that is not borne out later. A clue may emerge from the question, "Who initiated this referral?" A positive answer would be that they did so together after discussion; negative answers could include pressure from a general practitioner; a referral sought by one partner, without informing the other; or a referral initiated by the nondysfunctional partner threatening to leave because of the problem.

Motivational factors can be assessed, and unmotivated couples excluded, by the requirement to complete a general history sheet to be returned by mail before the definitive appointment is given. By this approach, one can reduce the number of initial appointments missed and assess more accurately the motivation of the couples when they attend.

The best guide to motivation is, however, the level of compliance with early homework tasks. This is assessed in the first few sessions, and the contrast is between couples who cooperate well with relaxation and sensate focus and those who bring up various reasons why they were unable to do so. Curiously enough, the practical reasons (visitors or overtime) seem to have worse implications for cooperation than reasons connected with arguments or resentment during attempts at sensate focus and related exercises. In these latter cases, one can work concurrently on marital issues, whereas there is little to be done for the others except homilies on trying to make more time for what they claim is important work on their sexual problem.

Sexual dysfunction treatment involves a delicate balance of cooperation with therapy and the spontaneity that is necessary for a good sex life. Motivation in both partners is a vital component in any sexual therapy: some blocks can be overcome by marital therapy techniques, but others require great therapeutic skill and patience to keep the partners cooperating with the therapist and each other; sometimes the task proves too great.

CASE HISTORY

The case described here is of interest in several ways. The problem originally presented was of marital arguments in which the parents were worried that their three children were suffering. Thus, the family attended for the first few sessions, while the couple attended alone for most of the later visits. The focus gradually shifted from marital to sexual problems.

The couple, in their late 30s, had been married for 12 years and had sons of 10 (John) and 8 (Sam) and a daughter of 5 (Jane). The husband (Ralph) was a commercial artist who felt he had failed in his profession and who was working in a deadend job. The wife (Laura) was a teacher who also counseled disturbed children and who had a history of depression. John was described as overemotional and as taking responsibility when his parents had rows. Sam was the overactive member of the family, who woke everyone in the morning and created scenes and diversions. Jane was a quiet girl who was close to mother and who had threatened to leave home.

The couple complained that their sexual relationship had been almost zero for some years, with the wife refusing any contact. The wife also felt that she had to make all the decisions about the house and family and objected to her husband's tantrums and possessiveness. In fact, she had sometimes threatened to leave home, but her recent full-time employment had made this less urgent, as the husband was looking after the children for some hours each day in her absence.

In the first session, the therapists complimented the whole family on adjusting well to a difficult situation: Ralph for carrying on his job and also nurturing the family, Laura for being able to resign her central role by going out to work, John for his responsible attitudes, Sam for keeping everyone's attention diverted from other problems, and Jane for saying what mother really wanted to say about leaving home.

The second session was with the parents alone, by arrangement. They spoke at first about John's tantrums and Sam's vulnerability but quickly moved into the sexual problem. Laura had very rarely experienced orgasm and never with her husband. Now she always rejected sexual advances and most nonsexual contact. Both partners admitted their inexperience, and the female therapist asked them if they could enjoy any aspects of sex play, to which they said yes. They were asked to spend 20 minutes talking each night, with some nonsexual physical contact.

This homework task progressed for a few days, but then Laura unexpectedly left home: Ralph spent half the night complaining bitterly about her to John, who was naturally upset. In the morning, Ralph locked Laura out and changed the locks, but later he allowed her in. She asked for a divorce, but after a further mixed family–marital session, Laura and Ralph decided to stay together as friends, with no sexual contact. In this session, Laura explained to the children that the parental troubles were not the children's fault.

It is not unusual for a family crisis to be provoked by attempts to alter the distance between family members such as by suggesting nonsexual touching: in this case the crisis was unexpectedly powerful. But after the crisis, the parents settled down and began to act as a team in dealing with the children, while at the same time having separate bedrooms themselves. From this safe "distance," over the next few sessions of marital therapy they both began to take responsibility for their own shortcomings, and each recognized the other's insecurity. Laura realized that she had a lot of unexpressed anger against Ralph because he was weak, dependent, and unassertive. The male therapist was able to support Ralph in asserting himself against Laura in the session. Laura in turn began to be less responsible, shouting at Ralph and leaving more family duties to him, while he reported a growing confidence in himself.

The therapists emphasized the seriousness of the crisis Laura and Ralph had weathered and warned them against trying to rebuild the marriage too quickly. After this session, Ralph began to take more initiative, but Laura continued to undermine him by interpreting all his actions and inadequacies; the therapists asked her to try and draw out his opinions instead of commenting on his behavior and suggested to him that if Laura analyzed him he should tell her to stop it.

They continued to have separate bedrooms, but during another session in which Laura admitted that she respected Ralph's qualities, and at the same time said she needed to have a "barrier" to protect her from his possessiveness, he expressed impatience about the lack of sex. The therapists decided on a gamble and suggested that once a fortnight Laura should go to his bedroom and ask for sex. Saturday was specified. This "sex rota" often breaks through the habitual power struggle that some couples experience in sexual relations, and although this couple had gone for such a long period without sex, it was successful. Laura approached Ralph on the appropriate Saturdays and felt a new sense of freedom and abandonment in knowing that she had made the initiative but could retreat to her own territory after the event.

On the last visit they reported successful sex once a fortnight. They retained their separate bedrooms. They were committed to the marriage. They reported that all three children seemed more settled.

There were, altogether, nine sessions with this case—two family and seven marital. The problems with the children might have needed intervention directly, but it was clear after the first session that marital difficulties were the primary problem. Regarding the marital sessions, it had seemed possible at first to help this couple to negotiate and to go ahead with behavioral sexual tasks. However, this was undermined because of the negative feelings the wife had toward the husband for reasons not directly to do with sex. It only became possible to work on the sexual problem after the "false start" had led to the crisis and to an adjustment of the marital distance from which the wife could safely contemplate the transient intimacy she needed to have sexual relations and avoid being possessed. The husband's increased assertiveness also helped him to be more successful in his sexual approaches and allowed the wife to respect him sufficiently to want him sexually. It was no surprise that, with the marital relationship improved and the parents working as a team, the children's mild behavior problems abated.

SUMMARY AND CONCLUSIONS

It will be seen, both from the introductory and the later sections of this chapter, that my approach is not one of uncritical enthusiasm for family, marital, or sexual therapy. It is, of course, quite possible to see almost any psychiatric or sexual problem in the light of interpersonal factors, just as it is possible to focus entirely on the individual; the decision on which way to look at a problem is often arbitrary. What I have tried to do is to identify some of the guidelines for choosing to see more than one person in treatment; the lists that follow are an attempt to summarize the position. They are not to be seen as rules to be followed slavishly but as general indicators of possible usefulness.

Family Therapy Indications

1. The younger the child who presents problems, the more one should be swayed towards the family approach.
2. Problems that present through one family member but focus on another (the worried mother and the teenage son, for instance) are involved.
3. Problems such as bullying, rivalry, child abuse, and incest are involved.
4. Neurosis, depression, anxiety, school refusal, anorexia nervosa, delinquency, truanting, etc.,—especially in younger children—are seen.
5. Some cases of alcohol or drug abuse—depending how severe the dependency is—warrant family intervention.
6. Psychosis does not demand family therapy as such, but a combined educational and emotional "cooling" approach will probably help to reduce relapses.
7. Family life cycle stages and transitions can indicate family therapy; problems presenting at these times can respond well.
8. One should be prepared to be flexible and include family, marital, or individual sessions according to availability and therapeutic need.

Marital Therapy Indications

1. For problems defined as marital, or involving both partners, including arguments, resentment, and coolness, reciprocity negotiation and communication training are suitable approaches.
2. In problems more located in one partner, whether unacceptable behavior or neurotic symptoms, and marital problems that do not respond to reciprocity negotiation or communication training, structural or strategic approaches may be effective.
3. Psychosis, as in family therapy, can be dealt with in couple therapy by a combined educational and emotional cooling approach.
4. When one partner will not attend, when the marriage is over, or when psychiatric symptoms can be dealt with more expeditiously in the individual, marital therapy should probably not be used.
5. In divorcing couples, counciliation is a useful way of reducing bitterness and improving cooperation.

Indications for Sexual Therapy

1. The specific sexual dysfunctions are a positive indication for sexual therapy.
2. The presence of anxiety is a strong pointer to sexual therapy being successful, but organic problems are not a total contraindication.
3. Relationship factors can often be dealt with successfully but are sometimes so severe as to render therapy impossible.
4. Psychiatric problems are not a contraindication, but psychotic and severe personality problems can render therapy ineffective.
5. Relationship break-up can be a fairly strong contraindication (even for individual sexual therapy).
6. Sexual deviations and outside relationships can increase the difficulty of sexual dysfunction work.
7. Social and housing problems can similarly increase the difficulty of the work.
8. Motivation in both partners in couple work is vital, and its absence can sabotage therapy.
9. Individuals can often be helped though not to the same extent as couples.

The benefits of family, marital, and sexual therapy, although clear to those who practice them at the clinical level, remain largely unproven in terms of outcome research. In an ideal world, the indications and contraindications would depend on outcome figures in terms of both symptom removal and system change, analyzed according to the effect of prognostic variables. We have some of these in the marital, sexual, and family therapy fields but, unfortunately, *very* few. In place of this ideal, I have attempted to compile a series of indications based on the literature (such as it is) and on clinical experience. The best advice to be given at this stage is to try the approaches in suitable cases and to attempt to record results in order to confirm or refute the rather tentative indications given in the present chapter.

REFERENCES

Ackerman, N. (1966). *Treating the troubled family*. New York: Basic Books.

Annon, J. S. (1975). *The behavioural treatment of sexual problems: Vol. 2. Intensive therapy*. Honolulu: Enabling Systems.

Ansari, J. M. A. (1976). Impotence: prognosis (a controlled study). *British Journal of Psychiatry, 128*, 194–198.

Bancroft, J. H. J. (1983). *Human sexuality and its problems*. London: Churchill Livingstone.

Beavers, W. R., & Voeller, M. N. (1983). Family models: Comparing and contrasting the Olson circumplex model with the Beavers systems model. *Family Process, 22*, 85–98.

Bennun, I. (1985). Prediction and responsiveness in behavioural marital therapy. *Behavioural Psychotherapy, 13*, 186–201.

Brindley, G. S., & Gillan, P. W. (1982). Men and women who do not have orgasms. *British Journal of Psychiatry, 140*, 351–356.

Cobb, J. P., McDonald, R., Marks, I. M., & Stern, R. (1980). Marital vs exposure therapy: Psychological treatments of co-existing marital and phobic-obsessive problems. *Behavioural Analysis and Modification, 4*, 3–16.

Crowe, M. J. (1978). Conjoint marital therapy: A controlled outcome study. *Psychological Medicine, 8*, 623–636.

Crowe, M. J. (1983). Marital and family therapy. In G. F. M. Russell & L. Hersov (Eds.), *Handbook of psychiatry: Vol 4*. Cambridge: Cambridge University Press.

Crowe, M. J. (1985). Marital therapy, a behavioural-systems approach. In W. Dryden (Ed.), *Marital therapy in Britain: Vol 1*. London: Harper & Row.

Crowe, M. J. and Ridley, J. (1986). The negotiated timetable. A new approach to marital conflict involving male demands and female reluctance for sex. *Sexual and Marital Therapy, 1*, 157–173.

Crowe, M. J., Czechowicz, H., & Gillan, P. W. (1977). *The treatment of sexual dysfunction: A report of 75 cases*. Presentation at VI World Congress of Psychiatry, Honolulu, 1977.

Falloon, I. R. H., & Liberman, R. P. (1983). Behavioural family interventions in the management of chronic schizophrenia. In W. R. McFarlane (Ed.), *Family therapy in schizophrenia*. New York: Guilford Press.

Furniss, T. (1983). Family process in the treatment of intra-familial child sexual abuse. *Journal of Family Therapy, 5*, 263–278.

Glick, I., & Kessler, D. (1974). *Marital and family therapy*. New York: Grune & Stratton.

Gurman, A. S., & Kniskern, D. P. (1981). (Eds.), *Handbook of family therapy*. New York: Brunner/Mazel (a).

Gurman, A. S., & Kniskern, D. P. (1981). Family therapy outcome research: Knowns and unknowns. In A. S. Gurman & D. P. Kniskern (Eds.), *Handbook of family therapy*. New York: Brunner/Mazel (b).

Jacobson, N. S. (1978). A review of the research on the effectiveness of marital therapy. In T. J. Paolino & B. S. McCrady (Eds.), *Marriage and marital therapy*. New York: Brunner/Mazel.

Jehu, D. (1979). *Sexual dysfunction*. Chichester: John Wiley.

Kaplan, H. S. (1974). *The new sex therapy*. New York: Brunner/Mazel.

Kempe, C., & Helfer, R. (1972). *Helping the battered child and his family*. Philadelphia: Lippincott.

Leff, J., Kuipers, E., & Berkowitz, R. (1983). Intervention in families of schizophrenics and its effect on relapse rate. In W. R. McFarlane (Ed.), *Family therapy in schizophrenia*. New York: Guilford Press.

Loader, P. (1985). Personal communication.

Masters, W. H., & Johnson, V. E. (1970). *Human sexual inadequacy*. London: Churchill.

McFarlane, W. R. (1983). (Ed.), *Family therapy in schizophrenia*. New York: Guilford Press.

Minuchin, S. (1974). *Families and family therapy*. Cambridge, MA: Harvard.

Minuchin, S. (1978). *Psychosomatic families: Anorexia nervosa in context*. Cambridge, MA: Harvard.

Minuchin, S., Montalvo, B., Guerney, B. G., Rosman, B.L., & Shumer, F. (1967). *Families of the slums*. New York: Basic Books.

Olson, D. H., Russell, C. S., & Sprenkle, D. H. (1983). Circumplex model of marital and family systems: VI: Theoretical update. *Family Process, 22*, 69–83.

Robinson, M. (1982). Reconstituted families: Some implications for the family therapist. In

A. Bentovim, G. Gorell Barnes, & A. Cooklin (Eds.), *Family therapy: Complementary frameworks of theory and practice*. London: Academic Press.

Russell, G. F. M. (1985). Personal communication.

Sager, C. J. (1974). Sexual dysfunctions and marital discord. In H. S. Kaplan (Ed.), *The new sex therapy*. New York: Brunner/Mazel.

Selvini Palazzoli, M. (1974). *Self-starvation: From the intrapsychic to the transpersonal approach to anorexia nervosa* (translated by Arnold Pomerans). London: Chaucer.

Selvini Palazzoli, M., Boscolo, L., Cecchin, G., & Prata, G. (1978). *Paradox and counterparadox*. New York: Aronson.

Skynner, A. C. R. (1974). *One flesh, separate persons*. London: Constable.

Walrond-Skinner, S. (1976). *Family therapy: The treatment of natural systems*. London: Routledge and Kegan Paul.

Wynne, L. (1965). Some indications and contraindications for exploratory family therapy. In I. Boszormenyi-Nagy & J. L. Framo (Eds.), *Intensive family therapy*. New York: Harper & Row.

4

Behavioral Family Assessment

ANGELA ARRINGTON
MEGAN SULLAWAY
ANDREW CHRISTENSEN
University of California, Los Angeles

While proper assessment is useful in most forms of psychotherapy, it is vital to the precise application of behavior therapy techniques. Perhaps more than any other type of therapy, behavior therapy relies on assessment data not only to guide and focus intervention efforts but also to provide feedback regarding the success of these efforts so that appropriate modifications can take place. Consequently, the assessment activities that take place within a behavioral family therapy framework are quite important. This chapter describes these assessment activities, first from a traditional or classical point of view. The limitations of this point of view are then explored. Finally, a broader based assessment model that addresses the limitations of the more conventional approach is proposed and illustrated with actual case material. It should be noted that this chapter is oriented toward the clinician and its aims are therefore practical. However, it does not provide a cookbook approach to doing family assessment, since the state of knowledge in this area does not justify such specific recommendations. Instead, this chapter provides a heuristic approach, offering a framework and guidelines for assisting clinicians in considering the various elements integral to a comprehensive assessment.

CLASSICAL BEHAVIORAL FAMILY ASSESSMENT

Traditionally, the goal of behavioral family therapy has been to change child behaviors. Those child behaviors that occur excessively are reduced in frequency or eliminated entirely, and those child behaviors that are absent or deficient are shaped into the child's behavioral repertoire. Classical behavioral family assessment serves the needs of behavior change by selecting and defining the behaviors that need changing (target behaviors), by measuring the occurrence of these behaviors so that changes in them can be determined, and by assessing the causal factors eliciting and maintaining these behaviors so that appropriate behavioral change techniques can be adopted.

Definition and Selection of Target Behaviors

Parents are the primary source of information about child disorders. While teachers, the identified child patient, and other family members can also provide information, their roles are usually secondary. Like most lay persons, parents are usually trait theorists rather than behavior theorists. That is, they are more likely to mention generalized, trait-like adjectives than specific behavioral descriptors when discussing their child's problems. For instance, parents are more likely to say that "Johnny is immature," "Susie is out of control," and "Harry has a real mean streak," than to say that "Johnny never does his two assigned daily chores of taking out the garbage and feeding the cats," "Susie has tantrums by yelling and pounding the table with her hands," and "Harry slaps his little sister on the face and behind."

Therefore, the therapist must assist the parents in translating their general complaints into specific target behaviors. This process of behavioral specification is often called "pinpointing" (Gordon & Davidson, 1981; Patterson, Reid, Jones, & Conger, 1975). The term itself suggests the precise objectification involved in defining general complaints as detailed behaviors. The criterion for an adequate definition is a description of sufficient objectivity that independent observers could agree on the occurrence of the behavior in question. A definition of Jenny's aggressiveness that included only hostile remarks and provocative acts would probably not meet this criterion, while a definition that specified hitting baby brother and calling him names would.

Besides trait-like descriptions, parents are also likely to mention a diffuse array of problems in describing the identified patient. For instance, they might comment that Bill has problems in school, he doesn't get along with his peers or do his chores, he throws tantrums, he hits his sister, and he acts like a bully. The therapist assists the parents not only in defining these problems but in categorizing them. Perhaps Bill's problems at school with his peers and with his sister, as well as his "being a bully," all center around his aggressiveness—his tendency to yell and hit to get what he wants from others. What the parents described as several problems might be subsumed under one category with each of the behaviors as exemplars of that category. Additionally, the therapist helps the parent separate the important from the unimportant problems and the primary from the secondary. Perhaps Bill's temper tantrums are a response to being punished for his aggressiveness and thus should be considered secondary to that problem.

Parent interviews are the most common method for selection and definition of target behaviors. Sometimes the child is included in these interviews (e.g., Patterson *et al.*, 1975) but often not. Direct questioning of the parents by the therapist is often sufficient to provide the necessary information. However, special techniques may be necessary if parents have difficulty generating specific target behaviors. The therapist may ask the parents to focus on recent instances when they were upset with the child. The therapist may also ask the parents to describe what some neutral observer (for instance, the therapist or a Martian) would see if that observer were present when the child was misbehaving. The therapist may even have the parents make notes during the coming week of instances of child misbehavior that are upsetting to them.

Sometimes questionnaires are useful in the selection and definition process. Patterson *et al.* (1975) have developed the Referral Problems Checklist, which consists of 32 common child problems such as aggressiveness, destructiveness, fearfulness, and lying. Each problem has a behavioral definition and behavioral examples. For example, destructiveness is defined as "rough treatment or the actual destruction of property." Examples are "throwing toys, messing up a game that someone else is playing, jumping on the sofa" (p. 155). Keefe, Kopel, and Gordon (1978) developed another measure, called the Checklist for Problematic Areas, which is organized by time of day: morning, after school, and after dinner. Possible problem areas in the morning include, for example, getting up, dressing, and eating breakfast.

If the process of selection and definition is done correctly, the therapist will have achieved two objectives. First, the parents will have selected a limited number of important child behaviors that will be the focus of treatment efforts; second, the parents will have defined the behaviors in such a way so that measurement of them is possible.

Measurement of Target Behaviors

Measurement is necessary to determine whether the target behaviors change as a result of treatment. A baseline measurement is conducted prior to treatment to establish the current rate of the behavior, and measurement is extended throughout treatment in order to determine the amount, if any, of change in the behavior. Measurement has, however, other functions than simply the assessment of change. The process of monitoring behavior may, by itself, have a positive reactive impact on behavior. Also, the obtained data may correct parental misperceptions about how frequently the child exhibits the behavior. Finally, measurement during the treatment period may serve to motivate parents as they see gradual changes in the child's behavior that they might not have otherwise noticed.

While parents are sometimes asked to estimate the frequency of a target behavior during the intake interview, these reports are not believed to be accurate enough to serve as an adequate baseline assessment. Furthermore, single estimates do not have any reactive or motivational effects. Therefore, parents are usually asked to measure the target behaviors by monitoring their occurrence at home. Patterson *et al.* (1975) assume that systematic observation is difficult and train parents during the session in this skill. They provide wrist counters to the parents, discuss a behavior that occurs frequently throughout the session, and have the parents independently record it for several minutes. This practice, with the discussion and feedback afterward, prepares the parents for home observation. Patterson *et al.* recommend daily phone calls to parents during the first few days of their data collection. These calls reinforce the importance of the monitoring and provide assistance for any difficulties with observation procedures.

Hall (1971) discusses specific methods for observing behavior that parents and teachers can use. Event recording, probably the most common method, involves a simple counting or tally of the frequency of a behavioral event (e.g., the number of times Bill hits his sister). In contrast, duration recording assesses the elapsed time of a behavior (e.g., amount of time crying during the night). Interval recording and time sampling are similar in that both involve a simple decision as to whether the behavior occurs or not at a particular time. In interval recording, the parent makes this decision in each of a series of continuous and usually short intervals (e.g., a series of 10-sec. intervals); in time sampling, the parent makes this decision only at the end of a longer interval (e.g., at the end of each 3 min.). To use an interval recording for measuring appropriate eating behavior during dinner, a parent might record the child as either eating appropriately or not during each 10-sec. interval during some part of the dinner time. To use a time-sampling procedure, the parent might note whether the child was eating appropriately or not at the end of each 5 min. of dinner time. Another procedure known as "direct measurement of permanent products" refers not to observations of behavior but to observations of the remains of behavior. For example, in using this procedure parents might count the number of toys left in the room or the number of math problems completed correctly.

The characteristics of the behavior and the convenience to the parent are the major factors in the selection of observational methods. If a behavior is discrete and easily observed, then event recording is usually the method of choice. If the behavior is not always observed but if it leaves a clearly observable product (such as clothes laying around the house), then the direct measurement of permanent products is preferable. Interval recording and time sampling are more complex since they both require timing cues, but they are often useful when a number of complex problem behaviors occur and one is interested in reducing this complexity to a simple appropriate–inappropriate dichotomy. Parents are also often asked to chart or graph the data that they collect (Hall, 1971; Patterson, 1971). This visual representation of the data provides clear and simple feedback about the course of the target behaviors throughout treatment.

Sometimes therapists themselves conduct observations of the target behaviors. They may go to the home or classroom (e.g., Keefe *et al.*, 1978; Patterson *et al.*, 1975) or may set up equipment for recording in the home (e.g., Christensen, 1979; Johnson, Christensen, & Bellamy, 1976). The expense of such procedures limits their use except for clinical research. Even when these procedures are used, therapists' observations are done in addition to, rather than instead of, parent monitoring. Therefore, in traditional behavioral assessment, parents are responsible for most measurements of target behaviors.

Functional Analysis of Target Behaviors

The above-described selection, definition, and measurement of target behaviors provide the therapist with information about what should be changed and gives the therapist a basis for evaluating that change. However, a functional analysis of the targeted behaviors is necessary to tell clinicians *how* to change those behaviors. A functional analysis examines the dynamic relationship between behavior and the stimulus events that control the behavior (Skinner, 1953). If done successfully, this analysis reveals the environmental conditions that elicit and maintain the target behaviors, thereby revealing which conditions must be altered if the behaviors are to be changed.

A simple way to conceptualize a functional analysis is in terms of a "three-term contingency" of antecedents, behaviors, and consequences (Bijou, Peterson, Harris, Allen, & Johnson, 1969). An antecedent–behavior–consequence or ABC analysis examines the events that regularly precede the target behavior and the events that regularly follow the target behavior. Therapists initially assume that these antecedents and consequences are functionally related to the behavior by serving as discriminative and reinforcing stimuli, respectively. In treatment, these assumptions can be evaluated by altering the antecedent and consequent events and examining whether the baseline rate of the behavior changes accordingly.

A functional analysis is typically conducted through a parent interview. Therapists' questions about the history of the target behavior (when it first started, how it developed), recent instances of the target behavior, and parents' efforts to cope with the behavior often provide revealing information about the events that elicit and maintain the behavior. Parents may be asked to describe a typical day in order to discover the sequence and context within which the target behavior occurs. Sometimes therapists ask parents to monitor the sequence of events around the target behavior for a few days in order to provide information for a functional analysis (Gelfand & Hartmann, 1984; Keefe *et al.*, 1978). Keefe *et al.* (1978) provide an example of such a recording in which parents noted what happened before and what happened after occasions of jealousy on the part of their older son.

LIMITATIONS OF THE CLASSICAL ASSESSMENT MODEL

Although the techniques of classical behavioral assessment and traditional behavioral family therapy (or parent training) have been developed through years of both clinical experience and empirical investigation, these approaches have a variety of limitations that may at times affect their clinical utility. For instance, when looking at the family as an entire system, it becomes apparent that conventional parent training focuses exclusively on one particular subsystem within the family—the parents and the target child, often only one parent (the mother) and the child. Factors affecting other subsystems of the family, for instance, the marital dyad or individual family members, are not systematically addressed. Further, while traditional parent training is limited in its focus on the parent and target child, it is also limited in its perspective within this subsystem. It is the parent's perspective, his or her definition of the problem, that is generally acknowledged and accepted. Additionally, it is the parent who is given responsibility for measuring and modifying the child's behavior; children are rarely asked to monitor or change their parents. While this rather one-sided approach may be justified in some cases, its potential problems and limitations must at least be acknowledged.

Due to these limitations of focus and perspective, factors arise that could interfere with the smooth, proper functioning of the traditional parent-training approach. These interfering factors can operate in two ways. They can interfere with the clinician's ability to assess the scope and complexity of a problem. They can also interfere with the effectiveness of a treatment intervention. These interfering factors fall into three categories: individual factors, marital factors, and familial factors.

Individual Factors

The traditional model makes a number of assumptions regarding the individual functioning of both the parents and the target child. Specifically, it is assumed that parents can make use of a fairly structured approach in dealing with their children and are able to accept the responsibility of measuring and modifying their own and their children's behavior. In order to accomplish this, the parents must be reasonable, logical, fairly well-organized, and amenable to change. Consequently, parental personality characteristics that are not consistent with these requirements or parental psychopathology might interfere with effective treatment. For instance, a parent who is psychotic would probably not be capable of meeting the requirements for parental involvement necessary to carry out a behavioral assessment and treatment program. At a less extreme level, a parent with a characteristically rigid view of the world (or of the child) might not be able to function adequately in a parent-training program. Some recent research also suggests that individual factors such as parental depression (Christensen, Phillips, Glasgow, & Johnson, 1983; Griest, Wells, & Forehand, 1979; Rickard, Forehand, Wells, Griest, & McMahon, 1981) or parental psychological adjustment (Griest, Forehand, Wells, & McMahon, 1980) may be related to the parent's tendency to perceive the child as deviant; these factors may therefore affect the ability to adequately report on the child's behavior.

Other important individual interfering factors relate to the target child. A rather obvious assumption involved in behavioral assessment of this sort is the belief that the child's behavior can be affected through a change strategy based on behavioral principles. The reasonableness of this assumption must obviously be evaluated for each individual child. Clearly, there are some classes of child pathology that are less amenable to this approach than others. For instance, some might argue that the severely disturbed, such as psychotic or affectively disordered children, might be better assessed individually rather than just in the context of their relationships with their parents. Failure to acknowledge such pathology on the child's part, just as failure to acknowledge pathology on a parent's part, might cause the clinician to underestimate the complexity of the family's situation in the assessment stage of treatment and/or might prevent effective treatment from taking place.

Marital Factors

In addition to the individual functioning of the parents and target child, the functioning of the marital dyad in the family must also be considered in assessing the applicability of a conventional parent-training program. There are at least two reasons for this, both of which have been substantiated through empirical investigation. First, a failure to assess marital factors can interfere with a proper conceptualization of the child's problems. Christensen *et al* (1983) and Oltmanns, Broderick, and O'Leary

(1977) have found that the state of the marital relationship may be related to deviance in the target child. Because the classical model attends only to the parent–child relationship, a major contributory factor to the child's problems (the marital relationship) may be ignored. Second, a poor marital relationship can affect treatment effectiveness since a cooperative set among the parents is necessary to carry out the essential aspects of the parent-training program, such as measurement of the child's behavior and a coordinated approach towards child care. Research indicates that a poor marital relationship precludes this cooperative set, which is necessary for the parents' work together during parent-training efforts (Miller, 1975). An additional finding that mothers with marital problems had more difficulty with parent training (Reisinger, Frangia, & Hoffman, 1976) lends more support to the notion that the state of the marital relationship can adversely affect behavioral treatment outcome.

Familial Factors

Certain family issues are excluded by the limited perspective and focus inherent in the classical model. Perhaps the most important of these issues relates to patient identification, the process by which the target child becomes defined as the source of the problem. There is some research evidence that this process often constitutes scapegoating. For instance, Arnold, Levine, and Patterson (1975) found no difference in the rate of deviant behavior between the identified patient and the other children in the families they studied. Other investigators have found that children who were referred for treatment were not necessarily more deviant in their behavior than a group of children who were not referred for treatment (Delfini, Bernal, & Rosen, 1976; Lobitz & Johnson, 1975). In addition, Christensen *et al.* (1983) showed that parental perceptions of child behavior are associated with the presence of marital discord and parental negative behavior toward the child but not with the actual behavior of the target child. These findings suggest that child behavior is not always the most important factor in the labeling and referral process and that the child may be the scapegoat for parental distress in the marriage. This, in turn, would suggest several things, including that, for some reason, parents (or the entire family) may single out one child to be defined as pathological even though he or she is not truly disturbed or is no more disturbed than other children in the family. A failure to assess both the functioning of the nonreferred siblings and the familial factors that account for the selection of the target child can interfere with the clinician's appreciation of the complexity of both the target child's problems as well as the family's problems.

Other Limitations

There are other potential limitations of the conventional behavioral approach. Specifically, there is some evidence that improvements through this method are very specific. For instance, improvements may be evident in the child's behavior at home but not at school (Johnson, Bolstad, & Lobitz, 1976; Wahler, 1975). While some of these aforementioned limitations have been acknowledged by proponents of the classical assessment model, a comprehensive framework for addressing these limitations has been absent. In an attempt to provide such a framework, we offer a new model of assessment—contextual assessment—that includes important aspects of the traditional model but also considers other factors, such as individual parent problems and marital discord.

CONTEXTUAL ASSESSMENT

The contextual assessment model retains central principles of the classical model but broadens the focus dramatically. As in the classical model, the emphasis remains on contemporaneous, proximal, and systems factors. Contextual family assessment focuses on contemporary rather than historical factors (as does classical behavioral assessment). While the importance of historical events is not denied, it is assumed that these events exert their influence through contemporary structures such as emotional tendencies and interpretative biases. For example, Dad's childhood history of rejection may account for his current punitive stance toward his children, but it is this current stance that is viewed as important.

The emphasis in contextual family assessment is also on the proximal factors of immediate experience rather than the distal factors of sociocultural forces. As with historical factors, it is assumed that sociocultural factors manifest themselves in the individual's immediate affective–cognitive–behavioral experience. For example, the differing expectations for men and women may explain, in part, Mom's poor assertiveness skills, but it is this lack of skills, not societal views, that is of immediate therapeutic concern.

Finally, contextual family assessment is systems oriented in that each potentially causative factor is considered in relation to other factors. Nothing is viewed as happening "out of the blue." While mentioning Mom's lack of assertiveness or Dad's punitiveness, the therapist also notes familial factors that maintain or enhance these tendencies. For example, Dad's punitiveness is so intimidating that it is hard for Mom to be assertive, while Mom's lack of assertiveness reinforces Dad's punitiveness by allowing it to go unchecked.

However, unlike classical behavioral assessment, contextual family assessment goes beyond the immediate, dyadic, behavioral context. First, it includes cognitive and affective factors as well as behavioral factors. While there is still interest in the sequence of antecedent–behavior–consequence, the focus is on the affective, behavioral, and cognitive events at each of these three levels. For instance, antecedents can refer to feelings, actions, or thoughts. Behavior is viewed broadly as emotional, cognitive, or motoric behavior. Likewise, consequences can be affective, behavioral, or cognitive events. For example, is the parent fearful of disobedience so that he or she makes a request in a commanding tone (affective and behavioral factors)? Is the child threatened or embarrassed by the manner of the parental remark (affective factors)? Does the parent interpret the disobedience as a personal insult and thus spank the child harshly (cognitive and behavioral factors)?

Second, contextual family assessment extends the focus beyond the immediate context of the problem. Compared with traditional behavioral assessment, it uses a wider angle lens and can see a longer sequence of events. What were the antecedants for the antecedant? Is Dad so often frustrated when he comes home that he yells at Susan to stop her usual energetic behavior? What are the consequences of the consequence? Does Mom's punishment of Billy's disobedience lead him to withdraw from her?

Finally, contextual family assessment extends the focus beyond the dyad of parent and child. The social context of the marriage and the entire family system are considered. Does Dad selectively respond to Frank's misbehavior while ignoring Julie's misconduct? Does Frank therefore disobey Dad's command, partly out of a sense of being treated unfairly? Does Mom order Ben to clean up when she is really angry at Dad for leaving so many messes? Does Dad spank Mary as a way of punishing Mom?

While broadening the focus, contextual family assessment retains the emphasis on sequence. The logic of functional analysis, illustrated by the antecedent–behavior–consequence paradigm, is simply applied in a larger context. The search for causes of the behavior of interest covers more locations, but the methodology is the same.

A contextual family assessment refocuses the problem even more dramatically than does traditional behavioral assessment. A family presenting with a child's problem often views the problem as residing totally in the child. In the traditional behavioral assessment, the therapist tentatively accepts the parents' view but directs them to look at how they may be unwittingly eliciting and reinforcing the child's symptomatic behavior. In a contextual family assessment, the therapist may also initially accept the parental view but then directs their attention to the preceding, concurrent, and consequent factors in the broad sequence of their family's interaction. If successful, the family begins to see that the problem is *the context*. Rather than being a case of Bill's noncompliance, which the parents in part elicit and reinforce, it is a case of Dad's intolerance, Mom's anger with Dad, Susie's effort to be the favorite child, and Bill's resistance.

The danger in conducting a contextual family assessment is seeing so much at so many different levels that confusion results. The intricate, multidimensional patterning of the family makes the problem of not seeing the forest for the trees all too common. What the therapist must do, of course, is discern the important factors, the ones that are most influential in the family's problems. If the wife's problems at work or the couple's sexual difficulties are not exerting important influences on the difficulties for which the family is seeking help, they should be ignored. There is never time to address all of a family's problems; furthermore, the family members rarely give us license to do so.

The key to determining what are important family factors is consistency. If something is a problem, it will happen repeatedly. If Mom's difficulties at work leave her so frustrated that she lashes out at the children repeatedly, then these difficulties warrant attention. If Jeff regularly plays Mom against Dad so he can get his own way, then this behavior should command therapist's attention. Because of the repetitious nature of human problems, the therapist need not be anxious about missing any important factors. If they are important, he or she will see them again and again and again.

In a contextual assessment, problems are organized by the units in the family—individuals, dyads, triads, and larger units building up to the entire family system. In most families, the most important units will be individuals, the marital dyad, and the entire family system. In some families, however, a sibling dyad or a grandmother–mother–daughter triad might be an important unit. Different problems will be associated with particular family units. For example, at the individual level, Susie gets fearful about performing well in school. At the marital level, Mom and Dad can't agree on how strong discipline should be for the kids. At the family systems level, Dad and Joe gang up on Mom.

When problems are attributed to an individual in the family, they should be described in such a way that the individual's reaction seems a natural one to the circumstances in which he or she exists. For instance, Susie gets anxious about school because she is afraid she won't be liked if she doesn't perform at the top of her class. James gets so upset when Debbie teases and tattles on him because he feels she and his parents gang up against him. Dad gets so angry with the kids because he feels Mom won't support him.

When problems are attributed to a dyad or larger system, they should be described in such a way that each person's role in the system is clarified. For example, on the marital level, a wife might be angry at not getting enough support from her husband so she criticizes him and ignores the things he does do. Feeling criticized, the husband withdraws further support in a "well, let her do it" attitude. A family systems example might be as follows: Mom feels Dad is too strict with the kids so she lets them do things he wouldn't. The kids naturally go to Mom for permission rather than to Dad, since they are more likely to get what they want. Dad gets angry at Mom for undermining his authority and puts even heavier restrictions on the children.

CONDUCTING A CONTEXTUAL ASSESSMENT

Procedurally, a contextual family assessment begins with the presenting problems of the family. As in classical behavioral family assessment, this assessment examines the immediate antecedents and consequences of these problems, but the examination includes affective and cognitive as well as behavioral and environmental events. Next, the focus broadens to include less immediate antecedent and consequent events related to the presenting problem, as well as a screening assessment of other family members, the marital dyad, and the family system as a whole. When the contemporaneous interaction of the entire family system, covering the multiple levels of affect, cognition, and behavior, has been examined in relation to the presenting problems, then the assessment is complete.

In the course of conducting a contextual assessment of a family, the therapist should keep a number of goals in mind. As mentioned above, he or she will want to understand the presenting problem, including the behaviors and their immediate antecedents and consequences. A related goal is to gain enough information to decide whether to accept the family's definition of the problem. A third goal is to assess the family's capacity to cooperate in treatment. For example, if the parents are seriously disturbed as individuals or as a couple, can they be expected to learn the skills presented in behavior therapy? It is also important to attend to other potential impediments to successful therapy. For example, if a family member is unemployed, declaring bankruptcy, and trying to find work, the therapist must be aware of these factors and decide whether behavioral family therapy is appropriate at this time. Finally, there are goals pertaining more to the process, rather than the content, of the initial session. These include establishing a relationship between family and therapist, instilling a sense of hope, and providing a beginning sense of what therapy will be like.

The Screening Procedure

The initial family assessment may consist of one to three interviews. The entire family should be present for the first interview, although it may be desirable to see the parents as a couple at some point during the assessment for at least two reasons. First, parents are often reluctant to discuss their concerns and observations in front of the child being discussed. Second, there may be issues between the parents that they prefer to discuss privately. All family members should, however, be present at the beginning of the first interview. This includes everyone living in the home, including immediate family, grandparents, and cousins. There are at least three reasons for this. First, it allows the therapist to meet the full cast of characters involved in the family problem. He or she can become acquainted with their perceptions of and feelings about the presenting problem and the identified patient. Second, the therapist can observe the interaction of individuals and dyads within the family system. Finally, by insisting that the entire family be present, the therapist plants the notion that the problem and its solution lie in the family as a whole rather than solely within the identified patient.

As the family is seated, introductions are made and some few minutes can be spent in small talk. This seemingly trivial social ritual provides an important transition period for the family members, allowing them to become acquainted with the therapist's style and to prepare to discuss what may be difficult and revealing topics. This is also a valuable time for the therapist. He or she can begin to get a sense of the psychological adjustment of individual family members, of the family style, and of the relationships of individuals to the family as a whole: Who is the family spokesperson? Who is the family disciplinarian? Who is the family comic? Additional information can be gained from noticing the family's seating arrangements: Who sits next to whom? Do parents sit together or are they separated by children? Hunches based on these observations can be pursued during the formal part of the assessment.

Initial Focus

Typically, the initial focus of the meeting will be the presenting problem as it involves the parent–child dyad. The therapist may begin by simply asking the family the reason for coming to therapy, perhaps by referring to a previous phone conversation: "Mrs. Gordon, I understand you are concerned about Lois's truancy. Perhaps you could tell me more about it?" The therapist can then encourage each family member to contribute their perspective: "I want to hear from all of you."

Further information is gathered about the behavior of interest itself, about concurrent cognitions and feelings of those immediately involved, and about the proximal antecedents and consequences of the behavior. At this stage of the interview, it is important that information be gathered without therapist collaboration in familial blaming or attacking of the identified patient. Instead, the message should be conveyed that the child is behaving a certain way for a reason (rather than because he or she is "bad") and that the therapist is interested in everyone's point of view, including that of the identified patient. This nonblaming message is conveyed implicitly when the therapist cuts short critical statements attacking the identified patient and encourages the identified patient to present his or her point of view.

Expanding the Focus

Once information about the antecedents, behavior, and consequences of the presenting problem as it involves the parent–target child dyad is collected, the therapist may widen the focus of the interview. At this point, he or she moves beyond immediate, proximal antecedents and consequences and beyond the parent–child dyad. In order to do this, the therapist may ask about thoughts, feelings, and behaviors preceding the immediate antecedents and following the immediate consequences. For example, the therapist might say, "OK, so Walter swears at Mom when he is asked to do his chores. Does this always happen? It sounds as if it only happens when he has been teased by his brothers earlier." Or, "Dad, after you punish Mike for playing with matches, it sounds as though you continue to feel really angry. What happens with that anger?" In doing this, the therapist begins to link familial factors to the problem behavior of the identified patient.

The therapist will also want to widen the focus beyond the parent–child dyad to other family members, including nonidentified siblings, as in the following examples. "Kathleen, when your parents and Stephen are upset at each other, what do you do? Do you get involved in their fighting? How does it make you feel?" "John, how does the conflict between Colleen and your folks affect your relationship with your parents and with your brother?" "Sally, it seems as though when your sister ran away you thought she did it on purpose to hurt the family. Could you tell us more about that?"

As the focus widens and family members become involved in the discussion, it is critical that the therapist maintain control of the interview. If a family begins fighting, they may leave the session feeling discouraged. They may also suspect that the therapist cannot break their powerful and destructive patterns of interaction and consequently is not strong enough to implement change.

At the end of this phase, the therapist should have an understanding of the problem in its larger context. He or she should know something about the proximal and distal antecedents and consequences, about the effect of conflict on other family members and dyads in addition to the parent–child dyad, and about the feelings and thoughts family members have about the conflict.

Assessing Individual Family Members

The process of assessing individual family members will have begun during the initial introduction period of the interview, as the therapist obsevers how each member handles the stress of the first session. It continues throughout the assessment interview, as the therapist more formally assesses the individual's social and school or occupational functioning. For instance, the clinician might say, "Now that I have a sense of what brought you here, I'd like to get to know each of you a little better." Subsequent questions may relate to school or job performance, social activities with friends, and so on, with the goal being to determine whether problems exist that will interfere with treatment of the family or that will require a redefinition of the presenting problem, thus necessitating further assessment.

Assessing the Marital Dyad

To assess the parental couple, the therapist should begin with an assessment of their functioning with respect to the identified patient and progress to questions about more general marital functioning. For example, "Sometimes parents disagree about how to handle a child's problems. Does that happen to the two of you?" "How has the conflict between Mom and Marc affected your relationship as a couple?" "What happens when the two of you fight? How is that related to the family conflict overall?"

At the same time, a great deal of information will be gained from the couple's behavior in the interview. Do they begin to fight over problem definition or over how to discipline their children? If they are unable to present a united front to the therapist, it is unlikely that they are able to do so at home with their children. During this phase of the interview, the therapist will usually want to see the couple alone and may also wish to observe the couple discuss an issue from behind a one-way mirror or from a corner of the room, in order to get a sense of the couple's general style of interaction.

Assessing the Family System

By this point, the therapist should have some sense of the larger family context and the roles played by individuals and dyads within the family. In order to understand the relationship of individuals and dyads within the system, it is helpful to think in terms of family structure: Where are the alliances in the family? Who defends them? Who speaks for whom? Is the identified patient being scapegoated while his or her sibling is the family star? Questions should be asked in order to clarify relationships as in the following examples: "It appears that Billy began to be a problem when his big brother left home. Before this, the brother was the family problem. Are these two things, brother leaving home and Billy's temper tantrums, related?" It also may be helpful for the therapist to observe the family unobtrusively as they talk, through a one-way mirror if possible.

After completion of the contextual assessment screening phase of contact with a family, the clinician is faced with a number of choice points. The clinician may feel satisfied that this procedure has helped to elucidate all of the relevant factors for understanding and thus treating the problem(s) at hand. If so, the clinician may provide a brief summary of what has been observed. However, in some instances, the clinician becomes concerned about something other than what the family has presented as the problem that warrants intervention. This concern can take two possible forms. The clinician may become concerned about a subsystem of the family other than the subsystem that the family has isolated as the source of the difficulty. For instance, while the family might seek treatment because of their son's school problems, the clinician might become concerned about the state of the marital relationship. Thus, while the family has focused on an individual as the subsystem of the family in need of attention, the clinician might wish to focus on a dyadic subsystem (in this case, the marriage). Another form that the clinician's concern may take is interest is a construct other than that on which the family has focused. Additionally, the clinician may believe that the family has correctly identified the problematic subsystem but has not identified the right problem within the subsystem. For example, while the family might be concerned about Joey's seeming disobedience, the therapist might become concerned that Joey is depressed.

FURTHER ASSESSMENT

This section provides a guide for the clinician in terms of further assessment should either or both of the above situations arise. The specific issues addressed include how to determine whether the family has identified the appropriate problem or whether further assessment is necessary; which subsystems, constructs, perspectives, and methodologies to utilize during assessment; and how to conduct the redefinition process that frequently ensues. Each of these issues are discussed within the framework of dealing with individual, marital, and family problems.

The issue of how to determine whether or not an issue should be pursued by further assessment is necessarily a difficult one. There are two general guidelines in this regard. First, the presenting problem should always be fully assessed in order to determine whether the problem actually exists at all and also to understand the specifics of the problem in detail. Second, any other apparent pathology in the family should at the least be acknowledged by the clinician. Pathology should be pursued by further formal assessment in any of the following three instances: (1) if left untreated, the particular pathology will interfere with the successful course of treatment for the presenting problem; (2) if an assessment of the issue of interest is necessary for an adequate conceptualization or understanding of the presenting problem; or (3) if the family member (or subsystem) of interest requests aid. Therefore, given the guidelines above, in a family seeking treatment for a child's oppositional behavior, should the therapist suspect that the mother in the family is depressed, he or she would at least acknowledge this to her. However, the mother's psychological functioning would not be assessed further unless (1) the clinician suspected that her depression would interfere with the treatment of her child's difficulties; (2) assessment of her functioning would contribute greatly to an understanding of the causes of the child's problems; or (3) she requested treatment for this problem.

Assessment issues, such as which subsystem to focus on and which construct to use, depend largely on the problem at hand and are addressed subsequently. However, a few general words about perspective and methodology will be useful in further assessment of any problem. In assessing any subsystem, one can gather information from a variety of perspectives. For example, in assessing children, one could gather information from the children themselves, their parents, their siblings, their friends, and their teachers. This would constitute an assessment that utilizes a variety of perspectives. The advantages of such a practice are obvious, including primarily the ability to gain a more multidimensional view of the subject of the assessment. The disadvantages involve the limitations of practicality. Obviously, the advantages gained from a multiple perspective assessment must be weighed against the demands of time and effort involved in conducting such an assessment.

As always with assessment, any number of assessment methodologies are available: for example, questionnaires, structured interviews, observational techniques, etc. The use of a variety of methodologies is best since it provides different ways of viewing the construct of interest. The overall aim, through attention to perspective and methodology, is to provide if possible a cross-perspective, cross-methodology convergence with regard to the construct being assessed. For instance, if a child is judged to be depressed from the point of view of his parents, teachers, and the clinician based on data gained from observational techniques, questionnaires, and a structured interview, then one's confidence in the validity of the findings is greatly enhanced.

Assessing Individual Problems

Individual problems that warrant further assessment could involve any individual in the family, including either parent, the target child, or non-target siblings. In making judgments about which individual problems should be pursued beyond the initial contextual assessment, clinicians have their own standards of individual pathology that they use, probably on a daily basis, in making these decisions. In addition, it should be noted whether an individual's belief system, emotional styles, and/or behaviors extend beyond the immediate antecedent–consequence structure of the presenting problem. For instance, does mother only scream and become enraged when Johnny does not obey her (consequence to presenting problem) or does she react this way in a variety of situations, in and outside of the family? If the latter is true, then this reaction may have more to do with mother's style than with Johnny's behavior. In such a situation, one might decide to assess mother's personality characteristics further.

The decision regarding which construct to focus on through further assessment is complex. Obviously, the possible range of individual constructs to assess is broad and includes the full scope of individual factors, including the individual adult and child psychopathologies, such as autism, schizophrenia, affective disorders, personality disorders, etc. Personality factors chosen often depend on the theoretical system to which the clinician ascribes and could include factors that are emotional (for example, mother's excitability), behavioral (son's stealing) or cognitive (father's paranoia).

The perspective chosen for assessment of individual problems is quite important. In assessing the individual parent, the perspectives most often selected include the parent (self-report) and possibly an adult significant other, for instance, a mate. Rarely are children asked for impressions of their parents, although this would at least theoretically be interesting information to obtain. Unfortunately, most of the assessment instruments pertaining to adults utilize self-report, thus limiting the options available for multiperspective assessment.

In assessing the individual child, the perspective most often chosen is that of the child's parent. While this information is important, another possible option, especially in assessing more subjective symptoms (for instance, depression), is to utilize the child as a reporting agent. While the great number of measures relating to child problems assess the child from the parent's perspective, a few measures, most notably those relating to depression and self-esteem, value the child's perspective. Rarely are siblings asked to report on one another's behavior through formal assessment tools, although this could be done through interview. For instance, they could be interviewed about one another's behavior, while keeping in mind the limitations of each child's developmental level. Last, if another adult's perspective on a child construct is desired, information from teachers could provide another source of data.

The range of methodologies available for assessing individual adult factors include, of course, questionnaires, observation techniques, and structured interviews. The appropriate methodology for assessing child problems depends partly on the age of the child. With younger children, monitoring and observing their behavior is more practical and convenient than administering questionnaires. This changes as a child ages and is better able to respond to questionnaires and it becomes harder to monitor behavior since the child is less frequently in the parents' presence. Also, the usefulness of interview techniques depends on the child's verbal capacity and developmental level.

Example

The Smiths bring in their son, Alan, for treatment because he is "unruly and disobedient." In the initial screening, the therapist, based on his own standards of normal child functioning, begins to suspect that another sibling in the family, Joyce, seen by her parents as the "good" child, is depressed and withdrawn. Because the therapist is uncertain what role Joyce's seeming depression may play in understanding Alan's problems, the therapist decides to do further assessment of Joyce's psychological functioning. Aware of the parents' tendency to see this child in a flattering light, the clinician asks for the parents' perceptions of Joyce on both an objective and subjective measure of child adjustment. Since some depressive symptoms are also experienced subjectively, a self-report questionnaire regarding depression is given to Joyce. Last, the clinician interviews the child using questions drawn from a standardized interview procedure. In this assessment scheme, the perspectives utilized included those of both the parents and the child, and the methodologies chosen included questionnaires, clinician observation, and interview.

Assessing Marital Problems

Whether or not marital issues should be assessed beyond the initial screening assessment should depend on the severity of any perceived marital problems, of course, and at least two other factors. First, it is important to determine to what degree the marital difficulty seems related to the presenting problem(s); second, and most importantly, it is important to determine whether these difficulties will interfere with the parents' ability to maintain a collaborative set in the treatment of the presenting problem.

While there exists a variety of marital functioning constructs that could be pursued through further assessment, perhaps the most commonly investigated of these include marital satisfaction, conflict, communication styles, and sexual functioning and satisfaction. However, the most important of these is marital satisfaction since this global concept usually correlates highly with the other, more specific indices of marital distress. The perspective of most of the standard marital assessment devices is that of the couple themselves. While one could argue that for subjective constructs like marital and sexual satisfaction, self-report is most appropriate, the perspectives of others in the environment, for instance, the children, might also be considered. The range of methodologies available for assessing couples is similar to that for assessing individuals. However, interviews and questionnaires are used most often in assessing marital satisfaction.

Example

The Jones family comes in for therapy with their son, George, who is a fire-setter. During initial screening, it becomes apparent to the clinician through her own observation that the parents have a marriage marked by distance and voiced dissatisfaction. In her opinion, these problems would interfere with the parents' ability to cooperate in treating their son's difficulties. The clinician also suspects that the parents' relationship may be directly related to George's behavior since on almost every occasion that he has started a fire, the parents had been arguing just beforehand (established through the contextual assessment). To further assess the marital situation, the clinician administers several questionnaire measures to the parents that focus on marital adjustment and satisfaction. Note that in this example, both the perspectives and methodologies employed are somewhat limited.

Assessing Family Problems

Issues involving the entire family unit should be pursued by further assessment when the causal sequence that links family members' behaviors to the presenting problem becomes quite complex. For instance, consider the following causal sequence: Father's stressful day at work is followed by Mother's ignoring of his complaints, which leads to his reported feelings of frustration and subsequent screaming at his daughter, Mary. This is, in turn, followed by Mary's temper tantrums (the presenting problem), which are reinforced by attention from Mother. This results in an angry response by Father (who is again feeling ignored by his wife) and by disruptive behavior from the other children in the family. In this case, the causal sequence involving the presenting problem is quite complicated and involves all family members. In cases such as this, it might be wise to consider assessing the family as a unit. Additionally, assessing a problem in family unit terms becomes more efficient both conceptually and practically. For instance, it is more straightforward to conceptualize a problem as related to a family's "lack of cohesion" rather than to Father's unwillingness to be involved in child care, the daughter's sense of isolation, Mother's distance from the marital unit, and the son's sense of being an abandoned child. It is also more efficient to assess only one construct than to assess four different ones.

There are any number of theoretical constructs that could be assessed on the family unit level. They include such issues as family structure, schism and skew, enmeshment, and disengagement, although family structure (that is, who is allied with whom, the characteristics of intrafamilial boundaries, etc.) is probably the most vital of these. In terms of perspective, it is important to gain information from all family members in assessing family unit issues. Methodology choice does present something of a problem in this area since the field of family assessment is still somewhat primitive. However, there are questionnaire measures as well as some observational techniques that do assess family functioning (e.g., Benjamin, 1974, 1977; Moos & Moos, 1976; Olson, Russell, & Sprenkle, 1980; Olson, Sprenkle, & Russell, 1979).

Example

The Everson family comes into therapy because their daughter, Lily, is reportedly anxious and withdrawn at school. As is typical of most families in this situation, the family assumes that the problem lies within the individual child. In the course of the initial screening, the therapist finds that, in fact, all family members show signs of anxiety difficulties, most notably the mother, who suffers from agoraphobia. It is additionally revealed that, while not meeting the formal criteria for psychiatric illness, other family members are relucant to engage in relationships outside of the home. This information, as well as the clinician's observations of "mind-reading" behavior on the part of family members, leads the therapist to believe that the concept of enmeshment characterizes this family's functioning and that further family unit assessment should be undertaken.

The Process of Redefinition

Once the clinician has completed the process of extended assessment discussed above, the question of redefinition arises. The clinician may choose to redefine the problem from that which the family has pinpointed as the presenting problem. This redefinition can occur for a number of reasons.

For one, it could be that the clinician has determined that the presenting problem does not exist at all or does not exist at the level of severity initially described by the family. For example, it could turn out after fuller assessment that Johnny doesn't have school problems as his parents believed. Second, it could be that further assessment has uncovered dimensions of the problem not considered by the family. For instance, contextual assessment of the sequencing of behavior might reveal a more complex causal chain than what was previously recognized. For example, when the parents fight, Johnny doesn't do his homework. Third, other problems might be uncovered that might not be directly related to the presenting problem (for instance, Mother's depression or Father's alcoholism).

The conventional redefinition that takes place in classical behavior family therapy is to reframe the parent's initial complaint ("our son is disobedient") as a parent–child problem ("your son doesn't receive the proper consequences for being obedient"). During contextual assessment, this redefinition can take any of a variety of forms. For instance, while the family is likely to present problems in terms of an individual child, the clinician is free to redefine these problems in terms of another child, either parent, the marital dyad, or the entire family unit. Once a redefinition has taken place, the way is cleared for the clinician not only to conceptualize issues in a different way but also to reflect this new conceptualization in the forms of assessment chosen. For instance, in the typical redefinition case referred to above, the clinician will now be interested in examining a new construct created by the redefinition, namely a parent–child construct rather than a construct tapping individual child behavior.

The above process becomes particularly important in a behavioral treatment framework since the process of assessment, treatment evaluation, and treatment modification is a continual one. Therefore, in the typical case, redefinition generates a new construct of interest to be assessed, addressed through some intervention effort, and then further assessed in order to determine the effectiveness of treatment. A family may come into treatment due to concerns about their child's anorexia. After full assessment, the clinician decides to redefine the problem from the child's anorexia to the family's overinvolvement with one another. Family overinvolvement then becomes the construct of interest. At this point, a treatment plan is devised to solve the problem of family overinvolvement, and measures to assess family overinvolvement are used throughout treatment to track the success of the intervention and to lead to modification in the treatment plan, if necessary. Finally, measures of family overinvolvement are used to evaluate treatment outcome when treatment is completed. The following case example illustrates the various points regarding contextual assessment and problem redefinition that have been highlighted throughout this chapter.

CASE EXAMPLE

Peter and Jane Williams entered therapy to discuss problems they were having with one of their two children. Peter, aged 35, was a corporate lawyer in a large law firm, while Jane, aged 32, was a full-time homemaker. Their two sons, Mark and Josh, attended a private religious school. Mark was 7 at the time of the interview; Josh, aged 6, was the identified patient. An attractive family, they lived in an upper-middle-income suburb of the city.

During the interview, Jane was energetic, highly verbal, and sarcastic. She described herself as disciplined and competitive. Peter was quiet and more passive. He displayed a quiet, self-deprecating style of humor and described himself as "more laid back" than his wife. Both children were friendly and active during the interview. They appeared to compete for parental attention.

Presenting Problem

The parents had indicated in the initial telephone contact that they were most concerned about Josh. As they elaborated in the initial screening session, Josh was often disobedient at school and at home and used "bad words." This was especially troubling in public. Lately, Josh had begun to swear at Jane and Mark at home. The parents were also concerned with the brothers' "constant bickering, although they rarely hit each other." Jane thought that Josh provoked Mark until a fight began. She also worried that she responded too inconsistently and occasionally too harshly. She was beginning to feel helpless to control Josh. Another problem mentioned by Jane was her unhappiness that Peter was not more involved with the children.

Initial Focus

Both parents defined the presenting problem as Josh's behavior—his disobedience, swearing at family members at home and in public, and picking fights with his brother, Mark. This latter behavior often consisted of wandering into his brother's room when Mark was involved in homework or his hobbies and refusing to leave. In order to assess this problem, Peter and Jane pinpointed two of Josh's worst problem behaviors: swearing and refusing to obey after a request was made of him. They were asked to record the occurrence of these behaviors, noting the time of day and immediate circumstances of their occurrence.

Upon further discussion and examination of the data collected by Peter and Jane, it appeared that there were clear immediate antecedents to Josh's problem behaviors. All of these behaviors occurred more frequently when Josh was tired and when he had been teased at school. He was most likely to swear when Jane or Mark were absorbed in something that excluded him: for instance, when Jane was cleaning house or cooking, when Mark was working in his room, or when Jane helped Mark with his homework.

When Josh misbehaved, a fairly predictable sequence of events followed. At first, Jane would try to ignore him. When she found herself unable to ignore him, she would speak sharply to him. Sometimes she would take him by the hand to scold him; other times she would take him to his room and tell him why his behavior was wrong. Peter was generally not involved in discipline. His job required long hours, and by the time he came home the children were often ready for bed and somewhat calmer. When Josh provoked Mark, Mark would first protest quietly, then yell at him, and finally call for Jane to intervene.

Based on this brief assessment, it appeared that Josh had his mother under good stimulus control. When he misbehaved, he was eventually reinforced with one-on-one attention from his mother. He had habituated to his mother's yelling; in fact, her eventual attention after first ignoring him reinforced his continued disobedience. As Josh was accustomed to one-on-one attention in his classes at school, he found it difficult to share his mother's attention with his brother. He was also unlikely to want to play by himself.

Expansion of Initial Focus

The initial analysis appeared fairly straightforward. However, when the focus of the interview was expanded, it became clear that the problem was actually rather more complex. The decision was made to see the parents alone for this part of the interview, as they appeared hesitant to talk frankly about their sons in front of them.

As Josh's misbehavior increased when he was teased at school, the therapists wondered how often this teasing occurred and how severe the problem was. Josh was teased for several reasons, among them his erratic school performance and his attendance at the "special education class" at his school. He had been diagnosed as having "delayed perceptual development of unknown etiology." According to tests, he had few skills in reading or arithmetic and virtually no spelling ability. He also had a very short attention span. These clear intellectual deficits were coupled with a low-normal IQ. He was also extremely frustrated with failure and competed with his brother's more adequate school performance.

Jane spent much of her day taking her boys to various activities. Both children received special tutoring. While Mark did not have Josh's intellectual deficits, he had been diagnosed as hyperactive. Jane preferred to keep him off Ritalin, and his tutor worked with him on improving concentration. There were also tennis lessons for Mark. As a result of all this activity, Jane was often tired and resentful of her husband. This, in turn, aggravated her lack of consistency in disciplining her children. Marital tension often preceded fights between Josh and Mark. Jane and Peter described several incidents in which they had begun to loudly disagree over something, only to hear Mark calling them from his room because "Josh won't leave me alone."

Jane felt resentful of the demands made on her by the children and guilty for her often erratic responses to them. Peter felt unappreciated as a money-earner; it was his hard work, after all, that paid for all of the boys' lessons. There were also underlying tensions concerning the cause of Josh's learning problems and Mark's hyperactivity. Peter had been exposed to Agent Orange before the children were conceived. Although Jane had never directly blamed Peter for the children's problems, the question of blame was raised indirectly after an incident involving Josh's misbehavior and school problems. Another consequence of Josh's fights with Mark was that they temporarily interrupted marital discord. However, this was a short-lived respite; in the long run, it only added to an already tense situation.

When the entire family was present for the screening procedure, both children were somewhat overactive, yet both were fairly easily influenced by social reinforcement and punishment (ignoring) when these responses were consistently delivered. When the parents were interviewed in the children's absence, they were more likely to begin overt fighting over marital issues.

Evaluation of Other Family Subsystems

Individuals

Mark had some academic problems at school, and it had been suggested that he was dyslexic. However, his grades were satisfactory (with tutoring), and he had several good friends at school. He was less happy at home and volunteered (to his parents' surprise) that, "I don't like it when they [his parents] fight."

Josh had had a full intellectual and perceptual test battery administered within the past year to which the parents allowed the therapist access. Josh had few friends and was beginning to become increasingly aware that he was different from the other children at school and was being left behind. He was continually frustrated in his attempts to succeed at school.

Information gathered from the interview and from observation of Jane's behavior during the screening sessions suggested that Jane was a bright, articulate woman without any major psychopathology or character disorder. She tended to be overinvolved in multiple projects, to feel continually under time pressure, and to be highly impatient with delays and interruptions. Her days were occupied with her house, with the children's numerous activities such as tutoring and sports, with parent groups related to her children's school, and with her own activities such as tennis and jogging. Concommitant with these activities was a feeling of resentment toward her husband for not being more involved with the family.

During the interview Peter appeared to be a quiet, rather sensitive man who tended to be self-critical and sometimes lacking in confidence. As a younger member of a prominent law firm with a family and household to support, he felt very pressured to do well and rise within the firm. As a result, he worked long hours and often weekends. Peter felt his wife's accusations of lack of involvement in the family were highly unfair. However, he felt helpless to adequately express these feelings in a direct, assertive fashion. In interactions with the therapist, Peter was articulate, amusing, and intelligent; in interactions with his wife he became quiet, withdrawn, and sullen.

Marital Dyad

Based on the couple's self-report and on observations made in the interview, it was clear that there was extreme marital discord. Individually they were very pleasant people; they socialized frequently with other couples and were active in the community. As a couple, however, they were barely civil to one another. A repetitious interaction pattern occurred that consisted of Jane's attacks on Peter followed by his attempts at defense and his eventual withdrawal. His silence only angered Jane further, prompting more sarcastic remarks.

Family System

During the session, it appeared that the children increased their activity levels and quarreling as the parents escalated their arguments. Mark appeared frightened by his parents' raised voices, and Josh responded by seeking his mother's lap. Sometimes the two children would begin to argue, too. The parents, distracted, would stop their argument temporarily. This in turn, reinforced the children's misbehavior.

Further Assessment and Redefinition

Based on the screening interview, the therapist began to entertain the hypothesis that the marital issues were the primary problem in the family and that they might warrant further assessment. This idea was further supported by the results of initial, exploratory attempts to change Josh's behavior by altering the immediate antecedents and consequences. These attempts were largely successful; however, Peter and Jane's ability to effectively collaborate in behavior change efforts were hampered by their marital conflict. For example, Peter sometimes sabotaged Jane's use of time-out to punish Josh for swearing. In addition, as noted earlier, parental conflict was a powerful antecedent to Josh's misbehavior.

A session devoted to further marital assessment utilized interviews and standardized questionnaires, such as the Areas of Change Questionnaire (Weiss, Hops, & Patterson, 1973) and the Dyadic Adjustment Scale (Spanier, 1976). On both of the questionnaire measures, Peter and Jane scored in the "distressed" range. Based on interviews and questionnaire data, the therapist suggested a redefinition of the problem—that the most critical issue was the marital relationship rather than Josh's behavior. This redefinition was accepted by Jane and Peter with some relief, and marital therapy was begun immediately.

SUMMARY

Clearly, a behaviorally based family assessment relies on context as a way of understanding the phenomena of interest. A traditional behavioral assessment procedure focuses on the behavior of interest and the behavioral antecedents and consequences that initiate and maintain it. However, the variety of limitations that are associated with such conventional assessment and treatment procedures suggests that a broader based contextual assessment would be more appropriate. This revised assessment procedure includes broader perspectives on a number of levels. First of all, the phenomena of interest, as well as any antecedents or consequences related to them, are not restricted to just behaviors but also include emotions and cognitions. Additionally, the causal chain (antecedents and consequences) of interest is made more complex by the introduction of "antecedents to antecedents" and "consequences to consequences." A broader based contextual assessment also allows for extensive focus on a variety of subsystems in the family or on constructs that may not be directly related to the presenting problem. Last, this procedure provides for the redefinition of the problem from a purely individual (child) or strictly dyadic (parent–child) focus to include any subsystem that is deemed appropriate.

The area of family assessment is still in its infancy; consequently, future empirical and theoretical work in this field should add tremendous clarity and flexibility to assessment endeavors. For instance, the development and refinement of measures of family unit functioning will provide the clinician with better—that is, more valid and reliable—ways of assessing the many family unit constructs that have been proposed by the various family functioning theories. To the extent that new developments are made in the area of measurement, clinicians will be faced with more choices and a greater ability to produce assessments that are specific to their interests and needs. This chapter has attempted to provide a framework that does not dictate to the clinician a specific set of instruments to be utilized in conducting assessments but rather suggests a set of issues to be considered, as well as guidelines that will help focus and define assessment efforts.

REFERENCES

Arnold, J. E., Levine, A. G., & Patterson, G. R. (1975). Changes in sibling behavior following family intervention. *Journal of Consulting and Clinical Psychology, 43*, 683–688.

Benjamin, L. S. (1974). Structural analysis of social behavior. *Psychological Review, 81*, 392–425.

Benjamin, L. S. (1977). Structural analysis of a family in therapy. *Journal of Consulting and Clinical Psychology, 45*, 391–406.

Bijou, S. W., Peterson, R. F., Harris, E. R., Allen, K. E., & Johnston, M. S. (1969). Methodology for experimental studies of young children in natural settings. *The Psychological Record, 19*, 177–210.

Christensen, A. (1979). Naturalistic observation of families: A system for random audio recordings in the home. *Behavior Therapy, 10*, 418–422.

Christensen, A., Phillips. S., Glasgow, R. E., & Johnson, S. M. (1983). Parental characteristics and interactional dysfunction in families with child behavior problems: A preliminary investigation. *Journal of Abnormal Child Psychology, 11*(1), 153–166.

Delfini, L. F., Bernal, M. E., & Rosen, P. M. (1976). Comparison of deviant and normal boys in home settings. In E. J. Mash, L. A. Hamerlynck, & L. C. Handy (Eds.), *Behavioral modification and families*. New York: Brunner/Mazel.

Gelfand, D. M., & Hartmann, D. P. (1984). *Child behavior analysis and therapy* (2nd ed.). New York: Pergamon Press.

Gordon, S. B., & Davidson, N. (1981). Behavioral parent training. In A. S. Gurman & D. P. Kniskern (Eds.), *Handbook of family therapy*. New York: Brunner/Mazel.

Griest, D. L. Forehand, R., Wells, K. C., & McMahon, R. J. (1980). An examination of differences between nonclinic and behavior-problem clinic-referred children and their mothers. *Journal of Abnormal Psychology, 89*(3), 497–500.

Griest, D., Wells, K. C., & Forehand, R. (1979). An examination of predictors of maternal perceptions of maladjustment in clinic-referred children. *Journal of Abnormal Psychology, 88*(3), 277–281.

Hall, R. V. (1971). *Behavior modification: The measurement of behavior*. Lawrence, KS: H & H Enterprises.

Johnson, S. M., Bolstad, O. D., & Lobitz, G. K. (1976). Generalization and contrast phenomena in behavior modification with children. In E. J. Mash, L. A. Hamerlynck, & L. C. Handy (Eds.), *Behavior modification and families*. New York: Brunner/Mazel.

Johnson, S. M., Christensen, A., & Bellamy, G. T. (1976). Evaluation of family intervention through unobtrusive recordings: Experiences in "bugging" children. *Journal of Applied Behavioral Analysis, 9*, 213–219.

Keefe, F. J., Kopel, S. A., & Gordon, S. B. (1978). *A practical guide to behavioral assessment*. New York: Springer.

Lobitz, G. K., & Johnson, S. M. (1975). Normal versus deviant children: A multimethod comparison. *Journal of Abnormal Child Psychology, 3*(4), 353–374.

Miller, W. H. (1975). *Systematic parent training: Procedures, cases, and issues*. Champaign, IL: Research Press.

Moos, R. H., & Moos, B. S. (1976). A typology of family social environments. *Family Process, 15*, 357–371.

Olson, D. H., Russell, C. S., & Sprenkle, D. H. (1980). Circumplex model of marital and family systems II: Empirical studies and clinical intervention. In J. P. Vincent (Ed.), *Advances in family intervention, assessment, and theory: An annual compilation on research*. Greenwich, CT: JAS Press.

Olson, D. H., Sprenkle, D. H., & Russell, C. S. (1979). Circumplex model of marital and family systems: I. Cohesion and adaptability dimensions, family types, and clinical applications. *Family Process, 18*, 3–28.

Oltmanns, T. F., Broderick, J. E., & O'Leary, K. D. (1977). Marital adjustment and the efficacy of behavior therapy with children. *Journal of Consulting and Clinical Psychology, 45*, 724–729.

Patterson, G. R. (1971). *Families: Applications of social learning to family life*. Champaign, IL: Research Press.

Patterson, G. R., Reid, I. B., Jones, R. E., & Conger, R. E. (1975). *A social learning approach to family intervention: Vol. 1: Families with aggressive children*. Eugene, OR: Castalia.

Reisinger, J. J., Frangia, G. W., & Hoffman, E. H. (1976). Toddler management training: Generalization and marital status. *Journal of Behavior Therapy and Experimental Psychiatry, 7*, 335–340.

Rickard, K. M., Forehand, R., Wells, K. C., Griest, D. L., & McMahon, R. J. (1981). Factors in the referral of children for behavioral treatment: A comparison of mothers of clinic-referred deviant, clinic-referred non-deviant and non-clinic children. *Behavioral Research and Therapy, 19*, 201–205.

Skinner, B. F. (1953). *Science and human behavior*. New York: Free Press.

Spanier, G. B. (1976). Measuring dyadic adjustment: New scales for assessing the quality of marriage and similar dyads. *Journal of Marriage and the Family, 38*, 15–28.

Wahler, R. G. (1975). Some structural aspects of deviant child behavior. *Journal of Applied Behavior Analysis, 8*, 27–42.

Weiss, R. L., Hops, H., & Patterson, G. R. (1973). A framework for conceptualizing marital conflict: A technology for altering it, some data for evaluating it. In L. A. Hamerlynck, L. C. Handy, & E. J. Mash (Eds.), *Behavior change: Methodology, concepts, and practice*. Champaign, IL: Research Press.

5

Functional Family Therapy

STEPHEN B. MORRIS
Comprehensive Psychological Services, Salt Lake City
JAMES F. ALEXANDER
University of Utah
HOLLY WALDRON
Rivendell of Utah, Salt Lake City

Functional family therapy (FFT) initially represented an integration of two perspectives of human behavior and change. The first perspective is an ecological one, which views deviant behavior as a systems-relevant interactional phenomenon. According to this perspective, deviant behavior has meaning only in terms of direct (e.g., interacting dyads) and indirect (e.g., coalitions, scapegoating, pseudomutuality) relationships. The second perspective is based on learning theory and targets specific stimuli and responses for change. This second perspective has a history of careful operationalization, empirical validation, and a concern for generalizability (Wahler, Berland, & Coe, 1979).

A third perspective, more recently formalized in the model, is the cognitive perspective, which emphasizes the attributional–information-processing components of change. This perspective has a rich conceptual and theoretical base and was adopted by FFT as a way to answer clinical questions that arose from the limitations of systems and behavioral perspectives and techniques (described below).

Because FFT is an evolving model that reacts to and spawns research questions and clinical experiences, a brief examination of its history will help clinicians understand its current practice.

HISTORY

Functional Family Therapy was initially identified as systems–behavioral family intervention (Alexander & Parsons, 1973). It was based on a matching-to-sample philosophy (Parsons & Alexander, 1973) in which the development of clinical technology involves four steps:

1. Identify behavioral patterns that distinguish deviant from nondeviant populations. This identification will ideally reflect careful empirical study, but if that is not possible it should at least represent a hypothetical–conceptual set of distinctions. To give one example, if one hopes to develop a treatment program for deviant single-parent populations, one should study, or at least try to understand, the major variables that distinguish between that population and a well-functioning single-parent population. Even if one cannot be an experimental social psychologist, one can at least attempt to be an informal anthropologist.

2. From the many variables that potentially distinguish between the adaptive and maladaptive populations, the matching-to-sample philosophy then identifies those variables that may cause or maintain deviant behavior.

3. Since an intervention program obviously cannot modify all distinguishing variables, a subset of potentially modifiable variables is identified. For example, if a particular subculture or ethnic group seems to have a high rate of delinquency, it would be inappropriate to target race, ethnicity, or culture as a variable. In reality, behavior change agents cannot, nor should they, attempt to change such factors. Within a particular culture or ethnic group, however, variables could be identified (e.g., attitudes, decision-making patterns) that distinguish between adaptive and maladaptive families. Intervention would then focus on these potentially modifiable variables.

4. Finally, an intervention program would be designed to change those modifiable variables that distinguish between adaptive and maladaptive populations. The program would then apply those techniques and evaluate the results. For maximum confidence, this step would be an "experiment" involving adequate controls to account for maturation, attention–placebo, and other alternative hypotheses.

This sequence was followed with a population of status delinquents (Alexander & Barton, 1976) in several studies. A variety of family interaction patterns was identified, including defensiveness, supportiveness, dominance, submission, and density–equality of talk time (Alexander, 1973; Parsons & Alexander, 1973). Techniques described below were designed to modify these patterns, and intervention was instituted with a sample of status delinquents. Intervention emphasized behavior change techniques such as communication training, contracting, and assignments (Parsons & Alexander, 1973). The programs were effective in reducing recidivism by one third to one half when compared with no-treatment controls and alternative treatments (Alexander & Parsons, 1973). The program also demonstrated impressive temporal generalizability (Wahler *et al.*, 1979) within families by significantly reducing subsequent delinquency in siblings by one third to one half and by reducing such delinquency significantly better than no-treatment controls and alternative treatments (Klein, Alexander, &

Parsons, 1976). Comparisons with individually based behavior therapy showed a similar beneficial effect (Shostak, 1977), as have numerous replications of the expanded model in several sites (Barton, Alexander, Waldron, Warburton & Turner, 1983; Gordon, Arbuthnot, & McGreen, 1983).

Limitations of Technology: Resistance

Though results were impressive in early evaluations of the program, not all the relevant phenomena were adequately described in the research reports. With the status delinquency population, and particularly with other more severe populations (e.g., Barton, Alexander, Waldron *et al.*, 1983), it became apparent that behavior change technologies often led to resistance, which was rarely described and certainly not conceptualized as a formal part of intervention models. Early clinical feedback and intuition and later empirical work (Barton, Alexander, & Turner, 1983) led to an expansion into a more complete and integrative model (Alexander & Parsons, 1982; Barton & Alexander, 1981). This expansion identified and took into account two major sources of resistance and lack of change: the function of behavior and the meaning of behavior. However, in order to describe the importance of these sources of resistance in the FFT model, we must first provide an overview of the major components of FFT.

COMPONENTS OF FUNCTIONAL FAMILY THERAPY

Functional family therapy is based on the interdependence of two basic components, cognitive change and behavioral change. Cognitive change occurs in the therapy phase; behavior change occurs in the education phase.

Therapy

The therapy phase of intervention, in which cognitive change is accomplished, is designed to modify attitudes, assumptions, expectations, labels, and emotions of the family. Family members typically enter treatment with punitive, blaming explanations for their problems. This view often interferes with the therapist's attempts to institute behavioral changes. Therefore, the therapist must move the family members from an individualistic focus to a nonblaming, relationship focus. The therapist must help family members to see themselves and one another as recipients rather than malevolent causes and to recognize that change can benefit everyone. In the FFT model, relabeling, as described below, is a primary method of establishing these new perspectives within the family.

Education

Behavior change is accomplished in the educational phase of intervention. Through the relabeling process, the therapist may already have begun to create adaptive change in the family. As Barton and Alexander (1981) have pointed out, however, the reattribution process is often a fragile one. Positive, relational views of their problems alone may not be sufficient to maintain long-term change in families; family members must also learn to behave differently if therapeutic gains are to persist. For this reason, it is important that education follow therapy. Education will allow family members to learn new behaviors that will substitute for old ones and thus prevent old maladaptive patterns from resurfacing.

The type of education families receive depends on (1) the functional outcomes of family members' behavior and (2) the relabels that the therapist has created within the family. The essence of FFT is its attempt to fit the educational strategy to family members' functions and attributions (Barton & Alexander, 1981). As a central concept in FFT, this notion is discussed in more detail in a separate section below.

Given that functional family therapists are aware of this complicated set of "fit" issues, they are trained to use a variety of techniques that promote overt behavior change. Before applying any given technique, the therapist offers a rationale to the family members so that they can see how it will help them. The rationale must be consistent with their goals and values.

Behavior change techniques include communication skills, technical aids, and interpersonal tasks. Communication skills, including negotiation skills, facilitate the appropriate expression of family members' feelings, thoughts, ideas, desires, and needs. Successful communication or negotiation typically requires brevity, source responsibility, directness, specificity, feedback, and active listening. The elements of adaptive communication are described in detail in the research literature and elsewhere (e.g., Alexander & Parsons, 1982; Jacobson & Margolin, 1979; Rimm & Masters, 1974; Stuart & Lott, 1972).

Technical aids are structural props that facilitate change, including time-out procedures (Patterson, 1971), reminder cards and message centers, (Alexander & Parsons, 1982), token economies (Ayllon & Azrin, 1968), recording charts (Patterson & Guillion, 1971), and contingency contracting (Stuart, 1971). By and large, these procedures are products of social learning research and are capable of producing changes in behavior when family members' functions are taken into account.

Interpersonal tasks are therapist-directed activities designed to enhance communication and family relationships. They may include practicing communication skills at home, taking a family outing, beginning a project together, or scheduling transition "space" into the day. Interpersonal tasks, derived from an assessment of functions, allow the therapist to create new learning patterns in the family (Alexander & Parsons, 1982).

Education is not restricted to the techniques listed above; there are many options. The only restriction is that any technique must be consistent with family functions.

THE MEANING OF BEHAVIOR

The brief overview of FFT presented above is at best a highlighting of major phases and techniques and at worst a horrible oversimplification of the nuances and difficulties involved in producing change. As mentioned above, family intervention often involves impediments to change, impediments that are often seen by clinicians as inadequacies on the part of the clients (e.g., lack of intelligence) or active resistance. Functional family therapy, however, sees these impediments as natural consequences of the inappropriate application of technology and the failure of clinicians to understand the meaning of behavior.

Family therapists, perhaps more than any others, have adopted meaning-change techniques as a way to reduce resistance, alter interactional patterns, and catalyze behavior change. These therapists call this process "relabeling," "reframing," or "positive connotation." For example, structural family therapists (Aponte & VanDeusen, 1981; Minuchin, 1974) suggest that relabeling restructures transactions and opens pathways for change. Strategic family therapists (Bandler & Grinder, 1982; Haley, 1963; Madanes, 1981; Watzlawick, 1978; Watzlawick, Weakland, & Fisch, 1974) suggest that reframing alters the class membership of events and makes it difficult for family members to return to former meanings and that this alteration leads to a change in behavioral consequences. Functional family therapists (Barton & Alexander, 1981) suggest that relabeling reduces resistance and motivates change by providing reattributions for the causes of family members' behavior that do not require the use of pejorative trait labels.

Thus, it appears that many therapies attempt to communicate a new meaning for symptomatic behavior to the client. Some of these, including FFT, contend that a change in meaning is a necessary precursor to behavior change. Functional family therapy attempts to explain the phenomenon of meaning change and its consequences in terms of a well-established body of psychological research (Barton & Alexander, 1981). As in other family therapies, however, relabeling in FFT was at first a technique in search of a theory. Functional family therapy's interest in the relabeling phenomenon developed out of clinical experiences in which behavior change technology alone failed to produce lasting change or in which clients made dramatic emotional and attributional shifts. Experimental research (Barton, 1983) has since demonstrated empirically the power of the attributional shift in the family context. The next section expands a previous attributional explanation of the relabeling phenomenon (Barton & Alexander, 1981) and suggests some guidelines for its effective use.

RELABELS: A DESCRIPTION AND EXAMPLES

A relabel can be described as the verbal portrayal of any "negative" family (or individual) behavior in a benign or benevolent light by describing the "positive" antonym properties of the behavior and by portraying family members as victims rather than perpetrators (Barton & Alexander, 1981). For example, the uninvolved father may be portrayed as someone who is lonely, afraid, and wants to protect his family from his unpleasant emotions. The wife abuser may be portrayed as someone who is frustrated, desperate, and never learned appropriate ways to vent his feelings. The delinquent may be portrayed as someone who is confused about her identity, who is struggling to be independent, and who is afraid to attempt more productive or socially acceptable behavior.

Relabels appear to operate on at least three levels: the interactional level, the motivational level, and the systemic level. At the interactional level, the relabel may provide a benign description of the interpersonal impact of behavior: "So, Mom, when Dad gets discouraged and throws things, you generally try to calm him down by leaving the room. John, where are you and what are you doing while all of this is going on?" At the motivational level, the relabel may recast motives in a benign or benevolent (rather than malevolent) light: "Mr. Jones, it seems from what you have said that you really care for your son, and that by grounding him you are simply trying to protect him." At the systemic level, the relabel emphasizes the similarities between people, or family "themes": "For various reasons you all seem to be crying for attention, but doing it in different ways. Dad, your bid for attention is to go off into the study and hope that someone will come and ask you why you are angry. Mom, you ask for attention by telling people how abandoned you feel when people forget their chores. John, you signal your parents that you need attention by having problems at school. Even though you each express it in your own unique way, all of you seem to want the same thing from each other." (Notice that plausibility is an important component of the effective relabel, an issue discussed in greater detail below.)

In order to give the reader a more accurate feel for how relabels operate in practice, the following excerpt from a therapy session is provided. In this session, the functional family therapist is working with a teenage girl and her parents.

Mother: Well, I . . . I just think we've got a real problem on our hands . . . you know, an incredible problem . . . with Heidi here. She's started staying out late, and, uh, I'm just really worried. We've got to do something about her. This can't go on any longer.

Father: The basic problem here . . .

Therapist: It sounds like you are worried about Heidi. That's . . .

Mother: Well, I am. She's going to get herself killed.

Father: And with good reason. She's staying out all hours of the night, all night long . . . not coming home, running around with friends that we don't know anything about and, uh, she's got to shape up.

Therapist: Sounds like both your folks are concerned about what's going on with you. Can you share a little bit of that with me?

Daughter: All right. They are getting real concerned, I guess. I don't know. I don't think I am doing anything wrong.

Therapist: Yeah, okay, so the way you see it you are just fitting in with your friends, doing what everybody else is doing.

Daughter: Sure.

Therapist: (*To father.*) So you don't see it the same way.

Father: Yeah, that's the problem with these friends, you know. Since she started hanging out with the friends, you know, she doesn't talk to us any more. She doesn't come home or anything like that. She is out all night with the friends. Now . . . and we don't know anything about these people. (*To mother.*) Do you know these kids?

Mother: No, and I am just worried.

Therapist: One way that I could maybe try to understand what you all three are struggling with is that you almost have a sense of loss, that you used to be important to her and now you don't feel as important to her as you think her friends are. Is that a fair thing to say? Heidi, did you realize that your parents were feeling bad that you hadn't, you know, that you hadn't been showing the same kind of being a part of the family? Did you realize that some of that was that they were hurt?

Daughter: No, I hadn't really seen it that way. It's more like they're mad.

Therapist: Yeah, so what you've been hearing . . . what they have not made clear, is that they're hurt and they're worried. What's been coming through is that they are mad. But how does it feel to you when you realize that a lot of it isn't the mad . . . it's the hurt?

Daughter: It feels a lot better . . . that they are not so upset about the things I do. If I thought they were really worried, maybe I'd take more time to worry about them.

Therapist: What's your reaction to that, Mom?

Mother: Well, I thought I told you one hundred times, honey, that what I get scared about is your getting in an accident, that about 11:00 I start worrying that something has happened to you.

Daughter: But then when I come home, you just yell.

Mother: Well, by the time three o'clock comes . . .

Daughter: (*Sarcastically.*) You say, "You've been out with your friends and la-de-da."

Therapist: Now, do you see what happened here? When I was talking about the fear and the hurt, everybody got quiet . . . Heidi kind of . . . her eyes kind of got teary and she said, "Well, gee, maybe I could try to worry more about them, too." Then I asked you about it and you notice what happened? You two started arguing about eleven o'clock again. That's one of the things I think it's important for us to keep in mind that sometimes when you express your fear in terms of like rules, then she responds to the rules and starts pushing away. Do you want her to pay attention to your hurt for awhile or would you rather talk about eleven o'clock? I know that is a tough question. It may be unfair, but . . .

Father: Well, I think we've got to talk about the rules. We still got to have rules. I mean you know, she is still, you know, our daughter and, you know, we can't have her be out all night, you know, doing heaven knows what, you know, with people we know nothing about.

Therapist: Okay. Does it seem like it's tough to be able to talk about the rules and the feelings you have for one another at the same time? It almost sounds like in this family it's hard for you to be able to do both. You see, I gave you a choice and you acted like, "Gee, the choice is rules."

Mother: I think we should talk about feelings because that is where I come in.

Therapist: Okay, you want to talk about feelings; you want to talk about rules.

Thirty second pause:

Therapist: Okay, let's see if I hear this right. So when you don't pay as much attention as you would like to the rules, that's what hurts you?

Father: That's right.

Therapist: And when they pay attention to the rules but not your feelings, that's what hurts you?

Daughter: Yes.

Therapist: So both of you, it sounds like, are sending out messages, "Here's what is important to me," and the other one is saying, "Yes, but here's something different that's important to me," and it's like two ships passing in the night. They keep missing and you end up arguing about things which aren't really what's going on. You know, you're arguing about rules, and she is saying, "That's not what's going on." You're arguing about feelings and you are saying, "That's not what's going on."

In this therapy session, the therapist provides interactional, motivational, and systemic relabels. An interactional relabel occurs when the therapist points out how the behavior of the daughter is not independent from, but interactive with, the parents' behavior: "when you express your fear in terms of rules, then she responds to the rules and starts pushing away." The motivational relabels occur when anger is described as "hurt" and when confrontations at three o'clock in the morning are portrayed as stemming from fear and worry. A systemic relabel occurs near the end of the dialogue when all family members are described as wanting to communicate but failing to do so, like "ships passing in the night." Again, the purpose of the relabels is to defuse resistance and drain away unproductive affect in order to set the stage for behavior change. The affective reactions of the daughter demonstrate how this can occur.

AN ATTRIBUTIONAL EXPLANATION OF FAMILY CONFLICT

Before describing how relabels might interrupt family conflict, let us consider how meanings might operate to maintain it. This explanation borrows heavily from attribution theory and information processing theory and focuses on conflicted families only. Future research may reveal that similar processes operate in healthy families as well.

According to attribution theory, all people have a "need" to explain, predict, and control events, especially the interpersonal events, that happen around them (Heider, 1958). People therefore engage in analysis of causation. However, economy of effort requires that a single sufficient cause be discovered, and dispositional, "trait-label" explanations are seen as sufficient (Jones & Davis, 1965). For example, in the delinquent family, people have a need to explain, predict, and control the behavior of the delinquent. Trait explanations are often used: "He is just a lazy, good-for-nothing, irresponsible young criminal," or "She is a chronic liar and thief," or even "He is a juvenile delinquent." Such labels, though pejorative, serve as sufficient "explanations" of the child's behavior and indeed may have some predictive utility.

Attribution researchers (Jones & Davis, 1965; Jones & Nisbett, 1972) have shown that people do not always engage in a rational, controlled search for all the relevant data, as some theorists have suggested (Kelley,

1973), but that they pay most of their attention to salient stimuli. At least two conditions may increase salience: hedonic relevance and personalism. An event is hedonically relevant to me if I perceive that it has some outcome for me. Thus, the war in Afghanistan, though important on the world scene, does not appear to affect my life directly and is not hedonically relevant. However, my delinquent son's behavior is hedonically relevant because it directly affects my life; if he steals my lunch money I must go hungry. His behavior is even more salient if it involves personalism, that is, if I believe he intends to hurt me personally through his behavior. If he steals my money to buy drugs, his behavior is salient because it is hedonically relevant; if he deliberately steals my money to get even with me for punishing him, his behavior is both hedonically relevant and personalized.

Other attribution researchers (Taylor & Fiske, 1978) have suggested that arousal may increase attention to salient stimuli. That is, if I am angry, in pain, or frustrated, I am more likely to pay more attention to things that are salient. Since it is apparent that family conflict often leads to a high degree of arousal, any behavior that is unacceptable will "pull" inordinate amounts of attention, especially if the behavior is hedonically relevant and personalized. In addition, delinquent families often experience significant stresses unrelated to direct family interaction, such as financial problems, which may create a background of additional stress and arousal. Under these conditions, it is not surprising that one member of a troubled family is often identified as the patient when he or she exhibits deviant behavior. The often-cited phenomenon known as scapegoating (Napier & Whitaker, 1978) could be viewed as the phenomenon that occurs when, under conditions of conflict and arousal, one member of a family comes to be blamed for family difficulties because his or her behavior is unacceptable. Because the behavior deviates from family norms, it takes on a figure-to-ground relationship to the rest of family behavior; that is, unacceptable behavior stands out against the backdrop of all family members' acceptable behavior and thus becomes highly salient. Because the behavior serves to meet a function and is reinforced, it continues and increases the stress and arousal in the family. Thus the scapegoat or "identified patient" label persists, in part, because of interactions between arousal and salience.

Taylor and Fiske (1978) suggested that people often respond to salient stimuli with little thought. They pointed out that the top-of-the-head phenomenon may be an example of automatic processing (Schneider & Shiffrin, 1977). "Automatic processing" refers to the way in which information coming in through the senses may be processed quickly and lead to an interrelated set of cognitive, emotional, and behavioral responses with little attention or conscious thought. For example, the busy executive drives his car to work without thinking much about it. He may listen to the radio, dictate a letter, look at the scenery, or even shave while still processing enormous amounts of data coming in through his senses. But he did not always drive this way; as a student driver he had to concentrate very hard on each aspect of the process in order to master it. This conscious attention to a task or event represents another kind of processing—controlled processing. Taylor and Fiske (1978) suggested that people engage in both kinds of processing, depending on the familiarity of the situation at hand. In conflicted families, individuals may be very familiar with a pattern of conflict or symptomatic behavior that has been repeated many times. The onset of such behavior, all too familiar, may trigger automatic processing, complete with well-practiced thoughts, feelings, and behavioral responses: "John, I've told you a thousand times that . . ." becomes a cue for enactment of a script that is extremely well-rehearsed.

It appears that conflicted families are likely to engage in a great deal of automatic processing. Family members have a heightened need to find a sufficient causal explanation for someone's behavior, and they invoke traits and dispositions to do so. The deviant nature of the symptomatic behavior increases its salience, as does the emotional arousal inherent in family conflict. The automatic processing of one individual serves as a salient stimulus for another individual to engage in automatic processing also, ad infinitum.

THE RELABELING MECHANISM

Clinical experience with families suggests that the power of the relabel as a therapeutic technique may lie in its apparent ability to disrupt automatic processing and require family members to engage in controlled processing, either by searching for existing response alternatives or by forming new ones. Appropriate relabels applied in timely fashion seem to have the effect of stopping people in midsentence, evoking puzzled or surprised looks, and prompting them to say things like, "Hmm. I never thought of it that way before." These responses often lead to the melting away of counterproductive affect and to the willingness to consider new alternatives.

In order to give the reader a better intuitive feel for the phenomenon we are describing, we turn to some examples from everyday experience and clinical work. Suppose you live in a neighborhood where several robberies have occurred in the last month. One night you are awakened by a scratching noise at the dining room window. You get up to investigate and suddenly remember the recent robberies. As you do so, your heart begins to pound, your palms feel sweaty, and your knees begin to shake. Carefully you tiptoe into the dining room and peek through the curtain, only to discover the branch of a nearby tree scratching against the glass. A feeling of relief sweeps over you, and your pulse begins to return to normal. In this situation, intense physiological arousal, as well as its removal, were precipitated by the respective cognitive appraisals of the situation.

To take a clinical example, consider the case of the married couple who enter therapy. The wife's main complaints are that her husband is distant, inconsiderate, never spends time with her, never wants to talk any more, and has quit doing his chores. He complains that she is just a nag and that he never gets any time for himself. They have engaged in numerous angry exchanges in which she bursts into tears and he retreats to the garage. In taking the history, the therapist learns that the man was largely raised by a stepmother, who became angry with him at the slightest provocation. This was in contrast to his natural mother, with whom he had a close relationship. His usual reaction to his stepmother was to leave the house and attempt to vent his emotions alone. The therapist suggests to the wife that this man has difficulty expressing his emotions to women, characterizing him as a lonely, sad individual who never resolved his pent-up grief over the death of his natural mother and who learned to retreat from conflict in order to protect others from his emotions. The wife's reaction to this relabel is to quickly become much calmer and to express a modified view of her husband's actions.

Another example involves a delinquent teenage boy and his father. The father, a single parent, is extremely frustrated and angry over his son's behavior. The son is frequently truant, is never home at predictable hours, and has been arrested for burglary. After several hours of therapy and numerous attempts to change their perceptions of each other, the father begins to shed silent tears when the son is portrayed as a lonely, confused, hurt young man who is still grieving over his parents' recent divorce.

To reiterate, the attributional explanation for the dramatic "simmering down" of affect described in these examples is this: certain events, due to their frequency or other factors, have come to elicit a certain class of thoughts, emotions, and behaviors virtually automatically. Each new instance of the event triggers automatic processing, leading to highly probable outcomes. The relabel interrupts this process by requiring the individual to consider alternative explanations. These alternative explanations activate different repertoires of thoughts, emotions, and behaviors, which are then substituted for the former ones. In certain cases, no alternatives are available because the new meaning is outside the individual's experience, and he or she is required to learn an entirely new repertoire. This "plugging in" of alternatives or the learning of new ones proceeds through controlled processing and represents the "education" or behavior-change component of FFT and other therapies.

Our clinical experience with families suggests that developmental crises, such as the birth of a new child, the exiting of a young adult, or the remarriage of a parent, provide useful opportunities for relabeling. For example, one set of relabels that is useful with delinquent families views delinquent behavior as the inappropriate attempts of a youngster to establish his or her identity and become independent from the family. The parental attempts to change the behavior through restrictive discipline may be viewed as ineffective efforts on the part of frustrated, confused, untrained individuals to protect the child from pain. Since the desire to be independent and the desire to protect one's children are often seen as benevolent and adaptive, these labels can evoke alternative responses and help set the stage for negotiation and constructive behavior change.

Although preliminary research (Fincham & O'Leary, 1983; Jacobson, McDonald, Follette, & Berley, 1985) has begun to examine the dimensions of relabels, most of our information about them comes from clinical experience. While awaiting further research we are prepared to offer some speculations about the dimensions of a relabel that may contribute to its effectiveness. First, we think a relabel must be as *plausible* as possible. Our experience suggests that relabels go down more easily if they invoke meanings and response repertoires already available to the individual rather than stretching his or her credulity. This means that the therapist will need to be creative in inventing relabels. While there usually exists a very large number of useful ways to conceptualize and relabel a behavior, the most effective relabels will need to be individually tailored to fit the needs and world views of the particular family. For example, in the case of the parent who uses harsh physical discipline, it may be more useful to relabel him or her as frustrated, inept, or discouraged than to expect family members to buy the idea that hitting is a way to be close to the children. Second, we believe relabels work better if they attribute *benign or benevolent motives* to the actor. The nonblaming attitude emphasized by this approach allows family members to let go of their defensiveness and take the risks necessary for change. For example, the teenager who shoplifts can be portrayed as having an intense need to belong to the group, a need so intense that it led her to forget her better judgment. If nothing else, it may be possible to portray an individual as a victim of influences beyond his or her control. Third, it seems that good relabels often point out the *benefits of symptomatic behavior* to the identified patient or others. For example, delinquent behavior could be characterized as a last-ditch attempt on the child's part to protect the parents' marriage by focusing attention on himself or herself and thereby keeping the parents distracted from their own pain.

It is well to bear in mind that the absolute "truth" of a relabel is not the most important issue. The role of the therapist is not necessarily to focus on objective reality but rather to understand and operate within the phenomenological experience of family members. Relabels may be used in a hypothesis-testing way to discover the family's world view and appreciate their experience. This does not mean that the therapist must be a professional prevaricator; however, the therapist must be willing to attempt several relabels in the search for the one(s) that finally achieves the desired results. Even an inaccurate relabel may be serviceable, since it could disrupt automatic processing through simple confusion. The "right" relabel, then, is the one that works: it disrupts automatic processing and invokes a new or different class of feelings, thoughts, and behaviors.

THERAPY FOR THERAPISTS

Clinicians sometimes notice that something inside *them* seems to rebel when a relabel for symptomatic behavior, especially extremely asocial or "sociopathic" behavior, is proposed. For example, many clinicians find that their own antipathies interfere with or prevent them from helping clients who are child molesters, spouse abusers, larcenists, and the like. Other, milder disorders or personal characteristics of certain clients may also trigger unproductive automatic processes in the therapist, processes that were learned, perhaps, in unpleasant experiences of the past. We believe, not too differently from other approaches (Beier, 1966; Rogers, 1951), that one requirement for effective therapy is that the clients, no matter how disturbed, feel that the therapist is willing to accept them in spite of their behavior. Feelings of blame and anger within the therapist may be a signal that he or she may need to do some personal relabeling. First, the therapist searches for a plausible relabel that fits the world view of the family and that feels believable. Next, the unproductive affect dissipates, leaving the therapist to be congruently accepting of the client. Then the therapist communicates the relabel to the client, on whom (it is hoped) it will have a similar effect. As with clients, the draining away or "simmering down" of the therapist's unproductive affect is the signal that the relabel has been successful.

FUNCTIONS

The cognitive change produced in the therapy phase sets the stage for behavior change. Education is the second major part of the intervention process in which behavior change technology (e.g., contingency management, communication training, self-control technology, modeling, role-playing) is used to provide the family with new behaviors. During this phase, a wide variety of tools is available to produce change.

However, clinical experience has shown that it is not always obvious which behaviors to change and which tools to use. The literature is replete with examples of success stories with numerous techniques—just as we know of clinical folklore also replete with examples of failures of those same techniques. Functional family therapy argues that this unevenness of success and of long-term maintenance in many behavioral programs derives from a lack of appreciation of the *interpersonal functions* of behavior. These interpersonal functions can lead to rapid change or to therapeutic resistance depending on how well the therapist can adapt educational technology to the interpersonal functions of behavior in families.

The FFT model considers functions to be concepts comparable with such descriptors as "maturity," "personality," "style," and "wisdom." Concepts such as these are not generally thought of as being *things* (e.g., a structure in the cerebral cortex) but instead describe patterns of behaving, thinking, and feeling. The patterns that these words describe seem organized and relatively consistent within a given context and are often used as explanatory or dynamic principles, as in "he's too immature to be able to handle that."

Functions in the FFT model represent a similar concept. Functions are defined as a person's pattern of behaviors, feelings, and thoughts that mediate the amount of psychological relatedness in a relationship with another person. Because of the regularities of these patterns, we assume they reflect the sort of organizational strategy described earlier as controlled and (more often) automatic processing. Like these other concepts, functions can and do change—for example, people do change in ways that we call more or less "mature." However, except for relatively dramatic events (e.g., suddenly losing one's parents, becoming unemployed after years of stable income) and natural developmental epochs (e.g., adolescence), people retain fairly stable levels of maturity, wisdom, and style in particular contexts for relatively long periods of time.

Functions may be described at many levels, because behaviors, feelings, and thoughts influence or define relationships in many ways. For example, if I cry in your presence my behavior can (1) produce tear stains on your clothes; (2) elicit nurturance from you; (3) embarrass you in front of others; (4) make it difficult for you to hear the stereo; and (5) make the floor wet so you slip. These effects, of course, depend on your reaction to them, since crying produces different reactions in different people in different contexts.

According to FFT, however, all of these reactions represent a degree of psychological association consisting of a blend of two independent dimensions: distance (separateness, autonomy) and closeness (intimacy, merging). These are orthogonal dimensions that can vary in intensity and amount. For example, a person we describe as "highly dependent" and "clinging" with respect to another person behaves in ways that create considerable closeness with that person—closeness that may or may not be acceptable to the other person. In contrast, a traveling salesman who loves his work creates, in an average working week, considerable autonomy from his wife and family. This form of distance may or may not be acceptable, depending on the other participants. Finally, a two-career marriage can represent a blend of both closeness and autonomy, in forms that can be highly rewarding or highly disturbing to the participants.

The FFT model makes a number of important assumptions about functions. As a preferred level of psychological relatedness, functions are not good or bad *per se*, though their expression may be. For example, FFT would argue that closeness in the form of symbiosis or parent–child incest is bad, but the same level of closeness, when manifested in other more acceptable forms (e.g., attentive parenting that fosters competence), can be good. Similarly, distance in the form of an adolescent's running away may be considered bad, while the same level of distance may be quite acceptable if it takes the form of joining several clubs, having a job after school, or going away to college. In these instances, the teenager interacts at a low rate with parents in terms of absolute frequency. However, the different forms of distance are valenced quite differently by parents and society. Nowhere is this issue more evident than in cross-cultural relationships, where, for example, touching can be a form of respect and caring in one culture but a major insult in another. Functional family therapy therefore argues that it is not the function that is "good" or "bad"; it is the expression of the function in terms of certain thoughts, feelings, and behaviors that may be unacceptable and should represent the target for change.

A second assumption of FFT is that functions are unique to each participant in each relationship. Functions are not "traits"; many people demonstrate a wide range of functions in different relationships. For example, a teenager simultaneously may be increasing closeness to a boyfriend and two girlfriends; vacillating between distance and closeness with one parent ("midpointing"); distancing from the other parent and another old boyfriend; and so on. Therapists must therefore assess each relationship individually.

Therapists must also recognize that their reality of functions is phenomenological not observational. As therapists, we can observe the impact people have on one another, and we can attempt to use this observation as a basis for inferring the nature of the interpersonal function. For example, if whining always produces contact from a parent, we can infer that the function of the whining is to produce closeness. On the other hand, if whining always produces disgust and long periods of avoidance on the part of a parent, we can infer that the function of whining is distance. However, we must remember that functions do not objectively exist but are phenomenologically experienced by participants. This experience may be nonconscious, reflecting the automatic processing described earlier. Nevertheless, participants will experience a configuration of behaviors, thoughts, and emotions in a particular way depending on their perceptual capabilities and their attributional schemata. Thus, therapists must be constantly reminded to adapt change techniques to the phenomenological reality of clients, not to the "objective" reality as therapists see it.

Of course, therapists can attempt to change phenomenological reality as described in the preceding section on relabeling. But if therapists also attempt to change the nature of functions as a vehicle for changing behavior, thoughts, and feelings, they will find that change becomes exceedingly difficult and requires considerable motivation, time, and resources. Changing behaviors, thoughts, and feelings while maintaining original functions, in contrast, can be an efficient way to produce change. To provide a concrete example, consider the husband and wife who experience a midpointing relationship in their marriage. Midpointing is a blend of both distance and closeness, sometimes called the "come here–go away" message. Across time, this relationship includes a pattern of coming together, then distancing (e.g., through fighting), then responding to the fighting by making up, then once again distancing. A change program based solely on increasing intimacy and decreasing distance would represent not only a change in behavior but also an attempted change in functions. For example, having the couple perform more joint projects, spend most of their free time together expressing various forms of intimacy, and go on weekend trips without the kids would all serve to increase contact/closeness. According to FFT, such changes would *not* be maintained in a couple whose functions were midpointing because the changes would not allow the couple to maintain their autonomy as well as their closeness. Instead, other programs would have to be instituted that would legitimize the distance as well as the closeness component of the couple's midpointing functions. For example, the couple could sometimes use message centers and letters to express affection. This would allow them to be independent at times, yet maintain a commitment to the relationship. Midpointing can be facilitated through other techniques, including social events such as bridge clubs, dance clubs, double-dating, and mixed-doubles tennis. These activities involve considerable expressions of affiliation but at the same time include the constraint (i.e., distance) imposed by the presence of others. For a midpointing couple, these solutions will be adopted and maintained as legitimate vehicles for change, while techniques that require too much contact and intimacy will be resisted.

It must be remembered that these same solutions may not work for other couples, since other relationships can have very different blends of distancing, midpointing, and closeness.

The therapist adopts interventions to fit the phenomenological reality and functions of each relationship. It is clear that FFT attempts to recognize individual differences and avoid the ethical problem of changing people as a vehicle for changing behavior. When clients are self-referred it may be palatable to "help" or "force" them to change their functions in order to attain therapeutic cure. However, in many coercive relationships (e.g., children referred by parents, families referred by the court), it is questionable that peoples' functions should be changed in order to modify unacceptable behaviors, thoughts, and feelings. FFT argues that on a short-term basis the functions attained by family members should be legitimized and maintained, though the behaviors that are expressed may be changed dramatically. For example, consider a mother who creates midpointing or distance from her family by pursuing a career in addition to being a homemaker. As part of the solution to her child's delinquency, FFT would not attempt to require more contact with her family and make attainment of her career role more difficult. In the same way, FFT would not force a woman whose function is contact closeness with her family into adopting a career, even if the therapist strongly believes in career options for women. Either of these approaches would be tyranny. However, with the first woman we may want to substitute more acceptable forms of midpointing or distance, such as telephone monitoring or surrogate parenting, for frequent nagging. With the second woman, we may want to substitute more acceptable forms of closeness, such as mother–child shopping trips and letter writing, for incessant snooping. In FFT, then, each person's functions are legitimized, not changed, but the behavioral expressions of functions are changed.

As mentioned previously, functions are not always stable throughout life. People can and do make changes in their behavior that redefine the nature of their relationships. For example, FFT may help an adolescent learn that he can create distance/autonomy by working at a job and providing his own income rather than by running away and stealing. As the members of his family respond positively to these new expressions of autonomy, he may desire to become "closer" to them and they to him. At this point, FFT would not insist that distance be fostered but would attempt to institute behaviors consistent with the new function of closeness. In other words, after we have helped all family members legitimize and maintain their functions and express them in adaptive ways, we can offer them the option of changing. We emphasize, however, that the desire and decision to change functions must come from the family, not the therapist, and that changes in functions must follow the legitimization and adaptive expression of existing ones.

An additional important consideration is the polydyadic nature of functions. Functions are unique to each relationship but do not operate in isolation. For example, if one parent is close to one child, the very behaviors that represent closeness to that child at the same time may represent distance from another child. In a similar way, if a parent is heavily invested (i.e., close) in work relationships, these very same behaviors (being on the job) may represent a form of distance from the person's family. Change in one relationship must not be initiated without consideration of how the effects of this change will reverberate through other relationships. Applying change technology without the consideration of this complexity can lead to the problem often encountered by naive therapists, who propose "obvious" solutions to families and are dismayed when they elicit vehement resistance. For example, a father said, "I refuse to pay my kid to be a member of this family. They don't bribe me to be a father, and I'm not going to bribe him to be a good kid!" Another parent had this familiar complaint: "Now the other kids all want to get this too. My 12 year old used to do the dishes just to make me happy. But since we started this stuff with Paul, John demands money, too. Am I gonna have to pay them all for everything? I'm not sure it's worth it."

To summarize, the myriad educational strategies and techniques noted earlier cannot be applied in a random manner. The new behaviors, feelings, and cognitions targeted by therapists must be consistent with the values of all family members. Positive change is more easily produced, and more reliably maintained, if the educational technologies are fitted to the values and functions of family members. On the other hand, resistance is more actively elicited if we try to change peoples' functions to fit our technologies.

SUMMARY

Functional family therapy is an evolving model that integrates principles of learning theory, systems theory, and cognitive theory. The recently formulated Anatomy of Intervention Model (AIM; Alexander, Barton, Waldron, & Mas, 1983) suggests that psychotherapy comprises several steps, each tapping certain therapist skills and working toward certain goals. While awaiting the results of research into these variables, the clinician is required to apply what is already known as he or she intervenes in family problems. This chapter has focused on the two core steps in intervention—therapy and education—and the meaning change and behavior change techniques involved in executing them. Functional family therapy has demonstrated its effectiveness with delinquent populations and will continue to evolve as clinical experience and applied research contribute to its growth.

ACKNOWLEDGMENT

The preparation of this chapter was supported in part by a University of Utah Eccles Foundation Graduate Fellowship to Holly Waldron. The authors wish to thank Dr. Charles W. Turner for his helpful comments on earlier versions of this chapter.

REFERENCES

Alexander, J. F. (1973). Defensive and supportive communications in normal and deviant families. *Journal of Consulting and Clinical Psychology, 40*, 223–231.

Alexander, J. F., & Barton, C. (1976). Behavioral systems therapy with families. In D. H. Olson (Ed.), *Treating relationships* (pp. 167–187). Lake Mills, IA: Graphic.

Alexander, J. F., Barton, C., Waldron, H., & Mas, C. H. (1983). Beyond the technology of family therapy: The anatomy of intervention model. In K. D. Craig & R. J. McMahon (Eds.), *Advances in clinical behavior therapy* (pp. 48–73). New York: Brunner/Mazel.

Alexander, J. F., & Parsons, B. V. (1973). Short term behavioral intervention with delinquent families: Impact on family process and recidivism. *Journal of Abnormal Psychology, 81*, 219–225.

Alexander, J. F., & Parsons, B. V. (1982). *Functional family therapy*. Monterey, CA: Brooks/Cole.

Aponte, H. J., & VanDeusen, J. M. (1981). Structural family therapy. In A. S. Gurman & D. P. Kniskern (Eds.), *Handbook of family therapy* (pp. 310–360). New York: Brunner/Mazel.

Ayllon, T., & Azrin, N. H. (1968). The token economy: A motivational system for therapy and rehabilitation. New York: Appleton-Century-Crofts.

Bandler, R., & Grinder, J. (1982). *Reframing: Neurolinguistic programming and the transformation of meaning*. Moab, UT: Real People Press.

Barton, C. (1983). *Communications, cognitions, and contingencies in delinquent and control families*. Unpublished doctoral dissertation, University of Utah.

Barton, C., & Alexander, J. F. (1981). Functional family therapy. In A. S. Gurman & D. P. Kniskern (Eds.), *Handbook of family therapy* (pp. 403–443). New York: Brunner/Mazel.

Barton, C., Alexander, J. F., & Turner, C. W. (1983). *Family members' attributions and communication exchange*. Poster session presented at the meeting of the World Congress on Behavior Therapy/Association for the Advancement of Behavior Therapy, Washington, DC.

Barton, C., Alexander, J. F., Waldron, H., Warburton, J., & Turner, C. W. (1983). *Family intervention, alternatives, and seriously delinquent youth: A program evaluation study*. Poster session presented at the meeting of the World Congress on Behavior Therapy/Association for the Advancement of Behavior Therapy, Washington, DC.

Beier, E. G. (1966). *The silent language of psychotherapy*. New York: Aldine.

Fincham, F. D., & O'Leary, K. D. (1983). Causal inferences for spouse behavior in distressed and nondistressed couples. *Journal of Social and Clinical Psychology, 1*, 42–57.

Gordon, D. A., Arbuthnot, J., & McGreen, P. (1983). *Short-term family therapy and school consultation with court-referred delinquents*. Paper presented at the 19th Annual Meeting of the Society of Policy and Criminal Psychology, Cincinnati, OH.

Haley, J. (1963). *Strategies of psychotherapy*. New York: Grune & Stratton.

Heider, F. (1958). *The psychology of interpersonal relations*. New York: Wiley.

Jacobson, N. S., & Margolin, G. (1979). *Marital therapy*. New York: Brunner/Mazel.

Jacobson, N. S., McDonald, D. W., Follette, W. C., Berley, K. A. (1985). Attributional processes in distressed and nondistressed married couples. *Cognitive Therapy and Research, 9*, 35–50.

Jones, E. E., & Davis, K. E. (1965). From acts to dispositions: The attribution process in person perception. In L. Berkowitz (Ed.), *Advances in experimental social psychology* (Vol. 2, pp. 220–266). New York: Academic Press.

Jones, E. E., & Nisbett, R. E. (1972). The actor and the observer: Divergent perceptions of the causes of behavior. In E. E. Jones, D. E. Kanouse, H. H. Kelley, R. E. Nisbett, S. Valins, & B. Weiner (Eds.), *Attribution: Perceiving the causes of behavior* (pp. 79–94). Morristown, NJ: General Learning Press.

Kelley, H. H. (1973). The processes of causal attribution. *American Psychologist, 28*, 107–128.

Klein, N. C., Alexander, J. F., & Parsons, B. V. (1976). Impact of family systems intervention on recidivism and sibling delinquency: A model of primary prevention and program evaluation. *Journal of Consulting and Clinical Psychology, 45*, 469–474.

Madanes, C. (1981). *Strategic family therapy*. San Francisco: Jossey-Bass.

Minuchin, S. (1974). *Families and family therapy*. Cambridge, MA: Harvard University Press.

Napier, A. Y., & Whitaker, C. A. (1978). *The family crucible*. New York: Harper & Row.

Parsons, B. V., & Alexander, J. F. (1973). Short term family intervention: A therapy outcome study. *Journal of Consulting and Clinical Psychology, 41*, 195–201.

Patterson, G. R. (1971). *Families: Application of social learning to family life*. Champaign, IL: Research Press.

Patterson, G. R., & Gullion, M. E. (1971). *Living with children: New methods of parents and teachers* (rev. ed.). Champaign, IL: Research Press.

Rimm, D. C., & Masters, J. C. (1974). *Behavior therapy: Techniques and empirical findings*. New York: Academic Press.

Rogers, C. R. (1951). *Client-centered therapy*. Boston: Houghton-Mifflin.

Schneider, W., & Shiffrin, R. M. (1977). Controlled and automatic human information processing: Detection, search, and attention. *Psychological Review, 84*, 1–66.

Shostak, D. A. (1977). *Family versus individual oriented behavior therapy as treatment approaches to juvenile delinquency*. Unpublished doctoral dissertation, University of Virginia.

Stuart, R. B. (1971). Behavior contracting within the families of delinquents. *Journal of Behavior Therapy and Experimental Psychiatry, 2*, 1–11.

Stuart, R. B., & Lott, L. A. (1972). Behavioral contracting with delinquents: A cautionary note. *Journal of Behavior Therapy and Experimental Psychiatry, 3*, 161–169.

Taylor, S. E., & Fiske, S. T. (1978). Salience, attention, and attribution: Top of the head phenomena. In L. Berkowitz (Ed.), *Advances in experimental social psychology* (Vol. 11, pp. 250–288). New York: Academic Press.

Wahler, R. G., Berland, R. M., & Coe, T. D. (1979). Generalization processes in child behavior change. In B. B. Lahey, & A. E. Kazdin (Eds.), *Advances in clinical child psychology* (Vol. 2, pp. 35–69). New York: Plenum.

Watzlawick, P. (1978). *The language of change: Elements of therapeutic communication*. New York: Basic Books.

Watzlawick, P., Weakland, J. H., & Fisch, R. (1974). *Change: Principles of problem formation and problem resolution*. New York: Norton.

6

Handling Resistance to Change

GARY R. BIRCHLER
VA Medical Center and University of California at San Diego

The concept of resistance is increasingly enigmatic in the fields of behavioral marital and family therapy. Resistance has only recently been discussed by behaviorally oriented relationship therapists (e.g., Barton & Alexander, 1981; Birchler & Spinks, 1980; Jacobson & Margolin, 1979; Weiss, 1979). It is still hotly debated as to whether (1) resistance is an inevitable and central phenomenon that provides the major grist for the mill in the therapeutic process (as psychoanalytic and family systems theorists would suggest); (2) resistance is an occasional phenomenon to be ignored or dealt with in order to return to the basic objectives of treatment (as most cognitive–behavioral and behavioral–systems therapists would suggest); or (3) almost in its entirety, what is called "resistance" is therapist- and therapy-generated rather than client- or couple-generated (as hard-line behaviorists would suggest).

Given that resistance, whatever its prevalence and source, is a real phenomenon, the objectives of this chapter are to broadly define the concept, to explore its functions, sources, and causes, and to outline both preventative and remedial intervention strategies for its management.

DEFINITIONS OF RESISTANCE

In order to handle resistance to change in marital or family therapy, we must first make a determination of what resistance is. A review of the literature on the topic is beyond the scope of this chapter; however, entire books have recently been devoted to contrasting psychodynamic and behavioral approaches to resistance (Wachtel, 1982) and to mastering resistance in family therapy (Anderson & Stewart, 1983). A variety of definitions of resistance exist, from the general to the specific, from psychodynamic to strict behavioral, and from an individual trait base to resistance as a property of the family or the entire therapeutic system. Following are a number of definitions that illustrate the scope of the issue.

Resistance is

- "the occurrence of behavior patterns that seem to be contradictory to the patients' avowed purpose in seeking treatment" (Dewald, 1982)
- "a basic reluctance to explore, to understand, to grow, and to change" (Blatt & Erlich, 1982)
- "client behavior that the therapist labels antitherapeutic" (Turkat & Meyer, 1982)
- "probably the most elaborate rationalization that therapists employ to explain their treatment failures" (Lazarus & Fay, 1982)
- "not so much something that periodically comes up to disrupt therapy, as it is the way in which the sincere desire to change confronts the fears, misconceptions, and prior adaptive strategies that make change difficult" (Wachtel, 1982)
- "any phenomenon that arises to thwart or hinder the change process" (Luther & Loev, 1981)
- "all behaviors of the family, the therapist, and the therapeutic system that operate to inhibit the family from becoming involved in therapy or, once the family is engaged, that prevent or delay change" (Anderson & Stewart, 1983)
- "often little more than rejection of the client's goals by the therapist" (Stuart, 1980)
- "a bad fit between therapist and family, often involving fundamental differences in purpose, goals, values, and/or style" (Heyman & Abrams, 1982)
- "patterns and transactions in family therapy that prevent change" (Glick & Kessler, 1980)

Consistent with a behavioral orientation, resistance phenomena are conceptualized as observable behaviors or patterns of behavior versus unconscious processes or anxiety defense systems that remain hidden within the individual. It is probable that all of the above definitions of resistance have some validity. Any given behavior or pattern of behaviors, whether a function of the clients, the therapist, or the interaction of the two, may or may not constitute resistance. As Turkat and Meyer (1982) wrote, "there are no behaviors that can universally be labeled 'resistance,' and the range of specific behaviors that can be labeled 'resistance' is infinite." It is generally the therapist who labels a behavior resistant, and to do so, he or she must fully determine the meaning or function of the behavior in the total context of the clients' problems and the therapeutic relationship. This functional analytic process will occur differently for each individual therapist and will certainly depend on one's prior experiences, training, and orientation.

In the present context, I believe that resistance in behavioral marital therapy is not inevitable, but that the potential for cognitive and behavioral manifestations of resistance is great. Moreover, resistance is frequently caused by the therapist or the therapy method. Therefore, when resistance is encountered, one must consider therapist factors first for the cause of difficulties. However, as is discussed below, cognitive and behavioral manifestations of resistance may also derive from the client(s) and from the environment external to the client–therapist interaction.

FUNCTIONS OF RESISTANCE

It is tempting to think of client and therapist resistance behaviors as negative, disruptive, and unwanted. However, their presence indicates that something is blocking therapeutic progress. Therefore, it behooves the therapist to take an investigative, hypothesis-testing approach once resistance is detected. Several positive functions can be served by resistance. First, note that the central nervous system in most organisms is slow to change. This is a conservative, adaptational property of organisms that is largely protective and survival oriented. Accordingly, resistance to change may serve the needs of stability and security, or it may represent just plain good judgment.

Second, resistance can serve as a regulating, pacing mechanism to keep change from occurring too quickly or in an overwhelming magnitude that is beyond the adaptive capacity of the individual or the family system. Resistance can serve as the safety brake for a potentially out-of-control change process.

Third, resistance may signal a misfit between the client's goals and those of the therapist. In fact, psychodynamic and family systems theorists often acknowledge and expect such a therapist–client discrepancy in defining therapeutic goals, while behaviorists claim such a discrepancy is unnecessary if not ill-advised. Perhaps this philosophical difference is why the former groups see resistance as inevitable; the latter group does not (Ransom, 1982). In any case, the emergence of resistance phenomena can serve to alert the therapist that treatment rationale, methods, short-term objectives, and outcome goals may not have been sufficiently explained to and accepted by the clients.

The fourth positive function of resistance behavior is that its presence can provide important information about the couple or the therapy process. For example, it can suggest that the timing of a particular intervention is inappropriate, that a particular topic or therapeutic intervention is too threatening or anxiety producing, that a negative cognitive set exists that may interfere with behavior change, that an important issue has been missed, or that the therapist has neglected to consider the influence of a significant person outside the context of therapy. There are many other possibilities; ultimately, however, resistance is first and foremost a signal event that should alert the therapist to determine the functional meaning of the resistant behavior.

Finally, resistance behavior by the therapist can also serve a positive function. For example, failure to call a client, to reschedule an appointment, or to follow up on a critical homework assignment, etc., may indicate excessive stress in the therapist or therapist burn-out. Repeated instances of such behaviors can alert the therapist to assess these factors.

Many behaviorally oriented clinicians, if they acknowledge the phenomenon of resistance at all, limit its conceptualization and utility to the positive functions noted above. Viewing resistance as an inevitable, negative, client-based phenomenon is too susceptible to *post hoc* rationalizations for unsuccessful treatment. Moreover, the presumption that all couples will resist change has the potential of becoming a self-fulfilling prophecy (Jacobson & Margolin, 1979).

On the other hand, it is hard to ignore definite clinical experience that some couples, or individual partners, despite initiating marital therapy, seem intent on and often successful in defeating the mutually defined goals of therapy. In these cases, from a prorelationship point of view, client-based resistance serves a negative function. One or more of the following factors are presumed to be involved: (1) one or both partners lack sufficient motivation to change; (2) there are conscious or preconscious hidden agendas regarding entrance into therapy, for instance, one client really intends to divorce but wants the spouse to accept it without a fight (or without falling apart); (3) there are persistent struggles for control that include the therapist as well as the couple; and (4) there are attempts to maintain or reestablish the dysfunctional status quo (i.e., homeostasis) in the relationship. Ultimately, the client may be reluctant to accept and assume responsibility for the conduct of his or her own life (Blatt & Erlich, 1982). Note once again, however, that presumptions of these negative functions of resistance are highly controversial and should be considered as last resort explanations for resistance behavior.

SOURCES AND CAUSES OF RESISTANCE

Three major variables cause resistance: the client(s), the therapist, and the extratherapeutic context (environment). As suggested earlier, nonbehavioral (psychodynamic and family systems) writers focus mainly on client-based factors; behaviorists focus mostly on therapist- and technique-generated factors. Often, however, the cause of resistance phenomena is an interaction between the couple and the therapist. In a general sense, resistance can be conceptualized as a consequence of a failure to be understood, that is, of the clients' failure to communicate clearly and the therapist's failure to understand effectively (Blatt & Erlich, 1982). More specifically, a number of behavioral- and family systems–oriented variables can account for resistance. They implicate the therapist, the clients, and the therapeutic system as all being critical to the overall process of assessment and modification of resistance.

In order to avoid resistance at the very outset of treatment, many writers describe the necessity for therapists to skillfully create a positive context for change (e.g., Alexander, Barton, Waldron, & Mas, 1983; Epstein, 1985; Goldfried, 1982; Jacobson & Margolin, 1979; Weiss, 1984). If, due to lack of competence or motivation, the therapist fails to establish (1) rapport and trust with the clients; (2) the clients' expectations of their own and the therapist's potential for success; and (3) the clients' understanding and faith in the assessment and intervention methods, then the likelihood of resistance behavior is great.

Next, particularly in the case of behavioral approaches, resistance can be caused by the therapist's failure to (1) successfully explain the rationale for treatment techniques; (2) reach consensus with the clients on goals and priorities for intervention; (3) effectively manage the critical homework assignments; or (4) use the appropriate techniques at the appropriate times to facilitate change.

Finally, resistance can be caused or exacerbated by the therapist's failure to understand the potentially disrupting role of significant others and other important environmental variables outside the context of therapy or to observe and react promptly to the emerging patterns, sequences, and meanings of behavior that constitute resistance to therapy.

Munjack and Oziel (1978) have presented five categories of resistance that are useful in a behaviorally oriented approach. In their view, resistance refers to certain types of obstacles encountered in the treatment process that oppose or hinder therapeutic change.

1. *Type I resistance: the client does not understand what to do*. The client's role in the situation is to be an assertive, active listener. When preoccupied, the client may fail to attend to rationales and instructions for assignments.

2. *Type II resistance: resistance due to deficit in skills*. In this situation, the client may understand rationale and instructions but be unable as yet (or permanently) to perform the necessary behaviors. Inabilities to discriminate feelings, to pinpoint problems and desires, and to communicate clearly may result in the emergence of behaviors that appear resistant in nature.

3. *Type III resistance: lack of motivation or expectations of success*. It is debatable who is responsible for correcting this situation: the therapist or client. However, various fears, previous negative experiences and treatment failures, and feelings of hopelessness and depression may predispose the client to resist change. In some cases, therapists are unable to reverse negative client expectations.

4. *Type IV resistance: resistance due to anxiety or guilt.* According to Munjack and Oziel (1978), a likely cause of the most severe kinds of resistance involves relationship problems where resentments, anxieties, and lack of trust prevail. Spouses may even collude to resist progress because they have experienced or anticipate negative consequences to their interactional behaviors. Open communication about feelings and problem-solving in threatening areas of conflict are frequently inhibited when clients are ashamed of their feelings or impulses or are fearful of outcomes.

5. *Type V resistance: resistance due to positive reinforcement (secondary gain).* However uncomfortable some strict behaviorists might be with types II or IV resistance noted above, all are familiar with type V. Lack of therapeutic progress may well be due to some positive reinforcement (secondary gain) for the patients' symptoms or self-defeating interactions. Munjack and Oziel's list (1978) includes (1) monetary gains pursuant to disability or other legal issues; (2) the avoidance of work or stress through special consideration given to the sick role; (3) attention and sympathy that comes with being sick or in pain; (4) continuing visits with the therapist if change is slow in coming; and (5) relationship gains. This latter factor is often operative in marital therapy. Clients may manipulate for personal gain in the context of the relationship, for instance, to make an alliance with the therapist, to control the content or pace of therapy, etc.

Behavioral marital therapists have suggested that many so-called resistance behaviors are part of a normal testing process. Partners are ambivalent and insecure about the interpersonal change process (Jacobson & Margolin, 1979), so they test the commitment levels of their spouses by engaging in resistance-type behaviors (Stuart, 1980). At one extreme, partners may actually appear to sabotage positive change by punishing one another for changing. It is sometimes unclear whether this phenomenon occurs as a result of a partner's skill deficit in failure to shape new behavior or whether it is motivated by profound or long-term resentment toward the spouse.

Brehm (1966) developed a theory of psychological reactance that posits that most people will resist change and exhibit noncompliance when faced with (1) external influence attempts; (2) barriers between them and a freely chosen behavior; and (3) self-imposed losses of freedom (i.e., mutually exclusive choices). If the theory is valid, most clients would manifest some degree of resistance to change in a behaviorally oriented therapy context and the therapist would have to work to minimize the degree of the clients' psychological reactance.

Obviously, unspoken anger toward the therapist, a common source of resistance, is due to an interaction between therapist and client variables. Nevertheless, many couples are unable or unwilling to express anger or resentment directly toward the therapist. When such anger is expressed indirectly, it can have the effect of blocking therapeutic progress.

Family systems theorists (Watzlawick, Beavin, & Jackson, 1967) suggest that the principle of homeostasis operates to keep dysfunctional family systems and their family rules intact. Familiar patterns of behavior, even though maladaptive and painful, can represent the couple's predominant attempts at interaction. Consequently, new and unfamiliar behaviors can be threatening to the *status quo* and are resisted.

Finally, it has been noted (Jacobson & Margolin, 1979; Spinks & Birchler, 1982) that a number of couples resist progress in treatment because at some level a determination has been made that the costs, in terms of personal time, energy, and marginal expectations for success, are just too high. Initially, these couples can appear motivated for the therapy program, but individually or as a couple they fail to instigate change. Unfortunately, these partners are often not assertive enough to tell the therapist of their implicit decision to maintain the *status quo*. In any case, resistance is evident.

MANIFESTATIONS OF RESISTANCE

As discussed above, any given behavior may or may not represent resistance. The therapist labels resistance as a function of his or her own experience and orientation. Resistance may be seen as inevitable or largely avoidable. If resistance is believed to be ever present (e.g., Anderson & Stewart, 1983) or very likely to occur in most cases or in some populations (see Chapter 5), then one's therapeutic approach will be designed to anticipate and to minimize resistance in a proactive fashion. On the other hand, if resistance is conceptualized as largely due to therapist error or as a client-generated block to therapeutic progress that sometimes occurs (Jacobson & Margolin, 1979; Meichenbaum & Gilmore, 1982; Spinks & Birchler, 1982; Weiss, 1984), then one's primary therapeutic approach will be designed to identify significant resistance when it occurs and to deal with it in a remedial fashion.

The behavioral–systems marital therapy model (see Figure 6-1) was originally developed (Birchler, Spinks, & Gershwin, 1978) because the early behavioral marital therapy (BMT) approach seemed to be of limited value for some couples (Birchler & Spinks, 1980). Other proponents of BMT also suggested the need to broaden the formulation. It was thought that the overall efficacy of BMT could be improved by integrating into it both family systems and cognitively oriented principles and techniques of intervention (Barton & Alexander, 1981; O'Leary & Turkewitz, 1978; Weiss, 1980). Most recently, cognitive–behavioral marital therapy (C-BMT) has been proposed as an important if not necessary variation of BMT. C-BMT is designed to incorporate clients' facilitative and nonfacilitative cog-

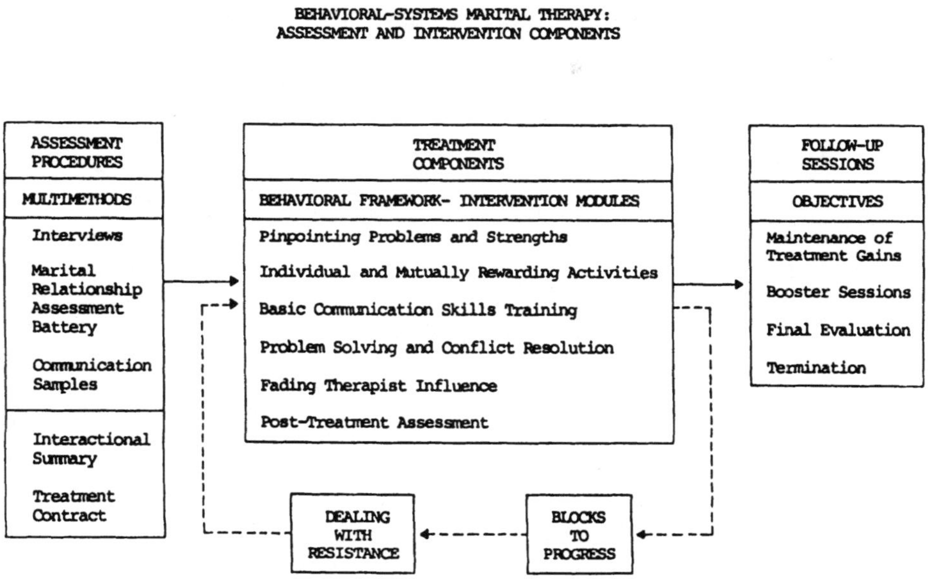

6-1. Behavioral–systems marital therapy: Assessment and intervention components. Reprinted with permission from Birchler, G. R. (1983). Behavioral–systems marital therapy. In J. P. Vincent (Ed.), *Advances in family intervention, assessment and theory* (Vol. 3, pp. 1–40). Greenwich, CT: JAI Press; and from Spinks, S. H., & Birchler, G. R. (1982). Behavioral–systems marital therapy: Dealing with resistance. *Family Process, 21*, 169–185.

nitions into the assessment and intervention model (Epstein, 1985; Jacobson, 1984; Weiss, 1984). In a sense, these various integrative models have been developed to handle resistance to BMT (i.e., to increase the outcome efficacy of the approach).

It should be noted that the basic treatment components that characterize BMT (Figure 6-1) are the most empirically validated procedures in the field of marital therapy (Jacobson, Follette, & Elwood, 1984). Nevertheless, resistance does occur while applying the BMT technology to distressed marriages. The indications of resistance listed in Tables 6-1–6-5 are consistent with a behavioral orientation and the behavioral–systems marital therapy model (Spinks & Birchler, 1982). From this behavioral frame of reference, resistance behaviors are defined as client- or couple-generated behaviors or behaviors generated by therapist–client interaction that block therapeutic progress in a significant way. Typically, resistance phenomena occur in repetitive, patterned sequences and, as Anderson and Stewart (1983) have categorized, they occur in one or more of the following con-

Table 6-1. Indications of Resistance during the Initial Contacts

- Requests for individual appointments (for marital therapy)
- Taking none of the blame or all of the blame
- Persistent tardiness or repeated cancellations
- Denying there is a problem
- One partner dominates
- One partner will not participate
- Couple insists on past history focus

texts: (1) during the initial contacts; (2) as a challenge to the therapist's competence; (3) during the assessment period or while making the initial contract; (4) in keeping the contract and following through with treatment procedures; and (5) while terminating treatment. Selecting from among the specific resistance behaviors noted by several writers (Anderson & Stewart, 1983; Glick & Kessler, 1980; Spinks & Birchler, 1982), Tables 6-1–6-5 provide lists that are not exhaustive but represent a considerable number of commonly observed resistance phenomena.

Table 6-2. Indications of Resistance by Challenging the Therapist's Competence

- Challenging qualifications, age, marital status, sex, race, experience with the problem, etc.
- Challenging process of therapy
- Challenging therapist's fairness or level of caring
- Challenging therapist's selection of assessment or treatment procedures

Table 6-3 Indications of Resistance during the Assessment Period and while Making the Initial Contract

- Scheduling problems
- Only one partner shows up
- Failure to comply with assessment procedures
- Partners disagree about the problems
- Lack of client–therapist consensus on the problems
- One partner wishes to continue, while one does not
- Withholding important information from the therapist
- Separation is a hidden agenda

Table 6-4. Indications of Resistance through Lack of Compliance with the Contract and Treatment Procedures

- Habitually late to appointments; missed appointments
- Failure to complete homework assignments
- Failure to recognize and shape desired behaviors
- Recurring crises between sessions
- Failure to progress in basic communication skills training
- Recurring escalation of conflict within sessions
- Regression (the emergence of original or new symptoms)
- Wrong focus or inconsistent focus on problem areas
- Flight into health: denial of problems
- Intellectualization, rationalization, or withdrawal of affect
- Inability to adopt a collaborative set
- Persistant hopelessness
- Scapegoating or focusing on an absent significant other

Table 6-5. Indications of Resistance during the Termination of Treatment

- Lack of generalization and maintenance of treatment gains
- Relapse to baseline dysfunctional interaction
- Emergence of new problems
- Noncompliance with postherapy assessment procedures
- Premature termination

STRATEGIES FOR HANDLING RESISTANCE TO CHANGE

The remainder of this chapter focuses on preventative strategies for minimizing resistance to change and remedial strategies for dealing with resistance as it emerges during three phases of BMT: the initial contacts and assessment phase, the ongoing treatment phase, and the termination phase. For illustrative purposes, the preventative versus remedial dichotomy that follows and the stipulation of phases of assessment and treatment are somewhat arbitrary punctuations in the overall process of BMT. In practice, assessment and treatment, anticipating client responses, and responding to them are fairly integrated operations. However, to the extent that some mild and intermittent resistance to change is expected, good preventative practice dictates designing therapist intervention procedures that preclude major problems. On the other hand, some clients and certain cases present or interact with the therapist to create significant, unanticipated resistance phenomena. In these cases, the therapist should be prepared to deviate from the standard BMT approach in order to identify and deal with the resistance. In the following sections, an attempt is made to review a variety of therapist skills and intervention options that can be used on a preventative basis and others that may be used on a remedial basis to handle resistance to change. Unfortunately, it is not possible in this chapter to suggest specific therapist responses to each of the indications of resistance listed above (Anderson & Stewart, 1983).

Initial Contacts and the Assessment Phase

First, let us consider the role of the therapist in preventing resistance before it occurs. Remember that our first line of thinking is, as Goldfried (1982) suggests, that the client is never wrong and, as Lazarus and Fay (1982) assert, that resistance is generally a function of the limitations of the therapist's knowledge and methods. Accordingly, the therapist has several tasks during the initial contact and assessment phase of BMT, and the presence and degree of client resistance are often a direct function of how the therapist proceeds to accomplish these objectives.

The first objective is for the therapist to establish his or her credibility as a knowledgeable, competent professional who can create the context for change. As Alexander *et al.* (1983) point out, the important skill here is impression management: that is, for the clients to perceive therapist credibility and competence (regardless of the therapist's actual therapeutic skills). At this point, anything that can increase the clients' initial expectations of a positive outcome serves to minimize resistance behavior. This includes such things as good recommendations from referral sources, appropriate office decor and location, appropriate therapist dress, and courteous, receptive introductory contacts, whether by phone or in person.

A second objective is to establish rapport with the couple. The therapist's abilities to demonstrate empathy, warmth, understanding, and control are important here. These qualities are demonstrated throughout the third objective of the assessment phase: information gathering. Practitioners of BMT typically employ several methods to gather data about the interactional problems and strengths of the marital dyad, that is, clinical interviews, questionnaires, samples of communication, and information collected in the home environment (Figure 6-1). Clinical interviews are designed to elicit the presenting complaints, the perspectives of each partner, and information about such things as (1) past experiences in therapy;

(2) typical styles of communication and conflict resolution; (3) perceived problems and strengths of the relationship in terms of occupations, household management, child management, demonstration of affection and recreation, etc.; and (4) clients' goals for therapy.

In conducting the initial interviews, several therapist activities facilitate client confidence and minimize resistance (Birchler & Spinks, 1980; Jacobson & Margolin, 1979). These interventions include (1) modeling good listening behavior, that is, clarifying and paraphrasing partners' statements, validating and empathizing with their feelings; (2) regulating and balancing the verbal participation of each partner by roughly equating their talk time and opportunity to be heard; (3) recognizing and allowing for each partner's ventilation of negative feelings in a supportive but controlled fashion; and (4) providing clear rationale and encouragement regarding the planned assessment procedures.

An additional recommendation, which encourages kept appointments and compliance with assessment procedures, is to gain an explicit commitment from the couple at the end of the first interview to complete the assessment phase of therapy. Contemplated assessment procedures are outlined and rationales are provided. The couple is told that during the next few meetings no one will be asked to change in the relationship, no blame for existing problems will be assigned, and only after the assessment phase is complete will the couple (and the therapist) make any decision regarding the commencement of therapy. The couple's commitment to seek understanding of the problems without abruptly changing things improves attendance while the therapist assesses the relationship and establishes credibility.

Paper-and-pencil questionnaires have always been an integral part of the behavioral marital therapist's assessment techniques (Weiss & Margolin, 1977). In addition to providing self-reported clinical information and documenting pre- and posttherapy changes in marital satisfaction and interaction, questionnaires can also serve the purpose of acquainting the couple with the therapist's theoretical orientation, concepts, and language. The types of questionnaires selected, for instance, the Marital Relationship Assessment Battery (Birchler, 1983b), can also help the couple focus on important relationship issues that they may not have considered. Occasionally, mild resistance is encountered regarding the completion of these questionnaires. However, when the questionnaires are administered and then interpreted in an encouraging, cooperative manner, the clients' confidence in the therapist's skills increases and subsequent resistance is minimized.

Information obtained during the assessment phase can be further enhanced by the collection of a sample of marital problem-solving (communication sample) and spouse observation data obtained from the home environment. Occasionally, mild resistance results from the therapist assigning these two enactive procedures. Concerning the communication sample, some couples are shy or otherwise reluctant to demonstrate their conflict resolution skills on videotape or while being observed. However, this is usually a momentary resistance that dissipates once the procedure is begun. In contrast, relative to the more controlled in-session assessment procedures, the daily collection of spouse observation data at home (Jacobson & Margolin, 1979) is more likely to meet with client resistance. Therapist support for this assessment (and treatment) technique is often needed in the form of midweek phone calls, mail-in postcards, and considerable in-session reinforcement for successful data collection. Nevertheless, when done effectively, the impressive ability of these data to account for partners' variations in daily marital satisfaction ratings usually justifies the effort expended by clients and therapist. That is, once clients learn about the functional relationship between their daily exchanges of pleasing and displeasing behaviors and their sense of satisfaction with the marriage, resistance to the behavioral approach in general and to this assessment technique in particular tends to dissipate.

Finally, the initial contacts and assessment phase are completed when the therapist presents his or her formulation to the couple and a decision is made regarding treatment. Considerable therapist skill is called for during this meeting since the therapist must integrate all of the assessment data into an effective summary and treatment recommendation. The formulation of marital dysfunction is presented in a clear and systematic fashion, using language and examples that can be understood and appreciated by each partner. Resistance to engaging in treatment is minimized to the extent that the therapist has translated each partner's concerns, hopes, and fears into the assessment summary and treatment proposal.

Occasionally, significant resistance to change emerges during the assessment phase and the therapist must deal with it using remedial action. If the initial instance is a mild occurrence, or if it is the first occurrence of such behavior (e.g., being late to the session, failure to complete an assigned assessment task, etc.), one possible option is to ignore it until it is repeated. A second option for mild resistance is to institute the three R's (Stuart, 1980), that is, provide *reassurance, redirection*, and *repetition* of the needed rationale and directives. Often, mild resistance can be overcome without having to label the behavior as resistive.

If the resistance behavior is repeated or becomes a significant block to therapeutic progress, planned departures from the behavioral framework may be necessary. The therapist must first make a determination of what the resistance behavior means, what purpose is being served, and what its function is. To accomplish this, most therapists label the behavior explicitly and discuss it with the client or couple. An explorative evaluation of cognitions and emotions (Spinks & Birchler, 1982) often uncovers important information as to why the clients were late (repeatedly), why assignments were not completed, and so forth. Typically, even when clients deny resistance *per se*, compliance improves.

Should this approach fail to resolve assessment-phase resistance, the next step is to set appropriate limits. For example, the therapist may indicate to the couple that he or she will be significantly handicapped in helping them if they are not able to complete the assessment procedures (or are not able to get to the sessions on time to allow enough time for assessment). Perhaps it would be best to make the next appointment after the assessment homework task is completed, or to call and cancel the next meeting if the couple cannot be on time. Depending on the clients' reasons for seeking treatment, such limit-setting may well resolve the resistance if the alternative is to terminate therapy. Note, however, that this intervention is most successful when instituted using a combination of empathy and firmness and after possible reasons for the resistance behavior are explored and addressed.

Another, sometimes frustrating, form of resistance encountered early on is a challenge to the theapist's qualifications. Clients may suggest that the therapist is too inexperienced, too young, too old, the wrong race, the wrong sex, has the wrong degree, etc. Reasons for such challenges range from genuine and appropriate concerns, to manipulations for control, to early signs of lack of intention to constructively participate in the therapy process. Possible therapist responses to these type of challenges are discussed at length by Anderson and Stewart (1983) and include the following: (1) do not be defensive; (2) be prepared for such questions and the contexts in which they might arise; (3) help the client or couple make their concern explicit so the issue can be addressed directly; (4) admit to differences and suggest advantages to them or appeal for the couple's help; (5) ask for a trial run; (6) use humor to diffuse a tense situation; and (7) if all else fails, explore the issue of referral. Note that clients' concerns are sometimes valid, and the problems can and should be solved. For example, an older, younger, more experienced, or different sexed cotherapist or appropriate supervisor could be added to the case. In this situation, only rarely must a referral to a different therapist be made; usually problems of this type that cannot be resolved have been exacerbated by an inexperienced therapist's responses.

Most of the resistance encountered during the two or three assessment-phase sessions can be handled by the methods discussed above. Sometimes major, therapy-threatening resistance behaviors do emerge during these first few meetings; therapist options for intervention in these situations are discussed below. The most likely period for encountering client resistance is during the treatment phase, that is, during the initiation of relationship behavior change procedures.

Ongoing Treatment Phase

Once again, there are a number of standard techniques that therapists can use to prevent resistance before it occurs. These include (1) assessing and maximizing clients' efficacy expectations as a prerequisite to instituting behavior change operations; (2) relabeling current behavior and functions of behavior in positive terms; (3) establishing a relationship focus and collaborative set; (4) paying particular attention to the complexities of assigning homework; and (5) predicting relapse and normalizing periods of interpersonal testing.

Meichenbaum and Gilmore (1982) have suggested that failure to comply with treatment procedures can be caused by a deficit in the client's knowledge of what is appropriate, the presence of knowledge but lack of skills, or the presence of both along with doubt and fear. This third cognitive factor can significantly affect the willingness to risk change. Stimulated by the work of Bandura (1977), behavioral marital therapists have encountered the assessment and modification of clients' dysfunctional cognitions and expectations regarding the process and outcome of treatment (Epstein, 1985; Jacobson, 1984; Weiss, 1984). The issue is whether clients believe that they, the therapist, and the therapeutic method have the potential to effect a desired treatment outcome. Enhancing the therapist's credibility (discussed above) is one facilitative technique. Another cognitive enhancement procedure consists of providing clients with a convincing rationale (and, if appropriate, empirical evidence) for each assessment and treatment intervention. Resistance is reduced to the extent that clients participate in the treatment process by understanding what and why certain requests are being made of them. Finally, behavioral clinicians are typically optimistic about prospects for change; if they communicate this enthusiasm and high hope for success, this generally increases clients' faith in BMT.

A cognitive restructuring technique that is often used to prevent resistance before it occurs and to prepare clients for behavioral change operations has been called relabeling (see Chapter 5) or reframing (Watzlawick, Weakland, & Fisch, 1974). The objective is to get couples to alter their dysfunctional or change-inhibiting attributions about the meaning of their partner's behavior, about their distressed marriage, and about prospects for change. For example, most couples enter marital therapy blaming their partners for relationship difficulties and sometimes attributing malevolent intent to their partner's behaviors. This cognitive set, by itself, serves to influence perceptions and interpretations of the spouse's intentions and behavioral responses (Gottman, 1979). Using the relabeling technique, such a generalized attribution might be challenged by the therapist suggesting that, for example, the husband's persistent argumentativeness is not negatively intended but rather is evidence of significant investment in the relationship; if the husband did not care about the relationship, he would hardly spend hours arguing over issue after issue. As much of the family systems literature has illustrated (e.g., Madanes, 1981; Minuchin, 1974), most symptoms, maladaptive behaviors, and ineffective styles of interaction can be relabeled in such a way to challenge, if not change, the meaning of these behaviors. Once the basic meaning is questioned, partners then have an opportunity to observe and modify both the functions and performance of such behaviors. As a general preventative measure, resistance to therapeutic progress may be minimized by preemptively relabeling negative behavior as positive or at least well-intended. If relabeling is effective, spouses are less intent on blaming each other and more open to adopting a collaborative set.

Establishment of a collaborative set (Jacobson & Margolin, 1979) is another early objective in BMT. It is achieved when partners make the transition from primarily blaming their partner (or themselves) for distress in the marriage to viewing the problems as interactional in nature. The problems and strengths and the success or failure of the relationship are seen as the shared responsibilities of both partners. Achievement of this relationship focus (win–win) versus an individual focus (win–lose) is critical in the progress of BMT. Once this is achieved, many forms of resistance seem to be resolved or more easily managed.

The collaborative set is sometimes elusive, especially with significantly or chronically distressed couples. Therapist strategies to achieve it include educational indoctrination at every opportunity. For example, using their own clinical material, couples are taught that a problem for one of them is a problem for both. The marital relationship is an entity different from and greater than each individual, but if nurtured, it has significant potential to benefit each individual. Reciprocity in the marital system means that positive investments reap positive rewards, negative inputs reap negative responses, and, in a caring relationship, doing things with the purpose of improving the marriage almost guarantees satisfaction to the individual. Behavioral assignments (Stuart, 1980) and cognitive restructuring techniques (Jacobson, 1984) can be employed to foster a collaborative set.

Resistance to BMT is most often encountered as noncompliance regarding homework assignments. BMT, obviously oriented toward behavior change, emphasizes skill acquisition and behavioral practice both during and between sessions. During the ongoing treatment phase (Figure 6-1), assessment and intervention activities carried out in the home environment are a major if not the critical part of the therapy. Therefore, behavioral marital therapists should be experts in directing homework assignments; as noted earlier, many behaviorists still consider most client resistance (i.e., noncompliance to therapist directives) to be the result of therapist error. Accordingly, as good practice and as an effective way to prevent resistance to progress before it occurs, therapists would do well to follow several guidelines concerning homework assignments (cf. Birchler & Spinks, 1980; Hartman, 1983; Lazarus & Fay, 1982; Martin & Worthington, 1982). Briefly, these include the following:

1. Initiate homework assignments only after having established rapport with the couple. Compliance will be increased to the extent that the therapist has value as a reinforcer to the client.
2. Ensure that the homework assignment fits with the couple's therapeutic goals. Induce the expectation that completion of the task will help alleviate presenting problems.
3. Involve the couple in planning the assignment. Maximize the appearance of clients' choice and volunteerism and minimize the appearance of the therapist's influence.
4. Make sure that the assignment does not exceed the partners' motivation levels. Consider factors such as the time, energy, and other costs involved in completing the task.
5. Make sure that the assignment does not exceed the partners' competence levels. When possible, observe practice efforts in the session and make homework assignments at or below the observed level of performance.
6. Minimize any threatening or anxiety-provoking aspects of the assignment. Pursue ultimate goals with small, attainable increments. Shape the desired behaviors.
7. Make sure the assignment is specific and clear. Obtain client paraphrases of the assignment and verbal commitments to complete the tasks. Consider giving written assignments and telling clients to post them on the refrigerator.
8. Consider carefully the possibilities for secondary gains to the partners if they do *not* carry out the assignment. Consider the assignment's impact on significant others and the supportive or sabotaging responses others may have.
9. For some couples, explicitly anticipate problems and setbacks regarding specific assignments and normalize these as part of the learning process.
10. Finally, it is critically important to follow up and review homework assignments. Support, shape, and acknowledge positive efforts. In subsequent sessions, do not extinguish homework compliance through inatten-

tion; do not punish efforts by responding negatively to failure or incompletions. Find some aspect to reinforce and build from there.

It cannot be overemphasized that if these ten guidelines are carefully followed, most of the homework noncompliance problems (i.e., the resistance) associated with BMT can be avoided.

A fifth technique designed to minimize resistance to change is therapist anticipation and prediction of relapses, setbacks, and periods of interpersonal testing (Stuart, 1980). Applied more broadly than homework assignment guideline 9 above, the therapist monitors the interactional process and therapeutic gains made by the couple and suggests that as part of the normal process of changing, setbacks and reversions to former, familiar styles of interaction are expected to occur. First of all, this phenomenon is most likely to occur following sudden instances or significant periods of improvement. Second, predicting relapses enhances both the therapist's credibility and control of the situation and the couple's ability to cope once setbacks occur. In the rare event that relapses do not occur, the therapist is pleased to be wrong.

Dealing with Resistance after It Occurs

Let us now consider therapist options for dealing with significant resistance to progress after it occurs. There are a number of standard techniques and others being developed that are innovative to the field of marital therapy. The choice of intervention strategy will depend on the form that the resistance takes (see the lists above) and on what the therapist already suspects regarding the cause and function of the resistance behaviors. The following set of techniques incorporates both progressive and specific use features. That is, the first therapist options described tend to be more commonly and easily used, while the latter ones tend to be more complicated and less often used (at least by behavior therapists). However, once a given resistance problem is fully understood, any of these interventions may be specifically indicated. Unfortunately, the decisions as to which techniques to use at which points are not yet empirically determined; clinical judgment is the rule.

When significant resistance to progress is first recognized, the therapist must next determine how the clients' cognitive, behavioral, and affective factors are involved and to what extent the therapist–couple interaction is implicated. The simplest way to start is to explore and evaluate the clients' cognitions and emotions regarding the resistance behavior (e.g., Spinks & Birchler, 1982). That is, label the behavior and ask the client or couple to help you understand its meaning. Many times an empathic approach helps the client to uncover and assert his or her concerns. Once identified, the issues can then be addressed through therapist support, education, or problem-solving. Sometimes clients deny the resistance, but it dissipates nevertheless. On other occasions, this technique does not resolve the problem because the clients will not or cannot identify the problems.

A related therapist option that can be used when resistance has been identified, its cause is unknown, and dysfunctional cognitions or attributions are suspected, is the so-called search-and-destroy cognitive restructuring technique described by Epstein (1985) and Jacobson (1984). The idea is to inquire into and elicit clients' beliefs about the therapy process and their attributions concerning their partners. Usually, this inquiry is done on a one-to-one basis, sequentially, as the alternative spouse observes. Common dysfunctional cognitions associated with the process of relationship change in general and BMT in particular include (1) my partner will never (or cannot) change; (2) effective therapy should fully revive romantic passion in the relationship; (3) positive feelings for spouse (love) must precede behavior change; (4) my partner should "know" how I feel; I should not have to express my feelings; (5) change that is not spontaneous is not real or made for the right reasons; (6) the existence of marital conflict means our relationship will not work; and (7) my spouse is acting positively only because of therapist directives.

All of these beliefs are likely to be counterproductive to the objectives of behavioral marital therapy. Once identified, the therapist first attempts to educate the client as to the erroneous or change-inhibiting nature of the cognitions. In addition, it may be helpful or necessary to design a hypothesis-testing (i.e., cognition-challenging) behavioral experiment. For example, clients who have thought that feelings of intimacy should precede actions of intimacy have often changed their minds as a function of Stuart's "Caring Days" (1980) assignment or Weiss's "Love Day" (1984) or "Cookie Jar" assignment (Weiss & Birchler, 1978). In general, by virtue of structured homework assignments that emphasize self and spouse observation procedures, spouses are asked independently to behave "as if" they especially care for their partner over a period of several days. When successful, these assignments demonstrate the partners' commitment to the relationship and their abilities to risk and bring about change. Usually, renewed feelings of respect and caring are experienced.

A third therapist option to handle resistance after it occurs has been discussed above. It consists of relabeling or modified interpretation of the couple's maladaptive behavior or interactional process. This technique is effective when the therapist already has a fair understanding of the underlying issue and wishes to suggest alternative, more benign explanations for expressed feelings or observed behaviors. The objective is to move the couple toward recognition and discussion of otherwise obstructive, underlying, unspoken issues or feelings. If the therapist's interpretation is relatively speculative or if the partners are sensitive to the therapist control issue, the couple is invited to simply entertain the possible validity of the new ideas. The interpretations can be rejected if not useful. Consider the following examples, in which, due to persistent lack of progress in a session, the therapist attempts to relabel the problem: "I wonder, Karen, if your anger about Chuck not helping you more around the house isn't really another way of asking for more attention and affection from him? Wanting to be close is different from wanting more help in the kitchen. What do you think?" Or, to a couple who seem to bicker constantly and malign each other's commitment to the marriage: "As much as you two talk about it, I really doubt that commitment is the issue here. The fact that you both spend huge amounts of time and energy arguing with one another demonstrates a degree of investment and commitment that few couples enjoy. I wonder if there isn't some other basis for your frustration."

More extensive interpretations of blocks to progress can be designed to effect major shifts in the focus of treatment or in the understanding the couple has about a certain problem (e.g., Spinks & Birchler, 1982). When an act of relabeling or interpretation seems effective, it is helpful to follow up by asking the couple to discuss the exposed issue while the therapist observes and facilitates the communication process by coaching and providing feedback.

A fourth therapist option for helping couples to identify and move beyond hidden issues that are causing resistance to progress is the use of interpretive modeling (Spinks & Birchler, 1982). This procedure is most effective when enacted by cotherapists, but it is also possible to use it as a single therapist. The innovative feature of interpretive modeling is that the two therapists role-play the parts of the husband and wife. Using good communication skills, self-disclosure, and feeling statements, they discuss the potential underlying issue as accurately as possible. The therapists interpret and represent the particular viewpoint of each partner. This technique is effective for several reasons. Unspoken issues that are out of clients' awareness are made explicit and overt. The expression and management of the underlying issues are modeled with particular skill, which imparts to clients a sense of confidence and reduced anxiety. Finally, catastrophic expectations are diffused as the client observers experience the therapists dealing with their critical issues without exacerbations or the development of overwhelming conflict.

The following is an example of interpretive modeling. The case involves a newly retired college professor and housewife who sought therapy because the husband had previously been involved (affectionately, but not sexually) with one of his female graduate students. This "affair" had hurt and angered the wife tremendously, and she insisted on marital therapy (or else!). However, after several sessions, her righteous anger continued to impede the development of a collaborative therapeutic set for the couple.

The husband appeared to be genuine in his desire to improve the relationship, but he was perceived by the wife as extremely distant, nonloving and noncaring.

W:* And ever since we've moved to California we've been having house guests. We came out here to retire and I've been cooking, doing dishes, and making beds since I arrived.

T: Would you prefer to have fewer visitors?

W: Well, I enjoy having someone else around. Ron's body is there, but emotionally and mentally he's off in space. At least I can talk to the guests.

T: Ron, do you agree that you do not talk much with Rene when you're at home?

H: Yes, to some extent. Although I've been very busy getting the new yard in shape, and also, it's hard to talk to someone who's always biting your head off.

T: OK, let's try something for a moment. I think there has been a fairly consistent pattern to your transactions lately, at least during your discussions in these sessions, if not at home. We are going to roleplay the two of you talking. Basically, we're going to make some guesses about some of your thoughts and feelings which may be hard for each of you to identify or express. Please watch and listen to us and be ready to correct our misperceptions. OK?

T(H): Rene, I am really struggling lately with what's been happening between us. I know my fling with Kim has hurt and angered you. I really don't know how it happened. And I'm working on getting past that issue altogether. But, these days I can't seem to do anything right in your eyes. It's like you're very angry at the least little thing that I do . . . or don't do.

T(W): Well, you're right. I feel tremendously rejected, like I'm an old bag you've carried around for over 40 years, and now I'm only needed to wash your clothes and cook your meals. We haven't had sex but once or twice in two years. I feel like I'm completely alone and on my own. I've got to survive this, all alone.

T(H): I'm sorry you feel that way, but I can see how you would. The thing is, I don't really understand what you want from me. My feeling for Kim,

*In this dialogue, the following abbreviations are used: W, wife; H, husband; T, therapist; T(W): the therapist role-playing the wife; T(H), the therapist role-playing the husband.

or for you for that matter, can't change over night. You keep asking me to share things, but when I tell you how I'm feeling you blow up. I feel like I can't win.

T(W): Well, I guess I am very depressed . . . and irritable. It's real frightening to feel abandoned after 40 years. But why can't you just treat me like you do any other friend or acquaintance. You can be so nice and attentive to someone you barely know. I guess we have to start somewhere. I'm going to start taking care of myself . . . and have some fun. If you want to join me, fine. If not, I'm still going to have some fun.

T(H): OK. I'd like to plan a few more things together, but not if we're going to get into big fights. I hope we're still in this together.

At this point, the therapists stop the role-play and ask for the couple's reactions. Frequently, if the content of the interpretive modeling is sufficiently well-considered, the couple's response is a stunned and emotional confirmation. But even in cases where the husband or wife expresses the need to correct or modify the therapists' presentation, the goal of uncovering and dealing with the obstructive covert issue has been achieved. After the interpretive modeling sequence is clarified and confirmed, the usual procedure is then to ask the couple to talk about the exposed issue using good (previously taught) communication skills. Interpretive modeling requires considerable advance planning and, usually, behavioral rehearsal on the part of the therapists. However, when the couple are spinning their wheels, it is an efficient and powerful technique to move the focus of therapy to much more profound and critical issues in the relationship.

Interpretive modeling is effective in BMT because the therapists model metalevel communications. Since the intervention is often made during the basic communication skills and problem-solving training phases of treatment, couples are immediately encouraged to further this type of leveling communication at home. Because of the fairly in-depth interpretive and intrusive nature of this technique, however, therapists are well-advised to be confident about their proposed content and to practice their delivery before using this approach. The clients should always be told that the content is speculative and is open to their modification or outright rejection. To avoid inadvertent misuse of this technique, beginning therapists should be carefully supervised; live supervision (Birchler, 1975) is advised.

Next, we come to the management of significant resistance to progress as manifested in clients' persistent noncompliance with homework assignments. Beyond the ten preventative guidelines noted above, there are three additional therapist options that may be effective in gaining compliance. These consist of antisabotage procedures, contingency management, and the use of paradoxical prescriptions.

Antisabotage procedures (Spinks & Birchler, 1982) improve the prospects of couples following through with homework assignments related to

(1) basic communication skills; (2) problem-solving; (3) negotiated plans for behavior change; (4) the development of individually and mutually rewarding recreational activities; and (5) posttherapy relationship maintenance skills (Figure 6-1; Birchler, 1983b). Both partners sometimes find ingenious ways to sabotage homework assignments. Following repeated failure to comply with agreed-upon assignments, the antisabotage procedure is instituted. It consists of four steps: (1) brainstorming with the clients all conceivable ways and reasons that there might be noncompliance with the plan; (2) isolating high-probability obstructive attitudes and behaviors for each person (for example, it is determined that husband tends to watch TV evenings and weekends and thus "inadvertently" fails to practice communication skills with wife as planned; wife notices this neglect but suffers angrily in silence throughout the week rather than assert herself); (3) assisting the couple to discuss how the identified high-risk sabotage behaviors will be modified to allow successful follow-through with the assignment; and (4) socially reinforcing the partners for taking the time to anticipate potential interactional problems and presenting a minilecture on the advantages to the relationship of prevention of problems versus more costly remedial actions. When used systematically and selectively, the antisabotage procedure is effective in gaining compliance with specific assignments.

Implementing principles of contingency management to facilitate homework compliance is not new. However, when the therapist has reasonably good rapport with the couple and other attempts to gain compliance have not been successful, making further contact (e.g., the next session) contingent on completing the assignment is often successful. The therapist should empathically but firmly explain the rationale for such a contingency and be willing to terminate therapy if compliance does not occur. While this procedure is most often used during the assessment phase, it can also be instituted during ongoing treatment. Some therapists have also used a response-cost paradigm where certain amounts of fees are refunded (or charged) depending on the couple's compliance with agreed-upon assessment or intervention tasks.

Paradoxical techniques should not be ruled out when resistance to homework assignments is significant and persistent and the therapist is determined to gain control over the situation. The use of paradox in general (Hare-Mustin, 1976; Soper & L'Abate, 1977) and in conjunction with BMT (Birchler, 1981) has been previously discussed. Suffice it to say that paradox consists of presenting a rationale or prescribing a set of symptoms or exercises that are designed to put clients into a therapeutic bind or to help therapists gain leverage over resistant behavior. The effectiveness of paradox depends on two main criteria: that the therapist's functional analysis of the symptom or interactional system be plausible and that follow-through with the assignment (or condition) be unacceptable to the clients.

Thus, assigning an oppositional couple the task of bickering and arguing three times a day during the next week because marital conflict represents intimacy to them probably satisfies both criteria.

Generally, behaviorists have found that paradoxical techniques are difficult to administer and should be used carefully and sparingly, especially by inexperienced therapists. However, such strategic techniques can sometimes offer therapeutic leverage that is otherwise difficult to obtain.

Another therapist option for dealing with resistance to progress is to assess and confront the resistance behavior in individual sessions. The conjoint therapy approach is temporarily suspended as the therapist meets with each partner in a separate or split session to address the lack of progress privately. In general, such individual sessions are used when something is blocking treatment progress, and conjoint techniques have not identified or resolved the problem. In these meetings, the therapist's objectives are to evaluate critically the individual's attitudes and feelings, to assess for hidden agendas, and to determine the partner's ultimate commitment to change in the relationship. If obstructive issues are identified, and if it is appropriate, clients are confronted with the self-defeating aspects of their cognitions and behavior. Not infrequently, the therapist learns (or confirms suspicions) that one partner's hidden agenda has been to terminate the relationship. When used strategically, individual confrontations can be effective because they are usually an unexpected departure from the conjoint meetings. The sudden shift in format gets the attention of the resistant partner(s). Moreover, it can be suggested implicitly or explicitly that if progress is not made soon, therapy will be terminated. This is the time for the therapist to use his or her best empathic–assertion skills. If successful, treatment progress and the conjoint therapy approach are resumed.

The last option the therapist has in the face of intractable resistance is a discussion with the couple concerning termination of therapy and a possible referral to someone else. Anyone who has worked extensively with significantly distressed couples does not always view this situation as a defeat. Certainly, there are some couples who progress quite far in marital therapy and then one partner decides to terminate the relationship. If the therapeutic contract remains "save the marriage," unrelenting resistance to progress is inevitable. To be sure, there are a certain number of cases where marital therapy evolves into divorce therapy. In other cases, couples can define an ambitious set of goals but seem to reach a certain plateau beyond which movement toward increased intimacy does not occur. Termination or at least an extended break in therapy may be indicated. Finally, there are cases where the therapist and clients, or the therapeutic orientation and the client's preferred approach, is simply mismatched. In these situations, referral to another qualified therapist is appropriate.

TERMINATION PHASE

Preventing resistance to termination before it occurs is usually well-accomplished by a number of common sense procedures, many of which should be performed throughout therapy. First of all, at the beginning of the treatment phase, there should be a clear understanding of the specific objectives and goals of treatment. Thereafter, periodic reviews should be made concerning the progress of therapy relative to the accomplishment and/or modification of these goals. Then, several weeks before the regular therapy sessions are terminated, the therapist purposefully begins to fade his or her direct influence over the process of therapy and the homework assignments (Figure 6-1). Clients are encouraged, indeed, taught, to take responsibility for more and more of the agenda and action plan during and between sessions.

At the beginning of the assessment phase and again several sessions before the end of treatment, couples are reminded of the importance of conducting comprehensive posttherapy evaluations. Assessment batteries are handed out to be completed a week or two before the last weekly meeting. Communication samples are once again obtained, usually at the penultimate regular meeting. Thus, at the last regular meeting, couples are given the benefit of comprehensive evaluative feedback, including data from the multimethod assessment procedures.

Finally, it is highly recommended to have a review or "booster" session 4–6 weeks after the regular meetings terminate. This procedure helps couples to monitor their posttherapy progress and to maintain their gains by knowing that they will have a return visit. These several procedures usually minimize resistance to termination.

However, significant resistance to termination can emerge despite preventative attempts to minimize it. Typically in such cases, new symptoms emerge, a relapse to former destructive interactional patterns occurs, or there is some other crisis that makes termination seem ill-conceived. In all of these termination-phase situations, therapists are advised to label and confront the resistance phenomenon directly. It may be helpful to relabel the meaning of the symptoms and to interpret relapses or crises as related to anxiety and fears about termination. Treatment gains can be reviewed and relationship strengths emphasized. In some cases, it is in the couple's best interest to normalize resistance at this stage as typical of the termination process. Afterward, the therapist should proceed with termination, albeit on a more gradual schedule, that is, meet every 2 weeks, then after a month, etc. Rarely is the termination-phase relapse so profound that earlier treatment gains are lost and therapy must begin anew.

CONCLUSION

Handling resistance to change in BMT, even more than BMT itself, is still very much more art than science. As is suggested in this chapter, the therapist is confronted with a number of fundamental and highly controversial issues. What *is* resistance? Is it a property primarily of the client, as psychodynamic theorists insist? Of the therapist, as strict behaviorists insist? Of the therapeutic system, as many family systems theorists insist? Is resistance the fundamental business of therapy, an inevitable component of therapy, or largely avoidable in therapy? What does resistance mean? What role does resistance play? What function does it serve? How do therapists identify resistance to change and, if it exists as a real obstructive phenomenon, how do we handle it to minimize its debilitating influence?

This chapter has not been definitive in answering these questions. However, from a behavioral perspective, an attempt has been made to expose the reader to these issues and to offer a compendium of observations that behavioral marital therapists and like-minded family systems therapists have made concerning the definitions, functions, and manifestations of resistance to change.

Handling resistance includes cognitive and behavioral strategies designed to prevent or minimize resistance before it occurs and somewhat more specialized techniques to modify and resolve resistance after it occurs. The actual resistance behaviors observed and the modification strategies employed can also vary as a function of the phase of therapy.

The task that remains for the reader (and the current literature suggests that this is an ongoing challenge for most of us in this field) is to determine one's philosophy about resistance to change. It is hoped that the set of values and strategies for intervention that we adopt will be of maximal benefit to our clients. As the clinical and investigative field of BMT evolves into behavioral–systems marital therapy (Birchler, 1983a), strategic–behavioral marital therapy (Weiss, 1980) and, most recently, cognitive–behavioral marital therapy (Hahlweg & Jacobson, 1984), the future may well hold a variation of BMT that obviates the need for a special chapter on handling resistance to change.

REFERENCES

Alexander, J. F., Barton, C., Waldron, H., & Mas, C. H. (1983). Beyond the technology of family therapy: The anatomy of intervention model. In K. D. Craig & R. J. McMahon (Eds.), *Advances in clinical behavior therapy* (pp. 48–73). New York: Brunner/Mazel.

Anderson, C. M., & Stewart, S. (1983). *Mastering resistance: A practical guide to family therapy*. New York: Guilford Press.

Bandura, A. (1977). Self-efficacy: Toward a unifying theory of behavioral change. *Psychological Review, 84*, 191–215.

Barton, C., & Alexander, J. F. (1981). Functional family therapy. In A. S. Gurman & D. P. Kniskern (Eds.), *Handbook of family therapy* (pp. 403–443). New York: Brunner/Mazel.

Birchler, G. R. (1975). Live supervision and instant feedback in marriage and family therapy. *Journal of Marriage and Family Counseling, 1*, 331–342.

Birchler, G. R. (1981). Paradox and behavioral marital therapy. *American Journal of Family Therapy, 9*, 92–94.

Birchler, G. R. (1983). Behavioral-systems marital therapy. In J. P. Vincent (Ed.), *Advances in family intervention, assessment and theory* (Vol. 3, pp. 1–40). Greenwich, CT: JAI Press. (a)

Birchler, G. R. (1983). Marital dysfunction. In M. Hersen (Ed.), *Outpatient behavior therapy: A clinical guide* (pp. 229–269). Orlando, FL: Grune & Stratton. (b)

Birchler, G. R., & Spinks, S. H. (1980). Behavioral-systems marital and family therapy: Integration and clinical application. *The American Journal of Family Therapy, 8*(2), 6–28.

Birchler, G. R., Spinks, S., & Gershwin, M. (1978). *A behavioral-systems approach to marital and family therapy*. Symposium presented at the Western Psychological Association Meetings, San Francisco.

Blatt, S. J., & Erlich, H. S. (1982). A critique of the concepts of resistance in behavior therapy. In P. L. Wachtel (Ed.), *Resistance: Psychodynamic and behavioral approaches* (pp. 197–203). New York: Plenum Press.

Brehm, J. W. (1966). *A theory of psychological reactance*. New York: Academic Press.

Dewald, P. A. (1982). A psychoanalytic critique of the behavioral contributions. In P. L. Wachtel (Ed.), *Resistance: Psychodynamic and behavioral approaches* (pp. 205–217). New York: Plenum Press.

Epstein, N. (1985). Structural approaches to couples' adjustment. In L. L'Abate & M. Milan (Eds.), *Handbook of social skills training and research*. New York: Wiley & Sons.

Glick, I. D., & Kessler, D. R. (1980). *Marital and family therapy* (2nd ed.). New York: Grune & Stratton.

Goldfried, M. R. (1982). Resistance and clinical behavior therapy. In P. L. Wachtel (Ed.), *Resistance: Psychodynamic and behavioral approaches* (pp. 95–113). New York: Plenum Press.

Gottman, J. M. (1979). *Marital interaction: Experimental investigations*. New York: Academic Press.

Hahlweg, K., & Jacobson, N. S. (1984). *Marital interaction: Analysis and modification*. New York: Guilford Press.

Hare-Mustin, R. T. (1976). Paradoxical tasks in family therapy: Who can resist? *Psychotherapy: Theory, Research and Practice, 13*, 128–130.

Hartman, L. M. (1983). Resistance in directive sex therapy: Recognition and management. *Journal of Sex and Marital Therapy, 9*, 283–295.

Heyman, D. S., & Abrams, V. (1982). The interface of family and therapist values in "resistance." In A. S. Gurman (Ed.), *Questions & answers in the practice of family therapy* (Vol. 2, pp. 11–14). New York: Brunner/Mazel.

Jacobson, N. S. (1984). The modification of cognitive processes in behavioral marital therapy: Integrating cognitive and behavioral intervention strategies. In K. Hahlweg & N. S. Jacobson (Eds.), *Marital interaction: Analysis and modification* (pp. 285–308). New York: Guilford Press.

Jacobson, N. S., Follette, W. C., & Elwood, R. W. (1984). Outcome research on behavioral marital therapy: A methodological and conceptual reappraisal. In K. Hahlweg & N. S. Jacobson (Eds.), *Marital interaction: Analysis and modification* (pp. 113–129). New York: Guilford Press.

Jacobson, N. S., & Margolin, G. (1979). *Marital therapy: Strategies based on social learning and behavior exchange principles*. New York: Brunner/Mazel.

Lazarus, A. A., & Fay, A. (1982). Resistance or rationalization? A cognitive-behavioral perspective. In P. L. Wachtel (Ed.), *Resistance: Psychodynamic and behavioral approaches* (pp. 115–132). New York: Plenum Press.

Luther, G., & Loev, I. (1981). Resistance in marital therapy. *Journal of Marital and Family Therapy, 7*, 475–480.

Madanes, C. (1981). *Strategic family therapy*. San Francisco: Jossey-Bass.

Martin, G. A., & Worthington, E. L. (1982). Behavioral homework. In M. Hersen, R. M. Eisler, & P. M. Miller (Eds.), *Progress in behavior modification* (Vol. 13, pp. 197–226). Orlando, FL: Academic Press.

Meichenbaum, D., & Gilmore, J. B. (1982). Resistance from a cognitive-behavioral perspective. In P. L. Wachtel (Ed.), *Resistance: Psychodynamic and behavioral approaches* (pp. 133–156). New York: Plenum Press.

Minuchin, S. (1974). *Families and family therapy*. Cambridge: Harvard University Press.

Munjack, D. J., & Oziel, L. J. (1978). Resistance in the behavioral treatment of sexual dysfunction. *Journal of Sex and Marital Therapy, 4*, 122–138.

O'Leary, K. D., & Turkewitz, H. (1978). Marital therapy from a behavioral perspective. In T. J. Paolino & B. S. McCrady (Eds.), *Marriage and marital therapy: Psychoanalytic, behavioral, and systems theory perspectives* (pp. 240–297). New York: Brunner/Mazel.

Ransom, D. C. (1982). Resistance: Family- or therapist-generated? In A. S. Gurman (Ed.), *Questions & answers in the practice of family therapy* (Vol. 2, pp. 3–10). New York: Brunner/Mazel.

Soper, P. H., & L'Abate, L. (1977). Paradox as a therapeutic technique: A review. *International Journal of Family Counseling, 5*, 10–21.

Spinks, S. H., & Birchler, G. R. (1982). Behavioral-systems marital therapy: Dealing with resistance. *Family Process, 21*, 169–185.

Stuart, R. B. (1980). *Helping couples change: A social learning approach to marital therapy*. New York: Guilford Press.

Turkat, I. D., & Meyer, V. (1982). The behavior-analytic approach. In P. L. Wachtel (Ed.), *Resistance: Psychodynamic and behavioral approaches* (pp. 157–184). New York: Plenum Press.

Wachtel, P. L. (Ed.). (1982). Resistance: Psychodynamic and behavioral approaches. New York: Plenum Press.

Watzlawick, P., Beavin, J. H., & Jackson, D. D. (1967). *Pragmatics of human communication: A study of interactional patterns, pathologies, and paradoxes*. New York: Norton.

Watzlawick, P., Weakland, J., & Fisch, R. (1974). *Change: Principles of problem formation and problem resolution*. New York: Norton.

Weiss, R. L. (1979). Resistance in behavioral marriage therapy. *American Journal of Family Therapy, 7*, 3–6.

Weiss, R. L. (1980). Strategic behavioral marital therapy: Toward a model for assessment and intervention. In J. P. Vincent (Ed.), *Advances in family intervention, assessment and theory* (Vol. 1, pp. 229–271). Greenwich, CT: JAI Press.

Weiss, R. L. (1984). Cognitive and strategic interventions in behavioral marital therapy. In K. Hahlweg & N. S. Jacobson (Eds.), *Marital interaction: Analysis and modification* (pp. 337–355). New York: Guilford Press.

Weiss, R. L., & Birchler, G. R. (1978). Adults with marital dysfunction. In M. Hersen & A. Bellack (Eds.), *Behavior therapy in the psychiatric setting* (pp. 331–364). Baltimore: Wilkins & Wilkins.

Weiss, R. L., & Margolin, G. (1977). Marital conflict and accord. In A. R. Ciminero, M. S. Calhoun, & H. E. Adams (Eds.), *Handbook for behavioral assessment* (pp. 555–602). New York: Wiley & Sons.

PART TWO

SPECIFIC APPLICATIONS

7

Parent Training: Clinical Application

ROGER McAULEY
Royal Belfast Hospital for Sick Children, Belfast

The hallmarks of parent-training behavioral intervention strategies include careful observational analysis of problematic parent–child interactions; formulation based on operant and social learning theory; and treatment that aims at correcting observed abnormalities through training parents in "theoretically correct" management skills.

The objective nature of the assessment and the educational approach to treatment appear at first glance to contain a good deal of common sense; the many successful applications of this approach that have been reported in the literature support this notion (Fleischman, 1981; Wahler, 1975). However, other reports (Dumas & Wahler, 1983; Forehand & Atkeson, 1977; Johnson & Christensen, 1975; Wahler, 1980) indicate that parent training in its present form has limitations in terms of therapeutic impact. Interestingly, the therapy tends to be less effective in families in which correlates of child deviance are observed—for instance, the presence of marital disturbance and parental separation (Cox & Rutter, 1985; Wolkind & Rutter, 1985). Recently, Dumas and Wahler (1983) examined the relationship between various measures of socioeconomic disadvantage and social isolation (or insularity) and treatment success. Their general findings seem to suggest that the higher the level of family social disadvantage and insularity, the greater is the likelihood of treatment failure. Thus, it is now becoming apparent that parent-training successes occur most readily in families in which the parent–child interaction is the only major family problem.

Many behavior therapists have added components to parent training, such as Parent Enhancement Therapy (Griest *et al.*, 1982), problem-solving (Patterson, Cobb, & Ray, 1973), and self-control training (Wells, Griest, & Forehand, 1980), in an attempt to sidestep limitations; such efforts probably do help. However, it seems to me that what will ultimately be required is a much broader way of assessing family and individual functions; from such assessments, more accurate and precise treatment plans can be generated. This, of course, will involve a much better understanding of how various family variables (for example, marital problems, social isolation, etc.) interact. Recent publications indicate that this type of research is underway. For instance, Patterson (1980) has demonstrated how family coercion disrupts family life; Wahler and Graves (1983) have shown how aversive extrafamilial contacts affect child management; and McMahon, Forehand, and Griest (1981) have elicited a relationship between parental depression and child management. In spite of these studies, we still have some way to go before we can produce the sort of broad assessment and treatment model that might be useful to behavioral clinicians.

In the meantime, how does the clinician overcome the limitations inherent in the parent-training approach? Other theoretical and therapeutic approaches address some of the very issues that parent training tends to neglect. Family therapists (for example, see Haley, 1976) view individual problems as part of the whole-family interactional matrix; behavioral difficulties may be caused or maintained by family interactional networks. Change is conceptualized as family change rather than as individual change. Functional family therapists (see Alexander & Barton, 1980) emphasize the importance of assessing individual behavioral styles and attempt to accommodate the findings into treatment designs. Cognitive therapists (Beck, 1976) have shown that an individual's appraisal may be closely linked to the same person's behavioral performance, which is obvious in persons with emotional disorders. In therapy, faulty appraisals become the focus of change. Aspects of each of these approaches (all of which sympathize with general behavioral principles of assessment and measurement) can easily be accommodated into a parent-training approach—perhaps with the effect of improving the rate of treatment success.

This chapter discusses some practical and clinical aspects of my approach to parent training—an approach that has evolved over a 10-year period and has been influenced by other approaches such as ones mentioned above. The focus is mainly on aspects of assessment.

ASSESSING PROBLEM BEHAVIOR

An accurate case formulation involves an understanding of the key factors in the presenting problem. This requires an assessment not only of the presenting problem but also of the interactional and constitutional contexts affecting and surrounding the problems. Attempts to understand how these broader contexts are connected can be instigated by examining behavioral sequences not only at a detailed interactional level but also at a much broader level—for instance, on a day-to-day basis. Some aspects of this assessment are discussed below.

Detailed Analysis of Problem Parent–Child Interaction

Observing Behavior

In spite of the fact that skilled interviewing can elicit a good deal of accurate information about families, it is recognized that recall about interactional sequences is particularly prone to systematic bias (Cox & Rutter, 1985). Many parent trainers will recognize this fact. This is exemplified in the following example.

> John, a rather immature 12 year old, presented with a number of behavioral difficulties, including homework and bedtime problems. His mother, who was a single parent (and reasonably well-adjusted), reported that John had frequent tantrums at these times. Focused questioning about the interactional sequences around the problem suggested that the mother was quite firm but to no effect. The reported problems were not observed during two observational assessments at homework time nor from the mother's own observational records. Mother was asked to tape-record the problems; the recordings revealed an interesting story. In one sequence, following the mother's initial request to complete homework, the child successfully sidetracked the mother into discussing five different topics. Arguing and irritability escalated in the mother and child. The treatment that followed involved teaching the mother more accurate observational skills and a firmer manner in approaching potential problem areas. There was no need to teach her to apply effective consequences.

This case illustrates the importance of obtaining accurate and clear interactional details. The importance of observation is underscored. (General aspects of observational methods are discussed elsewhere [McAuley & McAuley, 1977; Patterson, Cobb, & Ray, 1973]).

Gathering accurate observational information often presents difficulties for clinicians. Only the most dedicated will be willing to go and view the handling of nighttime or early morning problems. Older children (in my experience, those over 8 or 9 years old) will often respond to the observer's presence by failing to emit the types of behaviors complained of by the parents. While parent records coupled with focused inteviewing may help, alternative solutions are required in other cases. Tape-recording has been mentioned. Another solution is to role-play with the parent(s) the particular interactional sequences. I have found this particularly useful in studying the early morning interaction in school refusers. The therapist acting as the child gets the parent to go through the process step by step until an accurate picture of the complete sequence has been achieved. Frequently, an escalating sequence of increasing anxiety and irritability (typified by fewer firm assertions, dithering, and fussing) is seen in parent and child. The sequence, once elicited, is replayed and taped. The detail that this sort of approach adds to information derived in the interview is enormous. Further, the treatment ramifications are obvious.

Observation and Nonverbal Aspects of Behavior

Over the years, behavior therapists working with parent–child problems have produced observational coding systems for general research and treatment research purposes (Forehand & McMahon, 1981; Patterson, Ray, Shaw, & Cobb, 1969; Wahler, House, & Stambaugh, 1976). In general, many of the categories of behavior within each of these systems pertain to the verbal content of behavior and to simple descriptions of overt motor behavior (for example, sustained attention; play, etc.). Certain nonverbal aspects of behavior, such as voice tone, voice volume, facial expression, and space between interacters, receive much less attention. There is no doubt that such aspects present enormous difficulties for researchers in terms of construct validity and measurement reliability. That the problems are probably ones of measurement is further suggested by the references to nonverbal dimensions (such as facial expressions, firm stance, etc.) in the treatment reports of parent trainers. However, we are still in a situation of uncertainty about the importance of nonverbal dimensions in parent–child interactions. For example, Forehand and McMahon (1981) drew a distinction between instructions that are verbally clear in content (alpha commands) and those that are vague or unclear (beta commands). These two types of instructions apparently discriminate between distressed and nondistressed families. I suspect that, regardless of verbal content, the way in which the instruction is given (in terms of facial expressions, gestures, voice tone, and physical proximity or distance) would also accurately discriminate between these sets of individuals.

In clinical practice, it is often not so difficult to teach parents to give verbally clear messages. Demonstrating the importance of nonverbal components is often more difficult. One possible way around this problem is provided in the following case example.

> The mother of a 9-year-old aggressive girl was having difficulty in appreciating the importance of eye contact, voice tone, and physical proximity when giving instructions to her daughter. The therapist selected a typical problem sequence and asked the mother to role-play her child, while a cotherapist adopted the mother role. The sequence was reenacted with the cotherapist adopting three different parental styles: anger, apathy, and firmness. At the end, the mother was asked to describe her experience of each approach. In the angry exchange, she had felt apprehensive but in control of the interaction. When the interaction was apathetic, she felt she could do what she liked. In the firm sequence, she felt that she had little alternative but to comply. Following this demonstration, the therapist had little difficulty in getting the mother to approach her daughter with an air of firmness.

I have used the sort of technique described above not only with parents but also with therapists in training. The results are almost always similar to those in the case example. Role reversals of the type mentioned here, in which the parent or therapist acts as the child, are often useful when exploring or illustrating different styles and strategies of management during assessment and treatment.

Parent Appraisals: The Neglected Aspects of Parent–Child Interactions

Parental attitudes and expectations color and influence child-rearing practices. For instance, the initiation of a child psychiatric referral is often related more to the parents' perception of the child than to the actual level of deviance (Shepherd, Oppenheim, & Mitchell, 1971). Child-abusing parents frequently have inappropriately high expectations of their child's behavior; for instance, they may expect their 2 year old to display total obedience. Finally, studies have revealed that current parent emotions and attitudes can result in distortion in the information given about child development and child-rearing practices (see Cox & Rutter, 1985).

More specifically, research into the relationships between attitudes, appraisals, or thoughts and behavior has demonstrated that the way in which we view events should not be ignored (Nisbett & Ross, 1980). Generally, the findings suggest that behavior can be markedly enhanced or disrupted by performance appraisals. In fact, Bandura (1977) indicated that among the most reliable predictors of behavioral performance in specified situations are the belief statements that individuals make with regard to their ability in those situations.

Among many parent trainers, there has been an implicit assumption that attitudinal change will readily follow behavioral change. In some cases (and especially those where the sole problems are ones of child management), this is true, but in many it is not. Seligman's work on "learned helplessness" demonstrates the difficulty that some individuals have in changing even after many repeated behavioral accomplishments (Seligman, 1975). Cognitive approaches have shown that assessing, tracking, and analyzing individual thoughts can, along with continued behavioral accomplishments, have dramatic effects in persons suffering from emotional disorders (Beck, 1976). In terms of new repertoires, other cognitive therapists have demonstrated that individuals can be taught productive self-instructional skills (Meichenbaum, 1977).

In the light of such weighty evidence, it would seem that a failure to include evaluation of behavioral appraisals into problem assessment will often lead to inferior formulations and treatments. The following case example illustrates this point.

> A woman with a history of six psychiatric admissions over the previous 2 years was referred because of management difficulties with her two young children. Assessment revealed that, among other problems, she was a compulsive home-

> maker. She often did not complete her daily tasks until 10 or 11 P.M. A careful review indicated that this problem was worst when she was menstruating. Interviews with the mother suggested that she was mislabeling her physical symptoms (tiredness, irritability, and lethargy) as signs that she was again becoming psychiatrically ill. These signs triggered off anxiety; in an attempt to avoid unpleasant worries, she would work harder. When she stopped working, the worries returned. A vicious circle was initiated. Sometimes the process abated; on other occasions it ended in panic. On rarer occasions, the process ended in her taking an overdose. Among many other things, the mother was taught to label her symptoms more appropriately.

The two most common types of parent appraisal that are important in early assessment relate to the parents' perception of the child and their perception of their own interactional capability. These are examined below.

Perceptions of the child—such as "he's just like his father" (implying that the problem may be genetic in origin), "he has a head abnormality," "he has a medical problem," or, sometimes stated by foster parents or careworkers in childrens' homes, "he's much too disturbed for us to do anything with,"—can frequently be elicited from caretakers on their first visit to a psychiatric or psychological clinic. Such appraisals will often color the parent–child interaction, and a failure to elicit them may cause obvious problems in the therapist–parent relationship and consequently in later treatment.

> A 9-year-old boy with aggressive behavior problems was referred for assessment and treatment. At the first interview, the therapists interviewing the parents gathered information suggestive of marked handling abnormalities. At the end of the first assessment appointment, the therapist discussed his findings with the parents and also suggested conducting some home observational assessments. At this point, the father became angry, stated that the child was abnormal, and said he had only come to the clinic looking for a medical solution: "Aren't there some drugs you can give him?" The family did not agree to further assessment! (A careful examination of what the parents thought about their child's problem and what their expectations were in seeking help might have avoided their failure to cooperate in therapy.)

How might we deal with such problems? Take, for example, a situation in which a single parent complains that her 6-year-old son is "just like his father." There are a number of possibilities. First, we might conduct a careful study of what the father was actually like. (In probing this area, it is important to remember that the mother's appraisals of the father may be in the form of thoughts or visual images.) Following this study, we can then progress to comparing the findings with elicited descriptions (or, if necessary, parent records) of the child. Probably, differences will arise, which can be used constructively to weaken the mother's appraisal. Second, recognizing that these appraisals often have a global all-or-none quality, we could ask the mother for other examples of children being just like their father (or mother) in families that she knows or has known. This approach has the advantage of beginning with a subject that may not be associated with a great deal of subjective distress. As evidence for similarities and dissimilarities accrues, the discussion can be steered back to the central topic.

Third, an exploration of the ramifications of the mother's appraisal may suggest that the father was unresponsive to the mother and that the child is now viewed in the same light. A careful analysis of day-to-day events will often reveal areas of responsivity (for example, "he brings me coffee when I'm sick") that do not concur with the overall appraisal. Fourth, another meaning of the appraisal for the mother may be that she views her life as being ruined. It is hoped that an exploration of day-to-day events and life in the future will reveal other interactions and life events that do not fit in with this view. In turn, the mother might eventually relabel her statement: "He causes difficulties and problems for me; however, this only restricts my life in some ways." Once this position is reached, then the mother may begin to view the child differently. Last, the therapist might adopt a paradoxical stance: "As you say, in many ways, he seems just like his father and that must be very hard for you. Maybe we might spend our time thinking about how you can cope with and manage the inevitable consequences." The expectation here is that the mother will, as she begins to work on other tasks, start to view the boy differently. Generally, a resort to paradoxical techniques will only be required in the most resistant cases.

Frequently, we see children referred by pediatricians following negative physical investigations for problems such as headaches or stomachaches. Many parents remain preoccupied by the physical complaints, as evidenced by statements such as, "Look at her. You can tell she is ill. How can it be psychological?" The following case example illustrates the handling of such a problem.

> An 11-year-old girl was referred with a 4-month history of headaches. She had been off school and had also been housebound since the complaints began. She was admitted to the hospital on two occasions for physical investigations and also for trials of various medical treatments. Physical causes were not found, and treatments did not work. At our initial assessment, we noted several findings. First, the girl looked ill; second, the parents were convinced that there must be a physical cause; and last, there appeared to be considerable evidence that the child gained an enormous degree of parental attention from her physical symptoms. Prior to progressing to a contingency management solution, it was deemed essential to alter the parents' view of the situation. This was done as follows: first, we accepted that there might be a physical cause but suggested that it was probably not serious, in view of the extensive physical investigations; second, we got the parents to explore the future consequences of their child remaining housebound (for example, academic and social failure); and third, we examined instances of how family members had

coped with pain in the past (for example, the mother had coped well with past back pain). Following these steps, the parents were ready to discuss a contingency management approach. Within 6 weeks, the girl was back to normal, and the headaches were markedly reduced in frequency and intensity.

Granted, there are limitations in the conclusions that can be drawn from case reports such as the one above; however, it would still not be unreasonable to suggest that the preliminary handling of parent appraisals is an important element in overall case management.

Frequently, parents' descriptions of their problem interactions with their children are interspersed with evaluative statements such as, "I have tried lots of things and nothing works," "I can't help it," "I was just not cut out to be a parent," and "It's all my fault." Such beliefs probably pervade many of the parents' interactions with their child and probably influence the consistency and the assertiveness of their management efforts. Unless these attitudes or appraisals are dealt with, parent-training efforts may be hindered.

There are a variety of ways in which negative appraisals can be managed. First (and perhaps the most constructively), we can examine many interactional sequences and inevitably find ones that demonstrate areas of parental success. By repetition and perhaps also through parent record-keeping, we might be able to demonstrate the relative inaccuracy of negative appraisals. Second, by a careful and detailed analysis of a problem interaction, we could trace the sequential relationships in behavior, appraisals, and emotions and then later add constructive problem-solving appraisals and actions (Table 7-1). This technique is most effectively used with the parents imagining their interactions in an initially relaxed state. The differences between their own approaches and the more constructive approach can then be discussed at the end of the process. Third (and perhaps not very satisfactorily), we might approach treatment of the problematic appraisal indirectly. For instance, we could state that it seems that there is not much that we can do and then go on to project the potentially catastrophic implications of deviant child behavior in the future. This may cause the parents to reappraise their contribution to the interaction. Fourth (a technique not used often enough), we can get the parent to talk to another parent who has learned to successfully manage a child's behavior problems. Also, paradoxical techniques might be employed in resistant cases (see above).

Many parents express statements of guilt with regard to their failure to effectively manage child behavior. A major problem with the parent-training approach is that it can enhance this view. In other words, the covert message in teaching management techniques is, "you've done it all wrong in the past." At a general level, sensitivity to this issue is advisable in all cases; however, in some cases it may be necessary to deal with the guilt problems prior to engaging in management training. It may be possible

Table 7-1. Two Different Ways in Which a Parent Might Handle the Same Problem with Her Child[a]

Non-Coping Interaction		Coping Interaction	
Interaction	Parent Thoughts	Interaction	Parent Thoughts
P[a] asks C why	Oh no not again	P asks C why	Oh no not again
↓	↓	↓	↓
P gets no response	Why does he do it	P gets no response	Why does he do it
↓	↓	↓	↓
P asks again	It makes me angry	P realizes he is becoming angry	It makes me angry . . . hold on that does not help
↓			
C says I don't know	↓	↓	↓
↓			
P and C argue	He has no right to do this to me	P leaves the situation to calm himself	Right, keep calm . . . think
↓	↓		↓
P shouts at C	I dislike him	↓	Okay, what's the problem
↓	↓		↓
C cries	Sometimes I really want to hurt him	P returns and states that C will not be allowed out tomorrow evening	Thinks about and selects method
↓			↓
P hits and shouts at C			All right, that's better

[a]P, parent; C, child. The problem is that the child has come home late.

to deal with this by conducting a careful review of the developmental history of the problems. Take, for instance, the following case example.

> The mother of a 7-year-old child complained of his slowness and irritability. The child was apparently slow in getting dressed, slow in finishing his meals, slow in completing his homework, and often slow to settle at nighttime. The mother noted that the child became irritable when pressed to speed up. There were often several parent–child arguments each day. Further, the mother was of the opinion that it was in some way her fault that the child was like this. A developmental history revealed that the child as a baby had been colicky, slow to adapt to new routines, and slept poorly and irregularly. The mother had consulted several doctors (including two pediatricians). In each instance, she recollected being informed that the baby was quite normal in every way. We stressed to the mother that this advice was probably misleading and that the difficulties with the child at that time were very real. We informed the mother that the difficulties were more related to the child's temperament than to her own handling. In other words, her child was more difficult to handle

than many others. This understanding began a process in which the mother was able to begin to reappraise her own feelings and look more objectively at her child's problems.

It is not uncommon to find this type of history in children presenting with behavior problems. In some cases, family life events (for example, parental illness) may have triggered off poor handling, which then grows and escalates.

Within this section, the concentration has been on modifying singular appraisal abnormalities. This kind of approach can also be adopted to deal with circumstances in which appraisal abnormalities are more extensive. In fact, in cases in which the parents present with marked depression or anxiety, an undefined number of sessions devoted to cognitive therapy may be required prior to detailed work on child management skills. In socio-economically deprived and insularized families, abnormalities in situational and personal appraisals of a global and widespread nature may be identified even in the absence of marked depression or anxiety. I believe that, in many instances, problems are probably long-standing and reflect a state of helplessness.

Broad Analysis of the Relationships between the Problem Behavior and Other Behaviors

All units of interaction are embedded within a social system and may be affected by, or may influence, a wide range of other interactions within this system. It is probable that one of the major differences in families that do well in parent training, as compared with those that don't, is that their tracking and observing abilities are sufficiently accurate to allow separate family problems to be assessed and dealt with in a separate fashion. Conversely, in families who respond least well, tracking may be poor; thus, the effects of one problem may come to affect or influence another one (Wahler & Graves, 1983). A particularly pertinent example relates to the effects of divorce on children (Parke, 1981). When parents have separated because of their own disharmony, but can still agree on child management, then the effects of the separation on the children will be less than in circumstances where disagreement spreads into child management. Below are some examples drawn from clinical experience of situations in which interactions influenced one another.

1. A mother of a 3-year-old child with extensive behavior problems was often exhausted and irritated when her husband returned from work. The husband, who was supportive and distressed by his wife's difficulties, frequently took over the management of household chores and the child.

Usually, he did this successfully. The problem in doing so was that he unwittingly undermined his wife's confidence in her own abilities. His role in parent training was to help his wife via feedback and constructive suggestions with regard to her child handling. The mother's confidence and skills were successfully built up in a gradual manner.

2. A parent training program was initiated to help a single parent manage her 5 year old's noncompliance and tantrums. After relatively good progress with these two problems occurred, the next target behavior for change was the 5 year old's frequent fighting with his 8-year-old sibling. The problem was carefully analyzed via parent records and interview discussions. Following fights, it often appeared that the 5 year old was frequently reprimanded (and in fact the mother had begun to use time-out with the child), while the 8 year old was comforted. We were unable to identify the immediate antecedents to fights since they frequently occurred out of mother's sight. However, based on the general knowledge that deviant children frequently receive the lion's share of attention, we speculated that the 8 year old was probably instigating fights in order to redress this balance. Consequently, the mother was asked to ignore fights (and, where necessary, to transfer the fights to another room if they were found to be annoying). Within 10 days, the frequency of fights had reduced remarkably.

3. A 6-year-old child was removed from home after his mother had beaten him severely following an encopretic episode. We were asked to help. After assessment, a highly successful parent-training program in which both parents cooperated was completed. The child was returned home. Shortly afterward, the child's school teacher began to complain that the child was highly disruptive in class. A classroom observation supported this. Unfortunately, the classroom teacher was unwilling to instigate classroom management procedures. However, she did agree to cooperate in a detailed home–school report system. On return from school each day, the mother scored the report and awarded appropriate privileges. The reports indicated an immediate dramatic improvement! The mother became suspicious when the child had difficulties with his homework and when she could find little evidence of classwork in his exercise books. She visited the teacher but did not gain any further insight; further, she felt uncomfortable in the teacher's presence. We visited and found that the child's behavior had not changed. The teacher was apprehensive that if she sent a bad report, the child would be severely punished. The parents changed the child to another school where the classroom problems were quickly and successfully resolved.

There are many other examples that could be given that would illustrate how child management may influence and be influenced by other family and social situations (including unsupportive husbands, interfering relatives, undefined child management roles of boyfriends and stepparents, busy parental routines, noncommunicating parents). If parent training is to be successful, then such influences must be assessed and considered in an overall treatment plan, rather than being considered as a later adjunct to parent–child management work.

Clinically, there are several ways that such influences might (where relevant) be uncovered. First, by broadening the assessment of target behaviors, the therapist may discover setting events, that is, earlier antecedents and later consequences, that are influential. This, of course, may lead to the detection of other significant parent–child interactions or to discovery of other quite different family or social interactions. Further, there can be no fixed limitations about how far back in time or how far forward this analysis should go, other than might be suggested by the nature of the problem, as illustrated by the following example.

> A 10-year-old child was referred with an episodic stealing problem. The stealing, which took place at home and in school, occurred roughly once every 3–5 weeks. An analysis revealed a cyclical situation in which behavioral difficulties (talking back, lying, and fighting) gradually escalated up to the time of each stealing incident. During each escalation, the mother became increasingly distressed and eventually demanded that the father (who was rather uninvolved with the child) should intervene. He often did this and remained involved for a few days. During these occasions, the child's general behavior improved. As the father then decreased his involvement, the cycle repeated itself.

An investigation of other day-to-day relationships, including parent–parent, child–child, parent–relative, parent–friends, etc., should be made. Combined with the first approach, potential links between problems may be established or eliminated. Also, a study of the changes that resolution of the child management problems would cause may help reveal factors contributing to child handling difficulties; in other words, what would family members do that they don't do now? Obviously, if the child's problems do cause family social restrictions, then such effects may contribute to the family's irritability toward the child. Further, the establishment or reestablishment of a range of lost activities may help ensure maintenance of child management gains at a later stage (for a further discussion, see Haley, 1976; Lazarus, 1968). The following brief case description helps to illustrate to some degree all of the above suggestions.

Case Report

A 4-year-old boy was referred with multiple behavior problems. He lived at home with both natural parents and a 2-year-old sister. A typical day was as follows: he often got up early and demanded parental attention or else created a "mess" downstairs. He refused to cooperate with dressing and was often dressed forcibly. He often refused the breakfast or else messed about with his food. In the mornings, he went to nursery school, where his behavior did not appear to cause problems. His behavior at lunch time was often similar to that at breakfast time. During each afternoon, he demanded his mother's attention, followed her around, fought with his younger sibling, and often disrupted mother's attempts to play with him. Mother rarely took him out because his behavior was embarrassing. Tea time was similar to other meal times. Last, he often refused to go to bed, and, when his parents insisted, he cried, screamed, and returned downstairs until they "gave in."

Both parents had similar difficulties with the child and frequently argued about his management—one blaming the other. The parents rarely went out (since they were reluctant to leave this child with anyone because of his behavior). Episodes of general intimacy between parents were rare. The wife had also become sexually frigid. In addition, she had sought help for depression. Increasingly, the father sought solace in his work, and he often dreaded coming home. The younger child did not appear to cause any difficulties.

Parental relationships with the child's grandparents had deteriorated; the parents resented advice from one set about firmness and from the other about love and attention.

A history of the problem development revealed that the mother had had a difficult and long labor ending in a cesarian section and later followed by a wound infection. Additionally, the child was difficult to manage; he slept and ate poorly. Over time, the child management difficulties increased, marital problems developed, and eventually the mother became depressed. Some preliminary treatment of the mother's self-appraisals was undertaken but is not discussed here.

This case presented with multiple problems, and the first decision to be taken was where to begin. It was hypothesized for several reasons that the best place to begin was with child management. The marital, social, and depressive problems seemed to have arisen out of the child management difficulties; one of the main causes of parental rows was child management; and both parents appeared willing to engage in treatment.

The next decision was what area of child management should be tackled first: to teach observational and management skills to cover all of the problems and expect the parents to carry them out immediately would have an enormous task. Rather, it seemed sensible to look for one problem area that, if changed, would have beneficial effects on other child–parent interactions. The nighttime problems were selected, since they offered several advantages. First, both parents were available for the treatment; second, if the child went to bed early, then the parents would have time to themselves; and third, parents and child would be better rested and better able to cope with the next day.

The child management program was spread over eight sessions over a 3-week period. The child improved, the parents reported increased intimacy, and the mother's mental state also improved.

A review at 3 months revealed that the problems occurring during the day (but not the nighttime ones) had reemerged. An analysis of the situation indicated that the mother knew exactly what was happening within her interactions with the child. We could find no reasons for the relapse, other than the fact that the mother was bored. Consequently, we got the mother to change her daily routine so that she had some housework to do in the afternoon and also to become engaged in some activities outside the home. The situation again improved dramatically and remained improved at a 9-month follow-up.

The necessity for a wide case analysis is underscored. Unfortunately, as we move away from a discrete analysis of a specific behavior, we also move into systems of extreme complexity, which are scientifically very difficult to measure. Given this, our hypotheses at times will often tend not only to be unreliable but also to be oversimplistic. To some degree, the potential for error can be reduced by experience and by a good working knowledge of the findings of research into child and family psychopathology.

Constitutional Factors

Research has now demonstrated quite clearly that children differ temperamentally (Thomas & Chess, 1977). The differences are most noticeable in the first few years of life. Thomas and Chess found that 10% of babies studied had a difficult temperament, 15% were "slow to warm up" (especially with regard to new situations), 40% had an easy temperament, and the remainder presented with a mixed temperament. Over the first few years of life, individual temperaments showed some continuity; however, these continuities tended to disappear as the children became older. In spite of this, it is probably true that temperamental characteristics may contribute to the development of later child behavior problems (Rutter, 1982; Thomas & Chess, 1977), as in the case example detailed above. The important point to establish here is that, unless therapists have knowledge of such potential effects, they will almost certainly fail to pick them up either in interviews or observations.

The observation that children differ in such ways is often comforting to parents, who may have viewed themselves as responsible for the behavior problems; many theories of psychopathology have all too often put the blame on the mother's lap!

In the following case examples, temperamental factors were thought to play a part. While this is almost impossible to prove, it does appear that part of the success in treatment relates to employing solutions adapted to the child's style.

1. The parents of four children aged from 4 to 10 years presented because of difficulty with their 6-year-old son. He was described as active, aggressive, and noncompliant. A review of the parents' management style revealed that they liked to discuss and reason with their children after their children had broken rules. This method appeared to work for three of the children but not for the problem child. We hypothesized that since the child was more active, it was possible that he would respond to a more action-orientated management style—for instance, time-out for rule violations, with explanations later. This worked very effectively.

2. Interview with the parents of a 4-year-old child revealed that the child became heavily engrossed in activities. Much of his noncompliance was probably related to the fact that he just did not hear his parents' requests. The treatment involved getting the parents to keep records of the child's activities and their own daily events. Changes were made to accommodate the sets of routines. There was no longer a noncompliance problem!

3. An 18-month-old child was referred because he apparently spent up to 5–6 hours a day crying and whining. During three observational sessions lasting 1 hour each, the child spent approximately 60% of the time exhibiting these behaviors. We examined the mother–child interaction and could find no explanation in terms of attentional mechanisms. Going through the records again, we speculated that the mother was forcing the interaction; she attempted to influence the content of play, and she seemed to force the child into cuddles and close bodily contact. With the knowledge that some babies do not like such close contact and that mothers can adapt considerably to their child's behavior, we planned treatment as follows. We had the mother respond more to the child's initiation of play and physical contact. Within 2 days, the situation had completely reversed; contrary to our hypothesis, the child was enjoying physical contact! A review 6 months later indicated that everything was still well.

The relationship between behavior and food allergies has received much public interest (Randolph & Moss, 1981). In particular, the Feingold diet, which supposedly contains only those foods that are free of synthetic additives, has in some quarters received popularity as a treatment for hyperactivity and behavior problems. However there is no scientific evidence as yet about the utility or validity of this procedure. Further, the degree of relationship between potential allergies and behavior problems is as yet unknown. One of the major problems is that, given so many potential allergens in food, it is difficult to see how this subject can be researched, let alone assessed, in a clinical setting. In 12 years of practice, I have only come across one case in which an allergy seemed to play a clear part!

> A 4 year old with a wide range of behavior problems was assessed, and the parents were then trained to employ more effective management techniques. The success was limited, and we were unable to work out why. A few months later, the mother made the discovery that the child's behavior improved dramatically when the child received natural orange juice as opposed to concentrated juice. A simple reversal procedure demonstrated the effect.

Family Style

The parent-training literature I have examined gives little consideration to the general style that families and individual family members adopt in their day-to-day interactions. Some families favor physical closeness; others are very emotionally expressive; some favor well-defined individual roles; others favor a democratic approach to daily living. The number of possible styles is limitless. Alexander and Barton (1980) drew attention to the potential importance of gearing treatment to fit in with family style. They suggested that if this can be done, then change may occur more easily and also may be more likely to generalize over time. These researchers conceptualized family style on the basis of two dimensions: physical distance and personal closeness. The parent–child interactions of overprotected children can often be summarized as high in terms of personal closeness and low in relation to physical distance. Ambitious, hard-working fathers may tend to maintain a high distance and low level of closeness with their families. Treatment formulations can be designed to allow individuals to maintain their relative positions. For instance, in the case of an overprotected child, the mother might be asked to maintain a high level of interactional closeness but change the way in which such contact is expressed—perhaps by talking about and emphasizing the importance of the child's independent social interactions. At first sight, this approach has appeal; however, the clinical applications of this stylistic concept is far from simple. For instance, each family member may vary positionally, not only across interactions with other family individuals but also within their interactions with specific individuals. For example, a father may, because of a very busy work schedule, have little time for family matters during the week, but then at weekends he may devote his time closely to his family. Alexander (1983) acknowledged these difficulties; nevertheless, the idea appears to make good clinical sense and is almost certainly worth pursuing. Two examples of cases in which style was considered to be important in the overall treatment are described below.

1. A 14-year-old girl was referred as a result of a number of serious problems. These included drinking alcohol, staying out late, sexual promiscuity, and several acts of vandalism. At home, she was described as surly, argumentative, unsupportive, and noncompliant. Some initial contracts were set up between the girl and her parents. These appeared to contain the situation. Next, we attempted to teach the family negotiating skills. The mother and daughter were able to assimilate these skills reasonably rapidly. The father (in spite of repeated "patient" coaching, including video feedback) remained vague, global, and unspecific in terms of describing problems and suggesting solutions. The result was that he frequently disrupted effective problem-solving. Given his general verbal style, it was decided that he should monitor and keep notes of interactions, which he could later discuss with his wife. Thus, he maintained his style and family position without hindering the mother–daughter problem-solving. The girl remained difficult, but at least there was a massive reduction in her antisocial activities.
2. A 12-year-old girl who refused to attend school appeared to have a close relationship with her mother. Prior to the school refusal, they had talked a lot about day-to-day events, and each often worried about the other's problems. The girl was rather timid and shy. Following a bullying incident at school, the girl had begun to refuse to go to school. The mother had done a great deal of worrying; however, when the refusal persisted, the mother and daughter interactions became very negative in the mornings and full of concern and worry at other times. The treatment entailed first getting the mother to be much more assertive in the mornings (she was taught these skills in role-play situations). Second the mother was taught to maintain interactional contact with her daughter. Discussion of the school refusal difficulties was barred at all times except for a set 15-min. period each day. The treatment in this case included some skill change, but it also attempted to continue interactional style. In the successful outcome that followed, it was difficult to ascertain the relative importance of each of the two treatment components.

Finally, added to the conceptual problems mentioned above, it is worth noting that clinicians will probably often be in a dilemma about whether or not style should be changed or modified. (The same could also be said about many of those factors discussed in the preceding section.)

THE APPLICATION OF PARENT TRAINING

A successful outcome will entail not only an accurate assessment but also skill in carrying out the treatment procedures. The literature abounds with examples of what to do when training parents, but it often neglects issues about how to conduct the treatment or how to get the best out of parents in their efforts as therapists for their children. A number of salient topics related to this issue are discussed below.

Therapist Variables

Alexander, Barton, Schiavo, and Parsons (1976) drew attention to the important contribution of therapist variables. They demonstrated that improvements in delinquent children and their families were often significantly related to therapist variables such as warmth, empathy, self-disclosure, use of humor, and the ability to reframe problems in a more positive light. Interestingly, structuring skills (such as setting clear goals, giving clear messages, etc.), which one would assume were highly important behavioral skills, contributed less to the outcome variance than expected. In spite of this, the importance of these skills is probably essential in many therapeutic situations—especially those involving more difficult families. It would not seem unreasonable to conclude that therapists are more likely to succeed in helping families if they can conduct treatment with clarity and also relate positively to their clients. In practical terms, this may, among other things, entail the capacity to empathize with distressed clients; the ability to reframe aggressive interactions in a more positive manner; and the skills to draw out an undertalkative adolescent or quiet an overtalkative parent. Further detailed information about these skills can be obtained from a series of six research papers summarized in Cox and Rutter (1985).

Nonspecific Techniques

Prior to actual parent training, therapists ideally should have given consideration to the implication of their assessment formulations and consequent treatment hypotheses, such as the number and frequency of treatment sessions. Many of these issues are dealt with elsewhere (Herbert, 1981; McAuley & McAuley, 1977). Here the focus is on the management of some roadblocks to successful training.

Anticipating Problems

Therapists who have established a good rapport with their clients will obviously tend to have fewer problems during the treatment period: the child will be aware of what's going to happen, the parents will know how to put procedures into effect (the importance of role-played practice and actual ongoing observational supervision cannot be overstressed); the parents will feel that they have made a considerable contribution to the techniques being applied (the therapist will have facilitated a discussion of the different techniques that might be of use); and common problems that might arise during therapy will have been anticipated, including the following:

1. "It's so mechanistic." Applying new contingencies in a consistent manner will often feel very unnatural in the early stages of treatment. A discussion with parents about the feelings they have in learning any new skill should be helpful.
2. "The treatment has made things worse." Extinction bursts are common; if clients are led not only to expect them but also to understand that they probably indicate progress, then they may approach management more positively at these times.
3. Time restraints. Time schedules may need to be reorganized. For example, in managing a bedtime problem, it is wise to have parents view this management as their prime task in the next few days. When viewed in this manner, then interruptions of TV viewing or other routine activities may become less irritating.
4. Problems in withdrawal of attention. For some people, ignoring a child is not easy. It is usually wise to ask people to engage in a particular activity when ignoring a particular child behavior.
5. Problems in application of time-out. Many children are very skilled manipulators. They may cry in a heart-rending fashion, smile when being sent to time-out, say they don't care about it, or stay in time-out after the parent has indicated it is completed. Many parents may interpret such behavior as indicating that time-out won't work. Prior warning to "soldier on" and ignore such behaviors will often be helpful.

The answers to many therapeutic problems such as those above lies in forethought and experience. Every case presents different combinations of problems and some novel ones; for example, one child continually upset his mother when she was applying time-out by pointing to a picture with some writing on it and chanting, "ha ha ha you can't read," which was true!

Three other points should be kept in mind.

1. The process of change is painful; if there are ways in which this pain can be eased, then the chances of success may be heightened. The family contracting game designed by Blechman (Blechman, 1980) is probably helpful in introducing an element of fun and lightheartedness to the management of problem interactions. Similarly, I have on some occasions set up simple contracts between parents, in which they observe, evaluate, and then reward or fine each other on the basis of their adherence to agreed-upon contingencies. Subtly, this may also have the affect of dem-

onstrating a firm parental togetherness to the child. There are probably many other ways in which imagination and ingenuity can be brought to bear on relieving the pain of change.

2. The process of change is tiring; if planned breaks can be arranged, then the anticipation of weariness can be reduced. Asking parents to plan a special outing together at the end of the first (and perhaps subsequent) weeks' treatment provides them with something to which they can look forward. Further, the break may covertly increase the motivation to succeed; many people do not like to do something special without good reason! This idea is referred to by Kozloff (1979) as "scheduled breaks."

3. This process of change is often lonely; frequent therapist contact in the early stages of treatment (by telephone for instance) helps to alleviate uncertainty and encourages persistance. In addition, I have sometimes found that leaving my case records with the parents promotes an atmosphere of sharing between therapist and clients. This sharing is further promoted by also getting the parents to make notes about their own progress in the case records. Thus, the records reflect a continuous flow of therapist and parent entries. The idea for this procedure originated with Hutchins (1982) who used the procedure with different intentions. In her work with the families of physically and emotionally abused children, the case records were left to ensure that the many professionals from different agencies were clear about treatment directives when they made home visits.

CONCLUSION

Parent-training procedures are not in themselves difficult to learn or practice; in many cases, therapists can expect rapid and easy successes. After all, a large proportion of the treatment research papers refer to graduate students as being the main therapists, although, as a group, many of these people probably have very limited therapeutic experience. The two main difficulties for parent trainers in many other cases are (1) getting clients to the stage at which they will be able to successfully employ more effective child management skills and (2) helping clients maintain any gains that have occurred. The reasons for resistance lie within the wider context of the child's actual problems.

In this chapter, I have attempted to address some of these issues from a clinical perspective, including family systems, parents' thoughts, individual styles, and therapist variables. The area covered is vast, and most topics have only received superficial coverage; for example, the use of paradoxical procedures is a much more difficult and complex "art" than might appear from its brief mention. However, the main aim of this chapter is to suggest some possible ways in which our success rate in managing problem children might be improved. Ongoing research may in the future indicate more precise means for resolving these painful family problems.

REFERENCES

Alexander, J. F. (1983). Personal communication.

Alexander, J. F., & Barton, C. (1980). *Function family therapy*. Workshop at Association for Advancement in Behavior Therapy's Annual Conference, New York.

Alexander, J. F., Barton, C., Schiavo, R. S., & Parsons, B. V. (1976). Systems-behavioral intervention with families of delinquents: Therapist characteristics, family behavior and outcome. *Journal of Consulting and Clinical Psychology, 44*, 656–664.

Bandura, A. (1977). *Social learning theory*. Englewood Cliffs, NJ: Prentice-Hall.

Beck, A. T. (1976). *Cognitive therapy and the emotional disorders*. New York: International Universities Press.

Blechman, E. A. (1980). Family problem-solving training. *American Journal of Family Therapy, 8*, 3–22.

Cox, A., & Rutter, M. (1985). Diagnostic appraisal and interviewing. In M. Rutter & L. Hersov (Eds.), *Child and adolescent psychiatry: Modern approaches*. Oxford: Blackwell.

Dumas, J. E., & Wahler, R. G. (1983). Predictors of treatment outcome in parent training: Mother insularity and socioeconomic disadvantage. *Behavioral Assessment, 5*, 301–313.

Fleischman, M. J. (1981). A replication of "intervention for boys with behavior problems" (Patterson, 1974). *Journal of Consulting and Clinical Psychology, 49*, 342–351.

Forehand, R., & Atkeson, B. M. (1977). Generality of treatment effects with parents as therapists. *Behavior Therapy, 8*, 575–593.

Forehand, R., & McMahon, R. J. (1981). *Helping the noncompliant child: A clinician's guide to parent training*. New York: Guilford Press.

Griest, D. L., Forehand, R., Rogers, T., Breiner, J., Furey, W., & Williams, C. A. (1982). Effects of parent enhancement therapy on the treatment outcome and generalization of a parent training program. *Behaviour Research and Therapy, 20*, 429–436.

Haley, J. (1976). *Problem-solving therapy*. New York: Harper Colophon.

Herbert, M. (1981). *Behavioural treatment of problem children*. London: Academic Press.

Hutchins, J. (1982). Personal communication.

Johnson, S. M., & Christensen, A. (1975). Multiple criteria follow-up of behavior modification with families. *Journal of Abnormal Child Psychology, 3*, 135–154.

Kozloff, M. A. (1979). *A program for families of children with learning and behavior problems*. New York: Wiley-Interscience.

Lazarus, A. (1968). Learning theory and the treatment of depression. *Behaviour Research and Therapy, 6*, 83–89.

McAuley, R. R., & McAuley, P. E. (1977). *Child behaviour problems: An empirical approach to management*. London: MacMillan.

McMahon, R. J., Forehand, R., Griest, D. L., & Wells, K. C. (1981). Who drops out of treatment during parent behavioural training? *Behavioral Counseling Quarterly, 1*, 79–85.

Meichenbaum, D. (1977). *Cognitive–behavior modification: An integrative approach*. New York: Plenum Press.

Nisbett, R., & Ross, L. (1980). *Human inference: Strategies and shortcomings of social judgements*. New York: Prentice-Hall.

Parke, R. D. (1981). *Fathering*. London: Fontana.

Patterson, G. R. (1980). Mothers: The unacknowledged victims. *Monographs of the Society for Research in Child Development, 45*(5, serial no. 186).

Patterson, G. R., Cobb, J. A., & Ray, R. S. (1973). A social engineering technology for retraining the families of aggressive boys. In: H. E. Adams & I. P. Uniket (Eds.). *Issues and trends in behavior therapy*, Springfield, Illinois: Charles C. Thomas.

Patterson, G. R., Ray, R. S., Shaw, D. A., & Cobb, J. A. (1969). *A manuel for coding family interactions*. New York: Microfiche Publications.

Randolph, T. G., & Moss, R. W. (1981). *Allergies: Your hidden enemy*. Northampton, England: Turnstone Press.

Rutter, M. (1982). Temperament: Concepts, issues and problems. In R. Porter & G. M. Collins (Eds.), *Temperamental differences in infants and young children*. London: Pitman.

Seligman, M. E. P. (1975). *Helplessness: On depression, development and death*, San Francisco: Freeman.

Shepherd, M., Oppenheim, A. N., & Mitchell, S. (1971). *Childhood behavior and mental health*. London: University of London Press.

Thomas, A., & Chess, S. (1977). *Temperament and development*. New York: Brunner/Mazel.

Wahler, R. G. (1975). Some structural aspects of deviant child behavior. *Journal of Applied Behavior Analysis, 8*, 27–42.

Wahler, R. G. (1980). The insular mother: Her problems in parent–child treatment. *Journal of Applied Behavior Analysis, 13*, 207–219.

Wahler, R. G., & Graves, M. G. (1983). Setting events in social networks: Ally or enemy in child behavior therapy? *Behavior Therapy, 14*, 19–36.

Wahler, R. G., House, A. E., & Stambaugh, E. E. (1976). *Ecological assessment of child problem behavior*. New York: Pergamon.

Wells, K. C., Griest, D. L., & Forehand, R. (1980). The use of a self-control package to enhance temporal generality of a parent training program. *Behaviour Research and Therapy, 18*, 345–358.

Wolkind, S., & Rutter, M. (1985). Separation, loss and family relationships. In M. Rutter & L. Hersov (Eds.), *Child and adolescent psychiatry. Modern approaches*. Oxford: Blackwell.

8

Families of the Developmentally Disabled

SANDRA L. HARRIS
Rutgers, The State University of New Jersey
CAROLYN THORWARTH BRUEY
Private Practice, Marlton, New Jersey

THE CASE OF THE C FAMILY

Mr. and Mrs. C, their developmentally disabled daughter Allie (age 21) and son Paul (age 16) sought help because of Allie's behavior, which included tantrums, self-abuse, and public masturbation. Although Allie's behavior had always been of concern to the family, their distress increased as she entered adulthood and continued to pose major management problems.

Allie had a number of unusual, autistic-like behaviors. She rarely maintained eye contact, insisted on predictable routines, and at times appeared oblivious to her environment. Her speech was often echolalic and she rarely initiated conversation. Nonetheless, she was capable of answering questions in full, coherent sentences. Although her developmental disability was notable, Allie was also quite capable in many ways. She worked full time in an adult workshop, completed many household chores, and could go on independent shopping trips.

One prong of the intervention with Allie and her family focused on reducing the frequency of her problem behaviors. Her parents were asked to collect baseline data on the targeted problems, including how often the behavior occurred and the antecedents and consequences of the behaviors. After baseline data were collected, a comprehensive treatment program was initiated; first, a response-cost system was implemented within which Allie gained and lost points for appropriate and inappropriate behaviors. Allie was required to self-record her own behavior, and points were exchanged for money at the end of each week. Second, Allie was taught to use relaxation techniques (E. Jacobson, 1964) to reduce the muscular tension and increased agitation that were antecedents to her tantrums. Finally, she was trained in communication skills to reduce the attention-seeking quality of her self-abusive behavior.

The second prong of the intervention package for the C family focused on understanding them as a system. It became evident that Mrs. C was the person whose life was most affected by Allie and who was nonetheless the most resistant to change. Initially, Mrs. C was apathetic and depressed, answering questions in one-word responses and showing a limited range of emotion. She often appeared on the verge of tears, but she would not acknowledge feelings of sadness. She contended that the rest of the family spoiled Allie, arguing that Allie needed stricter discipline.

In contrast to his wife, Mr. C was an inevitably cheerful man who prided himself on his ability to "see the silver lining." He stated that he rarely became upset with Allie because "she couldn't help it." Superficially, Mr. C appeared well-adjusted to Allie's developmental disability. Nevertheless, as therapy progressed, it became evident that he was overinvolved with his daughter and did not accept the full extent of her handicap. He had sought professional help with the hidden agenda of finding a miracle cure.

Both Mr. and Mrs. C were emotionally exhausted by Allie's disability. They had mustered enough energy to handle her disability for 21 long years, and they currently found it difficult to motivate themselves to do more. They were also beginning to worry about their daughter's future after they died. During one session, Mr. C indicated that he expected Paul to take care of Allie when he and Mrs. C were dead.

This expectation was not at all consistent with the relationship between Allie and Paul. Although they had gotten along well in earlier years, the brother–sister relationship had deteriorated as Allie's behavior became increasingly intrusive. The situation was intensified because Allie's inappropriate behaviors sometimes followed Paul's attempts to interact with her. By the time the C family sought treatment, Paul and Allie rarely spoke to one another, and Paul appeared sullen and uninterested.

In light of these issues within the family, it was decided that it would be helpful to (1) decrease Mr. C's overinvolvement with Allie; (2) increase Mrs. C's interactions with her daughter; (3) improve Allie's relationship with her brother; and (4) help the whole family increase their awareness and acceptance of Allie's disability while exploring the options for her adult life.

In carrying out this treatment plan, the therapist worked to develop a stronger relationship with Mrs. C by supporting the notion that Mr. C could help Allie by adopting a "tougher" approach to Allie. At the same time, Mr. C was told that he "worked too hard" with Allie. He was instructed only to review Allie's negative points in the response-cost system while Mrs. C was assigned the task of reviewing Allie's positive points. This reversal of their usual roles helped Mr. C adopt a somewhat less involved relationship with his daughter while Mrs. C was guided into a more positive, rewarding interaction with the young woman.

As therapy progressed, sessions began to address broader, affective issues. Mr. and Mrs. C talked of the daily realities of having a developmentally disabled child. Gradually, Mr. C was able to express his feelings of anger toward Allie. Although initially ashamed of these feelings, he soon recognized that they were understandable—and healthy. In a similar fashion, Mrs. C began to express her sad feelings and to recognize that a sense of worthlessness and incompetence underlay her depression. She described herself as a failure, blaming many of Allie's problems on "poor mothering." In order to boost her sense of self-efficacy, Mrs. C was encouraged to adopt much of the executive decision-making role in Allie's care. Mrs. C was also given realistic feedback about the biological basis for Allie's disability.

For his part, Paul also began to discuss his emotional needs. After 3 months of therapy he was able to express how much he missed his past relationship with his sister. His frustration and feelings of rejection were examined in an open and supportive fashion. While these discussions were helpful, some direct behavior change was also required. To that end, Paul reinitiated a "secret code" that he and Allie had used to write notes to each other as children. Both young people used their coded messages as the grounds for reestablishing contact.

After 7 months of therapy, Allie's behavior problems had been completely eliminated. The response-cost system was slowly faded until her weekly allowance was based on overall behavior rather than being closely linked to target behaviors. Changes had occurred in the C family's transactional patterns as well. Mr. C's overinvolvement with Allie had diminished significantly, Mrs. C became increasingly involved, and the interactions between Paul and Allie were greatly improved. All the family members had increased their communication skills and they tended to use a problem-solving strategy when approaching difficult situations (e.g., planning for Allie's future living arrangements). The therapy was rated by all participants as having met or exceeded their initial goals.

INTRODUCTION

The present chapter focuses on the application of behavioral family intervention with families of developmentally disabled children. Many of the behavioral techniques used with these families are the same as those used to facilitate functioning in families struggling with other issues. Nevertheless, there is specific information not typically learned in clinical practice with other populations that one should know in order to be optimally helpful to families of the developmentally disabled. It is our goal in the present chapter to share with the reader some of this information based on our research and clinical activities with the families of developmentally disabled children.

We chose to open this chapter with the case of the C family in order to illustrate how a therapist with a behavioral orientation might integrate the use of behavioral child management techniques with training in problem-solving strategies and communication skills to provide a broad-based intervention for the family of a developmentally disabled person.

The C family offers a striking example of a family for whom the developmentally disabled child's needs posed special problems and whose interactions with that child may have served to intensify some of the problem behaviors. It was necessary not only to modify Allie's strikingly maladaptive target behaviors but also to help all the members of the family change their interactions with her and with one another. Changing the family's interaction patterns without teaching them new ways to manage Allie's behavior would have done little to provide them with real relief; trying to change Allie's behavior without helping the family to modify their roles in relation to her might simply have intensified the mother's depression, the father's failure to recognize his own feelings, and the brother's alienation from his sister.

In the pages that follow, we examine the potential and limits of training parents in behavioral techniques, review the literature describing what is known about the impact of a handicapped child on the family, discuss various family styles that we have identified among the families of developmentally disabled children, and address ourselves to a series of specific clinical questions such as the inclusion of the handicapped child in family sessions, the value of home visits, the treatment of siblings, the inclusion of the extended family in the change process, and ethical issues.

It is important for us to add that, although we believe behavioral family therapy can be very helpful to the family of the developmentally disabled child, we do not view the family environment as being at fault in the creation of the child's disability. Rather, it is our hypothesis that the raising of an autistic or mentally retarded child is a source of considerable stress for every family and that the dysfunction we see can most frequently be attributed to this stress. This does not rule out the likelihood that some families were dysfunctional prior to the introduction of their handicapped member. Although such dysfunction may intensify the stress inherent in having to cope with the child's handicap, we have not seen any persuasive data that a previous dysfunction is sufficient to play a causal role in the child's disability. We expect that few people will dispute this statement in regard to mental retardation, but we recognize that some other views have been proposed to account for the existence of infantile autism. Since these explanations are remote from our own view, and since space is limited, we will confine ourselves here to describing the kinds of interventions we have found helpful from our behavioral perspective.

PARENT TRAINING: SCOPE AND LIMITS

One of the most significant contributions of behavior therapy to the treatment of developmental disabilities has been our repeated demonstration of the feasibility of parent involvement in the behavioral treatment of their children. Parents have been shown capable of implementing a full range of treatment procedures within the home (Harris, 1983; Howlin, 1981; Koegel, Schreibman, Britten, Burke, & O'Neill, 1982). It therefore seems entirely appropriate to begin a discussion of behavioral interventions for families of developmentally disabled children by considering the scope and limitations of parent training in behavior modification.

Several years ago, when our interest in families of developmentally disabled children was in its formative stages, we undertook a series of studies on training parents of these youngsters to work with their child at home (Harris, 1983). This research, supported by the National Institute of Mental Health, enabled us to work closely with the families of more than 40 preschool children with autistic behavior.

The Sample

Our sample primarily included intact, white, middle-income families, from suburban communities in New Jersey and New York, who were highly motivated to work with their child and who were willing to cooperate with a research protocol that called for repeated videotaped assessments of their interactions. Thus, they were not a random sample of families of developmentally disabled children but rather a group whose relatively high educational level and motivation enhanced the likelihood of successful outcome. The children as a group were relatively impaired, with most of them meeting the American Psychiatric Association's diagnostic criteria (1980) for infantile autism. The majority were cognitively impaired, and all exhibited pronounced language deficits. A detailed description of the research population is available in Harris (1983).

Curriculum

Training the parents consisted of 10 evening meetings during which we taught them the basic concepts of behavior modification and operant speech training. The meetings lasted about 2 1/2 hours each and consisted of a blend of didactic material, demonstrations, and role playing by parents. Time was allotted for each couple to discuss the programs they were carrying out with their child at home and to make plans for their interventions for the following week. The curriculum included the basics of reinforcement, punishment, prompting, chaining, shaping, data collection, graphing of data, developing new programs, and issues of generalization and maintenance. As concepts were introduced, they were defined in simple terms and applied in concrete ways to the problems encountered by the parents.

The groups were led by psychologists, special education teachers, and graduate students in clinical and school psychology. Each of the leaders had extensive experience in classroom work with developmentally disabled children; at least one of the leaders of each group had lead a similar group in the past. Each group included five or six families, with both mothers and fathers expected to attend all sessions. It is testimony to the motivation of the parents that the absentee rate was very low and the drop out rate almost nonexistent. This level of participation was made all the more striking since the groups typically met in the middle of the winter, and many families traveled an hour each way to attend the meetings.

During the 10-week training phase, each family was expected to carry out at least two home programs. One program was aimed at teaching their child a new skill or controlling an unwanted behavior while the other was aimed at teaching prespeech and speech skills. Among the home-management programs were such goals as teaching the child to come when his or her name was called and various self-care skills, along with the elimination of self-injury, tantrums, and dangerous climbing. Prespeech and speech skills included establishing eye contact, nonverbal and verbal imitation, and the use of the full range of functional language.

Parents conducted daily teaching sessions in their homes and collected trial-by-trial data on these sessions. Although the group leaders were initially very active in helping parents design new programs, our level of input was faded over time to facilitate independent program development by parents after training ended.

Along with the evening seminars, each family received five 1-hour home visits by one of the group leaders. These visits focused on observation of the parents as they worked with the child, feedback on their teaching techniques, and demonstration of new skills. It was not the purpose of the visits for the group leader personally to bring about substantial changes in the child, but rather to create changes in the parents as teachers and thereby indirectly to benefit the child. Our experience has been that acting as the expert who performs "magically" with a child in the presence of the parents can serve to undermine the parents' confidence in themselves as teachers. We therefore kept our own work with the child to a minimum, focusing instead on the parents' performance.

In addition to the lectures, demonstrations, and home visits, each family read several books on behavior modification. We found that *Behavior Problems* (Baker, Brightman, Heifetz, & Murphy, 1976a), *Early Self-Help Skills* (Baker *et al.*, 1976b), and *Teaching Speech to a Nonverbal Child* (Harris, 1976) were well-received by the parents and provided a useful reference source for them. We encountered a few parents who were learning disabled and for whom reading was a chore. We therefore were cautious about relying on books as a primary source of information. Videotapes of effective parent–child interactions from previous groups were also a useful tool for highlighting the application of behavioral techniques.

Outcome

Clinically, we were satisfied that our program was effective in teaching parents the basics of behavior modification and enabling them to facilitate their child's speech. The groups were typically cohesive, elicited strong interest and cooperation on the part of parents, and led in some cases to the creation of friendship among parents. Our subjective feeling at the end of most sessions was enthusiasm and pleasure at the progress the parents and children were making. The groups seemed not only to meet the parents' need for didactic instruction but, by providing other people who shared the problems, to create a sense of support and comfort.

One cannot, of course, rely exclusively on a subjective sense of change in order to document a research program. Videotape assessments were made of the children and their parents before and after treatment and were coded for a variety of different skills. One set of tapes recorded the parents' efforts to teach their child a new skill such as nonverbal or verbal imitation, noun labeling, or the use of more complex grammatical forms. Another set of tapes depicted the parents playing with their child in the presence of a standardized set of preschool toys including a truck, doll, book, and blocks. The teaching tape was scored along a number of dimensions defined as important to efficient and effective teaching such as the proper use of reinforcement, presentation of discrete trials, use of prompts, and so forth. The play tape was coded for the kinds of speech attempts made by the children and the ways in which the parents attempted to facilitate their child's speech.

Both the parents and the children showed distinct changes in their behavior after the training program was completed as compared with before training. As a group, the children engaged in more frequent and complex speech after their parents completed the program than they had before (Harris, Wolchik, & Milch, 1983; Harris, Wolchik, & Weitz, 1981). Not surprisingly, the children with some speech made more progress than those children who were mute before training began. The parents showed themselves to be more skillful behavior modifiers after training (Harris, 1983; Weitz, 1982) and to engage in a wider range of behaviors intended to facilitate their child's use of language (Harris, 1983; Harris *et al.* 1983). Every family completed at least one successful behavior modification program in addition to the speech training (Harris, 1983).

We have offered this extended discussion of our training program to make clear that this was a careful, rigorous training program held in an atmosphere that was warm, supportive, and concerned with the experiences of individual families. In spite of the documented success of our program, when we conducted follow-up evaluations of the parents and children 1 year later, we found little evidence of continued growth on the part of the children. Thus, while the parents remembered how to perform their teaching tasks, they often were not doing so; also, while the children could perform the skills they had learned a year earlier, they typically had not progressed far beyond that point in the intervening time (Harris *et al.*, 1981). Similar reports of lack of continued change were made by Baker, Heifetz, and Murphy (1980) with families of mentally retarded children. These failures to find continued progress, along with the subjective reports of parents that they had run out of enthusiasm, were no longer very motivated to continue formal teaching, other family needs had taken precedence over the teaching, and so forth, led us to reflect on the limits of our didactic approach to parent training. In order to extend our efficacy, we began to examine the other needs that families may have, beyond those that can be met using parent-training techniques.

IMPACT ON THE FAMILY

Although one of the central assumptions of the present chapter is that the families of the developmentally disabled child do not differ in fundamental ways from other families, it is nonetheless important to acknowledge the special issues that confront these families and that pose distinctive problems for them. While the coping mechanisms used by the families of developmentally disabled children resemble those of other families, some of the ingredients that create their distress are unique to the child's disability.

Anyone who has visited a family with a self-injurious, autistic child; talked with the mother and father of a Down syndrome child shortly after their child's birth; met with a group of parents of retarded adolescents planning for their adult children; or watched the family of a profoundly retarded woman visit with her on the back ward of a state hospital has had some opportunity to witness the potential for anguish created by having a developmentally disabled child in the family.

There have been a number of moving literary attempts to describe the lives of these families. For example, both Park (1967) and Greenfeld (1973, 1979) wrote in graphic detail about the experiences of raising an autistic child. Helen Featherstone (1980), a professional educator and the mother of a severely handicapped boy, wrote a compelling book from the perspective of a social scientist who was forced to become an active participant in the reality of life with a handicapped youngster. These books convey a vivid taste of the experiences of families of developmentally disabled children.

The subjective sense of understanding acquired through clinical contact with families with handicapped children or through reading books by parents of these youngsters is a valuable source of therapeutic sensitivity. Nonetheless, it is important to turn to the research literature to examine these problems systematically.

THE RESEARCH FINDINGS

There exists a relatively small, and often methodologically weak, research literature addressing the impact that a handicapped child has on his or her family. Among the important design problems that permeate this literature are a failure to use a control group of families without a handicapped member, to parcel out the impact of having children *per se*; the absence of comparison groups of families with children having various kinds of handicaps; a primary reliance in much of the literature on mothers as informants for the entire family; and a failure to examine the impact of the child's disability on the family as a unit as well as on individual family members. In spite of these decided limits, there have emerged some consistent trends in the research on families of handicapped children.

There is almost no evidence to support the notion that families of developmentally disabled or physically impaired children exhibit higher rates of severe psychopathology than do other families. Most recently, Koegel, Schreibman, O'Neill, and Burke (1983) found no differences on Minnesota Multiphasic Inventory profiles for parents of autistic children and a normal comparison group. Similar findings of the absence of significant clinical disorder for parents of autistic and mentally retarded children were reported by DeMyer (1979), Carr, (1975), and Gath (1978).

Parents

Ruling out gross psychopathology or family disintegration does not mean that the presence of a handicapped child fails to produce significant sources of stress for members of the family. For example, Cummings (1976) and Cummings, Bayley, and Rie (1966) noted that parents of developmentally disabled children experience considerable stress, with the stress being greater for the parents of autistic than mentally retarded youngsters. Likewise, Holroyd and McArthur (1976) found that mothers of autistic children reported greater interference with their personal and family activities than did mothers of Down syndrome children.

DeMyer (1979), in an extensive study, found that mothers and fathers of autistic children experienced substantial effects in their daily lives from having a handicapped child. Mothers in the study reported more feelings of guilt, physical complaints, tension, and doubts about their ability to be effective parents than did fathers. Similarly, Gath (1978) found more depressive symptoms among mothers than fathers of Down syndrome infants. The Down syndrome mothers also complained more of feelings of depression than a control group of mothers of normal infants. In contrast to DeMyer (1979), Gath (1978) found that the mothers of Down syndrome children viewed themselves as no less competent in coping with their child than did the control group mothers. This difference between the reports of mothers of autistic and Down syndrome children may be due to differences of age of the children, or diagnosis, or both. In general, fathers have been studied much less than mothers, and we know less about their experiences with their handicapped child than we do about mothers' reactions.

Marriage

Although there is little evidence to suggest that the presence of a handicapped child leads directly to the deterioration of a marital relationship (Koegel *et al.*, 1983), some studies have suggested that having a handicapped child may intensify the stress inherent in child-rearing. For example, DeMyer (1979) noted that while general ratings of marital happiness do not differ in the families of autistic and normal children, the parents of the autistic youngsters described more frequent extremely unhappy marriages while the parents of the normal control children had more frequent extremely happy marriages. Gath (1978), who found significantly more poor marriages among the parents of Down syndrome children than normal control families, indicated that it was weak or moderate marriages that were most vulnerable when a baby with Down syndrome was born.

Siblings

Siblings as well as parents react to the presence of a handicapped child (Lobato, 1983; McKeever, 1983). Several studies have suggested that it is more difficult to be the sibling of a physically handicapped child than a normal brother or sister (Lavigne & Ryan, 1979; Tew & Laurence, 1973). It may be especially difficult to be a girl rather than a boy with a developmentally disabled sibling (Cleveland & Miller, 1977; Gath, 1973, 1974). Recently, Breslau (1982) reported that the sex of the sibling interacts with birth order; there was greater stress for older sisters and younger brothers in a sample of siblings of physically handicapped children.

Changes over Time

The age of the handicapped child has some impact on family distress. Carr (1975), in discussing the effects of the Down syndrome child on the family, pointed out that caring for the infant or toddler with Down syndrome is not a radically different experience than caring for the normal preschooler in that parents expect to provide a great deal of direct physical care and supervision for the very young child. Hence, her finding of little differences in day-to-day routine for these two groups was not surprising. Differences may emerge with more force as the child grows older. For example, Holroyd, Brown, Wikler, and Simmons (1975) found some evidence that it was more difficult to have an older autistic child at home than a younger one. Suelzle and Keenan (1981), in an extensive study of 330 families of developmentally disabled children, found that the parents of the older youngsters had less social support, were more isolated, and needed more services than did the parents of the younger children.

Although the nature of the stressor may change over time, there is good evidence that raising a handicapped child continues to be a source of distress for families over the years. Thus, Wikler, Wasow, and Hatfield (1981) considered the question of chronic sorrow in parents of mentally retarded children and found that this sorrow appeared intermittently in response to various significant developmental events such as the child's initial diagnosis, placing the child in a special facility, entering puberty, and so forth.

This brief review of the literature suggests that overall, although families of handicapped children do not exhibit more evidence of severe disability than do other families, they are at risk for more stress and subjective discomfort than the population at large. A sensitivity to these findings is useful to the clinician in understanding the kinds of issues presented by the family of a handicapped child in an educational or clinical setting.

DIFFERENT AND YET THE SAME

In a chapter on families of developmentally disabled children, there is an understandable tendency to focus on what makes these families unique. Nonetheless, it is important to keep this emphasis balanced by a recognition that families are families—these individuals function in accordance with the same basic principles as all other families. If we focus exclusively on what makes them different, we run the risk of failing to recognize that many of the same basic issues that trouble other families trouble these units as well. While the content of the family sessions may differ, the process of change may not.

Functional and Dysfunctional Family Styles

We have worked with families of developmentally disabled children in a variety of settings, including a day school for autistic children, parent-training groups, residential group homes for autistic and other developmentally disabled children, and a private outpatient practice for families with developmentally disabled children. Each of these contexts gave us a somewhat different perspective on this diverse population; the combination of perspectives has generated a picture of several different family styles ranging from the highly effective family to the markedly dysfunctional family.

Well-Functioning Families

In both day and residential schools for developmentally disabled children, we have worked with many families of handicapped children whom we could best describe as ordinary folks who have been forced to learn to cope with an extraordinary challenge. Most of these families have done a competent job of integrating their handicapped child into the daily routine of their families or, in the case of the residential setting, have come to terms with the notion that their child's extraordinary needs preclude keeping him or her in the home.

Our clinical involvement with most of these families can best be described as focusing on didactic training, short-term help with problem-solving, and support through especially difficult crises such as family illness, placement of the child in a new setting, dealing with the sadness created by the passing of a developmental milestone, the transient troubled responses of a sibling, and so forth. Our strategy in such cases focuses on mobilizing the existing family resources and minimizing our own involvement since the family is a healthy, well-functioning unit that requires assistance in the resolution of a relatively focused and specific problem.

Moderately Dysfunctional Families

In addition to the normally functioning families, who constitute the majority of people with whom we deal in educational settings, we also encounter some families in these settings, as well as in private practice, who exhibit a moderate level of dysfunction. Problems are of a chronic, ongoing nature and require a more extensive and prolonged intervention. Unlike the focused, highly specific issues of the well-functioning family confronting a crisis, these families have generated a long-term, chronic pattern of family interaction that ultimately creates stress for family members over time.

An example of such a distressed family was one in which the mother was defined for many years as the primary child care provider. Such a role was satisfactory to all family members in the retarded child's early years, but as time passed and the child's level of functioning changed very slowly, it became increasingly clear to the mother that her responsibilities for child care were going to be unrelenting. She envisioned herself at age 70 still cutting the meat, washing the face, and zipping up the jacket of her now fully grown retarded son. The mother's vision of herself eventually going into her own business or returning to school for training as a computer programmer was diminished by her need to care for her child. Her husband, picking up on her distress with her role, reacted with some initial effort to reassure her, but he was driven away by the anger and sadness he discovered when he attempted to explore the issue with his wife. His response was to attempt to ignore the issue, then to feel overwhelmed by it and to feel trapped himself by a similar image of his own perpetual burdens within the family. In such a setting, the other children as well as the handicapped child reacted in their idiosyncratic ways, and a reverberating pattern was set up within the family.

Confronted by such a family, we attempt to help all the family members redefine their goals, set realistic expectations, redistribute responsibilities, and consider alternatives to the once-adaptive and now-destructive patterns that have emerged over the years. Changes in such chronic patterns, although sometimes slow to emerge, follow the same paths as do changes in other families who have become stuck in maladaptive modes of interacting with one another. The child's handicap, while a reality that must be considered as an integral part of the planning and change process, is not the only factor to be considered in the therapy. We typically enter into a more long-term and active role in our work with these families than we do with the normally functioning family in an acute crisis.

Training families in techniques of problem-solving and contracting (e.g., Baucom, 1982; N. S. Jacobson, 1977, 1978, 1979; O'Leary & Turkewitz, 1978) can provide them with the kinds of skills they need in order to negotiate with one another more effectively and share their feelings. Improved problem-solving skills and more open communication help to decrease the likelihood of the perpetuation of maladaptive patterns within the family.

Markedly Dysfunctional Families

A third group of families with whom we have dealt are families in whom there exists a dysfunctional pattern based on pathological interactions, which in all likelihood would have emerged as dysfunctional regardless of the presence of the developmentally disabled child. For these families, while the child's handicap is not irrelevant, it usually turns out not to be the primary focus of our intervention. Rather, such families require help in understanding that the child's handicap may have become a distracting focus that has led them away from more fundamental issues in the family. Such issues may include serious psychopathology in one or more family members, disrupted marital relationships, and seriously maladaptive interactions among members of the family.

When these families present themselves for help, it is often based on their concern for their developmentally disabled child. Such concerns must be respected and can be used to facilitate establishing a good working relationship. Our credibility in issues of management may make it easier for the family to accept the notion that the problems extend beyond that child to include other members of the family as well. In these families, the developmentally disabled child often serves as the "identified patient." The reality of the child's disability may make the clinician vulnerable to accepting this presenting problem as the full picture since the child is, indeed, clinically disordered. We make a grave error on behalf of the entire family if we fall into the trap of accepting that portion of the picture as the entire scene. In some families who are resistant to change, we may have to realize that our efforts at change will be confined to dealing with the family's interactions with the developmentally disabled child; however, such therapeutic decisions must be made on an informed basis and not through an error in assessment.

An example of a family with a markedly dysfunctional pattern is one in which the father, a highly successful physician, worked 60–80 hours a week. He presented himself as a cool, aloof figure who had little time at home to respond to the needs of his mentally retarded son or those of his three other children. The oldest son was about to graduate from high school and had decided not to apply for college, preferring to remain at home and help his mother care for his retarded younger brother. Pressed about this he declined to explain his behavior and became sullen and withdrawn. His mother, in describing her oldest son, stated that she knew they were too close but that he was her best support and friend. The mother, a poised and articulate woman who graduated from a very fine Eastern college, had been drinking excessively since the birth of her retarded son. She felt isolated and remote from her husband and found her oldest boy a central source of emotional support. The retarded child, an attractive boy of 7, posed a myriad of management problems. Although developmentally capable, he was not yet toilet trained and did not use a spoon or fork to feed himself. The issue that brought the family for therapy was that the retarded son's behavior problems had recently deteriorated, and he had become actively destructive and aggressive at home. The family sought help for training in child management at the suggestion of the child's teacher, who reported only minimal management problems within the classroom.

Confronted by such a family, one's clinical responsibilities include the assessment of the retarded boy, each of the family members, the marital unit, and the family as a whole. Failure to consider these dimensions and to intervene with multiple levels of help will doubtless minimize the benefits to any member of the family. The family's dysfunction is likely to decrease the extent to which they can implement the behavioral teaching methods the child requires. It is also immediately clear that while this family needed help in the management of the retarded son's behavior, there existed a set of problems that extended far beyond his handicap. We find that we have to call on the full range of behavioral techniques in order to help these families. Fortunately, in this particular case, both parents were concerned about their older boy's reluctance to go to college, and this provided a port of entry for a closer look at the family as a whole.

SOME THERAPEUTIC ISSUES

Including the Handicapped Child

Clinicians who work with families of developmentally disabled children wonder whether they ought to include that youngster in family sessions. We believe that flexibility is a key to success in this process. Although some clinicians might argue that they would only see an entire family, we find it necessary to be far more adaptable. While including the handicapped child in at least some of the sessions is very important for purposes of assessment, we also find that the presence of this youngster can be disruptive to the discussions of other family members and may serve to slow down progress of the family. By virtue of his or her handicap, this child's responsibilities and contributions to the family will differ from those of others in the family, and the child's role in the therapy must be viewed within these constraints.

The child's level of cognitive functioning, age, ability to benefit from the ongoing family discussion, need for supervision, and similar factors must all be considered in deciding to include him or her. The nature of the problem is also important. When issues focus on the management of the child, more samples of his or her impact on family interactions are important than when the focus is on issues beyond the handicapped child. We do not find it essential for the child to be present for all sessions; with more severely impaired youngsters, we tend to involve them more for purposes of assessment than to bring about direct changes in their behavior during sessions. We find that as the family and their view of the child changes, they are able to implement the kinds of behavior management programs that create enduring changes in the developmentally disabled child as well as themselves.

Home Visits

While home visits may always be a useful source of information about a family and their physical environment, we find at least one home visit to be especially valuable with the family of a developmentally disabled child. Such a home visit offers a realistic view of the family's living quarters and of the kinds of behavioral programs that are feasible in light of physical constraints and gives us a chance to see the child in the natural environment. We have typically found that the developmentally disabled youngster ignores our presence and provides a rather uninhibited sample of behavior. Other family members are forced to cope with the youngster, and we thus are often given a compelling view of the reality of existence for the family. We try to conduct a visit early in therapy; we may return at a later time to evaluate progress or to gain a new perspective when changes are not occurring as we had expected.

Didactic Training

Training parents in behavior management is one of the special skills of behavior therapists. Working with the family as a unit certainly does not preclude the training of parents and siblings in behavior management techniques. We regard this kind of training as an integral part of the family change process. Not only does it help to improve the developmentally disabled child's behavior as the family had requested, but it also sets the stage for allowing the family to perceive therapy as a credible experience based on their initial success. We have yet to meet a family of a developmentally disabled child who cannot benefit from some instruction in child management. For some families, this may be the focal point of therapy, while for others it is merely one component. Although some families may receive this training at their child's school or similar setting, others may not have already had such instruction when they come for therapy. We have discussed the full details of our parent-training program elsewhere (Harris, 1983).

Marital Intervention

For some families, the focus of behavioral intervention may be the relationship between the parents. Observation of the family as they attempt to initiate change in the child using behavioral techniques may reveal tension between the parents that precludes their being effective teachers for their child. It may become evident that a couple actually promotes failure on the part of their developmentally disabled child in order to unite against their "unmanageable" child. Some couples may point directly to their distress with their marriage as the primary reason for seeking help. Couples who are raising a handicapped child may need more effective patterns of communication than other parents in order to compensate for the stress created by the child's extraordinary needs. Communication training (O'Leary & Turkewitz, 1978), while it cannot insure that all needs will always be met, does increase the likelihood that spouses will understand each other's desires.

In dealing with the couple, it is important to be sensitive to the possibility of issues concerning sexuality (Harris, 1983). Couples may be concerned about the risk of conceiving another handicapped child or may be so exhausted from the demands of child care that their sexual relationship suffers. The decrease in sexual activity can reduce the couple's opportunities for intimacy and comfort and thereby serve to weaken the marital relationship. For some couples, of course, diminished sexual activity may reflect a decline in the quality of their emotional relationship. Accurate assessment of cause and effect in these instances may well dictate intervention. For example, if a couple rarely has sex because both are exhausted from lack of sleep created by their autistic child's nocturnal wanderings, teaching their autistic child to remain in bed at night might be the most direct intervention. If, on the other hand, the couple is moving away from one another because of significant anger about issues in their relationship, this would require a very different focus of intervention. Such difficulties might be expected to respond to marital therapy addressed to such skills as communication training and problem-solving techniques.

Siblings

As we noted earlier, there are special sources of stress involved in being the sibling of a developmentally disabled child. The retarded or autistic child is typically not capable of becoming a fully contributing member of the sibling subsystem of the family. He or she always requires special care and consideration from siblings. In spite of these acknowledged differences, we typically attempt to integrate the handicapped child into the sibling group as fully as possible and to help the family identify ways to create a reinforcing bond between the handicapped child and his or her brothers and sisters. This may include encouraging such a child to assume responsibility for household chores like setting and clearing the table, taking out the trash, or sorting laundry. It may also include development of leisure time activities, such as jogging or bike riding, that can be shared by sibs and allow the handicapped child to compete in a competent fashion.

Training brothers and sisters in behavior modification techniques has been shown to be a feasible component of family treatment. Both Colletti and Harris (1977) and Schreibman, O'Neill, and Koegel (1983) taught siblings of developmentally disabled children to use behavioral techniques in their interactions with their handicapped brothers or sisters. Such training—while doubtless of potential value in that it can relieve parents of some demands on them, increase the likelihood of generalization of responding by the developmentally disabled child, and enhance the normal siblings' sense of efficacy—must nonetheless be done with a sensitivity to the normal siblings. Our experience has been that even well-functioning children have mixed feelings about their role as behavior managers and may express some distress about their relationship with their sibling. Both the therapist and the parents must be sensitive to these issues to ensure that they are discussed and respected.

The factual education of siblings can also be important in family treatment. McKeever (1983) suggested that siblings of handicapped children often do not ask questions about the disability and may not understand fully the nature of the problem. It is a responsibility of adults to initiate communication about the handicapping condition, to explain it in terms appropriate to the sibling's developmental level of understanding, and to provide increasingly fuller information as the child's cognitive ability matures and he or she is able to integrate more complex information. Like sex education, the teaching of moral values, or the imparting of other complicated and abstract information, this educational process does not end until the sibling reaches an adult level of understanding.

Extended Family

Behavioral family therapists, like other family therapists, find that they cannot ignore the presence of family members beyond the immediate nuclear unit. The need to involve the extended family is at least as urgent with families of developmentally disabled youngsters as with other families. Gath (1978) described the value of strong support from the maternal grandmother to the family of the Down syndrome child. The need for emotional and physical support felt by these families highlights the importance of involvement of grandparents, aunts, uncles, cousins, and others. Openness to sessions with these family members is therefore essential.

Including members of the extended family in therapy sessions can serve several different functions. One of these is to allow the extended family to share some of their own grief and move beyond such activities as blaming others in the family for being "responsible" for the defect in the handicapped child. There might, for example, be a tendency to blame the relatives on the "other side" for bad genes or bad influence. The pain of grandparents and others in the family may have led them to pull away from the nuclear family and to fail to provide the emotional support so urgently needed by the mother and father of the handicapped child.

If members of the extended family have regular child care responsibilities, they may also benefit from training in behavior modification. We often try to channel such training through the child's parents since it is important for all involved to perceive the parents as the experts on the child's care. When necessary, we have added our weight to parental demands that members of the extended family conform to their requirements for consistency in management techniques.

In cases where the relationships among family members were poor prior to the birth of the handicapped child, it may be necessary to intervene in much the same way as one would to solve problems in any troubled family. This can include such activities as communication skills training (Alexander, Barton, Schiavo, & Parsons, 1976; Guerney, 1977; Phillips, 1975; Robin, 1981) and contracting and problem-solving (e.g., N. S. Jacobson, 1981; N. S. Jacobson & Margolin, 1979), which can be adapted from marital and nuclear family intervention to work with the extended family as well.

Ethical Issues

In contrast to most clients, developmentally disabled people are less able to protect their own rights (McClannahan & Krantz, 1981). Indeed, they may not even understand the abstract concept of "rights." Such lack of understanding places the developmentally disabled person in a very vulnerable position. Consequently, the clinician must heighten his or her sensitivity about client rights when treating this population.

Certain strategies may be helpful in this regard. For example, questions to the client must be phrased in concrete terms to enhance the likelihood of truly informed consent. It is sometimes helpful to ask the developmentally disabled client to explain the treatment program independently to assess degree of understanding. In addition, behavioral techniques, especially those that involve any aversive component, need to be understood by all participants (Martin, 1975). In order to clarify behavioral programs, it is useful to write down operational definitions of behaviors and clear descriptions of treatment strategies. The family can post these written programs in an accessible location where they can be reviewed by everyone. Likewise, data collection offers a powerful tool for accountability since it allows all participants to monitor treatment progress. Adherence to these kinds of procedures will increase the probability that the developmentally disabled client's rights are protected by therapist and family alike.

SUMMARY

We have attempted to demonstrate that working with families of the developmentally disabled demands a blend of two themes. First, it is essential to remember that these families are more like other families than they are different. Second, it is equally important to remember that the presence of a developmentally disabled child creates a special set of very real problems that must be understood by the therapist if he or she is to establish a credible treatment relationship with the family. To this end, the therapist should understand the nature of developmental disabilities and be familiar with behavioral procedures necessary to teach new, adaptive skills and to control disruptive behavior. Given that context in which to operate, the therapist will then be able to provide the multiple levels of intervention necessary to aid the comfortable functioning of the family of the developmentally disabled child.

REFERENCES

Alexander, J. F., Barton, C., Schiavo, R. S., & Parsons, B. V. (1976). Systems-behavioral intervention with families of delinquents: Therapist characteristics, family behavior, and outcome. *Journal of Consulting and Clinical Psychology, 44*, 656–664.

American Psychiatric Association. (1980). *Diagnostic and statistical manual of mental disorders.* (3rd ed.). Washington, DC: American Psychiatric Association.

Baker, B. L., Brightman, A. J., Heifetz, L. J., & Murphy, D. M. (1976). *Behavior problems.* Champaign, IL: Research Press. (a)

Baker, B. L., Brightman, A. J., Heifetz, L. J., & Murphy, D. M. (1976). *Early self-help skills.* Champaign, IL: Research Press. (b)

Baker, B. L., Heifetz, L. J., & Murphy, D. M. (1980). Behavioral training for parents of mentally retarded children: One-year follow-up. *American Journal of Mental Deficiency, 85*, 31–38.

Baucom, D. H. (1982). A comparison of behavioral contracting and problem-solving/communications training in behavioral marital therapy. *Behavior Therapy, 13*, 162–174.

Breslau, N. (1982). Siblings of disabled children: Birth order and age-spacing effects. *Journal of American Child Psychology, 10*, 85–95.

Carr, J. (1975). *Young children with down's syndrome: Their development, upbringing, and effect on their families.* New York: Butterworth.

Cleveland, D. W., & Miller, N. (1977). Attitudes and life commitments of older siblings of mentally retarded adults. *Mental Retardation, 15*, 38–41.

Colletti, G., & Harris, S. L. (1977). Behavior modification in the home: Siblings as behavior modifiers, parents as observers. *Journal of Abnormal Child Psychology, 1*, 21–30.

Cummings, S. T. (1976). The impact of the child's deficiency on the father: A study of fathers of mentally retarded and chronically ill children. *American Journal of Orthopsychiatry, 46*, 246–255.

Cummings, S. T., Bayley, H. C., & Rie, H. E. (1966). Effects of the child's deficiency on the mother: A study of mothers of mentally retarded, chronically ill, and neurotic children. *American Journal of Orthopsychiatry, 36*, 595–608.

DeMyer, M. K. (1979). *Parents and children in autism*. New York: Wiley.

Featherstone, H. (1980). *A difference in the family*. New York: Basic Books.

Gath, A. (1973). The school age siblings of mongol children. *British Journal of Psychiatry, 123*, 161–167.

Gath, A. (1974). Sibling reactions to mental handicap: A comparison of the brothers and sisters of mongol children. *Journal of Child Psychology and Psychiatry, 15*, 187–198.

Gath, A. (1978). *Down's syndrome and the family—The early years*. London: Academic Press.

Greenfeld, J. (1973). *A child called Noah*. New York: Warner.

Greenfeld, J. (1979). *A place for Noah*. New York: Pocket Books.

Guerney, B. G., Jr. (1977). *Relationship enhancement: Skill-training programs for therapy, problem prevention, and enrichment*. San Francisco: Jossey-Bass.

Harris, S. L. (1976). *Teaching speech to a nonverbal child*. Lawrence, KS: H & H Enterprises.

Harris, S. L. (1983). *Families of the developmentally disabled: A guide to behavioral intervention*. Elmsford, NY: Pergamon Press.

Harris, S. L., Wolchik, S. A., & Milch, R. E. (1983). Changing the speech of autistic children and their parents. *Child and Family Behavior Therapy, 4*, 151–173.

Harris, S. L., Wolchik, S. A., & Weitz, S. (1981). The acquisition of language skills by autistic children: Can parents do the job? *Journal of Autism and Developmental Disorders, 11*, 373–384.

Holroyd, J., Brown, N., Wikler, L., & Simmons, J. (1975). Stress in the families of institutionalized and non-institutionalized autistic children. *Journal of Community Psychology, 3*, 26–31.

Holroyd, J., & McArthur, D. (1976). Mental retardation and stress of the parents: A contrast between Down's syndrome and childhood autism. *American Journal of Mental Deficiency, 80*, 431–436.

Howlin, P. A. (1981). The effectiveness of operant language training with autistic children. *Journal of Autism and Developmental Disorders, 11*, 89–105.

Jacobson, E. (1964). *Anxiety and tension control: A psychobiological approach*. Philadelphia: Lippincott.

Jacobson, N. S. (1977). Problem solving and contingency contracting in the treatment of marital discord. *Journal of Consulting and Clinical Psychology, 45*, 92–100.

Jacobson, N. S. (1978). Specific and nonspecific factors in the effectiveness of a behavioral approach to the treatment of marital discord. *Journal of Consulting and Clinical Psychology, 46*, 442–452.

Jacobson, N. S. (1979). Increasing positive behavior in severely distressed marital relationships: The effects of problem-solving training. *Behavior Therapy, 10*, 311–326.

Jacobson, N. S. (1981). Behavioral marital therapy. In A. S. Gurman & D. P. Kniskern (Eds.), *Handbook of family therapy* (pp. 556–591). New York: Brunner/Mazel.

Jacobson, N. S., & Margolin, G. (1979). *Marital therapy: Strategies based on social learning and behavior exchange principles*. New York: Brunner/Mazel.

Koegel, R. L., Schreibman, L., Britten, K. R., Burke, J. C., & O'Neill, R. E. (1982). A comparison of parent training to direct child treatment. In R. L. Koegel, A. Rincover, & A. L. Egel (Eds.), *Educating and understanding autistic children* (pp. 260–279). San Diego, CA: College-Hill Press.

Koegel, R. L., Schreibman, L., O'Neill, R. E., & Burke, J. C. (1983). The personality and family-interaction characteristics of parents of autistic children. *Journal of Consulting and Clinical Psychology, 51*, 683–692.

Lavigne, J. V., & Ryan, M. (1979). Psychologic adjustment of siblings of children with chronic illness. *Pediatrics, 63*, 616–627.

Lobato, D. (1983). Siblings of handicapped children: A review. *Journal of Autism and Developmental Disorders, 13*, 347–364.

Martin, R. (1975). *Legal challenges to behavior modification*. Champaign, IL: Research Press.

McClannahan, L., & Krantz, P. (1981). Accountability systems for protection of the rights of autistic children and youth. In G. T. Hannah, W. P. Christian, & H. B. Clark (Eds.), *Preservation of client rights* (pp. 83–106). New York: Free Press.

McKeever, P. (1983). Siblings of chronically ill children: A literature review with implications for research and practice. *American Journal of Orthopsychiatry, 53*, 209–218.

O'Leary, K. D., & Turkewitz, H. (1978). Marital therapy from a behavioral perspective. In T. J. Paolino & B. S. McCrady (Eds.), *Marriage and marital therapy* (pp. 240–297). New York: Brunner/Mazel.

Park, C. C. (1967). *The seige*. Boston: Little, Brown.

Phillips, D. (1975). The family council: A segment of adolescent treatment. *Journal of Behavior Therapy and Experimental Psychiatry, 6*, 283–287.

Robin, A. L. (1981). A controlled evaluation of problem-solving communication training with parent-adolescent conflict. *Behavior Therapy, 12*, 593–609.

Schreibman, L., O'Neill, R. E., & Koegel, R.L. (1983). Behavioral training for siblings of autistic children. *Journal of Applied Behavior Analysis, 16*, 129–138.

Suelzle, M., & Keenan, V. (1981). Changes in family support networks over the life cycle of mentally retarded persons. *American Journal of Mental Deficiency, 86*, 267–274.

Tew, B. J., & Laurence, K. M. (1973). Mothers, brothers, and sisters of patients with spina bifida. *Developmental Medicine and Child Neurology, 15*, (suppl 29), 69–76.

Weitz, S. (1982). A code for assessing teaching skills of parents of developmentally disabled children. *Journal of Autism and Developmental Disorders, 12*, 13–24.

Wikler, L., Wasow, M., & Hatfield, E. (1981). Chronic sorrow revisited: Parent vs. professional depiction of the adjustment of parents of mentally retarded children. *American Journal of Orthopsychiatry, 51*, 63–70.

9

Anxiety Disorders

R. JULIAN HAFNER
Dibden Research Unit, Glenside Hospital, Eastwood, Australia

In spite of attempts in the recent DSM-III to elucidate the classification of anxiety disorders, the area remains controversial (Tyrer, 1984). In my own clinical practice, particular problems are presented by "panic disorder" and "generalized anxiety disorder." I very rarely see patients who fit neatly into these DSM-III categories. However, I do see many patients who show a variety of features that are listed in *both* categories and who also describe symptoms listed in a third DSM-III category, "somatoform disorder," which is not classified as an anxiety disorder. Such patients often also complain of symptoms compatible with a DSM-III diagnosis of "agoraphobia." Since their agoraphobic symptoms are generally the most troublesome or obvious ones, these patients are commonly diagnosed as agoraphobic.

Thus, in routine clinical psychiatric practice, patients with agoraphobia usually present with a wide range of additional anxiety symptoms. Agoraphobia is therefore a useful clinical model for anxiety disorders in general, and I use it as such in this chapter. Obsessive-compulsive disorder, however, is treated separately; although Salzman (1982) has argued persuasively that severe agoraphobia is in reality a manifestation of obsessive-compulsive disorder, the two disorders are usually very different at a clinical level.

AGORAPHOBIA

Observing that a great majority of agoraphobics present with many additional symptoms and problems, Goldstein and Chambless (1978) suggested that in these cases the term "complex agoraphobia" should be used. In complex agoraphobia, depression, hypochondriasis, obsessive-compulsive symptoms, personality disorders, and marital and interpersonal problems often overshadow the agoraphobic symptoms. For that minority of patients who present with agoraphobia as their sole or major problem, Goldstein and Chambless suggested the term "simple agoraphobia." Both disorders occur most commonly in married women, who comprise at least 60% of agoraphobics who present for treatment (Vose, 1981). The agoraphobic component of both simple and complex agoraphobia is well summarized in the DSM-III: "The essential feature is a marked fear of being alone, or being in public places from which escape might be difficult or help not available in case of sudden incapacitation". In both conditions, a fear of incapacitation by panic attacks is the most common reason for phobic avoidance.

Simple Agoraphobia

Women with simple agoraphobia generally have a good premorbid adjustment. Indeed, there is evidence that before the development of agoraphobia these women experience *less* psychological symptoms than the normal population; they are also unusually extroverted and extrapunitive (Hafner, 1983a; Marks & Herst, 1970). Family or marital interaction is not usually a major factor in precipitating or perpetuating simple agoraphobia, although it often makes a minor or indirect contribution to the disorder.

In at least one third of cases, the panic attacks that lead to the development of simple agoraphobia occur after clearly definable psychological traumas. Of these, the most common is the death of a close relative. In such circumstances, panic attacks emerge as part of an unresolved or abnormal bereavement.

In a majority of cases of simple agoraphobia, there is no clear-cut precipitant. However, many married women who develop simple agoraphobia experience an unusual degree of sex-role conflict while their children are young and very dependent on them.

Because these women are nearly always energetic, competent, well-organized, and highly conscientious, they generally do well in their employment, from which they obtain considerable personal fulfillment and a recognition that they are worthwhile members of the community. They bring their very high personal standards into marriage and motherhood, which they nearly always regard as a full-time job. However, they find it very difficult to adjust to the realities of a full-time domestic commitment, with its enforced socioeconomic dependency on the husband and restriction of personal freedom. Panic attacks often emerge from intrapsychic conflict about being independent and self-fulfilling versus being dependent, confined, and living for and through their children and husbands, relying on vicarious fulfillment of the need for achievement and recognition.

Whatever their precise origins, panic attacks are extremely frightening, and this intense fear becomes conditioned to the situation in which it occurs.

Subsequently, such situations, or even the thought of them, evoke fear. This fear seems irrational to the afflicted person, since the situations are harmless in themselves—thus, the problem is not easily discussed or defined.

Two-Factor Theory

Because women who develop simple agoraphobia are usually vigorous, active people who welcome a challenge, they attempt to overcome their fears by repeatedly entering the situations that evoke them. Paradoxically, this *worsens* their fears, in a way that is explained by "two-factor theory" (Tarpy, 1975). This theory proposes that escape–avoidance is self-perpetuating because the consequent anxiety reduction reinforces the escape–avoidance response. For example, when a woman with simple agoraphobia experiences a panic attack in a crowded store, she is very likely to escape as soon as possible and may actually run out. As soon as she leaves, her anxiety levels fall sharply, and this powerfully reinforces the escape–avoidance response. Subsequently, her anticipatory anxiety increases. This is present in nearly all simple agoraphobics, and, when fully established, it is characterized by a progressive buildup of fearfulness hours or even days before confronting feared situations. Anticipatory anxiety has been called "fear of fear," and it is generally recognized as central to simple agoraphobia.

Once agoraphobic symptoms become established in these women, their intrapsychic conflicts about autonomy versus dependence are sharply reduced; they have no choice but to remain confined to the domestic. Any marital conflict over wives' autonomy and power within the marriage is also reduced. Conflict reduction decreases anxiety and, in accordance with two-factor theory, this further reinforces the escape–avoidance response, helping to consolidate the agoraphobia. Thus, the agoraphobic symptoms are reinforced by the conflict reduction that they engender. There is good evidence to support the idea that agoraphobia often emerges from and protects against sex-role conflict. Burns and Thorpe (1977) surveyed nearly 1,000 agoraphobics and found that 83% said they would take a job outside the home if they did not have agoraphobia. Marks and Herst (1970) compared "discontented" agoraphobic wives who wished to work outside the home with "contented" ones who said they were happy to remain full-time housewives. The discontented wives were significantly more phobic, depressed, irritable, and exhausted than the contented wives. However, "Somewhat surprisingly, discontented housewives rated their premorbid personality as more sociable ($p < .001$), less anxious ($p < .05$) and more independent ($p < .001$) than did the contented housewives. Discontented housewives were also more extroverted at present ($p < .01$) as well as in the past" (Marks & Herst, 1970, p. 21). From a sex-role perspective, these findings, far from being surprising, are entirely logical.

Simple agoraphobia often responds adequately to behavior therapy aimed at helping patients to reenter their feared situations gradually and systematically (graded exposure *in vivo*). In such cases, the intrapsychic conflicts or interpersonal problems that originally precipitated and subsequently perpetuated the agoraphobia have resolved, so that the agoraphobic symptoms can be regarded simply as learned or conditioned responses.

Supplements to Exposure in Vivo

The average duration of agoraphobia prior to entering specialized treatment programs is at least 10 years (Burns & Thorpe, 1977; Doctor, 1982; Marks & Herst, 1970). During these years of comparative social isolation, women with simple agoraphobia are likely to become depressed and deficient in self-confidence and social skills. While overcoming phobias reduces depression and enhances self-confidence, it does not necessarily improve patients' capacity to socialize. Probably the most rapid and effective way to achieve this is to treat simple agoraphobics in groups of four to six people. Patients in such groups generally socialize vigorously with each other during and after treatment and give each other practical support and encouragement in overcoming their fears. Directly comparing the outcome of group versus individual therapy for agoraphobia, Hafner and Marks (1976) found that group-treated patients had improved significantly more on measures of general symptoms and leisure activities and had required significantly less additional treatment by the 6-month follow-up visit.

Where it is impractical to treat patients in small groups, the therapist should devote sufficient time to enhancing patients' capacity for socializing. Because most simple agoraphobics are basically fairly sociable and extraverted, this is not usually a major problem, and referral to specialized social skills treatment programs is rarely necessary. When, as is usually the case after successful behavior therapy, simple agoraphobics return to work, they are nearly always able to spontaneously reestablish an adequate social network.

In a significant proportion of cases, husbands develop adjustment problems in relation to improvements in their wives' agoraphobia. Husbands' problems generally become evident only after large, rapid improvements in wives' agoraphobia and related symptoms (Hafner, 1984). Just as wives have adapted to agoraphobia over the years, so have their husbands. In particular, wives' agoraphobia consolidates and prolongs the husbands' role as sole family income earner, with its built-in assumptions of meaning and purpose in life. Thus, when wives seek to return to work after rapidly successful behavior therapy, husbands are forced into a major reappraisal of their lives. For some, this is accompanied by the development of transitory depression or other psychological symptoms.

Often, the situation is more complex. Years of marriage to a woman disabled by agoraphobia usually restricts husbands' leisure and social life. It also limits opportunities for promotion at work, since wives' needs for practical help and support not infrequently prevent husbands from attending business meetings or traveling. Thus, to preserve their self-esteem, husbands become unusually dependent on their role as family providers. Confronted with wives who almost overnight have become sociable and energetic, and who wish to acquire a substantial measure of social and economic independence from the husbands, it is not surprising that a significant proportion of husbands develop adjustment problems. Fortunately, most of these problems are transient, but they undoubtedly have an adverse impact on wives' progress in overcoming their residual symptoms. If wives relapse in the face of their husbands' problems, it is often very difficult for them to make up lost ground.

It is not yet clear whether husbands' adjustment problems can be avoided without reducing the level or pace of wives' improvement. However, a logical way of ameliorating husbands' adjustment difficulties is to involve them in wives' therapy. Barlow, O'Brien, and Last (1984) randomly allocated 28 married agoraphobics to individual or couple therapy. They found that couple therapy was significantly more effective as judged by a composite measure of phobic symptoms. Furthermore, patients receiving individual therapy reported a *deterioration* in work, family, and leisure activities after six treatment sessions, whereas at that point couple therapy had yielded substantial improvements.

Thus, there is tentative scientific evidence that couple therapy for agoraphobia is not only more effective than individual therapy but may also ameliorate adverse marital repercussions. At a clinical level, I have found couple therapy to be effective in most cases of simple agoraphobia, and I now use it routinely unless it is clearly impractical or inappropriate. My own approach, which I call "spouse-aided therapy" (Hafner, 1981), is illustrated by the following case.

Spouse-Aided Therapy for Simple Agoraphobia

Rachel, 30, presented with a 4-year history of severe agoraphobia. Her first panic attack had occurred while she was traveling to work on a crowded bus: "I was standing up because there were no empty seats. Suddenly, I felt this numb feeling come over me. I thought I was going to faint, and I started to panic because there was nowhere to sit. My heart began to pound and I became hot and dizzy. Somehow I managed to get off the bus at the next stop, and fairly soon I began to feel better. I waited for a less crowded bus and eventually got to work about 45 minutes late."

Over the next few weeks, Rachel had several similar attacks, usually on the way to or from work. Fearing that she had some sinister physical illness, she went to her family physician. After a thorough physical examination and some routine blood tests, he told her that there was nothing wrong with her. This made Rachel think that her very real and distressing symptoms were psychological or perhaps "imaginary," and she began to fear for her sanity. She saw a local psychiatrist who prescribed propranolol, an antianxiety drug. This made her feel worse, and she withdrew from therapy.

Over the next 4 years, Rachel became progressively more restricted by her agoraphobia. It was only with great difficulty that her family physician persuaded her to come and see me. When I interviewed her, Rachel was virtually housebound. She was able to walk unaccompanied a maximum of 400 meters away from her home. On most days, even much shorter distances were a major ordeal because of feelings of dizziness, unreality, and unsteadiness while she was walking.

Background and Precipitating Factors

Although Rachel's upbringing had been reasonably harmonious, it was characterized by a major inconsistency: on one hand, Rachel's parents had urged her to work very hard at school, with the aim of a career, and to excel in her music, at which she was gifted; on the other hand, they had prepared her by word and example for an exclusively domestic life, emphasizing the central importance of marriage and motherhood and the need for married women to be subordinate to their husbands.

Shortly after marriage at the age of 20, Rachel had relinquished her full-time music studies to become a full-time housewife and had started work in a local shop at the age of 25 only because of family financial problems. At this time, her son was 3 and her daughter was 4. She felt extremely guilty and worried about leaving her children in the care of others but nonetheless greatly enjoyed her work.

About 4 months before her first panic attack, she had a voluntary termination of pregnancy about which she felt profoundly guilty. A few days before the first attack, a female acquaintance died suddenly of a heart attack at the age of 48.

Thus, two major factors precipitated Rachel's first panic attack. First, there was unresolved grief about the loss of her unborn child, compounded by the sudden, unexpected death of an acquaintance who was almost the same age as Rachel's mother. Second, there was sex-role conflict; Rachel's upbringing emphasized full-time motherhood; hence, she was tormented by anxiety and guilt about resuming full-time work while her children were young. The fact that she enjoyed her work—even though it was beneath her original professional aspirations—increased her guilt.

Three months after her first panic attack, Rachel stopped working because of her anxiety symptoms. While this reduced aspects of her conflict over her sex role, it created new problems. She felt acutely the loss of her work and the social network, economic independence, and sense of being involved, useful, and worthwhile that it had given her. She began to regret her earlier resignation from the music school. Together with increasingly frequent and severe panic attacks outside the home, these and other background problems and worries caused Rachel to become moderately depressed. The depression and the anxiety symptoms were mutually reinforcing, and this contributed to the chronicity of Rachel's condition.

The Husband

Having obtained Rachel's consent, I interviewed her husband David, who was 2 years her senior. Like Rachel, he had a reasonably harmonious upbringing. However, his family of origin had been characterized by a rigid adherence to sex-role stereotypes, and he had been brought up to believe in a strict division of labor within marriage. In his view, a wife should be devoted exclusively to her husband and children, and a husband should be freed of all domestic responsibilities so that he can concentrate on his role as breadwinner.

When financial problems had forced Rachel back to work, David had been profoundly distressed and humiliated. It emerged that he had been trying to persuade Rachel to stop work for about a month before her first panic attack, since by then their financial problems had largely resolved.

It became clear that although David was thoroughly familiar with Rachel's symptoms, he believed that they were "imaginary" in nature and that they could be overcome by the correct application of "willpower." He was highly critical of Rachel for her failure to overcome her symptoms, and he deeply resented the measure of role-sharing that the agoraphobia had forced upon the couple. For example, David had to do much of the shopping because Rachel's symptoms prevented her from traveling alone to the nearest shopping center. David felt that shopping for the family was unmanly and undignified, and that it prevented him from getting on with more important things.

Nonetheless, there was evidence that David was ambivalent about the idea of Rachel's increased independence. For example, Rachel was unable to drive the family car because it did not have an automatic gearbox. For 3 years David had been promising to exchange it for a car with automatic gears, which Rachel was confident about driving alone within 2–3 miles of home. David's repeated failure to keep his promise not only frustrated Rachel and kept her virtually housebound but also suggested that at some level David welcomed her enforced confinement to the home.

Therapy

As is usual in such cases, David insisted that their marriage would be "perfect" if it was not for Rachel's agoraphobia; he could see no value in any therapy that did not focus directly on her symptoms. Marriage therapy was clearly unacceptable, so I outlined the principles of spouse-aided therapy to the couple, with the aim of securing David's constructive involvement in the treatment process. David willingly agreed to join me as a cotherapist in his wife's treatment.

The first conjoint therapy session focused on clarifying the precise nature and extent of Rachel's symptoms. I emphasized that they were very real and distressing and that David's criticism of Rachel's failure to "pull herself together" only added to her guilt and self-blame, indirectly perpetuating her symptoms. Hitherto, David had mistakenly believed that his criticism of Rachel would enhance her motivation to overcome her symptoms.

The second session was devoted to treatment goals. We had already agreed that Rachel's symptoms should be the initial focus of therapy, and during this session and the next I outlined the principles of graded exposure *in vivo*. Of these, the following are most important.

1. A hierarchy of fears should be constructed. Ideally, a list of 10–15 feared situations is drawn up. The least feared situations are placed at the bottom of the list, progressing systematically to the most feared situations at the top.

2. Exposure *in vivo* should commence in the least feared situation. The next situation on the list should not be tackled until fear and avoidance of the preceding situation have been overcome or substantially reduced. Progressing systematically up the fear hierarchy requires a great deal of time: a *minimum* of 4 hours a week practicing exposure *in vivo* is recommended. Patients should not be pushed into feared situations before they are ready. It is important for spouses to help patients to resist social or personal pressure to enter feared situations prematurely: this is likely to cause panic attacks, which may impede or reverse the progress of therapy, particularly if they lead to precipitant escape and reinforcement of the escape response by anxiety reduction.

3. The "75% rule" is a useful overall guideline. It states, "No phobic situation should be entered during systematic exposure *in vivo* unless there appears at least a 75% chance of the patient remaining in it long enough for anxiety levels to peak and then subside." Adherence to this rule minimizes the likelihood of escape from a feared situation while anxiety levels are very high or rising. If this escape does occur, it usually leads to an increase in anticipatory anxiety as explained by two-factor theory.

I also lent Rachel and David a copy of the treatment manual written by Mathews, Gelder, & Johnston (1981), which most couples find helpful in the initial stages of exposure *in vivo*.

At the end of the third session, I suggested that the couple begin to implement what they had learned. All went fairly smoothly until the sixth therapy session, during which Rachel became distressed and weepy. With great reluctance she explained that her distress was attributable to David's attitudes and behavior. Her initial success with exposure *in vivo* had considerably improved her mood and self-confidence. As a result, she had expressed a wish to return to music school on a full- or part-time basis, working if necessary to pay the fees. Now that her children were aged 8 and 9, she felt that they should be able to cope with her return to work, particularly if David offered emotional and practical support.

To her surprise, David had been totally against the idea. When she had persisted with her plans, he had become enraged and the couple had come to blows for the first time in their marriage. David had threatened to leave her unless she relinquished her "silly ideas." After the fight, Rachel had relapsed completely.

Fortunately, I had developed a good working relationship with David and was able to gently but firmly confront him about his unhelpful attitudes and behavior. The next three sessions focused on David and ways of helping him to relinquish the rigid sex-role stereotypes that hitherto had governed his attitudes toward Rachel and their marriage. As a result, David was able to reappraise his views, although he became moderately depressed for several weeks as the full implications of this reappraisal dawned upon him.

Sessions 10 and 11 focused on practical ways in which Rachel might be supported in her goal of resuming her music studies. David now understood how important this was for her, and he was able to give her a measure of encouragement. Since Rachel's agoraphobia was still a major problem, sessions 12–14 were devoted to exposure in vivo, while concurrently Rachel made enquiries about attending music school. By the 15th conjoint session, Rachel was able to travel fairly freely within 4–5 miles of home in the automatic car that David had finally bought, although she still had trouble coping with public transportation and crowded stores. Formal therapy, which had occupied a period of 19 weeks, was terminated after the 15th session; Rachel and David felt they had learned as much as they could, and they were confident that they could solve future problems by working at them together.

I followed the couple informally for 18 months. Rachel started music school about 3 months after the end of therapy. Once she had settled in, she greatly enjoyed it, and she became virtually symptom free after about 5 months.

Complex Agoraphobia

Hallam (1978) has suggested that agoraphobia is not a definable syndrome, but a variable feature of patients whose neurotic anxieties have many different sources.

Sheehan, Ballenger, and Jacobsen (1980) suggested that the DSM-III category, "agoraphobia with panic attacks," should be replaced by a new category, "endogenous anxiety." Because of the good response of endogenous anxiety to "antidepressant" drugs, Sheehan *et al.* emphasized the likelihood of a biochemical basis for the disorder. However, Tyrer (1984) cautioned against a tendency to base ideas about etiology and classification on response to drugs. Salzman's suggestion (1982) that agoraphobia should be regarded as a form of obsessive-compulsive disorder underlines the confusion that surrounds contemporary psychiatric views about the classification of agoraphobia.

Given this confusion, this chapter uses a pragmatic approach; the clinical problems presented by patients with complex agoraphobia are outlined. In this respect, a recent factor-analytic study by Hafner and Ross (1984) is helpful. These authors obtained questionnaire data on symptoms and personality from 160 female patients who had been diagnosed by experienced clinicians as meeting the DSM-III criteria for agoraphobia. All were actively seeking psychological or psychiatric treatment and were therefore representative of a clinical population. In contrast, previous large-scale factor-analytic studies of agoraphobia have been based on mainly nonclinical populations drawn from phobic organizations run by lay volunteers.

The first-order analysis showed that a large general symptoms factor (factor 1, 28% of variance), a social fears factor (factor 2, 11% of variance), and an illness phobia factor (factor 3, 7% of variance) existed *independently* of each other and of three agoraphobia factors (factors 3, 6, and 9, totaling 16% of variance). Second-order analysis revealed two factors. Factor 1 (56% of variance) comprised the first-order factors 1 and 2 plus factor 11 (fear of criticism, 3% of variance). Factor 2 (19% of variance) comprised first-order factors 3, 6, and 9. Scores indicating personality abnormalities correlated significantly with the higher-order factor 1 but not with factor 2.

These findings give objective support to the clinical impression that complex agoraphobia is a syndrome characterized by a very wide range of anxiety symptoms and general and social fears found in association with abnormal personality traits. During therapy, as much or more attention must be paid to these problems as to the agoraphobia.

Sex-Role Stereotyping and Complex Agoraphobia

Just as sex-role conflict is a major theme in simple agoraphobia, so is sex-role stereotyping in complex agoraphobia. Fodor (1974) has pointed out that the general fearfulness, timidity, emotional lability, dependency, and confinement to the home that characterize many agoraphobic women also represent an extreme example of the female sex-role stereotype. Goldstein and Chambless (1978) have emphasized the profound dependency on their husbands of women with complex agoraphobia.

Strikingly often, women with complex agoraphobia are brought up in families characterized by an absent or behaviorally withdrawn father (not uncommonly with alcohol problems) and a mother who raises her children virtually single-handedly. In such families, young agoraphobics-to-be have little opportunity to learn about nonpathological male–female relationships. They are anxious, at a conscious level, to avoid marrying men with the undesirable traits of their fathers, but they have had little or no experience of relating to "normal" men. Thus, their view of desirable men is based not on the reality of functioning male–female dyads, but on a composite image created by romantic and media-determined fantasies that have filled the vacuum left by the absence of an adequate father. These fantasies about men come to coincide with the male sex-role stereotype.

Women who later develop complex agoraphobia tend to marry while young, often to escape from their unsatisfactory families of origin. Marriage usually represents a transfer of ambivalent dependency from their mothers to their husbands. Because their "ideal man" is based on a sex-role stereotype, they tend to select husbands whose own attitudes and behaviors are strongly influenced by sex-role stereotypes. These men very often come from families of origin similar to that of the agoraphobic-to-be, and, in the absence of an adequate father, they have replaced a true sense of gender identity with a sex-role stereotype. This means that they may totally identify with the stereotype and cannot relinquish this identification without risking a major personal crisis and even the development of a psychosis (Hafner, 1979, 1986).

The Emergence of Panic Attacks

As Goldstein and Chambless (1978) have pointed out, the panic attacks that initiate complex agoraphobia generally emerge from a background of marital conflict. In my view, this conflict usually revolves around sex-role stereotypes. Whereas women with complex agoraphobia have a sex-role stereotyped view of men, their own private self-images are not based on a female sex-role stereotype. These women strongly identify with their mothers, who, as women who struggled virtually alone and usually in difficult economic circumstances to bring up their children, represent the antithesis of the female sex-role stereotype. Thus, women who later develop complex agoraphobia conform to a female sex-role stereotype in large part to please their husbands and to preserve marital stability.

Because of their disturbed families of origin, these women generally have very low self-esteem and find it extremely difficult to be assertive or to appropriately express their feelings. Thus, although they crave a measure of the strength and independence shown by their mothers, they lack the confidence to take any practical steps in this direction. Instead, they fantasize about escaping from their dull, constricting, stereotyped marriages into more romantic and fulfilling liaisons. They are full of suppressed rage about being "trapped," a rage that cannot be expressed directly but that emerges in the form of panic attacks.

Once panic attacks emerge, they compound the problems of these women, who almost always become concerned that the panics are a sign of some sinister mental or physical illness. Out of this concern emerges a constellation of fears that is usually termed "hypochondriasis" and that is probably represented by the illness phobia factor in Hafner and Ross's study outlined above.

In complex agoraphobia (unlike simple agoraphobia), panic attacks occur inside the home almost as frequently as they do outside. Those that occur inside the home reinforce patients' fears of illness, injury, and death. In severe cases, patients are very fearful of spending any time alone because they fear losing consciousness, being injured, or even dying during a panic attack. In such circumstances, generalized anxiety symptoms are understandably prominent, and great marital or family tension is created by the patients' profound reluctance to be alone.

Those panics that occur outside the home lead to avoidance much more rapidly than in the case of simple agoraphobia. Indeed, patients with complex agoraphobia sometimes give a history of total avoidance of a situation after experiencing one major panic attack in it. Thus, they do not always invoke two-factor theory, and anticipatory anxiety is much less evident in complex agoraphobia than it is in simple agoraphobia, although it may still be a problem.

Personality Factors

Patients with complex agoraphobia score at very high mean levels on measures of hostility (Hafner, 1977). Two independent studies (Hafner & Ross, 1983; Thomas-Peter, Jones, Sinnott, & Scott-Fordam, 1983) have shown that a high level of outward-directed hostility in patients is the best predictor of *poor* response to behavior therapy. Criticism and blame of others probably reflects an unwillingness to take personal responsibility for problems and symptoms, and this may explain the poor outcome. At a clinical level, it is often very difficult to form a constructive therapy relationship with complex agoraphobics, mainly because of their expectation that the therapist will unilaterally deliver a "cure" while the patient remains a passive agent. Failure to promise or deliver such a cure increases patients' hostility and ambivalence, further reducing the likelihood of a working relationship with the therapist.

Treatment of Complex Agoraphobia

To be successful, the treatment of complex agoraphobia must deal with the following areas:

- The panic attacks and associated symptoms and fears
- The patient's reluctance to accept personal responsibility for the symptoms
- The patient's habitual avoidance of feared situations
- Reinforcement of the patient's symptoms by stereotyped marital interaction and expectations
- Any personal problems of the spouse; since the great majority of patients presenting for treatment of complex agoraphobia are women, the spouse is usually male

In my view, these areas can be optimally dealt with only in a conjoint marital setting, and I have found spouse-aided therapy a generally effective way of initiating this.

The Role of Drugs in Treating Complex Agoraphobia

If patients are too depressed to formulate appropriate treatment goals, then spouse-aided therapy cannot proceed. Severe depression in such circumstances often responds to antidepressant drugs. Personally, I have found the monoamine oxidase inhibitors more useful in this context than the tricyclics, and this appears to be the concensus among experienced clinicians.

Where patients are unwilling to proceed with behavioral or spouse-aided therapy, they often respond to monoamine oxidase inhibitors. Occasionally, symptomatic improvement improves the marriage relationship, but more commonly it simply shifts the focus of marital dissatisfaction elsewhere. If progress during spouse-aided therapy or exposure *in vivo* is hindered by overwhelmingly severe panic attacks and related symptoms, the use of monoamine oxidase inhibitors is often of great value.

There is controversy about the role of benzodiazepines in treating complex agoraphobia. In a thoughtful review of the literature, Sartory (1983) concluded that they were unhelpful or detrimental when used in combination with behavioral treatments. At a clinical level, I believe that benzodiazepines should generally be avoided in the treatment of complex agoraphobia, not only because of the high risk of dependency but also because they hinder the process of fear reduction during exposure *in vivo*.

In spite of the claims of Sheehan *et al.* (1980) that panic attacks are primarily biochemical or genetic in origin, and therefore require chemical treatment, there is good evidence that exposure *in vivo* alone substantially reduces the frequency and severity of panic attacks, a benefit that is maintained during follow-up (Hafner & Marks, 1976). At a clinical level, it is usual for panic attacks to improve without the use of drugs if spouse-aided therapy is appropriately conducted.

Spouse-Aided Therapy for Complex Agoraphobia

Panic attacks and related symptoms and fears powerfully reinforce wives' dependency on husbands, leading to an instability of the marital system as eloquently described by Holmes (1982): "Rather than assuaging her fears his reassurances serve only to augment them. She becomes more and more anxious, rings him continually, insisting that she cannot cope, and that she needs him. No sooner has she rung off than her doubts redouble, she must contact him again. He becomes more and more of a 'superman,' hiding his worries, helping his wife, protecting her from stress, distancing himself from her all the while. He rings her at work, 'just to see how she is.' The more he tries to reassure her, the more desperate she becomes. The stronger he seems, the more helpless she feels" (p. 140).

Although the subsequent labeling of wives' fears as agoraphobia helps to stabilize the marital system, it consolidates the husbands' position as the wives' caretakers. Years of attempting to cope with wives' problems means that these husbands often ignore their own personal problems, at the same time struggling to express or deny feelings of anger and frustration about the burden of looking after a disabled wife. The idea that their wives are suffering from an illness for which they, the wives, have no personal responsibility is central to the husbands position: it justifies and makes laudable their years of inconvenience and self-sacrifice. Thus, attempts during therapy to show the couple that they can and should take personal responsibility for the disorder confront a fundamental aspect of their marital and personal adjustment.

During spouse-aided therapy it is often more difficult to alter husbands "overprotective" attitudes to wives than it is to get wives themselves to take more personal responsibility for overcoming their agoraphobia and related symptoms. An important task of therapy is to help husbands to relinquish a long-standing identification with the male sex-role stereotype that has been powerfully reinforced by years of marriage to a profoundly dependent woman.

Systematic exposure *in vivo* is often fundamental to the process of change within the marital system. If fear and avoidance are very severe and long-standing, it is sometimes necessary for the therapist to accompany the couple during the first one or two sessions. This not only helps the patient to enter feared situations, but it creates an opportunity to demonstrate to the husband optimal ways of facilitating exposure.

As in simple agoraphobia, marital problems are often exposed by the wives' early progress in overcoming fear. For years, these couples have endured a "compulsory" marriage: the wives have no choice but to remain married to their caretaker husbands, and the husbands feel compelled by a sense of loyalty, obligation, and duty to continue caring for their disabled wives. Furthermore, the wives' symptoms create a constant source of shared concern for these couples and generate a "pseudointimacy" within the marriage that partially obscures the lack of true intimacy. However, because husbands believe that their wives are unable to leave them, they feel free to treat them as they please, and it is very common for husbands to express in various overt or indirect, disguised, or subtle ways their resentment about being caretakers. Wives feel compelled to supress or deny their anger about their husbands' treatment of them, because they dare not risk alienating them and being abandoned.

Thus, wives' symptomatic improvement during exposure *in vivo* is often a profound challenge to marital equilibrium. Sometimes, it allows wives to express openly years of pent-up resentment and anger about their husbands, to which husbands respond by retreating further into their passive–aggressive posture of repression and denial. In such circumstances, husbands are unable to give their wives the emotional and practical support they need in order to continue systematic exposure *in vivo*, and they may even undermine wives' progress in various overt or subtle ways. Thus, wives partially relapse, and this partially restores marital equilibrium. In particular, it protects husbands from a fear that their wives might leave them if they achieve sufficient symptomatic improvement.

Dealing with issues such as these is central to spouse-aided therapy for complex agoraphobia. If they are not dealt with, wives may acquire a premature conviction that their husbands will never be able to meet their needs for warmth, emotional support, genuine intimacy, and companionship. If wives' symptoms improve enough, this conviction may lead to separation or divorce causing distress to both partners that might have been avoided by careful, informed, and sympathetic attention to the repercussions of successful exposure *in vivo*. In my own experience, such attention is usually rewarded not only by a sustained improvement in wives' agoraphobia and related symptoms but also by longer term improvement in the marriages and in the husbands' personal adjustment.

Agoraphobia in Men

Most clinical and research reports overlook the possibility of gender-related differences in agoraphobia. However, I have published data (Hafner, 1981b, 1983b) suggesting that the symptoms of agoraphobic men are different from those of agoraphobic women and that men respond relatively poorly to behavior therapy. The latter finding was also reported by Liotti and Guidano (1976), who added valuable clinical comments about the marital interaction of men with agoraphobia.

From the limited data available, it appears that agoraphobic men who fail to respond to behavior therapy differ in other ways from those who show a satisfactory response. The poor-outcome group is characterized by severe obsessive-compulsive symptoms, high levels of fear about illness, injury, and disease, a preoccupation with bodily symptoms relating to respiratory and cardiovascular function, and an intense fear of being alone. The good-outcome group is characterized by relatively high levels of generalized anxiety and a fear of losing control of inwardly or outwardly directed aggressive impulses. This latter group probably represents simple agoraphobia in men.

Most of those in the good-outcome group described repeated attempts to enter feared situations, and anticipatory anxiety was a prominent clinical feature, suggesting that two-factor theory was a major contributor to the disorder. Thus, behavior therapy was successful because it allowed those men to extinguish their acquired fear–avoidance responses systematically. Overt marital conflict was very common in this group and was usually related to sex-roles. Many men with simple agoraphobia found it difficult to identify with the traditional male role of breadwinner and sought greater involvement in domestic and child care activities. This was generally resisted by wives, who considered their husbands to be poaching on their territory.

In simple agoraphobia, spouse-aided therapy focusing on clarifying sex-role issues is generally successful in improving the marital climate and consolidating or extending the benefits of exposure *in vivo*.

The poor-outcome group can be broadly equated with *complex* female agoraphobics, although the determinants of the condition in men appear to be quite different from those operating in women. Exposure *in vivo* appears to be of little value in treating complex agoraphobia in men. Instead, therapy should focus on the marriage relationship and on the profound separation anxiety of these men.

Spouse-Aided Therapy for Men with Complex Agoraphobia

Almost all the men I have seen with complex agoraphobia came from families of origin that were dominated by their mothers. Strikingly often, their fathers' contribution to family life had been minimized through illness or the demands of work. About one third of the men had lost their fathers in childhood through death, separation, or divorce.

These men acquired a strong primary identification with their mothers and had no opportunity to develop a true sense of gender identity in the context of a relationship with their fathers. Thus, as in the case of the husbands of women with complex agoraphobia, they identified with the male sex-role stereotype as a substitute for true gender identity.

Through marriage, they sought women onto whom they could transfer the strong, ambivalent dependency that characterized their relationships with their mothers. However, at the same time, they expected their wives to complement the male sex-role stereotyped images that they had of themselves. Thus, they expected their wives to be both powerful and protective and dependent and submissive. These totally incompatible expectations produced profound marital conflict, which contributed to the emergence of panic attacks. Often, these panic attacks were associated with and compounded by unresolved grief about lost or absent fathers.

Wives powerfully reinforced husbands' panic attacks and related symptoms by responding to them with the care, concern, and nurturing behavior that was otherwise virtually absent from these marriages. Once the agoraphobia was consolidated, the basic marital dilemma was resolved or ameliorated: wives were powerful and protective in relation to their husbands' panic attacks and related symptoms, but, at the same time, husbands were able to control their wives by insisting that their lives revolved around their panic attacks and related symptoms and disabilities. Indeed, these men were able to exercise almost total control over their wives through their symptoms and, in particular, through their profound fear of being alone. If, as was often the case, it was impossible for husband and wife to be together constantly, husbands insisted on knowing exactly where their wives were at all times, so that they could contact them *in extremis*. Thus, in relation to the symptoms, wives were profoundly submissive to their husbands.

An extra dimension is added to these observations by the work of Fry (1962), who noted that "spouses reveal, upon careful study, a history of symptoms closely resembling, if not identical to, the symptoms of the patient. Usually, they are reluctant to reveal this history." (p. 248)

Thus, men from mother-dominated families with absent or uninvolved fathers may develop complex agoraphobia only if their wives refuse to conform with the female sex-role stereotype. If these men are successful in securing a posture in their wives that is submissive and dependent as well as nurturing, then their wives sometimes develop agoraphobia as part of adjusting to the marriage. This protects the husbands from having to deal with their own separation anxiety and identity problems. If, however, their wives refuse to be submissive and dependent, then the husbands themselves may become agoraphobic.

Spouse-aided therapy for men with complex agoraphobia is a difficult and challenging undertaking. Where unresolved grief about the loss of a father is contributing to the symptoms, grief work is essential. This is greatly facilitated if the couple are able to tackle the problem together. But the main focus of therapy is usually on the couple's sex-role stereotypes; getting them to relinquish or modify these generally requires at least 8–10 hours of careful, informed therapy. As much or more time is subsequently required to facilitate the couple's attempts at making the practical and attitudinal changes in their lives that are a prerequisite to a lasting and worthwhile improvement in the husband's symptoms.

Behavioral Family Therapy for Unmarried Agoraphobics

The family therapy literature describes many different approaches to the treatment in a family setting of psychologically disabled children and young adolescents. Usually, these approaches are extremely complex and require an intimate understanding of relevant theory and technique. They are often inappropriate for treating young adults who are still living with their families of origin, and this applies to most unmarried agoraphobics. The principles of spouse-aided therapy are particularly appropriate for treating this population because of the pragmatic emphasis on treatment goals. This encourages the family to work together without the need for a complex theoretical and technical framework.

It is increasingly recognized that severe psychological symptoms in young unmarried adults living at home usually provide a displaced focus for family conflicts and problems. Often, these problems revolve around the parental relationship: for example, the parents' shared concern about their offspring's agoraphobia gives them something to discuss and helps to preserve a marriage that might otherwise appear empty or frustrating. As the patient's agoraphobia and related symptoms improve with systematic exposure *in vivo*, the parents' problems are often exposed. This evokes fears in the patient about the possibility of parental separation or divorce. These fears are usually associated with the patient's partial relapse, which is reinforced by the increased parental cohesion it engenders. This vicious cycle can be prevented by encouraging the parents to deal with their marriage problems directly, thereby relieving the patient of the unfair burden of keeping his or her parents' marriage intact.

OBSESSIVE-COMPULSIVE DISORDER

Although obsessive-compulsive disorders are relatively uncommon, they have received a disproportionately large amount of attention in the psychiatric literature because they are bizarre and fascinating as well as disabling and persisting. Patients with these disorders crave relief from the tyranny of their symptoms, which often dominate and disrupt their entire lives. In such circumstances, it is not surprising that modern behavioral treatments for obsessive-compulsive disorders have come to focus almost exclusively on the patient alone, largely ignoring the family or marital context of the disorder.

For example, the behaviorists Foa and Steketee (1979) cite only two references, out of some 200 quoted, concerned with the treatment of obsessive-compulsive disorders in a family or marital setting. They suggest that treatment aimed at reducing interpersonal problems does not affect obsessive-compulsive symptomatology.

A similar reluctance to examine or modify the family setting is found in the psychoanalytic literature. For example, Rice (1974) described a married woman who received 7 years of psychoanalytic psychotherapy that actually resulted in a worsening of her obsessive-compulsive symptoms, although her anxiety and depression were lessened. Strikingly, her symptoms ceased immediately after the death of her husband and did not return. The patient subsequently continued in therapy for 9 months, leaving against the therapist's advice. Rice's exclusive preoccupation with the patient's *personal* psychopathology persisted throughout therapy, to the extent of his refusal to discuss the patient's rage toward her husband. He ignored the possibility that the patient's rage toward her husband may have been justified. Instead, the patient's husband is *her* victim: "One potent way that she was able to express the negative side of her ambivalence to her husband was by including him in her rituals and making him suffer thereby" (p. 65).

The preoccupation of behaviorists and psychoanalysts alike with treating the patient alone is not the only obstacle to a wider application of family and marital therapy in the treatment of obsessive-compulsive disorders. An additional obstacle is the absence of relatively straightforward family-oriented approaches of proven value. For example, Cobb, McDonald, Marks, and Stern (1980) showed that conjoint marital therapy was *unhelpful* in relieving severe obsessive-compulsive and phobic symptoms, although it significantly improved the marriage relationship. In contrast, conjoint behavioral therapy for the patient's symptoms significantly improved both the marriage and the symptoms.

These findings are not surprising. As in the case of agoraphobia, both marriage partners generally prefer that treatment focuses directly on the patient's symptoms. Offers of marital therapy are nearly always regarded as irrelevant or misguided, particularly by the spouse, although a surprising number of couples will go along with them initially, especially when nothing else is available. If, as is commonly the case, the obsessive-compulsive symptoms persist, couples indicate their dissatisfaction by dropping out of therapy.

By focusing initially on the patient's symptoms, spouse-aided therapy encourages both partners to become constructively involved in therapy. However, it is but one way of achieving this: for example, Hand, Spoehring, and Stanik (1977) have described a technique called "hidden couple counseling," which appears very similar to spouse-aided therapy.

Unlike agoraphobia, obsessive-compulsive disorder appears to be only slightly more common in women than in men (Rachman & Hodgson, 1980). However, men and women differ greatly with regard to the precise pattern of symptoms. Nearly 90% of women, but only 10% of men, are compulsive cleaners of the home. Men are more likely to be compulsive ritualizers and checkers. Only if these marked sex differences are taken into account can obsessive-compulsive disorders be adequately comprehended and treated.

Obsessive-Compulsive Disorder in Women

In order to illustrate the most common type of presentation, I outline the symptoms of three women with severe long-standing obsessive-compulsive disorders below.

Case 1

Yvonne, aged 46, had an 8-year history of compulsive cleaning and obsessional ruminating. Her life was dominated by cleaning and checking rituals. Often, she would collapse into bed at 3 or 4 A.M., exhausted by repeated compulsive washing of windows, stairs, and even walls. Many domestic tasks were repeated over 50 times until they were performed "perfectly" or until exhaustion occurred.

Case 2

Cathy, aged 22, had developed a severe obsessive-compulsive disorder shortly after her marriage at 18. Her symptoms had been exacerbated by the birth of her son, now 18 months old. He was a focal point of her rituals and obsessions, which were aimed ostensibly at protecting him and herself from contamination by germs. Cathy spent all day cleaning and disinfecting the house and insisted that her husband remove his shoes and clothing as soon as he entered their home. No other visitors were permitted.

Case 3

Fiona, aged 48, developed severe obsessive-compulsive symptoms about 6 years prior to referral. These related to fears of contamination by dogs' feces and urine, and in particular by dogs' saliva, because of its undetectability. She spent all day repeatedly washing clothes, carpets, and curtains in order to protect herself and her children against contamination. When her husband or children entered the house, Fiona insisted that they step into a large cardboard box, remove their shoes and outer garments, and then change into decontaminated indoor clothing. She even rang her husband at work to inform him of the precise location of dogs' feces on his walk home from the station, which route she carefully surveyed each afternoon.

Overdetermination of the Female Sex-Role Stereotype

The all-consuming preoccupation of these three women with washing, cleaning, and other domestic tasks is a classical feature of obsessive-compulsive disorders in women and may be regarded as an overdetermination of the female sex-role stereotype, with which such women strongly but ambivalently identify. Unconsciously, they hate their enforced domesticity and economic dependency on their husbands. They loathe boring, repetitive domestic tasks. They cope with their unconscious rage by using the psychological defence mechanism of reaction formation, attacking with detergents, disinfectants, mops, and scrubbing brushes the most immediate and obvious source of their rage: the home itself. By working themselves into a state of exhaustion, they diffuse their pent-up anger. By keeping constantly busy, they are able to ward off feelings of rage, guilt, and despair. And in their constant struggle to be perfect housewives, they are able to obscure from themselves their profound ambivalence to the role.

Spouse-Aided Therapy

Although wives' stereotyped view of marriage is a potent contributor to symptom maintenance, husbands' contributions are generally of equal importance. These men usually adhere very rigidly to a sex-role stereotyped perspective and believe that their wives should be subordinate to them, devoting themselves exclusively to their children, husbands, and domestic duties. Haley (1963) admirably illustrated this marital dynamic:

> If her case were written up from the classic point of view, she would be described in terms of her history, her fantasies, her guilts, and so on. If her husband were mentioned, it would probably be only in a passing statement that he was understandably unhappy about her compulsion. . . . However, in this case her husband was brought into therapy. . . . He demanded his own

> way, wanting his wife to do what he said and do it promptly. Although the wife objected to her husband's tyrannical ways, she was unable to oppose him on any issue—except her hand washing. . . . [A]s a result of her hand washing she actually managed to refuse to do anything he suggested (p. 13).

During spouse-aided therapy, as much time and effort should be devoted to changing husbands' attitudes and behavior as to those of wives. Because husbands' views of wives as essentially subordinate or inferior to them are often deeply ingrained (Hafner, 1982), altering these views is often the most challenging aspect of spouse-aided therapy.

The Role of Drugs

There is controversy about whether tricyclic antidepressants exert a direct effect on obsessive-compulsive symptoms, or whether improvement is secondary to an elevation of the patient's mood. My own clinical experience suggests that many patients recognize that they were seriously depressed only *after* a positive response to tricyclics, and this may partly explain the controversy. However, there is no doubt that a significant proportion of patients experience worthwhile symptom relief from tricyclics, of which clomipramine is probably the most effective (Thoren, Asberg, Cronholm, Jornestedt, & Traskman, 1980). Nonetheless, the value of tricyclics alone is very limited: patients often relapse unless sufficient attention is paid to the interpersonal and attitudinal aspects of the disorder. In my view, drugs should be used primarily when patients fail to respond adequately to properly conducted spouse-aided or behavioral family therapy.

Behavioral Diary

The use of a behavioral diary allows patients to record their progress during therapy and to clarify some of the determinants of their obsessive-compulsive symptoms. I recommend that patients obtain a notebook, which should be ruled into six vertical columns. In the first column are recorded date, time, and duration of significant symptom episodes. In the second, troublesome situations and events are outlined and related symptoms and coping behaviors described. In the third, anxiety levels before, during and after each symptomatic episode are rated on a simple 0–4 scale. In the fourth, the time spent *resisting* compulsions is recorded. In the fifth, patients enter their self-talk before, during, and after significant episodes. Self-talk, or verbal self-instruction, is important because it is generally very negative and reinforces the patient's poor self-image. If patients are encouraged to exchange negative self-talk for positive self-instruction, their progress in overcoming symptoms is usually facilitated. In the sixth column, patients enter the behavior of significant others in relation to noteworthy symptomatic episodes. This enables the interpersonal context of symptoms to be clarified.

Specific Behavioral Techniques

Marks (1980) has admirably described the basic principles and techniques of behavior therapy for obsessive compulsive disorder. In brief outline, the following methods are available.

1. Exposure *in vivo* and response prevention. These are best achieved during spouse-aided therapy by encouraging patients to proceed at their own pace. The role of husbands may in some cases be limited to general support and encouragement. If they are more directly involved, conflicts between spouses are almost inevitable, but these conflicts create an opportunity to examine unhelpful marital interactions and modify them.
2. Thought-stopping and thought habituation. I have found thought-stopping for obsessional ruminations and intrusive thoughts to be generally unhelpful, particularly in severe cases. Thought habituation appears to be a much more promising technique. Basically, patients are encouraged to deliberately retain in consciousness for as long as possible their unwanted or unpleasant thoughts. If they are successful in this, the power of such thoughts to distress them or to invoke counterrituals or counterthoughts is gradually diminished.

Whatever behavioral techniques are being used, it is vital to stress that progress will be slow, with repeated setbacks, and that many hours of regular application of different techniques is necessary before even modest improvement occurs. Constant reminders about this reality protect patients from self-blame about lack of progress and reduce the likelihood of husbands expressing their frustration and impatience in an unhelpful manner.

Obsessive-Compulsive Disorder in Men

The symptoms of the disorder in men are more varied and heterogeneous than in women and cannot be regarded primarily as an overdetermination of the male sex-role stereotype. Nonetheless, sex-role stereotyped themes are common, particularly with regard to levels of achievement. Very often, men with severe obsessive-compulsive disorder reveal (in the context of a supportive therapeutic relationship) totally unrealistic hopes and expectations about professional, academic, business, or social status and achievements. These ideas and fantasies are usually long-standing and may be fundamental to patients' self-esteem and sense of hope. Failure to achieve or even to approach these unrealistic goals is attributed by patients (and their wives) to the obsessive-compulsive symptoms. Thus, unless a great deal of concurrent attention is given to modifying unrealistic goals and aspirations, the application of behavioral techniques is unlikely to be fully successful. Symptom removal *per se* is sometimes followed by a sense of personal failure or existential despair that can lead to severe depression. While a proportion of patients emerge from this depression free of obsessive-compulsive symptoms, others relapse, and suicide has been reported (Hafner, 1981a). Tricyclics are sometimes useful in treating such depressions.

Marital factors are frequently central in preserving patients' unrealistic aspirations. The wives of men with severe obsessive-compulsive disorders often have a rigidly sex-role stereotyped view of marriage. In return for their selfless devotion to their children, husbands, and domestic duties, they expect their husbands to be highly successful in their reciprocal roles as family breadwinners and providers. Wives' anger about husbands' failure to achieve original aspirations in this regard is constrained only by the idea that their husbands are suffering from an illness for which the husbands have no personal responsibility.

Once the obsessive-compulsive disorder is confirmed as an illness, wives' anger and frustration are partially transformed into nurturing and caregiving behavior toward the patient. Where such behavior is overdetermined or highly ambivalent in origin, it may serve to perpetuate husbands' symptoms and interfere with behavioral therapy. Thus, it is vital to help wives modify their attitudes and expectations about their husbands and about sex roles in general. If this is not done, husbands remain in an impossible position: in order to please their wives, on whom they rely, they must be either "sick" or "successful." Since "success," in traditional, stereotyped terms, is beyond them, "illness" may be their only viable option.

Hostility and Obsessive-Compulsive Disorder

I have emphasized sex-role stereotypes not only because they are potent background factors in perpetuating symptoms, but also because they are given very little attention in the literature on obsessive-compulsive disorders. However, attention to stereotyped attitudes and expectations should not preclude discussion of other areas of marital interaction and communication, which is just as relevant as the concurrent attention to specific behavioral techniques.

Particularly important is the expression of anger and resentment within marriage. Barnett (1969) has suggested that "Aggression permeates the experience of the obsessional, playing a major role in the aetiology of the condition. . . . Depression, rumination or withdrawal replace anger in the patient's repertoire of responses. . . . As a hostile operation, withdrawal is most effective in an interpersonal situation where anger or criticism exists, delivering the final blow by disengagement" (p. 48).

Couples therapy usually reveals that *both* marriage partners are full of suppressed rage toward each other. This anger emerges in numerous direct and indirect ways, but particularly problematic are sudden outbursts of rage of enormous intensity. If expressed by the spouse, these outbursts usually cause a major setback in the patient; if expressed by the patient, the spouse tends to withdraw his or her emotional support, and this undermines the patient's progress. Couples are naturally reluctant to discuss such outbursts, because they are frightening and seem totally irrational. However, it is important to identify them and to teach both partners more appropriate ways of managing their anger and frustration.

Treating Obsessive-Compulsive Disorder in Unmarried Patients

When patients with obsessive-compulsive disorders live alone and are substantially free of close family ties, a combination of individual psychodynamic psychotherapy and behavior therapy is the logical treatment approach, with the addition of drugs if appropriate. Discussion of such cases is beyond the scope of this chapter.

While it is now usual to treat children with severe psychological disorders in a family setting, young adults are still treated mainly on an individual basis, even though family interaction may be critical in maintaining their symptoms. Nonetheless, there is some concensus in the literature that the following problems must be negotiated during the family therapy of young adults with severe obsessive-compulsive disorders (Hafner, Gilchrist, Bowling, & Kalucy, 1981):

1. The family's inability to express or discuss feelings. The parents I have worked with were characterized by a profound reluctance to reveal or discuss sad or angry feelings. Often, this reluctance was underpinned by a deep fear of the consequences of expressing such feelings. For example, the direct expression of anger was often regarded as likely to lead to a complete loss of control and perhaps the injury of others, with consequent destruction of family relationships. Similarly, it was feared that expressions of sadness would lead to uncontrollable depression with the possibility of self-injury or even self-destruction. These attitudes were incorporated by the obsessive-compulsive patient, who, finding that the direct

expression of feelings was impossible, expressed them indirectly through rituals and ruminations, which also served to ward off feelings of sadness and anger. Often, the obsessive-compulsive symptoms were precipitated by an event that heightened feelings of sadness and anger, such as the loss of a close relative or family friend.

2. The family's unrealistic aspirations for the patient. In one family, the father said that he "might as well be dead" if his son, the patient, did not get well and become a successful professional man. It was clear that the patient *needed* his symptoms to protect himself and his parents from a profound sense of failure.

3. The family's idea that the patient is medically ill. Once this idea is consolidated, the family feel powerless to manage the problem themselves. Instead, they hand it over to "experts" who, by treating the patient on an individual basis, simply consolidate his or her position as a displaced focus of the family's conflicts and problems.

Sometimes, the early stages of therapy seem to confirm the parents' worst fears: episodes of enormous, uncontrolled rage are common, and it is also common for the parents to develop psychological or "psychosomatic" symptoms of their own. Warning the family beforehand of the likelihood of such events is very helpful in managing them when they do emerge. After the initial, stormy phase of therapy—which is profoundly challenging to all concerned—it becomes possible to teach the family new patterns of interaction and to modify their expectations of each other. Surprisingly often, the patient's symptoms improve spontaneously in parallel with changes in family relationships, so that the application to the patient of specific behavioral techniques is unnecessary.

CONCLUSION

In writing this chapter, I could have put more emphasis on specific techniques and strategies, but I have avoided doing so for the following reasons. First, anyone who seeks to intervene in the marriages or families of patients with severe, persisting anxiety disorders is a pioneer. We know very little for certain about the factors that initiate and maintain these disorders and even less about optimal techniques and strategies for treating them. Too much emphasis on techniques might lead prematurely to the idea that they are the best available. Only by embarking on therapy in a flexible manner, with the need for innovation and dialectic held firmly in mind, will optimal strategies be developed and ultimately evaluated.

Second, I believe that there is a general overvaluation of the idea that therapy should be concerned primarily with the correct application of specific techniques, whether behavioral, cognitive, or psychodynamic. While techniques are very important, it is often as important to identify and alter attitudes and expectations that are mainly unconscious but that are nonetheless fundamental as background factors in perpetuating patients' symptoms.

Sex-role stereotypes are an almost universal, mainly unconscious, basis for attitudes and expectations about marriage and family life. Because they are so deeply ingrained in patients and therapists alike, they are rarely perceived as relevant, let alone central, to symptom maintenance. In emphasizing sex-role stereotypes, I do not wish to minimize other contributors to the genesis and maintenance of anxiety disorders. Hereditary, biological, chemical, and intrapsychic factors all contribute to a greater or lesser degree in individual cases. Spouse-aided or behavioral family therapy does not preclude attention to these other factors. Indeed, it creates a framework within which they may be examined and modified as part of the overall multimodal treatment process, if necessary.

REFERENCES

Barlow, D. H., O'Brien, G. T., & Last, C. G. (1984). Couples treatment of agoraphobia. *Behavior Therapy, 15*, 41–58.

Barnett, J. (1969). On aggression in the obsessional neuroses. *Contemporary Psychoanalysis, 6*, 48–57.

Burns, L. E., & Thorpe, G. L. (1977). Fears and clinical phobias: Epidemiological aspects and the national survey of agoraphobics. *Journal of International Medical Research, 5*, 1–7.

Cobb, J. P., McDonald, R., Marks, I. M., & Stern, R. (1980). Marital vs exposure therapy: Psychological treatments of co-existing marital and phobic-obsessive problems. *Behaviour Analysis and Modification, 4*, 3–16.

Doctor, R. M. (1982). Major results of a large-scale pretreatment survey of agoraphobics. In R. L. Dupont (Ed.), *Phobia: A comprehensive summary of modern treatments*. New York: Brunner/Mazel.

Foa, E., & Steketee, G.P. (1979). Obsessive-compulsives: Conceptual issues and treatment interventions. In M. Hersen, R. Eisler, & P. Miller (Eds.), *Progress in behavior modification* (Vol. 8). New York: Academic Press.

Fodor, I. G. (1974). The phobic syndrome in women: Implications for treatment. In V. Franks & V. Burtle (Eds.), *Women in therapy*. New York: Brunner/Mazel.

Fry, W. F. (1962). The marital context of an anxiety syndrome. *Family Process, 1*, 245–252.

Goldstein, A. J., & Chambless, D. L. (1978). A reanalysis of agoraphobia. *Behavior Therapy, 9*, 47–59.

Hafner, R. J. (1977). The husbands of agoraphobic women and their influence on treatment outcome. *British Journal of Psychiatry, 130*, 233–239.

Hafner, R. J. (1979). Agoraphobic women married to abnormally jealous men. *British Journal of Medical Psychology, 52*, 99–104.

Hafner, R. J. (1981). Spouse-aided therapy in psychiatry: An introduction. *Australian and New Zealand Journal of Psychiatry, 15*, 329–337. (a)

Hafner, R. J. (1981). Agoraphobia in men. *Australian and New Zealand Journal of Psychiatry, 15*, 243–249. (b)

Hafner, R. J. (1982). Marital interaction in persisting obsessive compulsive disorders. *Australian and New Zealand Journal of Psychiatry, 16*, 171–178.

Hafner, R. J. (1983). Marital systems of agoraphobic women: Contributions of husbands' denial and projection. *Journal of Family Therapy, 5*, 379–396. (a)

Hafner, R. J. (1983). Behaviour therapy for agoraphobic men. *Behaviour Research and Therapy, 21*, 51–56. (b)

Hafner, R. J. (1984). Predicting the effects on husbands of behaviour therapy for wives' agoraphobia. *Behaviour Research and Therapy, 22*, 217–226.

Hafner, R. J. (1986). *Marriage and mental illness: A sex-roles perspective*. New York: Guilford Press.

Hafner, R. J., Gilchrist, P., Bowling, J., & Kalucy, R. (1981). The treatment of obsessional neurosis in a family setting. *Australian and New Zealand Journal of Psychiatry, 15*, 145–151.

Hafner, R. J., & Marks, I. M. (1976). Exposure *in vivo* of agoraphobics: Contributions of diazepam, group exposure and anxiety evocation. *Psychological Medicine, 6*, 71–88.

Hafner, R. J., & Ross, M. W. (1983). Predicting the outcome of behaviour therapy for agoraphobia. *Behaviour Research and Therapy, 21*, 375–382.

Hafner, R. J., & Ross, M. W. (1984). Agoraphobia in women: Factor analysis of symptoms and personality correlates of factor scores in a clinical population. *Behaviour Research and Therapy, 22*, 441–444.

Haley, J. (1963). *Strategies of psychotherapy*. New York: Grune & Stratton.

Hallam, R. S. (1978). Agoraphobia: A critical review of the concept. *British Journal of Psychiatry, 133*, 314–319.

Hand, I., Spoehring, B., & Stanik, E. (1977). The treatment of obsessions, compulsions and phobias as hidden couple-counselling. In J. Boulougouris & A. Rabavilas (Eds.), *The treatment of phobias and obsessive-compulsive disorders*. London: Pergamon Press.

Holmes, J. (1982). Phobia and counterphobia: Family aspects of agoraphobia. *Journal of Family Therapy, 4*, 133–152.

Liotti, G., & Guidano, V. (1976). Behavioural analysis of marital interaction in male agoraphobic patients. *Behaviour Research and Therapy, 14*, 161–162.

Marks, I. M. (1980). *Cure and care of neuroses*. New York: Wiley.

Marks, I. M., & Herst, E. R. (1970). A survey of 1,200 agoraphobics in Britain. *Social Psychiatry, 5*, 16–24.

Mathews, A. M., Gelder, M. G., & Johnston, D. W. (1981). *Agoraphobia: Nature and treatment*. London: Tavistock.

Rachman, S. J., & Hodgson, R. J. (1980). *Obsessions and compulsions*. Englewood Cliffs, NJ: Prentice-Hall.

Rice, E. (1974). The compulsive companion: A case study. *International Journal of Psychoanalytic Psychotherapy, 3*, 183–194.

Salzman, L. (1982). Obsessions and agoraphobia. In D. L. Chambless & A. L. Goldstein (Eds.), *Agoraphobia: Multiple perspectives on theory and treatment*. New York: Wiley.

Sartory, G. (1983). Benzodiazepines and behavioural treatment of phobic anxiety. *Behavioural Psychotherapy, 11*, 211–217.

Sheehan, D. V., Ballenger, J., & Jacobsen, G. (1980). The treatment of endogenous anxiety with phobic, hysterical and hypochondriacal symptoms. *Archives of General Psychiatry, 37*, 51–59.

Tarpy, R. M. (1975). *Basic principles of learning*. Glenview, IL: Scott, Foresman.

Thomas-Peter, B. A., Jones, R. B., Sinnott, A., & Scott-Fordam, A. (1983). Prediction of outcome in the treatment of agoraphobia. *Behavioural Psychotherapy, 11*, 320–328.

Thoren, P., Asberg, M., Cronholm, B., Jornestedt, L., & Traskman, L. (1980). Clomipramine treatment of obsessive-compulsive disorder. *Archives of General Psychiatry, 37*, 1281–1285.

Tyrer, P. (1984). Classification of anxiety. *British Journal of Psychiatry, 144*, 78–83.

Vose, R. H. (1981). *Agoraphobia*. London: Faber & Faber.

10

Obsessive-Compulsive Patients and Their Families

IVER HAND
Psychiatric University Clinic, Hamburg

This chapter mainly relies on 10 years of clinical experience and observation, on hypotheses drawn from this experience, and on guilty feelings (as a behavior therapist) resulting from the lack of hard data with which to evaluate the concepts presented.

The term "systemic–strategic behavior therapy" is introduced to include recent changes in behavior therapy, integrating concepts and techniques from systems-oriented treatment "schools" (Friesen, 1985) and elaborating the functional–behavioral analysis toward a clinical strategy that equally refers to intraindividual and interactional functions of illness behaviors—and even to "hidden intentions" (Hand, 1986a). Thus, these changes have also improved the analysis of motivation for change.

Family variables are discussed in a more general systems approach, with particular attention to dyadic communication styles of the patient in family, spouse, and therapist contacts.

From a behavior therapy point of view, this chapter is premature. From a clinician's point of view, it is hoped to stimulate development of shared concepts and of meaningful questions for joint new research in systems and cognitive aspects of obsessive-compulsive symptoms (OCSs). An extended period of doubting preceded and followed the decision to let the clinician win over the research worker when confronted with the opportunity to write this chapter. As the conflict has been noted from the beginning, writer's cramp could be avoided.

SYSTEMIC AND INDIVIDUAL FUNCTIONS OF OCS AND TREATMENT OUTCOME

"Normal" obsessive-compulsive behavior (OCB) may turn into "pathological" obsessive-compulsive symptoms (OCSs) in the context of different somatic or psychiatric disorders or within an obsessive-compulsive disorder

(OCD). For OCD, behavior therapy is currently regarded as the "treatment of choice." Yet there exists a huge body of psychoanalytic experience and publications in this field (Jenike, Baer, & Minichiello, 1986; Nagera, 1976), as well as a variety of studies from a more biological orientation (Yaryura-Tobias & Neziroglu, 1983). Among the latter, several are concerned with the effects of psychotropic medication on obsessive-compulsive behaviors and accompanying depression (Marks, 1987; Mavissakalian, Turner, & Michelson, 1985a, 1985b). Regardless of their orientations, almost all of these publications rely on an individual disease model, largely neglecting systems variables.

Generally, behavioral treatments for OCD are less successful, more time-consuming, and more interactionally demanding than behavioral treatments for phobic patients. This may be due to a variety of reasons, including the following: (1) longer delay between onset of illness and first contact with therapist when compared with phobics; (2) more severe deficits in early individual development, in particular in the development of social skills (these often appear connected with impaired communication skills, which affect private and professional contacts as well as communication with the therapist); (3)stronger adherence to symptom behaviors that in many ways resemble socially reinforced virtues (orderliness, cleanness, etc.)—even in a normal population there is a much higher prevalence of OCBs than of other neurotic symptoms (Hand & Zaworka, 1982)—unlike phobias, many OCSs are not qualitatively new behaviors; and (4) frequently, OCSs seem to bring about reduction of general anxiety (dependent on internal, cognitive triggers) rather than of phobia-like anxiety responses to external triggers.

Published treatment studies with behavior therapy vary extremely in outcome (Beech, 1974; Foa, Steketee, Grayson, & Doppelt, 1983; Marks, 1987; Mavissakalian, 1985b; Rachman, 1983; Rachman & Hodgson, 1980). To some extent, outcome may depend on the types of obsessive-compulsive subsymptoms treated: washing and cleaning rituals seem to respond positively in 75%–95% of obsessive-compulsive patients (OCPs), whereas the same only holds true for 50%–70% of compulsive checking, counting, touching, or speaking rituals. The positive results for isolated obsessions go down close to 0% (Rachman, 1983). On average, with unselected clinical OCPs, one may expect success rates of 50%–70%, depending on the distribution of the mentioned subgroups in any given sample.

Separation of these three subgroups of OCSs seems useful also with regard to intrapersonal functions. For instance, washing and cleaning much more resembles phobic (avoidance) behaviors than the other groups of OCSs. Patients with these behaviors usually have a phobia-like anticipatory anxiety, the triggers of which can either be avoided or removed by the rituals. The main intraindividual function of these symptoms appears to be a reduction of trigger-focused anxiety.

Orderliness and checking—in particular, counting, touching, and speaking—are often connected with magical thinking. These rituals seem to have the intraindividual function of reducing more generalized anxiety. They are often induced by cognitions of anticipated disasters, which are hoped to be prevented by means of their magical power. With regard to magical thinking, there are overlaps of these OCPs with a subgroup of gamblers who are hooked on magical indicators for "luck," including numbers, melodies, and a wide range of external events (Hand, 1986b). In both of these groups, there is a certain delusional quality in the magical thinking; however, unlike in schizophrenia, there is little if any generalization of this kind of thinking into everyday life. The magical belief system appears unchangeable in spite of these patients' ability to differentiate clearly between a logical stream of thought and their irrational, magical expectations. Of course, in some patients, other intraindividual functions may be more important: checking and orderliness may be connected to primary low self-esteem with the aim to assure social approval, or they may result from the attempt to reduce mistakes resulting from impaired short-term memory—which itself may be the consequence of severe depression or of organically impaired brain functions.

Ruminating appears more closely connected to depression than the other two groups of OCSs (the level of depression ratings do not allow conclusions about causal connections between depression and OCSs). The ruminator frequently has the expectancy of unavoidable disaster; in fact, sometimes he or she is even convinced that the disaster has already happened and that he or she unfortunately cannot prove this to anyone. Cognitions in this subgroup are much closer to psychotic delusions than in the other two groups; these OCPs have by far the closest links to major depression or schizophrenia.

From a cognitive point of view, these three subgroups can be divided according to their concepts (guiding cognitive principles) of mastery or helplessness when faced with subjective threats of disaster: (a) The washer is characterized by the certitude of mastery—either by avoidance of anxiety-inducing triggers or by "undoing" the triggers with the rituals; (2) the OCP with counting, touching, or speaking rituals is guided by the expectation of mastery due to belief in the magical power of rituals preventing disaster from him- or herself or significant others (checkers are somewhere between these two groups); and (3) the ruminator, in contrast, anticipates disaster out of a certitude of helplessness, with symptom behaviors frequently even increasing rather than decreasing the negative expectations (as well as anxiety, guilty feelings, or depression). This separation of cognitions in the three subtypes of OCSs may to some extent "explain" the clinical impression that depression will improve usually in successful treatment of OCSs in the first group, frequently in the second, but rarely in the third. Of course, in the individual patient with mixed OCSs, we will find overlaps among the described cognitions and intraindividual functions. For a recent, but different cognitive-structural approach to OCBs, see Reed (1985).

With regard to differences in interpersonal functions, it appears that somewhere between the first and the third subgroups of OCPs, there is a cutoff point between "easy" and "tight" interaction styles, particularly with regard to interactional power struggles. We assume that primary impaired social skills have led to low self-esteem and high interpersonal vulnerability, for which pseudocompensation, by obsessional-dominating anancastic[1] interaction patterns, has been developed (see below).

We must strive for a combination of psychological (intraindividual as well as interactional) and biological variables in conceptionalization and treatment of OCDs. The relative importance of each of these variables in any given individual patient needs to be assessed before meaningful interventions can be derived and applied. In the context of this chapter, the family and system variables are given priority, but in the individual OCP, they are not the decisive ones *per se*! Also, it must be mentioned that for many OCPs with complex additional problems, mere exposure treatment may have better symptomatic and generalized effects than interventions in the other problem areas (Hand & Sauke, 1985). The following considerations therefore refer to those patients who are failures in traditional symptom-directed behavior therapy and for whom family and systems variables have to be considered as major sources of resistance to change.

Behavioral Treatment Strategy

Treatment of a person with OCSs requires complex pretreatment analyses, including psychopathological classification. Only with obsessions and compulsions in the context of a neurosis or psychosomatic disorder can the symptom-directed techniques of behavior therapy be applied. Even then, careful evaluation of motivation and intraindividual as well as interactional functions of the symptomatology is necessary to avoid erroneous application of exposure (Hand, 1986a).

OCS and Motivation for Change

From a combined individual and systems point of view, one can find a variety of obstacles for the development of "real" motivation for change. Neither do patients' explicit statements that they want their OCSs to be treated really indicate that this is so. Similarly, relatives' opposite statements about the patient also don't necessarily reflect the truth (Hand, 1981a). Common obstacles to motivation for change include the following.

Patients may hide symptoms. These behaviors may have been an important precondition for a professional career (meticulousness, orderliness, cleanness) or subjective well-being (magical rituals); their escalation has not been judged adequately by the OCP, and attempts from others to get him or her to reduce the behaviors are perceived as a threat to his or her personality. A feeling of shame about the subjectively meaningful but logically "silly" OCSs may additionally increase the tendency to hide the symptomatology. The experienced clinician will detect hidden OCSs in a variety of psychiatric patients as well as in normals.

Before trying to reduce a patient's OCBs, the therapist ought to keep in mind that many compulsions resemble "normal" behavior patterns that may have been severely enforced and reinforced in education, religion, and working conditions in industrial- or religion-oriented societies. These behaviors also resemble rituals in children's games and in everyday adult life, which seem to be a precondition for healthy individual development (Erikson, 1978). These behaviors seem to serve two major functions: (1) to facilitate the development of adaptive stereotypes to constant external overstimulation and (2) to reduce anxiety induced by such distinct triggers as unknown rules in spontaneous social encounters or a fear of death. Magical rituals in several aspects resemble religious rituals for reduction of generalized anxiety and feelings of guilt; these rituals also can go far beyond the desired levels, then to be called an illness.

Many patients with OCDs suffer from severe social deficits unknowingly and without displaying them immediately to the unexperienced observer. Over the years, these OCPs have developed pseudocompensation for these deficits—a latent aggressive, anancastic style of interaction (Donath, 1987; Yaryura-Tobias & Neziroglu, 1983)—that leads to a "winning the battle but losing the war" mode of social interaction. These OCPs have developed skills to dominate others in dyadic interaction, giving the immediate impression that they are socially "overskilled." Peers at work as well in private life will soon tend to avoid such people; the OCPs then receive yet more reinforcement that others don't like them and they don't like others. The resulting avoidance of dyadic closeness is motivated by the desired avoidance of any risk of being hurt when getting close. As a "coping" strategy for severe social deficits, such a pattern unfortunately appears subjectively successful; therefore, these patients are very reluctant to give up this skill and be exposed to their deficits. In treatment, it may take a long time until such patients are ready to acknowledge their deficits and to learn more adequate coping strategies. In this context, and from a systems point of view, one also has to help spouses of such patients with their own deficits, which have made them tolerate this interactional style for extended periods of time.

In the therapist–patient relationship, this interaction style is probably one of the main reasons for high dropout and failure rates. The therapist needs specific training to detect the reasons for this communication style and to learn to cope with it in a therapeutic way, rather than responding with increasing aggression and rejection.

Initial aggressive interaction from these OCPs may not only result from their typical communication pattern, but it may also come from the above-mentioned feeling of being threatened by any attempt of the therapist to reduce the OCBs. On the basis of such experiences, therapists have developed a very specific interaction style with these patients (see below). With such patients, "successful" treatment often seems to introduce mutually acceptable compromises of the OCPs with their social environments regarding OCBs and communication styles. On rating scales (Zaworka, Hand, Jauernig, & Lünenschloss, 1983), such reductions of OCSs may look impressive and prove statistically significant, and subjective suffering of all individuals within a family system may also be considerably reduced, yet general social functioning of the OCP may remain severely impaired.

Obsessive-compulsive symptoms may become one of several weapons in interactional power struggles in couples, families, and larger systems. Sometimes the "intervention" of the OCS weapon by one family member may even be followed by the invention of "anti-OCS OCSs" in another member. To make matters even more complicated, both fighters may agree to hide the existence of these weapons in front of the therapist. Much like the previously described pseudoassertive interaction style, the use of OCSs as an interactional weapon usually results from primary interactional deficits. The following three case examples illustrate these interactional functions.

Case 1

A housewife and her husband both complained about her severe OCSs in the home. The wife expressed a strong desire to receive treatment for the OCSs and not for her considerable depression, social anxiety, and functional somatic complaints. Exposure treatment failed to help. Subsequent reanalysis of her pretreatment ratings on multisymptomatic self-rating scales (Hand & Zaworka, 1982) revealed that, in spite of the high scores in OCSs, the patient had rated highest in "behavioral resistance" (Zaworka & Hand, 1981)—the degree to which a person continues everyday activities in spite of intermittent symptomatology—against her social phobic symptomatology. According to our model of motivation, this should have indicated that motivation for change was actually highest in the area of social anxiety.

Repetition of the behavioral analysis—on the basis of a much more trustful relationship having resulted from the exposure treatment—revealed that the patient lived in an increasingly unhappy marriage. She felt suppressed by her husband, a successful businessman. Because of her social deficits and dependency on her husband, she had been unable to make her point in marital power struggles. Thus, she eventually developed exaggerations of those behaviors that her husband originally had requested from her, including cleanliness and orderliness in the house (opposition by paradox). When these behaviors had reached a "pathological" level (according to the norms of her husband), they had also led to new restrictions in the family that increasingly limited the husband's freedom of behavior and power at home. The wife defended her new power by insisting that she had developed an illness for which she was not responsible. The husband finally accepted this interpretation and then concluded that there should be a cure. Thus, the wife's paradoxical communication was attacked by the husband's paradoxical communication. She had no logical reason to refuse his proposal of treatment, again finding herself in a trap. Since she had insisted on the illness quality of her hidden power strategy (i.e., OCSs), she had to pretend motivation for illness (i.e., power) reduction. She was defeated again by her husband, who was now using the paradoxical strategies that she originally had introduced into the battle. Thus, marital problems and her social deficits remained the couple's secret when they first asked for treatment. The wife had not dared to mention these problems in the early stages of treatment, and the therapists had not sufficiently used their strategy of behavior therapy and their imaginations to question her request for symptom (i.e., power) reduction.

Such a failure of exposure, here due to the hidden systems function of OCSs, can sometimes be avoided by the results of a behavioral analysis *in vivo* always preceding exposure *in vivo* interventions.

Case 2

Wife and husband together requested treatment for her extensive OCSs in and around the kitchen. No mention was made of marital or other problems. Only the *in vivo* analysis at the couple's home revealed that the living and sleeping rooms were stacked with hundreds of copies of the husband's professional journals; that is, he had been a compulsive journal collector years before the compulsions of his wife had started. Only at this point were the couple able to admit to years of arguments about the husband's compulsion, which had totally destroyed the previous *gemütlichkeit* at home. From a power point of view, when the husband had established his obsessive-compulsive empire in the sleeping and living rooms, the wife prevented his invasion into the kitchen by developing her own OCSs there ("fighting the enemy with his own weapons"). Under the heavy pressure of her husband, she eventually came to agree that only her OCSs were an illness. As in the previous couple, she gave in to his demand to get treatment and did not dare to tell the truth even in individual interviews at the hospital office.

Assessment of motivation may also be necessary in a broader systems approach (Wynne, McDaniel, & Weber, 1986), as the following example may illustrate.

Case 3

A woman came to the intake interview because her neighbors had become intolerant of her noisy ways of checking whether or not the entrance door to her apartment was locked (referral for treatment because of interactional function of one OCS). She herself did not suffer at all from this habit, and, rather than reducing this OCS, she wanted to discuss strategies to use to calm down the neighbors. When she had developed some trust in the therapist, she started talking about her intraindividually most important OCS, which also had become her major purpose in life: compulsive bible translating. As a young woman, she had joined a monastery to withdraw from normal social contacts. At entry she had bestowed a large amount of inherited money on this institution. A year later, she left the place in disappointment but was refused refund of her money. After these experiences, she had started her private bible translations with the "hidden intention" (Hand, 1986a) of demonstrating to her (holy) father in Rome that something had to be wrong in the existing bible translations, since they were the guide for those people who had treated her so badly. Further, she indicated that monks in monasteries had not been able to deliver proper bible translations over a period of almost 2,000 years. So she had dedicated her life to bible translating.

Every year she worked as a part-time secretary for some months; for the rest of the year, she lived on this money like a nun in the solitude of her flat, devoting her time to translating. She had sent several preliminary translations to the Pope, with the hidden intention of getting father's help to educate his daughters in the monastery properly. The therapist's help was only wanted to get the Pope to respond in the desired way.

Here, in a broader systems context, social deficits—and a pseudocoping strategy for them (with latent, hidden aggressiveness or resentment)—created a vicious circle of mutual reinforcement of OCSs and of social deficits. The OCSs turned into an ultimate purpose in life.

As has been shown, OCSs can become weapons in interpersonal power struggles. Such power struggles may occur as intermittent developmental stages of a relationship, but they may also turn into a chronic exchange of hostility.

Case 4

A housebound female "washer" gained total control over her husband's behavior in the apartment. The apartment was divided into several zones of cleanness, with the husband only being allowed to move in the least clean zones, which amounted to some 20% of the total space. When entering the house, the husband had to follow the wife into the bathroom, there to undress and to get a wash from head to toe. This, among other submissions, was the result of severe power struggles earlier in the marriage; some 15 years earlier, the wife had called the husband a "dirty pig" for having an affair with another woman (which had never been confirmed then or thereafter). In this context, she had developed a brief psychotic episode with delusional jealousy. This was successfully treated by neuroleptics, but the wife had since developed her excessive "dirt-phobia," with extreme cleaning rituals of husband and apartment. (More information is given on case 4 later on in this chapter.)

Case 5

A male compulsive "speaker" developed the idea that a message is only sent properly when certain words or sentences are spoken with the "correct" sound and intonation. Only the patient could decide whether these standards for correctness were met, although he sometimes pretended to consider other persons' judgments. At home, his wife was forced to listen to him until he felt satisfied. Any attempt from her to push him to finish increased his irritation, leading to more interruptions and repetitions, and severely extended the time needed for finishing the ritual. The husband sometimes locked the wife in the bathroom, repeating his words from outside and allowing his wife out only after he decided to stop talking. If the wife then attempted to leave the house, he would lock the front door, immediately starting new words and forcing her again to listen for another extended period of time. For years this marital interaction was also characterized by the wife's constant threat to seek divorce.

Such an interaction may end in physical violence. If such a patient is then admitted to the hospital—due to pressure from his wife and a doctor—he will soon start this type of communication with the ward staff. Eventually he will provoke so much aggression on the ward that he will be discharged, against his wife's will. The best kind of help for a couple like this may be to change the wife's behavior in terms of her specific symptom-related and general interaction with the husband.

The explanation of the development of such complex OCSs on intraindividual as well as interactional levels needs to consider "pathology" in spouses who accept this kind of chronic symbiotic existence (Hafner,

1986). If, in treatment, spouses are not sufficiently involved and changed, the patient may be successfully treated, in the hospital, but the spouse will respond with deep dissatisfaction and aggression toward the patient and therapist, complaining about other deficits or problem behaviors in the patient.

If therapists do not pay attention to interpersonal functions of OCSs in couples or families, and if they neglect the impact of such functions (in particular, the expression of hostility via OCSs) on the patient–therapist relationship, they may not be able to separate real from pretended motivation for change. In such a situation, short-term symptom treatment may be wrongly applied and may result in the patient turning a treatment technique into a new OCS, as we have seen in a "licking" ritual, resulting from exposure and modeling in a dirt-phobic compulsive washer. By this, the patient constantly expressed his aggression toward the therapist, who—from the patient's point of view—caused pain to him and needed to be publicly blamed for what he did.

BEHAVIORAL TREATMENT TECHNIQUES

In behavior therapy, by far the most frequently applied treatment technique for OCSs is the combination of exposure *in vivo* and response prevention. In clinical work, there is no logic in separating these elements. Usually, exposure is only seen as a means to reduce symptomatology. But exposure can potentially serve three functions.

1. Exposure can extend the behavioral analysis in a state of higher emotional arousal. In addition to office interviews, exposure may reveal more details of symptom behavior and other problem areas. The patient may discover feelings and cognitions that he or she didn't recognize before, having avoided this state of prolonged emotional arousal. Before exposure, the patient may feel afraid of anxiety, whereas under exposure he or she may discover that the feelings provoked by confrontation with the stimulus are actually depression or anger. Tolerance of such strong feelings may then provoke "hidden cognitions" or "suppressed memory," and the patient may achieve access to highly relevant information about other problem areas, which may then become the new focus of treatment (see the continuation of case 4 below).
2. When the conduct of exposure has been done in an interactionally proper way, it can enhance the therapist–patient relationship. Trust in the therapist may increase so much that previously conscious but hidden information is now communicated to the therapist (see cases 1 and 2).
3. Effective exposure may result in response management and symptom reduction. Response management is particularly important to prevent

intermittent relapses by increasing self-help capacity. In this context, training of depression management should be applied in an identical way to anxiety management (Hand *et al.*, 1974; Hand *et al.*, 1986). In this concept, exposure to an external trigger 1 usually is much more an exposure to or confrontation with the patient's internal—cognitive–emotional–physiological—responses (i.e., trigger 2), induced by prevention of external, motor behavior responses (avoidance).

If we conceive of behavior as composed of motor, cognitive, emotional, and physiological activities constantly interacting with one another, the term "exposure response prevention" is clearly misleading, as response prevention only occurs for the motor behavior. Therefore, I have proposed (Hand, 1981c; Hand *et al.*, 1986) to rephrase the term into "exposure response management." "Response management" refers to learning coping strategies with anxiety, depression, anger, or guilty feelings, the exposure to which has become possible by prevention of the initial motor or mental avoidance response.

The latent aggressiveness of many OCPs can easily get the therapist involved in power struggles at any stage of treatment. The exposure *in vivo* sessions are the most intensive intrusions into the OCP's autonomy. They include the most threatening questioning of the obsessive-compulsive or anancastic pseudocoping strategies. Therefore, my colleagues and I have developed a very particular interaction style with these patients while conducting the exposure sessions in their homes.

We only initiate the first home visit after patients have made a clear decision that they are ready to take the risk of destroying the obsessive-compulsive concepts, thus facing any and all possible risks that might result. Once this decision has been made in the office, we tell the patients that at any point during exposure at home, they will be free to change their mind, interrupt exposure, and return to the rituals. Before doing so, however, they will be asked to reevaluate the decision, with a discussion of its consequences, before indulging in the rituals again. Having entered the first few square yards of the home, each further step will be explained to the patients and will need their approval. With this motor behavior the therapists submit themselves entirely to the control of the patients. In the first hour of exposure in the home, patients check whether the therapists know about obsessive-compulsive concepts and whether the therapists make "mistakes" in behavior in the home—due to a lack of knowledge or of caring.

The most difficult aspect of the first 4-hour contamination session at home with washers and cleaners is the mutual agreement between patients and therapists that they are to contaminate virtually every square centimeter of the flat with "dirt" or "germs." Before starting, patients and therapists have also agreed that this full contamination cannot be undone, as it would take months of work. So the patients, when following through the whole session, are taking an extreme risk; they do not know what their responses will be, but they do know that their usual coping behaviors will no longer be available. This means that the patients have to take the risk of parting from the certitude of mastery based on the rituals. This decision to let go of a long-established cognitive concept will not be helped by pushing the patients beyond the actual state of motivation. Each interruption of the exposure by patients is therefore accepted by therapists in order to teach new coping strategies. Exposure is done in self-conduct under self-control, the therapist mainly being there to make adequate suggestions and for expert dialogue when doubt arises. With this concept, few patients drop out of the exposure treatment. Therefore, we never applied 24-hour supervision of response prevention in a hospital setting.

For the following reasons, it may become necessary to engage other family members in one or more of the exposure sessions at home: (1) successful symptom reduction in one session may be very irritating for relatives, who for years have obeyed to the OCS rules in the house; they may respond with anger or aggression, suspecting that they have been cheated if OCSs can be solved in a 1-day session; (2) the relatives may be able to profit from teaching and modeling (by observing the therapists' interaction style with the patient) of new interaction styles; training of new interaction and communication patterns regarding the symptom behavior may generalize into other relevant areas of couple and family communication (Hand, Spoehring, & Stanik, 1977); and (3) involvement of the spouse and other family members is an additional opportunity to assess family norms with regard to OCBs; sometimes other family members may show clearly pathological OCSs, even more than the designated patient.

Exposure to an external trigger is believed to work via induction of exposure to the internal cognitive–emotional–physiological responses; therefore, *there is no apparent reason to look for different treatment techniques in ruminations*! As for compulsions, one has to identify what patients try to avoid by ruminating, and then one has to expose them to these feelings and cognitions. These may be feelings of anxiety, depression, guilt, or even emotional closeness as well as confrontation with conflict situations. As in compulsions, the avoidance of insecurity with the concommittant desire for 100% predictability of future events is an additional important intraindividual function. These intraindividual functions of ruminations are often combined with the "winning the battle, losing the war" type of interactional function.

Case 6

A saleswoman from a childrens' shoe shop suffered from the rumination that, in spite of her meticulousness, she might have sold shoes that did not fit the children. The children might then have fallen while running across roads, and they may have been killed by cars passing by. She asked, "Doctor, how can you prove to me that I am wrong?" The most frequent simplistic response to a question of this type is to try reasoning with the patient that these are clearly wrong assumptions. The outcome of such an attempt usually is an increasingly emotional and finally aggressive interaction. This "game of reasoning" is always won by the patient—and she knows it in advance (the reader is advised not to try to role-play this particular case history with friends among his colleagues or family members—afterward they may not be friends anymore). Therefore, we did not give in to that demand to supply security.

We have also never seen thought-stopping to work with this kind of ruminator. Two alternative techniques or therapist responses do appear helpful, however.

The first technique is prescribing the symptom. With this approach, the patient and the therapist get the chance to control the occurrence of the symptom (Hand, 1981b). Prescriptions seem to work particularly well when they impose frequent ruminations (e.g., every 30 minutes for 5 minutes), with constant writing of the ruminations into a little booklet in order to control mind wandering. There are several speculations as to why this works. Perhaps for the patient who follows this prescription, the rumination soon becomes a terribly boring activity. Patients learn that the more they talk about the ruminations, the more prescriptions they will get. From this, it is easy to understand that the positive effects of such prescriptions rely entirely on the therapeutic relationship. If the therapist's motivation was anger rather than benevolence, such a prescription is a dangerous weapon in the therapist–patient communication and may lead to violent counterattacks by the patient who correctly feels hurt.

When it works—and this will only happen on the basis of a trusting patient–therapist relationship—the greatest relief for the therapist is the immediate reduction in time required by the patient to discuss the rumination; this reduces the risk for the development of a power struggle, and it allows more treatment time for more important issues.

Another helpful technique is exposure to the feeling of insecurity: a request for reassurance by the patient will be answered by the therapist as follows: "I'm sorry; you may be right or you may be wrong with your worry; there is no way for me to decide." Many patients will then emphasize the therapist's responsibility to find a solution. The therapist may now argue that there is no way to find an answer that is 100% sure. The therapist can even say that it is only 100% sure that questions of this kind can never be answered for sure and, when discussed, are bound to lead to severe anger because of the lack of a possible solution.

Apart from such direct dealing with ruminations, we usually find it more important to establish alternative behaviors than to deal too directly with the symptom behavior—which is in contrast with our and others' experiences with symptom techniques in compulsions.

FAMILY BEHAVIOR THERAPY

Behavior therapists need to integrate elements of systems-oriented treatment without leaving the paradigm or the strategy of behavior therapy. Family-oriented interventions can be derived from two basically different groups of systems-directed interventions: the psychoeducational and the systems-proper approaches.

The psychoeducational approach has been best developed in the treatment of schizophrenia (Anderson, Reiss, & Hogarty, 1986). The main emphasis is on the teaching of a certain disease model, not only to the patient but also to significant others. This approach is supposed to improve illness management by patient and family, thus reducing risks for relapse. The teaching refers to biological as well as to psychological and interactional aspects of the disease and its impact on every family member. A clear differentiation is made between the sane family member and the sick. It is still not known whether the content of the teaching material or the emotional experience of being taken care of is most helpful for the relatives. Another unresolved question is whether the teaching material is best presented in a few workshops or whether it is better to spread the information over many sessions in order to make it easier to grasp.

In a similar though much less elaborate manner, spouses and other family members have been employed in individual behavior therapy (Matthews, Teasdale, Munby, Johnston, & Shaw, 1977), including home-based exposure treatment for OCPs. In the therapist-guided approaches, the therapist remains *the* expert, comparable with the doctor in medicine. The relative is taught to become a mediator between therapist and patient. By this, the relative's understanding of the disease of the patient is hoped to improve responses to disease behaviors of the patient. This ideally might lead to reinforcement of "healthy" behaviors rather than opposition to "illness" behaviors of the patient.

Apart from the potential benefits, the therapist-assisted attribution of "sick" and "sane" roles to different family members may also be harmful in the long run—especially when interactional functions of illness behaviors are more important than intraindividual ones. Often, it seems more desirable to see the spouse as a copatient rather than a cotherapist, for instance, as with parents who bring their child with OCSs for treatment. Once a primary organic or psychotic disorder is excluded in the child, the parents are included in the patient role (see case 7, below).

Relatives who are initially reluctant to accept the patient role may enter treatment as the "helper" of the therapist in order to develop trust before daring to attempt the next step. This can be achieved in a systematic way, in a behavioral group therapy model for obsessive-compulsives (Hand & Tichatzki, 1978) or in individual therapy. If, initially, spouse and patient refuse a joint patient role but accept the spouse as cotherapist in treatment of the patient's OCSs, and if there is a severe but denied communication problem in the everyday interaction of the couple, "hidden couple counseling" is used (Hand *et al.*, 1977). Communication training becomes part of the symptom treatment, but it is designed to affect the more general communication problems—without the couple being told so.

A family setting is regarded healthy when it is organized according to a generation hierarchy with level-specific roles, responsibilities, and power distribution (Haley, 1971). The occurrence of symptoms in a child is expected when at least one parent has settled on the child level, and at least one child has done the reverse in order to stabilize the family unit. The first aim of treatment, then, is to relocate each family member back to the appropriate hierarchical level. Parents are taught to act as a unit with the child to reestablish role-specific rules, rights, and duties. The experience of newly established joint parental power is assumed to reassure the child that both parents don't need his or her help anymore to keep the family going. Means to achieve such changes may be derived from family therapy, as well as from behavioral interventions for deficits in the parents that may have led to this mix-up of role behaviors.

We also teach parents to separate their parental from their marital problems and role expectations. If the marital relationship is impaired, but each individual parent's contact with the children is good, we frequently encounter the following problem: both spouses had successfully acted as parents, leading one spouse subsequently to demand "rights" (e.g., sexual) on the marital level; in a vicious circle, the one spouse who didn't want to intensify marital interaction therefore did not dare to show joint parental behaviors in fear of subsequent new marital demands. Provided there is good will on both sides, teaching of separation of parental and marital role expectations, rights, and duties can have immediate beneficial effects. Treatment thereafter consists of separate training in parental behavior and couple counseling. The decreases in the child's symptom behavior are indicators of treatment progress with the parents (see 7, below).

In systems theories, symptoms are believed to serve primarily interpersonal functions in social micro- and macrosystems. Whenever behavior is changing in one person, this affects the behavior of others close to him or her. Essentially, such an interactional feedback loop model appears to be similar to the operant learning theory paradigm, although in the latter, such a feedback loop was never explicitly formulated in family or systems terms. The smallest interpersonal unit is dyadic and the smallest family unit triadic. Such couple or family units may be treated as *one* systems unit with regard to bonds to a variety of other systems units.

The therapist must to some extent join this complex combination of interacting micro- and macrosystems. He or she has to reflect the role as a participant in the systems. Like a judo master, the therapist will not oppose the powers of the family but will use them to induce change. Especially in families with more than one highly vulnerable member, we have learned that direct attempts to induce major changes in the "pathological" bonds are perceived with a shared panic that these attempts might constitute a threat to the existence of the family. This panic may then mobilize resistance and even increase suffering (see case 4). Therefore, the therapist must first reassure the system that he or she, like all the family members, will help insure the family's survival. This is a strategy of "join the system where it is," in extension of Kanfer's "join the patient where he is" (see case 8, below).

The next technique is the opposite of the judo approach. It is an important element in the work of the Milano group (Selvini Palazzoli, Boscolo, Cecchin, & Prata, 1977), derived from treatment of families with a "symptomatic" child. The main emphasis is on the detection of unhealthy family communication stereotypes, which supposedly serve the family to keep a balance in spite of internal disruptions. Although the theoretical concept is similar to the above-mentioned ones, therapists draw different consequences. In this dynamite approach, the family appears to be interpreted as an unhealthy communication castle, surrounded by strong defensive walls and almost inaccessible to therapeutic attacks from outside. The intervention is then to smuggle communication dynamite into this system, using a Trojan horse–like strategy called "prescription." Destruction of the pathological communication structure is the aim, with the very optimistic assumption that thereafter the family members will return to healthy communication patterns.

For the experienced behavior therapist, this may be a helpful technique with some families. Before using it, however, the therapist must always assess each family member's potential to return to healthy communication patterns. In adults with OCSs, who frequently suffer from long-lasting primary deficits along with impaired communication skills, such interventions without behavioral treatment for the deficits appear extremely risky. Just cutting the "pathological" bonds will leave the family without any bonds at all, and the family's individuals will be without the capacity to form new bonds in alternative social settings.

Application of the Trojan horse approach should therefore only be considered by very experienced therapists with constant peer supervision. Note that home-based exposure may unintentionally turn into such a "dynamite" approach (see case 4).

Family-directed individual behavior therapy can be tried whenever analysis reveals spouse or family problems as a major contributing factor to an individual's pathology, and other relevant family members refuse to participate in treatment. The patient will then be taught to become the mediator for family therapy—that is, how to induce desired changes in other family members by changing his or her own behavior.

SUMMARY

Behavioral family therapy with OCPs and their relatives must be tailored to the specific needs of a given family unit. Based on the individual, familial, and systemic functional hypotheses regarding OCSs, and with the basic available family interventions in mind, three final case examples are provided to demonstrate systematic application of the various possible combinations of these elements in clinical practice. In contrast to the usual procedure, this summary will therefore not be based on an abstract comprehension of detailed clinical or research material. Rather, it provides a practice-oriented comprehension of the application of multiple, complex concepts by detailed case descriptions.

Treatment of a family with a child as the identified OCP is fairly easy as long as there are no major primary deficits in the parents and both mainly suffer from a breakdown in marital communication (see case 7 below). If there are additional individual deficits in one or both parents, treatment may become more complicated and less successful (case 8 below). The most difficult family unit to treat is one in which both family problems and severe OCSs have coexisted for a very long period of time (case 4 continued.)

Case 7

The identified patient was the 7-year-old son. He displayed OCSs ("magical" checking, touching, counting, and covert speaking of magical words) at age 3 for about 1 year; OCSs reappeared 6 months before the family sought help. The son lived with both parents at home.

The following hypotheses were developed from family and individual interviews. The main family problem was a severe marital tension with a hidden contract between parents to avoid open communication about the wife's desire to leave marriage. Symptoms in parents included the following: the wife showed severe depression and sexual withdrawal; the husband showed regular, though moderate, long-term use of alcohol in the evenings; both spouses showed signs of severe but still "normal" OCBs or obsessionality. Acting as a parent, the son tried to relieve mother's depression by sticking close to her and keeping her busy with his symptomatology. Additionally, OCSs for the son had the intraindividual function of a coping response (by magical rituals), with his own increasing anxiety and insecurity resulting from confrontation with mother's depression and from the lack of affection between his parents, which severely threatened the existence of the family. Son responded similarly to his father, who, under professional and interactional stress, showed increased OCBs (collecting and ruminating).

The treatment plan included treatment interventions with the parents only. There was separation of two treatment areas: parental role behavior and the marital relationship. Both parents showed clear motivation to improve parental behavior and, at the beginning, marital interaction. They accepted the interpretation that their son had acted as a parent, managing to bring both child-parents into the badly needed treatment.

The treatment goals were as follows: On the parental level, both were jointly to replace the child on the child level and to resist his initial protest behaviors against such a move. They were to accept that successful joint parental efforts gave no "rights" on the marital level.

On the marital level, the couple was trained in risk-taking communication regarding the marital problems. They were to accept the risk that marital counseling might lead to improvement of marriage (not the initial aim of the wife) or to its termination (not the initial aim of the husband). Motivation to accept these opposite risks resulting from opposite marital goals was due to joint willingness to reduce the son's suffering from their marital indecisiveness.

In this context, the parents were also to accept their own symptom behaviors as indicators of mistakes in daily conduct; the sexual withdrawal of the wife and the regular use of alcohol by the husband in the evening were directly linked. The couple were to follow a new therapist-induced communication style that was designed with the intention of using their obsessionality to induce change. Every day, one is to tell the other for 1 hour how he or she experiences reality in the marriage. The listener was to learn not to feel hurt but to stay curious and to respond only on the following day when given his or her opportunity to express personal reality.

The treatment effects over five sessions were as follows: The wife experienced immediate relief and decrease of her depression since her fantasies of leaving her husband were out in the open. She felt she had gotten back choices for future conduct of her life. The husband concommittantly developed increasing depression after his initial "shock" about the extent of his wife's inner withdrawal. In spite of this shift of depression from wife to husband, a variety of important changes occurred. The couple jointly reported a substantial increase in mutual understanding resulting from the communication exercises in the evenings. The husband stopped drinking completely a couple of days after abstinence had been suggested as an experiment to find out how it might affect family life. Between sessions 4 and 5 (at 3-week intervals) the couple had taken up sexual intercourse again for the first time in years (without any direct interventions in this area in treatment) and had repeated this interaction with mutual satisfaction. The wife felt generally much freer to respond positively to the husband, which was clearly appreciated by him. In spite of all these improvements, which were also described by the husband, the husband's depression and anxiety with regard to the potential breakdown of the marriage seemed to remain. Yet he fully agreed with treatment aims and the family development since its start.

The son showed a severe reduction in OCSs after the second treatment session and greatly increased his peer contacts outside home without any pushing from his parents. This was interpreted to the parents as a consequence of him having realized that responsibility for the parents was taken over by the therapists and that since the beginning of treatment mother's depression had lifted almost completely. The parents were no longer worried about the son's health, and they gradually forgot the threat of a child psychoanalyst that the son would need daily analysis for a couple of years.

About 90% of treatment time was devoted to marital problems, training of open communication, and mutual listening rather than defending. Parental training needed little attention after both had accepted the family model of the son's OCSs. Separation of marital and parental problems enabled the parents to use their originally existing parental skills quickly.

Case 8

The identified patient was the 15-year-old son. His multiple, somewhat bizarre OCSs had started around age 13. He developed a complex system of "good" and "bad" motor and cognitive-verbal behaviors, believed to indicate or prevent disasters. He largely restricted his food intake to a rare, difficult to buy fish and insisted on being fed by mother in a highly ritualized manner. Parents were allowed to talk to each other only in his presence, using a very restricted vocabulary regarding restricted topics, controlled by him. Mother and father were separately to conduct specific cleaning and checking rituals under his supervision (usually from his preferred recliner), he claiming to be too sick to do his rituals himself. In other areas he "regressed" to the behavioral level of a 2-year-old boy: He stopped washing and dressing himself and frequently urinated and defecated into his bed at night, forcing mother to get up to clean him. He explained these behaviors as due to certain obsessions that would not allow him to behave differently. Within half a year, he was unable to go to school. Since then, he had been housebound and alone while his parents were at work and extremely close to his mother when parents were at home. The symptoms started when his father had had an intimate relationship with a female neighbor and threatened to leave the family. When the son got "very sick," the father separated from his girlfriend.

The following hypotheses were developed after family and individual interviews: The function of the OCSs for the son was to cope with a threat of a breakdown of the family. This threat arose when the patient had entered puberty and realized that, since his very few friends had started dating girls and not seeing him anymore, he had to face growing isolation. His social deficits—resulting from a single-child role and a family atmosphere characterized by the obsessional–depressive interaction styles of his unhappily married parents—severely impaired his capacity to relate to the opposite sex. The initial "coping" response—in a vicious circle feedback loop—resulted in more pathology; the total loss of peer contacts and the now exclusive relationship with his unhappy parents increased his social deficits and reinforced his strong OCSs.

For the mother, the son's illness brought her husband back into the home, though not into the family or marriage. The mother's emotional needs then became entirely served by devoted care to her increasingly sick child; she "had to" cook strange meals of only very rare fish and vegetables; she "had to" provide sexual education, for instance, by reading to the son from pornographic journals; she "had to" get up at night from her connubial bed (with open doors to son's sleeping room), where no sex had happened for years, to follow the son's demands to be cleaned when he had urinated or defecated in his bed. The mother complained about these demanding tasks, but she had never seriously tried not to do them, even when husband or relatives had tried to stop her. She also refused discussion of her primary deficits or problems.

The father felt lost in a "responsibility trap." He failed to respond to his son's challenges (who finally even tried to provoke him by sexual closeness to the mother) to be a "strong," responsible husband and father. Yet he kept feeling responsible for his son and was trapped by the belief that he could only help the son by staying with his wife. Thus, with sad resignation, he stayed in the family, waiting for the day when the son would be sane again and he could run away.

The son's falling ill saved family from being left by the father. The son's staying ill prevented possible repetitions of the father's escape attempt. The chronically unhappy marriage deteriorated constantly, and the son's illness got increasingly worse. For the initial function of saving the family, the son had to pay an increasing price when his behavior turned against him by severely increasing his social deficits—making him even more dependent on the further existence of the family. This dependence increased his irritation and anxiety, and he totally dominated his parents with his symptoms. He forced them to talk and to move according to the laws of his OCSs—he even forced them to carry out his rituals, while he gave instructions from a wheelchair. Through this behavior, he did not leave his parents any time to talk or act out or improve their marital or individual problems.

Finally, the family was characterized by deep distrust among its three members, hidden aggression between the parents, and a total lack of open communication. The illness in each of the family members had developed self-reinforcing properties and kept all three together and possibly even alive.

A long-term multimodal treatment plan appeared necessary. When the parents had first contacted us, they had already tried various individual treatments for the son elsewhere. We insisted on initial family therapy, thereafter splitting the family for marital treatment of the parents and peer group treatment for the son. The son immediately was excited about the idea of family therapy, whereas it took the parents 1 year to accept this. During this year, they made several attempts to force us and other therapists to try yet another individual treatment of the son. Eventually, they accepted our offer and the son supported us by self-induced, far-reaching changes in his OCBs in order to enable outpatient family treatment. He stopped urinating and defecating in his bed at night, and for the first time in a year he agreed to have his long hair washed and cut and to leave home with his parents in order to come to the outpatient sessions. The parents felt very insecure about these unexpected changes.

Since the OCSs, almost like a spiritual power, had controlled the otherwise chaotic family interactions, we wanted to replace them initially with therapist control over family interaction. We had gained trust of the son during the 1-year waiting period, and we eventually won the power struggle with the parents regarding family treatment. We had gained some trust from the parents when, to their great surprise, the son reduced his OCSs dramatically at the beginning of treatment. This seemed a sufficient precondition to get each family member to accept our claim for control over family communication for a limited period of time.

Training of new communication rules was started with the exchange of "behavioral presents" among the individual family members. We purposely avoided "reciprocity counseling" (Stuart, 1980), as this is poison to obsessive-compulsive families; reciprocity counseling would result in endless debates among family members as well as between family and therapists with regard to the "fairness" of the exchange of behavioral presents (see similar criticism of reciprocity counseling by Jacobson, 1984). We demanded the right to decide whether each individual's behavioral presents to the others were acceptable or not. Previously, family communication had been governed by the rule "demand a lot to get a little." Each member was to learn that "one gets by giving and not by demanding." When this communication "game" was accepted and started to work, we additionally introduced couple sessions for the parents. Through these, we also tested our hypothesis that the son wanted to get rid of his responsibility for the parents' marriage; if we were right, the son would respond to the additional marital therapy by another clear reduction of his OCSs, which did occur.

Only thereafter did we apply a few individual and family sessions of exposure *in vivo* for the OCSs. However, the major amount of symptom reduction had already occurred during the previous treatment sessions, which did not deal with this symptomatology!

The multimodal approach, though including few and simple interventions in an apparent chaos of multiple problems, led to the establishment of new marital behaviors of the parents (except for sexual contact). The son's symptomatology was lowered to such an extent that after 3 years of a housebound life he went back to school, got his driving license, and started dating girls his age. All this took 1 year; treatment started with sessions once a week, decreasing in frequency to monthly and bimonthly intervals.

Unfortunately, the son always refused to participate in the final intervention that we had planned for him—peer group therapy for his primary social deficits and their symptomatic pseudocompensation by anancastic interaction. Without such treatment, we had predicted gradual relapse because of his primary social deficits and their increase resulting from peer isolation during the years of puberty. He would almost have to get into trouble when peer contacts at school or contacts with girls became closer.

The son managed to go to school for about a year after termination of treatment. Then gradual relapse started, first with OCSs in the son, which were soon accompanied by the mother's escape from her reestablished marital behaviors to help the son again. Another year later, the old interaction scheme was reestablished in the family. Had the son joined the peer communication training group and eventually become independent of his parents, they would probably have had to work out a mode of separation, with subsequent individual help for each of them and their deficits.

Case 4 Continued

In case 4, it was already demonstrated how OCSs can serve to express chronic anger and hate in a relationship that both spouses are unable to break up. Exposure and family therapy of this patient are particularly suited to demonstrate how powerful and dangerous intervention techniques can be if change is not really wanted by the treatment-complaint patient.

This patient, with excessive dirt-phobic cleaning rituals in her apartment, had stopped using her phone—her last communication link to the outer world (apart from her husband and one daughter who lived with her). This was to avoid contamination with the dirt that she thought would be there after her daughter had used the phone.

In exposure, when asked to touch the phone, she hesitated more than with other objects in the flat, asking the therapist, "Are you aware that I had a psychotic breakdown 15 years ago?" Only when the therapist had asked back, "Do you really want me to get as scared as you seem to be?" did she reluctantly start this particular exposure exercise. While touching her ear and her hair with the phone, she initially reported fearfulness, then anger, and finally hate. Accompanying cognitions at this point were thoughts about her youngest daughter. First, the patient didn't know how to link the feelings of hate with the thoughts about her daughter; this particular daughter was the only person in her entire life that she had felt close to over the past 15 years. In extended exposure, the patient then recalled her most traumatic family event 15 years ago, when she had developed psychotic jealousy. For the first time in many years, she now remembered that almost worse than the assumed infidelity of her husband had been the experience that her then 6-year-old daughter, her favorite child, had not taken her part in the marital war but had continued to express her love for her father. In later years, she had suppressed her deep disappointment about this daughter to save the illusion that there was one stable, trusting relationship in her life. Only in exposure to the phone did she realize this illusion. She immediately felt sad, at the same time losing her problems with the phone completely. She apparently accepted subsequent exposure to the reality of the mother–daughter relationship in an intense prolonged treatment session with mother and daughter. Proposition of such intense family intervention in the very situation in which the family conflict had been uncovered proved a therapeutic mistake, resulting from insufficient exploration of the patient's "real" motivation for such a painful step.

Real-life exposure to the hidden mother–daughter conflict induced a highly emotional interaction between mother and daughter—including tears and exchange of resentment, aggression, disillusionment. After two sessions, the mother–daughter confrontation had to be stopped, when the patient developed clinical signs of rheumatoid arthritis in her knees. She went to the hospital, but even with the most sophisticated laboratory investigations, the clinical diagnosis could not be confirmed. It was nevertheless decided to try antibiotic treatment. The patient responded with an immediate allergy to the medication. Eventually, she was discharged with the clinical symptoms unchanged. She was then offered long-term interruption of the behavior therapy—which she gladly accepted.

Some 8 months later, we learned that the patient had made great improvement; she had stopped most of the excessive cleaning rituals in the flat—not because of behavior therapy but because of the involuntary "response prevention" of her arthritis, which hindered her from moving around in her home (this being her personal explanation). Then the arthritis miraculously improved, without the OCSs increasing. The patient then persuaded her husband to join a dancing class with her (after 15 years of OCS-induced confinement to the flat). Her expressed reason for this was not an attempt to improve marriage; instead, she wanted to exercise her knees so that they would regain full functioning.

With this development, from the therapist's point of view, the patient, who had always been treatment-compliant, proved that the aims of therapy had been correct. However, the speed of confrontation with the family conflict—accidentally uncovered by exposure for rituals—had been too fast. When left alone, the patient continued her treatment at her own speed.

This extremely vulnerable patient, with her totally dependent husband, had responded over 15 years to interactional traumata with acute psychosis, followed by chronic, severe neurotic symptomatology. Later the patient evidenced painful psychosomatic complaints when the OCSs were reduced and a traumatic past experience was uncovered. Nevertheless, short-term behavior therapy seemed to have induced changes on relevant levels, and the patient continued treatment at her own speed with limited goals to make life a little more enjoyable.

Had the accidental Trojan horse intervention not happened, a much slower paced treatment would have included interventions to improve the severe individual deficits in both spouses.

CONCLUSION

We are only in the beginning of a systematic integration of family- and systems-oriented interventions into a general strategy of behavior therapy. Among the neurotic disorders, application of such strategic–systemic interventions appears very difficult and at the same time very needed in the area of OCSs—especially with regard to the as yet unsatisfactory global outcomes of more individually centered interventions like exposure *in vivo*.

On the other hand, we have to be careful not to throw out the baby with the bathwater. As our own data show (Hand and Sauke, 1985), for the majority of the OCPs in a clinical outpatient setting, exposure-based treatment still remains the "treatment of choice." Exposure *in vivo* also remains an essential element in a variety of family-centered behavioral treatments, mainly in patients who fail to respond to exposure alone or who show a clear indication that family or couple intervention is essential and sufficient.

We hope soon to be able to delineate predictors for treatment outcome with the application of symptom- and/or family-directed modes of treatment. We feel currently that, in families where (nonpsychotic and nonorganic) OCSs occur in a child, only the parents need individual or couple treatment.

We conceive exposure *in vivo* (to trigger 1) as a technique to induce internal cognitive–emotional–physiological response sets, which are the essential trigger (trigger 2) for motor, cognitive, or emotional avoidance or undoing. Thus, exposure *in vivo* is assumed to work by exposure to and tolerance of trigger 2, for which coping (management) srategies then need to be taught. In such a concept, one can apply identical exposure principles to compulsions and obsessions. Such an integrative concept also avoids the academic dispute on the nature of behavioral versus cognitive-behavioral treatments.

The various possible intraindividual and interactional functions of OCSs need to be analyzed for any individual patient and to be integrated into all treatment steps, including the application of exposure. The frequent interactional vulnerability of OCPs—with the difficult pseudocompensation by an anancastic interaction style—is a decisive variable in most individual as well as in systems-oriented interventions.

NOTE

1. The term *anancastic* is used in European psychopathology for OC *trait* variables, being separated from OC *state* variables.

REFERENCES

Anderson, C., Reiss, D., & Hogarty, G. (1986). *Schizophrenia and the family*. New York: Guilford Press.

Beech, H. (1974). (Ed.). *Obsessional states*. London: Methuen.

Donath, J. (1897). Zur Kenntnis des Anankasmus (psychische Zwangszustände). *Archiv für Psychiatrie und Nervenkrankheiten, 29*, 211–224.

Erikson, E. (1978). *Toys and reasons: Stages in the ritualization of experience*. London: Marion Boyars.

Foa, E., Steketee, G., Grayson, J., & Doppelt, H. (1983). Treatment of obsessive-compulsives: When do we fail? In E. Foa & P. Emmelkamp (Eds.), *Failures in behavior therapy*. New York: Wiley & Sons.

Friesen, J. (1985). *Structural-strategic marriage and family therapy*. New York: Gardner Press.

Hafner, R. (1986). *Marriage and mental illness: A sex roles perspective*. New York: Guilford Press.

Haley, J. (1971). (Ed.). *Changing families*. New York: Grune & Stratton.

Hand, I. (1981). Motivationsanalyse und Motivationsmodifikation im Erstkontakt. In B. Crombach-Seeger (Ed.), *Erstkontakt—prägender Beginn einer Entwicklung*. Wien: Facultas. (a)

Hand, I. (1981). Symptomverschreibung: Negative Übungen, negative Praxis, paradoxe Intention. In M. Linden & M. Hautzinger (Eds.), *Psychoterapie-Manual*. Berlin, Heidelberg, New York: Springer/Verlag. (b)

Hand, I. (1981). Expositions behandlung. In M. Linden & M. Hautzinger (Eds.), Psychotherapie-Manual. Berlin, Heidelberg, New York: Springer/Verlag. (c)

Hand, I. (1986). Verhaltenstherapie und kognitive Therapie in der Psychiatrie. In K. Kisker, H. Lauter, J. Meyer, C. Müller, & E. Strömgren (Eds.), *Psychiatrie der Gegenwart* (Bd. 1). Berlin, Heidelberg, New York: Springer. (a)

Hand, I. (1986). Spielen, Glücksspielen, krankhaftes Spielen ("Spielsucht"). In D. Korczak (Ed.), *Die betäubte Gesellschaft*. Frankfurt: Fischer Taschenbuch. (b)

Hand, I., Angenendt, J., Fischer, M., & Wilke, C. (1986). Exposure *in vivo* with panic management for agoraphobia: Treatment rationale and long term outcome. In I. Hand & H. V. Wittchen (Eds.), *Panic and Phobias: Empirical evidence of theoretical models and long-term effects of behavioral treatments*. Berlin: Springer/Verlag.

Hand, I., Lamontagne, Y., Marks, I. (1974). Group exposure (flooding) *in vivo* for agoraphobics. *British Journal of Psychiatry, 124*: 588–602.

Hand, I., & Sauke, G. (1985). *Exposure in vivo versus problem solving in behavior therapy of obsessive-compulsive disorders*. Presented at the 15th Annual Meeting of the European Association for Behavior Therapy Congress, Munich.

Hand, I., Spoehring, B., & Stanik, E. (1977). Treatment of obsessions, compulsions, and phobias as hidden couple counseling. In J. Boulougouris & A. Rabavilas (Eds.), *Phobic and obsessive-compulsive disorders*. New York: Pergamon Press.

Hand, I., & Tichatzki, M. (1978). Behavioral group therapy for obsessions and compulsions. In P. Sjöden, S. Bates, & W. Dockens (Eds.), *Trends in behavior therapy*. New York: Academic Press.

Hand, I., & Zaworka, W. (1982). An operationalized multisymptomatic model of neuroses (OMMON): Toward a reintegration of diagnosis and treatment in behavior therapy. *Archiv fur Psychiatrie und Nervenfrankheiten, 232*, 259–279.

Jacobson, N. (1984). Clinical innovations in behavioral marital therapy. In K. Craig & R. McMahon (Ed.), *Advances in clinical behavior therapy*. New York: Brunner/Mazel.

Jenike, M., Baer, L., & Minichiello, W. (1986). (Eds.). *Obsessive-compulsive disorders*. Littleton, MA: PSG Publishing.

Marks, I. (1987). *Fears, phobias, and rituals*. New York/Oxford: Oxford University Press.

Mathews, A., Teasdale, J., Munby, M., Johnston, D., & Shaw, P. (1977). A home based treatment program for agoraphobia. *Behavior Therapy, 8*, 915–924.

Mavissakalian, M., Turner, S., Michelson, L., & Jacob, R. (1985). Tricyclic antidepressants in obsessive-compulsive disorder: Antiobsessional or antidepressant agents? II. *American Journal of Psychiatry, 142*, 572–576. (a)

Mavissakalian, M., Turner, S., & Michelson, L. (1985). *Obsessive compulsive disorder: Psychological and pharmacological treatment*. New York, London: Plenum Press. (b)

Nagera, H. (1976). *Obsessional neurosis*. New York: Jason Aaronson.

Rachman, S. (1983). Obstacles to the successful treatment of obsessions. In E. Foa & P. Emmelkamp (Eds.), *Failures in behavior therapy*. New York: Wiley & Sons.

Rachman, S., & Hodgson, R. (1980). *Obsessions and compulsions*. Englewood Cliffs, NJ: Prentice-Hall.

Reed, G. (1985). *Obsessional experience and compulsive behavior: A cognitive-structural approach*. New York: Academic Press.

Selvini Palazzoli, M., Boscolo, L., Cecchin, G., & Prata, G. (1977). Family rituals: A powerful tool in family therapy. *Family Process, 16*, 445–453.

Stuart, R. (1980). *Helping couples change*. New York: Guilford Press.

Wynne, L., McDaniel, S., & Weber, T. (1986). *Systems consultation: A new perspective for family therapy*. New York: Guilford Press.

Yaryura-Tobias, J., & Neziroglu, F. (1983). *Obsessive-compulsive disorders: Pathogenesis, diagnosis, treatment*. New York: Marcel Dekker.

Zaworka, W., & Hand, I. (1981). Ein individuelles Verlaufs- und Indikationsmodell (IVIM) für (zwangs-) neurotische Symptombildungen. In U. Baumann (Ed.), *Indikation zur Psychotherapie*. München, Wien, Baltimore: Urban & Schwarzenberg.

Zaworka, W., Hand, I., Jauernig, G., & Lünenschloss, K. (1983). *Das Hamburger Zwangsinventar, HZI*. Weinhelm: Beltz Verlag. (Hamburg Obsessive-Compulsive Inventory, HOCL; English translation available from I. Hand.)

11

Behavioral Marital Therapy in the Treatment of Depressive Disorders

WILLIAM C. FOLLETTE
Memphis State University
NEIL S. JACOBSON
University of Washington

Until recently, depressive disorders have been treated primarily using individual therapy. The depressed client presents for therapy or someone close to the patient facilitates the initial contact with the therapist. From that point forward, the depressed client and the therapist are left to their own devices to resolve the depression. The people with whom the depressed client most commonly interacts are not included in therapy. For many clients, this approach is relatively successful. The treatment outcome literature to date has provided evidence for the efficacy of several treatment approaches based on individual therapy strategies. These include pharmacotherapy and psychotherapy (e.g., Bellack, Hersen & Himmelhoch, 1983; Kovacs, 1980; Kovacs, Rush, Beck, & Hollon, 1981; Weissman, Prusoff, DiMascio, Neu, Goklaney, & Klerman, 1979; also see Steinbrueck, Maxwell, & Howard, 1983).

But not everyone responds to treatment. For those who do respond, recurrence of episodes of depression is common (Kovacs, *et al.*, 1981; Rush, Beck, Kovacs, & Hollon, 1977). For some individuals, we may be overlooking important factors in the acquisition, maintenance, and resolution of depression. Until recently, interpersonal, social, and relationship factors seem to have been overlooked.

But now there is a growing interest in the importance of these factors. Strong arguments have been made stating that the social interactions of the depressed person act to maintain depression. It has been suggested that interactions with a depressed individual are aversive and that the interacter's negative reaction is subtly communicated to the depressed person, thus exacerbating the depression (Coyne, 1976a, 1976b). Lewinsohn (1974) has described how people can inadvertently reinforce depressive behaviors when they interact with someone who is depressed.

Only recently have researchers begun to rethink how therapy could best address the social and interpersonal factors related to depression. Several investigators are examining the importance of involving family members in the actual therapy with the depressed patient (Beach & O'Leary, 1986; Coyne, 1984; Jacobson, 1984a; Rounsaville, Klerman, Weissman, Chevron, & Merikangas, 1983). One particular aspect of the social network that has received particular attention is the marital relationship of the depressed patient.

It is easy to understand why the marital relationship is becoming a focus of treatment in depression. There are some cases where the marital relationship is apparently the direct cause of depression. In other cases, the marital relationship may have become distressed as a result of the depressive episode, and the distressed relationship may maintain the depression in a variety of ways.

The spouse is obviously an important part of the depressed person's social environment. During conjoint therapy, couples are likely to emit specific instances of clinically relevant behaviors that cause or maintain depressed mood or interpersonal discord. The therapist can directly observe these interactions and functionally analyze the variables controlling or moderating the depression. Interventions that focus on behaviors that occur naturally during therapy can often be extraordinarily useful (Kohlenberg & Tsai, 1987).

Marriage *per se* seems to offer some protection against depression for men but not for women (Weissman & Klerman, 1977). However, women who describe the presence of an intimate and confiding relationship with a male partner do appear to show a decreased vulnerability to depression (Brown & Harris, 1978). For many depressed women, marriage does not protect against depression. In fact, the marriage may be a major factor in the onset of depression. If it is true that confiding, intimate relationships, but not marriage in general, help decrease the incidence of depression, then trying to improve the marital relationship seems most appropriate. Such an intervention might well reduce the recurrence of depressive episodes.

Several studies provide evidence that depression and marital conflict can and do occur simultaneously. Investigators looking primarily at marital distress have noted high rates of concomitant depressive symptoms (e.g., Beach, Jouriles, & O'Leary, 1985). Likewise, investigators focusing on depression have noted similar high rates of marital distress in depressed subjects (e.g., Rounsaville, Weisman, Prusoff, & Herceg-Baron, 1979). Marital conflict can persist even after the episode of depression has ended (Bothwell & Weissman, 1977; Hinchcliffe, Hooper, & Roberts, 1978; Rounsaville *et al.*, 1979). Other studies have suggested that in those instances where marital conflict exists, the prognosis for sustained resolution of the depression is poorer (Klerman & Weissman, 1982; Rounsaville &

Chevron, 1982). Briscoe and Smith (1973) provided evidence suggesting that one possible consequence of depression is divorce. It would certainly be desirable to reduce the likelihood of subsequent divorce by increasing marital satisfaction and thereby reducing the stress that accompanies divorce.

This chapter outlines the rationale for a marital intervention for the treatment of depression and the marital distress that may have either resulted from or contributed to the depression. When we talk about depression in this chapter, we are referring to major depressive episodes as defined in DSM-IIIR (APA, 1987). The clinical experience we refer to is based on a study currently in progress in which female subjects are thoroughly screened to meet this diagnostic category. We focus on depressed women for three basic reasons. First, the prevalence of depression in females is estimated to be approximately twice that of males (Boyd & Weissman, 1981; Robins, Helzer, Weissman, Orvaschel, Gruenberg, Burke, & Regier, 1984; Weissman & Klerman, 1977), and, as we mentioned above, the marriage itself may be one of the causes of depression in women. Second, much of the empirical research studying depression within the marital context has used subjects where the wife was the member of the dyad who was depressed. Third, we have begun an outcome study using behavioral marital therapy and cognitive therapy for the treatment of women with major depression. Some of ideas presented here come from our clinical experience on this project.

For the reasons stated above, we will present our clinical examples with the wife as the identified client. Using sex-specific pronouns makes the clinical discussion less awkward and easier to understand. However, we have no reason to think that the therapy presented in this chapter would not be effective for a wide variety of cases including those when the husband is the identified client, or both spouses are wage-earners, students, geriatrics, or when partners are the same sex. Certainly the specific issues would change as demographic features changed, but the basic techniques would still be applicable. These are empirical questions that should be answered through clinical research.

Most behavioral formulations of depression relate the affective experience of depression to some sort of extinction phenomenon or shift in reinforcement contingencies. Skinner (1953) recognized that the social environment was the primary mediator of positive reinforcement and that disruption of this reinforcement could lead to depression. Ferster (1965, 1973) suggested that there might be a significant degree of punishment or aversive control in the environment of the depressed person. He speculated that someone who was depressed could be quite passive with respect to his or her social environment, frequently failing to act in ways that would alter the environment to increase reinforcers or decrease aversive stimuli.

Lewinsohn (1974) pointed to the importance of social contingencies in the maintenance of depressive behaviors. By at first supplying sympathy and concern when depressive behaviors are emitted and then by avoiding aversive interactions with the depressed person, people close to the depressed person strengthen and maintain depression. Given the evidence of the reciprocal influence the depressed person and persons around the depressed person have on one another, a therapy for depression that focuses on the interpersonal and social environment of the depressed person may facilitate improvement while reducing the likelihood of relapse. Since so much of a married person's social and reinforcement (including punishment) environment centers around the home and marriage, it makes sense to treat the depression within the context of the marital relationship.

TREATMENT

Introducing Conjoint Treatment

Often, the depressed woman comes to therapy alone. Sometimes husbands bring in their depressed wives (Vaughn & Leff, 1976). In either case, the problem is usually labeled as depression. Little or nothing is said about the effects of the depressive behavior on the relationship, nor is much said about how the relationship contributes to the onset or maintenance of the depression.

The first task is to present treatment as a joint undertaking. There are two main obstacles to overcome. The first problem is to get the nondepressed husband to participate in treatment. The common inclination is for him to believe that the problem rests solely with his wife and that everything will be all right once the depression is cured. The therapist must present treatment in a way that allows the husband to participate without feeling that he is being blamed for the depression. A nonthreatening rationale that justifies the inclusion of the husband must be provided. The rationale depends on the individual features of the couple. When marital distress exists, is openly acknowledged by both spouses, and is one of the presenting complaints, it is usually easy to justify the participation of the husband. At other times, we emphasize the social support function of marital relationships in helping depressed people recover and refer to the relationship-enhancing aspect of our program as a means of facilitating improvement.

The specific form of this rationale varies from couple to couple. At times we use a social learning explanation that emphasizes the relationship between depression and existing contingencies in the environment. The paucity of reinforcers experienced by depressed people may reflect an actual scarcity in the environment (MacPhillamy & Lewinsohn, 1973) or, in some cases, the depressed person is unable to recall them accurately when they do occur (DeMonbreun & Craighead, 1977; Nelson & Craighead, 1977). In either event, the benefit gained from the cooperation of the husband in using the relationship as a springboard for increasing pleasant events is made apparent.

At other times, we emphasize the difficulties that nondepressed spouses have coping with the depressive behavior of a partner. We explain how depression can create frustration, resentment, and marital discord, which in turn exacerbates the depression (Coyne, 1976a). Typically, even when husbands deny the existence of marital discord, they admit to frustration at their inability to help. At times, they are even willing to admit to the anger and resentment that often colors the intimate relationships of depressed people.

A third rationale emphasizes the families' preoccupation with the depression. We explain that, quite often, family interaction is restructured in such a way that the depression becomes the center of activity. This preoccupation with the depression can easily serve to reinforce the depression. Thus, a vicious cycle is created in which preoccupation leads to more depression, which in turn leads to even more preoccupation. We often explain to couples that the depression has led them to "forget about having a relationship." When marital therapy can shift attention to the business of enhancing the marriage and away from the depressive episode *per se*, the cycle is broken.

Once the husband has agreed to participate, the second problem with conjoint therapy for depression must be addressed. This is the problem of developing a collaborative set where the therapist and the couple work on all aspects of the problem without the husband and therapist forming an alliance to make the wife feel inferior and powerless. This is especially difficult when doing conjoint therapy for depression. The depressed patient is usually willing to define herself as "defective." This is part of the negative self-perception experienced by depressed individuals. The idea that the patient is defective is frequently supported by the spouse so that he does not have to feel responsible for his partner's depression.

The therapist deals with this problem throughout therapy. There is no standard solution to it, nor is it a problem for all depressed couples. If both partners are complaining of marital problems in addition to depression, a formulation of their situation that emphasizes reciprocal responsibility is much less of a problem than in those instances where one or both spouses insist that the only problem is the wife's depression. Generally, we do not attempt to force-feed a dyadic rationale on spouses who resist such a presentation. To impose such a conceptual framework onto skeptical couples would probably meet with resistance and perhaps even result in the couple dropping out of therapy. Instead, we have found any one of a number of alternative rationales to be more benign: for instance, using the notion that the husband is a valuable resource whose social support can help fight the depression; emphasizing how the depression effects the relationship rather than vice versa; and using the idea that the husband can learn more effective ways to cope with his wife's depression by coming to therapy. We believe that all of these justifications may be true.

We do not try to enlist the cooperation of the clients by providing a convenient rationale for treatment. In fact, we present those justifications for doing conjoint therapy that we believe have empirical or clinical support. There are circumstances in which the justification for conjoint, maritally focused therapy becomes obvious to the depressed woman and her spouse even if they were not obvious initially. It has been our experience that if individual cognitive therapy sessions with the depressed spouse alone dominate the early stages of therapy, the marriage often deteriorates as the wife's depression lifts. As the wife becomes less depressed, she becomes angrier at her husband. For many couples, this intermediate stage of marital distress forms a natural transition into making the marriage the primary treatment focus. The denial of marital distress becomes more difficult to maintain as the conflict becomes more overt. Not all couples are initially willing to accept the need for or the desirability of marital therapy in the treatment of depression. For many depressed couples, it almost seems as if the marital problems must become more pronounced before marital therapy can be used effectively.

Assessment

A detailed discussion of the assessment of depression in the context of marital and family therapy is beyond the scope of this chapter. However, we briefly describe some of the procedures that are helpful in conducting therapy and engaging the dyad in the treatment program. Because the assessment procedures can be cumbersome, it is important for the therapist to explain the rationale for each instrument and make use of the instruments during the course of therapy. Different considerations apply to therapy conducted in a research setting.

Both members of the dyad should be assessed for depression. The severity of depressive symptoms can be assessed using the Hamilton Rating Scale for Depression (Hamilton, 1967). Standardized clinical interviews such as the NIMH Diagnostic Interview Schedule or the Schedule for Affective Disorders and Schizophrenia can be used to determine whether or not clients meet research diagnostic criteria or DSM-III criteria for depression if such information is required. Beyond that, some quantifiable instrument that assesses the current severity of depression should be administered prior to every session. Most of the self-report inventories for depression can be used, with each having advantages and disadvantages. For a more complete discussion of the assessment of depression and related issues, see Lambert, Hatch, Kingston, & Edwards (1986) or Mayer (1977). The Beck Depression Inventory (BDI; Beck, 1978), the Zung Self-Rating Depression Scale (SDS; Zung, 1965), and the Center for Epidemiological Studies Depression Scale (CES-D; Radloff, 1977) are easily administered and scored and are face valid. Both members of the dyad should fill out the depression scale.

The status of the marital relationship should be assessed at the beginning, in the middle, and at the end of treatment. This can easily be done with the Dyadic Adjustment Scale (DAS; Spanier, 1976) or the Marital Adjustment Scale (MAS; Locke & Wallace, 1959). Both scales are short and easy to score with well established norms and discriminant validity. We favor the DAS because of its slightly better psychometric properties but the correlation between the two instruments is approximately 0.85.

Prior to therapy, conducting a communication assessment is useful. There is evidence that communication patterns involving depressed subjects may be a factor in maintaining depression. Linden, Hautzinger, and Hoffman (1983) suggested that depressed persons emit higher rates of statements of negative well-being along with statements of negative views of the self and the future during conversation. Hinchcliffe, Hooper, and Roberts (1978) also noted negative nonverbal behaviors in dyads with a depressed spouse. We have observed that during unstructured conversations between couples where one partner is depressed, the discussion quickly focuses on the depression.

We suggest that couples be given the task of talking about their day for 10 min. while being videotaped. For instance, the husband is instructed to begin the conversation by asking the wife "How was your day?" This process can be repeated at the end of therapy. This serves a number of purposes. The behavioral sample can be used to determine the extent to which depressive or hostile interactions pervade the relationship. The tape can be played to the couple to show that even though the depression might be considered to affect only the wife, in fact, it clearly affects each partner. Finally, the "How was your day?" interaction provides a window into patterns of power and dominance in the relationship (Jacobson & Holtzworth-Munroe, 1986). Many depressed couples have extremely skewed conversations, in which the husband demonstrates dominance by not listening to his wife and/or by focusing on himself for the bulk of the conversation.

We also have couples discuss and come to an agreement about a problem area in their relationship. From this the level of conflict resolution skill in both spouses can be assessed. Conflict-resolution discussions also reveal the extent to which depressive behavior leads to concessions from the husband and the degree of hostility he expresses. Research by Biglan *et al.* (1985) found several differences between depressed and nondepressed couples while they engaged in problem-solving tasks. This work suggested that problem-solving when the wife was depressed had unique features. The depressed wives tended to emit depressive behaviors, which resulted in a reduction of aversive behavior shown by their partners. Such couples also tended to exhibit less self-disclosure than nondepressed couples and wives emitted fewer actual problem-solving behaviors.

Perhaps one of the more important aspects of the assessment process for the conjoint treatment of depression is a behavioral assessment of shared activities. For this purpose, a modified version of the Spouse Observation Checklist (SOC; Patterson, 1976; Weiss & Perry, 1983) is useful. This 408-item list of activities represents a large sample of behaviors that each spouse can emit either alone or together. A shortened, individualized version has been proposed and validated (Atkinson & McKenzie, 1984; Follette, Jacobson, & Follette, 1984), so that the SOC contains only relevant items for the couple. Each person keeps this daily log for the first 2 weeks of therapy. Each event that occurs is noted along with whether that event was positive, neutral, or negative in impact. At the end of each day, after the SOC is completed, the observer rates his or her daily satisfaction with self, satisfaction with the relationship, and daily mood ratings on nine-point scales. Other informal questionnaires that sample the same domain of behaviors but have a shorter format seemly likely to be useful as well.

The information gathered through these methods is used in the behavior-exchange component of treatment described below. The daily satisfaction ratings and mood ratings are plotted against the number of positive and negative behaviors that occurred each day. This has many uses. By the time couples enter treatment, they may feel quite hopeless about affecting the depression or their own relationship with each other. The inability to detect the relationship between behaviors and mood or satisfaction is seen in distressed marriages. The sense of powerlessness and lack of control is a hallmark of depression. Except in very rare circumstances, by using some type of activity record couples can see that what they do influences how they feel about the marriage and their own affect.

By the end of the assessment period, the therapist should have a picture of the level of depression in both partners, an indication of the satisfaction with the relationship, evidence of the communication patterns within the dyad, and a detailed picture of the daily activities of the couple. Any relationship between mood and spouse activity can also be documented.

Initial Treatment

The goals of the initial sessions are to (1) further the collaborative set between the couple and the therapist; (2) quickly structure the environment to increase the number of pleasant activities that the couple and each individual experiences; and (3) demonstrate the association between what occurs in the relationship and both partners' moods.

We explain that many different factors may affect depression. Some people become depressed when they are not engaging in enough pleasant and satisfying experiences in their lives. Others become depressed because they are incorrectly perceiving what is happening around them. Still others are depressed because they are not satisfied with the way they relate to people.

Our initial challenge to the couple is to teach them to be scientists and detectives studying themselves. We tell them that they are the ones who can best determine what influences the depression and the relationship. We help them gather information, plan ways of testing ideas, and implement changes in their lives. We acknowledge that not everyone is the same and that they may have special problems that no one has noted before. But if that is the case, then it is especially important that they document how they are different.

If it seems relevant for a particular case, we will discuss common reactions to a depressed person that others are likely to experience. This discussion explains that others often are sympathetic, but they may inadvertently reinforce depressive actions by not helping the patient resume normal activities (Lewinsohn, 1974). Also, people sometimes come to find interacting with someone who is depressed to be aversive, and they subsequently withdraw (Coyne, 1976a).

It is useful to have clients feel they are active collaborators in control of their own treatment. They can gather the data on how therapy is working and what is most effective for them. Presenting multiple influences on the depressed mood can reduce the threat to both partners. Defining them both as detectives or scientists can keep them, especially the depressed client, from feeling inferior to the therapist.

Since therapy often focuses on interaction issues, it naturally validates the reasons for including the spouse. We assure the husband that it is legitimate to have negative reactions to the behaviors of a depressed spouse. This is useful since it reduces the guilt he may be feeling. It also provides hope by implying that his response is transient. It may also be reassuring for the wife to learn that the conflicting messages that she has been receiving from her partner are not unique to their relationship.

During the initial sessions, daily ratings of satisfaction with self, relationship, and mood, along with information about what actually occurred, serve as the primary focus. The homework assignments are basically those used in behavioral marital therapy (BMT; see Jacobson, 1984a, 1984b; Jacobson & Margolin, 1979). Initially, each person is given the assignment of increasing the partner's daily satisfaction rating with the relationship. The couple are told that often this can be done by increasing the number of positive behaviors each emits and decreasing the number of aversive behaviors. At this point, the emphasis is on increasing satisfaction, not mood. This is so that both spouses are working for the other, with neither perceiving that he or she is giving while getting nothing in return.

Before each session, the therapist calls the couple and collects data on the three daily ratings and the number of positive and negative behaviors that have occurred. These are plotted before therapy so that the data can be presented during the session. These data are used to emphasize two major points. First, there are almost always some changes in satisfaction and mood. This is highlighted so that couples (and especially the depressed member of the dyad) can see that the responses do vary. Sometimes it appears to the clients that things never change and there is no hope of improvement. The actual data provide evidence that the situation *does* change. Second, the data are explored to see whether there is an obvious relationship between ratings and events. The therapist may point this relationship out but underplay the significance, saying that it is interesting and consistent with what we know but suggesting that more evidence is needed. The couple are asked to generate hypotheses about what things seem to influence their responses and to go home and test those hypotheses.

Note that a firm foundation for the empirical testing of cognitive distortions is being laid during the behavior-exchange portion of therapy. The couple are told that they can ask each other for suggestions of how to behave, if they wish, but they can also feel free to experiment unilaterally for a while. As the initial sessions go on, more and more emphasis is shifted to collaboration instead of unilateral action.

The initial sessions, although originally derived from a model of marital distress, also follow directly from a social learning theory of depression. Behavior-exchange exercises are designed to increase the frequency of positive reinforcers; it is precisely a paucity of such reinforcers that is hypothesized to be causally related to depression. Because much of the affective improvement seen in the treatment of depression comes in the first six to eight sessions, we want the couples to track the improvement daily and note how these improvements covary with particular actions.

Middle Sessions

During the middle portion of therapy, emphasis shifts from behavioral-exchange methodologies to two additional areas: (1) cognitive distortions and (2) communication and problem-solving skills.

There are several factors that we have considered in deciding to emphasize communication training in our treatment program. If her interactions with her husband are perceived by the wife as critical and punishing, then it is difficult to foster a confiding relationship that may reduce future relapse (Brown & Harris, 1978). Hautzinger, Linden, and Hoffman (1982) studied the communication patterns of two groups of distressed couples. In one group, the couples were distressed but neither person was depressed. In a second matched group, the wives were clinically depressed. The investigators found that communications where one partner was depressed were quite different; they were characterized as being uneven, negative, and asymmetrical when compared with communications of the group where neither spouse was depressed. Specifically, the nondepressed partners expressed positive and healthy feeling, mood, and self-esteem when describing themselves, while being more negative and demanding in their partner evaluations. On the other hand, the depressed persons talked about their own person, feeling, and future negatively while evaluating their partner positively and excusing their partner's behavior. This study and our clinical experience underscore the need for communication training in these couples.

Problem solutions that are arrived at where one partner views herself negatively seem likely to be inequitable and unsatisfying in the long run. If problem solutions are, in fact, poor, then the depressed person may find that the only way of successfully affecting the environment is through the use of aversive control strategies. Hautzinger *et al.* (1982, p. 313) suggested that therapy to reduce uneven and negative interactions is an important part of the psychotherapeutic approach to the treatment of depression.

There is a growing body of evidence indicating that communication between depressed subjects and others is dysfunctional, although it is not clear as yet whether these communication difficulties are unique to depression (Holtzworth-Munroe, Schmaling, & Jacobson, 1986). However, the literature seems to suggest that the quality of communication among depressed couples is a good—perhaps one of the best—predictor(s) of relapse (Hooley & Hahlweg, 1986). It has been observed that depressed women and their nondepressed spouses continue to manifest dysfunctional communication patterns even after the wife has recovered from a depressive episode (Hinchliffe *et al.*, 1978; Weissman & Paykel, 1974). It is possible that such communication patterns contribute to the recurrence of episodes of depression.

As for the actual treatment for the middle phase of therapy, we make use of a slightly modified version of our standard communication training and problem-solving program (CPT; Jacobson & Margolin, 1979) while also borrowing heavily from Beck's cognitive therapy (Beck, Rush, Shaw & Emery, 1979). Communication training begins with teaching how to clearly express ideas, wishes, and feelings, while the listener learns to give evidence that he or she clearly received the message without distortion. The clear sending and receiving of information is important in the treatment of distressed couples and crucial in the treatment of couples in whom depression exists.

In the course of communication training, the listener is encouraged to paraphrase often and to frequently state his or her affective status as a result of the previous communication. The paraphrasing serves several purposes. By hearing the listener rephrase what was just said, without interjecting value judgments about the content, the sender can be certain that what was said was, in fact, heard. This can be especially important when the depressed person is the listener. Beck *et al.* (1979) have described how negative cognitive schemas may distort information and experiences. Though experimental evidence in support of the pervasiveness of negative distortions is inconsistent (Coyne & Gotlib, 1983; Segal & Shaw, 1986), it is clear that depressed subjects tend to perceive comments directed toward them as more negative than do nondepressed subjects (Gotlib, 1983). Therefore, we use communication exercises as an opportunity to introduce the idea of cognitive distortions when it occurs during paraphrasing exercises.

During this portion of therapy, the therapist closely observes the husband who is also taught to self-monitor so that he is aware of the message he is sending. McClean, Ogston, and Grauer (1973) have reported that nondepressed spouses are prone to offer "constructive criticism," when, in fact, independent observers identify this communication as hostile. We emphasize watching for distortions by both spouses.

It is important to be certain that each partner is aware of the impact of his or her communication. After paraphrasing, spouses should summarize their feelings and reactions. We encourage people to use phrases such as "I feel ______when you ______" as a way of promoting accurate feedback. When treating a depressed spouse it is especially important to avoid the use of phrases such as "You always" or "You make me." These global statements are characteristic of depressed individuals, who tend to make global, inaccurate inferences when, in fact, specific behaviors often lead to specific outcomes. We have noted this type of distortion in almost every distressed marital case we have ever treated, regardless of whether either spouse was depressed. It is crucial to teach couples to recognize and correct these overgeneralizations.

By requiring the couple to use more positive, nonaccusatory structures, we try to make it simple for the nondepressed spouse to give specific feedback to the depressed spouse. For example, if the husband is able to say, "I get angry when I suggest that we do something together and you answer 'Who would want to be around me' and then walk away," much has been accomplished. First, the depressed individual receives some validation for the perception that the partner is angry. Second, the antecedents of the anger are clearly specified, which acts against the tendencies on the part of depressed people toward arbitrary inference and overgeneralization. In therapy, if the depressed spouse distorts the message, the therapist is present to point out the distortion; also, if the nondepressed spouse is hostile and angry, but unaware of such feelings, the therapist can validate the wife's reaction to the style of the comments.

This illustrates an aspect of marital therapy with depressed couples that fits particularly well with cognitive therapy for the depressed spouse alone. By focusing on marital interactions, and clarifying both the intent and impact of communication, the therapist provides fertile ground for testing depressogenic beliefs. Since cognitive activity in depressed people often revolves around significant others, the marital communication setting provides a perfect laboratory for testing beliefs. Conjoint marital therapy provides the therapist with an opportunity that rarely exists when treatment focuses solely on the depressed individual: the opportunity to see whether the problem is distorted thinking or whether most interactions are really negative. The therapist can even intervene directly to correct negative interactions when they seem to be the source of the problem. Thus, by including the spouse and focusing directly on marital communication, the therapist can test beliefs about the depressed person's thinking and intervene as indicated.

Another step in communication training with depressed couples is to have the listener supply information about positive aspects of a situation following a negative statement. This is not an attempt to sugarcoat criticism but rather it is a way to make such exchanges as nonpunitive as possible. As applied to the above comment, the result might be "I get angry when I suggest that we do something together and you answer 'Who would want to be around me' and then walk away. But I feel much better when you agree to come along or offer another suggestion for things we can do together."

Combining communication skills and cognitive therapy techniques, the therapist asks the depressed spouse to identify her underlying beliefs so that they can be validated or refuted. For example, the depressed spouse might say, "I feel like such an unlovable person. When you ask me to go for a walk I think that you are just saying that because you have to. No one would really want to be with me right now. Do you really want to go for a walk?" The spouse might learn to answer "I really do want to go for a walk. I find the times when we do things together to be more fun for both of us. Even if you don't want to go for a walk right now, it is especially nice if you suggest something else we could do together."

As communication skills are learned and refined, the next step is to apply them to problem-solving tasks. There may be problems that need to be resolved as a result of the depression, as a result of marital distress, or simply because most of us find the need to solve problems in the normal course of life. In addition, successful problem-solving can be therapeutic for someone who is depressed, because it is a mastery experience. Solving a problem demonstrates that events can be controlled and altered. The nondepressed spouse also has an opportunity to see his partner as an active, competent member of the relationship.

Problem-solving skills are taught in two stages. The first is proper problem definition. The person initiating a complaint is taught to state the problem in clear and concise terms. Specific statements that describe one and only one problem are encouraged. The listener is not allowed to interrupt nor to raise cross-complaints or otherwise sidetrack the discussion. The listener is also encouraged to start his or her response with a paraphrase of what was just said.

This pinpointing of the target complaint is useful in that it defines problems that are of manageable size. For the depressed person, this pinpointing reduces the problem from a global, amorphous complaint to specific behavioral statements. This encourages the depressed partner to see problems as being more circumscribed and not part of a generally negative world. Early problem statements may be of the form, "You don't care how I feel about anything." Such a statement would be typical of a distressed relationship even if neither partner were depressed. As communication and problem-solving skills are acquired, the statement might eventually be expressed as, "I feel unimportant when you come home and begin reading the paper without asking me how my day went." The differences between these two statements are important. The first statement is a global, stable attribution about some aspect of the spouse's behavior that might be expected to exacerbate depression (Abramson, Seligman, & Teasdale, 1978). In addition, it provides little useful information to the receiver about what to do in response to the complaint. The second statement solves both of these problems.

As the couple's problem-solving skills are strengthened, we also encourage the person initiating a problem-solving session to begin the complaint by acknowledging his or her role in contributing to the problem, as well as by pointing to something that the partner does that is positive: for instance, "I really enjoyed it last week when you brought me some flowers as a surprise. And I realize that sometimes I don't let you know how I feel about things, but I've been feeling that I am not very important when you come home and begin reading the paper without asking about how my day went." The listener would paraphrase, in a nonjudgmental way, while accepting the legitimacy of the complainer to have the complaint. This does not require accepting responsibility for being a bad or thoughtless person. But the listener does acknowledge that the complainer has the right to react. The topography of the reply might be of the form, "When I come home and start reading the paper without asking about your day, you feel as if I think you are not important, is that right?"

Now the actual problem-solving portion of problem-solving begins. The couple must find a solution that is a compromise for both parties and is behaviorally specific. The compromise portion of the solution is included so that neither party has to take total responsibility for a problem; interpersonal problems, by definition, involve both people. The compromise can be especially useful for the depressed person who is often too willing to take blame for everything that goes wrong. Also, the need for specificity stems from the emphasis in therapy on testing what factors influence satisfaction and mood.

After both members of the dyad agree on the problem, they begin to work toward a mutually acceptable solution. Couples are instructed to generate potential solutions. The more possible solutions the better. During the solution-generation phase, ideas are not critically examined; no idea is judged too absurd or impractical at this time, and neither party is allowed to criticize solutions. This encourages novel ways of examining problems.

After a potential list of solutions is generated, the couple examines each alternative. Solutions that both people consider absurd are eliminated first. The remaining items are evaluated. The person proposing the solution explains why it was offered and how it solves the problem. Items are often eliminated at this point because they simply do not solve the problem. Items are also rejected if they require too much emotional effort by the person against whom the complaint is lodged. It would serve little purpose to implement a solution that caused resentment.

The remaining solutions are examined, and an agreement is formed. The specific behaviors of the solution are detailed, with each person taking responsibility for his or her part. It is important to emphasize the point raised earlier about problem-solving being a procedure in which the individuals compromise. Often, a perfect solution that is mutually agreeable is not apparent. In such cases the task is to find a solution that will improve the problem. The remaining portion of the problem can be addressed in future problem-solving sessions once both parties have seen how each of them affects the situation. Frequently, partial solutions to problems are useful. Couples come to see that what was thought to be a huge problem was, in fact, more manageable than originally felt. It is not uncommon for major problems to become minor annoyances once the most upsetting part of the problem is removed. An analysis of client reactions to behavioral marital therapy suggested that if a couple's major complaints were not addressed during therapy, clients were likely to report that omission as a shortcoming that may contribute to relapse (Holtzworth-Munroe & Jacobson, 1985). We therefore emphasize that the therapy must attempt to address significant problems even if the result is not a complete resolution. We feel that a series of even partial successes in dealing with a major problem can make a significant impact on marital satisfaction and depression.

The partners alternate initiating problems for the problem-solving sessions. This helps keep both spouses aware that each has a legitimate right to request change. They are strongly encouraged to generate equal numbers of potential solutions. This is monitored rather closely by the therapist since there is evidence that the nondepressed partner tends to dominate problem-solving sessions (Biglan *et al.*, 1985).

While we might like to believe that all problems can be solved with these techniques, there are some problems that couples seem less able to handle. In these cases, altering the most aversive aspects of the problem can be helpful. Many problems can be eliminated. The result is that there are fewer total problems, and those that remain seem more tolerable.

Thus far, we have emphasized the behavioral marital aspects of our intervention. Throughout these middle sessions we also use the cognitive techniques in the same manner that Beck has proposed (Beck *et al.*, 1979). But throughout therapy, we make use of the marital relationship as the natural laboratory for applying the cognitive and behavioral skills that are being taught.

Ending Therapy

In the first part of therapy, we focus on increasing positive behaviors and activity. In the middle sessions, we address the communication training and problem-solving techniques while calling attention to the difficulties that may arise from cognitive distortions. In the final phase of therapy, we emphasize generalization of the skills learned during therapy. We teach couples to be aware of the possibility of recurrence of depression and how it might be handled using the skills just acquired.

Less time is spent talking about specific homework tasks. Homework is debriefed rather quickly, with the therapist fading out suggestions as time goes on. Much of the time is spent reviewing what the couple have learned about how their actions and beliefs affect their mood and marital satisfaction. The mood of the husband is examined so that he is aware of what factors influence him also.

Toward the end of therapy, each person also summarizes what personal behaviors are particularly useful in improving mood or strengthening the relationship. The wife may notice that engaging in new activities when she begins to feel blue is useful. Or she may take the time to compliment her family when they do something particularly pleasing. For the husband, more adaptive strategies may include being more responsive to reasonable requests for change and expressing more clearly what things he finds pleasurable about the relationship. Both spouses may find it useful to discuss individual perceptions of the relationship with one another.

The therapist can use the data gathered in therapy to highlight the skills and behaviors that were most associated with improvement for both people. The therapist may also have the couple review which specific strategies each used most effectively and which remain to be mastered. Therapy has taught the couple skills that were useful for the past episodes of depression, and the possibility of future episodes is openly discussed. The focus of therapy has been on developing joint solutions to the problem of depression, which both spouses share and to which they both contribute. Likewise, the credit for the successful resolution of this problem is shared. Depression is presented as being similar to most other relationship problems; it can be analyzed and managed by using the tools learned in therapy.

SPECIAL PROBLEMS

The above brief description of conjoint therapy where one partner is depressed is a modified version of behavioral marital therapy with an emphasis on additional cognitive techniques. It is modified in that it places emphasis on techniques that are proposed to be of special significance to the treatment of depression. We do not yet have sufficient data to predict which couples are likely to do best with this approach and which couples will not do well. We do have some initial clinical impressions that certain types of issues may require special attention.

Learning History and Control

One issue that must be attended to is that the nondepressed spouse may have acquired a learning history that interferes with useful collaboration. This is especially true when there have been repeated episodes of depression. A husband may have learned to avoid attending to the conversation of his depressed wife. Many studies have shown that it can be aversive to interact with depressed subjects (e.g., Coyne, Kahn, & Gotlib, 1984). The husband may not exhibit reasonable listening skills because avoidance of attending has been negatively reinforced by removal of the aversive affect that can arise from interactions with the depressed partner. If this is a problem, it is usually apparent during communication skills training. Paraphrasing exercises frequently help increase accurate attending.

However, the basic problem is that, for some depressed individuals, feedback is necessary to let them know in what ways they are making conversation aversive. One must help the depressed spouse become aware of which specific behaviors, both verbal and nonverbal, elicit aversive responses from the listener. This can be especially delicate because depressed individuals are particularly sensitive to criticism (Gotlib, 1983). It is also important to tell the listener that it is all right to have negative reactions.

A depressed person may have learned to control the actions of the spouse by coercion (Patterson & Reid, 1970). The depressed person is not necessarily being intentionally coercive. In most cases, the depressed person has learned subtle behaviors because they more effectively lead to desired outcomes. If we conceptualize coercion as control by the use of negative reinforcement, then the typical coercive interaction may be the result of positive contingencies not being effective. Reasonable requests by a wife for alterations in the relationship or role definitions may have been ignored or punished. For example, she may have asked for help with household tasks on several occasions but no help was received. Then, during a depressive episode when the wife was tearful and sad, the spouse may have helped around the house. This may have led to an improvement in the wife's mood, after which the husband no longer gave any assistance. The next time the wife's mood was sad, the same pattern continued, only this time the children may have been more polite as well. What the depressed person has learned is that requests for help don't affect her family's behavior, but behaving in a "depressed" manner *is* effective in getting help. Regardless of what initially provoked the depressed mood, it has been strengthened by environmentally mediated contingencies.

In this example, it is also clear that the spouse's helping behavior was not positively reinforced by the depressed person feeling better. We know that because when her mood improved, the helpfulness stopped. To be motivated to help again, the husband had to be controlled by the institution of more depression symptoms. Eventually, the maintenance of supportive behavior came under the control of the implicit threat of more depression if the helping decreased.

One cannot be certain where the exact source of the problem is in the above situation. It may be with the wife because she does not adequately express her wishes for help. Or she may ineffectively reinforce the help when it occurs (i.e., take it for granted) so that it does not become a strong response. Likewise, the husband may be unresponsive to reasonable requests for change but very sensitive to the depressed mood of his partner. Neither may be aware of the contingencies operating to control their behavior.

Therapy must focus on the functional relationships among the behaviors each spouse emits, the conditions under which they occur, and the contingencies in the environment. The above scenario is not rare. Special attention is needed to identify such styles of control, bring them to the attention of the couple, and substitute positive requests for change and positive contingencies when change occurs. Husbands of depressed wives may show a tendency to discount the wife's requests for change. Or they may see the requests as valid only for the duration of the depression. The depressed spouse may not feel like adequately reinforcing behavior change because it requires attention and energy that she may lack during a depressive episode.

Behavior-exchange and communication exercises are especially useful for identifying the relationship between events and mood changes. Initially, it is up to the therapist to make sure that the environment adequately reinforces desired behaviors and does not allow them to be under the discriminative control of the depression only.

Another issue that must sometimes be addressed is the use of depressive behaviors to maintain the relationship. The depressed wife may perceive that she is no longer a desirable partner. She may think that her partner is not likely to stay with her because he can easily find someone with more positive attributes and fewer liabilities. The depressed wife may also believe that she cannot make herself a more attractive partner because of her negative view of herself and the future. Therefore, in order for her to maintain the relationship, she must increase the cost to her partner of leaving the relationship. Borrowing from social exchange theory (Thibaut & Kelley, 1959), the depressed person adds to the cost of entering a new alternative relationship by increasing guilt for leaving a very dysfunctional spouse.

In such cases, the depressed person is exercising power in the relationship by increasing the costs to her spouse for not attending to her and maintaining commitment to the relationship. Unfortunately, once such power is exercised, it produces a great impediment to regaining normal functioning. If the depressed person begins to improve, then the guilt that the partner might feel over leaving the relationship lessens. The cost of engaging in an alternative relationship decreases, and the relationship is, ironically, at the greatest risk for failure when the depressive episode is beginning to lift.

But it would be a mistake to assume that only nondepressed spouses consider ending marital relationships with depressed mates. Actually, in our clinical experience, it is more common for the depressed spouse to consider divorce as she begins to recover from the depressive episode. We have frequently observed that recovery from depression is often accompanied by anger toward the spouse. Instead of blaming herself for whatever difficult life circumstances served as antecedents for the depressive episode, the recovering wife begins to blame the partner. The result is often deterioration in the marital relationship. It is at this stage where marital therapy can often have its maximal impact. It is almost as if the problem must be relabeled from depression to marital distress for marital therapy to be a credible treatment.

Suicide

Anyone who treats depressed clients must be aware of the potential risk of suicide. Suicide represents the leading risk for death among those with depression (APA, 1987). Feighner *et al.* (1972) include thoughts of suicide or the wish to be dead among the criteria to be considered in making the diagnosis of depression. We closely attend to suicidal ideation and suicide attempts when they appear. However, since it is not unusual for depressed clients to have such thoughts or even to attempt suicide, we try to address these issues in the most useful framework possible.

Let us stress that we do not underestimate the potential seriousness of suicidal thoughts and behaviors. But our general strategy for handling these occasions is to offer the following interpretation of suicidal behaviors (including thoughts) to our clients. First, we explain that this is a common part of the phenomonology of depression. In this explanation, we try to let both spouses know that the presence of such thoughts does not make a *prima facie* case for the depressed wife being unusually "sick" or "crazy." We also acknowledge that admitting to such thoughts is a scary experience but not indicative of being "disturbed."

Second, we tell the clients that, in our experience, the most common reason clients attempt suicide is that it is the only thing they can think of to deal with what seem like overwhelming and painful problems. That is, we interpret suicidal behavior as a type of problem-solving strategy. We are direct in saying that while we can view such behavior as problem-solving behavior, we think it is a poor strategy. It is easy to point out the obvious limitations of suicide as an effective means for solving problems.

By talking about suicidal thoughts and actions in this manner, we make suicidal ideation easier to discuss openly and help the attempter feel and be perceived by her spouse as less abnormal. Though a complete discussion of suicide is beyond the scope of this chapter, we think that this approach increases the likelihood that a client with such ideation will inform us when such thoughts occur without feeling hopeless. Since those people who attempt suicide or have such ideation may be at increased risk of actually completing suicide (Pokorny, 1983), we try to make it easy and normal for the person to inform us of such feelings. At the same time, we avoid stigmatizing the client.

The presentation of suicidal behavior as a problem-solving strategy has other therapeutic benefits. It immediately suggests an agenda for the session. We can analyze what problem or situation seemed to justify such a preemptory response. Clients are taught to generate and examine alternative solutions. The therapist does not underestimate the seriousness of the situation and is usually quite active in these sessions. But the way the problem is addressed is consistent with everything else about our behavioral marital approach to depression. The situation is presented as a joint problem, and both spouses are involved in the solution. From a paradigmatic perspective, our approach reduces the likelihood that suicidal behaviors will be operantly reinforced. It also changes the aversive and frightening nature of suicidal thoughts to a discriminative stimulus to recognize that a problem exists and begin looking for effective strategies.

Suicidal behaviors can be related to hopelessness and pessimism (Beck, Weissman, Lester, & Trexler, 1974). One advantage of our therapy approach is that we make continued reference to data collected during the course of therapy. We present to the clients the actual satisfaction and depression ratings they have collected during therapy. We are able to show the clients, using their own data, that the situation is not hopeless and that the depression does change in response to their actions. Since depression ratings do often improve substantially during the first 8 weeks of therapy, we can be optimistic without being patronizing.

Other Family Members

The rationale for including spouses in the treatment of depression centers around the assumptions that (1) the partners of the depressed client may be contributing to the development or maintenance of depression; (2) the partner can be especially useful in assisting the return to normal mood and reduce the likelihood of future depressive episodes; and (3) we reduce the probability that the client is seen as defective and incapable of being a productive and healthy part of the family. Conjoint therapy for depression might also have salutary effects for other family members and thus reduce the likelihood of environmentally induced relapses.

There are many family issues that may contribute to depression and may become the focus of some of the therapy. They are generally addressed within the context of problem-solving and communications sessions. Some solutions may manifest themselves during behavior-exchange exercises. Though our current research protocol makes including other family members in the session difficult, family topics are frequently addressed.

We have noted clinically that the depressed spouse frequently seems to feel considerable resentment during her recovery. Much of this resentment is directed toward her husband. Common themes include child-rearing responsibilities, resentment toward parents, social isolation, and anger about being taken for granted. At the moment, we address these issues using cognitive and behavioral techniques. In the future, as research constraints diminish and we develop more clinical experience with the relevant issues, other modalities may be developed.

When the wife finds herself becoming isolated and disillusioned about having to manage the entire burden of child-rearing, we seek to establish behaviorally specific remedies that frequently involve the husband and children accepting more responsibilities in these domains. This allows the wife to function more autonomously during her free time. When others have to accept some of the responsibilities that were previously the wife's, there may be an increased appreciation for what she does. On those occasions when the wife does enjoy more free time, we encourage the development of activities that minimize the frequently reported sense of social isolation.

There is no doubt that some husbands resent some of the shifts in responsibilities. They may feel that they are working hard to earn the family a living and that at the end of the day they do not feel like helping with other family responsibilities. However, by gathering data on daily depression versus the amount of cooperation that occurs, we can empirically show the link between how helpful the husband is and the impact it has on the depression and the relationship. The same is true for the cooperation of older children.

It is interesting to note that in families in which both spouses work, the wife almost always works *and* runs the house with relatively little assistance from the spouse. Often, little has been said about this arrangement prior to therapy, but the issue quickly emerges as discussion about household duties begins.

Many of the couples we treat seem to have sex-role stereotyped relationships. Altering some aspects of the relationship is frequently necessary and encounters some resistance. Our best strategy—albeit not always successful—is to point out (again, using the couple's own daily data) that by altering roles, the wife's mood improves and both people often report increased satisfaction with the relationship. These adjustments are not easy to make, and much of our time in therapy can be centered around strictly marital issues such as these.

When a wife has been depressed and functioning at a lower level in the family, she may see herself as worthless and not deserving of respect. Children may learn to treat their mothers in that same disrespectful manner. Since a major emphasis in our approach is to avoid labeling the client as defective, it is important that both spouses attend to the issue of having the children maintaining a positive attitude toward the mother. Children can be encouraged to be helpful without having to define the mother as failing at the task of being a mom. In our research, we rarely have the opportunity, given the time constraints of our program, to bring the children into the sessions. But the issue of the children's behavior and attitude is frequently part of the problem-solving homework.

It may also be appropriate to raise these same issues about the grandparents' behaviors. If the parents of the couple have helped out while the wife was depressed, it may be necessary to take active steps to signal to them that, though the depression was disruptive, normal function and relationships are again possible and appropriate.

We mentioned earlier that sex-role stereotyping seems to be a significant problem that may somehow contribute to depression. Clients with sex-role stereotyped views are likely to have parents that help foster those views. It is sometimes necessary to help couples learn to redefine aspects of their own relationships while at the same time keeping the attitudes of their parents from creating guilt or resentment. This can be accomplished by behavioral rehearsal or brief assertion training around specific areas of disagreement. It can be quite disruptive to negotiate more cooperation around the house, more free time for the wife, and increase her outside activities with the cooperation of her husband and children only to have the wife's parents or in-laws announce that they think the wife is failing her family somehow.

Depression in Other Family Members

In cases where both members of the marital dyad are depressed, our treatment intervention is essentially the same as described above. Initially, the therapist has to be more structured and directive than usual. This is because the symptoms of depression can include lower behavioral output and decreased cognitive functioning. In a case where neither spouse is active, the homework is initially more behavioral and focuses on increasing both shared and individual positive reinforcement. The therapist may find it useful to make frequent telephone contacts to be sure homework is being done; twice-weekly sessions for the first 3–4 weeks are helpful.

It is uncommon for both partners to experience concomitant full-blown major depressive episodes. It is more common for the partner without the complete depressive syndrome to show signs of depressed mood, including elevated depression scores and pessimism. The therapist must be careful not to construe the couple's inactivity and lack of initial engagement as signs of treatment failure. The restricted affect and activity that the depressed clients show requires more effort and energy on the part of the therapist than usual.

In the cases where both spouses are depressed, the therapist must be careful not to be fooled by rapid but incomplete progress. Where marital discord and depression are present, relief of the depression can be interpreted as restoration of marital harmony (and vice versa). The therapist and couple must continue to attend to the remaining problems in the treatment program. Things may look and feel so much better to the couple as their mood improves that they do not fully learn all the appropriate skills necessary to continue to improve and to prevent relapse.

A more complicated problem exists when the wife has a major depressive episode and the husband exhibits one of the more common forms of psychopathology in males, either alcoholism or substance abuse or antisocial personality disorder. Without getting sidetracked on all the clinical possibilities, we will say that we see no reason to conduct conjoint marital therapy for a depressed wife when the husband evidences clinical sociopathy.[1] In such cases, individual therapy seems to us to be indicated. Where there is active substance abuse, referral to a substance abuse program for the husband is appropriate while beginning individual therapy for depression for the wife. When and if the substance abuse problem responds to treatment, conjoint therapy can be conducted. Conjoint therapy can be helpful to both spouses for their shared difficulties.

CONCLUSIONS

These clinical observations are anecdotal at this point. They need to be tested in a controlled research context. Other clinical observations are also worthy of more systematic inquiry. For example, there is an extremely traditional sex-role structure in many of the depressive marriages that we observe. It seems that quite often extremely self-confident, dominant men are paired with passive, dependent, powerless (and depressed) women. Rather than finding the depressive episode aversive, some of our nondepressed husbands say things such as, "I liked her better when she was depressed." It is our belief that many of the married depressed women we treat are in chronically oppressive relationships with a very low rate of reinforcement. Rather than emphasizing social skill deficits or other defects in the depressed women, we are moving toward a model that increasingly emphasizes the aversive family and social environmental context in which depression often occurs. This clinical observation that the family environment may be contributory to depression is part of a complex set of factors that may lead to depression. The need for further study in this area is crucial. It remains to be seen whether it would be useful to develop typologies of depression within the marital context. These typologies would assess family stressors, social, cognitive and interpersonal skills, behavioral and personal assets, and family structure.

In short, failure to emphasize marital and family therapy as a treatment for depression seems to us to be a glaring omission. For those depressed individuals who are married, a truly long-lasting recovery often requires changes in the family environment—changes that turn a depressogenic milieu into one that provides the social support and other rewards that can occur in intimate relationships.

NOTE

1. We are talking here about clinical sociopathy. This should not be confused with only an elevation on the Pd scale of the MMPI, which often occurs in spouses

with marital distress. This elevation is, in part, due to the family discord items on scale 4 of the MMPI.

ACKNOWLEDGMENT

We thank Victoria M. Follette for helpful clinical and editorial comments during the preparation of this chapter.

REFERENCES

Abramson, L. Y., Seligman, M. E. P., & Teasdale, J. (1978). Learned helplessness in humans: Critique and reformulation. *Journal of Abnormal Psychology, 87*, 49–74.

American Psychiatric Association. (1987). *DSM IIIR—Diagnostic and statistical manual of psychiatric disorders* (3rd ed., rev.). Washington, DC: American Psychiatric Association.

Atkinson, B. J., & McKenzie, P. N. (1984). The personalized spouse observation checklist: A computer-generated assessment of marital interaction. *Journal of Marital and Family Therapy, 10*, 427–429.

Beach, S. R. H., Jouriles, E. N., & O'Leary, K. D. (1985). Extramarital sex: Impact on depression and commitment in couples seeking marital therapy. *Journal of Sex and Marital Therapy, 11*, 99–108.

Beach, S. R. H., & O'Leary, K. D. (1986). The treatment of depression occurring in the context of marital discord. *Behavior Therapy, 17*, 43–49.

Beck, A. T. (1978). *Beck depression inventory* (rev. ed.). Philadelphia: Center for Cognitive Therapy.

Beck, A. T., Rush, A. J., Shaw, B., & Emery, G. (1979). *Cognitive therapy of depression*. New York: Guilford Press.

Beck, A. T., Weissman, A., Lester, D., & Trexler, L. (1974). Measurement of pessimism: The hopelessness scale. *Journal of Consulting and Clinical Psychology, 42*, 861–865.

Bellack, A. S., Hersen, M., & Himmelhoch, J. M. (1983). A comparison of social skills training, pharmacotherapy, and psychotherapy for depression. *Behavior Research and Therapy, 21*, 101–107.

Biglan, A., Hops, H., Sherman, S., Friedman, L. S., Arthur, J., & Osteen, V. (1985). Problem solving interactions of depressed women and their spouses. *Behavior Therapy, 16*, 431–451.

Bothwell, S., & Weissman, M. M. (1977). Social impairments four years after acute depressive episode. *American Journal of Orthopsychiatry, 47*, 231–237.

Boyd, J. H., & Weissman, M. M. (1981). Epidemiology of affective disorders. *Archives of General Psychiatry, 38*, 1039–1046.

Briscoe, C. W., & Smith, J. B. (1973). Depression and marital turmoil. *Archives of General Psychiatry, 28*, 811–817.

Brown, G., & Harris, T. (1978). *Social origin of depression*. London: Tavistock.

Coyne, J. C. (1976). Depression and the response of others. *Journal of Abnormal Psychology, 85*, 186–193. (a)

Coyne, J. C. (1976). Toward an interaction description of depression. *Psychiatry, 39*, 28–40. (b)

Coyne, J. C. (1984). Strategic therapy with married depressed persons: Initial agenda, themes, and interventions. *Journal of Marital and Family Therapy, 10*, 53–62.

Coyne, J. C., & Gotlib, I. H. (1983). The role of cognition in depression: A critical appraisal. *Psychological Bulletin, 94*, 472–505.

Coyne, J. C., Kahn, J., & Gotlib, I. (1984). Depression. In T. Jacobs (Ed.), *Family interactions and psychopathology*. New York: Pergamon.

DeMonbreun, B. F., & Craighead, W. E. (1977). Distortion of perception and recall of positive and neutral feedback in depression. *Cognitive Therapy and Research, 1*, 311–330.

Feighner, J. P., Robins, E., Guze, S. B., Woodruff, R. A., Jr., Winokur, G., & Munoz, R. (1972). Diagnostic criteria for use in psychiatric research. *Archives of General Psychiatry, 26*, 56–73.

Ferster, C. B. (1965). Classification of behavior pathology. In L. Krasner & L. P. Ullman (Eds.), *Research in behavior modification*. New York: Holt.

Ferster, C. B. (1973). A functional analysis of depression. *American Psychologist, 28*, 857–870.

Follette, W. C., Jacobson, N. S., & Follette, V. M. (1984). *Development and evaluation of a shortened, individualized version of the Spouse Observation Checklist*. Paper presented at the annual meeting of the Association for the Advancement of Behavior Therapy, Philadelphia, PA.

Gotlib, I. H. (1982). Self-reinforcement and depression in interpersonal interaction: The role of performance level. *Journal of Abnormal Psychology, 91*, 3–13.

Gotlib, I. H. (1983). Perceptions and recall of interpersonal feedback: Negative bias in depression. *Cognitive Therapy and Research, 7*, 399–412.

Hamilton, M. (1967). Development of a rating scale for primary depressive illness. *British Journal of Social and Clinical Psychology, 12*, 56–62.

Hautzinger, M., Linden, M., & Hoffman, N. (1982). Distressed couples with and without a depressed partner: An analysis of their verbal interactions. *Journal of Behavior Therapy and Experimental Psychiatry, 13*, 307–314.

Hinchcliffe, M. K., Hooper, D., & Roberts, F. J. (1978). *The melancholy marriage: A study of psychiatric disorder in women*. New York: Free Press.

Hinchcliffe, M. K., Hooper, D., & Roberts, F. J., & Vaughan, P. W. (1975). A study of the interaction between depressed patients and their spouses. *British Journal of Psychiatry, 126*, 164–172.

Hoehn-Hyde, D., Schlottmann, R. S., & Rush, A. J. (1982). Perception of social interactions in depressed psychiatric patients. *Journal of Consulting and Clinical Psychology, 50*, 209–212.

Holtzworth-Munroe, A., & Jacobson, N. S. (1985, November). *Predicting relapse following behavioral marital therapy*. Paper presented at the meeting of the Association for the Advancement of Behavior Therapy, Houston, TX.

Holtzworth-Munroe, A., Schmaling, K., & Jacobson, N. S. (1986). *Interpersonal aspects of depression*. Unpublished manuscript.

Hooley, J. M., & Hahlweg, K. (1986). The marriages and interaction patterns of depressed patients and their spouses: Comparing high and low EE dyads. In M. J. Goldstein, K. Hahlweg, & I. Hand (Eds.), *Treatments of schizophrenia: Family assessment and intervention*. New York: Springer-Verlag.

Jacobson, N. S. (1984). Marital therapy and the cognitive-behavioral treatment of depression. *The Behavior Therapist*, 7, 143–147. (a)

Jacobson, N. S. (1984). The modification of cognitive processes in behavioral marital therapy: Integrating cognitive and behavioral intervention strategies. In K. Hahlweg & N. S. Jacobson (Eds.), *Marital interactions: Analysis and modification*. New York: Guilford Press. (b)

Jacobson, N. S., & Anderson, E. A. (1982). Interpersonal skill and depression in college students: An analysis of the timing of self-disclosures. *Behavior Therapy, 13*, 271–282.

Jacobson, N. S., & Holtzworth-Munroe, A. (1986). Marital therapy: A social learning/cognitive perspective. In N. S. Jacobson & A. S. Gurman (Eds.), *Handbook of Marital Therapy*. New York: Guilford Press.

Jacobson, N. S., & Margolin, G. (1979). *Marital therapy: Strategies based on social learning and behavior exchange principles*. New York: Brunner/Mazel.

Klerman, G. L., & Weissman, M. M. (1982). Interpersonal psychotherapy: Theory and research. In A. J. Rush (Ed.), *Short-term psychotherapies for depression*. New York: Guilford Press.

Kohlenberg, R. J., & Tsai, M. (1987). Functional analytic psychotherapy. In N. S. Jacobson (Ed.), *Psychotherapists in clinical practice: Cognitive and behavioral perspectives*. New York: Guilford Press.

Kovacs, M. (1980). The efficacy of cognitive and behavioral therapies for depression. *American Journal of Psychiatry, 137*(12), 1495–1504.

Kovacs, M., Rush, A. J., Beck, A. T., & Hollon, S. (1981). Depressed outpatients treated with cognitive therapy or pharmacotherapy. *Archives of General Psychiatry, 38*(1), 33–39.

Lambert, M. J., Hatch, D. R., Kingston, M. D., & Edwards, B. C. (1986). Zung, Beck, and Hamilton rating scales as measures of treatment outcome: A meta-analytic comparison. *Journal of Consulting and Clinical Psychology, 54*, 54–59.

Lewinsohn, P. M. (1974). A Behavioral approach to depression. In R. M. Friedman & M. M. Katz (Eds.), *The psychology of depression: Contemporary theory and research* (pp. 157–185). New York: Wiley.

Lewinsohn, P. M. (1975). The behavioral study and treatment of depression. In M. Hersen, R. Eisler, & P. Miller (Eds.), *Progress in behavior modification* (Vol. 1). New York: Academic Press.

Libet, J., & Lewinsohn, P. M. (1973). The concept of social skill with special reference to the behavior of depressed persons. *Journal of Consulting and Clinical Psychology, 40*, 304–312.

Linden, M., Hautzinger, M., & Hoffman, N. (1983). Discriminant analysis of depressive interactions. *Behavior Modification, 7*, 403–422.

Locke, H. J., & Wallace, K. M. (1959). Short-term marital adjustment and prediction tests: Their reliability and validity. *Journal of Marriage and Family Living, 21*, 251–255.

MacPhillamy, D. M., & Lewinsohn, P. M. (1973). *Studies on the measurement of human reinforcement and the relationship between positive reinforcement and depression*. Unpublished manuscript, University of Oregon.

Mayer, J. M. (1977). Assessment of depression. In P. McReynolds (Ed.), *Advances in psychological assessment* (Vol. 4). San Francisco: Jossey-Bass.

McClean, P. D., Ogston, K., & Grauer, L. (1973). A behavioral approach to the treatment of depression. *Journal of Behavior Research and Experimental Psychiatry, 4*, 323–330.

Nelson, R. E., & Craighead, W. E. (1977). Perception of reinforcement, self-reinforcement and depression. *Journal of Abnormal Psychology, 86*, 379–388.

Patterson, G. R. (1976). Some procedures for assessing changes in marital interaction patterns. *Oregon Research Bulletin, 16*(7).

Patterson, G. R., & Reid, J.B. (1970). Reciprocity and coercion: Two facets of social systems. In C. Neuringer & J. Michael (Eds.), *Behavior modification in clinical psychology*. New York: Appleton-Century-Crofts.

Paykel, E., & Weissman, M. M. (1973). Social adjustment and depression. *Archives of General Psychiatry, 28*, 659–663.

Petzel, T. P., Johnson, J. E., Johnson, H. H., & Kowalski, J. (1981). Behavior of depressed subjects in problem-solving groups. *Journal of Research in Personality, 15*, 389–398.

Pokorny, A. D. (1983). Prediction of suicide in psychiatric patients. *Archives of General Psychiatry, 40*, 249–257.

Radloff, L. S. (1977, summer). The CES-D scale: A self-report depression for research in the general population. *Applied Psychological Measurement, 1*, 383–401.

Robins, L. N., Helzer, J. E., Weissman, M. M., Orvaschel, H., Gruenberg, E., Burke, J. D. Jr., & Regier, D. A. (1984). Lifetime prevalence of specific psychiatric disorders in three sites. *Archives of General Psychiatry, 41*, 949–958.

Rounsaville, B. J., & Chevron, E. (1982). Interpersonal psychotherapy: Clinical applications. In A. J. Rush (Ed.), *Short-term psychotherapies for depression*. New York: Guilford Press.

Rounsaville, B. J., Klerman, G. L., Weissman, M. M., Chevron, E. S., & Merikangas, D. R. (1983). *Interpersonal psychotherapy for depression: Conjoint marital*. Unpublished treatment manual, Massachusetts General Hospital.

Rounsaville, B. J., Weissman, M. M., Prusoff, B. A., & Herceg-Baron, R. L. (1979). Marital disputes and treatment outcome in depressed women. *Comprehensive Psychiatry, 20*, 483–490.

Rush, A. J., Beck, A. T., Kovacs, M., & Hollon, S. (1977). Comparative efficacy of cognitive therapy and imipramine in the treatment of depressed outpatients. *Cognitive Therapy and Research, 1*, 17–37.

Segal, Z. V., & Shaw, B. F. (1986). Cognitions in depression: A reappraisal of Coyne and Gotlib's critique. *Cognitive Therapy and Research, 10*, 671–694.

Skinner, B. F. (1953). *Science and human behavior*. New York: Free Press.

Spanier, G. B. (1976). Measuring dyadic adjustment: New scales for assessing the quality of marriage and similar dyads. *Journal of Marriage and the Family, 38*, 15–28.

Steinbrueck, S. M., Maxwell, S. E., & Howard, G. S. (1983). A meta-analysis of psychotherapy and drug therapy in the treatment of unipolar depression with adults. *Journal of Consulting and Clinical Psychology, 51*, 856–863.

Thibaut, L. M., & Kelley, H. H. (1959). *The social psychology of groups*. New York: Wiley.

Vaughn, C. E., & Leff, J. P. (1976). The influence of family and social factors on the course of psychiatric illness. *British Journal of Psychiatry, 129*, 125–137.

Weiss, R. L., & Perry, B. A. (1983). The Spouse Observation Checklist: Development and clinical applications. In E. E. Filsinger (Ed.), *Marriage and family assessment*. Beverly Hills, CA: Sage Publications.

Weissman, M. M., & Klerman, G. L. (1977). Sex differences and the epidemiology of depression. *Archives of General Psychiatry, 34*, 98–111.

Weissman, M. M., & Paykel, E. S. (1974). *The depressed woman: A study of social relationships*. Chicago: University of Chicago Press.

Weissman, M. M., Prusoff, B. A., DiMascio, A., Neu, C., Goklaney, M., & Klerman, G. L. (1979). The efficacy of drugs and psychotherapy in the treatment of acute depression. *American Journal of Psychiatry, 136*, 555–558.

Zung, W. W. K. (1965). A self-rating depression scale. *Archives of General Psychiatry, 12*, 63–70.

12

Acute Inpatient Settings

JAMES P. CURRAN

STEPHEN V. FARAONE
Brown University Medical School

DEBORAH J. GRAVES
University of South Florida

In this chapter we describe our behavioral family therapy program, which is initiated during a patient's hospitalization on our acute inpatient unit at the Providence Veterans Administration Medical Center. Before describing this program, we first describe the structure and philosophy of our inpatient unit. We also elaborate on our model of schizophrenia as it provides direction for our treatment program. After detailing our behavioral family therapy program, we discuss its aftercare component and our clinical assessment strategies.

Our inpatient unit is an acute (average length of stay, less than 30 days), moderate-sized (bed capacity, 30) treatment facility. It's a voluntary unit and treats a variety of psychiatric disorders, including personality disorders, major depressive disorders, and, of course, schizophrenia. Since ours is a veterans' hospital, the vast majority of patients on the inpatient unit are men, and the descriptions of patients in the chapter will reflect that preponderance.

Patients admitted to the unit are assigned to a clinical team. These clinical teams are derived from milieu treatment principles and are composed of both patients and staff members. Professional members of the clinical team consist of psychiatrists, psychologists, social workers, occupational therapists, and nurses. Although all treatment decisions are made in the context of the team, patients are assigned one primary therapist. Schizophrenic patients in our treatment programs are assigned to the psychologist on the team. The psychologist is responsible for developing individual treatment programs and for coordinating the efforts of other team members in a comprehensive approach to the patient. Treatment is truly a team effort. The psychiatrist on the team manages the patients' neuroleptic medication; medication compliance is an integral part of our behavioral family therapy program. The nurses on the team often serve as cotherapists in our behavioral family therapy program. The team's social worker assists the patient's primary therapist in discharge planning. The multidisciplinary team reflects the unit's biopsychosocial treatment model, which stresses that treatment reflects a comprehensive approach to a biological, psychological, and social factors.

Another philosophical principle that characterizes our treatment unit is that patients are not regarded as passive recipients of treatment but as coparticipants in their care. The patients on the team select a team captain who records patient levels and status. The patients are encouraged to participate in their treatment planning during team and community meetings and during care-planning rounds. Decisions regarding unit activities and policies are made at twice-weekly patient government meetings. For example, decisions regarding who is issued weekend passes are made at these meetings.

The other important structural component of our inpatient unit is our step level system, which operates as a gross contingency system. The objective behind the step levels is that patients should progress through them as a means of preparation for discharge. The earlier levels are more restrictive, while the higher levels are more consistent with community functioning. At each step, more is required from patients and more privileges are available. All patients are restricted to step level 1 when entering the unit. As a patient stabilizes, activities of daily living are addressed, such as eating, sleeping, personal hygiene, and basic socialization. The decision whether a patient has met the basic criteria in these activities of daily living, and may be advanced to step level 2, is made by the patient's clinical team and the patient government. Advancement to the highest level, level 3, requires not only appropriate behavior in daily living activities but also active involvement in the treatment plan. Again, the patient's team and the patient government make the decisions regarding entry into level 3.

Although the research personnel who guide our behavioral family treatment were not involved in developing the treatment philosophy and structure of our inpatient unit, we feel that they are not only compatible with but facilitate the behavioral family program. With a less helpful philosophy and structure, we would not expect as much success with our program. However, the infusion of our family program into the existing clinical unit was not without some difficulty. Our inpatient unit is a general clinical facility and not a specialized research unit. As such, there were initially some misgivings regarding the staff's acceptance of a structured research program. From the beginning, we made it very clear to the staff that we knew that if we were to impose our program on them it would fail. We told the staff that if the program was to be a success we would need their unqualified support. We spent time educating the staff, had workshops conducted for them by leading experts in the field, and paid for their tuition to attend workshops at several sites out of Rhode Island.

We listened to the issues they raised and worked out compromises. We also knew that if our program was to be a success that the research staff would have to become an integral part of the clinical unit. Consequently, our research personnel attend all staff meetings, are members of the clinical team, participate in treatment care planning of patients who are not part of the program, and attend general staff social functions (e.g, holiday parties). Basically, the program sold itself with the professional staff becoming converts.

Our treatment program is guided by the diathesis-stress model proposed by Zubin and Steinhauer (1981). The diathesis-stress model postulates that individuals inherit or acquire a degree of vulnerability that will make them more likely to demonstrate schizophrenic symptomatology. The vulnerable individual, the schizotrope, can possess any one etiological factor etiotype (genetic, biochemical, neurophysiological, developmental, ecological, or learning) or any combination of them. The model further states that no single etiotype is in itself a necessary and sufficient etiological agent but that the interaction among them can produce a schizotrope. Such an individual, although vulnerable, may never develop an episode or, under certain conditions, may develop one or more episodes. The vulnerability model stipulates that unless a triggering event occurs no episode will follow. The vulnerability model assumes that schizophrenia is not a continuous disorder but that vulnerability to it is. This vulnerability may remain latent for life, or it may be elicited by life event stressors. Since the etiotypes and their combinations have not yet been isolated, therapeutic intervention should be directed not at curing the disorder but at ameliorating the suffering and preventing the initial occurrence or a recurrence.

The diathesis-stress model of schizophrenia is somewhat analogous to our conceptualization of diabetes. Diabetes may be one or several diseases. We do not know all the possible etiological factors or combinations of factors that make an individual susceptible to acquiring diabetes. Some of these factors appear to be inherited, while some appear to be acquired. While we have no cure for diabetes, we are able to affect its course and ameliorate the suffering associated with it.

Our behavioral family program is modeled after the programs developed by Falloon and colleagues (Falloon, Boyd, & McGill, 1984; Falloon, Boyd, McGill, Ranzoni, Moss, & Gilderman, 1982; Falloon & Liberman, 1983). The two major differences are that the intensive phase is initiated during the patient's inpatient stay and there are few home visits.

When a patient is admitted to our treatment unit, he is assigned to a multidisciplinary treatment team. If the patient appears to meet the DSM-III criteria for schizophrenia, the psychologist on the team will conduct a structured interview—the Diagnostic Interview Schedule (DIS)—which was developed by the National Institute of Mental Health (NIMH) as a means to facilitate differential diagnoses. Even if the team is quite confident that the patient meets DSM-III criteria, the psychologist still conducts a DIS because we have found it helpful in providing information regarding other diagnostic issues; also, it greatly assists us in drawing up treatment plans.

The psychiatrist on the team begins aggressive neuroleptic treatment on the patient's initial entry into the unit. It is typical for the psychiatrist to choose the medication that seemed to work best during previous episodes. After an initial relatively high dosage, the patient's medication is titrated down during his hospitalization. Although we don't have a strong preference regarding medication choice, Prolixin Decanoate makes medication compliance problems much clearer.

Once it is apparent that the patient is "clearing" and the medication is having an effect (usually after several days), the psychologist on the team will approach the patient to discuss his illness and proposed treatment. Since our family therapy program is part of a research protocol, we need to obtain the patient's informed consent in order for him to participate in the program. Likewise, we need the patient's permission to recruit his family and their informed consent to participate in the program. During these initial interviews, the psychologist discusses the nature of the patient's illness with him, explains both the treatment protocols and assessment procedures utilized, and briefs him on the nature of his family's proposed involvement.

Once the patient has given his consent for the staff to attempt to recruit his family, an initial meeting is scheduled with the family. The details of the program are outlined for them, and an attempt is made to enlist their consent to participate in the program. In our program, family membership is broadly defined to include not only siblings, spouses, and parents but also roommates and girlfriends.

A special note of caution here: many families have been quite upset and/or angered by their previous contacts with mental health professionals. They have found these previous contacts unrewarding. Often the family members have been ignored and "kept in the dark" regarding their relative's condition. They have also been made to feel directly or indirectly responsible for this condition; many family members will tell you that the previous doctors made them feel that they caused the illness and that if it weren't for them the patient would not be sick. Previous therapists may have aligned themselves with the patient in order to rescue him from a perceived dysfunctional family. Hence, family members are often angry, distrustful, and suspicious regarding mental health professionals.

Most mental health professionals have been taught during their training that the families of schizophrenic patients are at least partially responsible for the condition. Although in most cases this message is not directly communicated to the relatives of the patients, it often is indirectly communicated. Because of the negative bias toward family members, it has been easy for mental health professionals to label families as dysfunctional if they did not fit the professionals' model of an ideal family. Mental health professionals are more likely to attribute the dysfunction and chaos found in some families of schizophrenic patients as being responsible for the illness rather than being the result of the illness.

It is difficult but necessary to shed this negative bias in working with families in a true alliance. The fact is that there are no data to indicate that any one family pattern is responsible for the development of schizophrenia (Goldstein & Rodnick, 1975). It is important to keep in mind the utter devastation to the family brought on by the illness; families experience genuine pain and disruption. Dr. Agnes Hatfield once said, "these kids just don't show well." By that, she meant that most parents take great pride in their children and in their accomplishments. However, in the case of schizophrenic children, parents are often rebuked by the community and stigmatized.

Although at times it may be difficult to work with some families, it should always be kept in mind that the families are our potential allies in the caring and treatment of the patient.

STRUCTURE OF THE PROGRAM

Our family treatment program consists of two stages, an intensive stage and an aftercare stage. The intensive stage consists of 12 sessions, which comprise three modules. Patients and their families can choose to meet either twice a week or once a week during the intensive stage. If the family chooses to meet twice a week, then the intensive stage is often completed during the patient's hospitalization. If the families choose to meet once a week, then the intensive stage is usually completed only after the patient has been discharged from the hospital. The aftercare stage begins after the 12-session intensive stage and continues for 1 year. For the first 2 months of the aftercare stage, bimonthly meetings are held, followed by monthly booster sessions. Family treatment sessions are generally conducted by cotherapists: a member of the research program and generally a nurse or a psychology intern from the clinical unit. All sessions within the intensive and aftercare phases last approximately 1.5 hours. Additional sessions can be scheduled if needed. Families also have the option of participating in a family support group, which meets on the first and third Wednesday of each month. (We describe the family support group later in the chapter).

As mentioned previously, the 12-session intensive phase is divided into three modules: education, communication, and problem-solving. The education module is covered in the first two sessions and has as its goal educating family members concerning the nature and treatment of schizophrenia. The next five sessions are devoted to communications skills training with the goal of improving family communication. The last module consists of five sessions devoted to helping families develop better problem-solving skills, Although we have organized the program into three modules, it should be noted that the material from earlier modules is often incorporated into later modules. For example, we frequently find ourselves discussing the materials presented in the educational module during the problem-solving module. During the aftercare stage, emphasis is on continuing to problem-solve, although some education and communication skills training is also conducted during these sessions.

Behavioral family therapy is different in many ways from traditional family therapy. The aim of the therapist is to build a solid alliance with all family members. Blaming family members for the patient's condition is countertherapeutic. The goal for many traditional family therapies is to make the family "normal," yet in many ways the goal of new behavioral family therapy is to create an "abnormal" family process (McFarlane, 1983). That is, the goal is to build a protective environment for the patient by keeping emotions at a low level and simplifying communication.

The temptation to try to "fix" the family to some ideal model must be resisted. For example, in one of the ethnic groups with which we work, there is a tradition of the family being governed by a strong patriarchal figure. There is a temptation to try to democratize these families; this temptation must be resisted. Imposing one's views on the family could carry the implicit message that their previous mode of functioning was wrong and caused the illness.

The therapist must join with the family and have them become part of the treatment team. The therapist must serve as a funnel of communication between the family and the inpatient hospital staff, and the therapist must work to prevent the alienation of the family from the inpatient treatment team. The family must be kept informed of decisions regarding the patient, and the therapist must be able to provide input to the clinical team regarding family concerns and needs in treatment planning. The family should be involved in important decisions such as medication and discharge.

Education Module

We had first planned to educate both the patient and the family during the same meetings. However, because many of our patients weren't ready for education when we began our first contact with the family, we decided to educate the family and the patient separately. The positive outcome of the independent educational sessions is that families are much more likely to talk about concerns regarding the patient when he is not present.

It has been our experience that families with a relatively young schizophrenic member with few admissions tend to be quite frightened and bewildered; families with older patients with numerous admissions tend to be more angry and distrustful. In either case, we have been amazed at how little knowledge regarding schizophrenia family members have been given in their prior contacts with mental health professionals. Family members have reported numerous attempts to obtain information from professionals only to be rebuffed. Although their relative may have been discharged to their care, no professional has ever sat down with them to talk about management issues.

We tell families that the patient has an illness for which, at present, there is no cure. Families are told that the goal of the family treatment program is not to produce a cure but to decrease the probability of relapse and increase the patient's social and occupational functioning. They are told that the course of the illness is quite varied. Some individuals demonstrate only a couple of episodes with good recovery while other individuals have frequent episodes with poorer outcome. Families are also told that mental health professionals are not able to predict the course of the illness for an individual patient but that they have begun to understand factors that seem to affect the course. Families are further told that they will be taught to respond to these factors with the hope of effecting a positive outcome.

Families are told that there are other diseases within the medical field that are in some ways analogous to schizophrenia; the example given is diabetes. We have no cure for diabetes but we have isolated factors that appear to affect its course. Proper management of diabetes can lead to relatively good prognosis and functioning, as can proper management of schizophrenia.

The goals of our overall program are as follows:

- Resolution of family guilt
- Realization of handicap
- Neuroleptic medication adherence
- Identification of stressors
- Management of disruptive behavior
- Keeping the family healthy

Actually conducting the educational presentation is nowhere as orderly as it is presented here. Questions by family members prompt discussions out of sequence, topics are intermeshed, and often the same topic is rediscussed. In fact, some of the same issues brought up in the education module will again arise during the communications and problem-solving phases of the program. Each phase is dependent on and builds on the other. For example, when attending to family members' communication patterns, it is not unusual for our therapist to return to the "dopamine hypothesis" discussed in the education module and explain once again how excessive dopamine cause the patient to be overwhelmed unless communication is direct and clear.

The style of our presentation is also important. Although parts of the presentation are quite didactic, a certain sense of informality must also be maintained. It is necessary for the members of the family to feel free to ask questions and interrupt at any point in the discussion.

Our educational presentation is based on the vulnerability-stress model of schizophrenia that we outlined in the beginning of this chapter. Schizophrenia is presented as a mental illness with a biological etiology. Family members are told straightforwardly that it is unlikely that they have caused the illness. Psychotic symptoms are explained as a part of a serious mental illness and not as a result of child-rearing practices. The "sick" family member is described as highly vulnerable to stress, and the family is told that although, it is unlikely they caused the illness, they can protect the patient by providing a home environment more accommodating to his handicap. Families are told that the patient will have a better chance of avoiding rehospitalization if they can lower the stress level in the home.

Two areas of information seem particularly helpful in resolving the guilt of family members. These areas involve the genetic basis of schizophrenia and the neurochemical problems associated with it. We tell families that we know schizophrenia is a disease for several reasons. One is that the incidence of schizophrenia is consistent across countries, races, ethnic groups, etc. Furthermore, the incidence of schizophrenia increases as the amount of shared common genetic variance increases. The genetic basis of schizophrenia is also supported with a description of the twin and adoption studies (e.g., Gottesman & Shields, 1972; Heston, 1966). The sophistication of presentation varies according to the family's prior knowledge, intelligence, and so on.

A genuine sense of relief comes to the family when they realize that they did not cause the illness. One mother stated that ever since her son's first hospitalization, she had tormented herself every night before going to bed by trying to determine what she did differently in rearing this one child out of ten that made him become schizophrenic. With an understanding of the genetic basis for schizophrenia usually comes a decrease in the amount of accusations and arguing in families. For example, before receiving this information, one father had blamed the mother for babying their son and causing him to be schizophrenic; he ceased blaming the mother on hearing the genetic explanation.

We have also found that a discussion of neurochemical problems associated with schizophrenia is useful in reducing a family's guilt, as a means to increase a patient's medication compliance, and as a rationale for lowering stress within a family. Families are told that the genetic predisposition to schizophrenia seems to create a chemical imbalance. This imbalance seems to manifest itself in the nervous system at the site of the neuronal synapses. Neurotransmitters are responsible for transmitting messages across the synapses. It is our best bet that an overabundance of one of these transmitters, namely dopamine, is responsible for faulty communication across these neurons (Snyder, 1976). Subjectively, this creates problems for schizophrenics because they cannot screen out competing stimuli as most of us do. This produces attentional deficit problems as well as stress because of the confusion resulting from overstimulation. Families are told that medications are prescribed to compensate for this chemical imbalance.

We have found it quite helpful in altering a family's communication patterns to return to the "dopamine hypothesis" to provide a rationale why messages have to be simpler and clearer. It also helps to return to the dopamine hypothesis when it is necessary to allow a patient to remove himself from an overstimulating environment. We explain to the family that even pleasant events (e.g., birthday parties) may be overstimulating and stressful to the patient.

It is not uncommon for family members to believe that the ill member's symptoms are volitional and can be brought under control by the patient. Repeated discussions of the phenomenology of the illness and the genetic basis for the etiology, excessive dopamine, and information-processing deficits are usually sufficient to dissuade family members from the belief the patient is "putting on the rest of the world." It is critical for family members to believe there is a true handicap in order for them to be supportive and caring during difficult times.

We realize that an emphasis on the handicap risks setting up the family for manipulation by the patient. However, we feel that this is a necessary risk. Attempts at manipulation can be brought under control during the communication and problem-solving phases of the program.

A family's realization of the schizophrenic's true handicap alters unrealistic expectations. For example, a mother of one of our patients had hoped he would enroll in law school on discharge from the hospital. This patient had been in special education classes during junior and senior high school and had failed in a community college. When the mother realized her son's handicap and the stress associated with law school, she changed her unrealistic expectations.

Many of our patients and their families try to push themselves or their loved ones too fast during the recovery period. We tell our families and the patient that schizophrenia is like any other severe illness in that it often requires a long recovery period (6 months to 1 year). During this period, patients often sleep a lot and are not highly motivated to do much of anything. This is a pretty difficult issue because most members of the family want what is "best" for the patient and feel that he will benefit by getting back into "the swing of things." However, rushing a patient can often precipitate a relapse. Discussions about this recovery period usually foster a "hands-off" attitude toward the patient and decrease the amount of stress.

Clearly, our most effective treatment for the symptoms of schizophrenia is antipsychotic medication (May & Simpson, 1980). Since medication compliance is a major goal of our program, a good amount of time is spent during the educational module providing information about medication. Families are informed of the prescribed drugs' purpose, effectiveness, dose requirements, and potential side effects. We feel that before the patient is discharged, it is important that a medication regimen equally satisfying to both the patient and the family be decided on. This decreases the probability that medication compliance will become a source of arguments in the family.

As we note earlier, we are developing a preference for intravenous Prolixin Decanoate as the medication of choice. It is our experience that families prefer Prolixin Decanoate over ingestables because they are assured that the patient is taking medication as prescribed. Many of our patients also like the increased contact with mental health professionals necessitated by their returning to the hospital for their shots every few weeks. The vast majority of our patients live within 45 min. of the hospital; hence, transportation is not a major problem.

Since the amount of stress experienced by schizophrenic patients appears to affect the course of the illness, it is important to identify stressors. One useful procedure in helping the patient and the family to discover stressors is having the patient describe his psychotic break. Describing the break helps the relatives gain awareness of how severe the patient's illness is and also helps them pinpoint stressors that they might not have been aware of. If a family member is part of a precipitating event, it is important to label the event rather than the relative as the stressor. For example, a sister of one of our patients used to take her brother out to nightclubs with her because he was rather shy and she felt that this would do him good. When her brother started to discuss his psychosis, she was astonished to learn that when she took him to these nightclubs he became excessively paranoid and felt the urge to kill everybody in the club before they killed him. We used this event to underline the fact that patients, because of their low suspectibility to stress, can find events stressful that others regard as positive or neutral.

We capitalize on the fact that patients have the most expertise regarding whether they are experiencing stress. That is, we often tell the family that the patient is a "good detective" in spotting events that he feels are stressful. The family should attempt to listen to the patient and perhaps make alternate plans. One of the difficulties we have experienced with patients is that, although they are experiencing stress, they are reluctant to tell others for fear that they may hurt their feelings. This reluctance is a major issue that we try to work through in the communication skills portion of the program.

Work on "expressed emotion" (Brown, Birley, & Wing, 1972) provides evidence that the family may play a role in the relapse of schizophrenics. Family members are told that the manner in which they behave toward the patient can decrease the probability of relapse. In particular, family members are told that research indicates that high levels of criticism and too much emotional involvement with the patient may precipitate relapse. Since the discussion of criticism and overinvolvement can elicit guilt in family members, we have carefully thought out ways of teaching these concepts without making the family feel too defensive. Family members will often be perplexed as to how their behavior can affect the course of the illness without having caused the illness. We respond to their puzzlement through the use of a metaphor; that is, floods are caused by something beyond human control, but we can have an effect on how much damage floods cause by building strong dams. We tell families that because of the patient's previous predetermined vulnerability, we need to build a protective environment around him.

We also let families know that overinvolvement and criticism are natural responses to a sick person and are often the result of concern and love. We tell families that when a child is ill, we often shower him or her with affection (e.g., alcohol rubs, reading stories, taking the temperature, etc.). We may also admonish a child to stay in bed, rest, take medication, dress warmly, or drink fluids. When a child is not getting well, family members often feel frustrated and angry at their own helplessness. Sometimes this anger is displayed at the sick child.

Our explanations seem to help family members accept their own past behavior and allow them the freedom to modify their current behavior by attempting alternative strategies. Obviously, lectures and discussions are often not enough to create significant change in fixed behavioral patterns. Therefore, we regard our didactic presentation as an important *beginning*, which lays the groundwork for future efforts in the communication skills and problem-solving modules.

Families are told not to confuse the patient's need for a low-stress environment with permissiveness. Intolerable behavior is not to be permitted. Families are told that setting reasonable limits helps maintain a low-stress environment and provides structure for the patient. We try to teach family members to respond effectively to undesirable and threatening behaviors. For example, family members are told that violence cannot be tolerated and are urged to call the police if such behavior is exhibited. On the other hand, families are told not to argue with or confront paranoid thinking but rather to take a benignly indifferent attitude toward it and accept it as a part of the illness.

For most of our families, the schizophrenic illness has caused a major disruption in their lives. In many cases, the disruption has been so severe that family life is completely centered around the sick patient. Families are made to realize that in the case of acute illnesses, it is often necessary for families to center their attention on the sick patient, but in the case of long-term illnesses the patient's life and the lives of other family members must go on. The patient and the family must learn to live with the illness. They must learn to manage the illness as effectively as possible without sacrificing the needs of the other members of the family.

If family functioning centers too much on the sick individual, the family's physical and emotional health will suffer. For example, the spouse of one of our schizophrenic patients was so afraid that her husband would hurt or kill himself during the middle of the night that she would refuse to sleep. When she was told that it was unlikely he would harm himself, that her own health was suffering, and that she needed to be strong for long-term care, she moved into a separate bedroom and was able to enjoy a good night's sleep.

We try to encourage the patient and family to develop their own social support networks independently of each other. Having support systems to lean on can be very therapeutic for the patient and family. With few support systems, it is no wonder that the family members become overinvolved with each other. Increasing the support systems decreases the enmeshment.

Communication Training Module

For some families, it is not unusual to be unable to make simple statements to one another without creating an all-out confrontation. Communication deficits have long been identified in distressed families (Jacobson & Martin, 1976) and in families of schizophrenic patients (Singer & Wynne, 1966). Interest in communication and interactional patterns of schizophrenic families was refueled by Brown, Birley, and Wing's work (1972) on "expressed emotion." Their work indicated that high levels of critical comments and overinvolvement might affect the course of schizophrenia by precipitating relapse. One of the primary goals of the communication skills training module is to decrease the level of critical comments by teaching families more appropriate strategies, such as developing constructive feedback and increasing the use of positive reinforcement.

For families who have severe communication deficits, the communication skills module is a necessary prerequisite for the problem-solving module since effective communication is necessary for effective negotiation. Likewise, the communication skills module is dependent on an effective education module because it is difficult for families to communicate if they believe the patient is a malingerer or if one of the spouses believes that the other spouse caused their child to be schizophrenic.

Our communication skills module consists of five sessions approximately 1.5 hours long. This module is almost always completed during the patient's hospital stay. However, even after this module is completed, many of the postdischarge sessions still involve communication skills training.

One of the disadvantages to training families while the patient remains in the hospital is the problem of fostering generalization to the natural environment. However, one clear advantage in completing this program while the patient is in the hospital is that the therapist has some control over the discussions, some of which might result in angry confrontations between the family and the patient if they were to be continued at home.

The content of the communication skills module (i.e., the actual skills taught) is determined by the clinical team on the basis of an assessment of the family's communication patterns. One assessment instrument we find particularly useful is the Direct Family Interaction Test developed by Goldstein, Judd, and Rodnick (1968), which is discussed in a later section. If the family does not appear to have any communication deficits, then this module could be abbreviated. However, it has been our experience that few families (less than 10%) do not have serious communication deficits. Skills we and others (Falloon & Liberman, 1983) have generally found lacking in families include listening skills, giving and receiving positive feedback, giving and receiving criticism, feeling talk, making requests, assertive behavior, and reciprocity of conversation.

The training routine for each skill includes the following: (1) a didactic presentation regarding strategies and rules for the deployment of the skill with its accompanying rationale; (2) either videotaped or live modeling of the major components of the skill; (3) a discussion of, and quizzing of family members on, the major points of the lesson; (4) behavioral rehearsal and role-playing; (5) videotape and family members' feedback; (6) mastery of the skill via repeated trials; (7) practice assignments to promote transfer of learning; and (8) review of the skill at subsequent sessions. In order to illustrate how we teach family communication skills, an explanation of one of our lessons (giving criticism) follows.

Rules for a skill are presented by the therapist by writing them on a blackboard and also by distributing a copy of the rules to each family member. For example, rules for giving criticism are as follows:

1. State the criticism in terms of your own feelings, not in terms of absolute statements.
2. Try not to criticize the entire person; rather, try to direct the criticism at specific aspects of his or her behavior.

3. Try to request a specific behavior change. If there is something specific the other person can do to improve the situation, try to request that specifically. Don't assume that he or she will know how to please you.
4. Within the conversation, try both to start and finish on a positive note. In other words, try to diminish the overall negativeness of your conversation by sandwiching statements with either compliments or some type of positive regard.
5. Don't let your tone of voice become angry. Your goal is to actually change someone's behavior; a heated argument probably will not result in obtaining this goal.

The rationale for effective criticism skills is derived from the previous discussions in the educational module regarding the expressed emotion literature. That is, it appears that high levels of critical comments may precipitate relapse in schizophrenic patients. Since the goal of the program is to prevent relapse, it is necessary to decrease high levels of critical comments. This is not to be interpreted as meaning the patient has a license to do anything he wants without family members being critical. It simply means that families must learn to give feedback in a more constructive fashion.

Modeling demonstrations are provided by the therapists themselves or by videotaped examples. To illustrate any particular skill, several demonstrations are undertaken. Sometimes, for a change of pace or to produce a little bit of humor, the therapist will demonstrate inappropriate behavior and ask group members for feedback.

Family members are next requested to rehearse the skills depicted in the lesson. If the lesson is particularly difficult and/or the family members are particularly unskilled, we may have them imitate the same situation that was modeled for them. However, we are more likely to ask them to describe a family situation in which it would be appropriate to display such behaviors. Often the situation nominated is one that occurred recently and that ended in failure or a confrontation.

These role rehearsals are obviously critical; they give the therapist an idea of how well the family members have mastered the skills and how likely they are to carry out these skills in future situations. At times during these role rehearsals, therapists may request that family members switch roles. For instance, the patient may be asked to role-play his father while the father then becomes the patient. This is done in order to let both parties know what it is like being in one another's shoes.

These role rehearsals are videotaped and played back for the family. We have found the video feedback to be particularly helpful in allowing family members to see how they come across. Family members often comment (and we think, in most cases, sincerely) that they had no idea that they seemed so confrontive. Family members and therapists also provide verbal feedback regarding the execution of the skills in the rehearsal. In the initial lessons, therapists usually direct feedback in order to provide a good role model for how feedback should be structured. It is important that family members learn how to give positive feedback in high dosages and how to give negative feedback in an appropriate and constructive fashion.

At the end of each skill lesson, we provide practice assignments to promote transfer of learning to the family environment. We ask the family members to practice these skills in the family context and to audiotape the practice so that we can monitor it for the next session. Family members are also given homework sheets outlining the major points of the lesson. Space is also provided on these sheets for them to write in the results of their practice.

The therapist tries to insure that before the family leaves, they have formulated a plan to practice the homework. For example, if the patient is going home for the weekend, then the family may decide to practice the homework after breakfast on Sunday morning. The homework assignments are reviewed during the next session. Families are praised for any attempt to complete the homework assignment. The therapists give constructive feedback and, when necessary, try to shape more positive approaches.

Communication skills training can be difficult at times with families that have been devastated by such a serious illness. These families have suffered a great deal of frustration, bewilderment, and grief. Some members of the family have been exhausted by the illness and have isolated themselves. Others have blamed themselves or other members of the family. However, we have been pleasantly surprised that, in most cases, beneath all this disarray, confusion, and anger lies a genuine caring for each other. As a result, we are often able to reinterpret inappropriate behaviors as natural responses and as indicators of caring.

As an example, a not uncommon family style is an overinvolved mother and a highly critical father. Each of them may blame the other for their son's illness. The father may say that the reason their son is ill is because the mother has babied him, while the mother may feel that the father's constant criticism led to the illness. Parents are first reminded that there is no evidence that family interactional patterns cause schizophrenia. Genetic predispositions and biochemical imbalances are again stressed. Parents are told that overinvolvement and high levels of criticism are natural responses to a sick child suffering from a severe illness. They are told that both interactional strategies indicate a real love and commitment on their parts. In other words, they are told that we understand that they are well intentioned, but that both strategies do not work with someone suffering from this illness and need to be changed. We have found that placing such past interactional patterns in the context of a family commitment leads to more mutual efforts by family members to facilitate change.

Problem-Solving Module

Falloon, Doane, and Pederson (1985) have found that relapse in schizophrenic patients is strongly associated with the family's ability to solve problems effectively. Our problem-solving module uses the six-step approach to teaching families proposed by Falloon *et al.* (1982). The six steps are to (1) pinpoint and specify problems; (2) develop several options or alternative responses; (3) evaluate each option in terms of possible consequences; (4) choose the option that maximizes positive consequences and minimizes negative consequences; (5) plan and implement the option as a family; and (6) review the problem after the selected option has been implemented.

These steps appear simple; however, effective use of this model requires organization, commitment, and an ability to compromise—skills that are often deficient in schizophrenic families. The therapist needs a fair amount of experience and skill in order to help the family implement the model. In contrast to more traditional insight-oriented approaches to family treatment, however, behavioral problem-solving offers a clear direction during treatment for both patient and therapist. The goal for problem-solving is not for the therapist to solve all the problems within a family; rather, the goal is to teach the family the model so that they may solve their current problems and problems that arise in the future.

In our program, problem-solving training is conducted during the five sessions of the intensive stage of the program and continues throughout the follow-up period. Each session begins with an update on the implementation of previous solutions. As the family becomes more adept at problem-solving, homework assignments are completed by the family without the therapist being present. A regular time is scheduled in order for the family to constructively deal with problems and solutions. These sessions are audiotaped in order for the therapist to monitor the family's attempt at problem-solving. The family appoints one member to keep a record of the problem and plans for its solution.

The first step in successful problem-solving, and perhaps the most difficult, is for the family to pinpoint and specify problems. One of the reasons this step proves so difficult is that family members, like most individuals, are not used to operationalizing problems. That is, they state the problem in nonbehavioral terms: for example, "John shows no interest in me." A more operationalized definition might be, "When I come home from work John does not ask me how my day went."

A second reason the problem definition phase tends to be so problematic is that it requires cooperative efforts from family members. In many families, members may be used to handling conflicts in a more competitive manner. In order to get families to shift from a competitive to a collaborative problem-solving set, the therapist must be very direct and forceful. This does not mean the family members cannot ever argue or get angry with one another. However, arguing or fighting is counterproductive to problem-solving, and we do not allow it during this step.

Another problematic issue when defining problems is the natural tendency for people to suggest solutions before adequately defining the problem; these premature solutions generally reflect the bias of the family member issuing the proposal. It is imperative to disallow solutions until the problem has been adequately defined.

A fourth deterrent to adequate problem definition is the tendency for families to be defensive during this phase and essentially to "cross-complain." It is again the therapist's responsibility to keep just one problem on the table at a particular point in time. Family members need to be told that when someone is attempting to state a problem, it is their responsibility to be good listeners and to understand the complainer's problem and acknowledge that person's concerns. Family members are told that listening does not imply an admission of guilt and that they will have an opportunity to address their own concerns later.

The complainer is asked to present complaints using the communication skills learned in the earlier module. The complainer is told to begin with something positive, to be specific about the complaint, to express it in terms of feelings, and to admit that he or she may have some role in the generation of the problem.

Interestingly enough, it has been our experience that while initial problem-solving sessions seem to focus on problems relevant to the schizophrenic patient, later sessions seem to revolve around broader family issues.

The second phase of problem-solving, developing options or alternate responses, can prove difficult. We try to get families to use a brainstorming approach, but for some concrete families, this freewheeling approach is difficult. The therapist tries to model brainstorming by presenting some obviously absurd solutions. Brainstorming has the benefit of disinhibiting family members who may have felt inhibited during previous family discussions.

One caution: during the solution-generation stage, family members often make comments regarding the quality of the solutions. Therapists should ask members to refrain from passing judgment on solutions during the brainstorming phase. It is also important for the family member who is appointed secretary to list each and every proposed option, because family members have selective memories regarding potential solutions.

The third stage is for the family to evaluate each option in terms of its consequences. It has been our experience that some family members are quite adept at seeing the positive consequences for themselves while neglecting the negative consequences for other members of the family. Likewise, some family members can see immediate consequences but not long-term consequences.

The fourth stage of effective problem-solving is to choose the option that maximizes positive outcome and minimizes negative outcome. During this stage, there is a tendency for one or two dominant family members to try to exercise their wills and choose the option that they feel is best for the family. We have witnessed a tendency in our therapists to try to democratize the option-choosing stage. However, it should be noted that some members within the family appear to exercise better judgment than other members, and this should be kept in mind. Also, the cultural context in which a family makes a decision should be a consideration. That is, some families are patriarchial or matriarchial, and it may not be wise to attempt modifications in such systems. Again, it has been our experience that the best solutions seem to be those involving change by several members of the family, with each party *willing* to sacrifice for the good of the whole.

In order to implement the option chosen, we often have the family draw up a contract. The contract should be clear, precise, and represent the option chosen. We often have the families place the contract in a visible place so all can see it and be reminded of it. Violations of the contract should be noted and brought into the treatment session.

The last step in problem-solving is reviewing the contract. All contracts are regarded as tentative until they have been proven effective. If family members are dissatisfied with the contract, then renegotiation is initiated.

It has been our experience that, at the beginning of problem-solving training, it is not a good idea to come up with solutions that require a lot of effort on the part of the patient. Most patients at this point have a low energy level, and it is difficult for them to sustain very much effort. This obstacle should be discussed directly during the option-selection phase. If the solution selected does require a lot of effort from the patient, both the patient and the family might be very disappointed.

AFTERCARE PHASE

During the aftercare phase of the behavioral family therapy program, index patients and their families are seen by their primary family therapists for at least 12 months following the completion of the intensive phase. In general, families meet at least twice a month for the first 2 months and once a month thereafter, unless they experience some problems that require unscheduled visits.

Aftercare therapy sessions are consistent with treatment received during the intensive phase. The format incorporates modeling, behavioral rehearsal, and feedback. In these sessions, problems and difficulties that the family encounters or expects to encounter in the near future are presented and discussed. The therapist facilitates the family's coping strategies through the principles taught in the modules during the intensive phase.

Information and/or advice presented during the psychoeducational sessions is repeated and reinforced whenever necessary. Briefly, this information includes the following: (1) definition of schizophrenia; (2) description of the illness, including symptoms and their interference with daily functioning; (3) biological as well as environmental components of schizophrenia; (4) importance of compliance with the medication regimen, including side effects and other dangers; (5) importance of creating a less stressful environment; and (6) course of illness (the approach should be guarded but hopeful). Some direct advice given to the families includes to (1) tone down unrealistic expectations; (2) forget about guilt; (3) provide structure for the patient but not to push; (4) make sure the patient stays on medication; and (5) to utilize strategies for coping with delusions, hallucinations, threats, violence, and so on.

During the aftercare phase, the family's attention should be redirected to social communication skills if the therapist perceives that difficulties in problem-solving are directly or indirectly related to continued deficits in communication skills. These communication skills include (1) active listening skills, including nonverbal behavior; (2) reciprocity of conversation; (3) giving and receiving positive feedback; (4) giving and receiving negative feedback; (5) expression of feelings; and (6) assertive behavior and making requests.

If additional difficulties impinge on the family's coping and problem-solving strategies, then additional treatment might be offered by the therapist as an adjunct to the family therapy. For example, if the therapist feels that severe marital problems are interfering with the family's ability to effectively problem-solve, then marital therapy is recommended.

The therapist's role during this phase of treatment is facilitative. There is minimal therapist input unless obstacles to effective problem-solving are noted. It is hoped that the family will continue the shift from competitive to collaborative solutions. The therapist interrupts family members if they are being competitive to remind them of the rules and to reinforce behaviors that are consistent with collaboration; however, every therapist has to remember not to stifle the family tendency toward fighting or arguing. Remember that the goal is not to eliminate arguing or fighting but rather to establish problem-solving as a viable alternative.

In addition to our aftercare therapy program, relatives of our schizophrenic patients are encouraged to participate in a family support (self-help) group that meets twice monthly (Atwood, 1983; Hatfield, 1983; Wasow, 1982). Here relatives (spouses, siblings, parents, and/or other significant others) share their difficulties and develop strategies to solve their problems. Relatives who once believed themselves to be alone are introduced to others who suffer similar difficulties with their "mentally ill" relatives. In addition to this type of support, participants are also provided with education about the nature and course of the illness by a nurse and psychologist who sit in on the group. Other more structured programs are available for these relatives if they request them. For example, one program involved the veteran's benefits counselor, who answered questions about how relatives could insure that patients were receiving benefits due to them.

The support groups and behavioral family therapy share a similar approach. They clearly identify the patient and *not* the family member as the ill person, which is different from psychoanalytic and traditional family system approaches. While these traditional approaches emphasize that schizophrenia is causally related to family upbringing and relationships, research has *not* confirmed any such causal relationship.

CASE ILLUSTRATION

Charles B was a 33-year-old unemployed black male with a diagnosis of chronic paranoid schizophrenia, participating in our behavioral family therapy with his parents, Charles Sr. and Bernice. The parents also attended the family support group and have become extremely active mental health advocates and members of the Mental Health Association.

At the time of Charles's admission his predominant symptoms were blunted affect, homicidal delusions (e.g., assassinating various members of the Mafia using his martial art skills), and auditory hallucinations. He was hospitalized at the request of his parents because they feared he would be harmed due to his threats against various Mafia figures. It should be noted that since his first break, the patient was always reported as delusional. However, he did not verbalize delusions when he was not acutely psychotic.

Charles was the older of two children. It was reported by both parents and patient that Charles was an A and B student in high school, but he was socially introverted. After attending a private college for a year, he dropped out, entered the army, and served for 2 years prior to his honorable discharge. He returned to live with his family. His first psychotic break occurred 1 year after his discharge from the service in 1972. Both parents were employed. At the time of his first break, his younger sister was still in junior high school. She now attends a pharmacy school in New England.

Charles could be described as an alert male who looks his age, with a sturdy build. He maintained good hygiene habits and appeared well-kempt. His cognitive functions and memory were unimpaired. He possessed above-average intelligence and had good insight into the nature of his problems. Even though he was mentally competent, he was declared financially incompetent. His father was appointed conservator of his Veteran's pension. The patient was extremely helpful and was liked by hospital staff. He was socially outgoing, but he did not form intimate or close relationships with people.

Charles had at least eight prior psychiatric hospitalizations. For a period of time, he was incarcerated in the adult correctional institute for robbery. Two weeks prior to admission, he became more preoccupied with his paranoid and homicidal delusions. During his recent hospitalization, his Prolixin was increased to 25 mg intramuscularly every 2 weeks. After discharge his medication was increased to 37.5 mg intramuscularly every 2 weeks because observers, including his parents, noted that his behavior had deteriorated.

Charles's case provides an example of the flexibility that exists within our treatment program. His parents joined the family support group prior to their participation in the behavioral family therapy. In fact, they learned of the treatment program during one of the guest lectures by our staff and requested to be included in the program. Family treatment with the B family has been quite effective and rewarding. In the initial assessment of the family, particular problems were noted in basic communication skills, especially giving and receiving negative feedback, nonverbal listening skills, and feeling talk (i.e., the ability to share emotions). Also, the family needed to learn how to solve problems collaboratively.

Prior to their participation in the family support group, the parents stated that they had minimal understanding of schizophrenia and how to cope with their son's unusual behavior. They were guilt ridden and felt very alone. They received minimal support from their relatives and the community at large, leading to their social isolation. In response to the son's difficulties, the mother became increasingly overprotective and overinvolved. (This response is not atypical of relative's attempts to deal with physically/emotionally ill patients). The father, on the other hand, became increasingly more critical of his son's behavior.

During both the family support group and behavioral family therapy, the parents learned to respond more effectively to Charles's illness. Some of the guilt feelings and social isolation subsided. Of particular importance was the reduction of the mother's overinvolvement. There was also a reduction in the frequency of critical statements made by the father; he is presently working on how to communicate negative feedback more constructively. Interestingly, the father and son were able to point out nonverbal behavior in the mother, of which she had been totally unaware.

This surprised her, and she worked diligently on correcting these behaviors, particularly a lack of eye contact during social interaction. The mother and father learned to monitor their behavior and gained some insight into the factors that influenced their behavior as well as Charles's behavior.

The family reported that the home environment became less stressful and tense after they began the total treatment program. Minor problems existed, but they have been able to bring these situations into therapy. Considerable progress was made with this family. Recently, Charles began coaching a boys' basketball team at a local recreation center.

ASSESSMENT

The principle that "effective treatment requires careful assessment" is particularly relevant for clinicians who work with schizophrenic patients and their families. The multivariate phenomenology of schizophrenia, in combination with the complexities of family interaction, results in a situation that is confusing and at times overwhelming. This state of affairs can be clarified by the careful and systematic use of two tools: psychiatric evaluation of the patient and behavioral assessment of the family.

Psychiatric Evaluation

The assessment of psychopathology has three major goals: (1) establishing a correct diagnosis; (2) evaluating prognosis; and (3) monitoring the course of the disorder. The first two goals are best achieved through a comprehensive structured psychiatric interview. An excellent review of available interviews is given by Hedlund and Vieweg (1981). A good example of a completely structured interview is the National Institute of Mental Health's Diagnostic Interview Schedule (DIS). The DIS diagnoses a variety of psychiatric disorders according to criteria specified by three major diagnostic systems: DSM-III, Research Diagnostic Criteria (RDC), and Washington University criteria (Robins, Helzer, Croughan, & Ratcliff, 1981). DSM-III diagnoses can be scored with a publicly available computer program.

The 263 items of the DIS ensure that the interviewer inquires about symptoms unrelated to schizophrenia that may have prognostic significance. For example, the prevalence of problem drinking among schizophrenics may be as high as 63% (Gottheil & Waxman, 1982). Concomitant alcoholism bodes poorly for prognosis and has significant implications for treatment planning. The presence of affective symptoms prior to or during a schizophrenic episode predicts good outcome (Taylor & Abrams, 1975; Vaillant, 1964). Better outcome is also found for paranoid as compared with nonparanoid schizophrenics (Tsuang & Winokur, 1974), and the former benefit more from phenothiazine than the latter (Goldstein, 1970). The detailed knowledge of the symptom profile generated by the DIS can aid the clinician's preparation of long-term case management and rehabilitation plans.

For the purpose of monitoring the longitudinal course of psychopathology, an evaluation instrument should permit a relatively brief assessment of severity along multiple dimensions of symptomatology. A thorough review of rating scales that meet these requirements is available (Endicott & Spitzer, 1980). One scale that has been used extensively is the Brief Psychiatric Rating Scale (BPRS). A comprehensive review of the BPRS was given by Hedlund and Viewig (1980). The version we use consists of 21 seven-point scales of psychopathology, which are rated based on the information collected during a semistructured 20–40 min. interview. Dimensions of psychopathology that are broader than individual scales can also be derived from the BPRS. Goldstein, Rodnick, Evans, May, & Steinberg (1978) gave rules for summing scales into four factors: (1) anxiety and depression; (2) schizophrenic symptoms; (3) hostility and suspiciousness; and (4) withdrawal. Periodic BPRS ratings can be used to document patient responsiveness to therapeutic interventions and to explore the functional relationships between psychopathological behavior and the environment. The BPRS can also be used to define relapse. Since no one definition can do justice to the multivariate, clinical phenomenology of relapse, we use three different sets of BPRS relapse criteria. "Psychotic relapse" is considered positive if any of the following scales are rated 6 or 7: hallucinations, unusual thought content, and conceptual disorganization. "Psychotic exacerbation" is considered positive in the presence of any 3-point total increase across the above three scales, excluding changes at or below point 3. "Behavioral relapse" is considered positive if any of the following scales are rated 6 or 7: bizarreness, self-neglect, hostility, depression, suicidality, or anxiety.

In addition to the standard BPRS, our assessment program includes the Target Symptom Ratings suggested by Falloon, *et al.* (1984). For each patient, we specify three schizophrenic symptoms that are characteristic of his or her disorder. During the BPRS interview, questions are asked to enable the interviewer to rate these "target symptoms." Since these three scales are individualized, the ratings can be based solely on the unique phenomenology of each patient's symptoms. Although the incremental validity of using target symptoms in addition to the BPRS has yet to be established, their sensitivity to treatment-induced changes has been demonstrated (Falloon, *et al.*, 1984).

Both the DIS and the BPRS should be administered at the beginning of the patient's hospitalization because they will serve as the foundation for important aspects of treatment planning. The DIS will take 3 or more hours to administer to inpatient schizophrenics. Thus, for most patients, several sessions are required to complete the DIS. In many settings, the length of the interviews will be too costly for use by professional staff. However, the structure of the interview makes it feasible to use nonprofessional staff members after they have been appropriately trained. In fact, Robins *et al.* (1981) report high levels of diagnostic agreement between nonprofessional interviewers and psychiatrists. The BPRS can also be administered by a nonprofessional after appropriate training. A useful schedule of BPRS assessments is the following: at the beginning of hospitalization, the end of hospitalization, and every 3 months thereafter on an outpatient basis.

Behavioral Family Assessment

There is a substantial body of evidence indicating that patients who live in a stressful family environment characterized by high "expressed emotion" (EE) have an increased risk for relapse (e.g., Vaughn & Leff, 1976; Vaughn, Snyder, Freeman, Jones, Falloon, & Liberman, 1982). EE measures the degree of criticism and/or emotional overinvolvement expressed about the patient during the Camberwell Family Interview (CFI; Brown & Rutter, 1966). The CFI is a semistructured interview that encourages relatives to discuss the impact that the patient's disorder has had on them and the emotional atmosphere of their home while the interviewer probes for details of the onset and course of the disorder. Complete descriptions of bothersome episodes, along with the family's reactions, are elicited with the goal of allowing relatives to ventilate negative feelings about the patient without explicitly urging them to do so. Interviews are audiotaped for later coding by a trained rater who (1) counts the number of criticisms the relative makes about the patient and (2) rates the degree of emotional overinvolvement on a five-point scale. Unfortunately, the implementation of the correct procedure for rating EE requires intensive training, lengthy interviewing, and careful, time-consuming coding. For many practitioners, this limits its usefulness as a clinical tool. Nevertheless, an accurate evaluation of the stress level in the home environment is necessary to faciliate the implementation of behavioral family therapy. For this purpose, the clinician should become familiar with the structure and style of the CFI so as to be able to interview relatives in a manner that allows expression of criticism and emotional overinvolvement without directly eliciting such expression and become familiar with the definitions of criticism and overinvolvement used in the EE studies and use these dimensions to structure the evaluation of the patient's relatives.

An alternative to the CFI that provides additional information about communication and problem-solving skills is the Direct Family Intervention (DFI) procedure used by the UCLA family project (Doane, West, Goldstein, Rodnick, & Jones, 1981; Valone, Norton, Goldstein, & Doane, 1983). The major difference between the DFI and the CFI is that, whereas the CFI rates attitudes that the relative expresses about the patient to an interviewer, the DFI rates the actual behavior of the relative in the presence of the patient. In addition, the DFI enables the clinician to directly assess the communication and problem-solving skills of patients and their families. Briefly, the DFI is composed of four steps. First, each family member is asked individually to identify two family problems. The patient identifies problems created by other family members, and they in turn identify problems created by the patient. Each respondent is asked to role-play a statement that describes the issue to the offending party. These statements are audiotaped. The second step requires family members to respond to audiotaped problem statements about their behavior. Their responses are audiotaped contiguous to the original problem statement. Next, the audiotapes corresponding to the two most emotionally laden problem areas are played for the entire family as a stimulus for two separate 10-min. family discussions, which are videotaped. Finally, these two discussions are coded for affective style (AS) and problem-solving style (PSS). The AS codes have been described by Doane *et al.* (1981). They include supportive, critical, guilt-inducing, and intrusive statements. PSS includes codes such as statement of problem, solution proposals, plan for implementation, paraphrase of feelings, and seeking clarification.

The DFI shares with the CFI a complexity of administration and coding that results in limited clinical utility. However, it should be effective for the clinician to do the following: (1) observe the entire family attempting to resolve one or more problems and (2) become familiar with the AS and PSS codes and use them to structure evaluations of the family interaction.

A more detailed assessment of communication skills can be made by incorporating assessment devices that have been developed for the evaluation of social competence. Our assessment program incorporates two modes of evaluating social competence: self-report inventory and videotaped role-play interaction. For self-report of social skill, Lowe and Cautela (1978) have developed the Social Performance Survey Schedule (SPSS). This 100-item inventory has been demonstrated to be a reliable and valid measure of social competence (Lowe, 1982; Miller & Funabiki, 1984).

Our role-play measure of social competence is the Simulated Social Interaction Test (SSIT). Research supporting the reliability and validity of the SSIT has been discussed in detail by Curran (1982). The SSIT differentiates normals from psychiatric patients, is significantly related to hospital personnel ratings, and is sensitive to changes brought about by social skills therapy. The SSIT procedures are straightforward. The patient is videotaped while responding to a series of eight standardized situations. Each videotaped situation is then rated for social competence and anxiety by trained judges. There are two major advantages of the SSIT. First, it is free of the biases inherent in self-report inventories such as the SPSS. It is impossible for patients to "fake good" on the SSIT and unlikely that they will "fake bad." Second, the SSIT assesses social behavior in the context of specified situations and is thereby sensitive to patient–situation interactions. Furthermore, as Curran (1982) noted, the eight situations used cover the range of situations reported to be most difficult for psychiatric patients (Goldsmith & McFall, 1975). Thus, the SSIT can be used by a clinician to determine which situations are most difficult for a given patient. Social competence programs can be designed in accordance with this assessment by using knowledge of patient–situation interactions to choose role-plays during therapy sessions and to assign between-session practice tasks.

The disadvantage of the SSIT is that most clinicians do not have the resources needed to administer it. In addition to videotape equipment and trained raters, the SSIT requires a narrator, who describes the scenes, and two confederates who take turns role-playing with the patient. For the practicing clinician, a less rigorous but practical approach may be taken. First, the clinician should become familiar with the range of situations covered by the SSIT (Curran, 1982). The clinician can then use these situations to engage in role-plays with the patient and family. The informal observation of these role-plays can provide the clinician with a guide for assessing the situation-specific skill needs of patients and their families.

The usefulness of these observations can be increased if the observers learn a conceptual structure within which observations can be organized. A useful organizational scheme is provided by Curran's minimodel (1979) of social skills performance. The minimodel requires the observer to answer two questions: Are communication skills present? Are interference mechanisms present? An interference mechanism is a response that "inhibits and/or disrupts the effective application of social response capabilities" (Curran, 1979, p. 60). Examples include anxiety, cognitive distortion, and aggression. Based on answers to the minimodel questions, patients can be classified into four groups: (1) adequate skills, interference absent; (2) adequate skills, interference present; (3) inadequate skills, interference absent; and (4) inadequate skills, interference present. Ideally, such a classification should be made specific to each of the range of situations covered by the SSIT. The implications of the classificatory system are obvious. Individuals from the first group do not require skills treatment. Neither do group 2 members, but they probably need some other treatment (e.g., exposure therapy, cognitive therapy). Group 3 patients are candidates for skills therapy, and group 4 patients require skills training in conjunction with some other therapy. When assessing a family, this model can be applied to all family members. If rigorously applied, it will help the clinician decide how to treat maladaptive family interaction.

Educating families about the nature of schizophrenia is an integral part of our treatment program. For assessing family knowledge about schizophrenia, we have developed a 24-item true or false questionnaire that covers a variety of issues, including symptoms, course, prognosis, etiology, and medication side effects.

The knowledge questionnaire can be used to assess a family's need for the educational treatment. The results will also give the clinician clues as to which areas of the education program should be emphasized for particular families. We also use the knowledge questionnaire to assess the effectiveness of the educational intervention by giving it to family members after the intervention and at 3-month intervals during the aftercare phase of treatment.

SUMMARY

Our behavioral family therapy program is initiated during a patient's hospitalization on our acute inpatient unit at the Veterans Hospital in Providence, Rhode Island. Our inpatient unit is a moderate-sized facility that treats a variety of psychiatric disorders. When admitted to the unit, patients are assigned to multidisciplinary clinical teams. Although all treatment decisions are made in the context of the team, patients in behavioral family therapy are assigned to a psychologist on the team who acts as the primary therapist. After the patient has stabilized on the unit, the psychologist approaches the patient to discuss his illness and proposed treatment. Since our family treatment program is part of a research protocol, we obtain both the patient's informed consent and the informed consent of the family.

Our family treatment program consist of two stages, an intensive stage and an aftercare stage. The intensive stage consist of 12 sessions comprising three modules: education, communication, and problem-solving. The aftercare stage begins after the 12 sessions of intensive stage and continues for 1 year. During the first 2 months of the aftercare stage, bimonthly meetings are held followed by monthly booster sessions. Family treatment sessions are generally conducted by cotherapists: a member of the research program and, generally, a nurse or psychology intern from the clinical unit. All sessions within the intensive and aftercare phases last approximately 1.5 hours. Additional sessions can be scheduled if needed. Families also have the option of participating in a support group that meets twice a month.

Our family program is based on the philosophy that families are major caregivers in the treatment of schizophrenia and should be perceived as allies. During the education module, we try to inform families what is known about schizophrenia and what isn't known. A diathesis-stress model of schizophrenia is presented to the family. Families are told that the patient has an illness for which, at present, there is no cure. They are told that the goal of the program is not to produce a cure but to decrease the probability of relapse and to increase the patient's social and occupational functioning. Psychotic symptoms are explained as part of a serious mental illness and not a result of childrearing practices. The patient is described as being highly vulnerable to stress, and the family is told that although it is unlikely that they have caused the illness, they can protect the patient by providing a home environment more accommodating to his handicap. Information is given during the education module in such a fashion as to be consistent with the following goals: (1) resolution of family guilt; (2) realization of handicap; (3) adherence to neuroleptic medication; (4) identification of stressors; (5) management of disruptive behavior; and (6) keeping the family healthy.

The communication skills training component of the intensive phase is seen in most cases as prerequisite for the problem-solving module since effective communication is necessary for effective negotiation. At times, communication training can be quite difficult. Some families cannot make even a simple statement to one another without creating an all-out confrontation. The skills taught during the communication skills module are determined by the clinical team based on the assessment of the family's communication patterns. Skills typically taught are listening skills, giving and receiving positive feedback, giving and receiving criticism, expression of feelings, making requests, assertive behavior, and reciprocity of conversation. Skills training procedures include didactic presentation, modeling, discussion, behavioral rehearsal, feedback, repeated trials, practice assignments, and review.

The goal of the problem-solving module is not for the treatment team to solve all the family's problems but rather to teach the family a problem-solving model. The problem-solving module presented is a six-step process including (1) problem definition; (2) developing options; (3) evaluating options; (4) choosing options; (5) implementation; and (6) review.

The aftercare phase of our behavioral family therapy program is consistent with the treatment received during the intensive phase. Problem-solving is stressed, with continued communication skills training and information provided. During the aftercare phase, families meet twice a month for the first 2 months and monthly thereafter. Family members may also choose to attend a family support group that meets twice monthly.

Our assessment consists of psychiatric evaluations of the patient and behavioral assessment of the family. Our psychiatric evaluation of the patient centers on three themes: (1) providing a correct diagnosis; (2) evaluating a prognosis; and (3) monitoring the course of the disorder. We use the DIS to assist in diagnosis and evaluating prognosis. A variation of a BPRS (Endicott & Spitzer, 1980) and the Target Symptom Ratings (Falloon, *et al.*, 1984) are used to monitor the course of the disorder. Stress in the home environment is measured with the use of the CFI (Brown & Rutter, 1966). Communication and problem-solving deficits are measured by the DFI (Valone *et al.*, 1983; Doane *et al.*, 1981). The patient's social competency level is measured by a pencil-and-paper instrument (SPSS; Lowe, 1982) and a role-play measure (SSIT, Curran, 1982). Finally, family knowledge about schizophrenia is measured by an instrument that we have developed consisting of 24 true or false questions. We have found that the dictum "effective treatment requires careful assessment" is particularly relevant to clinicians who work with schizophrenic patients and their families.

REFERENCES

Atwood, N. (1983). Supportive group counseling for the relatives of schizophrenic patients. In W. A. McFarlane (Ed.), *Family therapy in schizophrenia*. New York: Guilford Press.

Brown, G. W., Birley, J. L. T., & Wing, J. K. (1972). Influence of family life on the course of the schizophrenic disorder. *British Journal of Psychiatry, 121*, 241–248.

Brown, G. W., & Rutter, M. (1966). The measurement of family activities and relationships: A methodological study. *Human Relations, 19*, 241–263.

Curran, J. P. (1979). Pandora's box reopened? The assessment of social skills. *Journal of Behavioral Assessment, 1*, 55–71.

Curran, J. P. (1982). A procedure for the assessment of social skills: The Simulated Social Interaction Test. In J. P. Curran & P. M. Monti (Eds.), *Social skills training. A practical handbook for assessment and treatment*. New York: Guilford Press.

Doane, J. A., West, K. L., Goldstein, M. J., Rodnick, E. H., & Jones, J. E. (1981). Parental communication deviance and affective style. *Archives of General Psychiatry, 38*, 679–685.

Endicott, J., & Spitzer, R. L. (1980). Evaluation of psychology treatment. In A. J. Kapland & B. J. Sadocks (Eds.), Comprehensive textbook of psychology. Baltimore: Williams & Wilkens.

Falloon, I. R. H., Boyd, J. G., McGill, C. W., Ranzoni, J., Moss, H., & Gilderman, A. M. (1982). Family Management in the prevention of exacerbation of schizophrenia. *The New England Journal of Medicine, 306*, 1437–1440.

Falloon, I. R. H., Boyd, J. L., McGill, C. W., *et al.* (1984). *Family care of schizophrenia*. New York: Guilford Press.

Falloon, I. R. H., Doane, J. A., & Pederson, J. (1985). Family versus individual management in prevention of morbidity of schizophrenia: III. Family functioning. *Archives of General Psychiatry, 42*, 34–42.

Falloon, I. R. H., & Liberman, R. P. (1983). Behavioral family intervention in the management of chronic schizophrenia. In W. R. McFarlane (Ed.), *Family therapy in schizophrenia*. New York: Guilford Press.

Goldsmith, J. B., & McFall, R. M. (1975). Developmental evaluation of an interpersonal skill-training program for psychiatry patients. *Journal of Abnormal Psychology, 84*, 51–58.

Goldstein, M. (1970). Premorbid adjustment, paranoid status, and patterns of response to phenothiazine in acute schizophrenia. *Schizophrenia Bulletin, 1*, 24–37.

Goldstein, M. J., Judd, L. L., & Rodnick, E. H. (1968). A method for studying social influences and coping patterns within families of disturbed adolescents. *Journal of Nervous and Mental Disorders, 147*, 233–251.

Goldstein, M. J., & Rodnick, E. H. (1975). The family's contribution to the etiology of schizophrenia: Current status. *Schizophrenia Bulletin, 14*, 48–63.

Goldstein, M. J., Rodnick, E. H., Evans, J. R., May, P. A. R., & Steinberg, M. R. (1978). Drug and family therapy in the aftercare of acute schizophrenia. *Archives of General Psychiatry, 35*, 1169–1177.

Gottesman, I. I., & Shields, J. (1972). *Schizophrenia and genetics: A twin study vantage point*. New York: Academic Press.

Gottheil, E., & Waxman, H. M. (1982). Alcoholism and schizophrenia. In E. M. Pattison & E. Kaufman (Eds), *Encyclopedic handbook of alcoholism*. New York: Gardner Press.

Hatfield, A. B. (1983). What families want of family therapists. In W. R. McFarland (Ed.), *Family therapy in schizophrenia*. New York: Guilford Press.

Hedlund, J. L., & Vieweg, B. W. (1980). The Brief Psychiatric Rating Scale (BPRS): A comprehensive review. *Journal of Operational Psychiatry, 11*, 48–65.

Hedlund, J. L., & Vieweg, B. W. (1981). Structured psychiatric interviews: A comparative review. *Journal of Operational Psychiatry, 12*, 39–67.

Heston, L. L. (1966). Psychiatric disorders in foster home reared children of schizophrenic mothers. *British Journal of Psychiatry, 112*, 819–825.

Jacobson, N. S., & Martin, B. (1976). Behavioral marriage therapy: Current status. *Psychological Bulletin, 83*, 540–556.

Lowe, M. R. (1982). Validity of the positive behavior subscale of the social performance survey schedule in a psychiatric population. *Psychological Reports, 50*, 83–87.

Lowe, M. R., & Cautela, J. R. (1978). A self-report measure of social skills. *Behavior Therapy, 9*, 535.

May, P. R., & Simpson, G. M. (1980). Schizophrenia: Evaluation of treatment methods. In H. I. Kaplan, A. M. Freedman, & B. J. Sadock. *Comprehensive textbook of psychiatry, III*. Baltimore: Williams & Wilkins.

McFarlane, W. R. (Ed.). (1983). *Family therapy in schizophrenia*: New York: Guilford Press.

Miller, L. S., & Funabiki, D. (1984). Predictive validity of the social performance survey schedule for component interpersonal behaviors. *Behavioral Assessment, 6*, 33–44.

Robins, L. N., Helzer, J. E., Croughan, J., & Ratcliff, K. S. (1981). National Institute of Mental Health Diagnostic Interview Schedule: Its history, characteristics, and validity. *Archives of General Psychiatry, 38*, 381–389.

Singer, M. T., & Wynne, L. C. (1966). Communication styles in parents of normals, neurotics, and schizophrenics. *Psychiatric Research Reports, 20*, 25–38.

Snyder, S. H. (1976). The dopamine hypothesis of schizophrenia: Focus on the dopamine receptor. *American Journal of Psychiatry, 133*(2), 197–202.

Taylor, M., & Abrams, R. (1975). Manic depressive illness and good prognosis schizophrenia. *American Journal of Psychiatry, 132*, 741–742.

Tsuang, M. T., & Winokur, G. (1974). Criteria for subtyping schizophrenia: Clinical differentiation of hebephrenic and paranoid schizophrenia. *Archives of General Psychiatry, 31*, 43–47.

Vaillant, G. E. (1964). Prospective prediction of schizophrenic remission. *Archives of General Psychiatry, 11*, 509–518.

Valone, K., Norton, J. P., Goldstein, M. J., Doane, J. A. (1983). Parental expressed emotion and affective style in an adolescent sample at risk for schizophrenia spectrum disorders. *Journal of Abnormal Psychology, 92*, 399–407.

Vaughn, C. E., & Leff, J. P. (1976). The influence of family and social factors on the course of psychiatric illness: A comparison of schizophrenic and depressed neurotic patients. *British Journal of Psychiatry, 129*, 125–137.

Vaughn, C. E., Snyder, K. S., Freeman, W., Jones, S., Falloon, I. R. H., & Liberman, R. P. (1982). Family factors in schizophrenic relapse: A replication. *Schizophrenia Bulletin, 8*, 425–426.

Wasow, M. (1982). *Coping with schizophrenia: A survival manual for parents, relatives, and friends*. California: Science and Behavior Books.

Zubin, J., & Steinhauer, S. (1981). How to break the logjam in schizophrenia: A look beyond genetics. *The Journal of Nervous and Mental Disease, 169*, 477–492.

13

Prevention of Morbidity in Schizophrenia

IAN R. H. FALLOON
Buckingham Mental Health Service, England

Family-based interventions have played a major part in the search for effective management of schizophrenia. Early efforts focused on observations that the patterns of family interaction with the person suffering from a schizophrenic disorder appeared distorted and confusing. As a consequence, family therapists sought to unravel these "abnormal" communication patterns and thereby reduce the cognitive distortions underlying the index patient's disturbed thought processes. Once the index patient could express him- or herself freely without resorting to the cognitive distortions inherent in delusions, hallucinations, and thought interference, it was assumed that these symbolic expressions would melt away. Schizophrenia was considered to be a coping response that the index patient learned to exhibit to deal with a "crazy-making" family environment.

Early attempts to enhance the clarity of family communication provided evidence to support this hypothesis. Several uncontrolled studies demonstrated improvement in the florid symptoms of schizophrenia after sessions of conjoint family therapy (Bowen, 1961; Esterson, Cooper, & Laing, 1965; Friedman *et al.*, 1965; Jackson & Weakland, 1961). Indeed, these early efforts were among the first systematic attempts to establish family therapy as a therapeutic approach to mental disorders. A lack of controlled outcome research at a time when powerful new pharmacological agents were being introduced probably contributed to relatively limited dissemination of these methods within the mainstream of psychiatric practice. However, the lack of general acceptance of the value of these methods may have suffered also from the rather excessive claims of their supporters, who sought to contrast the efficacy of family therapy with that of the phenothiazines in the management of florid schizophrenia. Claims for psychotherapeutic care were accompanied by elaborate theories of the psychosocial etiology and nature of schizophrenia that categorically denied the existence of any biological basis for the disorder. Many case reports of successful treatment appeared; they described persons who were labeled as "schizophrenic" but were probably suffering from severe personality disorders. In these cases the argument for a psychosocial etiology associated with inconsistent parenting behavior was more cogent.

The development of a behavioral family therapy approach to schizophrenia occurred at a much later stage and in a contrasting manner (Falloon & Liberman, 1982). The initial phase of its development consisted of educational workshops for patients and their families, who were invited to discuss the nature of the disorder, its diagnosis, and medical management with mental health professionals. Schizophrenia was described as a biological disorder associated with an imbalance of brain chemistry that was highly sensitive to environmental stress factors. Treatment consisted of long-term drug therapy and social support that aimed to maximize the potential for the individual's psychological development. This approach has been further refined as a treatment method known as psychoeducation (Anderson, Hogarty, & Reiss (1980) and has shown considerable efficacy in its own right (Hogarty *et al.*, 1986).

The second phase in the development of a behavioral approach to families with members suffering from schizophrenia involved in the addition of communication training to the educational workshops (Falloon, Liberman, Lillie, & Vaughn, 1981). Family members were taught to communicate their mutual feelings and needs in a direct, specific manner that would tend to facilitate efficient conflict resolution. This communication training module was based on the observations that the chronic course of schizophrenia was reliably associated with high levels of "expressed emotion" (EE) directed toward the index patient. The specific components of family interaction most closely associated with a chronic course were critical and hostile expressions of negative feelings, intrusive remarks indicating a highly overinvolved attitude, and a lack of expression of positive feelings and warmth (Vaughn & Leff, 1976). The behavioral family intervention strategy that was derived from this formulation attempted to train all family members in the effective expression of positive and negative feelings that reduced harsh criticism and intrusive communication and enhanced the expression of positive feelings.

The third phase involved the addition of structured problem-solving to education and communication training. A greater emphasis was placed on the manner in which stress appeared to trigger recurrent episodes of schizophrenia and on the fact that this stress was derived from threatening life events from sources outside of immediate family, as well as from high levels of expressed emotion within the family (Zubin & Spring, 1977). Problem-solving offered the potential for management of stress from extra- as well as intrafamilial origins (Liberman, Falloon, & Aitchison, 1984).

The final phase of the current development of behavioral family therapy for schizophrenia concerned the addition of a variety of validated behavior therapy strategies to the problem solving approach. These specific strategies included social skills training and operant conditioning strategies, including methods to modify persistent hallucinations and delusions as well as activation of individual suffering from severe "negative" symptoms (Falloon, Boyd, & McGill, 1984).

This increasing complexity of the behavioral family therapy approach has been accompanied by an increasing sophistication in assessment procedures, which constitute the empirical basis for this treatment method. Education, communication, and problem-solving issues are all addressed in the family assessment and serve to guide the therapist to tailor the intervention to the relative strengths and weaknesses of each family unit.

The next phase in the development of behavioral family therapy for schizophrenia is already under way; it seeks to examine specific strategies to counter inadequate transfer of skills trained in therapy sessions into the everyday life of families. This chapter attempts to outline each of these phases in detail with clinical examples of their applications and evidence for their specific and combined effects on the course of schizophrenia and the clinical, social, and family morbidity commonly associated with this disorder.

ASSESSMENT OF FAMILY COPING BEHAVIOR

Assessment of family behavior in established cases of schizophrenia has tended to focus on deficits of communication among family members or levels of emotional tension that have been postulated as causal factors in the etiology of the disorder. The "double-bind" interaction pattern, which is characterized by unclear communication and a discrepancy between verbal and nonverbal messages, is probably the most widely cited communication deficit (Bateson, Jackson, Haley, & Weakland, 1956). Other communication patterns considered deviant in families with persons suffering from schizophrenia include marital "schism" and "skew" (Lidz, Fleck, & Cornelison, 1965), "pseudomutuality" (Wynne, Ryckoff, Day, & Hirsch, 1958), "perceptual distortion" (Laing, 1967), and "communication deviance" (Wynne, Singer, Bartko, & Toohey, 1977). Only the latter has been extensively studied; it has been shown consistently that families of persons suffering from schizophrenia tend to speak in a less clearly focused manner. However, such family communication difficulties do not appear specific to schizophrenia (Hirsch & Leff, 1975) and are probably the result of the stress experienced by these families. Nevertheless, unclear interpersonal communication is likely to interfere with the efficiency of family problem-solving and the potential of the family to resolve stresses.

Patterns of family coping with schizophrenia have been extensively investigated in a series of studies of "expressed emotion" (EE). Where family members tend to take a highly critical stance toward the index patient, particularly at times when his or her behavior is overtly disturbed, the risk of major exacerbations appears to be increased. A similar but less striking increase in the risk of exacerbation is observed where one or more family members become overly concerned and distressed about the index patient's welfare and cope in a highly intrusive manner. These two coping styles have been combined in an index of "expressed emotion," which has been shown repeatedly to be a good predictor of the short-term clinical course of schizophrenia (Vaughn & Leff, 1976). Similar predictive power of EE has been observed in studies of other mental illnesses and stress-related disorders.

Vaughn (1977) observed that in families where criticism and overinvolvement appeared low (i.e., low EE), family members tended to solve their problems in a calm, objective, and sometimes highly creative manner. They tended to have a greater understanding of the nature of the index patient's disorder and to offer support rather than criticism or intrusiveness at times when the patient's disturbed behavior was prominent. This tended to foster effective problem-solving and stress reduction. Further support for the health enhancement potential of low-EE family coping was provided by physiological studies that suggested that the physical presence of a low-EE relative tended to reduce physiological concomitants of stress such as heart rate and galvanic skin responses (Tarrier, Vaughn, Lader, & Leff, 1979).

However, although low-EE families tend to cope more effectively with everyday household stresses, there is evidence that their coping functions can be overwhelmed by stressful life events, many of which derive from the social network outside the immediate family. These life events appear to account for the less frequent major exacerbations seen in low-EE cases (Leff & Vaughn, 1980). For this reason, it is important to assess the problem-solving functions of both high- and low-EE families and to attempt to enhance their stress management potential. An additional benefit of enhanced problem-solving efficiency is the potential for assisting all family members to achieve their goals and maximize their creative abilities. Guidelines for a behavioral analysis of family functioning include an assessment of the family on each of the following parameters.

- How much does each family member know about the nature of schizophrenia and its comprehensive management?
- How does the family cope with the burden of the illness?
- How effective is the interpersonal communication of family members, particularly concerning stressful issues?
- How efficient is family problem-solving?
- What are the short-term goals of individual family members?
- How does family problem-solving contribute to or detract from the achievement of these goals?

BEHAVIORAL ANALYSIS OF THE FAMILY SYSTEM

A comprehensive behavioral analysis of a family system is an extremely complex procedure and often entails between 10 and 20 hours of careful interviewing and observation. The precise nature of the analysis will be determined by the complexity of the presenting problems. Where multiple problems exist within a family, exploration of the functioning of the family unit is undertaken after behavioral analysis of each of the family members experiencing problems. Multiple problems are often found in families in which one member suffers from a distressing chronic disorder such as schizophrenia. In the approach adopted by Tarrier, Barrowclough, Vaughn, Bamrah, & Freeman, (1986), a list of target problems is derived from a behavioral analysis of each family member. A more limited approach is to focus on the generic problem-solving functions of the family unit and to pay less attention to the specific content of the family's presenting problems. In this chapter, we describe a method that primarily concerns the manner in which families conduct their problem-solving of stressful issues. We focus secondarily on the nature of the stressors themselves. In our approach, assessment begins with a series of interviews with individual family members before examining the family as a collaborating unit.

ASSESSMENT OF INDIVIDUAL FAMILY MEMBERS

Every family member, including the index patient, is interviewed to establish the unique assets and deficits that contribute to or detract from efficient family problem-solving. Family members are invited to describe their understanding of the nature of schizophrenia, including its etiology, characteristic features, antecedents and consequences of clinical exacerbation, the value of psychosocial and pharmacological interventions, and the expected prognosis. The manner in which they cope with any problems related to the disorder is explored, and they are asked to provide examples of their coping behavior (both good and bad). A survey is made of specific persons, activities, places, and material objects that are considered positively reinforcing, as well as of similar contexts in the social environment that are experienced as unpleasant and aversive.

Finally, short-term (3–6-month) goals are defined. Each family member is asked to define two specific goals that he or she would like to achieve, independent of any current constraints due to personal limitations or impediments attributed to any other family member, including the index patient and his or her disorder. The therapist assists each family member to define realistic goals that can be achieved readily with reasonable effort and that will result in a substantial improvement in that person's quality of life. Steps already taken toward achievement of these goals, the problems that may need to be overcome, and the levels of support and conflict likely to be provided by the family unit are all discussed.

Once all family members have completed individual interviews, the therapist will be able to assess the interrelatedness of the various goals and problems of family members. Areas of mutual support may be contrasted with areas of mutual conflict. For instance, an anxious mother may support goals that involve family members spending more time in her company and discourage progress toward goals that may increase her sense of isolation. Although extensive exploration of these intrafamilial dynamics is not a primary feature of the behavioral analysis, such an understanding of the potential conflicts and supports assists the therapist in directing the therapy with greater confidence. In particular, it may allow the therapist to steer the family away from major areas of emotional conflict during the early stages of therapy when addressing such issues may prove explosive and result in overwhelming stress, thereby precipitating an episode of schizophrenia in the vulnerable family member. This should not be misconstrued as indicating that behavioral family therapy for schizophrenia discourages families from addressing conflictual issues. Rather, it is considered important to delay problem-solving these issues until there is evidence that the family is capable of effectively resolving the problem in a constructive manner.

ASSESSMENT OF FAMILY PROBLEM-SOLVING FUNCTIONS

During the interviews with family members, the therapist may obtain reports of each person's problem-solving behavior. More comprehensive assessment of family problem-solving is gained through a meeting of all family members. The family members are asked to describe how they have attempted to deal with two or more everyday problems of general concern to the family. A detailed report of the specific behavior of each family member is elicited. In particular, details are sought about any discussions, where they occurred, who was included, how the discussion was structured, the style of communication, the manner in which problems were defined, the solutions derived, and the planning and implementation completed. The content of the problem-solving and the specific strategies employed is of less interest than the *structure*. However, note is made of the effectiveness of the plan in reducing long-term stress associated with the problem.

The next step involves observation of the family's attempt to conduct a problem-solving discussion. Several methods have been developed to obtain a natural display of family problem-solving behavior. Undoubtedly, the most objective of these methods is to observe families interacting in their own homes. However, lack of resources usually limits the clinical use of such an approach. Nevertheless, the value of home visits in the assessment of family functioning is considerable, and at least one home visit should be attempted whenever possible. In the absence of naturalistic observations of the family in unstructured time together at home, a number of structured tests of problem-solving have been devised that can be applied in a variety of settings.

The method we have employed successfully is a variation of the method developed by Michael Goldstein and his colleagues for studies with disturbed adolescents (Goldstein, Judd, Rodnick, Alkire, & Gould, 1968). The family members are invited to choose a current unresolved problem issue of concern to all family members. This need not be a major "hot" issue but may be an everyday difficulty, such as cleaning up the yard or planning a family activity for the weekend. Once an issue is chosen that seems likely to generate lively discussion among all family members, the family is instructed to discuss the issue for 10–15 minutes and to attempt to make some decision and plan about resolving the issue. The therapist tells the family that he or she will not take part in the discussion and withdraws to let the family conduct the discussion as naturally as possible. To aid this process, the therapist audiotapes (or videotapes) the discussion and may retire to the next room, take a seat in another part of the room, or watch through a one-way mirror. Before leaving, the therapist switches the tape recorder on.

From whatever vantage point, the therapist actively monitors the family discussion to ensure that he or she is able to intervene to stop the discussion should a heated argument seem imminent or to prompt further discussion where families dry up after a very brief conversation. At the end of the allotted time, the therapist provides positive feedback to the family about their effort and may assist in the resolution of any critical concerns that occurred.

After the session, the recording of the problem-solving discussion is reviewed for evidence of effective interpersonal communication and problem-solving skills as well as significant deficits that appear to detract from efficient problem resolution. These reports and observations of problem-solving, together with the individual assessments, place the therapist in a position to formulate a unique treatment plan to correct deficits in the family's ability to cope with their specific stresses and goals. Wherever feasible, the plan is designed to build on the preexisting strengths of the family, both as individuals and as a unit.

It must be emphasized that this initial assessment merely establishes a baseline of family functioning. It is likely to be only partially valid and, as such, forms the basis for the therapist's initial hypotheses. A highly skilled behavior therapist may be able to pinpoint one or two key deficits that may be remedied with minimal intervention and with maximal benefits to the whole family. However, with chronic disorders characterized by long-term vulnerability, such as schizophrenia, such formulations are seldom available and the course of behavioral family therapy is often a painstaking process of persistent evaluation, intervention, and review. Perhaps the most characteristic feature of behavioral family therapy is the manner in which each session always provides further opportunity for behavioral assessment and allows session-by-session modification of the formulation and intervention plan.

In order to provide an understanding of this process, we have chosen a case example to to illustrate the assessment process and to follow progress through the various components of a typical intervention plan.

CASE STUDY

George and Enid K and their 27-year-old son Arthur lived in a suburb of a large city with a family cat. (The Ks had another child also, Susan, aged 32, who lived nearby.) Arthur had first experienced symptoms of schizophrenia at age 19, just after he had been jilted by his first girlfriend. He heard menacing voices when he was alone at home telling him to kill himself and that he was a homosexual. The voices commented on his actions and his thoughts, particularly any sexual thoughts or behavior. He thought the voices were his ex-girlfriend's family but did not actually recognize them. He believed they were part of a conspiracy to kill him and was suspicious that his brother-in-law, Tony, was also involved. This had led to two family fights when Tony visited, which he did frequently to pick up his two children who stayed with George and Enid after school.

Arthur also experienced passivity delusions, believing that his thoughts were being controlled by telepathy. He occasionally experienced that his thoughts stopped unexpectedly and that thoughts coming into his head were not his own. At the time he was assessed for a behavioral family management program, he was symptom-free after a recent episode in which the symptoms described above were all prominent. He was taking 300 mg of chlorpromazine at night, with minimal unwanted effects.

George K had poor understanding of Arthur's disorder. He believed it was "some sort of depression," did not know anything that made it better or worse, and thought it was caused by Arthur's smoking marijuana. He tended to blame Arthur for his problems and to get angry with him and argue with him whenever Arthur mentioned his delusions or hallucinations. He criticized his wife for overindulging Arthur and for her lack of firmness with him. Mr. K was a retired salesman who drank heavily and frequently. He had few interests or friends and spent most of his time watching sports on TV, either at home or at a nearby bar. He had great difficulty defining any functional goals but finally agreed that he would like to go out to a movie or have pizza with his wife once a week.

Enid K was a rather timid woman who tended to do everything she could to please her husband and her son. She had not worked outside the home since her marriage 36 years earlier. Enid cared for her two grandchildren (Susan's children) four afternoons a week. She thought Arthur's illness was called "psychosis" and had heard the term "schizophrenia" being used on one occasion. She believed that he had always had the problem because he was "high-strung" and "always needed help as a child." She was very distressed and tearful when talking about Arthur's disorder, which she believed was helped by drug therapy and by "being kind to him." This meant doing everything for him and having no expectations that he would help in any constructive manner. For the "sake of peace," she tended to allow both Arthur and his father to have their own ways.

Homemaking activities and child minding absorbed the greater part of Enid's time. She had one friend she went shopping with once a month. It was extremely difficult to get her to set a personal goal that did not involve her husband or son in some way. However, she decided that she would like to visit her friend, May, once every 2 weeks for 1 hour.

Arthur K knew that his disorder was called "schizophrenia." He did not know what had caused it or what factors contributed to exacerbations or remissions. He believed that his drug treatment was for insomnia and admitted taking the drugs irregularly. He remembered being told that his was an "incurable" disease, and he had "given up after that." He spent much of his time lying on his bed and seldom left the immediate confines of the house or garden. He occasionally mowed the lawn or swept the paths.

Arthur's stated goals were to get a job and get married. These were broken down into achievable first steps of "researching all the vocational training schemes and sheltered workshop programs in the neighborhood," and "initiating a 2-min. conversation with a girl he found attractive."

Family-Reported Problem-Solving Assessment

The family described their attempt to organize a family dinner gathering to celebrate Mr. K's birthday. It was evident that Mrs. K had done most of the planning without involving her husband or son. She had hoped that they would assist her but had not specifically requested any help. When they failed to volunteer assistance, she began nagging them and a row ensued. This ended in Mr. K storming off; he reappeared intoxicated after the dinner had started. Arthur went to his room and refused to come out until all the guests had departed. Mrs. K was extremely distressed and blamed herself entirely for the behavior of her husband and son. The family reported this as a typical example of family problem-solving.

A second example of problem-solving was only slightly more successful. A large electricity bill had arrived by mail. Mr. K asked his wife if she could account for the excessive amount. She was preparing vegetables for the evening meal when he approached her. She told him she was surprised with the amount and said she would talk to him about it later. Meanwhile he checked the gas meter and found that the reading was substantially less than that on the bill. He asked his wife to phone the gas utility the next morning and seek an explanation of this discrepancy. She did this and was told this was an estimated bill and it would be best if she paid the bill without questions. She went ahead and did this without further discussion with her husband. When he saw the receipt he "blew his top" and became extremely hostile toward his wife. No further discussion was conducted on that subject.

These two reports of family problem-solving suggested major deficits in the communication and problem-solving skills of the family as a unit. In particular, they seemed to point to deficits in communication between Mr. and Mrs. K. There was no evidence that the three household members ever sat down to discuss a problem together in a structured manner. Mrs. K appeared to make decisions without consulting her husband or son, both of whom tended to withdraw, the former with the assistance of alcohol.

Observed Problem Solving

The therapist chose one of two unresolved problems volunteered by the family. This was the issue of "helping Mrs. K with the household chores." The K family were invited to discuss and resolve this issue in a 15-min. period, while the therapist retired into the adjacent dining area of the main family room.

A lively discussion ensued that moved immediately to listing suggestions about possible chores that could be undertaken by each household member. Agreement was reached that Mr. K would vacuum the floors, Mrs. K would wax the kitchen and bathroom tiles, and Arthur would clean his bedroom. This plan was reached without any clarification of the precise nature of the problem, discussion of alternative solutions, or any detailed planning. However, the family did appear quite resourceful in that each person chose one area in which they would offer specific assistance. The discussion remained calm throughout. Mother dominated the discussion and made several statements that seemed designed to induce guilt feelings in her husband and son. These included, "I do everything for you Arthur, now surely it's time you started pulling your weight to help around here" and "George, your idea of home is having me wait on you hand and foot without having to lift a finger." Both of these statements engendered lengthy responses as the two men attempted to justify their behavior. There was no evidence of clear expression of either positive or negative feelings or positive requests. Interruptions were frequent by all family members, not one of whom showed any evidence of effective listening behavior.

Formulation of Family Problem-Solving Functions

The following strengths of family problem solving were noted: Mrs. K was committed to the family and deeply concerned about the welfare of Arthur and Mr. K. She had a fair understanding of the nature of Arthur's disorder and its drug treatment. She was able to generate solutions to problems and showed competent planning skills and the ability to implement plans efficiently. Mr. K was able to identify Mrs. K's deficiencies in coping with Arthur. He used withdrawal to cope with family stress and delegated tasks to wife. He was able to generate solutions to problems. Arthur had a tendency to avoid or withdraw from stressful situations. He provided some assistance in household chores and was able to generate solutions to problems.

Significant deficits considered to detract seriously from family problem-solving efficiency included the following: Mrs. K exhibited overly emotional communication of needs, and she had a tendency to take over from others and to be intrusive. She used nagging criticism rather than direct communication through positive requests and the expression of specific negative feelings in a constructive manner. Mr. K displayed inadequate communication of needs and feelings with a tendency toward aggressive criticism and demanding behavior. He relied on alcohol to cope with stress. Arthur showed inadequate communication of needs and feelings.

Finally, there was a notable absence of any person in the family taking a chairperson's role in family discussions; consequently the discussion lacked structure and coherence. Specification of problem issues, evaluation of consequences of suggested solutions, and effective planning and review of efforts were all grossly deficient.

The limited understanding of the association between stress factors and drug therapy and the course of schizophrenia did not provide the family with a cogent rationale for the utility of long-term stress management and pharmacotherapy in the management of Arthur's disorder. In the subsequent section of this chapter, the implementation of a family management approach to schizophrenia is described with special reference to the K family.

EDUCATION ABOUT SCHIZOPHRENIA

Behavior therapy is based on learning theory strategies, with a strong emphasis on scientific evaluation of the strategies when they are applied to individual cases. Didactic instructions are an accepted part of all behavior therapy approaches, although the aim is not merely to achieve cognitive insight; rather, the aim is to extend insight to a full working understanding of the principles enunciated, as shown by the resultant changes of behavior (Falloon, 1986). Success in a smoking cessation program is not measured by evidence that smokers who participate in the program change their attitudes to smoking and argue that it is bad for their health; it is measured by evidence that participating smokers change their smoking behavior in a stable, enduring manner. Thus, the goal of educating patients and their families about schizophrenia is to facilitate change in their behavior in two major ways: to enhance compliance with prescribed medication regimens and to provide a rationale for family-based stress management.

Initial approaches to the education of patients and families were aimed merely at the goal of providing information that was considered important for patients to know from an ethical standpoint. The informed participation of the consumer was considered crucial. However, much to our surprise, the patients and families reported how useful they found this information as a guideline to coping with this mysterious disorder (Falloon & Liberman, 1982). This positive feedback led to subsequent incorporation of a brief educational component into many of the new approaches to schizophrenia (Anderson *et al.*, 1980; Leff, Kuipers, Berkowitz, Eberlein-Vries, & Sturgeon, 1982).

Although the mutual sharing of information about the nature, course, and treatment of schizophrenia is a continuous process, two or three sessions at the onset of behavioral family therapy are devoted entirely to discussion about the diagnosis, etiology, genetics, course, and drug and psychosocial management of the disorder. These initial sessions provide a rationale for the subsequent behavioral interventions and the drug treatment approach that is carefully monitored throughout.

The index patients are encouraged to play a major role in the education process. They are asked to describe their own experiences of the disorder, its symptoms, and its associated disabilities and handicaps, as well as their experiences of the treatment—particularly the beneficial and unwanted effects of drugs and the impact of stress on the florid symptoms. Generally, this is the first opportunity that family members have had to discuss their mutual experiences of schizophrenia. Not infrequently, other family members may reveal episodes of similar disorders, often previously undisclosed and untreated. During these discussions, written handouts and audiovisual teaching aids may be used to provide a framework for the sessions, but the family is encouraged to focus on their personal experiences, with the index patient clearly taking the role of the "expert" whenever feasible. Such a patient role is unlikely to prove possible until the index patient is stabilized and is able to distance himself or herself sufficiently to give a reasonably objective report of the phenomenology. Such informality and openness are seldom possible within a group setting of families who have not met one another previously. For this reason, we prefer to provide this educational module *initially* to families on their own; however, the family may join a group of other patients and families subsequently.

A questionnaire is given before and after these sessions to ascertain the knowledge acquired and to assist in targeting areas where further discussion may be required. Evidence from three studies suggests that a 50% increase in knowledge about the disorder and its management can be expected in most families. Furthermore, there is some evidence to suggest that the index patient's level of knowledge is associated with compliance with medication (McGill, Falloon, Boyd, & Wood-Siverio,1983).

Although it might be expected that this education process may have its pitfalls, there have been remarkably few reports of difficulties. The overwhelming response has been one of gratitude and bewilderment at why such education has not been widely available in hospital settings. Some criticism has been directed toward the booklets we have handed to families. Tarrier and Barrowclough (1986) have questioned the reading ability of consumers necessary to comprehend these handouts. The repetitive use of the word "schizophrenia" substantially increases the reading age on standardized tests. However, it should be pointed out that these sheets are designed to be used in conjunction with a therapist-led discussion and not to be handed to patients to read unaided. But it may be legitimate to question the use of a complex, confusing, and difficult-to-pronounce term like "schizophrenia" when one is attempting to provide a common sense understanding of the disorder. To date, no satisfactory alternative has been invented, but the search continues!

The K family appeared to have very limited understanding of the nature of schizophrenia or its management principles. However, on the positive side, they had relatively few misconceptions about the disorder—a somewhat more difficult problem to correct.

During the first session, which focused on the nature of schizophrenia, all three family members recalled being told that Arthur's illness was called "schizophrenia;" and they understood that it was a mental illness characterized by "being in a world of his own," "having weird ideas," and "not talking sense."

Mr. and Mrs. K expressed considerable surprise to hear that Arthur had stayed in his room playing his loud music as a way to "drown out" the voices he heard. Arthur described how, when tension was running high in the family, he got a feeling in the pit of his stomach that preceded hearing voices. Whenever he experienced this feeling, he quickly retired to his room and tried to relax on his bed, either listening to music or reading a magazine. This usually prevented the voices from appearing. Mrs. K told Arthur how sensible she felt he was to work this out himself and tearfully said that she wished his Dad would cope in the same way, without running off to a bar to get drunk. Mr. K said that the drink was his way of relaxing and getting away from it all.

The family had some difficulty grasping the concept that schizophrenia probably had a multifactorial etiology. They were unable to comprehend how brain chemistry could change and how such changes could lead to disturbed behavior. Although the therapist used the analogy of drugs and alcohol affecting the brain and producing changes in a person's mood and behavior, the family's lack of basic knowledge of physiology left them confused on this issue. However, they did acknowledge that drug therapy had improved Arthur's behavior substantially.

Because Mrs. K tended to blame herself for Arthur's disorder, the therapist spent some time clarifying current theories that link family stress with schizophrenia. He explained that there was no evidence that anything that families said or did could cause schizophrenia, no more than families could cause diabetes. However, just as cooking the right kind of food for a person with diabetes is a major part of the treatment, families can be a great help in reducing serious episodes of schizophrenia through careful management of major stressors impinging on the index patient.

When the genetic issue was discussed, Mrs. K mentioned that her daughter had had some mental disturbance after the birth of her first child and asked whether that might have been schizophrenia. The therapist briefly reviewed the symptoms and concluded that this seemed more likely to have been a depressive episode.

At the end of the session, the family appeared able to comprehend that Arthur had schizophrenia, that stress adversely affected this disorder, and that drug therapy helped. Arthur seemed very pleased that his parents now had some understanding of what he had been through—in particular, that his father realized that he had an illness and was not merely behaving badly.

The second session dealt with drug therapy. Mrs. K had reported a basic understanding of the importance of drug therapy in the management of schizophrenia. This contrasted with Arthur's misunderstanding of the prophylactic value of medication and his father's total ignorance of this aspect of treatment. This assessment led the therapist to focus on the rationale for the continued use of neuroleptic drugs in the prevention of exacerbations of schizophrenia. He emphasized that not taking these drugs regularly more than doubled the risk of a serious episode. He also pointed out that irregular drug taking tended to increase the severity of any side effects. Fortunately, Arthur had not experienced any serious side effects, so the issue of how to cope with unpleasant effects was not discussed in detail.

The manner in which any street drugs tend to make schizophrenia worse was of particular interest to Mr. K. With Arthur's help, the therapist enabled Mr. K to recognize that Arthur's illness had begun before he began abusing drugs. Arthur had attempted to use marijuana as a tranquilizer to help him cope with his voices. Unfortunately, he found that after some initial benefit the drug tended to make the hallucinations worse. Arthur agreed with his father that he would avoid such measures in future.

The latter part of the session provided an opportunity to list the three early warning signs that Arthur had shown before his florid episodes. They were fitful sleep, feeling tension inside his head, "as if it was about to burst," and spending more time in his room lying on his bed. Arthur and his parents were instructed to monitor each of these symptoms and to report any evidence of their reappearance at the earliest possible time.

Subsequent to this session, the regularity of Arthur's tablet taking increased markedly; it remained good throughout the subsequent year of treatment.

ENHANCING THE CLARITY OF FAMILY COMMUNICATION

Effective, clear communication of information, personal feelings, and needs is the basis for efficient problem-solving. At times of crisis, ineffective communication patterns impede coping efforts and may even exacerbate the stress, thereby contributing to further episodes of schizophrenia.

The components of family communication that are the basis for problem-solving include the ability to listen empathetically to a distressed person and to clarify the exact problem contributing to the distress; mutual expression of positive and negative feelings concerning the specific behavior of family members; and making constructive requests for behavior change in one another. The nonverbal and verbal components of interpersonal communication must be addressed, particularly where major deficits detract from the clarity of expression. It is assumed that all family members have the ability to receive and process verbal and nonverbal information without major impairments. Persistent psychotic symptoms, moderate or severe mental retardation, or drug or alcohol intoxication may impede this basic process and must be addressed before considering communication training for the family.

Communication training employs the skills-training procedures derived from social learning theory. After the major strengths and weaknesses of each family member's communication skills have been targeted during the baseline assessment, improved communication is shaped in repeated brief reenactment of family interaction. Clear instructions and guidelines are provided for each skill (*see* Falloon *et al.*, 1984) and family members take turns to demonstrate their competence in the skill. Coaching, supportive feedback, and modeling by other family members and the therapist are provided where performance is less than competent. By choosing to reenact communication that has previously occurred, the artificiality of role-playing is reduced. Each session usually provides a focus on one specific skill, for instance, expressing positive feelings or active listening. Initial sessions usually focus on more fundamental skills with later sessions dealing with increasingly more complex communication.

Almost all families can improve their skills in all areas of interpersonal communication, so that some time is usually spent on each skill area. In families where communication is good at baseline, such training is brief, and several skills may be reviewed on a 1-hour session. In families where many members have major deficits, several sessions may be devoted to those deficient skills. However, the key objective is to facilitate problem-solving and to enable families to sit down together and discuss a problem issue in a reasonable, calm, and respectful manner. This can often be achieved with less than optimal communication skills. Furthermore, many such families are burdened by multiple problems and are not motivated to spend hours of their time enhancing their communication skills unless there is an immediate effect on resolution of their overwhelming stressors. In such cases, the therapist may elect to focus initially on teaching the family the structured problem-solving approach and then to begin to shape those communication skills that appear to specifically limit problem-solving efficiency.

It is important to note that no attempts are made to discourage family members from expressing their negative feelings of anger, frustration, etc. Indeed, such communication is encouraged as the initial step in problem-solving. However, family members are trained to express their negative feelings in a clear, direct way that places the responsibility for the feelings and their subsequent resolution squarely on the shoulders of the person expressing them. In this manner, family members are discouraged from coercive nagging or hostility and rejection, all of which tend to result from attempts to blame other people for one's own unpleasant feelings.

Several aspects of effective communication are common to all skills. These include the importance of nonverbal aspects of communication, such as posture, proximity to the recipient, eye contact, voice tone, and facial expression, and the importance of making specific statements of feelings associated with the specific behaviors of others, rather than global statements of pleasure or displeasure.

The sessions tend to be structured as workshops during which family members are able to rehearse different communication skills with supportive coaching and feedback. The content of the issues raised is less important than the structure of the communication; in other words, "it is not what you say, but how you say it." The crucial step in communication training is achieved when family members show evidence that they have incorporated more effective communication strategies into their everyday discourse. Behavioral family therapists make a specific effort to ensure that this transfer of skills from therapy to the natural setting is achieved efficiently. The major way in which this is attempted is through homework assignments. After each skill is trained during sessions, each family member is requested to attempt to use the skill on every occasion possible during the next week and is provided with a weekly worksheet to record examples daily. At the beginning of the next session, the therapist reviews the worksheets and invites family members to reenact one or more occasions when they used the skill. Other family members observe this reenactment and comment on the effective elements displayed and give constructive suggestions for improvement.

Another major strategy to enhance generalization is to conduct sessions in the home. This avoids one step in the generalization process: that of transfer across settings (i.e., clinic to home). In addition, reenactment becomes more true to life, and prompt sheets reminding family members to practice each skill can be placed in strategic locations (e.g, refrigerator door) throughout the house. No apologies are made for the use of such unsophisticated strategies. They are demonstrably effective despite their lack of intellectual quality. It is the efficient manner in which results are achieved that is the greatest concern of behavior therapists and family members, not the elegance of the process!

The baseline assessment of the Ks revealed that all three members tended to avoid expressing negative feelings in a direct manner. Instead they tended to bottle them up and withdraw (Arthur), to drown them in alcohol (Mr. K), or to express them in a coercive, nagging way (Mrs. K). All of these coping methods contributed to explosive family arguments and ineffective problem-solving.

Recognizing the likelihood that each family member had many unexpressed strong negative feelings stored up over the years, the therapist chose to tread very delicately with this family. He did not introduce the issue of expressing negative feelings until the family had begun to develop more positive, respectful communications through increasing their exchanges of warm, positive feelings and until they showed competence in making noncoercive positive requests of one another. The family had also employed the structured problem-solving approach in one session to cope with the unexpected death of a close friend.

The therapist recalled several everyday negative issues that family members had reported during the baseline assessment and in subsequent sessions. He was prepared to structure the training around expression of these "not too hot" issues, if necessary.

After a brief introduction highlighting the value of expressing negative feelings in resolving problems, the therapist outlined and gave examples of the four steps involved with the aid of a handout listing them. Family members took turns, starting with Mrs. K (who appeared most likely to perform the skill competently), to demonstrate expressing a negative feeling toward another family member. Mrs. K said she was disappointed that her husband had come home late last night without letting her know. The therapist praised her for the direct expression of her feelings about a specific behavior. He prompted her to add a request for change in this behavior in the future. Mrs.K then told her husband that she would like him to phone her if he was going to be late so that his dinner would not be spoiled. The therapist stopped the action before Mr. K could respond and invited Arthur and Mr. K to comment on what particular aspects of Mrs. K's communication they liked. Arthur commented on his mother's firm voice tone, Mr. K on his wife's telling him just one thing he had done wrong rather than "flying off the handle."

Mr. K and Arthur had more difficulty expressing their negative feelings in this manner. Arthur found he could not look his father in the eye, and Mr. K required help in finding the right expression to describe his frustration at his son's seeming unwillingness to mow the lawn weekly. With coaching from the therapist and other family members, each man eventually managed to improve substantially on his initial efforts and was warmly praised for this improvement.

The therapist gave the family members a worksheet (Figure 13-1) on which to note their attempts to express negative feelings during the next week. He explained the precise nature of the assignment and invited Arthur to demonstrate exactly how he understood the task. The session was completed by briefly asking the family to express a positive feeling to each other family member about something pleasing they had done in the past few days.

At the start of the next session, the therapist reviewed the worksheets of Mrs. K and Arthur—Mr. K had misplaced his. After praising their efforts at attempting to use the approach introduced in the previous session (all three) and at completing the worksheets (Mrs. K and Arthur), the therapist invited each person to reenact one of the examples noted. Mr. K reenacted telling Arthur that he disapproved of his lying on the sofa watching TV all Sunday afternoon. He stood over Arthur, who was lying on the sofa, and said "Why don't you get up and do something, go for a walk or help your mother, rather than lie around all day?" The family were invited to give feedback on this: what they liked, followed by suggestions for improvement. Mrs. K pointed out that Mr. K did specify a behavior that upset him. Arthur said Mr. K had made a suggestion for something he could do. Both noted that a direct expression of feelings was missing, and the therapist later remarked on the postural discrepancy that made eye contact difficult. Mr. K repeated the reenactment twice: first, to incorporate a statement of his feelings and then to sit down on a chair so that he did not tower over Arthur in a threatening manner.

- SAY **EXACTLY** WHAT DISPLEASED YOU.
- TELL THE PERSON HOW IT MADE YOU FEEL.
- SUGGEST A WAY THIS COULD BE AVOIDED IN FUTURE.

DAY	PERSON WHO DISPLEASED YOU	WHAT EXACTLY DID THEY DO THAT DISPLEASED YOU?	HOW DID YOU FEEL? (angry, sad, etc.)	WHAT DID YOU ASK THEM TO DO IN FUTURE?
SUN				
TUES				
WED				
THURS				
FRI				
SAT				
MON				

Examples:

I feel angry that you shouted at me, Tom. I'd like it better if you spoke quieter next time.

I'm very sad that you did not get that job. I'd like to sit down and discuss some other possibilities with you after dinner.

I feel very anxious when you tell me I should get a job, it would help me a lot if you didn't nag me about it.

Figure 13-1. The unpleasant feelings worksheet.

Mrs. K appeared to have used the skill competently at home. Arthur required further coaching on his eye contact, voice tone, and feelings statements. Training continued throughout the session and part of the next, with further coaching provided during part of the each subsequent session. Five sessions later, each family member had achieved competence in the use of the skill, and the therapist was satisfied that they all expressed negative feelings at home in this manner on occasions and that Mr. K and Arthur used one or more elements of the skill frequently.

The ideal of expecting family members to deploy these skills with 100% veracity is unrealistic and appears unnecessary to achieve substantial improvements in stress management. The therapist should emphasize the importance of using communication skills in the optimal fashion at times of stress and the value of practicing them everyday so that they become habitual.

STRUCTURED PROBLEM-SOLVING

Problem-solving is a core component of behavioral family therapy for schizophrenia. In addition to providing a strategy for coping with stress, it can be applied to the achievement of functional goals. It can also be an aid to resolving therapist problems such as involvement of reluctant family members, resistance to homework, etc. The method we use involves six steps. However, before embarking on training the family in this structure, the therapist ensures that the family arrange a regular weekly meeting time of 30 min. or so, during which they will be expected to conduct their own problem-solving discussions. A person is nominated to chair the discussion and another to record notes on the discussion. Early establishment of this family meeting appears vital to the successful transfer of structured problem-solving to family life. After problem-solving this issue with the family, the therapist introduces the six-step approach.

Step 1 is to identify a specific problem or goal. This crucial step involves targeting an area of concern by employing active listening skills to clarify and eventually pinpoint a specific problem or goal. This frequently involves breaking down a complex issue into smaller, more manageable steps so that it can be specified in a fashion that is readily understood by all family members. For instance, an issue about "Jack not having anything to do all day" becomes "helping Jack to join the youth club."

Step 2 is to list alternative solutions. Once the problem or goal has been clearly specified, the family group is encouraged to brainstorm all the possible solutions. Discussion is minimized, particularly judgments about the relative merits of proposed solutions. Every idea is written down, including "good" and "bad" suggestions. This encourages reticent family members to contribute their ideas and prevents the dominance of one or more members. At least five suggestions are listed before moving to the next step.

Step 3 is a discussion of the merits of each suggestion. The specific strengths and weaknesses of *each* suggestion are highlighted in a brief discussion. Discussion about the comparative advantages of various suggestions is forestalled until the next step.

Step 4 is selection of the optimal solution. This involves a lengthier discussion about the relative merits of the various suggestions. Particular note is made of the ease in which they can be applied within the *current* resources available to the family. Thus, the "ideal" solution may prove difficult to implement at this point due to practical considerations such as finances, time commitments, state of health, etc. The "best" solution is usually one that can be readily applied immediately with moderate effort of family members. Straightforward solutions are favored over complex solutions that require extensive organization. The chosen solution may represent merely the first step in resolving the problem or achieving the goal.

Step 5 is to plan implementation of the solution. A detailed plan of action is drawn up to map out the steps that need to be taken to successfully implement the solution. Strategies to ensure effective implementation may need to be devised. Anticipated roadblocks are pinpointed and ways of coping with them planned. It is often useful to have the family rehearse overtly or covertly all, or selected, steps in the plan. Small, but crucial, details that are overlooked in planning often underlie failed attempts at implementation. The final part of every action plan is to set out a specific time to review progress.

Step 6 is to review all efforts. Problem-solving, no matter how skillfully conducted, carries no guarantee of success. At the review discussion, *all efforts* to implement the plan are praised, even where the implementation has fallen far short of expectations. Failure of any attempt is then examined in terms of the partial success achieved: What went wrong? Family members are encouraged to use the knowledge they have acquired in any partially successful attempts to construct a modified plan of further action. The therapist emphasizes that problem-solving or goal achievement is a continuous process and that worthwhile success is usually achieved only after multiple attempts and considerable persistence.

The therapist, again aware of the potential for explosive outbursts in the K family, prepared for the initial session of problem-solving training by recalling a number of problem issues reported by the family that seemed unlikely to create a highly emotive discussion. These included organizing a family activity at weekends and getting Arthur involved in a vocational rehabilitation program.

After reviewing the homework from the previous week, which involved continued practice of expressing negative feelings, the therapist gave a brief overview of the six-step problem-solving approach and handed each family member a worksheet (Figure 13-2). He invited the family to choose a family meeting time, which they readily agreed would be immediately after the evening meal on Mondays. Mr. K protested that he would have to miss the televised football game, but Mrs. K said she would have dinner ready at 6 P.M.; providing Mr. K was home punctually, there would be sufficient time for the meeting before the game. The therapist praised the family for their excellent planning skills and willingness to compromise and pointed out the value of having something to reward oneself with at the end of a problem-solving discussion. Watching football was a reward for Mr. K and Arthur; they still needed to consider how they could reward Mrs. K's efforts.

Mrs. K agreed to take the role of chairperson and Arthur agreed to take notes at the family meetings. The therapist then invited the family to

---

SOLVING PROBLEMS

Step 1: What is the problem?

Talk about the problem, listen carefully, ask questions, get everybody's opinion. Then write down *exactly* what the problem is.

____

____

Step 2: List all possible solutions.

Put down *all* ideas, even bad ones. Get everybody to come up with at least one possible solution.

(1) ____________________________________
(2) ____________________________________
(3) ____________________________________
(4) ____________________________________
(5) ____________________________________
(6) ____________________________________

Step 3: Discuss each possible solution.

Go down the list of possible solutions and discuss the advantages and disadvantages of each one.

Step 4: Choose the best solution or combination of solutions:

____

____

Step 5: Plan how to carry out the best solution.

Step (1) ________________________________
Step (2) ________________________________
Step (3) ________________________________
Step (4) ________________________________

Step 6: Review implementation and praise *all* efforts.

Figure 13-2. The problem-solving worksheet.

choose an everyday problem or goal. Mr. K chose the issue he had set as a goal during the initial assessment: to take his wife out once a week. Mrs. K protested that this was not a real problem, but the therapist reassured her that it was a good issue to practice and invited Mr. K to tell his wife how important he considered the issue. Mr. K spoke movingly about how much it would please him to be able to make her happy and do some of the things they had not done since the early years of their marriage.

The therapist handed the problem-solving discussion over to the family, interrupting only to provide further detailed instructions at each step in the process. The family agreed on a goal of Mr. K taking Mrs. K out once a week. The brainstorming focused on what the couple would do on their night out. Suggestions included letting Mrs.K choose, going to a movie, having dinner out, going to a nightclub, and visiting old friends. The therapist encouraged the family to come up with "bad" as well as "good" ideas and prevented Mr. K from closing the discussion prematurely when the suggestion of going to a movie was proposed. When the family found they could not think of a sixth alternative, the therapist suggested "you could do nothing, stay at home." All three family members looked aghast, and Mr. K exclaimed, "That wouldn't be right, would it!"

Further assistance from the therapist was needed to get the family to move quickly through step 3 of highlighting the pros and cons of each suggestion. Mrs. K was asked to keep a tight rein on the discussion and not to allow the family to become bogged down with detailed planning at this stage.

A consensus was quickly reached that Mr. and Mrs. K would enjoy going to a movie. Indeed, Mrs. K had already heard about a movie that that she was eager to see.

Planning was cursory until the therapist intervened to point out that in order to ensure that the goal was achieved, it would be necessary to organize the evening carefully: to nominate a day and a time; to arrange an early evening meal; to ensure that Arthur would be happy to stay at home alone; to ensure that Mr. K had sufficient cash to pay for the tickets, etc. It became evident that Mrs. K was deeply worried about leaving Arthur alone. When she suggested that Arthur come too, Mr. K angrily stated that he wanted to go out with his wife alone. The therapist noted the hostile expression of negative feelings and requested that Mr. K rephrase his expression in the manner he had learned in earlier sessions. He was able to do this successfully, and the tension subsided. The therapist suggested that Mrs. K's concern about leaving Arthur alone might be a useful topic to problem-solve at their next family meeting at home. Mr. K did not attend that meeting, but Mrs. K and Arthur sorted out a plan for how Arthur could cope with any problems that might occur while his mother was out.

The implementation was reviewed two sessions later. Mr. and Mrs. K had gone out as planned, only to find that the movie they planned to see was no longer showing. They attended another movie, which Mr. K enjoyed but Mrs. K considered too violent. The review revealed that the plan had worked well apart from the one hitch. In the future, they decided that one day before they would phone the cinema to check exactly what movie was showing.

Subsequent training in problem-solving focused on difficulties in defining problems and goals in exact terms and on detailed planning. The family was taught active listening skills, particularly the need for repeated use of clarifying questions when defining specific problems or goals.

Mr. K did not attend family meetings at home. This became a source of frustration for Mrs. K and the therapist. After several attempts to find a more convenient time, and repeated positive requests from Mrs. K, the therapist intervened and devoted a session to problem-solving Mr. K's noncompliance. Mr. K's response was to attend the next family meeting but to continue to avoid the meetings thereafter. Continued problem-solving of this issue proved relatively unrewarding for the next 3 months, but further success then ensued with Mr. K attending every second session on average.

Despite these problems, attendance at therapy sessions was excellent, and noticeable reduction in family tension was reported. At the 6-month review (after 20 sessions), the family showed evidence of a good understanding of the management of schizophrenia. On one occasion, Mrs. K had picked up the early signs of an episode a few days after Arthur had been rejected from a vocational rehabilitation program. A small increase in his drugs and problem-solving by the family combined to abort the episode. Arthur was taking his drugs regularly, forgetting only the occasional dose. He was spending much more time helping with chores about the house. He had contacted two old friends and had gone out with them on several occasions. He had achieved his goal of researching local rehabilitation programs—unfortunately, to little avail. His second goal of conversing with a girl he found attractive had been achieved, although he reported that the girl concerned was not really attractive.

Mr. and Mrs. K had improved their marital relationship substantially. Arguments were infrequent, and they were spending time together regularly. Mr. K still spent considerable time drinking heavily, and this remained a major concern to his wife. Both were pleased with the improvements they noted in Arthur. "It's as if a cloud has been lifted. He is his old self most of the time now," they reported. Mrs. K remained overprotective, but she was optimistic that Arthur could improve further. She despaired at the lack of local facilities for his rehabilitation and had met with a parents' group who were planning to set up their own program. She had not achieved her goal of visiting her friend May, but she had phoned her on several occasions. Mr. K's goal of taking his wife out once a week had been partially achieved; they went out every second week.

The problem-solving assessment revealed substantial reductions in ineffective communication patterns and a concomitant increase in problem-solving efficiency. These improvements in problem-solving were further accentuated at the 1-year review and were associated with further reductions in clinical, social, and family morbidity. A surprising finding was that Mr. K stopped drinking about 8 months of family therapy, began attending Alcoholics Anonymous, and remained abstinent at the 1-year review.

Space does not permit further details of this and other cases. The interested reader is referred to *Family Care of Schizophrenia* (Falloon, *et al.*, 1984) for further details of the application of behavioral family therapy in schizophrenia.

OTHER BEHAVIORAL STRATEGIES

The use of behavioral family therapy in the aftercare of schizophrenia described in this chapter is mainly as a stress-management framework. However, schizophrenia is a heterogenous condition, and its sufferers (and their families) may experience a wide range of behavioral disturbances in addition to the characteristic symptoms of the disorder. Phobias, obsessional symptoms, social skills deficits, and depression, as well as side effects of neuroleptic drugs, compliance difficulties, and persistent delusions or hallucinations, are commonly experienced. A broad range of behavioral strategies may be employed within the family problem-solving framework. Of course, the therapist may need to become more actively involved in training the family to employ behavior therapy strategies. The close collaboration between family members and therapist that is developed in behavioral family therapy facilitates the use of these methods.

However, the therapist is discouraged from proposing a validated therapeutic procedure until the family has had the opportunity to seek their own solution through the creative problem-solving process. It is surprising how often the family-generated solution resembles a validated therapuetic approach but tends to provide a more efficient answer to the specific family problem.

PROBLEMS IN THE APPLICATION OF BEHAVIORAL FAMILY THERAPY IN SCHIZOPHRENIA

One advantage of employing a problem-solving approach to therapy is that the identical approach can be employed to deal with the problems the therapist encounters in the therapeutic process. Commonly encountered problems, such as nonattendance of significant family members, noncompliance with homework tasks, lack of adherence to drug regimens, taking of illicit drugs, and hostility between family members, may all be subjected to the problem-solving process. In addition, the inexperienced therapist may find it helpful to conduct a problem-solving session with his or her supervisor before addressing the issue with the family.

It is crucial that the therapist adheres faithfully to the problem-solving and communication methods he or she has been teaching to the family. Deviation from these principles, especially the use of coercive statements (e.g. "now *I want* you to do this" or "it is *very important* that *you should* do that") or confrontation (e.g., "*why did you* do this?"), even in its mildest forms, frequently increases family members' reluctance to collaborate with the therapist—or with any other person, for that matter.

When addressing a therapist-related problem, it is important that the therapist defines the issue as his or her *own problem* and does not frame it as a family problem: for instance, "I am very disappointed that nobody in the family has completed their worksheets again this week. I would like to spend the first part of this session talking about this problem which has been bothering me a lot. Because it is my problem I'd like to chair this discussion myself and would be most grateful if you could all help me plan a solution. Is that O.K.?" Such an approach appears to facilitate resolution of problems in therapy and provides an excellent demonstration of the method for the family. Just as in families it is crucial to employ excellent communication skills when stress is high, the therapist may need to choose his or her words very carefully at these times. However, it is very beneficial for the therapist habitually to use the same communication skills that he or she is training the families to adopt throughout the course of therapy—and, arguably, to employ the same skills with colleagues, family, and friends as well!

In addition to employing the problem-solving model to resolve problems related to the therapeutic process, the therapist may choose to address family crises in a similar manner. If the crises occur prior to introducing structured problem-solving to the family, the therapist chairs the discussion and completes the worksheet personally. Once the family members have used the problem-solving format on a few occasions, the therapist may invite the family to attempt to problem-solve themselves; however, the therapist should be prepared to participate more actively should the family effort flag or should tensions threaten to overwhelm them.

In this manner, problems that emerge in the course of therapy are all subjected to continual problem-solving. Specific strategies are seldom necessary. Despite excellent problem-solving, resolution of most difficult issues is seldom straightforward. Persistence and patience are essential qualities of effective therapists. Where this problem-solving approach has been applied, remarkably few families have terminated their therapy prematurely, and most have shown significant benefits.

THE EFFICACY OF BEHAVIORAL FAMILY THERAPY IN THE PREVENTION OF MORBIDITY IN SCHIZOPHRENIA

The benefits of behavioral family therapy in the long-term management of schizophrenia have been examined in a series of studies. Several controlled studies have not yet been completed. To date, the strongest evidence for the value of combining behavioral family therapy with drug management is provided by the University of Southern California study (Falloon, 1985).

In this study, 39 index patients and their families were assigned at random to two treatment conditions: behavioral family therapy (BFT) or individual supportive therapy (IST). Three patients dropped out of the study in the early stages of therapy, leaving 18 closely matched patients and families in each group. Assignment was made after patients had been stabilized on optimal doses of neuroleptic medication after an acute episode of schizophrenia. The initial phase of intensive therapy consisted of weekly sessions for 3 months, tapering to biweekly sessions until 9 months, when monthly booster sessions continued until at least 24 months. In this way, each patient received 40 sessions during the 2 years after achieving stabilization. Throughout this period, doses of neuroleptic drugs were adjusted every month to minimize the dosage given. Therapists treated equal numbers of patients in each condition and were responsible for all case management, including emergency care, throughout the study.

A battery of measures was administered to patients and family members on entry to the study and after 3, 9, and 24 months. The measures included independent, blind ratings of communication and problem-solving behavior; clinical, social, and family morbidity; compliance with medication; plasma levels of neuroleptics; life stresses; and family coping behaviors.

Patient Characteristics

All patients studied were English-speaking, aged between 18 and 45 years, and had a diagnosis of schizophrenia according to DSM-III criteria. One third had experienced their first episode of schizophrenia at entry to the study. All lived in close daily contact with at least one natural parent and in stressful home environments, as determined by high-EE features or severe family burden.

Treatment Conditions

All patients received optimal neuroleptic management, crisis care, and rehabilitation throughout the study.

The BFT followed the outline provided in the early portion of this chapter. It was conducted predominantly in the home, although the booster sessions after 9 months were often conducted in a multifamily group in the clinic or a community hall.

IST was usually conducted in the clinic and was of similar duration and intensity, but it focused on patient-related problems. A problem-oriented approach was employed that aimed to reduce stress and promote social functioning. Problem-solving strategies as well as a range of behavioral approaches were employed but in a less systematic fashion than in the family therapy. Family members were counseled where appropriate but always in individual sessions. No attempt was made to teach problem-solving in a direct manner.

Results

The first issue that concerns a behavior therapist is whether the specific changes that were the key goals of the therapy were achieved. In this case, was there evidence that the BFT enhanced the problem-solving efficiency of the family units who received it? The answer was resoundingly positive. Not only was problem-solving behavior increased after the intensive training phase of BFT (Figure 13-3), but a measure of how well families coped with life stresses over the first year of the study also revealed a highly significant benefit for BFT that appeared to increase with time, leveling out after 9 months (Figure 13-4). These data provide impressive support for the specific effects of BFT in enhancing family stress management through communication and problem-solving training. However, of greater significance to clinicians, patients, and their caregivers is how this improved management of stress affects the course of schizophrenia and the quality of life of the patients and families.

BFT was associated with fewer major episodes of schizophrenia during the 2-year study period. Three BFT patients (17%) experienced a total of seven major episodes, while 83% of IST patients experienced 41 major episodes of schizophrenia and 11 major depressive episodes. These obser-

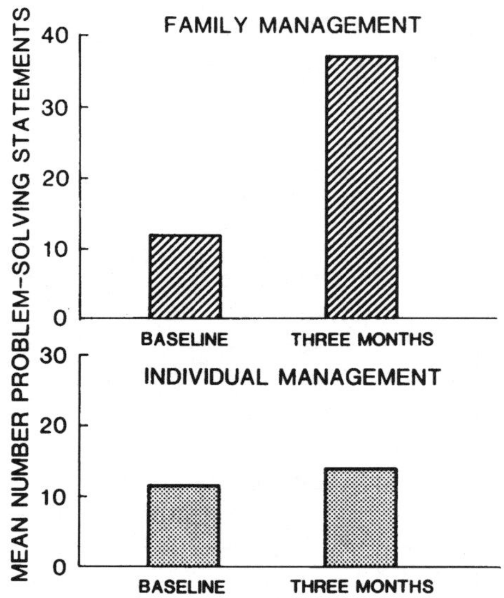

Figure 13-3. Problem-solving behavior increased after 3 months of behavioral family therapy.

vations were supported by blind ratings of psychopathology (Figure 13-5). The course of target schizophrenic symptoms of BFT patients was significantly more stable than for IST patients. Furthermore, despite entering the study at a period when maximum stability had been achieved with drug therapy and supportive care, the target symptom ratings of BFT patients tended to improve from this baseline, indicating a trend toward further remission. At the end of 2 years, only one third showed continuing evidence of schizophrenia, and one half showed no evidence of any symptoms of mental disorder whatsoever. A less stable course was evident for IST patients, with 83% continuing to show symptoms of schizophrenia at 2 years. Nevertheless, case records and family reports indicated that most of these patients had benefited from the treatment they received in the study and that their disorders had improved substantially when compared with the two years prior to entering this program. Thus, the comparative benefits of BFT could not be attributed to any deterioration associated with the patient-based approach.

Similar advantages for BFT were noted in the area of social functioning. BFT patients almost doubled the time they engaged in constructive work activities compared with the 2 years before the study. Rating scale measures of social role performance showed significant improvements over the 2-year period of the study as well as significantly greater improvement

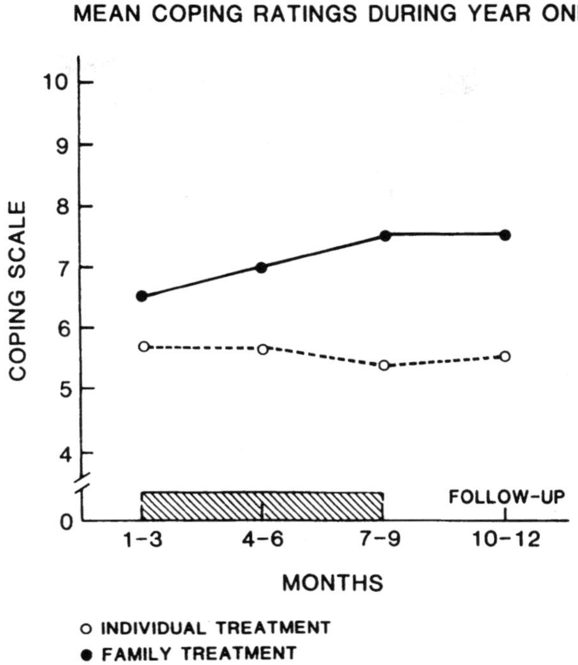

Figure 13-4. The benefits of behavioral family therapy on family coping behavior increased with time, leveling out after 9 months. *Note*. From *Family care of schizophrenia* (p. 403) by I. R. H. Falloon, J. L. Boyd, and C. W. McGill, 1984, New York: The Guilford Press. Copyright 1984 by The Guilford Press. Reprinted by permission.

than that rated for IST patients. The greatest benefits were noted in the areas of work activity, household tasks, and friendships outside the family.

Family members rated increased satisfaction with BFT patients' functioning, even when deficits were still evident. The burden family members associated with caring for the index patients was reduced over the 2 years of the study so that only 17% of families reported significant burden at this point. No change in family burden was associated with the patient-based approach, and almost two thirds of families continued to experience moderate or severe burden after 2 years. Benefits in terms of improved quality of life for families were difficult to rate, but improvements in the health and well-being of families appeared more evident in families who engaged in the family therapy.

An economic analysis demonstrated that the BFT approach, even when based in patients' homes, is extremely cost-efficient. The overall benefits achieved during the first year of the program were achieved with

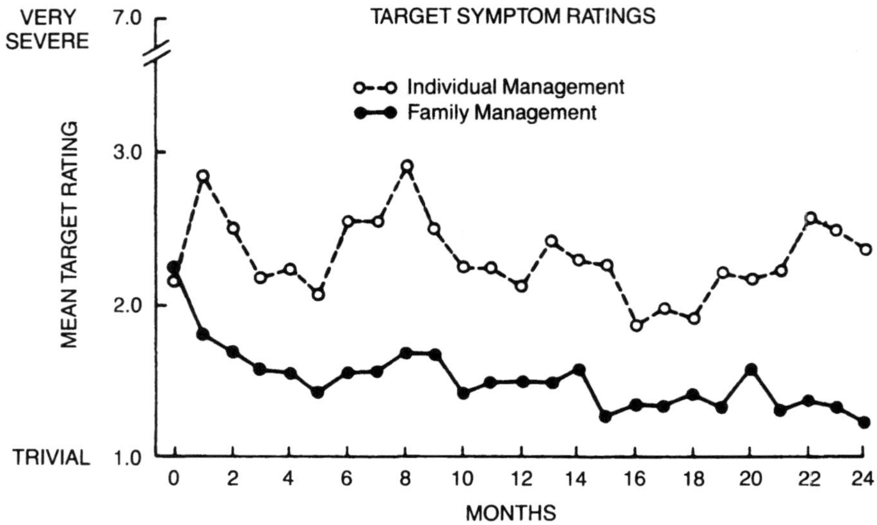

Figure 13-5. Blind psychopathology ratings supported that behavioral family therapy was associated with improvement of schizophrenia during the 2-year study period. *Note.* From "Family management in the Prevention of morbidity of schizophrenia: Clinical outcome of a two-year longitudinal study" by I. R. H. Falloon *et al.*, 1985, *Archives of General Psychiatry, 42*: 887–896. Reprinted by permission.

a cost saving of 19% and represented a 250% increase in cost efficiency (i.e., value-for-money).

Further analysis of the process of change showed close links between changes in the communication and problem-solving behavior of families and the clinical and social benefits associated with the BFT approach.

Impressive as this evidence may seem, it is essential that one or more replications are completed before BFT can be recommended as a treatment of choice for the prevention of morbidity in schizophrenia. Fortunately, those replication studies are underway, including a multicentered, NIMH-sponsored collaborative project.

In addition, behavioral family therapy is being employed in inpatient settings (see Chapter 12), in the rehabilitation of long-stay cases (at the University of Rochester), in family-based residential care (at the University of Vienna), and in the early intervention of preschizophrenic cases (in Buckingham, England). The preliminary results of the Buckingham project suggest that the combined use of BFT and low doses of neuroleptic drugs in the prodromal phase of schizophrenia may prevent the development of the disorder. This finding, together with indications that BFT may facilitate long-term remissions of schizophrenia, may offer hope that the prevalence of schizophrenia may eventually be reduced—or, at least, that the severe deteriorating outcome of many cases of schizophrenia may be eliminated.

CONCLUSIONS

It may be concluded that BFT is a very promising therapeutic approach in the long-term community-based care of schizophrenia. In this situation, it is used both as a prophylactic measure to modulate stresses impinging on the index patient, and to promote social adaptation of patient and family. The therapist coaches the family to develop highly efficient problem-solving methods that enhance their ability to cope with a wide range of stresses. The same problem-solving approach is employed by the therapist in crisis intervention and in handling difficulties in the process of therapy.

An additional component of this BFT approach is the education provided about the nature and management of schizophrenia. Although this is not substantially different from behavioral treatment of other disorders, for instance, anxiety and depression, greater structure has been imposed.

This BFT method has gained wide acceptance with clinicians, and the need for training has been overwhelming. A training manual (Falloon, *et al.*, 1984) has been published as have workbooks and training aids. Training can be fully accomplished within 6 months. This compares very favorably with other family therapies. The availability of efficient training provides hope that BFT will soon become available to the hundreds of thousands of sufferers of schizophrenia and their families who are likely to benefit from this approach.

REFERENCES

Anderson, C. M., Hogarty, G. E., & Reiss, D. J. (1980). Family treatment of adult schizophrenic patients: A psychoeducational approach. *Schizophrenia Bulletin, 6*, 490–505.

Bateson, G., Jackson, D. D., Haley, J., & Weakland, J. (1956). Toward a theory of schizophrenia. *Behavioral Science, 1*, 251–264.

Bowen, M. (1961). The family as the unit of study and treatment. *American Journal of Orthopsychiatry, 31*, 40–60.

Esterson, A., Cooper, D. G., & Laing, R. D. (1965). Results of family-oriented therapy with hospitalised schizophrenics. *British Medical Journal, 2*, 1462–1465.

Falloon, I. R. H. (1985). *Family management of schizophrenia: A study of the clinical, social, family and economic benefits*. Baltimore: Johns Hopkins University Press.

Falloon, I. R. H. (1986). *Informing the consumer: Developments in patient and family education*. Paper presented to the World Mental Health Federation conference on Mental Health Education, Dublin, September.

Falloon, I. R. H., Boyd, J. L., & McGill, C. W. (1984). *Family care of schizophrenia*. New York: Guilford Press.

Falloon, I. R. H., & Liberman, R. P. (1982). Behavioral family interventions in the management of chronic schizophrenia. In W. R. McFarlane & C. C. Beels (Eds.), *Family therapy in schizophrenia*. New York: Guilford Press.

Falloon, I. R. H., Liberman, R. P., Lillie, F. J., & Vaughn, C. E. (1981). Family therapy for relapsing schizophrenics and their families: A pilot study. *Family Process, 20*, 211–221.

Friedman, A. S., Boszormenyi-Nagy, I., Jungreis, S., *et al* (1965). *Psychotherapy for the whole family*. New York: Springer.

Goldstein, M. J., Judd, L. L., Rodnick, E. H., Alkire, A., & Gould, E. (1968). A method for studying social influence and coping patterns within families of disturbed adolescents. *Journal of Nervous and Mental Disease, 147*, 233–251.

Hirsch, S. R., & Leff, J. P. (1975). *Abnormalities in the parents of schizophrenics*. London: Oxford University Press.

Hogarty, G. E., Anderson, C. M., Reiss, D. J., *et al* (1986). Family psycho-education, social skills training and maintenance chemotherapy in the aftercare treatment of schizophrenia. One-year effects of a controlled study on relapse and expressed emotion. *Archives of General Psychiatry, 43*, 633–642.

Jackson, D. D., & Weakland, J. H. (1961). Conjoint family therapy: Some considerations on theory, technique, and results. *Psychiatry, 24*, 30–35.

Laing, R. D. (1967). *The politics of experience*. New York: Pantheon.

Leff, J., Kuipers, L., Berkowitz, R., Eberlein-Vries, R., & Sturgeon, D. (1982). A controlled trial of social intervention in the families of schizophrenic patients. *British Journal of Psychiatry, 141*, 121–134.

Leff, J., & Vaughn, C. (1980). The interaction of life events and relatives' expressed emotion in schizophrenia and depressive neurosis. *British Journal of Psychiatry, 136*, 146–153.

Liberman, R. P., Falloon, I. R. H., & Aitchison, R. A. (1984). Multiple family group therapy for schizophrenia: A behavioral problem-solving approach. *Psychosocial Rehabilitation Journal, 7*, 60–77.

Lidz, T., Fleck, S., & Cornelison, A. (1965). *Schizophrenia and the family*. New York: International Universities Press.

McGill, C. W., Falloon, I. R. H., Boyd, J. L., & Wood-Siverio, C. (1983). Family educational intervention in the treatment of schizophrenia. *Hospital and Community Psychiatry, 34*, 934–938.

Tarrier, N., Vaughn, C. E., Lader, M. H., & Leff, J. P. (1979). Bodily reactions to people and events in schizophrenia. *Archives of General Psychiatry, 36*, 311–315.

Tarrier, N., Barrowclough, C., Vaughn, C. E., Bamrah, J., & Freeman, H. L. (1986). *A controlled behavioural intervention to reduce schizophrenic relapse*. Paper presented at the Biennial Winter Workshop on Schizophrenia, Schladming, Austria, 26–31 January.

Tarrier, N., & Barrowclough, C. (1986). Providing information to relatives about schizophrenia: Some comments. *British Journal of Psychiatry, 149*, 458–463.

Vaughn, C. (1977). Interaction characteristics in families of schizophrenic patients. In H. Katschnig (Ed.), *Die andere Seite der Schizophrenie*. Vienna: Urban and Schwarzenberg.

Vaughn, C. E., & Leff, J. P. (1976). The influence of family and social factors on the course of psychiatric illness: A comparison of schizophrenic and depressed neurotic patients. *British Jounal of Psychiatry, 129*, 124–137.

Wynne, L. C., Ryckoff, I., Day, J., & Hirsch, S. (1958). Pseudo-mutuality in the family relations of schizophrenics. *Psychiatry, 21*, 205–220.

Wynne, L. C., Singer, M. T., Bartko, J. J., & Toohey, M. L. (1977). Schizophrenics and their families: Recent research on parental communication. In J. M. Tanner (Ed.), *Developments in psychiatric research*. London: Hodder and Stoughton.

Zubin, J., & Spring, B. (1977). Vulnerability: A new view of schizophrenia. *Journal of Abnormal Psychology, 96*, 103–126.

14

Alcoholism

MANFRED M. FICHTER

FELICITAS POSTPISCHIL
Department of Psychiatry, University of Munich

Alcohol abuse and dependence are highly prevalent disorders that cause much misery for patients and their spouses and children, not to mention the high financial burden on society for treatment and rehabilitation. According to preliminary results of the Epidemiologic Catchment Area (ECA) program—the largest psychiatric epidemiologic study of representative community samples in history—the highest prevalence rates of disorders in the communities studied were for substance abuse disorders, affective disorders, and anxiety disorders (Myers *et al.*, 1984; Robins *et al.*, 1984). According to these results, more than 9 million people in the United States suffer from alcohol abuse or dependence in any 6-month period; 23 million to 31 million people in the United States will suffer from alcohol abuse or dependence at some time during their lives. In this chapter, the term "alcoholism" is used to describe alcohol abuse and alcohol dependence.

The family system constitutes an important factor in the syndrome of alcoholism. The behavior of the alcoholic may disrupt and impair the funtioning of his or her family system. Alcoholism creates escalating crises in the family function; it causes economic drain on family resources, causes sexual dysfunction, impairs the marital interaction, threatens job security, brings about physical abuse of family members, leads to abuse of family members by neglect, and puts strains on the family system by the refusal of the alcoholic to take responsibility (Bailey, Habermann, & Alksne, 1962; Jackson, 1954; Orford, Oppenheimer, Egert, & Hensman, 1977). On the other hand, the family system may contribute to the development of alcohol problems in a member of the family. Although alcoholics marry at about the same rate as the general population, alcoholics' separation and divorce rates are four to eight times higher (Paolino, McCrady, & Diamond, 1978). There is also empirical evidence that continued heavy drinking in spite of treatment is positively correlated with further marital disruption and that marital dysfunctions, on the other hand, can contribute to the development of alcohol problems (cf. Polich, Armor, & Braiker, 1981). Follow-up reports have reached rather pessimistic results concerning the sobriety of patients treated for alcohol dependence (Polich *et al.*, 1981). However, previous treatment studies have widely neglected the family system and have focused primarily on the patient. In the 1970s and 1980s, there has been a growing interest in the important effects of alcoholism on the family as well as in the effects of the family on alcoholism (Ablon, 1976; Hanson & Estes, 1977; Janzen, 1977; Kaufman, 1984; Kaufman & Kaufman, 1979; Krimmel, 1973; Paolino & McCrady, 1979; Scott, 1970; Steinglass & Robertson, 1983).

CONCEPTS OF FAMILY INTERACTION AND ALCOHOLISM

There has been much speculation about the effects of the family on alcoholism. The personality structure of the spouses of alcoholics has been the focus of many early studies. Based on psychoanalytic concepts, the *disturbed personality hypothesis* was introduced in the 1930s to explain alcoholism in the male on the basis of neurotic conflicts of the spouse. The model was hard to test empirically, and those studies that did attempt to test it (assessing interpersonal perception, dependency, dominance, and general measures of psychopathology) produced conflicting results (Drewery & Rae, 1969; Kogan, Fordyce, & Jackson, 1963; Kogan & Jackson, 1963; Lanyon, 1973; Mitchell, 1959; Paolino & McCrady, 1977). A variant of the disturbed personality hypothesis is the *decompensation hypothesis*, which states that the spouse of an alcoholic will decompensate when the alcoholic successfully becomes sober. There is only limited support for this hypothesis, and the fable of the neurotic woman who chooses an alcoholic to fulfill her own neurotic needs is oversimplified; these earlier typologies of alcoholics and their spouses have little validity. The only conclusion that can be drawn with certainty from the existing data is that the common characteristic of spouses of alcoholics is that they are married to alcoholics.

Three decades ago, Joan Jackson proposed a *sociological stress theory*, which changed the focus from individual psychopathology to family interactions and role functioning in the family unit (Jackson, 1954, 1956, 1959, 1962). In this model, alcoholism in a family member was seen as a stressful experience, resulting in redefinition of family roles with the spouse taking over responsibility and control as a way to cope with the unpredictable behavior of the alcoholic family member. The process of the family members coping with the stress put on them by the alcoholic was described in five stages of family disorganization: (1) denial of the drinking problem by all family members; (2) disorganization of family relationships; (3) attempts at reorganization of family roles including the alcoholic; (4) separation from the alcoholic; and (5) reorganization of the partial family systems or—in the case of successful rehabilitation of the alcoholic—reorganization of the complete family unit as a dry system. Jackson's work was highly stimulating. However, because it was based on the study of members of the self-help organizations AA and Al-Anon, it may not be representative of alcoholic families in general.

Systems Theory of Family Interactions

Beginning in the 1970s, a paradigm shift took place from an individual perspective to a family system perspective. In family system theory, the unit of analysis is the whole family with its interaction patterns and roles. According to this view, a family system attempts to maintain its homeostasis. Symptoms such as alcoholic drinking can be seen as adaptive and protective for the whole family system, because they may maintain or reestablish homeostasis. The individual members of the family system are functionally interdependent. Each family member affects and is affected by the other members. System theory does not follow the usual concept of linear causality and deductive hypothesis testing. System theory is more sophisticated than previous theories focusing on the individual psychopathology, and the involvement of complex family interaction patterns leads to the concept of multicausality; this concept, however, brings about methodological difficulties for empirical testing and validation. Janzen (1977) analyzed 24 family-oriented studies concerning methodological soundness and found that none of the studies fulfilled all of his four methodological criteria (randomized allocation of patients, presence of control group, specification of patient characteristics, and sufficient measures of behavior change on various levels). Important contributions to the empirical assessment and validation of a system-based view of the alcoholic and the family have come from the work of Steinglass and associates (Steinglass, 1977, 1979, 1980, 1981; Steinglass, Weiner, & Mendelson, 1971). According to Steinglass, alcohol becomes the organizing principle for family interaction in the presence of an alcoholic.

The systems view of alcoholism is not restricted to the nuclear family and may be extended to older and younger generations of the family as well. The case example of family B (see below) shows how the grandmother's role of controlling and terrorizing the couple's marriage was delegated after her death to the couple's son Eric (isomorphism). The consequences for children of being raised by an alcoholic family member are often overlooked. Children may be abused by a drunk parent and grossly neglected by both parents. Children of alcoholics are subjected to chronic stress and tension in the family and often show developmental, emotional, and learning problems, behavior deficits, and/or antisocial behavior. In addition, alcoholism "breeds" alcoholism and drug abuse in the children of these marriages. A nonalcoholic wife may encourage an older son to take over responsibilities abdicated by the father, placing the son in overt competition with the father in both behavior and drinking. Daughters in such families may feel that the alcoholic father prefers them to their mother and that if the mother were more loving, the father would not drink. These daughters believe the ills of weak men can be cured by love and tend to marry alcoholics and repeat this pattern in multiple marriages (Kaufman & Pattison, 1982a).

Social Learning Theory

Based on the learning theories (especially on operant conditioning paradigms), social learning theory has served as a valuable model for the understanding and treatment of alcohol dependency. Almost everybody has experienced at least once the powerful and short-term reinforcing effect of alcohol. A theory based on the reinforcing characteristics of alcohol and alcohol-related social behavior has a high degree of plausibility and is also relevant for treatment. In a functional analysis, the antecedents (discriminative stimuli), the resulting behaviors (reactions), and the consequences of behavior must be explored. In the case of an alcoholic, the antecedent situation may be, for example, the subjective anxiety experienced in facing a vocational or interpersonal problem; the response is drinking; and the immediate consequence is the temporary cessation of anxiety. In all forms of addiction, we find an immediate positive consequence, which reinforces the behavior, and long-term negative consequences (such as the loss of job). The negative consequences usually occur slowly and therefore do not exert any notable influence on the addictive behavior. According to social learning theory, alcoholics and their spouses often have not developed sufficient skills of communication and problem-solving.

The empirical analysis of problem-solving behavior and the analysis of interactions in alcoholic families based on a social learning paradigm have been started quite recently. Gorad, McCourt, and Cobb (1971) found a responsibility-avoiding indirect style of communication in alcoholic couples in an experimental game situation. Clinical experience and some empirical studies (Ballings, Kessler, Gomberg, & Weiner, 1979) pointed to a high level of hostility and coercive verbal interaction using threats and nagging to exert control over each other in alcoholic couples. Moos and Moos (1984) compared recovered and relapsed alcoholics 2 years after completion of inpatient treatment with matched community controls on various sets of family-functioning indices. Families of recovered patients were functioning as well as families of the community controls. In families of relapsed patients, the authors found more family arguments than in families of recovered patients, less cohesion, less expressiveness, less recreational orientation, and less agreement about their family environment than in the community control families. Alcoholic couples with a high degree of hostility and coercive interaction patterns were shown to have the poorest prognosis (Moos, Bromet, Tsu, & Moos, 1979; Orford *et al.*, 1977). Alcoholic couples engage in positive exchanges at a low rate, show a low rate of friendly acts (Billings *et al.*, 1979), have ambiguous, vague and inconsistent ways of communication with a low rate of relationship-relevant messages emitted by the alcoholic (Klein, 1979), and show a low rate of intimate positive interactions (Djukanovic, Milosavcevic, & Jovanovi, 1976). Alcohol consumption also increases assertive or aggressive acts within the alcoholic couple and increase the amount of verbal output of the alcoholic (Billings *et al.*, 1979; Foy, Miller, & Eisler, 1975).

These data reveal poor communication and problem-solving skills in alcoholics and their spouses. They point to the necessity of focusing therapy on these deficits and dysfunctional ways of interaction, if the therapy effects are to be enduring. There are no basic contradictions between paradigms of family systems theory and social learning theory. An amalgam of both theories may be helpful for our understanding of alcoholism and for designing effective treatment plans. The laws of reinforcement not only apply to single individuals but also apply to a family system; also, symptoms that appear dysfunctional from an individual perspective may well be adaptive when viewed from the family systems perspective. Davis, Berenson, Steinglass, and Davis (1974) reviewed the adaptive consequences of drinking and showed reinforcement for continued drinking. Our present knowledge, however, also shows that dysfunctional interaction patterns seen in alcoholic couples are not unique and are in no way specific for alcoholism; it has been concluded that "basically, alcoholic marriages are not unique but rather neurotic marriages in which alcoholism is part of the neurotic interaction" (Kaufman & Pattison, 1982a, pp. 664–665). General systems theory and social learning theory provide a model that facilitates the assessment of interaction patterns in an individual couple. The model is flexible enough to incorporate new scientific evidence; it can be formulated with sufficient explicitness to lend itself to empirical validation, and it can be helpful in designing therapy.

Ethnicity, Gender, Stage of Illness, and Type of Family System

A family is a highly complex system embedded in an even more complex social system, including neighbors, colleagues, school friends, etc., and cultural values and sanctions. The therapists of alcoholics and their families should be open to these complexities and aware that typologies are always simplifications. For a differential analysis of the importance of the effects of the family system on alcoholism in a family member, the factors of ethnicity, gender, stage of alcoholism, and the type of family system have to be taken into account.

Patterns of alcohol consumption and the reactivity of the family will differ from one *ethnic group* to another and will not be the same, or instance, for an Irish American family, an Italian immigrant family, and a rural southern black family (Ablon, 1976; 1980; McGoldrick, Gioridano, & Pearce, 1982).

The *gender* of the alcoholic is of importance in drinking and interaction patterns. Drinking by women appears to be related to problems of women in our society in general. Most women drink because of conflicts about their sex role, because of feelings of inferiority, loneliness, and futility, and because of problems in self-expression and actualization. Women tend to hide their drinking from their family more than men; women also show a much higher prevalence of alcoholism in the family of origin than male alcoholics (Sandmaier, 1980). Female alcoholics often perceive their mothers as cold, bossy, and domineering. The prealcoholic daughter often rejects her mother and gravitates to her father for affection. The father often is warm and gentle but alcoholic and speaks up to his dominant wife only when drunk. Winokur and Clayton (1968) reported that 52% of the fathers and 35% of the mothers of female alcoholics were absent, mentally ill, or suffering from an affective disorder; for male alcoholics, this was true in only 32% of the fathers and 21% of the mothers. Female alcoholics also may give birth to impaired children, which may cause feelings of guilt, hostility, and rejection. The male spouse of the female alcoholic is more likely to leave his partner than a female spouse of a male alcoholic. Hence, the sex of the alcoholic family member is of importance for the design of family intervention strategies. According to our experience, it is more difficult to get the male spouse of a female alcoholic than the female spouse of a male alcoholic to participate in family sessions or groups for significant others.

The *stage of alcoholism* and whether the therapist is dealing with a dry or wet family system is of importance in family-oriented therapy. Family interactions and family structure show changes during the course of alcoholism of a family member (Steinglass, 1980). In early phases, we often find denial of the alcohol problem and overreaction to the alcoholic behavior. The family system then adapts to the alcohol problem, isolates the alcoholic, and forms a new homeostasis, partially excluding the alcoholic. Finally, the family may separate from the alcoholic or may get into repetitive cycles of neurotic and enmeshed engagement and chaotic disengagement (Steinglass, 1980). When working with a wet family system, the therapist must be ready to deal with the problems arising in this constellation (e.g., patient comes to sessions intoxicated). In a wet system, it is more fruitful to work with the sober spouse and to expect changes from him or her rather than from the drinking alcoholic. In this case, treatment should aim at helping the spouse to disengage and disentangle emotionally from the alcoholic and to obtain more independence. In wet family systems, it may be helpful to confront the family with the three choices suggested by Berenson (1976): (1) keep doing exactly what you are doing; (2) detach or emotionally distance yourself from the alcoholic; or (3) separate or physically distance yourself from the alcoholic. The family is thus confronted with three choices that at first seem impossible; the therapist thereby intensifies the crisis to induce change.

Families with an alcoholic member can react to this problem in many different ways; the reactivity patterns in one family also change over time. Kaufman & Pattison (1982b) described different *types of family systems* with an alcoholic member: the functional family, the neurotic enmeshed family, the disintegrated family, and the absent family. A differential analysis of alcoholic family systems may help to increase our understanding of structural and functional factors in the family system (see below).

DEALING WITH DIFFERENT TYPES OF FAMILY SYSTEMS IN ALCOHOLISM

The Functional Family System

In this type of family system, the alcoholic behavior in a family member usually is caused by life events or chronic difficulties originating outside the family, while the family system is functionally intact. Insight-oriented therapy and reconstructive family therapy are often resisted and may indeed be unnecessary. Clear information about the medical, psychological, and social consequences of further drinking, family contracts, and supportive measures (e.g., treatment with disulfiram) may often be sufficient. This was the case in family A:

Case Example: Family A

The alcohol-dependent patient was a 54-year-old traveling salesman. He showed a severe cirrhosis of the liver as a result of drinking. Because of a hepatic coma, he was admitted to a medical unit. After he had recuperated from this illness, a family session was initiated. The patient, his wife, and his daughter and son (both in the medical profession) participated in this session. Detailed information on possible further medical complications as a result of alcohol drinking was given, and support of the patient by the family members concerning the drinking problem was discussed. The patient was also encouraged to cut down on his workload and was helped to resolve some of his problems at work. In the absence of neurotic traits in the patient and other members of the family, a single session of family intervention was sufficient to induce complete and lasting alcohol abstinence in this patient.

The Neurotic Enmeshed Family System

This family system is characterized by neurotic traits in the family members, enmeshment of the family system, and dysfunctional family interaction patterns. Usually, we find indirect communication (e.g., through a third party), overreaction to the drinking behavior of a family member, a high degree of competitiveness, and endless fights about who is to blame. Coalitions take place between the nonalcoholic spouse and other family members (usually the children), alienating and distancing the alcoholic family member and driving him or her in a child-like status and passive–dependent behavior. Much has been written about the neurotic enmeshed family system, and findings have been inappropriately generalized to all alcoholic families. The reaction pattern of the nonalcoholic spouse in a neurotic enmeshed family system has been called "coalcoholism." The coalcoholic spouse is unable to disengage from the alcoholic, feels guilty and responsible for the alcoholic, takes over the parental role of the alcoholic, and manages the family through enmeshed coalitions with other family members. In the relationship, the coalcoholic fulfills a neurotic need for control and power over another person and reduces his or her own anxieties (of being left alone) and feelings of insufficiency. In many instances, neurotic family conflicts are not restricted to the nuclear family. Grandparents, children, and more distant relatives may contribute to the perpetuation of alcoholism in a family member.

Simple therapeutic measures will hardly be enough to induce change in a severely enmeshed, neurotic family system with an alcoholic. Often, the alcoholic and family are not ready to receive treatment before they have reached a later phase, when external threats have emerged (e.g., loss of job) and the coalcoholic spouse's overprotectivity has been replaced by hostility, disgust, and detachment. In working with these families, it is important to focus on the present and future rather than letting them recount the past in endless fights. The therapist should avoid being pressed into the role of a judge of family arguments and conflicts. With a neurotically enmeshed family system, an educational and supportive approach or treatment with disulfiram is not sufficient. Instead, it is necessary to involve the entire family system in the treatment, to offer the alcoholic family member intensive therapy (which often will include hospitalization), and to restructure the family system. It is also necessary to work on disengagement of the mutual enmeshment of family members and to clarify boundaries among family members.

Case Example: Family B

All members of the nuclear family—the 51-year-old father, 46-year-old mother, and 28-year-old son—showed substance abuse or dependence. Eric, the only son, was the first to show symptoms of alcohol and drug dependence. He started drinking at age 13 and soon became known to the youth authorities because of burglary and antisocial behavior. Because his parents always helped him out, Eric was never convicted. He had been hospitalized 13 times for alcohol detoxification, followed each time by immediate relapse. Disputes between father and son occurred often and usually resulted in fights. Once Eric almost killed his father with an axe during a dispute. Several times, Eric had begun to work but never for long. Then, at age 22–24, he stayed in one company, where his father had been working for almost 30 years as a locksmith and plumber.

During this time, the father's alcohol consumption increased, and arguments and disputes in the family occurred more often. After two decades of alcohol abuse, the father developed alcohol withdrawal symptoms, blackouts, loss of tolerance, and loss of control; in addition, he heavily abused nicotine and caffeine. Eric's slowness at work provoked his father, and Eric finally quit his job. He was unemployed for the next 4 years and started taking tranquilizers and hallucinogenics. Meanwhile, the father's alcohol dependence increased, and the mother started taking benzodiazepines. While the father went to work early and while the mother fulfilled her duties as a housewife, the son stayed in bed until noon, had breakfast when his parents had lunch, and lived an "oblomovistic" (irresponsible) way of life. Thus, Eric provoked his parents as well as neighbors by listening to loud music, smoking pot, and going out in the evening to partake of the night life of Munich.

Finally, the father was put under pressure from his employer to do something about his alcohol problem; he was the first of the family to come to our alcoholism treatment unit. After detoxification, he participated in a 6-week intensive inpatient behavioral family therapy treatment. In the course of this therapy, he participated in group therapy sessions with other alcoholics and took part in eight family therapy sessions; his wife attended a group for spouses of alcoholics. It became clear that there was a high degree of enmeshment in the family, mostly between the mother and the son. Between them, a coalition existed, tending to distance the father from the family.

Except for being the breadwinner, the father had little say in the family. In critical situations, the mother would always take the side of the son. The mother was highly dependent on signs of well-being from her son. If he did not call her when he was away from home, she would panic. Thus, the son could spoil a day or even a vacation for his parents, and he was well aware of this power. The father often criticized the son for not going to work and just playing around at home. This criticism functioned as negative reinforcement, perpetuating the behavior of the son it meant to change. When the father spoke up and asked for clear sanctions for the son's behavior, he was ridiculed by his wife. Aged 28 years, Eric still lived at home. In the course of therapy, the wish was expressed by all that he should become more independent and live by himself. In fact, he still lived in a room leading to his parents' bedroom, thus exerting power even over the parents' sexual sphere. We learned that the grandmother, a tyrannic and domineering woman, had occupied this room for many years before she died and had made it impossible for the couple to develop a normal and independent marital relationship. Immediately after her death, the son was moved into this room, and it is reasonable to assume that he was delegated the same function that the grandmother had had earlier: dominating the marriage of the couple, who were centered solely around Eric's needs and whose well-being was depending on his well-being. The boundaries of each family member were insufficient, and all had deficits in their personal individuation. When an apartment was found to which the parents intended to move, leaving the son in the old apartment, the mother developed intense fears about leaving her son.

Major aims of therapy were (1) to help each member of the family to build up his or her own feelings of identity and to increase individuation; (2) to support each member to live in a dry system; and (3) to restructure the balance of the family system by showing the son a better perspective for his own development and by helping the parents strengthen their own interests and (for the first time in their marriage) to develop a true partnership with mutual love and support. (It must also be mentioned that the father had become impotent five years earlier due to diabetes and alcoholism.)

After a first stage of improvement in the course of therapy, a stage of resistance developed, and family members reported that everything had become worse than ever before. Finally, the son asked for inpatient treatment, was detoxified and was referred to a drug-rehabilitation unit for long-term rehabilitation. The benzodiazepine dependency of the mother then came up as a problem that had not been recognized by the family before.

Case Example: Family C

Family C included a male alcoholic with a passive, depressive, dependent personality structure; his spouse was coalcoholic. Jim came for inpatient treatment at age 37 because his employer "asked" him to do so. Seven years earlier, when his mother, to whom he felt closely attached, had died, Jim had started drinking heavily (about 8 liters of beer each day). Jim became physically dependent and showed social withdrawal.

Jim's mother had been 15 when he was born as an illegitimate child. Jim was raised in a children's home for 4 years, then by his mother and his stepfather, whom he despised. He went to school for 10 years and was then trained as fiscal officer. A few weeks after the death of his mother, Jim met Cheryl. She reported that Jim appeared so helpless to her that she felt pity for him and decided to accept his proposal of marriage. Cheryl was an active, hectic, lively, and determined woman; she took care of a shop for clocks and watches that Jim had inherited from his mother. Cheryl also managed the household and took care of the two children. In the evenings, Jim drank and stayed in bed much of the time. There were frequent arguments between Jim and his spouse, each one blaming the other. Cheryl called Jim "a failure" and pitied herself for having married him.

Analysis of the interactions between the couple showed that Cheryl reinforced Jim's passive and dependent behavior. There were indications that Cheryl needed Jim the way he was to have a goal in life and to exert control. On the other hand, Jim had never learned to stand on his own feet, to take responsibility. Cheryl replaced the functions of his mother: she took over responsibility not only concerning him and the children but also concerning the management of the shop. The more dominant and hyperfunctional Cheryl behaved, the more passive and dependent Jim became.

During inpatient therapy, Jim acquired social skills in role-play sessions, increasing his competence and confidence. It was made clear to Jim and Cheryl that each of them contributed to the perpetuation of the drinking problem: Jim by remaining passive, dependent, and lazy and Cheryl by taking over his responsibilities and keeping him in child-like dependency. Early in therapy, there was a high degree of nagging and criticizing each other. In the course of therapy, it was attempted to increase positive exchanges and positive reinforcement and to build up more active recreational activities for Jim—especially activities that Jim and Cheryl could share together. It also became necessary to deal with the anxieties of the couple. Jim's anxiety was that Cheryl would leave him if he tried to become independent; Cheryl's anxiety was that Jim would not need her any more and would leave her when he has become capable of taking care of himself. It also was necessary to work with Jim's negative self-concept ("I am a loser," "I am incapable," "I'll never learn to look after me by myself"). Since neurotic needs were fulfilled in this couple, and since family systems of this type are often rather static, it could not be expected that behavior patterns that had been used for so long would change within a few days or weeks.

Therapeutically induced change must be a continuous process by which the family system becomes more flexible and through which the coalcoholic learns not to take over the alcoholic's responsibility. The alcoholic must also learn that taking responsibility and becoming more active improves the marital relationship, gives him or her more freedom, and makes him or her less dependent in every respect.

The Disintegrated or Absent Family System

In later stages, a functional or a neurotic family system may disintegrate. Usually, alcoholics lose their jobs, their families, and their self-respect and present to a therapist without any recent family contact. In other cases, the family system is virtually absent, and the alcoholic has never had close family ties, or the family system has over the years disintegrated so badly under the burden of the alcohol dependency that significant others can only be found in fellow drinkers and boarding home operators. At first glance, family therapy appears irrelevant when there is no family. Nevertheless, the therapist should explore former family ties early in treatment. At this stage, the aim should not be the reconstitution and reunion of the family but rather clarification and redefinition of personal roles and ties. Sometimes indifference, but more often rejection, hostility, bitterness, and ambivalence, toward the alcoholic will be observed in the former family members of a disintegrated alcoholic family. Initially, the therapy in a disintegrated family system should focus primarily on the patient, who must learn not to blame the others for the drinking but to take responsibility for him- or herself. The patient in the early phase of treatment needs support to achieve abstinence for a long period of time (at least several months). He or she also should be introduced to self-help groups, which can serve as a valuable social support system. When abstinence is achieved, vocational retraining can be initiated. The patient must learn in successive steps to be responsible, maintain abstinence, and solve problems in an adequate way without falling back into drinking. Only when this has been achieved, and when relatives and friends have had the opportunity to observe the process of individuation and stability in the patient, will it be possible to renegotiate the patient's role in the family system.

In many cases, it may not be possible to reconstitute the family system; in these cases, family sessions will be helpful to appropriately define separated roles, to reconcile each family member with the burden of the past, and to build up the basis for a mature and independent life of the patient separated from the family. When former family members are invited to family sessions, they often feel that again they have to give in to the patient after having had the burden of an alcoholic family member for so many years. It is therefore helpful to stress right in the beginning that the aim of therapy is not reunification of the family but rather reconciliation between family members and the support of independence and separation when it is desired. Healthy separation will be better than forced reunion of the family. In the case of disintegration of an enmeshed neurotic family system, the neurotic needs of the coalcoholic spouse of the alcoholic must also be taken into account. When a partnership was heavily based on the neurotic needs of the alcoholic and the coalcoholic (as in family C), all family members will have to change their previous roles if they attempt reunification in a new partnership. Working through dysfunctional family interactions during the course of therapy may help the patient and spouse to become more sensitive to irrational needs. Awareness and understanding of dysfunctional behavior patterns are important but not sufficient for changes in behavior. At first in role-play sessions, and later in real-life situations, functional interpersonal behavior and problem-solving skills must be taught. In cases where the family is practically absent or is unwilling to cooperate, the patient needs support in building up new social networks and friendships. In many cases, the alcoholic without any useful family ties has never acquired the social skills to build up a stable partnership and to communicate effectively when problems arise and need to be solved. Patients who previously did not use effective ways of problem-solving, either because of their own anxiety or because of lack of social skills, will profit much from social skill training, including role-play and homework assignments. Finally, the usefulness of participation in self-help groups such as AA for the alcoholic and Al-Anon for the non- or coalcoholic family members must be stressed.

Case Example: Family D

Family D included a lonely alcoholic housewife and her offended, narcissistic husband. Jane was admitted for detoxification at age 40 following a 4-year period of heavy but concealed drinking. Her mother had been dependent on tranquilizers, and Jane had been brought up as the only child, trying to live up to the high expectations of her parents. At age 18 Jane met her husband Hans, who appeared optimistic and independent. Jane married him to escape the restrictions and overprotectiveness of her parents' home. After 6 years of marriage Jane had a miscarriage, which resulted in depression, loss of self-esteem, and feelings of guilt. Two years later, she gave birth to a healthy child, and later a second child was born. This change made it necessary for her to stop working. At work she had been quite successful, and becoming a housewife resulted in a loss of social reinforcement and isolation from other adults. Meanwhile, her husband was successful at work, and Jane felt betrayed because Hans got the reinforcement for his work that she was denied.

Jane began to drink alcohol secretly. When her alcoholism became overt to her husband, he blamed and humiliated her and withdrew his love. In addition, Hans brought his mother into the household, and she took over the household duties, took care of the children, and even slept in the same room as Hans. Jane felt lonely, humiliated and guilty; she missed positive social reinforcement, felt overly controlled by her husband and her mother-in-law, and lost her self-confidence.

Hans formed a coalition with his mother against Jane. He felt betrayed by Jane, whom he thought was neither a proper wife for him nor a good mother for their children. He had high moral ideals for himself and his family members, felt that he gave more to his wife than he received from her, and became more and more harsh and hostile. A wall of ice built up between the two, and there was a constantly high level of tension in the family. They were unable to speak to one another without blame. The situation became unbearable. Hans behaved with more and more hostility toward Jane, and her feelings of guilt and self-depreciation increased.

Early in therapy, it became clear that Hans felt too betrayed and offended to reconstitute the marriage; he had decided to get a divorce. Whenever Jane was at home during inpatient treatment for a weekend, a tense situation built up; each blamed the other, each felt betrayed by the other, and Jane's desire to ease the tension by drinking increased. Hans reacted in an almost paranoic way to the attempts of a therapist to support Jane's self-esteem. Since reconciliation appeared impossible, Jane, after discharge from the hospital, moved in with her mother; during therapy, her skills to build up new social relationships were improved. Positive reinforcement from the therapist and other patients in her group helped improve her damaged self-confidence. In spite of heavy arguments with her husband concerning the children, she managed to remain sober after separation from her narcissistic, oversensitive, and hostile husband and his mother.

THERAPEUTIC STRATEGIES FOR ALCOHOLISM IN THE FAMILY CONTEXT

We have already pointed out that alcoholics and their families show a high degree of variation depending on age, sex, stage of illness, and ethnic background of the patient. This variation among patients affords a flexible treatment approach. Nevertheless, there are certain recurrent themes in the process of therapy, and certain therapy techniques have been found helpful. Recurrent themes in the family therapy of alcoholism are the following: (1) The alcoholism is denied, or there is denial that there is any other problem beside the alcoholism. In the initial stages, the denial of alcoholism and of marital problems is seen in the patient as well as the spouse. (2) The patient or the spouse may attempt to coerce the other to take the "first step." (3) There may be resistance on the part of the spouse to be included in therapy; the spouse may argue that he or she is not ill and has already carried so much of a burden. (4) There may be ambivalence from the spouse concerning the partnership and whether or not he or she will stay with the patient. (5) In many cases, feelings of bitterness, disappointment, and hostility can be observed in the spouse; these feelings of distress gradually have to be worked through in therapy and shared with others. Interaction between family members may show a high degree of negative criticism and nagging. (6) The spouse may express feelings of guilt concerning his or her role in the development of alcoholism. (7) The patient and spouse often express their fear of a relapse into drinking. This general fear may be counterproductive and serve as a self-fulfilling prophecy. The therapist should explain that a relapse may even have positive effects and that strategies must be learned to detect an imminent relapse and to stop drinking in an early stage of relapse. (8) Often, difficulties can be observed in expressing feelings, needs, and desires by both the patient and spouse. Neither may do what he or she would like to do, instead doing what he or she thinks the other would like. This kind of thinking soon leads to a "negative balance," anger, and bitterness. (9) Towards the end of therapy, the issue of dependence on the therapist and separation from other members of the therapy group becomes an issue. The facts and feelings of this process of separation must be dealt with.

Family therapy can be conducted in various settings: (1) sessions with a single family or conjoint marital counseling; (2) multiple-family therapy sessions or multiple-couples treatment sessions; (3) group sessions for significant others, in which the patients are excluded; and (4) sessions with alcoholics focusing on family issues in the absence of the family. It will make a difference whether the family system is dry or wet and whether the patient is treated on an in- or outpatient basis. Detailed descriptions of behavioral methods used in couples and family generally can be found in Azrin (1976), Gottman *et al.* (1976), Liberman, Wheeler, de Visser, Kuehnel, and Kuehnel (1980), Miller (1976), Miller and Heston (1980), O'Farrell and Cutter (1979), Weiss (1975), Weiss, Birchler, and Vincent (1974), and in other chapters of this book. The following intervention techniques are useful in the therapy of alcoholics and can be incorporated in any of the above-mentioned therapy settings.

Information, Education, and Teaching

Knowledge reduces helplessness! It may sound trivial that information on alcoholism and its consequences is necessary and helpful to build up a motivation for change, but this fact *is* often overlooked. We find it helpful to emphasize that alcoholism is an illness and that aggressive, disinhibited acts, unreliability, and denial of alcohol drinking are signs of this dependency. Giving the relatives booklets, books, and videotapes about alcoholism can be very effective. It should also be pointed out that the family's support of the patient and his or her goals in treatment is important.

Therapeutic Contracts

A therapeutic contract usually exists implicitly. The explicit formulation of the expectations of the patient, other family members, and the therapist and the formulation of the consequences of the achievement of certain goals are extremely helpful in the process of therapy. A therapeutic contract may help to reduce the emotional reactivity of family members when it includes what action is to be taken in the case of a relapse. A therapeutic contract may deal with attendance of therapy sessions, involvement in self-help groups (AA and Al-Anon, etc.), modification of disruptive behavior in the family, intake of medication etc. Since avoidance, inconsequent behaviors and unreliability are common features of alcoholics, a therapeutic contract is important. A therapeutic contract should be explicit, clear, and unequivocal, and it is most helpful when it is written out.

Homework Assignments

Task assignments help to extend the therapy session in time and space. Each assignment must be tailored to the patient's and family's needs and competence. It is the task of the therapist to transform the issues analyzed in the therapy sessions into a homework assignment for the patient and/or family members. The tasks must be well understood and compatible with the goals of therapy. They should be rehearsed in the session before being given as homework assignments. An assignment can be very simple (e.g., making a phone call to a friend or reading a certain book) or complex. Thus, the patient and the spouse may negotiate certain responsibilities (e.g., washing the dishes, making plans for leisure time) and privileges and may agree on a contingency contract stating that each has to do something to please the other at least, for instance, three times per week. Assignments of this kind help to increase the amount of positive exchange. Task assignment may also make use of paradoxical strategies such as symptom prescription (e.g., prescribing the patient to be passive, silent, and depressed each day from 9 to 10 A.M.). The completion of task assignments and possible difficulties in carrying out the assignment should be discussed in the next session. When patient and spouse repeatedly show noncompliance concerning homework assignments, the therapist may point out to the couple that the disturbance of their relationship is so severe that they will not be able to carry out homework assignments; a remark of this kind may induce paradoxical reactions. In group therapy, those who completed the homework assignment rather than those who did not comply should receive the therapist's attention.

Sharing Recreational Activities

Most alcoholic couples have difficulties in planning their recreational activities, especially when the time-filling alcohol consumption is withdrawn. It should be an aim in therapy to build up and reinforce active recreational activities in which the patient and spouse or the whole family is involved (shared rewarding activities). A list of possible rewarding activities should be explored, and certain activities can then be prescribed as homework assignments. Possible causes of failure (such as waiting until the last minute so that a babysitter cannot be found) should be anticipated.

Training of Communication Skills

The training of communication and problem-solving skills should preferably be conducted in groups. The therapist should make use of model learning, prompting, behavioral rehearsal, and feedback. Feedback should focus on the positive rather than on the negative. Important areas for the training of communication skills are (1) learning to listen to others; (2) increasing the frequency of positive interactions; and (3) learning the direct expression of emotions. Patients should be encouraged to talk to each other rather than to center their communication on the therapist, and they should be encouraged to actualize and to enact transactional patterns in their family rather than to describe them. It is the task of the therapist to help the patient and the family members to enact and resolve family conflicts in the session rather than to talk about disagreements of the past. The therapist should make it clear that blaming each other is counterproductive; instead of blaming ("You never helped me"), each person should learn to express his or her own feelings ("I felt angry and then sad and lonely when you did not help me"). In family role-play sessions, individual boundaries can be delineated, and each family member should speak personally ("I want," "I think"). The parental subsystem sometimes may need protection from intrusion by children (as in the case example of Family B).

Attentive Listening

For effective communication, it is important to listen attentively to the others. Many families will have experienced the "all are speaking and nobody listens" syndrome, where important messages get lost and communication drifts to other topics without resolution of the previous topic. Communication sessions should proceed from easy to difficult tasks, from the simple to the more complex. It is helpful to start communication sessions with sessions for attentive listening. A family or group member is asked to listen to another person's message and to repeat the message as accurately as possible. It can be pointed out that understanding the other's opinion does not necessarily mean agreeing with it. Only when the message of the other person has been listened to attentively (including eye contact, intonation of voice, facial expression, and gestures), and when the received message has been repeated accurately, should response to the message be made in these training sessions.

Increase of Rewarding Interactions

It should be a goal in the family therapy of alcoholics to change the general interaction patterns in the family so that they become more positive to the alcoholic than excessive drinking was previously. For this purpose, communication sessions to increase the frequency of positive interactions and exchanges of tenderness are helpful. Family and group members should be encouraged to increase the frequency with which they notice, acknowledge, and initiate caring behaviors; the homework "catch your spouse doing something nice" can be assigned. It is helpful to rehearse the task of directly praising and acknowledging something about another person. This simple task may be very difficult for some patients and their family members, and this task may need prompting, coaching, modeling, and practice.

Expressing Feelings Directly

Alcoholics often show nonassertive, indirect, responsibility-avoiding states of communication. Some have never learned to express their feelings and their point of view directly. Group members should be encouraged to use statements beginning with "I" rather than "you." Examples of direct ("I am angry at you because you are late") and indirect ("Why can't you come on time?") ways of communication should be given. Indirect communication within a family should be analyzed. Thus, some people may do something (household repairs or buying a present) instead of verbally and directly stating that, for instance, they feel guilty. The probability of being understood by others will be higher when the communication is more direct. A direct statement of feelings ("I feel uneasy and guilty because I came home very late last night") gives the other person a clearer understanding of the situation and a better chance to respond directly ("I was worried about you. You could at least have called") and makes it easier to resolve the conflict ("I promise to call you the next time I come late from work").

Negotiating and making agreements

An important communication skill is making positive and specific requests. The opposite—unspecific negative accusations—is found much more often in troubled families. In communication sessions, each group member should learn to say what he or she wants or needs (positive) and exactly where and when he or she wants it (specific). Requests should be formulated as requests and not as accusations or threats. Examples of positive and specific requests should be given (Weiss, Birchler, & Vincent, 1974). Thus, the statement "You should treat me better" is insufficient, while the statement "It made me feel good when you greeted me and gave me a kiss when I came home from work; I wish you would greet me this way every day" is specific and contains positive aspects. In the communication sessions and as homework assignments, the formulation of positive specific requests, the negotiation of compromises, and achieving solutions and agreements should be practiced.

Dealing with Resistance

The therapist must know how to deal with resistance and noncompliance in behavioral family therapy. The rationale of the therapy should be explained to the patients in advance. In behavioral group therapies, resistance to role-playing may be observed. It is important to keep the level of anxiety low, to start with easy situations and progress to the more complex, and not to talk extensively about role-playing but rather just to practice it. It is our experience that patients' resistance to role-playing will be minimal when the therapist is competent and has no personal resistance to role-playing. Behavioral rehearsal and role-playing are important and effective ingredients of behavioral family therapy because new behavior patterns need practicing before they can compete with old maladaptive habits. For this purpose, and to achieve generalization to the patients' natural environment, it is also very important that homework assignments are carried through. The therapist should assign homework in a clear, specific way, should rehearse the assignment briefly to make sure it is well-understood, and should ask about the homework assignment in the next session.

ACKNOWLEDGMENT

Preparation of this article was supported by the Wilhelm-Sander-Stiftung (Grant Number 82.011.2).

REFERENCES

Ablon, J. (1976). Family structure and behavior in alcoholism: A review of the literature. In B. Kissin & H. Begleiter (Eds.), *The biology of alcoholism: Social pathology* (Vol. 4). New York: Plenum.

Ablon, J. (1980). The significance of cultural patterning for the alcoholic family. *Family Process, 19*, 127–144.

Azrin, N. H. (1976). Improvements in the community-reinforcement approach to alcoholism. *Behaviour Research and Therapy, 14*, 339–348.

Bailey, M. B., Habermann, P., & Alksne, H. (1962). Outcome of alcoholic marriages. *Quarterly Journal of Studies of Alcoholism, 23*, 610–623.

Berenson, D. (1976). Alcohol and the family system. In P. J. Guerin (Ed.), *Family therapy: Theory and practice*. New York: Gardner Press.

Billings, A. G., Kessler, M., Gomberg, C. A., & Weiner, S. (1979). Marital conflict resolution of alcoholic and nonalcoholic couples during drinking and nondrinking sessions. *Quarterly Journal of Studies of Alcoholism, 40*, 183–195.

Davis, P. J., Berenson, D., Steinglass, P., & Davis, S. (1974). The adaptive consequences of drinking. *Psychiatry, 37*, 209–215.

Djukanovic, B., Milosavcevic, V., & Jovanovi, R. (1976). The social life of alcoholics and their wives. *Alcoholism, 16*, 67–75.

Drewery, J., & Rae, J.B. (1969). A group comparison of alcoholic and nonalcoholic marriages using the interpersonal perception technique. *British Journal of Medical Psychology, 115*, 287–300.

Foy, D. W., Miller, P. M., & Eisler, R. M. (1975). *The effects of alcohol consumption on the marital interactions of chronic alcoholics*. Paper presented at the meeting of the Association for the Advancement of Behavior Therapy, San Francisco.

Gorad, S. L., McCourt, W. F., & Cobb, J. C. (1971). A communications approach to alcoholism. *Quarterly Journal of Studies of Alcoholism, 32*, 651–668.

Gottman, J., Notarius, C., Gonso, J., & Markman, H. (1976). *A couples guide to communication*. Champaign, IL: Research Press.

Hanson, K. J., & Estes, N. J. (1977). Dynamics of alcoholic families. In N. K. Estes & M. F. Heinemann (Eds.), *Alcoholism: Development, consequences, and intervention*. St. Louis: Mosby.

Jackson, J. K. (1954). The adjustment of the family to the crisis of alcoholism. *Quarterly Journal of Studies of Alcoholism, 15*, 562–586.

Jackson, J. K. (1956). The adjustment of the family to alcoholism. *Marriage and the Family, 18*, 361–369.

Jackson, J. K. (1959). Family structure and alcoholism. *Mental Hygiene, 43*, 403–406.

Jackson, J. K. (1962). Alcoholism and the family. In D. J. Pittman & C. R. Snyder (Eds.), *Society, culture and drinking patterns*. New York: Wiley.

Janzen, C. (1977). Families in the treatment of alcoholism. *Quarterly Journal of Studies of Alcoholism, 38*, 114–130.

Kaufman, E. (1984). Family system variables in alcoholism. *Alcoholism: Clinical and Experimental Research, 8*, 4–8.

Kaufman, E., & Kaufman, N. (1979). *Family therapy of drug and alcohol abuse*. New York: Gardner Press.

Kaufman, E., & Pattison, E. M. (1982). The family and alcoholism. In E. M. Pattison & E. Kaufman (Eds.), *Encyclopedic handbook of alcoholism* (pp. 663–673). New York: Gardner Press. (a)

Kaufman, E., & Pattison, E. M. (1982). Family and network therapy in alcoholism. In E. M. Pattison & E. Kaufman (Eds.), *Encyclopedic handbook of alcoholism* (pp. 1022–1032). New York: Gardner Press. (b)

Klein, R. M. (1979). *Interaction processes in alcoholic and nonalcoholic marital dyads*. Doctoral dissertation, Washington University.

Kogan, K. L., Fordyce, W. E., & Jackson, J. K. (1963). Personality disturbance in wives of alcoholics. *Quarterly Journal of Studies of Alcoholism, 24*, 227–238.

Kogan, K. L., & Jackson, J. K. (1963). Role perception in wives of alcoholics and nonalcoholics. *Quarterly Journal of Studies of Alcoholism, 24*, 627–639.

Krimmel, H. E. (1973). The alcoholic and his family. In P. G. Bourne & R. Fox (Eds.), *Alcoholism: Progress in research and treatment*. New York: Academic Press.

Lanyon, R. I. (1973). *Psychological screening inventory manual*. New York: Research Psychologists Press.

Liberman, R. P., Wheeler, E. G., de Visser, L. A. J. M., Kuehnel, J., & Kuehnel, T. (1980). *Handbook of marital therapy: A positive approach to helping troubled relationships*. New York: Plenum Press.

McGoldrick, M., Gioridano, J., & Pearce, J. K. (1982). *Ethnicity and family therapy*. New York: Guilford Press.

Miller, P. M. (1976). *Behavioral treatment of alcoholism*. New York: Pergamon Press.

Miller, W. R., & Heston, R. K. (1980). Treating the problem drinker: Modern approaches. In W. R. Miller (Ed.), *The addictive behaviors: Treatment of alcoholism, drug abuse, smoking, and obesity*. New York: Pergamon.

Mitchell, H. E. (1959). Interpersonal perception theory applied to conflicted marriage in which alcoholism is and is not a problem. *American Journal of Orthopsychiatry, 29*, 547–559.

Moos, R. H., Bromet, E., Tsu, V., & Moos, B. (1979). Family characteristics and the outcome of treatment for alcoholism. *Quarterly Journal of Studies of Alcoholism, 40*, 78–88.

Moos, R. H., & Moos, B. (1984). The process of recovery from alcoholism: III. Comparing functioning in families of alcoholics and matched control families. *Quarterly Journal of Studies of Alcoholism, 45*, 111–118.

Myers, J. K., Weissman, M. M., Tischler, G. L., Holzer, C. E., Leaf, P. J., Orvaschel, H., Anthony, J. C., Boyd, J. H., Burke, J. D., Kramer, M., & Stoltzman, R. (1984). Six-month prevalence of psychiatric disorders in three communities. *Archives of General Psychiatry, 41*, 959–967.

O'Farrell, T. J., & Cutter, H. S. G. (1979). A proposed behavioral couples group for male alcoholics and their wives. In D. Upper & S. M. Ross (Eds.), *Behavioral group therapy: An annual review*. Champaign, IL: Research Press.

Orford, J., Oppenheimer, E., Egert, S., & Hensman, C. (1977). The role of excessive drinking in alcoholism-complicated marriages: A study of stability and change over a one-year period. *International Journal of the Addictions, 12*, 471–475.

Paolino, T. J., Jr., & McCrady, B. S. (1979). *The alcoholic marriage: Alternative perspectives*. New York: Grune & Stratton.

Paolino, T. J., Jr., McCrady, B. S., & Diamond, S. (1978). Statistics on alcoholic marriages: An overview. *International Journal of the Addictions, 13*, 1285–1293.

Polich, J., Armor, D. J., & Braiker, H. B. (1981). *The course of alcoholism. Four years after treatment*. New York: Wiley & Sons.

Robins, L. N., Helzer, J. E., Weissman, M. M., Orvaschel, H., Gruenberg, E., Burke, J. D., & Regier, D. A. (1984). Lifetime prevalence of specific psychiatric disorders in three sites. *Archives of General Psychiatry, 41*, 949–958.

Sandmaier, M. (1980). *The invisible alcoholics: Women and alcohol abuse in America*. New York: McGraw-Hill.

Scott, E. M. (1970). *Struggles in an alcoholic family*. Springfield, IL: Charles C Thomas.

Steinglass, P. (1977). Family therapy in alcoholism. In B. Kissin & H. Begleiter (Ed.), *Biology of alcoholism. Treatment and rehabilitation of the chronic alcoholic*. (Vol. 5). New York: Plenum.

Steinglass, P. (1979). Family therapy with alcoholics. A review. In E. Kaufman & N. Kaufman (Eds.), *Family therapy of drug and alcohol abuse*. New York: Gardner Press.

Steinglass, P. (1980). A life history model of the alcoholic family. *Family Process, 19*, 211–226.

Steinglass, P. (1981). Assessing families in their own homes. *American Journal of Psychiatry, 137*, 12.

Steinglass, P., & Robertson, A. (1983). The alcoholic family. In B. Kissin, & H. Begleiter (Eds.), *The pathogenesis of alcoholism. Psychosocial factors*. New York: Plenum Press.

Steinglass, P., Weiner, S., & Mendelson, J. H. (1971). A system approach to alcoholism: A model and its clinical application. *Archives of General Psychiatry, 24*, 401.

Weiss, R. L. (1975). *Spouse observation checklist*. Unpublished Questionnaire, Marital Studies Program, University of Oregon, Eugene, OR.

Weiss, R. L., Birchler, G. R., & Vincent, J. P. (1974). Contractual models for negotiation training in marital dyads. *Journal of Marriage and the Family, 36*, 321–331.

Winokur, G., & Clayton, P. J. (1968). Family history studies in comparison to male and female alcoholics. *Quarterly Journal of Studies of Alcoholism, 29*, 885–891.

15

Senile Dementia

STEVEN H. ZARIT
The Pennsylvania State University

Among the various problems of the later half of the life cycle, senile dementia is certainly the most devastating for patients and their families. Patients with dementia suffer a gradual loss of memory and other cognitive abilities. As they become cognitively impaired, they are unable to carry out the ordinary activities of everyday life, such as their work or leisure interests, and in time they need assistance with even basic activities such as dressing or bathing. When there is an available relative, the responsibility for supervision and care of dementia patients can often fall upon family members. While many families express a preference for providing assistance themselves, the care of patients with dementia can be extremely stressful. Caregivers often provide around–the–clock supervision, assist with activities of daily living, and must contend with a variety of behavior problems caused by the patient's cognitive impairment, including agitated or repetitive behaviors. The task of caregiving is further complicated in cases of dementia by the fact that the qualities that have made the relationship between patient and caregiver important in the first place are gradually eroded as the disease progresses. For many family caregivers, the situation gradually becomes overwhelming.

This paper will describe possible interventions to assist families of victims of dementia. While symptoms of dementia cannot currently be slowed or reversed, it is possible to enhance the quality of life for patients and to support family members so that they can manage the tasks of caregiving. By looking at dementia in a family context, rather than just as a disease, the impact on a particular family system can be considered, and strategies developed to reduce the stresses on caregivers.

DEMENTIA AS A SOCIAL PROBLEM

The pattern of cognitive decline in dementia stands in sharp contrast to the normal aging process. With normal aging, cognitive changes are gradual and do not generally interfere with successful completion of activities of daily life. Dementia, on the other hand, has catastrophic effects on a person's functioning. Characteristics of dementia are not simply accelerations of normal aging; rather, many abilities which are spared in aging, especially verbal skills, are affected in dementia (Botwinick & Birren, 1951; Goldstein & Shelly, 1975; Overall & Gorham, 1972; Schale & Schale, 1977).

There are several types of dementia, which can be distinguished by their underlying brain pathology, and, to an imperfect degree, by clinical characteristics (Hachinski, 1983; Liston & LaRue, 1983; McKhann, Drachman, Folstein, Katzman, & Stadlan, 1984). The most frequent dementia is Senile Dementia of the Alzheimer Type or Alzheimer Disease, which accounts for between 50 and 70 percent of the cases. Alzheimer Disease is characterized by specific changes in the cerebral cortex, including senile plaques, neurofibrillary tangles, and granulovacuolar structures. There is also an overall loss of brain neurons. This disorder was originally described as a "pre-senile" disease, that is, occurring before age 60, but research on the neuropathology of senile dementia revealed brain changes that are identical or nearly identical to "pre-senile" Alzheimer cases (Terry, 1978; Terry & Wiesniewski, 1977).

The second most common type of dementia is Multi-infarct dementia, which occurs when a person suffers a series of small strokes or "infarcts." Approximately 10 to 20 percent of dementia cases are of the Multi-infarct type (Terry, 1978). As in Alzheimer Disease, the resulting intellectual deficits are progressive, and while there are some initial differences in the pattern and type of symptoms between Alzheimer and Multi-infarct patients, both result in severe, global impairment that is difficult to distinguish in terms of cognitive functioning or behavior. (Hassinger, J. M. Zarit, & S. H. Zarit, 1982). Post-mortem studies have indicated that 10 to 20 percent of dementia cases have pathologies typical of both types of dementia (Terry & Wiesniewski, 1977).

Types of irreversible dementia that are encountered less frequently include the following:

- Pick Disease
- Jakob-Creutzfeldt Disease
- Kuru
- General Paresis
- Parkinson Disease
- Huntington Disease
- Progressive Supranuclear Palsy
- Wilson Disease
- Spinocerebellar Degenerations
- Idiopathic Basal Ganglia Calcification

For a more complete description of the clinical and pathological features of the dementias, see the text by Cummings and Benson (1983).

While epidemiological studies of dementia are hampered by inexact diagnostic critera, usual estimates are that between 4% to 7% of the population over age 65 is affected (Mortimer, Schuman, & French, 1981; Gurland, Dean, Cross, & Golden, 1981). Prevalence increases with age, to perhaps as high as 20% over age 80, although data on that age group is incomplete. Prevalence studies have been made in Northern Europe and the United States, and while there is some variability in rates, causes of these differences have not been identified. More women are affected than men, although it is not clear if sex differences are a function of women's greater longevity, or if they are more susceptible to the illnesses which cause dementia.

While the dementias affect only a small proportion of the older population, their importance is considerable. It has been estimated that one half of long term care patients in nursing homes or similar facilities have symptoms of dementia. The majority of dementia patients, however, are living in the community, although their impairments are often as great as those in nursing homes (Lowenthal, Berkman, & Associates, 1967; S. H. Zarit, Todd, & J. M. Zarit, 1986).

There is also evidence that the number of persons with dementia is rising. With the advances in medicine and public health in this century, a larger percentage of the population is living to old age. In 1900, only 40% of the population could be expected to live to age 65 or beyond, while currently it is estimated that 70% of a cohort will live to old age. Moreover, many people are living to age 80 and beyond (Bouvler, Atlee, & McVeigh, 1975; Brotman, 1982; Crimmins, 1984). In fact, people over 80 are the fastest growing age group in the population. One result of this aging of the population is that larger numbers of people are affected by the chronic diseases of aging, including the dementias.

At the same time that numbers of dementia patients are increasing, the pool of potential caregivers is decreasing. When there is no spouse to take on caregiving responsibilities, the role usually falls to a daughter, if there is one. But with women entering the workplace in record numbers, fewer can take on full-time caregiving responsibilities. Even part-time caregiving may place too much strain on someone who is working and has her own husband and children (Brody, 1985). With the overall aging of the population, it is also becoming common for caregiving children themselves to be older. A daughter caring for an elderly mother can be in her 60s or even 70s, facing limitations imposed by her own aging.

Despite these demographic changes, families still provide most of the help to older persons with chronic disabilities. Surveys have indicated that family members remain the major source of assistance when an older person is ill (Shanas, 1979; Morris & Sherwood, 1983; Stone, Cafferata,

& Sangl, 1987). With public concern about increased costs of long-term care for older people, there is likely to be more emphasis on the responsibility of families, even as the pool of caregivers is decreased.

TRADITIONAL MANAGEMENT APPROACHES

A custodial bias prevails in the management of dementia patients. Because the disease cannot be arrested, it is generally assumed that little can be done for the patient or family. As a result, families are typically advised to place their relative in a nursing home. Institutional care can have appropriate uses, especially for patients who are very difficult to manage in an uncontrolled environment or when family resources are not available to provide supervision and assistance (Knight & Walker, 1985), but placement needs to be considered in the light of all the options available for management of the patient and with an understanding of the problems that institutional care creates for patients and families.

Relocation to a nursing home is a traumatic event for any older person, but there is reason to believe it is even more catastrophic for dementia patients. Studies of the effects of relocation which included cognitively impaired individuals usually cite higher rates of morbidity and/or mortality following relocation, compared to groups that have not been moved (see S. H. Zarit & Anthony, 1986). Because of their difficulties learning new information, dementia patients have more problems adjusting to the new routines and surroundings of an institutional setting. Furthermore, because they are having adjustment problems, they are often tranquilized, although the drugs most commonly used, the phenothiazines, can sometimes exacerbate the problems they are meant to treat. The agitation, restlessness and bizarre behavior of nursing home patients can sometimes be traced to paradoxical reactions to tranquilizing drugs, or to other medication problems.

In addition to the benefits for patients of staying in familiar surroundings, families generally prefer to avoid institutionalization whenever possible. Rather than being abandoned by families, older persons are generally integrated into the family through interchanges of assistance and affection (Bengtson & Cutler, 1976). When an older person requires assistance, family members generally step in (Shanas, 1979). In fact, older persons with the highest risk of institutionalization are those without families (Branch & Jette, 1982; Bergmann, Foster, Justice, & Matthews, 1978).

Although families may prefer home care, nursing home placement is often recommended out of concern for the caregiver's health and well-being. Particularly in cases of dementia, it is widely believed that it is not possible to care for a patient at home without excessive stress or burden on the caregiver. Nursing home placement, however, often does not relieve the family's burden, but changes the type of burden they experience (George & Gwyther, 1986; S. H. Zarit, Todd, & J. M. Zarit, 1986). Instead of providing care in the home, caregivers must now travel to visit the patient, sometimes daily or more often. They interact with the staff to influence the patient's care and sometimes supplement the staff's activities. They may, of course, experience emotional distress over placing their relative in a nursing home. In the United States, long-term nursing home care for dementia patients is not reimbursed under Medicare or most private health insurances. Thus, placement can be an economic catastrophe, particularly for spouse caregivers who, depending on state regulations, may have to spend down to poverty levels before the patient becomes eligible for Medicaid. This can place severe financial pressures on the family.

Home care, of course, is not a viable alternative if it is achieved at the cost of the physical or emotional health of family caregivers. To insist that families ought to care for their demented elders, and then to provide no help or relief from the stresses that can result is irresponsible. In some situations, home care is not possible due to the patient's behaviors or the family's resources or preferences. For many families, however, the critical issue is whether home care can be made more tolerable through outside assistance in care of the patient.

DEMENTIA IN A FAMILY CONTEXT

How we conceptualize dementia affects our responses to patients and their families. If dementia is viewed as a medical problem which does not currently have a cure, the implication is that little can be done to alter the impact on families. In contrast, Kahn (1975) has proposed that dementia is a bio-psycho-social phenomenon. He argues that while the biological aspects are not currently amenable to treatment, psychological or social dimensions are.

By viewing the dementia patient's behavior in the family context, treatable aspects of the problem will become apparent. Families differ in their size, organization, values, solidarity, resources, and in the personalities of individual members. As a result, their responses to dementia will be variable. While some are overwhelmed early in the disease, others show amazing resiliency, and may keep patients at home even in the last stages of the disease. Learning about the sources of this variability can be useful for developing programs for reducing the caregiver's stress.

While most of the literature on the impact of caregiving remains anecdotal, empirical studies are now emerging. Most studies identify objective tasks which caregivers must perform, which are sometimes called "objective burden," and how these responsibilities have affected the caregiver's life, which is termed "subjective burden" (*see* Montgomery, Stull, & Borgatta, 1985, S. H. Zarit, in press). This distinction between objective stressors and subjective evaluations of their impact is important for developing clinical interventions. A common mistake is for clinicians to judge that the care demands are overwhelming, without considering how the family evaluates the situation.

Studies suggest the relation of objective care demands and subjective stress or burden is complex. In an early study, Hoenig and Hamilton (1966) distinguished between objective burden, which included behavior problems and the amount of adverse effects to the household, and subjective burden, which was the caregiver's perception of the impact, and found no relation between these two measures. Similarly, Lowenthal, Berkman, and their associates (1967) reported that the breakdown of a family support system was related to the caregiver's becoming exhausted, but not necessarily to an increase in an older patient's symptoms.

A series of recent studies have emphasized the distinction between objective indicators of impairment and subjective burden (S. H. Zarit, Reever, & Bach-Peterson, 1980; J. M. Zarit, 1982; Boutsells & S. H. Zarit, 1984). In these studies, all patients met current diagnostic criteria for dementia, and were living at home with a caregiver at the time of the assessment. Severity of impairment was measured in three ways: the extent of cognitive deficits, the number of functional problems that caregivers must cope with, and the duration of the illness. Subjective burden was measured both with a 22-item inventory, the Burden Interview, that asked caregivers to rate the extent to which they had experienced adverse changes in their health, well-being, social and personal life and finances (J. M. Zarit & S. H. Zarit, 1982), and by a measure of current psychiatric symptoms, the Brief Symptom Inventory (BSI) (Derogatis & Spencer, 1982). Both measures therefore reflect caregivers' own subjective appraisals of the impact of caregiving.

Subjective burden was found to be unrelated to severity of symptoms. Other factors, however, were significantly associated with burden. The strongest relation was with the caregivers' ability to cope with behavior problems caused by the disease. Caregivers who are able to manage problems more effectively reported less stress on both the burden measure and the BSI (J. M. Zarit, 1982; J. M. Zarit & S. H. Zarit, 1982).

Other determinants of burden include the type and quality of relationship between caregiver and dementia patient. Relatives who serve primarily as caregivers are the wives, husbands and daughters of patients. While clinical impressions have suggested that daughters experience more stress, empirical studies which focus on primary caregivers of dementia patients indicate that wives are the most burdened, followed by daughters, and with husbands reporting the least burden (J. M. Zarit, 1982; Boutselis & S. H. Zarit, 1984; Fitting, Rabins, Lucas, & Eastham, 1986). These results may partly reflect response styles, that wives more readily acknowledge the changes that caregiving has had on their lives. Another contributing factor may be that wives have more problems coping with typical dementia-related behavior problems, while husbands often take a more detached, problem-solving approach (J. M. Zarit, 1982; Fitting *et al.*, 1986). Whatever the caregiver's relationship to the patient, ratings of the quality of the relationship before the onset of the illness were associated with impact. Those caregivers who viewed the relationship as more positive reported less burden (J. M. Zarit, 1982; Woods, Niederehe, & Fruge, 1985).

Family support may also be an important mediator of burden. A preliminary report suggested that the frequency of visits by other family members was related to decreased burden for the primary caregiver (S. H. Zarit, Reever, & Bach-Peterson, 1980), though subsequent studies have not replicated this finding. Rather than the amount of interaction and assistance being important, the caregiver's perception of how adequate family support was had a strong relation to impact. When there was more perceived support, burden and psychiatric symptoms were less (J. M. Zarit, 1982). A more thorough investigation of family system variables is currently underway, although results are still preliminary (Niederehe & Fruge, 1984).

These findings are based on cross-sectional analyses, which might obscure the relation of severity of the patient's impairment and burden. To examine that possibility, two longitudinal studies have been made, which focus on determinants of burden at each time of testing, and factors associated with nursing home placement (S. H. Zarit, Todd, & J. M. Zarit, 1986; Hassinger, & S. H. Zarit, 1986). The first study involved a small sample of spouse caregivers who were followed for a two year period of time. Subjects were 31 husbands and 33 wives who at the time of the first interview were all caring in the home for a spouse with dementia. Patients had a moderate degree of impairment at the time of initial assessment, as indicated by years of duration of the illness ($\overline{X}$ = 5.5 years) and measures of cognitive impairment. The second study had a larger sample including husbands, wives, daughters, and small numbers of sons and other relatives who were in the primary caregiving role (Hasinger & S. H. Zarit, 1986). Characteristics of patients were similar to the first study.

The results indicated that both the patient's initial level of impairment and caregivers' subjective burden were associated with subsequent placement. As one would expect, patients with more severe impairments were more likely to go into nursing homes. After removing the effects of severity, subjective burden was also a significant predictor of placement. When asked about their decision, caregivers who placed their relative cited difficulties managing patients as one of the major reasons for their decision (along with advice from physicians and family members). The role of dementia-related deficits, however, has to be viewed in light of the fact that families who kept patients at home were coping with impairments as great as those who entered nursing homes. Thus, institutionalization would appear related to the ability to manage or tolerate the changes in the patient. It also should be noted that subjects' ratings of subjective burden did not increase over time, even though patients' had continued to deteriorate.

Other possible determinants of caregiver burden remain to be explored. No systematic findings are available on the relationship between burden and various demographic variables (caregiver's age, education, race, or ethnicity), with the exceptions of the caregiver's relationship to the patient and income. Families with lower incomes have been found to report higher burden (Sainsbury & Grad de Alarcon, 1970; Reece, Walz, & Hagenbrock, 1982). In the United States, the Medicaid program, which provides health care to the lowest income group, actually encourages placement by providing more consistent reimbursement for nursing home care than for community service, while middle income persons usually can obtain little or no reimbursement for either nursing home or in-home care (Knight & Walker, 1985).

Anecdotal evidence also suggests that programs such as day care or respite care may be useful in lowering the burden on caregivers, though controlled studies have not as yet been reported. Caregivers themselves frequently note the need for more assistance, especially respite care.

Taken as a whole, these studies suggest a complex relation between dementia and families' responses. Rather than a linear association between severity of patients' impairment and caregivers' reports of burden or stress, there appears to be considerable variability, even when patients have moderate to severe difficulties. These results are consistent with general models of stress, which posit that the impact of events is influenced by several factors, including the perception of the event as harmful, coping responses, and social support (Lazarus, 1966; Lazarus & Folkman, 1984). Areas for possible intervention to relieve burden include helping caregivers manage day-to-day problems more effectively and increasing the available support.

FAMILY INTERVENTIONS FOR DEMENTIA

The first programs to emphasize providing support to the families as a way of helping elderly patients with chronic psychiatric disabilities in the community were developed by some of the pioneers of the community mental health movement (Kahn, 1975; Macmillan, 1958, 1967; Perlin & Kahn, 1968). They viewed the role of the family as critical, and designed interventions to support the family's efforts, rather than shifting the burden of care. Early intervention was felt to be critical in order to relieve the stress on caregivers before they felt overwhelmed.

Building upon studies of caregiver burden, and principles of community and family treatment, a model of interventions with families of dementia patients has been developed. This model, which has been described in detail elsewhere (S. H. Zarit, Orr, & J. M. Zarit, 1985), emphasizes a short-term, problem-focused intervention to lower burden on caregivers by improving their skill at managing problem behaviors and increasing the amount of support and assistance they receive.

There are two phases in this model, assessment and treatment (Table 15-1). During the assessment phase, the diagnosis of dementia is confirmed and sources of burden identified. The treatment phase can be described heuristically as having an input, process, and output. The input is information about dementia and its effects on behavior. The process of treatment is problem solving. The output or goals are improved management of behavioral problems and increased social support. Treatment is implemented in three modalities, counseling the primary caregiver, family meetings, and support groups. The use of these modalities depends on the needs of a particular family. Major features of this model are described below.

Assessment Phase

Diagnostic Issues in Dementia

The starting point for interventions is accurate diagnosis. In the past the bias of many professionals about aging led them to label any mental changes as senility or hardening of the arteries, even when the patient's problem was potentially treatable, as in the case of late-life depressions. Although knowledge about the aging process and dementia has increased, the tendency for overdiagnosis has continued. One unintended effect of the recent publicity given to Alzheimer Disease is that diagnosis is now used in the same imprecise way that senility was in the past. Because the implications

Table 15-1. Comprehensive Interventions with Caregivers of Dementia Patients

Assessment Phase:

- Confirm diagnosis of dementia.
- Identify sources of burden on the family.

Treatment Phase:

- Input: Information about dementia and its effects on behavior
- Process: Behavioral problem solving
- Output: Increase management skills and social support

Treatment Modalities:

- Counseling the primary caregiver
- Family meetings
- Support groups

of dementia are radically different from other disorders that can be mistaken for it, and from the milder changes due to normal aging, successful interventions necessarily begin with correct diagnosis.

Accurate diagnosis of the dementias is a complex process. There are currently no procedures or tests that definitely diagnose Alzheimer Disease or other dementias, or which separate without error dementia patients from those whose cognitive changes are due to normal aging, or to some other cause. Diagnosis, in fact, can be confirmed only at autopsy, with microscopic studies of brain tissue, or in rare cases where a brain biopsy has been performed. While particular behavioral and cognitive deficits are hallmarks of the dementia syndrome, similar symptoms can be brought on by a variety of treatable problems. Possible causes of symptoms of dementia include: drug toxicities, infections, heart problems, malnutrition, fractures, surgery, metabolic and endocrine disorders, and stressful life events, especially relocation to a new environment (NIA Task Force, 1980). Delirium is also common among older persons, and has most of the same causes as reversible dementia (Lipowski, 1980; NIA Task Force, 1980). This relation of treatable disorders and cognitive impairment can also be noted in dementia patients. Any sudden worsening in cognition or behavior can often be traced to a treatable problem, such as drug toxicity. Depression can also be mistaken for dementia, particularly because some older depressed patients make extensive complaints about failing memory. The differentiation between dementia and depression can usually be made on the basis of cognitive assessment, because depressed patients, despite their complaints, generally have little or no actual impairment (Kahn, S. H. Zarit, Hilbert & Niederehe, 1975; S. H. Zarit, 1980). The possibility that a patient's cognitive symptoms are the result of mild changes associated with the normal aging process must also be considered.

Generally, it is advisable to diagnose dementia only when other possible causes have been conclusively ruled out, and no other explanation can account for the findings of impairment. To identify treatable causes of cognitive problems, a coordinated medical and psychological evaluation should be conducted, including evaluation of current symptoms, history of the patient's cognitive problems, psychological testing, and a thorough medical examination (for more information, see Cummings & Benson, 1983; McKhann *et al.*, 1984; NIA Task Force, 1980; S. H. Zarit, Orr, & J. M. Zarit, 1985).

In some instances, a family's report that an older person's memory is failing will not be verified in a clinical examination. While these cases represent a small number of families encountered in clinical settings, they indicate an important phenomenon. Mislabeling someone as demented often masks serious marital or family conflicts. The following example illustrates how mislabeling of an older person as having Alzheimer Disease can occur in the context of marital conflict (see also Gilewski, Kuppinger, & S. H. Zarit, 1985).

Mr. M was a 68-year-old man who had retired two years earlier. He was referred for an evaluation by a marriage counselor who had been seeing him and his wife conjointly for about two months. Both the therapist and Mrs. M felt that Mr. M had Alzheimer Disease, because he had not followed any directives given to him by the therapist, and because of his wife's reports that he often forgot to do things she asked him to do, such as to take out the garbage. When Mr. M was seen alone, he also reported having trouble with his memory. Psychological testing, however, was in normal ranges, with no evidence of dementia-like problems. Mr. M was very depressed (Beck Depression Inventory Score of 35), and he had virtually no interests or activities. He had spent most of the time since his retirement sitting at home. He and his wife both indicated the marriage had never been a happy one, but their conflict was intensified since Mr. M's retirement, because that placed them in contact with one another for most of the day.

Given these findings, Mr. M's memory problems are best understood as part of the marital system, and not as early signs of Alzheimer Disease. This type of mislabeling needs to be clearly distinguished from actual cases of dementia, with clinical interventions being directed toward the real problem which, in this example, was their marital conflict.

Assessment of Sources of Burden

After diagnosis has been confirmed, there needs to be an assessment of the patient's current functioning, the family's responses and the resources available for assisting the primary caregiver. The starting point is to determine the patient's current level of functioning, including ability to perform self-care tasks and any disruptive or disturbing behavior caused by the cognitive deficit. While there are some general trends in the course of dementia, individual differences are also considerable. The overall course of dementia involves gradual deterioration, with complex functions affected first and more elementary habits, such as dressing or bathing, later on. The general pattern of decline has been described as going through five stages (Reisberg, Ferris, & Crook, 1982). Patients will vary, however, in the rate of deterioration and in which abilities are impaired. Language, for example, may be more severely impaired early in the disease for one patient, and affected to a lesser degree in another. Similarly, some patients retain a particular complex ability, such as doing mathematical computations, for a long time, even though other intellectual abilities are impaired. Although there is some predictability in the order in which impairments develop, differences can occur, related to the patient's prior habits or experiences or the care situation. As an example, incontinence is considered to occur in middle to late stages of the disease, but it can occur fairly early, when there is some complicating factor, such as if the patient has been having urinary tract problems. Or it may not occur until fairly late in the disease, because of good management (e.g., helping the patient find the bathroom) or because of other individual differences in manifestation of symptoms.

In addition to the possibility that environmental and personality factors affect manifestation of symptoms, the variability among patients is likely due in part to differences between types of dementias, which affect somewhat different areas of the brain (see Cummings & Benson, 1983, for a review). A further source of variability is that there is some heterogeneity within each disease. For example, there have been several reports that Alzheimer patients differ in sites of the brain affected, pattern of presenting symptoms, and rate of change.

Assessment of the patient's current functioning should include four levels: 1) Instrumental Activities of Daily Living (I–ADL), 2) Physical Activities of Daily Living (P–ADL), 3) behavior problems associated with dementia, and 4) neuropsychological performance. As described by Lawton (1971), I–ADLs include some complex activities as shopping, cooking, and using transportation. P–ADLs involve more basic functions such as dressing, bathing, and using the toilet. There are several available measures of activities of daily living, but some modification should be made with this population. Specifically, the available scales focus on whether the patient can complete the activity. A common problem among dementia patients, however, is that they resist or struggle when the caregiver tries to provide assistance or to encourage them verbally to carry it out.

Behavioral problems include excesses and deficits that result from the patient's cognitive deficit, including, agitation, wandering off, talking a greatdeal, not talking at all, or asking the same question over and over again. The Memory and Behavior Problems Checklist, shown in Table 15-2, has been developed to assess typical behavior problems (J. M. Zarit & S. H. Zarit, 1982).

Finally, neuropsychological assessment can identify the extent to which different abilities have been affected, which can be helpful in planning interventions. As an example, a neuropsychological assessment might reveal that a patient has a significant naming deficit, which was not apparent from casual observations of speech. If that patient also was difficult to manage in some situations, those situations could be examined for the possibility that the language deficits might be a contributing factor. An intervention could be developed to try alternative explanations, or which encouraged caregivers to respond to what they felt the patient meant, rather than to the literal meaning of the patient's statements.

Another focus of the assessment is the family's response. To understand how families respond to the demands of caregiving, it is necessary

Table 15-2. Memory and Behavior Problems Checklist—Revised, 1987

INSTRUCTIONS TO CAREGIVER:

"I am going to read you a list of common problems. Tell me if any of these problems have occurred during the past week. If so, how often have they occurred? If not, has this problem ever occurred?" Hand the subject the card on which the frequency ratings are printed.

(Note: Ratings can also be made of the degree of difficulty of problems.)

FREQUENCY RATINGS

0 = never occurred
1 = occurred frequently in the past but no longer occurs
2 = has occurred recently, but not in the past week
3 = has occurred 1 or 2 times in past week
4 = has occurred 3 to 6 times in past week
5 = occurs daily or more often
7 = this problem would occur if patient wasn't supervised

BEHAVIORS	FREQUENCY						
1. Asking the same question over and over again	0	1	2	3	4	5	
2. Trouble remembering recent events (e.g., items in the newspaper, on television)	0	1	2	3	4	5	
3. Trouble remembering significant events from the past	0	1	2	3	4	5	
4. Mixing up past and present (e.g., thinking a deceased parent is alive)	0	1	2	3	4	5	
5. Losing or misplacing things	0	1	2	3	4	5	
6. Hiding things	0	1	2	3	4	5	
7. Unable to find way about indoors	0	1	2	3	4	5	
8. Unable to find way about outdoors, for example on familar streets	0	1	2	3	4	5	
9. Wandering or getting lost	0	1	2	3	4	5	7
10. Not recognizing a familiar place	0	1	2	3	4	5	
11. Not recognizing familiar people	0	1	2	3	4	5	
12. Not recognizing a familiar object	0	1	2	3	4	5	
13. Forgetting what day it is	0	1	2	3	4	5	
14. Unable to start activities by self (besides ADL's)	0	1	2	3	4	5	
15. Unable to keep occupied or busy by self	0	1	2	3	4	5	
16. Follows you around	0	1	2	3	4	5	
17. Being constantly restless or agitated	0	1	2	3	4	5	
18. Spending long periods of time inactive	0	1	2	3	4	5	
19. Being constantly talkative	0	1	2	3	4	5	
20. Talking little or not at all	0	1	2	3	4	5	
21. Being suspicious or accusative	0	1	2	3	4	5	
22. Doing things in public that embarrass you	0	1	2	3	4	5	
23. Waking you up at night	0	1	2	3	4	5	
24. Appears sad or depressed	0	1	2	3	4	5	
25. Appears anxious or worried	0	1	2	3	4	5	
26. Becomes angry	0	1	2	3	4	5	
27. Strikes out or tries to hit	0	1	2	3	4	5	
28. Destroying property	0	1	2	3	4	5	
29. Engaging in behavior that is potentially dangerous to others or self	0	1	2	3	4	5	7
30. Seeing or hearing things that are not there (hallucinations or illusions)	0	1	2	3	4	5	
31. Any other problems (specify):	0	1	2	3	4	5	

to assess the unique characteristics, resources and deficits of a given family. Notions that caregiving follows some sequence of stages or is guided by underlying dynamics may have some heuristic value, but greatly oversimplify the variability in families' responses. Families differ on a number of dimensions that are likely to affect caregiving, including size, emotional closeness, values, differentiation of roles, and past history of caregiving, to name a few. Who is designated as the primary caregiver (e.g., spouse, child) is also important, as discussed earlier. There will also be cases in which caregiving is shared, or where no one has clearly taken on primary responsibility. The role conflicts and emotional burden that caregiving places on the primary caregiver should be considered.

Of particular importance are the ways caregivers respond to problem behaviors, and the availability of help from within the family or from other sources. Caregivers vary considerably in how they manage specific deficits. As was discussed earlier, behaviors upsetting to one family are tolerated by another. Some caregivers try to hide or correct the patient's deficits. Others show increasing irritation when patients cannot correct their own errors or regulate their behavior. Still ohers learn effective ways of coping with the effects of memory loss or other disabilities. Although some problems, such as incontinence or violent behavior, are more difficult for families, responses are variable and some caregivers will manage even the most severe deficits effectively.

The amount of help actually or potentially available to the primary caregiver should also be determined. It is not uncommon to find family members who could potentially contribute, but who are not involved because they are unaware of the dimensions of the problem or do not want to become involved, or because they disagree with the primary caregiver's management of the situation. Even when they feel positive about the caregiver's involvement, they may view the problems and tasks of caregiving in a different way than does the primary caregiver. Availability and use of formal social services also should be determined, as well as the caregiver's attitudes about accepting outside help.

A more subtle dimension affecting caregiving has to do with the role the impaired elder played in the family in the past and how his/her illness has changed the family system. Instrumental tasks, such as housekeeping, transportation, or management of finances, which the impaired elder now needs help with, can readily be identified in an assessment. But there are certain functions that are less obvious to an outside observer, which involve maintenance of the family system, and which are more difficult to replace (S. H. Zarit, Orr, & J. M. Zarit, 1985). Consider the implications for a family if the person everyone turned to as a problem solver is now impaired, or if the patient had maintained contact among family members, organizing family gatherings and responding to others' emotional needs. Knowing what the impaired elder contributed to the family, and what gaps are created by his/her impairment is crucial for understanding the family's response to caregiving demands.

The major implication of the variability in family organization is that there is no single pattern of response to caregiving. Families will reach many different solutions to the task of caregiving, depending in part on how the elder's illness has disrupted the family system, and what resources and coping strategies are available. The key to successful interventions is to pinpoint the particular strengths and weaknesses of a family's response, and to target ways to bring out more of their assets, while minimizing their deficiencies (see S. H. Zarit, Orr, & J. M. Zarit, 1985).

Treatment Phase

Providing accurate information to families about their relative's dementia and its effects on behavior is the starting point for interventions. Having correct information is a necessary foundation on which other interventions are based, and may, in itself, lead to spontaneous improvements in the caregiver's mood or coping strategies.

Families will often have a lot of questions about the causes and treatment of dementia. In some cases, they may not even know what the diagnosis is, or its implications. Many families are searching for cures, and want information about current treatment alternatives. This must be done in a sensitive but frank way that brings out the limitations in current treatments. Successful interventions often depend on changing the family's treatment agenda from curing the patient to identifying what they can do to manage the stress they are experiencing.

Information is also used to help families understand and relabel problem behaviors. Families are often disturbed by problem behaviors, because they make incorrect inferences about the patient's motivations. For example, they may believe that a patient asks the same question over and over again deliberately to annoy them, or out of laziness. The family then responds with anger or frustration over what they see as the patient's intentional lack of cooperation. By understanding that these behaviors are the result of the patient's memory loss and other cognitive difficulties, families can often tolerate them better.

There are a variety of behaviors of dementia patients which are not harmful or dangerous, but merely annoying, and relabeling these as part of the patient's illness is helpful. Problems in which patients contradict the families' perceptions of reality, such as when they make accusations about things being stolen, are a good example. Families will often argue with patients about the facts, though with little success. A more effective strategy is to consider why patients make paranoid complaints in the first place.

Often these complaints serve to mask their memory problems. Families then can be asked to think about what the dementia patient must be feeling when making those accusations. Rather than trying to correct the patient's reality, they can respond empathically to what they think the patient is feeling, and avoid any direct confrontation over the "facts." An appropriate response might be to say, "It must be upsetting not to be able to find your money," and then to offer some reassurance that the caregiver will take care of the problem. Similar empathic responses can be used for other statements that contradict reality, such as if a patient insists on seeing a deceased parent or "going home." Patients are expressing important emotions with these statements, which caregivers can learn to acknowledge and channel in some appropriate way.

The main focus of treatment is to improve the caregiver's problem-solving skills in order to enable them to manage dementia-related deficits more effectively and to increase the assistance they receive from others. The problem solving process is shown below:

1. Identify the Problem
   a. Antecedents
   b. Consequences
2. General Alternative Solutions (no censoring)
3. Select a Solution: Pros and Cons
4. Cognitive Rehearsal
5. Carry Out the Plan
6. Evaluate Outcome (Zarit, Orr, & Zarit, 1985)

Problem solving is carried out in somewhat different ways, depending on whether the focus is the patient's behavior or support for the caregiver. When used to modify the patient's behavior, problem solving begins with a behavioral analysis. Caregiver and clinician identify the problem in operational terms, and then the caregiver is instructed to observe how often and under what circumstances it occurs. This record serves as a baseline against which subsequent changes can be measured, and also is useful for identifying possible antecedents and consequences of problematic behaviors, that is, events which trigger or reinforce behavior (Kanfer & Saslow, 1965). As an example, periods of agitation may be preceded by a stretch of time in which the patient is inactive (antecedent), or may be followed by more focused attention (consequence) than at other times of the day.

After the baseline period, the caregiver and clinician review the behavioral observations to identify antecedents or consequences and to propose possible solutions. In the example above, the problem behavior follows periods when the patient is inactive, so solutions might focus on increasing his/her level of activity. It is important, however, to encourage caregivers to generate solutions themselves. If they are unable to do so, they can be urged to brainstorm with the clinician and state any solution that might come to mind. They should not at this point rule out any possibilities prematurely because they do not seem practical. This approach helps overcome the feeling of hopelessness which afflicts many caregivers and prevents them from exploring possible alternatives.

After generating a list of possible solutions, the caregiver then chooses one. If a caregiver has trouble making a choice, the method of pros and cons is used, in which the advantages and disadvantages of each alternative is evaluated (Beck, Rush, Shaw, & Emery, 1979). This procedure demonstrates to caregivers that they have nothing to lose, and thus helps overcome the reluctance they might have to try something new.

When a strategy is selected, a cognitive rehearsal can be conducted (Beck *et al.*, 1979), in which the caregiver mentally rehearses the steps necessary for carrying out the plan. Potential obstacles can then be identified in advance, and the strategy refined. At that point the caregiver is ready to try out the strategy, while continuing to keep records on the occurrence of the problem. These observations will be useful for evaluating the strategy's effectiveness.

Problem solving can be contrasted to the use of drugs. Medications are frequently prescribed for problems such as not sleeping at night, agitation, and restlessness. Unfortunately, the medications used have variable results, and may even make the problem worse. A problem-solving approach, in contrast, identifies the specific context in which symptoms occur. For example, if a patient who is not sleeping at night is napping during the day, it may be more efficacious to keep him awake than to prescribe a medication. Problem solving can also be used in conjunction with medications. Before a medication is introduced, the family can obtain a baseline on the frequency of problem behaviors for which the medication is targeted. Then, after the drug has been started, continued monitoring of the patient provides feedback on effectiveness. This type of monitoring can lead to a more rational use of medications, as well as identifying possible behavioral approaches.

The other major use of problem solving is to identify additional assistance for the primary caregiver. This includes help from family, friends or social agencies. Record-keeping can pinpoint when help will be most beneficial by identifying when caregivers experience the most stress. In some cases, having the caregiver keep track of when he or she feels the most stressed reveals that no specific action on the patient's part is the cause; rather, there is a build up of stress to the point that the caregiver has trouble coping. This type of observation can be useful for identifying for caregivers the potential benefits of receiving help, so that they do not have to be pushed beyond endurance.

Formal services, such as someone to come into the house to care for the patient, day care, or overnight respite care, may be inconsistently available, or too costly for some families. Sometimes, too, services for "frail" elderly are reluctant to take on dementia patients. Families may need an advocate with agencies to provide assistance. Help from family and friends, when it can be arranged, tends to be more flexible and more readily accepted by the primary caregiver.

Despite these problems, additional support for the primary caregiver is usually available, but many caregivers are reluctant to ask. Among the reasons they give for not accepting help are that they ought to be able to do everything themselves, that no one else can do as good a job, or that the patient will not accept anyone else. It is important to identify these beliefs, and to explore alternative perspectives on accepting help (S. H. Zarit, Orr, & J. M. Zarit, 1985). As an example, a caregiver might be encouraged to consider the implications of trying to do everything for herself, how that will affect her ability to continue caring for the patient in the long run. As for the patient accepting a helper, that can sometimes be difficult. By gradually introducing a new person or program, however, these difficulties can be minimized.

Implementing Treatment

It is often useful to begin an intervention by holding several (3 to 10) counseling sessions with the primary caregiver. Caregivers often seek help when they are experiencing a lot of stress, and the relationship with a supportive, nonjudgmental clinician will relieve some of their feelings of distress and isolation. Caregivers will also be able to consider the information provided by the clinician about care alternatives, and begin to use a problem-solving approach. As their need for assistance is clarified, the clinician can begin planning for a family meeting.

One critical dimension affecting the course of the counseling is the caregiver's ability to use the problem-solving process. Some caregivers are excellent problem solvers, and quickly adopt useful strategies for managing the stresses they are under. Others, however, proceed more slowly, and the clinician must explore why they are having difficulty with this approach. In some cases, they may be too angry to try, saying they do not know why they have to be the one to change, when it is the patient who is ill. The clinician can respond empathically, while also pointing out that they have nothing to lose by trying some new approaches. In other instances, the caregiver may not have good problem-solving skills in the first place, and so the clinician must proceed more slowly to build up this ability. Learning to use problem solving is essential, however, because it provides the caregiver with alternatives, and also allows for some emotional distance in the relationship.

Family meetings can build on the gains made in counseling the primary caregiver. By involving those who can most directly assist the primary caregiver, the family meeting directly addresses the issue of support. It can also be used to clarify the nature of the illness for other family members and to resolve conflicts or misunderstanding about the patient's care. Planning for the family meeting, including who to invite and where to hold it, is done in the counseling sessions. Preparations should also include exploring dimensions of the family system, such as whether there are any long-standing conflicts, and what roles various family members play. As when treating any family, the clinician needs to be aware of the possible limitations of information provided by just one family member, and be prepared to change his/her beliefs about how the family functions based on observations made during the family meeting.

In most cases, only one family meeting will be necessary. The focus of the meeting is on providing information to family members about the patient's illness, identifying the caregiver's needs for assistance, and then encouraging the family to use their own problem-solving skills for assisting the caregiver. Families typically have less information about dementia than the primary caregiver, and may be focused on seeking a cure, rather than developing effective management strategies. By beginning the family meeting by answering questions about causes and treatment of the dementia, the clinician can redirect them to practical care issues. When they understand the patient's condition and its effects on behavior, they will often spontaneously identify ways of helping the primary caregiver. If there is no effective problem solver in the family, the clinician can play a more active role. Suggestions should be made in light of there being different things that each person can contribute. Family members should not be pressured into volunteering more than they want. The clinician should also note the person who might be overcommitting his or her services, and try to work out a more reasonable schedule.

Success of the family meeting depends on the clinician's figuring out how problems get solved in a particular family, and then supporting that process. This task is facilitated by creating a supportive atmosphere in the meeting. The clinician can acknowledge positive contributions, and redirect nonsupportive communications. The clinician should not take sides in any disagreements, and keep disagreements within boundaries, so that compromises might be reached.

An important dimension of the family meeting is to keep the focus on problems related to the dementia. Some families may have long-standing conflicts which potentially could erupt during the family meeting. While it would be difficult to resolve these issues in one or two family sessions, families can usually cooperate on problems around the dementia. The clinician, however, may have to differentiate clearly between the immediate, dementia-related concerns and other areas of conflict, and keep the focus of the meeting on the former.

On occasions, the family meeting may open lines of communication where there had previously been a troubled relationship. As an example, a husband who was caregiver for his wife was estranged from his two daughters. The daughters were still angry over their upbringing and the way their father dominated the family with his odd behaviors and ideas (he was a lifelong agoraphobic). When the family was first seen, the daughters actually believed their father's odd behavior had caused their mother's illness. A family meeting led to a greater understanding on their part both of their mother's illness and how much care their father was now providing. One result of the meeting was that the daughters stepped in to relieve their father on occasions. As part-time caregivers, they realized how much effort their father had been making. This awareness increased their appreciation of their father, and led to a major reconciliation between him and one of the daughters.

Follow-up of the family meeting is important to determine if everyone has carried out his or her part of the plan, or if some modifications need to be made. This can usually be done by telephone or in a session with the primary caregiver. If the plan that was agreed upon is not working at all, a second meeting could be held to explore what has interfered with carrying out the tasks. The clinician should take a positive and impartial tone. Rather than blaming the family or making them feel guilty for their failure, the clinician can relabel the plan as an experiment which showed them some arrangements that did not work out. The family's good intentions can be reinforced, and they can be encouraged to come up with a more realistic plan.

The type of assistance that is most frequently available for family members is the support group. Support groups, however, vary from one to the other in how they are organized and what they emphasize. For example, groups differ in the degree of professional involvement. Some follow a self-help model with minimal or no professional assistance, while others are professionally led, or have a mixed format with some professional guidance. Groups also differ in the amount of structure they maintain in meetings. Some are primarily didactic, with a speaker or topic for each session. Others have an unrestricted agenda, and allow freewheeling interactions among participants.

Within the treatment model proposed earlier, support groups are conducted by a trained leader. The group setting is used to enhance the interventions made in individual counseling and family meetings. Groups are an efficient way of sharing information, and participants often take the initiative to bring in articles or other material. Caregivers will also pool their knowledge about community resources, such as which doctors provide better care, or about informal channels for obtaining in-home help. Problem solving also takes on new dimensions in groups. Caregivers who will not follow suggestions from a professional will often try strategies when they are proposed by another caregiver. Caregivers often make creative suggestions for managing problem behaviors or obtaining support. For example, a caregiver in one group described how she used affection when she had trouble getting her husband to cross a busy street when the light changed. She had tried arguing with him and pulling him, but he would not budge. She then took a breath and thought about it a minute. When the light changed again, she gently took him by the elbow, and said in a soft voice, "Okay, honey, now it's time for us to cross." Other caregivers in that group then tried using affection in other situations when their relative was upset, and reported generally positive results.

One of the most important aspects of a support group is the opportunity to interact with people who are in a similar situation. Being a caregiver can be an isolating experience. Some will even regard the strong emotions they feel as signs of their own mental weakness. Hearing that others have gone through similar circumstances and have felt similar emotions helps normalize their experience, and creates positive ties among group members.

The leader's role is to maximize these positive changes by building cohesiveness in the group and fostering a supportive atmosphere where caregivers can speak freely without fear of censure. It is particularly important to set and maintain therapeutic norms in the group, such as allowing everyone a chance to talk and not letting one person dominate the conversation, or by intervening when one participant is overly critical of another.

There is as yet little consensus on the best composition of support groups. Clinical experience suggests participants are attracted to groups in which other members have a similar relationship with the dementia patient, that is, all the group members are spouses, or children. Another important dimension is severity of the illness. There will be more initial cohesion in the group if all the dementia patients are having similar problems. If there is a wide disparity, the person whose relative does not fit may feel isolated or left out. In cases where most group members have a severely impaired relative, someone caring for an early dementia patient may be frightened by what he or she hears. These problems of disparity can usually be resolved by noting how caregivers can learn from another, even while some aspects of their situations are different.

SUMMARY

Care of a dementia patient can place considerable stress on families. While the underlying disease cannot be treated, there are often treatable components of the situation. By changing their approach to the patient, caregivers may learn to modify some troubling behaviors. Obtaining assistance with caregiving tasks is also critical in relieving the caregiver's stress. Useful interventions include providing the caregiver with an understanding of the disease and how it affects the patient's behavior, and teaching a problem-solving approach for coping with problem behaviors and the demands of the caregiving routine. Counseling with the primary caregiver, family meetings, and support groups are all helpful, and achieve somewhat different objectives.

REFERENCES

Beck, A. T., Rush, D., Shaw, D., & Emery, G. (1979). *Cognitive therapy of depression*. New York: Guilford.

Bengtson, V. L., & Cutler, N. E. (1976). Generations and intergenerational relations: Perspectives on age groups and social change. In R. H. Binstock and E. Shanas (Eds.), *Handbook of aging and the social sciences*. New York: Van Nostrand Rinehold.

Bergmann, K., Foster, E. M., Justice, A. W., & Matthews, V. (1978). Management of the demented elderly patient in the community. *British Journal of Psychiatry, 132*, 44–49.

Botwinick, J., & Birren, J. E. (1951). Differential decline in the Wechsler–Bellevue subtests in the senile psychoses. *Journal of Gerontology, 6*, 365–368.

Boutselis, M., & Zarit, S. H. (1984, November). *Burden and distress of dementia caregivers: Effects of gender and relationship*. Paper presented at the meetings of the Gerontological Society of America, San Antonio, TX.

Bouvier, L., Atlee, E., & McVeigh, F. (1975). *The elderly in America*. Washington, D.C.: Population Reference Bureau.

Branch, L. G., & Jette, A. M. (1982). A prospective study of long term care institutionalization among the aged. *American Journal of Public Health, 72*, 1373–1379.

Brody, E. M. (1985). Parent care as a normative family stress. *Gerontologist, 25*, 19–29.

Brotman, H. (1982). *Every ninth American: An analysis for the chairmen of the select committee on aging*, House of Representatives. Ninety-seventh Congress. Washington, D.C.: Publication No. 97–332, U.S. Government Printing Office.

Crimmins, E. M. (1984). Life expectancy and the older population: Demographic implications of recent and prospective trends in old age mortality. *Research on Aging, 6*, 490–514.

Cummings, J. L. & Benson, D. F. (1983). *Dementia: A clinical approach*. Boston: Butterworths.

Derogatis, L. R., & Spencer, P. M. (1982). *The brief symptom inventory (BSI): Administration and procedures manual-I*. Baltimore: Clinical Psychometric Research Unit, Johns Hopkins University School of Medicine.

Fitting, M., Rabins, P., Lucas, M. J., & Eastham, J. (1986). Caregivers for dementia patients: A comparison of husbands and wives. *Gerontologist, 26*, 248–252.

George, L. K., & Gwyther, L. P., (1986). Caregiver well-being: A multidimensional examination of family caregivers of demented adults. *Gerontologist, 26*, 253–259.

Gilewski, M., Kuppinger, J., & Zarit, S. H. (1985). The aging marital system. *Clinical Gerontologist, 5*, 3–16.

Goldstein, G. & Shelly, C. H. (1975). Similarities and differences between psychological deficit in aging and brain damage. *Journal of Gerontology, 30*, 448–455.

Gurland, B. J., Dean, L., Cross, P., & Golden, R. (1981). The epidemiology of depression and dementia in the elderly: The use of multiple indicators of these conditions. In J.

O. Cole and J. E. Barrett (Eds.), *Psychopathology in the aged* (pp. 37–62). New York: Raven.

Hachinski, V. C. (1983). Differential diagnosis of Alzheimer's disease: Multi-infarct dementia. In B. Relsberg (Ed.), *Alzheimer's disease: The standard reference* (pp. 188–192). New York: The Free Press.

Hassinger, M. J., Zarit, J. M., & Zarit, S. H. (1982, April). A comparison of clinical characteristics of Multi-infarct and Alzheimer's dementia patients. Paper presented at the meetings of the Western Psychological Association, Sacramento, CA.

Hassinger, M. J. & Zarit, S. H. (1986, August). *Predicting institutionalization of dementia patients*. Paper presented at the meetings of the American Psychological Association, Washington, D.C.

Hoenig, J., & Hamilton, M. W. (1966). Elderly psychiatric patients and the burden on the household. *Psychiatria et Neurologia* (Basel), *154* (5), 281–293.

Kahn, R. L. (1975). The mental health system and the future aged. *Gerontologist, 15* (1, part 2), 24–31.

Kahn, R. L., Zarit, S. H., Hilbert, N. M., & Niederehe, G. (1975). Memory complaint and impairment in the aged. *Archives of General Psychiatry, 32*, 1569–1573.

Kanfer, F. H., & Saslow, G. (1965). Behavioral analysis: An alternative to diagnostic classification. *Archives of General Psychiatry, 12*, 529–538.

Knight, B., & Walker, D. L. (1985). Toward a definition of alternatives to institutionalization for the frail elderly. *Gerontologist, 25*, 358–363.

Lawton, M. P. (1971). The functional assessment of elderly people. *Journal of the American Geriatrics Society, 19*, 465–481.

Lazarus, R.S. (1966). *Psychological stress and the coping process*. New York: McGraw Hill.

Lazarus, R. S., & Folkman, S. (1984). Coping and adaptation. In W. D. Gentry (Ed.), *Handbook of Behavioral Medicine*. New York: Guilford.

Lipowski, Z. J. (1980). *Delirium: Acute brain failure in man*. Springfield, IL: Charles C. Thomas.

Liston, E. H., & LaRue, A. (1983). Clinical differentiation of primary degenerative and Multi-infarct dementia: A critical review of the evidence. Part II. Pathological studies. *Biological Psychiatry, 12*, 1467–1483.

Lowenthal, M. F., Berkman, P., & Associates (1967). *Aging and mental disorders in San Francisco*. San Francisco: Jossey–Bass.

Macmillan, D. (1958). Hospital–community relationships. In *An approach to the prevention of disability from chronic psychoses: The open mental hospital within the community*. New York: Millbank Memorial Fund.

Macmillan, D. (1967). Problems of a geriatric mental health service. *British Journal of Psychiatry, 113*, 175–81.

McKhann, G., Drachman, D., Folstein, M., Katzman, R., Price, D., & Stadlan, E. M. (1984). Clinical diagnosis of Alzheimer's disease. *Neurology, 34*, 939–944.

Montgomery, R. J. V., Stull, D. E., & Borgatta, E. F. (1985). Measurement and the analysis of burden. *Research on Aging, 7*, 137–152.

Morris, J. N., & Sherwood, S. (1983). Informal support resources for vulnerable elderly persons: Can they be counted on, why do they work? *International Journal of Aging and Human Development, 17*, 81–98.

Mortimer, J. A., Schuman, L. M., & French, L. R. (1981). Epidemiology of dementing illness. In J. A. Mortimer and L. Schuman (Eds.), *The epidemiology of dementia*. New York: Oxford University Press.

NIA Task Force, (1980). Senility reconsidered. *Journal of the American Medical Association, 244* (3), 259–263.

Perlin, S., & Kahn, R. L. (1968). A mental health center in a general hospital. In L. J. Duhl and R. L. Leopold (Eds.), *Mental health and urban social policy: A casebook of community action*. San Francisco: Jossey–Bass.

Popkin, S. J., Gallagher, D., Thompson, L. W., & Moore, M. (1982). Memory complaint and performance in normal and depressed older adults. *Experimental Aging Research, 8*, 141–145.

Overall, J. E., & Gorham, D. R. (1972). Organicity versus old age in objective and projective test performance. *Journal of Consulting and Clinical Psychology, 39*, 98–105.

Reece, D., Walz, T., & Hagenbroeck, H. (1983). Intergenerational care providers of non-institutionalized frail elderly: Characteristics and consequences. *Journal of Gerontological Social Work, 5*, 21–34.

Reisberg, B., Ferris, S. H., & Crook, T. (1982). Signs, symptoms, and course of age-associated cognitive decline. In S. Corkin, K. L. Davis, J. H. Growdin, E. Usdin, & R. J. Wurtman (Eds.), *Alzheimer's Disease: A Report of Progress in Research*. New York: Raven Press.

Sainsbury, P., & Grad de Alarcon, J. (1970). The psychiatrist and the geriatric patient: The effects of community care on the family of the geriatric patient. *Journal of Geriatric Psychiatry, 4*, 23–41.

Sanford, J. R. A. (1975). Tolerance of debility in elderly dependants by supporters at home: Its significance for hospital practice. *British Medical Journal, 3*, 471–473.

Schaie, K. W., & Schaie, J. P. (1977). Clinical assessment and aging. In J. E. Birren and K. W. Schaie (Eds.), *Handbook of the Psychology of Aging*. New York: Van Nostrand Rinehold.

Shanas, E. (1979). The family as a social support system in old age. *Gerontologist, 19*, 169–174.

Stone, R., Cafferata, G. L., & Sangl, J. (1987). Caregivers of the frail elderly: A national profile. *Gerontologist, 27*, 616–626.

Terry, R. D. (1978). Aging, senile dementia and Alzheimer's disease. In R. Katzman, R. D. Terry, & K. L. Bick (Eds.), *Alzheimer's Disease: Senile Dementia and Related Disorders*. New York: Raven.

Terry, R. D., & Wiesniewski, H. M. (1977). Structural aspects of aging of the brain. In C. Eisdorfer & R. O. Friedel (Eds.), *Cognitive and Emotional Disturbance in the Elderly*. Chicago: Year Book Medical Publishers.

Woods, A. M., Niederehe, G., & Fruge, E. (1985). A family systems perspective on the impact of dementia. *Generations, 10*, 19–23.

Zarit, J. M. (1982). *Predictors of burden and distress for caregivers of senile dementia patients*. Unpublished doctoral dissertation. University of Southern California.

Zarit, J. M., & Zarit, S. H. (1982, November). Measurement of burden and social support. Paper presented at the meetings of the Gerontological Society of America, San Diego, CA.

Zarit, S. H. (in press). Interventions with caregivers of dementia patients. In E. Light & B. Lebowitz (Eds.), *Alzheimer's disease treatment and family stress: Directions for research*. Washington: D.C.: National Institute of Mental Health.

Zarit, S. H. (1980). *Aging and mental disorder*. New York: The Free Press.

Zarit, S. H., Reever, K. E., & Bach-Peterson, J. M. (1980). Relatives of the impaired elderly, Correlates of feelings of burden. *Gerontologist, 20*, 649–655.

Zarit, S. H., Orr, N. K., & Zarit, J. M. (1985). *The hidden victims of Alzheimer's disease: Families under stress*. New York: New York University Press.

Zarit, S. H., & Anthony, C. R. (1986). Interventions with dementia patients and their families. In J. E. Birren, M. L. M. Gilhooly, & S. H. Zarit (Eds.), *The senile dementias: Policy and management*. Englewood Cliffs, NJ: Prentice–Hall.

Zarit, S. H., Todd, P. A., & Zarit, J. M. (1986). Subjective burden of husbands and wives as caregivers: A longitudinal study. *Gerontologist, 26*, 260–266.

16

Primary Health Care Settings

IAN R. H. FALLOON
Buckingham Mental Health Service, England
R. EDWARD HARPIN
Private Practice, San Diego
TERENCE PEMBLETON
Buckingham Mental Health Service, England

The rise of family therapy has occurred during a period that has seen the demise of the traditional family doctor. The family physician, in addition to providing for the physical health care of the family, often making visits to the home, also functioned as a major provider of family counseling, especially at times of crisis. Indeed, it was a general physician, Henry Richardson, who first expounded the concept of families as homeostatic systems, akin to those operating in the body's physiology (Richardson, 1948). In a volume entitled *Patients Have Families*, he entreated his fellow physicians to pay greater attention to the family-wide stress factors that he believed often underlay somatic illness in vulnerable family members. He described several intractable cases that he successfully treated by defining family stresses and counseling family members to resolve these stress factors effectively. Richardson drew the analogy between the reciprocity of family members' responses to stress and the physiological mechanisms of homeostasis that control neuroendocrine functions in the body. This analogy was adopted and further expounded by Don Jackson (1959) as one of the earliest conceptual frameworks upon which family therapy developed.

The notion that any family, when confronted with stress, tends to cope by adopting the mutually most satisfying pattern of interpersonal transactions was proposed. Where basic conflicts preexist in family relationships, this arrangement tends to place excessive strain on one or more family members. This strain, at times, is considered to be relieved when the vulnerable family member(s) develop an illness that expresses the emotional conflicts within the family as a whole. This illness often takes the form of a severe cognitive or emotional disturbance, such as schizophrenia. These notions that distorted family relationships are a primary factor in the etiology of schizophrenia are supported by a host of studies that showed abnormalities in the interpersonal communication in families in which one member suffered chronic schizophrenia (Goldstein, Rodnick, Evans, May, & Sternberg, 1978). Unfortunately, few of these studies controlled for the effects of having a chronic, handicapped member. The few that did control for this chronic illness variable found no pattern of communication that was specific to schizophrenia (Farina & Holzberg, 1968; Ferreira & Winter, 1965; Hirsch & Leff, 1975). It appeared that the abnormalities of communication are a feature of the excessive stress on the family of coping with a disturbing chronic disorder in one member. Unfortunately, despite abundant clinical evidence that interventions that involved conjoint meetings between the whole family and a psychotherapist were effective in improving the course of schizophrenia, disillusionment with the ability to discover a specific family communication deficit as the cause of the disorder resulted in a lack of enthusiasm for family therapy in this disorder.

Thus, the brilliant insights of Richardson concerning the potential benefits of stress-reduction strategies involving not merely the patient with a chronic illness, but also his or her entire family, were lost to a generation of physicians. Recently, these concepts have been revitalized. Studies have demonstrated that family stress reduction may result in benefits for conditions as disparate as asthma (Lask & Matthew, 1979) and chronic renal failure (Reiss, 1982). One implication of these findings is that family therapeutic approaches may be a particularly useful tool in the primary medical care setting and may prove especially effective when applied by the family practitioner. The health-promoting role of family care can be effectively supported by the family practitioner, who treats the patient and family at home. This contrasts with hospital care, where family members are considered a nuisance, cluttering up the wards, preventing effective nursing, and, at best, providing a diversion for patients during the brief, unwelcome visiting hours.

Behavioral family therapy (BFT) has been successfully employed in the management of several major mental disorders (schizophrenia, depression, anorexia nervosa, Alzheimer Disease). The goal has been the reduction of everyday family stress, as well as training family members and index patients to cope more effectively with the specific disabilities associated with their disorders. The core ingredients of this approach are as follows.

1. *Assessment of family behavior.* This includes individual family members' understanding of the index patient's disorder; the goals and problems of individual family members; the efficiency of the family unit in assisting each member to achieve those goals; and the efficiency of the family unit to achieve effective resolution of all problems that arise, both within and outside the family. The emphasis is on observable interactions among family members rather than their cognitive and emotional responses

to one another, although the latter are also considered extremely important.

2. *Establishment of a problem-solving milieu.* This involves the effective communication of emotionally charged issues within a family group discussion. Training in expressing specific positive and negative feelings about the specific behavior of family members, making constructive requests, and employing empathic listening methods may all assist in enhancing the cohesion and mutual trust of the family unit.

3. *Developing a framework for problem resolution.* A structured approach to family discussions about problems or goals is developed in workshop sessions with the family. This entails defining clear problems or goals, brainstorming potential solutions, evaluating each suggestion, choosing the most appropriate, planning and implementing that solution, and reviewing the process in a constructive manner.

4. *Specific behavioral strategies* have been developed for specific problems. Where the family members are faced with specific problems that they appear unable to resolve with their own problem-solving efforts, the therapist may instruct them in the use of validated behavioral procedures such as contingency contracting, social skills training, operant procedures, anxiety management, etc.

5. *Continuous monitoring of progress.* A crucial component of BFT is the continuous assessment of progress toward the goals of individual family members and the family as a unit. Self-monitoring with diaries and checklists enables progress to be charted on an everyday basis and also enables the therapist to validate the changes during the treatment sessions.

These methods were described in detail by Falloon, Boyd, and McGill (1984). They require very little modification when they are employed within a family practice setting. One major adaptation is that the time available to the therapist for a family practice service is usually more restricted and crisis-oriented. Therapy sessions tend to be no longer than 15–20 min. Although double or triple appointments are feasible, efforts to increase the efficiency of treatment are desirable. This goal can be achieved through the use of teaching aids in the form of written guidelines and worksheets for use during the sessions and at home. A greater focus on the specific goals of the intervention and emphasis on work carried out between sessions increases efficiency further without detracting from the quality of the therapy.

Over the past few years, we have treated families with BFT in primary care settings, often in collaboration with the physicians and nurses of the primary care team. The effectiveness of these methods in this setting has not been formally investigated. A number of typical cases are reported here that illustrate the broad-based utility of BFT in primary care.

CASE EXAMPLES

Bulimia and Weight Reduction

EG was a 28-year-old secretary, married for 5 years, without children. She was a well-built woman with a muscular frame. She had felt self-conscious about her large figure since puberty. Her mother prevented her from dieting and insisted on feeding her with cream cakes and cookies throughout adolescence. After EG left home at age 18, she began dieting and her weight dropped from 150 to 130 pounds. However, despite constant efforts to lose more weight, she was unable to achieve any further reduction. This frustrated her and made her feel miserable and suicidal. When EG felt depressed, she visited her mother, who fed her fattening treats. Although EG found solace in the food, this mood elevation was short lived; on returning to her apartment she felt guilty and ashamed of her behavior. She learned that she could induce vomiting, and this provided a partial solution to her problem of coping with visits home.

EG met her husband at the age of 22; they dated for a year before getting married. EG avoided premarital sex because she feared that her husband would see her body as grotesque. After marriage they established a satisfactory sexual relationship, but EG continued to cover her body as much as possible. Throughout the courtship, EG had desperately tried to lose weight through dieting and using laxatives. However, no stable weight reduction was achieved. EG continued to induce vomiting after visits to her mother and occasionally after excessive food intake at restaurants or parties.

EG was very keen to have children and went to a gynecologist for a checkup. She was told to lose weight in order to have a healthy pregnancy. This advice caused her considerable distress. She began to worry constantly about her weight. She continued to diet but was again unsuccessful. At times when she felt very depressed and suicidal, EG would visit an ice cream parlor or coffee shop and eat excessive quantities of high-calorie foods. On returning home, she relieved her guilt by induced vomiting. She began to induce vomiting after most meals and became increasingly depressed when she was unable to get her weight below 125 pounds.

EG consulted her family practitioner for advice on weight reduction. He observed that she appeared depressed and explored her problems. She told him about her self-induced vomiting and her concerns about not being able to get pregnant because she was overweight. After several counseling sessions, the family practitioner consulted the mental health service for further advice on EG's management. It was suggested that he involve the husband and conduct conjoint marital therapy. After three sessions, during which EG admitted to her husband her vomiting behavior and her worry about her weight, the appearance of her body, and wanting to get pregnant, some relief of her depression was noted. However, her bulimic behavior remained. At this time, the family practitioner left the health center and invited the first author (I. R. H. F.) to continue the treatment.

A functional analysis revealed that EG's husband cared for her deeply, shared her eagerness to have children, and found her body extremely attractive. He had found her depression difficult to cope with, largely because she had refused to discuss it with him. Husband and wife both appeared to have good communication skills but avoided discussion of emotionally charged issues. It was agreed to provide five sessions of behavioral marital therapy to improve mutual problem solving. EG initially had great difficulty expressing unpleasant feelings to her husband. However, after telling him that she worried most about her weight when he was away on business trips, they successfully established a plan that he would telephone every night he was away. EG felt much greater confidence in expressing her fears and concerns to her husband after this. The two of them worked out a strategy for preventing bulimic behavior. This involved EG speaking with her husband or a close friend, who knew about the problem, at times that she felt depressed and wanted to eat excessively. This plan proved very successful, and, although EG spoke with her husband on only one occasion, her self-induced vomiting was reduced from two to three times daily to less than one a week over three weeks; this led eventually to a sustained elimination of this habit.

The couple planned a holiday in Greece and decided that they would begin their attempt to get pregnant. They returned 2 weeks later in good spirits, despite both gaining several pounds. EG employed a straightforward weight reduction program over the next month and, with the support of her husband, began to accept that 130 pounds was her best weight. Six months later, she was half way through her pregnancy, appropriately concerned about her weight gain, and very happy. She had told her mother about her difficulties and had requested that her mother did not push food at her during visits. EG and her husband continued to convene weekly meetings at which they discussed problems or future plans. Over a year later, after the birth of her son, EG appeared to be coping well, with no recurrence of bulimia or depression despite weighing 142 pounds. She was attending a new mothers' group and using a diet and exercise program to achieve her prepregnancy weight. Her husband had managed to change his work habits to spend more time at home and enjoyed his role as a new parent.

Acute Obsessive-Compulsive Disorder

SJ was a 26-year-old married woman with children aged 5 and 8 years. She presented to her general practitioner complaining of feeling tense, anxious, and depressed. She described having "odd" thoughts that she could not get rid of. These included thoughts about suicide, although she did not feel she wanted to die, and thoughts of killing her children, although she loved them deeply. These thoughts made her extremely anxious and the harder she tried to put them out of her mind, the stronger they continued to bother her. Thus, these thoughts were consistent with obsessional ruminations.

A functional analysis revealed that these thoughts had begun 2 weeks ago at the time SJ's father had been diagnosed as having a terminal illness. She was extremely close to her father and was unable to contemplate how her life would continue in his absence. She worried that her mother would be unable to cope after father's death.

SJ spent most of her time doing the housework and caring for her two children. Her husband was supportive and concerned but could not understand her unwanted thoughts. He was working long hours as a self-employed carpenter. He did his best to reassure his wife, but he was very concerned that she might harm herself or her children and wondered if she was going mad.

A treatment plan was developed that initially involved education of husband and wife (and family doctor) about the nature of obsessive-compulsive disorders. SJ was encouraged to bring on her distressing thoughts and allow them to flow without attempting to resist them in any way. Her husband was instructed to encourage his wife to initiate this habituation process and to talk over these thoughts with her without reassuring her himself. Throughout this program, they were reminded about the nature of obsessive-compulsive thoughts, in particular, the tendency for them to be maintained by resistance and reassurance, as well as the unlikelihood that she would act upon these thoughts.

Within a week, SJ appeared much less distressed and reported that the unwanted thoughts had been greatly reduced in frequency and intensity. She was encouraged (with continuing support from her husband) to continue promoting her unwanted thoughts without resistance.

Three weeks later, SJ's father was readmitted to hospital and her thoughts became more intense. They now included intense fear that she would take an overdose of aspirin when her father died. She experienced feelings of panic with a fear that she would lose control. She felt unable to visit her father in the hospital and tried to avoid thinking about him. At this point, she and her husband were taught structured problem-solving and provided with several worksheets to continue using between sessions to begin to plan how to cope with all aspects of her father's death. It was suggested that they involve her mother, brother, and sister-in-law in some aspects of this problem-solving.

A week later, SJ and her husband reported having had several problem-solving discussions regarding visiting her father, coping with his death, and the major family adjustments that would be necessary. SJ was much less distressed and was spending more time taking her children out on activities during their summer holidays. SJ and her husband had experienced some minor difficulties with the problem-solving method and received guided practice during the session.

Two weeks later, SJ's father died. She experienced normal feelings of grief and coped exceptionally well with his funeral and events at the time of his death. Funeral plans were organized by herself, her husband, and her brother, using a problem-solving worksheet. SJ experienced the occasional suicidal thought but regarded this as a normal phenomenon. She remained concerned about her mother and continued to employ the problem-solving format to assist in dealing with her mother's practical and emotional difficulties. The day prior to her father's death, SJ had written a very moving poem that expressed how much he had contributed to her enjoyment of life and how his spirit would live on in her and all his many friends.

Six months later, SJ experienced a brief recurrence of her distressing thoughts, but she was able to cope with them through habituation and problem-solving with her husband. She remained a somewhat tense and anxious person but felt that she was coping 50% better than before therapy.

Several other cases of acute obsessive-compulsive symptoms associated with major life stressors have been treated in a similar fashion. The involvement of spouses and other key family members in providing assistance with specific behavioral strategies, as well as in problem-solving of the life stresses that appear to have triggered the behavioral disturbance, has been considered a major factor in the rapid and sustained recovery from these distressing disorders. Purists might argue that this type of intervention does not constitute family "therapy"; however, it is clear that the family involvement in this manner appears to improve the efficacy of treatment substantially.

Early Treatment of Schizophrenia

One of the advantages of working in a primary care setting is the potential for detecting serious mental illnesses at the initial or prodromal presentation of symptoms. At this stage, it is often relatively easy to intervene with drugs and psychosocial treatment to prevent the progression toward a full-blown condition.

JG was a 19-year-old man, living with his parents and two younger sisters. He had left school a year earlier, and the family had expected that he would enter a university. He was an excellent sportsman, but he found academic studies very difficult, despite obtaining average grades in most subjects. JG had not worked for several months after finishing school. Two months before he presented, he had obtained a job in a local gardening center. He was awkward and shy with customers and had great difficulty coping with them, especially when they asked him for advice about plants. In order to avoid contact with customers, he spent as much time as possible checking that the goods on the shelves were correctly displayed.

The first sign of any significant abnormality was noted at work when the manager found him staring at a geranium and chanting religious verse. When asked what he was doing, JG appeared embarrassed and said he was practicing for the church choir. He did not attend church and was not in the choir. Over the next few days, a further series of inexplicable bizarre acts occurred at work. Then, on the weekend, JG was expected to play tennis for his club team. He left home to attend the match but he did not arrive. That evening he was found walking in the middle of the main street of a town 10 miles away carrying his tennis racquets. When approached by the police he told them he was trying to find his tennis club. They returned him to his home, where he was greeted by his anxious parents. His father took him to the family doctor the following morning; after brief consultation with a psychiatrist, a provisional diagnosis of early schizophrenia was made. JG described a belief that people were talking about him wherever he went; he felt that he was being persecuted, and he suspected that some people were controlling his thoughts and actions. His family doctor prescribed a small dose of neuroleptic drugs and arranged for BFT to begin immediately.

A functional analysis of the family revealed considerable concern among all family members for JG's future, especially worries about his ability to succeed in a professional career. JG's father was disturbed by his son's failure to achieve since leaving school and described several attempts he had made to assist in finding suitable employment for him. JG's parents described difficulties in their own relationship resulting in constant bickering and arguments.

On the second visit to the home the therapist noted that JG was much calmer and had perceived many fewer comments referring to him on the TV or elsewhere. However, he remained anxious in social situations. The entire family was educated about the vulnerability stress-diathesis model of schizophrenia. JG was told that, in the light of his current symptoms, he might be expected to succumb to schizophrenia at times of high stress. The symptoms of schizophrenia, its course, and its management were all discussed in detail. The prodromal features of the presentation of the disorder were carefully defined, and a list was given to the index patient and his parents. Any evidence of these warning signs in the future were to be reported immediately to the family doctor so that early intervention could be provided without delay.

Because it was evident that the family were able to communicate their feelings effectively, it was decided that no additional training in this area was necessary. The family therapy moved immediately to training in structured problem-solving. The family mastered the use of this approach without difficulty and began to employ it at home to assist JG to resolve his immediate stresses. JG's father agreed that pushing JG toward a professional career was likely to create stress and was willing to consider much less stressful jobs based on JG's strengths. JG's strong interest and prowess in tennis and other sporting activities encouraged him to consider entering a training program for sports center management. At the same time, his parents reported that they had successfully employed the problem-solving format to plan ways to spend more time together and to reduce father's excessive time spent at work.

After three family sessions, JG appeared free from symptoms, and his family doctor began to reduce his neuroleptic medication, which was discontinued without incident after 3 months. One year later, JG was functioning well and had had two temporary jobs while awaiting entry to a 2-year course in sports center administration. His parents were pleased with his progress and were happier in their own relationship. They continued to employ the problem-solving methods to resolve stresses that arose from time to time.

The value of BFT in the prevention of major exacerbations of schizophrenia has been investigated in a controlled study (see Chapter 13). However, its efficacy in the prevention of the initial full-blown presentation of this disorder is not yet established. We have employed the approach described in this case report in 12 similar cases with similar results. Not one of these cases has developed a major episode of schizophrenia, and all have returned to normal functioning without long-term medical intervention. However, we plan to maintain continued contact with these individuals and their families for at least 5 years and remain readily available for further early intervention should the prodromal signs of the disorder emerge.

It is possible that these cases represent the substantial proportion of mild cases of schizophrenia that occur in the community and remit spontaneously without recurrence. Such cases are managed effectively by the primary care services without referral to mental health professionals. However, it is also possible that the timely application of effective drug therapy combined with stress management involving the patient and family may form the basis of a program of prevention for schizophrenia—currently one of the major public health problems in the developed countries.

Acute Agoraphobia

RN was a 27-year-old married woman who lived on a farm with her husband and children, aged 5 and 7 years. She had presented to her visiting community nurse complaining of a mixture of anxiety and depression. Her family doctor prescribed 150 mg of amitriptyline at night. After 6 months, RN decided to stop taking the tricyclic drugs without consulting her doctor. She stopped them abruptly. Over the next 2 weeks, she became increasingly tense and anxious. She visited her sister-in-law, who lived in an isolated farmhouse and was extremely fearful of being attacked by a rapist who had been widely publicized on the media as attacking women in a nearby area. RN reassured her sister-in-law, but on returning home realized that her own house was somewhat isolated; she began to experience similar fears for her own safety. RN experienced severe feelings of panic when she was alone in the house and persuaded her husband to stay with her when her children went to school. This anxiety generalized to driving the car or shopping on her own. Her mother was invited to stay, and RN became housebound. She again contacted her community nurse who arranged a consultation with her doctor.

Her family doctor instructed RN to restart the tricyclic drugs, but after 2 weeks no improvement had occurred, so he referred her to a therapist. RN appeared tearful and distraught when interviewed with her mother and husband and community nurse at her doctor's office. She expressed feelings of guilt and suicide, with constant worrying. Her sleep and appetite were minimal. She described panic attacks occurring five or more times daily. Her husband and mother were very supportive, caring for the home and children. They were concerned and wanted to help.

The initial treatment plan involved (1) educating the patient and family about anxiety disorders and their management (her depressive syndrome was considered secondary to the anxiety state); (2) training the patient and her family to develop a graduated program of exposure to her feared situations assisted by the community nurse; (3) a gradual return to home care and parenting functions; (4) continuation of tricyclic medication; and (5) continued functional analysis of family problems.

A week later, RN was much less anxious, with improved appetite and sleep. But she had spent most of the week at her mother's house and remained fearful of staying alone at her own home. A session of family problem-solving with RN and her husband, mother, and father enabled a clearly defined plan to be devised to implement graduated return home and resumption of expected activities. Each participant agreed on a specific responsibility and rehearsed aspects that they thought might prove difficult; for example, RN rehearsed how she would explain her absence from home to her children, while her mother rehearsed how she would cope if her daughter had a panic attack on the shopping trip they planned. During the next week, RN spent increasing time at home and began to undertake a substantial amount of housework. She went shopping for food with her mother. However, an argument with her husband resulted when he insisted that she drive the children to school each morning. She told him that she did not think she could cope with driving the car back from the school alone. He became angry and accused her of neglecting the children and himself. During the next session this argument was reenacted and both partners rehearsed alternative ways of expressing their feelings about the issue. It became apparent that RN's husband frequently criticized her parenting abilities and contributed relatively little to activities involving the children or the household. Problem-solving was carried out concerning the issue of increasing his participation in the family and assisting his wife with chores.

Two weeks later, RN had returned home and was staying on her own without panic attacks for long periods during the day. She was still unable to drive the car alone, but she had taken several bus trips to shop and visit friends on her own. Her husband, although not providing much tangible assistance, was more supportive of his wife's efforts. The couple practiced giving and receiving praise for small pleasing everyday activities. In addition, the plan to increase the husband's household participation was reviewed and some adjustments made; for example, RN practiced reminding him to take out the trash bins on Tuesday nights in a noncoercive manner.

A month later, family functioning had returned to normal. Further functional analysis revealed no significant stresses. RN was free of pathological anxiety or depressive symptoms. She continued to take tricyclics. The therapist reviewed the education about the management of anxiety, the problem-solving format, and the value of focusing on small positive behaviors rather than nagging about minor deficiencies.

Two months later, the tricyclics had been gradually reduced and discontinued, and a year later the patient and her husband were free of any major concerns.

In this case, the constructive collaboration of the extended family enabled the effective management of an acute affective disturbance, colored by a mixture of anxiety and depression. The level of distress at the initial presentation to the behavior therapist precluded detailed behavioral assessment of the family unit. Instead, the therapist conducted the assessment on an ongoing basis. The specific components of BFT were used in the management of the acute crisis so that some constructive changes in the marriage could be undertaken that might be expected to have long-term benefits. The problem-solving and communication skills of this couple showed several deficiencies after the acute crisis had been resolved, but none of these deficits appeared to detract from competent functioning or gave rise to concern to either partner. In such a situation, it is tempting for the therapist to impose his or her own concept of a "model couple" on the marriage and to seek changes he or she believes will prove beneficial. We believe it is important to assist families to make those changes that they desire for themselves. In the absence of specific client-centered goals, we prefer not to intervene.

Anorgasmia

Sexual problems are encountered frequently in family practice. There is a tendency to take a prescriptive approach to their treatment, based on the highly successful techniques pioneered by Masters and Johnson (1970). However, sexual difficulties may be signs of wider marital and family distress (see Chapter 3), and their successful management may be achieved only when a comprehensive analysis of family functioning has been conducted.

SF was a 38-year-old woman married to a 40-year-old accountant, RF. They had three children, 13, 15, and 17 years old, all living at home and attending a nearby high school. SF initially presented to her family doctor with concerns about continued use of oral contraceptive tablets. When her doctor discussed alternative methods of contraception, SF told him that she had stopped having sexual intercourse with her husband 6 months ago and had no desire to engage in further sexual activity. She said that she had never experienced an orgasm with any form of sexual stimulation but was not bothered about this.

SF's doctor referred her to a therapist for advice. Individual interviews with husband and wife revealed a conflict of sexual needs. RF preferred sexual intercourse at least two or three times a week. He found his wife physically desirable and fulfilling. He expressed concern that he was unable to excite her to orgasm and fears that her rejection of sexual activity might lead to him fulfilling his sexual needs outside the marriage, although he had not done so and did not wish to.

SF said she had enjoyed premarital sex but lost interest as soon as she married. Her decision to cease engaging in sex was not precipitated by any specific stress or event. SF complained that her husband was always too busy with his work to relax in the evenings with her or the children. He tended to go to bed early, whereas she preferred to stay up late and work on her many interests. She was a talented writer and had published two novels and numerous short stories. She also enjoyed needlework and dress design. Her husband appreciated these activities but had never shown much active interest or involvement with them. Occasionally, SF would wake RF when she came to bed and attempt to discuss some exciting idea with him. RF tended to cut short these discussions and to attempt to initiate sexual contact at these times.

A year earlier SF's father had died. She had been very close to him and continued to miss him greatly. She had found herself often comparing RF to her father in her thoughts and wishing RF could share her interests in the same intimate and rewarding way that her father had done.

Initially, five sessions of therapy were planned. The first step would be to enhance the enjoyment the couple experienced when they spent time together in joint activities—nonsexual at first, moving to sexual contact later. After the first session, they achieved the goal of spending 2 hours relaxing alone, without the children, playing a game of cards. They felt less tense and more cheerful. SF had enjoyed playing with RF and felt that he had loosened up and was less serious and more playful. She had previously found him uptight, obsessional, and always complaining of her messiness about the house. SF enjoyed playing games, including going to parties where she liked to flirt with other men in a fun-filled way. RF disapproved of this behavior, despite realizing that SF never carried her flirtations any further.

The therapist introduced the couple to the sensate focus technique, whereby they were instructed to engage in nongenital sexual "play," focused on touching one another and communicating pleasurable sensations in a mutual fashion. This proved very enjoyable to both partners. Despite instructions not to have intercourse, this had occurred spontaneously during one sensate focus session and both had found it highly enjoyable. SF said that because it was "wrong," she had found it extremely exciting but did not experience orgasm.

At the fourth session, a week later, SF and RF both appeared tense and frustrated. During the week, RF had been very busy with his work. They had spent no time relaxing together in any manner. On one occasion, RF had attempted to initiate sex with SF in his usual manner. She got out of bed and went to the sitting room. RF followed, and they had a discussion. They decided that they must solve the problem of planning sufficient time to spend together in a relaxed manner and went back to bed. During this session, the therapist conducted problem-solving on this issue and gave them several worksheets to use in a similar manner at home.

The final session found the couple happier. They had planned three occasions together during the week. During these times, they had spent time talking about their feelings toward one another and planning their future together. SF found she was able to tell RF when she felt like sex and when she did not. He found this very helpful and was likewise able to communicate his sexual needs in an open, direct manner. They enjoyed sex on two occasions. SF said it had become a game that she enjoyed playing, so she could relax and have fun. She continued to enjoy flirting at parties, but RF was now able to join in the fun in a spontaneous way.

Six months later, further improvement had occurred. Planning time together had become a family ritual, and both partners had become more efficient in their use of time, producing a more relaxed lifestyle. Their sexual contact remained mutually enjoyable, although SF remained anorgasmic.

It has often been said that the high rate of success of the Masters and Johnson clinic in St. Louis owed as much to the holiday environment as to the specific techniques of sexual counseling. The setting in which sexual activity occurs, including both the physical and emotional environment, is an important factor. The value of BFT approaches in the assessment and management of sexual problems is illustrated in this case example. It is worth commenting that this case was a complete success, despite the persisting anorgasmia of the wife. The goal targeted by husband and wife was to reestablish satisfying intimate and sexual contact, *not* to achieve orgasm. Both partners were fully satisfied with the outcome of therapy.

An Infertility Problem

The therapist was asked to consult with JB after she had come to her family doctor's office in a very distressed state. A week earlier she had been admitted to hospital with an ectopic pregnancy. She was 30 years old and had been married to her husband, TB for 7 years. For the previous 5 years, they had been attempting to conceive without success. Three years earlier, they had sought consultation at an infertility clinic. Since that time, almost all their energies had been channelled into achieving conception. No specific abnormality had been found, although JB's older sister had suffered similar infertility problems.

The ectopic pregnancy occurred 10 days after learning of the successful conception and the excitement associated with that event. The ectopic pregnancy and resulting removal of an ovary and fallopian tube came as a crushing blow. This had been compounded by a discussion with their obstetrician who had told them bluntly that their future chances of conception were now minimal. Both JB and TB were extremely angry at the insensitive manner in which the obstetrician had told them this news. They were also angry that throughout this episode, as well as the preceding 3 years, they had received no emotional support from him for their perceived burden.

Individual interviews revealed that husband and wife had both viewed having children as a primary goal in their lives. They were both social workers, but career goals were clearly of secondary consideration. They were very disappointed and frustrated at the loss of hope for parenthood. JB would not consider returning to her work with maladjusted adolescents. TB had recently started a new administrative job and hoped this would enable him to take his mind off his disappointment.

It was apparent that the couple communicated their deep affection to one another and were extremely supportive. However, they tended to avoid discussing difficulties and subsequently did not resolve their problems very efficiently. It was agree that two sessions of crisis-oriented problem-solving would be provided.

A week after the initial assessment, JB was feeling much better; she felt somewhat lethargic but was less tearful and preoccupied. The evening before the session, the Bs had had a long discussion about their future plans. They had not agreed on any specific plans but their mutual communication of feelings had produced considerable relief. During the session, the couple were trained in the use of problem-solving. They dealt with the issue of developing shared leisure interests. They agreed to organize two evenings a week when they would plan joint leisure activities for 2 hours. One evening would be organized by JB, the other by TB. They were left several worksheets to continue problem-solving themselves.

The next week, JB appeared fully recovered from her depressed state. The Bs had carried out their leisure activity plans successfully and felt very pleased and confident in their mutual support. The next day they had an appointment at the infertility clinic. TB was very concerned that they get the obstetrician to answer their many questions in a satisfactory manner. He described the difficulties they had experienced with this doctor on previous consultations. The therapist role-played the consultation with the couple and coached them to assert themselves effectively with the doctor and to carefully prepare their questions. They were instructed to continue using their problem-solving worksheets to work on problems and goals.

JB phoned after the appointment with the obstetrician. She was very distressed, complaining that once again he had been brutally frank in his manner, although answering their questions specifically. The obstetrician told them they had a 1 in 10 chance of another ectopic pregnancy. His only advice was to tell JB to relax. On their arrival home, the Bs sat down and had a problem-solving discussion. They decided that they would have another course of hormone therapy and try to conceive again, despite the discouraging statistics. If they were unsuccessful on this occasion they decided that they would consider adopting a child. They felt that they had dealt with their crisis effectively and would continue to resolve their difficulties on their own. The therapist offered future help at any time the couple requested.

Six months later they were midway through a hormone course, and both were working at satisfactory jobs and enjoying balanced social and leisure activities. They continued to use the structured problem-solving methods regularly with good results.

The stresses associated with health problems are considerable. These are most prominent in persons with chronic persistent or relapsing conditions, but the lack of concern for the psychosocial well-being of people with less serious health problems leads to considerable distress and morbidity that is largely dealt with by the family practitioner. BFT has a place in the efficient management of these stresses, and a few sessions may provide lasting benefits for families who lack major emotional conflicts and have no gross deficiencies in their interpersonal communication skills.

SUMMARY

These case reports typify the application of the BFT approach to the wide range of issues that confront the family practitioner. It is evident that the efficiency of these methods is such that they could be applied readily in this setting. All these cases were treated by a behavior therapist working in collaboration with family doctors and on occasions with community nurses. In several cases, the family doctors worked as cotherapists, and many reported using some aspects of the approach in their everyday practice. Comprehensive training in BFT is beyond the scope of most basic family practitioner training programs. However, several family practitioners have received extensive training in these methods and report considerable benefits from the use of these methods in dealing with family stress.

The question must be posed of whether it is more cost-efficient to provide family practitioners with skilled behavior therapists as collaborators in the primary care setting or to train the practitioners themselves to proficiency in these methods. In the Buckingham Project, we hope to facilitate both these goals (Falloon, Boyd, & McGill, 1984). Each family practice group has a team of skilled behavior therapists (nurses) who are available to see cases with the family doctor on a 24-hour basis. As well as providing specialized therapy within the primary care team, these therapists provide training and supervision for the family practitioner and associated professional staff. This enables early detection and prompt, effective management of conditions such as schizophrenia, major affective disorders, and anxiety states, thus preventing hospital care and chronic morbidity. Marital, sexual, and family problems, including those associated with physical health issues, are also dealt with using a family-based perspective.

Research is currently underway to examine the efficacy of this model of mental health care delivery, which clearly acknowledges the unique health-enhancing capacity of the family unit (Falloon, Wilkinson, Burgess, & McLees, 1987).

REFERENCES

Falloon, I. R. H., Boyd, J. L., & McGill, C. W. (1984). *Family care of schizophrenia*. New York: Guilford Press.

Falloon, I. R. H., Wilkinson, G., Burgess, J., & McLees, S. (1987). Planning, developing and evaluating community-based mental health services for adults. In D. Milne (Ed.), *Evaluating mental health practice*. London: Croom-Helm.

Farina, A., & Holzberg, J. (1968). Interaction patterns of parents and hospitalized sons diagnosed as schizophrenic or non-schizophrenic. *Journal of Abnormal Psychology, 73*, 114–118.

Ferreira, A. J., & Winter, W. D. (1965). Family interaction and decision making. *Archives of General Psychiatry, 13*, 214–223.

Goldstein, M. J., Rodnick, E. H., Jones, J. E., McPherson, S. R., & West, K. L. (1978). Familial precursors of schizophrenia spectrum disorders. In L. C. Wynne, R. L. Cromwell, & S. Matthysse (Eds.), *The nature of schizophrenia*. New York: Wiley.

Hirsch, S. R., & Leff, J. P. (1975). *Abnormalities in the parents of schizophrenics*. London: Oxford University Press.

Jackson, D. D. (1959). Family interaction, family homeostasis and some implications for conjoint family psychotherapy. In J. Masserman (Ed.), *Individual and family dynamics*. New York: Grune & Stratton.

Lask, B., & Matthew, D. (1979). Childhood asthma: A controlled trial of family psychotherapy. *Archives of Disease in Childhood, 54*, 116–119.

Masters, W. H., & Johnson, V. E. (1970). *Human sexual inadequacy*. London: Churchill.

Reiss, D. (1982). *The role of family in institutional rehabilitation of clients with behavioral and physical disabilities*. Final Report, National Institute of Handicapped Research, US Department of Education Grant Number G008003044.

Richardson, H. B. (1948). *Patients have families*. New York: Commonwealth Fund.

17

Recent Advances in Therapy and Prevention

KURT HAHLWEG
Max Planck Institute of Psychiatry, Munich
DONALD H. BAUCOM
University of North Carolina, Chapel Hill
HOWARD MARKMAN
University of Denver

"Marriage is one of the most nearly universal of human institutions. No other touches so intimately the life of practically every member of the earth population. . . . The beginning of marriage is lost in the preliterate past, but in recorded history, everywhere, its problems have enlisted the attention of religionists, moralists, poets, lawmakers, and social reformers. The scientist alone has hesitated, until recently, to make it an object of his professional concern" (Terman, 1938, p. 1). These are the introductory lines in Terman's book in which he describes the results of his questionnaire study with 1133 married couples, the first published psychological study of the determinants of marital happiness. Since then there has been a tremendous increase—a literature explosion, as Gurman and Kniskern (1978) pointed out—in research on marriage, divorce, and especially on marital therapy.

The reasons for this growing scientific interest in marriage and marital problems are manifold; to name just a few:

1. The rate of divorce in most Western countries, as well as in Eastern Europe, has shown a steady increase over the past 20 years (Carter & Glick, 1976). At the moment, about 40% of all marriages in the United States will end in divorce (Hetherington, Cox, & Cox, 1978). The estimated rate for West Germany is about 25% (Duss v. Werdt & Fuchs, 1980). The decision to divorce is often the result of many years of marital distress. Since the divorce rate represents only a portion of the population of couples who experience marital tension, the incidence of marital distress is significantly greater than that of divorce.
2. According to U.S. figures, about one million children per year are involved in the divorce process and in the marital conflict that precedes

and follows it. While we know how severe the negative consequences of divorce are for the children over a time period of two years following the divorce (Hetherington *et al.*, 1978), very little is known about the long-term consequences.

3. The data on family violence is compelling. In a study based on a representative U.S. sample, 12.1% of husbands and 11.6% of wives admitted that they had physically attacked their partner during the last year (Straus, Gelles, & Steinmetz, 1980). Since these figures are certainly conservative, we estimate that the real incidence rate is about 30% regardless of social class. Children are the targets of violence in about 63%–73% of the cases, with 3.6% of those cases resulting in severe, injury-causing child abuse. There is a strong association between family violence and marital conflicts. In high marital conflict families, the violence rate was 43.9% in contrast to only 2.3% in families with a low conflict rate. Straus *et al.* (1980) conclude: "even leaving aside the psychological damage that such violence can produce, just the danger to physical health implied by these rates is staggering. If any other crime or risk to physical well-being involved almost two million wives and two million husbands per year, . . . a national emergency would probably be declared" (pp. 49–50).

4. The negative impact of marital distress and divorce can only be estimated. About 50%–60% of patients seeking help in psychiatric services report their marital situation as the primary complaint (Overall, Henry, & Woodward, 1974). After reviewing the available evidence, Bloom, Asher, and White (1978) concluded that marital disruption is associated with an increased risk of psychopathology in the partners. Recently, Vaughn and Leff (1976), Hooley (1985), and Hooley, Orley, and Teasdale (in press) reported that the level of criticism expressed by the partner about hospitalized depressed spouse, during an interview without the patient present, significantly predicted relapse over a nine month period. Depressed spouses returning to a highly critical partner (high on expressed emotion [EE]) relapsed in about 60% of the cases while those who returned to a noncritical partner relapsed only in about 10% of the cases (Hooley *et al.*, in press; Vaughn & Leff, 1976).

When looking at these examples of how marital conflict influences the life of so many, the growing need for effective methods either to prevent or to treat marital problems is understandable. Perhaps as a consequence, Behavioral Marital Therapy (BMT) has developed rapidly over the past 15 years and is currently the most thoroughly investigated approach within the marital therapy field. Starting from a focus on operant conditioning (Stuart, 1969), it has broadened its theoretical background and now consists of a wide range of treatment techniques including measures to increase the reciprocal exchange of positive reinforcement in the couple, communication and problem-solving training, cognitive components, and strategic interventions (see Epstein & Williams, 1981; Jacobson & Margolin, 1979; Weiss, 1980). With a time lag of approximately 10 years, interest in the prevention of marital distress from a behavioral point of view has grown, producing an impressive but yet small body of evidence for its effectiveness (Markman, Floyd, Stanley, & Jamieson, 1984).

In this chapter we will describe the theoretical assumptions underlying the BMT approach, characterize the techniques used in BMT and in prevention programs, report on their empirical status, and discuss the future developments in this field.

THEORETICAL UNDERPINNINGS OF BMT AND RELATED PREVENTION PROGRAMS

The theoretical formulations of this approach are based on assumptions from Social Exchange Theory (Thibaut & Kelly, 1959) and Social Learning Theory (Bandura, 1974). Within marriage as well as other intimate relationships, each partner has certain ways he or she would prefer to be treated. That is, most spouses prefer to be shown respect through particular behaviors, to be loved and cared for in certain ways, and to be helped with tasks in a particular manner. Whereas people may choose their spouses in part because they initially behave toward them in these preferred ways, many if not all married persons attempt to alter their spouse's behavior such that the behavior more closely aligns with these preferences. To accomplish this goal, spouses rely upon operant techniques to alter their partners' behavior. That is, married partners reward and punish each other for engaging in or not engaging in specific behaviors.

However, distressed couples appear to encounter difficulty in at least two ways when attempting to alter partners' behaviors. First, many distressed spouses use very ineffective behavior change strategies or actually apply operant procedures in opposition to their desired goals. That is, some spouses reward behavior which they would like to see eliminated, or they punish behavior which they would prefer to maintain or increase. Second, distressed spouses often become involved in a "coercion process" in which both spouses use aversive tactics rather than more positive approaches to induce desired changes in their partner, that is, heavy reliance on punishment and extinction. Whereas these aversive strategies might be successful in achieving the immediately desired effect, the long-term effects of such strategies are frequently destructive to the relationship. For example, physically abusing a partner during an argument can quite effectively silence the partner's opposing point of view immediately, but such behavior is likely to induce fear, anger, and mistrust in the partner.

This high rate of aversive behaviors among distressed couples is important because, compared to the frequency of positive marital events, the frequency of negative marital events appears to be more highly predictive of daily relationship satisfaction (Jacobson, Waldron, & Moore, 1980; Weiss, 1980). Baucom (1987) has referred to this as the "splinter phenomenon": When one has a painful splinter in the finger, it is hard to focus on how well the rest of the body feels. Therefore the behavioral marital therapist must not only attempt to increase the rate of positive interactions between two partners but must also give rapid attention to decreasing negative interactions.

The rate of each person's positive and negative behaviors also appears to be related to the partner's behavior. In fact the concept of reciprocity is central to understanding and treating couples from a behavioral perspective. Reciprocity can be viewed as the behavioral version of the Golden Rule, "You tend to do unto others as they do unto you." More precisely, positive reciprocity implies that the probability of a positive behavior from one spouse increases following the occurrence of positive behavior from the partner; negative reciprocity is defined similarly (Gottman, 1979; Gottman, Markman, & Notarius, 1977). Reciprocity has been explored almost totally within the context of couples' communication. The findings indicate that both distressed and nondistressed couples exhibit positive and negative reciprocity, although distressed couples exhibit higher levels of negative reciprocity than do nondistressed couples (Billings, 1979; Gottman *et al.*, 1976; Margolin & Wampold, 1981; Rausch, Barry, Hertel, & Swain, 1974).

The existence of reciprocity is important from a treatment perspective. First, since many distressed couples become involved in negative reciprocal interactions which tend to spiral in intensity (Gottman, 1979: Gottman *et al.*, 1977), the therapist will attempt to break this sequence early in order to halt the rapidly escalating negative behaviors. Second, since each partner's behavior influences the other's behavior, this provides a means for each person to take control and responsibility for improving the relationship. Rather than waiting for the other person to change to improve the marriage, each person is challenged to behave more positively and less negatively himself or herself, because that is one of the most effective ways to alter the spouse's behavior. Thus BMT views the couple as a system in which behavior of one member affects the other.

Along with other theoretical approaches, BMT lays major emphasis on the couple's communication. This is not surprising since communication failure is the most frequent complaint of couples requesting marital therapy (Geiss & O'Leary, in press). Behaviorists view communication as important for at least two reasons. First, verbal and nonverbal communication is one of the major strategies which adults use to reward and punish each other. Thus many conversations become aversive and spouses avoid each other after they insult, belittle, and criticize each other. Second, communication is important because it is one means through which couples attempt to resolve noncommunication areas of conflict. Since many distressed couples have major difficulties in this area, training in problem-solving skills has become a major focus of BMT.

Up to this point, discussion has focused on the importance of behavior *per se*. Whereas the role of couple's cognitions and emotions toward the marriage have never been ignored within BMT, early BMT treatment approaches did de-emphasize these domains. The logic was that behavior, cognitions, and emotions are interrelated, and if one can be successful in altering behavior, then corresponding changes will occur in the couple's thought and feelings about each other. Although clinical observation supports that this at times does occur, researchers began to question whether this was the most effective way to address couples' cognitions and emotions. Consequently during the 1980s there has been an increasing emphasis on cognitive restructuring with couples. In particular BMT has begun to incorporate treatment procedures which focus on faulty attributions or explanations which couples provide for their marital events. Without focusing the couples' attention on attributions, the therapist found that couples at times minimize the importance of specific behavior changes which occur during therapy, attributing them solely to the therapist's directives. Also increasing attention has been given to spouses' high expectations of what a marriage should be. Such a focus has been important because difficulties in reaching solutions to problems or discontent with a partner's behavior are at times related to unrealistic expectations of what a partner should do and what a marriage should provide. In addition, cognitive procedures have been developed to assist the couple in maintaining behavioral changes when BMT procedures encounter difficulty. Therefore direct attempts to alter couples' cognitions have increased because some distorted cognitions have been shown to be related to marital discord (Baucom, Wheeler, & Bell, 1984; Eidelson & Epstein, 1982; Fincham & O'Leary, 1983; Jacobson, McDonald, Follette, & Berley, 1985; Kelley, 1979; Madden & Janoff-Bulman, 1981) as well as seemingly interfering with the behavioral changes sought in BMT. At present, however, there is only minimal data available indicating the effectiveness of these cognitive restructuring procedures.

The role of couples' emotions is also gaining increased attention within BMT. Whereas BMT has always hoped that couples would leave treatment happier and less angry or depressed, no interventions have been developed which directly alter the couples' emotions. That is, BMT traditionally has attempted to promote affective changes through decreasing negative behavior and increasing positive behavior which the couple defines as important; thus the behavior–emotion link has been maintained as the manner through which changes in affective *experience* occur.

However the *expression* of emotion has received more emphasis recently. Although communication training has always been central to BMT, overall BMT has, at least in the United States, focused on communication essential for problem-solving with a de-emphasis on communicating emotions. Since expressing one's feelings can either be a rewarding or a punishing experience for both the speaker and listener, helping couples master this type of communication requires no extension of the theoretical base of BMT. Recently BMT investigators have borrowed from treatment strategies such as those developed by Guerney (1977) to assist couples in their expression of both positive and negative emotions (Baucom, 1985; Hahlweg, Schindler, & Revenstorf, 1982).

BMT INTERVENTION STRATEGIES

Based on the above theoretical assumptions, BMT intervention strategies typically include four basic components: behavioral assessment of marital distress, techniques to increase the reciprocal exchange of positive reinforcement in the couple, communication skills training, and problem-solving techniques including specifying, negotiating, and contracting (e.g., Jacobson, 1981; Jacobson & Margolin, 1979; Lester, Beckham, & Baucom, 1980; Stuart, 1976; Weiss, Hops, & Patterson, 1973). In the following these components will be explained in more detail relying on a treatment program developed in West Germany (Hahlweg, Revenstorf, & Schindler, 1982; Hahlweg, Schindler, & Revenstorf, 1982). When there is great variability in approaches, alternative treatment strategies used in the U.S. are described.

Behavioral assessment. A unique feature of the BMT approach lies in its emphasis on behavioral analysis of the determinants of a couples' marital distress. Extensive interviewing, self-report questionnaires and behavioral observation by spouses or trained observers are used. Since a description of these instruments is beyond the scope of this chapter, the interested reader is referred to comprehensive reviews (e.g., Jacobson, Elwood, & Dallas, 1981; Weiss & Margolin, 1977) or books devoted to behavioral marital assessment (e.g., Filsinger & Lewis, 1981; Filsinger, 1983).

Establishing Positive Reciprocity. To enhance partner and self-observation with regard to positive verbal and nonverbal behaviors, a homework assignment developed by Liberman, Wheeler, & Sanders (1976, p. 387) is used in the beginning of the treatment: "Catch your spouse doing/saying something nice and let him/her know about it." From the following week onward couples are asked to perform "caring days" (Stuart, 1976). In this procedure each partner chooses one day of the week on which he or she is asked to emit caring behaviors (for example, doing the dishes, putting the children to bed, listening to partner problems, paying partner a compliment, smiling at him or her) independently of the actions of the spouse. Each partner records the planned and received caring behaviors. At the beginning of each treatment session the course of the "Caring days" is reviewed.

Communication Skills Training. Communication training can involve a number of specific skills, and behavioral marital therapists differ in which skills they emphasize with couples. As alluded to earlier, one area of emphasis is the expression of emotion. The two approaches developed for handling negative feelings are somewhat analogous to "controlled drinking" versus "abstinence" within the alcoholism treatment literature. Clearly, distressed spouses often have very negative feelings about many problem areas. The "controlled" approach teaches the couples to express these emotions adaptively and in moderation. Once these emotions are expressed, the couple is ready to seek a solution to the problem. The "abstinence" approach has assumed that due to the high degree of negative reciprocity and escalation in distressed couples, having them focus on expressing negative feelings about a problem area at the beginning of problem-solving can result in arguments and little desire to resolve a problem. Thus this later approach asks the couple to remain much more cognitive and in general to put negative feelings "aside" while attempting to solve problems. Whereas some expression of emotion is essential in stating a problem and preferred solutions, there is great variability in the extent to which couples are taught to focus upon and express emotions during communication skills training.

In the treatment program developed by Hahlweg *et al.* (1982a), couples were taught to express their emotions. In this component, specific speaker and listener skills are trained based on Guerney's (1977) intervention model.

Speaker skills:

1. Use I-messages (express your *own* feelings about the topic).
2. Describe specific situations (speak of specific situations in order to avoid generalizations like "always" or "never").
3. Describe specific behaviors (speak of specific behaviors in specific situations in order to avoid labels like "lazy" or "cold").
4. Stick to the "Here and Now" (discuss one problem at a time in order to avoid sidetracking).

Listener skills:

1. Listen actively (indicate by your nonverbal behavior that you are listening to your partner by body posture, facial expression, and assenting).
2. Paraphrase (summarize your partner's remarks and check their accuracy).
3. Ask open questions (when you do not understand your partner's feelings/thoughts).

4. Give positive feedback (for appropriate responses by your partner).
5. Give feedback of your own feelings (when hurt by a statement of your partner, respond with an I-message).

The basic assumption is that partners who employ the communication skills in turn should avoid blaming, criticizing and sidetracking, increase their mutual understanding, and generate specific solutions to their problems. The core skills are reciprocal *self-disclosure* of feelings, attitudes, and thoughts either about a specific problem in the relationship or about a general point of discussion, and *accepting* (not necessarily agreeing to) the speaker's utterances.

Until recently, BMT outcome studies in the U.S. have not emphasized expressing emotions (e.g., Baucom, 1982; Jacobson, 1977, 1978; Mehlman, Baucom, & Anderson, 1983). Instead a wide range of communication skills were taught to assist in problem-solving. Rather than deciding *a priori* what communication skills would be taught to every couple, each couple was taught specific skills depending upon that couple's communication weaknesses and strengths. Thus couples are taught to avoid the following communication difficulties which apply: interrupting; deciding who is at fault; trying to establish the truth; getting sidetracked onto other problems; dealing with multiple facets of a problem at one time; "guilting" the partner into a solution; giving ultimatums; using the terms "always" and "never"; using trait names; mind-reading; and giving discrepant verbal and nonverbal communication. In addition spouses are encouraged to make eye contact; praise the partner whenever possible; speak in terms of specifics rather than generalities; and state what one wants or prefers (Lester, Beckham, & Baucom, 1980).

Problem-Solving Training. To help the couple solve their own problems a structured discussion scheme can be used:

In *Step 1* both partners convey their views of the conflict, disclosing their feelings, thoughts, and attitudes toward the problem, and giving mutual feedback. In *Step 2* each partner describes his needs and wishes regarding the problem. In *Step 3* the couple generates specific solutions for the problem in a brainstorming fashion. In *Step 4* a balanced agreement is negotiated and an informal "good-faith" contract can be written.

In addition to these frequently used strategies, more formal contracts have been employed at times. One way to extend the above problem-solving approach into a contract is to have each spouse state a problem which involves a desired behavior change from the partner. Next the couple uses the above problem-solving steps to resolve each problem. Finally the two solutions are woven together into a *quid pro quo* contract of the nature: if the husband makes his agreed-upon behavior change, the wife changes her behavior as specified; and if the wife changes her behavior, the husband changes his behavior as specified. However, if either person does not comply with the agreed-upon behavior change, then the partner is not obligated to change his or her behavior.

STRATEGIES TO PREVENT MARITAL DISTRESS

As noted above, data from the United States and Europe clearly indicate that marital distress and its sequelae produce enormous social costs. The traditional response to marital distress by mental health specialists has been treatment for distressed couples. Treatment strategies from a behavioral perspective have already been described. An additional response to the problems of marital distress is to offer prevention programs to couples before problems develop and/or intensify.

Although interest in preventing marital distress has increased, preventive intervention programs for couples still receive inadequate attention from marital researchers and marital clinicians alike. Instead, religious organizations take the primary responsibility for offering prevention programs to couples. These programs (1) focus on current and future religious practices; (2) highlight areas of agreement and disagreement concerning intimate relationships and expectations for marriage; and (3) enlighten couples concerning current and potential personality differences. Then guidance is provided about current and future problems unique to each couple (Markman, Floyd, Stanley, & Lewis, 1985). It is interesting to note that the content of these traditional premarital counseling programs is similar to the same areas explored by early (and, in some cases, contemporary) marital researchers who focused on demographic and personality variables as predictors of marital success.

In contrast, prevention programs from a BMT perspective focus on issues relevant to all marriages (Markman *et al.*, 1985). Consistent with BMT, these programs attempt to modify relationship beliefs and behaviors that theory and research suggest are predictive of the development of marital conflict and dissatisfaction. The personality and demographic factors that are the focus of traditional premarital counseling programs and traditional research have not been found to account for future levels of marital satisfaction. Instead, it is the quality of the couple's communication and problem-solving skills that seems to be most related to future satisfaction or dissatisfaction.

Prevention programs must be distinguished from both treatment and relationship enhancement programs. In contrast to treatment, prevention programs are future oriented and do not directly focus on current problems. While prevention programs for couples clearly attempt to enhance current relationship quality, the overarching objective is to maintain already high levels of functioning and to prevent problems from developing or intensifying in the future. Prevention programs may include interventions that may be helpful in the future but are of little value currently. Essentially, successful relationship enhancement and enrichment programs achieve preventative goals for the subset of participating couples who are happy, and in turn we consider these programs to be a subset of prevention programs (Markman *et al.*, 1985). We will focus on prevention programs developed for premarital couples rather than postmarital couples for several reasons. One, couples who participate in marital relationship enhancement programs are likely to be experiencing relationship problems and dissatisfaction (Powell & Womper, 1982; Doherty & Walker, 1982). Second, despite some claims to the contrary (Gurman, 1980; Druckman, Fournier, Robinson, & Olson, 1980), we believe that the premarital, transition-to-marriage period is a time when couples are unusually receptive to intervention and are clearly happy (otherwise they wouldn't be planning marriage).

Implicitly or explicitly (Markman *et al.*, 1985) prevention programs for couples are based on family development theories that maintain that the degree of resolution in early family transition periods (transition to marriage, transition to parenthood) sets the stage for future relationship functioning (e.g., Carter & McGoldrick, 1980; Duvall, 1977). Thus, these transitions may be viewed as critical periods for relationship growth and development that provide an important opportunity for preventative interventions. Moreover, prevention and crisis intervention theorists suggest that people are more open to intervention during these periods (Bloom, 1977). Similarly, in the couples area, research has suggested that couples' interaction patterns are in transition during the premarital stage and stable afterward (Markman, 1981; Raush, Barry, Hertel, & Swain, 1974). Until recently most prevention programs for couples have been based on clinical intuition and common sense. However, contemporary programs have emerged that place prevention in the context of ongoing research and of treatment programs from a cognitive–behavioral perspective or consistent with this perspective. These programs include the Minnesota Couples Communication Program, Guerney's Relationship Enhancement Program, and the Premarital Relationship Enhancement Program (PREP). For all three of these major programs the focus is on modifying the couples' communication and/or problem-solving skills and in some cases on modifying relationship beliefs and expectations. The emphasis on modifying the couples' interaction is consistent with research indicating that this functional interaction pattern *preceeds* the development of marital problems and dissatisfaction and that these problems are somewhat independent of the couples' premarital level of satisfaction (Markman, 1979; 1984). Since communication deficits may be partially related to marital distress, young couples can clearly benefit from training skills taught in BMT programs. Thus, the major prevention strategy from a behavioral perspective is to use the

BMT techniques described above in order to enhance couples' current level of communication and problem-solving skills, and more importantly to help couples learn how to "engage these skills to deal with problems in the future." Techniques to achieve these goals are described in detail in Guerney (1977), Miller, Nunally, & Wackman (1975) and Markman *et al.* (1984).

THE EFFECTIVENESS OF BMT IN ALLEVIATING MARITAL DISTRESS

Since its beginning, the empirical status of BMT has been reviewed excellently by different authors (e.g., Baucom & Hoffman, 1986; Jacobson & Margolin, 1979; Margolin & Christensen, 1981) who conclude that BMT seems to be superior to nontreatment and nonspecific control groups and that the treatment effects are stable over time. However, Jacobson (1981) was careful to point out that "definite evidence regarding the effectiveness of BMT awaits the outcome of future research" (p. 587). Since 1981 a number of controlled outcome studies, especially in Europe, have been published which were not included in the former reviews. Therefore another review on the effectiveness of BMT seems justified. There are at least three different ways to conduct a review of multiple oucome studies:

1. Narrative reviews. After each study has been narratively described and criticized, the findings are implicitly summed up (e.g., Jacobson & Margolin, 1979).
2. "Box score" approach. The number of studies, or significance tests, are calculated in which one treatment or control group is significantly better or worse than another (e.g., Gurman & Kniskern, 1978).
3. Statistical meta-analysis. The so-called "effect-size" method was introduced by Smith and Glass in their 1977 review of the effectiveness of psychotherapy in general. They measured the magnitude of effect of any given therapy by following the formula: $ES = (ME - MCG) / SDCG$. The "effect-size" (ES) is therefore defined as the mean difference between the treated (ME) and nontreated (MCG) subjects after therapy (at posttest) divided by the standard deviation of the control group (SDCG).

In a recent paper by Hahlweg and Markman (in press) the ES approach was employed to review the empirical status of BMT. Included in this meta-analysis were all of the published treatment outcome studies in which some form of BMT was compared to a control group. To be included, the studies must have provided sufficient data to enable the calculation or estimation of effect sizes as described by Smith, Glass, and Miller (1980).

Using these criteria, 17 studies were included in the analysis (for a list of these studies see Hahlweg & Markman [in press]).

In eight studies BMT was compared only to a control group; in five studies the effectiveness of different BMT components was analyzed, and in four studies BMT was compared to other approaches such as Communication Skills Training, Systems Theory, or Interpretative Therapy.

Overall, 613 couples were included in the 17 studies. Four-hundred and twenty were treated either with BMT or another approach, and 193 served as control couples. Subjects were predominantly middle-class with a mean age of about 32 years, and had been married for approximately 7.5 years, with an estimated 70% of the couples having had at least one child. In terms of severity, couples were at least moderately distressed with an average prescore on the Marital Adjustment Scale (MAS; Locke & Wallace, 1959) or Dyadic Adjustment Score (DAS; Spanier, 1976) of 82, a score which is considered an indication of marital distress (Gottman *et al.*, 1976).

The internal validity of the studies defined in terms of random assignment and experimental mortality rates (Campbell & Stanley, 1966) was impressive. Eighty-eight percent of the clients were allocated randomly to the experimental conditions and the attrition rate was rather low (5.7%). When both criteria are combined, 77% of the studies can be judged as having a high internal validity.

There were 50 therapists involved in the outcome studies, with an average of three per study. The therapists had a rather low level of clinical experience, consisting of between 1 and 2 years of graduate psychology work. The mean length of treatment was 10.9 sessions, with the average session lasting an average of 75 minutes. When comparing the older studies (published before 1980) with the more recent ones (published since 1980), the mean duration differed significantly (8 versus 13 sessions). Thus, there appears to be a definite trend to prolong the treatment. This is probably due to the fact that an increasing number of clinicians and researchers recognize that BMT should be applied in a multi-component but more time-consuming modality in order to produce clinically significant changes and stabilize treatment gains.

Outcome of BMT

BMT versus control. The 17 studies yielded 81 effect-sizes (i.e., outcome measures). There was an average of 4.8 outcome measures per study, which demonstrates researchers' efforts to assess the effect of therapy in a multidimensional way. The effect-sizes per study were averaged, resulting in a mean ES of 0.95 for 17 studies. This means, in terms of the Smith and Glass interpretation, that the average person who had received BMT was better off at the end of treatment than 83% of the people who had received either no treatment or a placebo treatment. Rosenthal (1983) points out that the interpretation of the ES in this way is perhaps difficult to understand. He proposes a more transparent interpretation: the binomial effect size display (BESD) which displays the change in success or improvement attributable to the treatment procedure. In terms of BMT, the chances of improving for control couples is 28%, while the chances of improving for experimental couples is 72%.

Cross-cultural comparison. Seven studies were conducted in Europe and ten in the United States. The meta-analyses were performed separately for Europe and the United States, resulting in ES measurements of 0.81 and 1.05, respectively. This difference was not found to be significant. Thus, the United States results replicate the European results, and *vice versa*, providing strong support for the cross-cultural generalizability of the results of BMT.

BMT versus different control groups. Four studies included a nonspecific or placebo control group while fourteen studies compared BMT to a nontreatment control group. The comparison with the nontreatment controls yielded an ES of 1.03, while the comparison with the nonspecific (placebo) controls resulted in an ES of 0.63. Due to the small N, the difference between both effect-sizes were significant only on the 10% level. However, these data do underscore the need to examine the type of control group used when evaluating therapeutic effectiveness.

Self-report versus observational measure. Self-report data is regarded as being more prone to distortion than measures resulting from direct observation (Margolin & Weiss, 1978). Ten studies used observational measures, while all studies used self-report measures. Computing the ES for self-report and observational measures independently resulted in very similar ESs: 0.99 and 0.97, respectively. This result challenges the continued use of costly observational measures providing that one is mainly interested in measuring global improvement in various areas of marital functioning for which self-report instruments are available.

Different BMT approaches. BMT is not a unitary approach and one can differentiate between two major forms. The first approach is a generically labeled behavior exchange (BE) which is designed to increase the frequency of positive behaviors in the marital relationship. Much of the treatment is focused on instigating positive changes in the natural environment. Communication Skills Training (CT) and Problem-Solving Training (PST) are only briefly included, if at all. The other approach is a combination of CT, PST, and BE, and is far more process-oriented in teaching the couple interactive skills during the therapy sessions (Jacobson, 1984). Six studies used a BE approach, while thirteen studies used a combination of CT,

PST, and BE. The ES for the two approaches were nonsignificant (0.78 and 1.00, respectively).

Older versus recent studies. A reduction in treatment effectiveness has often been reported when attempting replication of early results or introduction of new treatment methods into the general clinical practice (Shapiro & Morris, 1978). This reduction has often been interpreted as the result of lowered optimism on the side of new experimenters/clinicians. Comparison of the older studies (published before 1980) with the more recent ones (published from 1980 on) resulted in effect sizes of 1.13 and 0.82, respectively. While this difference is not significant, perhaps the latter ES should be used as a more realistic estimate of BMT's effectiveness.

Stability of treatment gains. Eight studies had follow-ups between 3 and 6 months after therapy, while five studies had follow-ups between 9 and 12 months after therapy. When calculating the respective ESs, we could find no decrease in ES occurred from the posttest period to the different follow-ups. Therefore it seems that BMT produces long-lasting stable effects for those couples who *remain together*. The rate of *separations/divorces* after BMT is difficult to evaluate since many studies do not report data on this topic. However, looking at the published data it seems that about 10%–15% of couples separate/divorce after BMT (Hahlweg, Revenstorf, & Schindler, 1982a).

Clinical significance. Statistical significance is not the only issue of importance, and can certainly be very misleading when the achieved treatment gains are statistically significant but irrelevant to the couples' everyday life. One way to assess the clinical relevance of the changes in the couples' behaviors is to compare the posttest means with normative data (e.g., MAS and DAS scores of greater than 100 which are generally viewed as indicative of marital adjustment [Gottman *et al.*, 1976; Markman, 1979]). Ten studies provided sufficient data to calculate such normative effect-sizes resulting in an ES of 0.13. This small ES indicates that a substantive amount of couples after BMT are still describing their relationships as unsatisfying and distressful. In a recent re-analysis of four controlled outcome studies using stringent criteria for clinical significance Jacobson *et al.* (1984) found that the mean rate of clinically improved couples was about 55%. This result corroborates the finding based on the ES method.

BMT versus other approaches. In four studies BMT was compared to other approaches such as communication skills training, systems theory, and interpretative therapy. Separate calculations resulted in comparable effect sizes after therapy: 0.88 for BMT and 0.83 for "other". However, when calculating the ES for follow-up data (range: 3 to 9 months) the results yielded effect sizes of 0.98 for BMT and 0.72 for "other". Although not tested for significance due to the small N, these findings may support the notion that the results of BMT may be more stable than those of other approaches.

Four other important issues, namely those of the effectiveness of cotherapist treatment, the efficacy of BMT group therapy, the prediction of treatment outcome, and the effect of BMT on couples' communication and problem-solving skills, have been investigated only rarely. Therefore the application of the ES method is not appropriate. In the following the respective results will be discussed narratively.

Relative effectiveness of cotherapists versus single therapist. Many writers have extolled the virtues of cotherapy when treating couples. An obvious disadvantage of cotherapy, however, is the cost of additional therapist time required to treat a couple. Only if couples benefit more from treatment by cotherapists than by individual therapists can cotherapy be recommended. In a controlled outcome study by Mehlman, Baucom, and Anderson (1983), this issue was investigated for BMT. The findings indicate that a single therapist is as effective as cotherapists. This result is in line with findings from sex therapy, which also show no differences (Arentewicz & Schmidt, 1980).

BMT in a conjoint or conjoint group modality. BMT is predominantly applied in a conjoint modality (one couple is treated by one therapist). Given the growing need for marital therapy, it seems worthwhile to experiment with more cost-effective modes of delivery, namely a conjoint group approach (two therapists treating three or four couples in a group). There are a number of possible advantages in delivering BMT in groups (Liberman, Wheeler, & Sanders, 1976): (1) group members provide a wide variety of models for each other in demonstrating alternative ways of communication or problem-solving; (2) feedback and positive reinforcement can be more powerful coming from peers than from a therapist; (3) seeing fellow couples progress helps to maintain positive expectations; and (4) group cohesion may improve therapeutic outcome.

In two studies (Bennun, 1985; Revenstorf, Schindler, & Hahlweg, 1983) the effectiveness of a conjoint and a conjoint group BMT treatment were compared, showing no significant differences between the two modalities. However, Revenstorf *et al.* (1983) pointed out that from a clinical point of view a conjoint group treatment cannot be recommended without some qualifying remarks:

> If the couples are more or less equally improving, group treatment works well and is very beneficial for the participants because of the range of different models for problemsolving and the exchange of positive behaviors. But given that one or two couples are not or only mildly improving, group treatment can be a very difficult task for the therapist and may restrict the possible range of improvement for the rest of the group members. With such a constellation

> the sessions may last longer than the planned 2.5 hours, due to measures in order to increase group cohesion and cooperation.
>
> The group treatment therefore may not be cost-effective, at least not with two therapists (two therapists × four couples × 2.5 hours duration of session = 50 minutes per couple). If, however, a student (preferably of the opposite sex) is available as a cotherapist in a training situation, group therapy is worthwhile to consider. In general, the conjoint treatment seems to be the more conservative approach especially for the more "difficult" couples. It is our impression that the conjoint treatment leads more rapidly to the core problems of the couple, whereas the group treatment is more profitable with respect to the learning of positive behaviors by modeling and imitation. Moreover for many people, groups are attractive as a social event. So, largely, the choice of group treatment appears to be a matter of taste. (pp. 622–623)

Prediction of outcome in BMT. In spite of the established efficacy of BMT there is the need to refine the treatment strategies. One essential step along this line is to identify those couples (or individuals) who will not respond favorably to the treatment or will not maintain the achieved treatment gains over time. Results from prediction studies are not univocal. Crowe (1978) reported that couples referred from their general practitioner did significantly better than those referred by psychiatrists. In addition, sex of the referred showed a weak correlation with outcome: those situations where the husband was referred turned out a little bit better than those where the wife was referred. O'Leary and Turkewitz (1981) reported a negative correlation between age and duration of marriage and outcome. Baucom and Mehlman (1984) compared different models of combining husbands' and wives' outcome measures in order to predict marital status following BMT. The most consistent single predictors were self-reported marital satisfaction (MAT) and positive communication (negatively correlated!) as measured by the Marital Interaction Coding System (MICS; Hops, Wills, Patterson, & Weiss, 1972).

The importance of the quality of the couples' emotional affection for predicting outcome was stressed by Hahlweg, Schindler, Revenstorf, and Brengelmann (1984). In contrast to clinical lore, the amount of negative conflict behavior—that is, how often and how aversively the partners quarrel and how many unresolved problems they experience in their relationship prior to therapy—was not a useful predictor for long-term therapy outcome. Instead, the loss of intimacy or a low emotional–affective quality of the relationship was indicative of therapy failure. In Bennun's study (1985) problems of care and nonsexual affection were not changed by BMT. His results support the aforementioned findings by Hahlweg *et al.* (1984c), who concluded that clients with a combination of considering divorce, being longer married, having sexual intercourse very seldom, and experiencing their marriage as not affectional will be difficult to treat and will not profit much from BMT as it is currently practiced.

EFFECTS OF BMT ON COUPLES' COMMUNICATION AND PROBLEM-SOLVING SKILLS

Common complaints presented by couples who seek BMT are lack of communication and inability to solve problems. Accordingly, communication training (CT) and problem-solving training (PST) are integral parts of BMT. This focus on communication is due not only to the obvious needs of the clients but also follows directly from the theoretical assumptions borrowed from Social Learning Theory (Bandura, 1974). This model suggests that "a critical skill in determining a successful marriage is skill in conflict resolution" (Jacobson, 1981, pp. 559–560). As described above, there seems to be a general agreement on which specific communication skills should be taught to the couple. However, only recently Hahlweg, Revenstorf, and Schindler (1984) presented empirical evidence that couples successfully treated with BMT do acquire these skills and that the changes in their communication patterns are significant from a clinical point of view.

Three different samples were used in the study: 29 couples treated by BMT, 14 waiting-list control couples (WL), and 12 nondistressed couples (ND). Each couple was asked to engage in discussions about problems in their relationship which were videotaped: BMT and waiting-list couples twice (before and after treatment or waiting time), ND couples only once. Each discussion lasted for about 10 minutes and was later analyzed by trained observers using a behavioral coding system (Kategoriensystem für partnerschaftliche Interaktion* [KPI]; Hahlweg *et al.*, 1984b) designed to assess empirically the aforementioned speaker and listener skills. The KPI consists of ten verbal categories: (1) Self-disclosure (SD), (2) Positive solution (PS), (3) Acceptance of other (AC), (4) Agreement (AG), (5) Problem description (PD), (6) Metacommunication (MC), (7) Criticism (CRI), (8) Negative solution (NS), (9) Justification (JU), and (10) Disagreement (DG). In order to apply sequential analysis these categories can be collapsed into the following summary codes: SD plus PS = Direct Expression (DE), AC plus AG = Acceptance and Agreement (AA), PD plus MC = Neutral Information (NI), CRI plus NS = Critique (CR), and JU plus DG = Refusal (RF).

All the foregoing content categories receive a nonverbal rating (see Gottman, 1979; Notarius & Markman, 1981). In a hierarchical order, the facial cues of the speaker or listener are first evaluated as positive, neutral, or negative. If the coder is unable to code the utterance as positive or negative, the coder scans the voice-tone cues. If the coder is still unable to code the utterance as positive or negative, the body cues are scanned and then the appropriate rating is applied.

*Interacting Coding System

The *reliability* of the KPI codes was investigated in several studies (Hahlweg, Schindler, & Revenstorf, 1984; Hooley, 1985) showing that the interobserver reliability is acceptable for frequency and sequential analysis.

In Figure 17-1 the results of the *frequency analysis* are shown. An analysis of covariance revealed significant differences between BMT and WL couples after treatment or waiting time for all positive and negative variables in the predicted direction, but no differences for the neutral variables.

To evaluate the clinical significance of these results, the posttest means of the BMT couples were compared with the means of the ND couples. As evident from Figure 17-1, the treated couples almost reached or slightly exceeded the level of the ND couples in all verbal summary codes. "Thus not only did BMT significantly improve verbal skills relative to no treatment but the verbal behavior resulting from BMT was also essentially indistinguishable from that of ND couples" (Hahlweg, Revenstorf, & Schindler, 1984, p. 557).

With regard to the nonverbal behavior, treated couples did not reach the level of the ND couples despite the fact that the BMT couples nearly doubled the amount of positive reactions and decreased the amount of negative reactions by almost 50%. This is due to the very high base rate of positive responses in the ND couples.

When using base rate (frequency) analysis, one can only conclude that the treated couples showed significantly more positive and less negative behaviors than the control couples. This is a satisfying result in itself, but

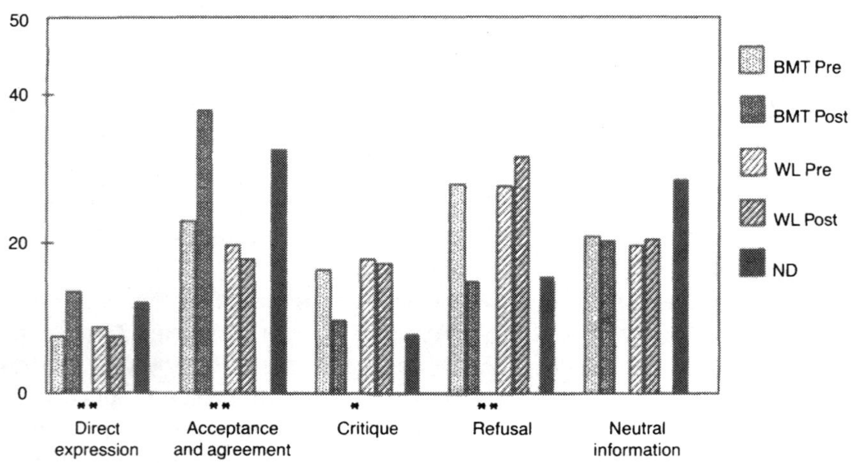

Figure 17-1 Means of KPI codes for BMT, WL, and ND couples.
Note. BMT = Behavioral Marital Therapy; WL = Waiting List; ND = Nondistressed.

it does not answer the more interesting question: do the partners also learn to respond adequately to the stimuli presented by their spouses; that is, do they change their interaction patterns? To answer this question sequential analysis of the interaction sequences is necessary.

A discussion of the various methods of sequential analysis is beyond the scope of this chapter (see, e.g., Gottman & Bakeman, 1979; Revenstorf, Hahlweg, Schindler, & Vogel, 1984). In this study the so-called "K-Gramm" method was used (Revenstorf *et al.*, 1984). The following behavior sequence demonstrates how the data are analyzed with the K-Gramm method. The first letter indicates the person: husband (H) or wife (W). The second and third letters represent the summary code. The observed behavior sequence was as follows: (1) HDE, (2) WAA, (3) HNI, (4) WCR, (5) HRF, and (6) WRF. The sequence is analyzed by looking at the frequency of the following patterns: 2-Gramm, HDE/WAA, WAA/HNI, HNI/WCR, and so on; 3-Gramm, (HDE, WAA)/HNI, (WAA, HNI)/WCR, and so on; 4-Gramm, (HDE, WAA, HNI)/WCR, (WAA, HNI, WCR)/HRF, and so on. For each K-Gramm pattern, the conditional probability is computed.

The rationale of communication training (Guerney, 1977) is that spouses should respond to a direct expression statement (i.e., self-disclosure) of the partner with acceptance or agreement in order to facilitate general communication and problem-solving. To visualize the course of the problem-solving attempts of the couples, the response chains following a direct expression statement are shown in Figure 17-2 for the various groups and assessment times (before/after). Partners 1 and 2 are alternating in the sequence (1, 3 = reaction of Partner 1; 2, 4 = reaction of Partner 2).

To explain Figure 17-2 in more detail, the response chain of the ND couples (Figure 2c) is considered. If Partner 1 emits a direct expression statement (DE), Partner 2 responds to this with an accepting or agreeing reaction (AA; p = .62). Partner 1 reacts to the sequence DE/AA either with an agreeing or accepting reaction (AA; p = .33) or a neutral information (NI; p = .27). Lack of data prohibits further analysis; at Lag 3 one positive and one neutral outcome can be seen in the ND group.

A comparison of the response chains of the WL couples before and after their waiting time reveals no important differences. Following a direct expression, Partner 2 is likely to react with a refusal (RF; p = .30) or an accepting or agreeing reaction (AA; p = .25). At both time points, one negative and one positive outcome is observed (see Figure 17-2a). The untreated BMT couples react slightly differently in that there are two negative outcomes and one positive outcome. After therapy the response chains are completely different and comparable to the ND couples: as assumed, the BMT couples react to a direct expression statement predominantly with an accepting or agreeing response (p = .60). No negative

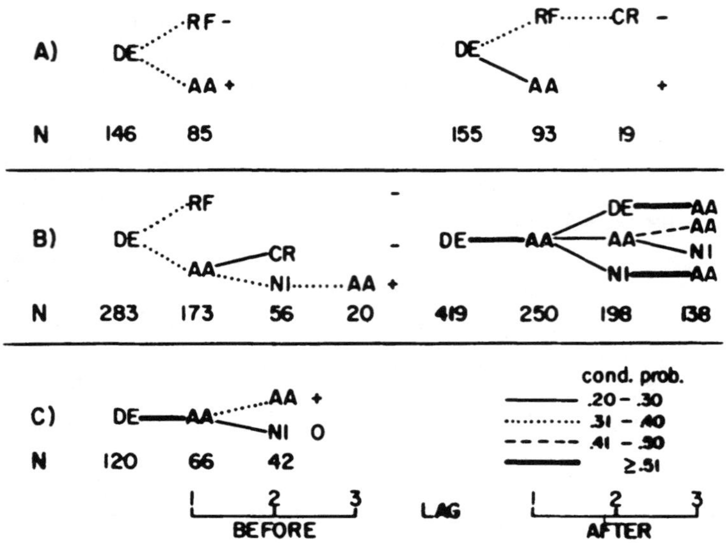

Figure 17-2. Probability trees of interaction sequences following a direct expression (DE) statement, p (x/y) ≥ 20: A) waiting-list couples before and after waiting period; B) Behavioral Marital Therapy couples before and after treatment; and C) nondistressed couples.
Note. NI = neutral information, AA = acceptance and agreement, CR = critique, and RF = refusal. N = absolute frequency of codes at each lag.

behaviors are observed in the chains ending with one neutral and three positive codes (see Figure 2b).

In the foregoing analysis using five summary codes, the longest observed sequence consisted of four alternating responses. In order to look at longer interaction patterns the summary codes DE plus AA were collapsed into Positive Communication (PC) and CR plus RF were collapsed into Negative Communication (NC).

When looking at positive or negative escalation processes, interesting results emerged. Negative Escalation (see Figure 17-3) is defined as a sequence of negative communication behaviors (NC-NC-NC-NC) of both partners. To explain Figure 17-3 the ND couples will be considered. The base rate of NC for ND couples is $p = .25$ (sequence length 1). Given that Partner 1 emits a negative communication behavior, Partner 2 will react negatively as well with a conditional probability of $p = .46$ (sequence length 2), Partner 1 will react negatively to that with $p = .50$ (sequence length 3), and Partner 2 negatively with $p = .44$ (sequence length 4). Nondistressed couples therefore also show a tendency to escalate but after four reactions they seem to "cool" or "slow down" the process.

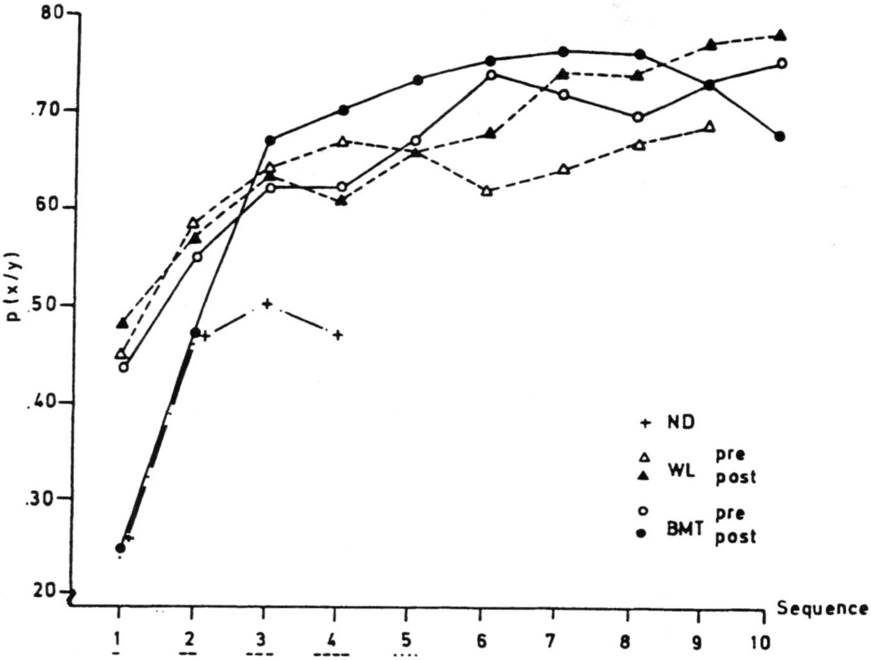

Figure 17-3. Generalized interaction pattern: "negative escalation."
Note. Ordinate indicates the conditional probability of the response after the foregoing sequence (n − 1). ND = nondistressed, WL = waiting list, and BMT = Behavioral Marital Therapy.

In contrast, the distressed and untreated couples show a clear-cut negative escalation process starting at a base rate of about .45 and increasing in conditional probability up to a maximum of .72 (BMT pre, sequence length 10).

Especially interesting are the results for the treated BMT couples. They start off with almost the same base rate and Lag 1 conditional probability as the ND couples (base rate = sequence length 1, $p = .24$; sequence length 2, $p = .46$), but at sequence length 3 they escalate even above their pretest level exchanging negative behaviors with a conditional probability well over .65 for a sequence length of 10.

When looking at the results of the Hahlweg, Revenstorf, & Schindler, (1984) study, it seems that BMT works satisfactorily in achieving the specific treatment goals: increasing the partners' self-disclosure, mutual understanding, and generation of specific and positive problem solutions, while decreasing blaming, criticizing, and sidetracking when discussing a topic relevant to the relationship. This is apparent from frequency as well as sequential analysis. At posttest there were highly significant differences between the WL couples and the BMT couples regarding the frequency of verbal and nonverbal behaviors. Treated couples showed a significant increase in the amount of direct expression, accepting/agreeing, and positive nonverbal behavior, and a significant decrease in the amount of criticism, refusal, and negative nonverbal behavior. A comparison with normative data showed that in all verbal codes, treated couples approximated the level of the ND couples. Changes became even more apparent when looking at the interaction patterns of the couples after BMT from a descriptive point cf view. When analyzing the problem-solving attempts of the treated couples, the response chains closely resembled the patterns exhibited by the ND couples, whereas the WL couples did not change at all from pre- to posttreatment either with regard to frequency or sequence.

However these positive results do not explain why a substantial amount of couples do not profit from BMT. Hahlweg, Revenstorf, and Schindler (1984) speculated about the possible reasons for this:

> A partial answer to this intriguing problem may be found in the generalized pattern "negative escalation" [see Figure 17-3]. After therapy, BMT couples started off with almost the same base rate and Lag 1 conditional probability as the ND couples. But given that Partner 2 was responding negatively to Partner 1, a full-blown aversive escalation process that escalated even above pretest level was inevitable. It seemed that Partner 1 was saying to himself or herself at Sequence Length 3: "The treatment didn't work—he/she is behaving like all the years before, but this time I won't give in!"
>
> It appears that BMT is sensitizing couples to the occurrence of negative stimuli and that the usual treatment techniques are not optimally suited to prevent these quickly occurring processes. The length of the escalation process as shown in Figure 17-3 is about 1 minute, so that interventions have to be very quick (within 10 seconds or so) to stop the escalation. Furthermore, in this case the basic aim of an intervention should be the individual partner. Taking this into account, BMT researchers and practitioners should explore in more detail the various options of cognitive interventions in order to (a) identify idiosyncratic stimuli that start the negative escalation and (b) train the partners in the use of alternative responses in order to prevent escalation. (p.p. 564–565)

A re-analysis of the Hahlweg, Revenstorf, and Schindler (1984) data shed light on the question whether all treated couples or only a subgroup showed this destructive pattern of negative escalation. BMT couples were assigned to a successfully or unsuccessfully treated group according to their level of marital quality *one year after* the end of therapy.

At pretest both groups show very similar patterns of negative escalation. At posttest very different patterns emerge: the group treated successfully (as rated one year later!) shows no negative escalation at all, while the unsuccessful couples portray a full-blown aversive cycle on a very high level (see Figure 17-4).

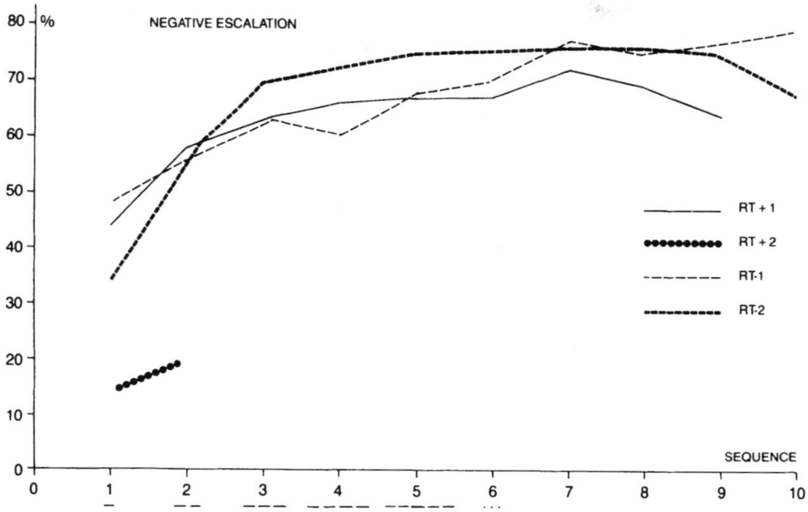

Figure 17-4. Generalized interaction pattern: "negative escalation" for successfully and unsuccessfully treated couples.
Note. Ordinate indicates the conditional probability of the response after the foregoing sequence (n − 1). Response Time (RT) +1 = successful couples, pre; RT +2 = successful couples, post; RT −1 = unsuccessful couples, pre; RT −2 = unsuccessful couples, post.

From this analysis it is evident that BMT as currently practiced is well suited for responders but that it needs to be extended in order to help the long-term nonresponders. Behavioral observation and methods of sequential analysis appear especially useful in identifying these couples at risk of not responding in the long term to the standard treatment.

EFFECTIVENESS OF PREVENTION PROGRAMS FOR COUPLES

In sharp contrast to our knowledge about the effects of treatment from a behavioral perspective, we know relatively little about the effectiveness of behaviorally oriented prevention programs for couples. The major reason for our ignorance is the lack of research designed to evaluate prevention programs. Furthermore, methodological and conceptual problems have marred the research that has been conducted. Most studies have evaluated the immediate or short-term longitudinal effects of the programs. These studies are inadequate because, in contrast to treatment programs, the goals of prevention programs (e.g., preventing dissolution, promoting satisfaction) are by definition long-term in nature and it sometimes takes years for serious marital problems to develop. In addition, the possibility of negative effects on couples due to participation in unevaluated prevention programs (Doherty & Walker, 1982; Gurman & Kniskern, 1978; Meadows & Taplin, 1970) highlights the imperative for well-designed long-term evaluations for prevention programs for couples.

Furthermore, without long-term follow-up, we may draw the wrong conclusions about the effectiveness of prevention programs for couples. One example will suffice. In one study we found that premarital couples who received communication training initially do worse than controls. At follow-up they are better off than controls (Markman, 1981). Without follow-up we would have accepted the initially disappointing results and drawn the wrong conclusion about the preventative possibilities of the program. As we have stated elsewhere (consider the current state of affairs), "literally thousands of premarital and married couples are taking advantage of a variety of intervention programs . . . and there are no data on the long-term positive or negative effects of these programs" (Markman & Floyd, 1980, p. 78).

When this research area was last reviewed (Markman, Floyd, & Dickson-Markman, 1982), most studies failed to meet even the least rigorous standards of experimental design. Due to reliance on single group designs (e.g., Meadows & Taplin, 1970) there was no random assignment to treatment and control conditions (Druckman *et al.*, 1980). Further, there were no studies with more than one follow-up and most relied on only self-report measures, lacking sensitive assessment in changes of interaction. However, the most recent review of the effectiveness of prevention programs (Hahlweg & Markman, in press) is more encouraging.

Evaluating the Effect-Size of BPI

In a recent paper we used the effect-size (ES) approach to review the empirical status of behavioral approaches to premarital intervention (BPI). Using the same criteria employed in the BMT review (summarized above), seven studies were included in the analysis (for a list of these studies see Hahlweg and Markman, in press).

Overall, 238 couples were included in the seven studies. Of these couples, 110 participated in a prevention program, and 128 served in non-treatment, waiting-list or placebo control groups (31 prevention couples initially participated in an attention-placebo control group). Subjects were generally middle-class, with a mean age of 22.3 years, and had been dating approximately 2¼ years. Consistent with the objectives of prevention programs (i.e., to keep happy couples happy), couples were predominantly in the nondistressed range on measures of relationship functioning.

The *internal validity* of the studies, defined by random assignment and mortality rates, was very good. Eighty-one percent of the subjects were randomly assigned to conditions, the pre-post attrition rate was 8% and the pre-follow-up rate (range: 6 months to 3 years) was 21%. When other criteria are combined, 71% of the studies can be judged as having high levels of internal validity.

There were 28 *consultants/leaders/instructors* involved in the prevention studies with an average of four per study. The use of these educational titles is consistent with the educational/preventative (vs. therapeutic) objectives of the programs. The leaders were predominantly graduate students and in some cases paraprofessionals who were trained specifically to deliver the program. All of the programs were delivered to groups of couples, with the average group size being four to five couples. There was one leader for each group, but two studies assigned each couple their own consultant. The mean length of the *intervention program* was six sessions, with the average session lasting 2½ – 3 hours.

Outcome of BPI

BPI versus control (pre-post). The seven prevention studies used yielded 38 effect-sizes. There was an average of 5.6 outcome measures per study. The effect sizes per study were averaged, resulting in a mean ES of 0.79 for the 7 studies. This means that the average couple who participated in BPI was better off at the end of the program than 79% of the nontreatment or attention-placebo couples. The BESD results indicate that the chances of improving was 33% for control couples and 67% for intervention couples.

BPI versus different control groups. Three studies included an attention-placebo control group, while 4 studies compared BPI with a nontreatment or waiting-list control group. The comparison with the nontreatment controls yielded an ES of 0.55, while the comparison with the attention-placebo controls yielded an ES of 1.12. This unexpected pattern of results clearly suggests that the positive impact of BPI is not due to nonspecific factors (e.g., attention).

Self-report versus observational measures. Six studies used self-report measures while all studies used observational measures. In contrast to the BMT studies, computing the ES for self-report and observational measures independently resulted in *very different* effect sizes: 0.52 and 1.51, respectively. Thus, findings suggest that BPI is changing the couples' interaction in a positive manner, but that these changes are not having the same large impact on the couples' perceptions of their relationship. Alternatively, since couples who participate in prevention programs are by definition already happy with their relationships, a ceiling effect may be operating that limits positive changes on the self-report measures.

Different BPI approaches. Similar to BMT, there are three major different approaches to premarital intervention. The first focuses on improving self-awareness and communication and is represented by the Minnesota Couples Communication Program (Miller *et al.*, 1975). The second focuses on improving communication and enhancing relationships, represented by Guerney's Relationship Enhancement Approach (Guerney, 1977). The third focuses on improving both problem-solving and communication skills as well as modifying expectations, represented by the Premarital Relationship Enhancement Program (PREP; Markman, Floyd, Stanley, & Storaasli, in press). Two studies evaluated the self-awareness approach, two the communication/enhancement approaches and three the problem-solving/communication expectation approach. The ES for the three approaches were 0.71, 1.14, and 0.57, respectively. The higher ES for the relationship enhancement programs is consistent with their objectives of enhancing the current relationship of couples, while other programs (e.g., PREP) are designed to teach skills that will help the couple cope with future problems.

Long-term follow-up. Despite the importance of long-term follow-up to evaluate the preventive goals of BPI studies, only 4 studies included follow-up measures. The follow-up periods ranged from 6 months to 3 years. The ES for the two studies with follow-up less than 1 year was 1.01, and for the two studies with follow-up of longer than 1 year was 0.65. Thus the positive effects of BPI are generally maintained over time and indicate that these programs may be *preventing* the development of marital problems for some couples, compared to controls.

RECOMMENDATIONS AND FUTURE DEVELOPMENT OF BMT AND BPI PROGRAMS

It seems safe to conclude that BMT's and BPI's empirical base is very sound. The results of the meta-analysis of the controlled studies can be summarized as follows:

1. BMT is more effective than nontreatment in reducing marital distress, and these changes remain stable for at least a 12 month period after therapy. The average rate of improvement after therapy which is attributable to BMT is about 40%. That is, the chance of getting better rises from about 30% (the estimated improvement rate for the control group) to about 70%. This seems a very reasonable increase. Furthermore the comparison between the European and the United States studies revealed that BMT is

about equally effective in different cultural settings. This provides strong evidence for the generalizability of the results of BMT.

2. BPI is more effective than nontreatment in improving the relationships of premarital couples and in preventing subsequent problems. The effects of BPI are not as strong as BMT, but this may be due to the difference in targets, happy versus unhappy couples, as well as methodological problems such as ceiling effects. Although the available data indicates that there are possibilities for preventing marital problems using cognitive-behavioral approaches premaritally, there is a clear need for additional, well-designed, longitudinal studies carried over longer time periods.

3. The rates of improvement for BMT and BPI vary depending on the type of control group used for comparison. However, even when compared to the most challenging control group (nonspecific), BMT is superior, resulting in a 26% increase in improvement. This finding illustrates the power of nonspecific factors which operate in BMT as well as other forms of therapy, but highlights the need to evaluate the type of control group used. Unexpectedly, for BPI, the effects were stronger when compared to attention-placebo versus nontreatment controls.

4. The comparison of BMT with other approaches resulted in an interesting finding: after therapy no apparent differences in the respective effect-sizes were observed. However, BMT seems to be more effective in stabilizing the achieved treatment gains than other approaches. While this difference in ES at 6 month follow-up is not statistically significant, the results may indicate that BMT works as expected in helping couples to function as their own therapists.

5. For BMT, similar effects are found for self-report and observational measures. Therefore, one can recommend against using the more costly observational measures when global improvement is the major outcome measure. However, as discussed earlier, observational measures may be critical to the evaluation of the question "Does BMT produce change in couples' interaction patterns in order to prevent relapse?"

6. For BPI, in contrast to the BMT results, stronger effects are found for behavioral versus self-report measures. Therefore, we recommend the continued use of observational measures when evaluating BPI programs. This is particularly important when evaluating the shorter-term effects, because the proximal goals of the program, to modify couples' interactions and ceiling effects, limit the changes that can be demonstrated by self-report measures.

7. For BPI the most important implication of these findings is the need for more well-controlled, longer-term outcome studies. Good models are now available of such designs, and future investigations will hopefully shed brighter light on such questions as "can we prevent marital distress?" and "what types of couples benefit most from such programs?"

8. For BMT the most important implication of these findings is that it seems no longer necessary to conduct more of this type of outcome research (comparing BMT to a control group) because the efficacy of BMT seems to be clearly established. This does, of course, not imply that any further outcome research is not necessary. When we consider the clinical outcome of BMT, it is obvious that a substantive number of couples or individuals are still distressed after therapy, indicating the need for further refinement.

EXTENSIONS OF BMT

In the following discussion we will note possible extensions of BMT which may be promising for future research and clinical application.

Cognitive Components

The possible value of integrating cognitive interventions into BMT has been discussed in relation to the phenomena of negative escalation. In order to stop these destructive processes, methods of "cognitive restructuring" (Meichenbaum, 1974) seem particularly useful. One possible strategy derived from Meichenbaum's principles is to train the couple in some form of crisis management as described by Schindler and Vollmer (1984).

This treatment component is intended to enhance generalization through facilitating the use of previously trained problem-solving skills, particularly in crucial situations. The term "crisis" describes a situation in which aversive exchanges tend to escalate. If one follows a progressive escalation process, one can identify four stages. For each of these stages an inner dialogue (Meichenbaum, 1974) is trained which can help to avoid the increase of an aversive exchange and support direct communication.

The *first stage* represents the period before one spouse points out a specific behavior pattern in the other which is particularly disliked. In such a case the following questions should preceed any overt behavior: (1) Do I think this behavior is really important enough to discuss or change? (2) Is this reaction only occasional, and am I usually content with this issue? (3) Have I contributed to the behavior?

In case the client decides that it is important to discuss the event, then he or she should consider whether it is appropriate to engage immediately in a discussion of the disliked behavior pattern of the spouse.

Stage two becomes relevant when the spouse decides that the conflict issue should be addressed now and that the situation is appropriate. At this point the communication skills as trained in BMT should become operational. This means to omit blaming and to express feelings directly. Although the other spouse may not at once react in a constructive manner, it should be remembered that responsibility for successful problemsolving discussions resides primarily with the dissatisfied partner.

Stage three represents coping with an imminent quarrel. In spite of all efforts to the contrary, a quarrel may ensue. In the case of an extended and hurting quarrel, the client should interrupt the conversation in order to avoid further escalation. He or she should directly express his or her fears, ask for a time lapse, and suggest the resumption of the discussion later.

If everything has gone wrong in that the prevention of escalation has failed, and communication has broken down (*Stage four*), then each spouse must feel responsible for again adopting positive interaction. Each one should consider whether he/she is prepared to tolerate a day or two of tension until the other gives in, or take the first step to have, for instance, an enjoyable weekend together.

The "weighing up" or appraisal is the essential characteristic of the cognitive training at all four stages. The clients are coached in anticipation of outcome and decision-making according to their individual priorities. The inner dialogues along the described rationale are trained by means of their typical conflict situations.

Attributional Components

Besides this rather circumscribed cognitive intervention, other strategies have been developed and are currently investigated in controlled experiments by research groups headed by Baucom and Epstein (Baucom & Lester, 1984; Epstein, Pretzer, & Fleming, 1982). As noted earlier, one of the major foci is couples' attributions for marital events. Various marital events are viewed as positive or negative, important or unimportant in part based on the spouse's understanding of why that event occurred or why the partner behaved as he or she did. Thus if a husband begins helping out more around the house, the wife might respond positively if she interprets his behavior as an act of love. However she might become annoyed if she views it as a prelude to his announcing that he has spent a large amount of money. Many distressed couples appear to make attributions which minimize the importance of their partner's intended positive behavior or even interpret it negatively; similarly, negative behavior is focused upon and given great importance through attributions. In order to maximize the meaningfulness of behavior changes which occur through BMT procedures, the explanations for these changes must be considered. Otherwise, for example, a husband might attribute the wife's behavior changes, which required significant effort, to the therapist's directives.

At times attributions for problem areas are also important in motivating a spouse to change his or her behavior. Frequently distressed couples tend to attribute primary blame to the partner for problems and consequently perceive little need for self-change. A more balanced perspective on the problem, including how one's own behavior and thoughts contribute to the difficulty, places responsibility on both persons to change to improve the relationship.

As a result, treatment procedures have been developed to focus on couples' attributions for marital events. For example, Baucom and Lester (1984) taught couples to select a marital problem and evaluate the various specific factors that contributed to the problem. Each spouse is instructed to focus on his or her own contributions to the problem rather than the partner's contributions. Any misinterpretations of either person's behavior is clarified. Each person also discusses possible changes he or she could make to improve the problem area. Thus, by considering the multiple factors contributing to a problem, the simplistic, blaming, attributional pattern is combatted. Similarly, by focusing on possible self-changes to improve the problem, each partner assumes responsibility instead of waiting for the other to change.

Weiss (1980) has proposed that intervention strategies from strategic therapy be viewed as attempts at cognitive restructuring to alter couples' attributions. His focus is on those instances in which couples are unwilling to comply with BMT procedures because of their explanations for their marital problems and their spouses' behavior. He suggests that the prudent use of paradoxical instructions can at times help the couple alter their perspective on a problem and thus change their behavior. Thus, instructing a couple to argue as frequently as possible can change the meaning of an argument since it is now an assignment. Under such circumstances the argument can loose its power since its context has changed, and it might decrease in frequency. Similarly the therapist can reframe a set of aversive interactions to shift the couple's attributions toward each other. Consequently, the therapist might emphasize to partners who argue frequently and hurt each other that one has to care a lot about someone to be so deeply hurt by that person and to spend so much time discussing relationship issues.

The major differences between these approaches from strategic therapy and those suggested by Baucom and Epstein is that in the strategic techniques the therapist is providing a different attribution to the couple or altering the meaning through a behavioral assignment opposite to the desired behavior. Baucom and Epstein attempt to alter attributions by having the couple nondefensively discuss a problem area and arrive at their own new attributions rather than having the therapist provide different explanations.

Couples' expectations of how each partner should behave and what a relationship should be like is another focus for cognitive restructuring. At times couples are distressed because they have unrealistic expectations of certain aspects of a relationship. For example, Eidelson and Epstein (1982) have noted that some couples expect sex to create a constant ecstatic experience. Under such circumstances, the couple's sexual behavior might not need to change, merely their expectations. Consequently the assumption that a problem always calls for problem-solving with a resultant behavior change is too simplistic. Including an opportunity for the couple to evaluate the appropriateness of their expectations can become an important aspect of dealing with a problem area. In such a context, the clinician will help the couple decide whether to change expectations and/or behavior. Whereas these treatment approaches seem logical based on clinical observation and basic research findings relating attributions and expectations to marital discord, exploration of the utility of these procedures is merely beginning. At present data does exist demonstrating that these approaches produce the intended cognitive changes in distressed couples (Baucom & Lester, 1984; Epstein *et al.*, 1982). However the most effective way to combine these approaches with more commonly used BMT procedures is unknown and is a major challenge for the 1980s.

REFERENCES

Arentewicz, G., & Schmidt, G. (1980). *Sexuell gestörte beziehungen: konzept und technik der paartherapie*. Heidelberg: Springer.

Bandura, A. (1974). *Social learning theory*. Englewood Cliffs, NJ: Prentice-Hall.

Baucom, D. H. (1982). A comparison of behavioral contracting and problem-solving/communications training in behavioral marital therapy. *Behavioral Therapy, 13*, 162–174.

Baucom, D. H. (1985). *Supplementing behavioral marital therapy*. Research in progress.

Baucom, D. H. (1987). Attributions in distressed relations: How can we explain them? In S. Duck & D. Perlman (Eds.), *Heterosexual relations, marriage, and divorce*. London: Sage.

Baucom, D. H., & Hoffman, J. A. (1986). The effectiveness of marital therapy: Current status and application to the clinical setting. In N. S. Jacobson & A. S. Gurman (Eds.), *Clinical handbook of marital therapy*. New York: Guilford Press.

Baucom, D. H., & Lester, G. W. (1984, November). *Augmenting behavioral marital therapy with cognitive restructuring*. Paper presented at the 18th Annual Convention of the Association for the Advancement of Behavior Therapy, Philadelphia.

Baucom, D. H., & Mehlman, S. K. (1984). Predicting marital status following behavioral marital therapy: A comparison of models of marital relationships. In K. Hahlweg & N. S. Jacobson (Eds.), *Marital interaction: Analyis and modification*. New York: Guilford Press.

Baucom, D. H., Wheeler, C. W. & Bell, G. (1984, November). *Assessing the role of attributions in marital distress*. Paper presented at the 18th Annual Convention of the Association for the Advancement of Behavior Therapy, Philadelphia.

Bennun, I. (1985). Prediction and responsiveness in behavioral marital therapy. *Behavioural Psychotherapy, 13*, 186–201.

Billings, A. (1979). Conflict resolution in distressed and nondistressed married couples. *Journal of Consulting and Clinical Psychology, 17*, 368–376.

Bloom, B. (1977). *Community mental health: A general introduction*. Monterey, CA: Brooks-Cole.

Bloom, B., Asher, S., & White, S. (1978). Marital dysfunction as a stressor: A review and analysis. *Psychological Bulletin, 85*, 867–894.

Campbell, D. T., & Stanley, J. C. (1966). *Experimental and quasi-experimental designs for research.* Chicago: IL: Rand McNally.

Carter, H., & Glick, P. C. (1976). *Marriage and divorce: A social and economic study.* Cambridge, MA: Harvard University Press.

Carter, E., & McGoldrick, M. (1980). *The family life cycle: A framework for family therapy.* New York: Gardner Press.

Crowe, M. J. (1978). Conjoint marital therapy: A controlled outcome study. *Psychological Medicine, 8*, 623–636.

Doherty, W. J., & Walker, B. J. (1982). Marriage encounter casualties: A preliminary investigation. *American Journal of Family Therapy, 10*, 15–25.

Druckman, J. M., Fournier, D. M., Robinson, B., & Olson, D. H. (1980). *Effectiveness of five types of preparation programs: Final report.* Grand Rapids, MI: Education for marriage.

Duss v. Werdt, J. & Fuchs, A. (Eds.) (1980). *Scheidung in der schweiz (Divorce in Switzerland).* Bern, Stuttgart: Haupt.

Duvall, E. (1977). *Marriage and family development.* Philadelphia: Lippincott.

Eidelson, R. J. & Epstein, N. (1982). Cognition and relationship maladjustment: Development of a measure of dysfunctional relationship beliefs. *Journal of Consulting and Clinical Psychology, 50*, 715–720.

Epstein, N., & Williams, A. M. (1981). Behavioral approaches to the treatment of marital discord. In G. P. Skobran (Ed.), *The handbook of marriage and marital therapy.* New York: Spectrum.

Epstein, N., Pretzer, J., & Fleming, B. (1982, November). *Cognitive therapy and communication training: Comparison of effects with distressed couples.* Paper presented at the 16th Annual Convention of the Association for the Advancement of Behavior Therapy, Los Angeles.

Filsinger, E. (Ed.). (1983). *Marital measurement sourcebook.* Beverly Hills, CA: Sage.

Filsinger, E., & Lewis, R. (Eds.). (1981). *Assessing marriage: New behavioral approaches.* Beverly Hills, CA: Sage.

Fincham, F. D., & O'Leary, K. D. (1983). Causal inferences for spouse behavior in maritally distressed and nondistressed couples. *Journal of Social and Clinical Psychology, 1*, 42–57.

Geiss, S. K., & O'Leary, D. (in press). Therapist ratings of frequency and severity of marital problems: Implications for research. *Journal of Marriage and Family Therapy.*

Gottman, J. M. (1979). *Marital interaction: Experimental investigations.* New York: Academic Press.

Gottman, J. M., & Bakeman, R. (1979). The sequential analysis of observational data. In M. E. Lamb, S. J. Suomi, & G. R. Stephenson (Eds.), *Social interaction analysis.* Madison, WI: The University of Wisconsin Press.

Gottman, J. M., Markman, H. J., & Notarius, C. I. (1977). The topography of marital conflict: A sequential analysis of verbal and nonverbal behavior. *Journal of Marriage and the Family, 39*, 461–478.

Gottman, J. M., Notarius, C. I., Markman, H. J., Banks, S., Yoppi, B., & Rubin, M. E. (1976). Behavior exchange theory and marital decision making. *Journal of Personality and Social Psychology, 34*, 14–23.

Guerney, B. G. (1977). *Relationship enhancement.* San Francisco, CA: Jossey-Bass.

Gurman, A. S. (1980). Behavioral marriage therapy in the 1980's: The challenge of integration. *American Journal of Family Therapy, 89*, 86–96.

Gurman, A. S. & Kniskern, D. P. (1978). Research on marital and family therapy: Progress, perspective, and prospect. In S. L. Garfield & A. E. Bergin (Eds.), *Handbook of psychotherapy and behavior change*. 2nd ed. New York: Wiley.

Hahlweg, K., & Markman, H. J. (in press). The effectiveness of behavioral marital therapy: Empirical status of behavioral techniques in preventing and alleviating marital distress. *Journal of Consulting and Clinical Psychology*.

Hahlweg, K., Revenstorf, D., & Schindler, L. (1982). Treatment of marital distress. Comparing formats and modalities. *Advances in Behavior Research Therapy, 4*, 57–74.

Hahlweg, K., Revenstorf, D., & Schindler, L. (1984). Effects of behavioral marital therapy on couples' communication and problem-solving skills. *Journal of Consulting and Clinical Psychology, 52*, 553–566.

Hahlweg, K., Reisner, L., Kohli, G., Vollmer, M., Schindler, L., & Revenstorf, D. (1984). Development and validity of a new system to analyze interpersonal communication (KPI). In K. Hahlweg & N. S. Jacobson (Eds.), *Marital interaction: Analysis and modification*. New York: Guilford Press.

Hahlweg, K., Schindler, L., & Revenstorf, D. (1982). *Partnerschaftsprobleme: Diagnose und Therapie. Handbuch für den Therapeuten* (*Marital Distress: Assessment and therapy Manual for the therapist*). Heidelberg: Springer.

Hahlweg, K., Schindler, L., Revenstorf, D., & Brengelmann, J. C. (1984). The Munich marital therapy study. In K. Hahlweg & N. S. Jacobson (Eds.), *Marital interaction: Analysis and modification*. New York: Guilford Press.

Hetherington, E. M., Cox, M., & Cox, R. (1978). The aftermath of divorce. In J. H. Stevens & M. Mathews (Eds.), *Mother–child, father–child relations*. Washington, DC: National Association for the Education of Young Children.

Hooley, J. M. (1985). *Criticism and depression*. Unpublished doctoral thesis, Oxford, GB.

Hooley, J. M., Orley, J. & Teasdale, J. D. (in press). Levels of expressed emotion and relapse in depressed patients. *British Journal of Psychiatry*.

Hops, H., Wills, T. A., Patterson, G. R., & Weiss, R. L. (1972). *Marital interaction coding system*. Unpublished manuscript. University of Oregon, Oregon Research Institute. (Available from ASIS/NAPS, c/o Microfiche Publications, 305 E. 46th Street, New York, NY 10017)

Jacobson, N. S. (1977). Problem-solving and contingency contracting in the treatment of marital discord. *Journal of Consulting and Clinical Psychology, 45*, 92–100.

Jacobson, N. S. (1978). Specific and nonspecific factors in the effectiveness of a behavioral approach to the treatment of marital discord. *Journal of Consulting and Clinical Psychology, 46*, 442–452.

Jacobson, N. S. (1981). Behavioral marital therapy. In A. S. Gurman & D. P. Kniskern (Eds.), *Handbook of family therapy*. New York: Brunner/Mazel.

Jacobson, N. S. (1984). A component analysis of behavioral marital therapy: The relative effectiveness of behavior exchange and problem-solving training. *Journal of Consulting and Clinical Psychology, 52*, 295–305.

Jacobson, N. S., Elwood, R. W., & Dallas, M. (1981). Assessment of marital dysfunction. In D. Barlow (Ed.), *Behavioral assessment of adult disorders*. New York: Guilford Press.

Jacobson, N. S., Follette, W. C., Revenstorf, D., Baucom, D. H., Hahlweg, K., & Margolin, G. (1984). Variability in outcome and clinical significance of behavioral marital therapy: A reanalysis of outcome data. *Journal of Consulting and Clinical Psychology, 52*, 497–504.

Jacobson, N. S., & Margolin, G. (1979). *Marital therapy: Strategies based on social learning and behavioral exchange principles*. New York: Brunner/Mazel.

Jacobson, N. S., McDonald, D. W., Follette, W. C., & Berley, R. A. (1985). Attributional processes in distressed and nondistressed married couples. *Cognitive Therapy and Research, 9*, 35–50.

Jacobson, N. S., Waldron, H. & Moore, D. (1980). Toward a behavioral profile of marital distress. *Journal of Consulting and Clinical Psychology, 48*, 696–703.

Kelley, H. H. (1979). *Personal relationships: Their structures and processes*. Hillsdale, NJ: Erlbaum Associates.

Lester, G. W., Beckham, E., & Baucom, D. H. (1980). Implementation of behavioral marital therapy. *Journal of Marital and Family Therapy, 6*, 189–199.

Liberman, R. P., Wheeler, E., & Sanders, N. (1976). Behavioral therapy for marital disharmony: An educational approach. *Journal of Marriage and Family Counseling, 2*, 383–395.

Locke, H. J., & Wallace, K. M. (1959). Short-term marital adjustment and prediction tests: Their reliability and validity. *Marriage and Family Living, 21*, 251–255.

Madden, M. E., & Janoff-Bulman, R. (1981). Blame, control, and marital satisfaction: Wives' attributions for conflict in marriage. *Journal of Marriage and the Family, 44*, 663–674.

Margolin, G., & Christensen, A. (1981). The treatment of marital problems. In R. J. Daitzman (Ed.), *Clinical behavior therapy and behavior modification* (Vol. 2). New York: Guilford Press.

Margolin, G., & Wampold, B. E. (1981). Sequential analysis of conflict and accord in distressed and nondistressed marital partners. *Journal of Consulting and Clinical Psychology, 49*, 554–567.

Margolin, G., & Weiss, R. L. (1978). Communication training and assessment: A case of behavioral marital enrichment. *Behavior Therapy, 9*, 508–520.

Markman, H. J. (1979). The application of a behavioral model of marriage in predicting relationship satisfaction of couples planning marriage. *Journal of Consulting and Clinical Psychology, 4*, 743–749.

Markman, H. J. (1981). The prediction of marital distress: A five year follow-up. *Journal of Consulting and Clinical Psychology, 49*, 760–762.

Markman, H. J. (1984). The longitudinal study of couples' interaction: Implications for cognitive/behavioral, social exchange, and social skills models of relationship development. In K. Hahlweg & N. S. Jacobson (Eds.), *Marital interaction: Analysis and modification*. New York: Guilford Press.

Markman, H. J., & Floyd, F. (1980). Possibilities for the prevention of marital discord: A behavioral perspective. *American Journal of Family Therapy, 8*, 29–48.

Markman, H. J., Floyd, F., & Dickson-Markman, F. (1982). Toward a model for the prediction and prevention of marital and family distress and dissolution. In S. Duck (Ed.), *Personal relationships 4: Dissolving personal relationships*. London: Academic Press.

Markman, H. J., Floyd, F., Stanley, S., & Jamieson, K. (1984). A cognitive/behavioral program for the presentation of marital and family distress: Issues in program development and delivery. In K. Hahlweg & N. S. Jacobson (Eds.), *Marital Interaction: Analysis and modification*. New York: Guilford Press.

Markman, H. J., Floyd, F., Stanley, S., & Lewis, H. (1985). Prevention. In N. S. Jacobson & A. S. Gurman (Eds.), *Clinical handbook of marital therapy*. New York: Guilford Press.

Markman, H. J., Floyd, F. J., Stanley, S., & Storaasli, R. (in press). The prevention of marital distress: A longitudinal investigation. *Journal of Consulting and Clinical Psychology*.

Meadows, M. E., & Taplin, J. F. (1970). Premarital counselling with college students: A promising triad. *Journal of Counseling Psychology, 17*, 516–518.

Mehlman, S. K., Baucom, D. H., & Anderson, D. (1983). Effectiveness of cotherapist versus single therapists and immediate versus delayed treatment in behavioral marital therapy. *Journal of Consulting and Clinical Psychology, 51*, 258–266.

Meichenbaum, D. (1974). *Cognitive behavior modification*. Morristown, NJ: Learning Press.

Miller, S., Nunally, E., & Wackman, D. (1975). *Alive and aware*. Minneapolis, MN: Interpersonal Communication Program.

Notarius, C. I. & Markman, H. J. (1981). The couples interaction scoring system. In E. Filsinger & R. Lewis (Eds.), *Assessing marriage: New behavioral approaches*. Beverly Hills, CA: Sage.

O'Leary, K. D. & Turkewitz, H. (1981). A comparative outcome study of behavioral marital therapy and communication training. *Journal of Marital and Family Therapy, 7*, 159–169.

Overall, J. E., Henry, B. W., & Woodward, A. (1974). Dependence of marital problems on parental family history. *Journal of Abnormal Psychology, 83*, 446–450.

Powell, G. S., & Wampler, K. S.(1982). Marriage enrichment participants: Levels of marital satisfaction. *Family Relations, 31*, 389–394.

Raush, H. L., Barry, W. A., Hertel, R. K., & Swain, M. A. (1974). *Communication, conflict, and marriage*. San Francisco, CA: Jossey-Bass.

Revenstorf, D., Schindler, L. & Hahlweg, K. (1983). Behavioral marital therapy applied in a conjoint and a conjoint-group modality: Short and longterm effects. *Behavior Therapy, 14*, 614–625.

Revenstorf, D., Hahlweg, K., Schindler, L., & Vogel, B. (1984). Interaction analysis of marital conflict. In K. Hahlweg & N. S. Jacobson (Eds.), *Marital interaction: Analysis and modification*. New York: Guilford Press.

Rosenthal, R. (1983). Assessing the statistical and social importance of the effects of psychotherapy. *Journal of Consulting and Clinical Psychology, 51*, 4–13.

Schindler, L. & Voller, M. (1984). Cognitive perspectives in behavioral marital therapy: Some proposals for bridging theory, research, and practice. In K. Hahlweg & N. S. Jacobson (Eds.), *Marital interaction: Analysis and modification*. New York: Guilford Press.

Shapiro, A. U., & Morris, L. A. (1978). The placebo effect in medical and psychological therapies. In S. L. Garfield & A. E. Bergin (Eds.), *Handbook of psychotherapy and behavior change* (2nd ed.; pp. 369–410). New York: Wiley.

Smith, M. L. & Glass, G. V. (1977). Meta-analysis of psychotherapy outcome studies. *American Psychologist, 32*, 752–760.

Smith, M. L., Glass, G. V., & Miller, T. I. (1980). *The benefits of psychotherapy*. Baltimore, MD: Johns Hopkins University Press.

Spanier, G. B. (1976). Measuring dyadic adjustment: New scales for assessing the quality of marriage and similar dyads. *Journal of Marriage and the Family, 38*, 15–28.

Straus, M. A., Gelles, R. J., & Steinmetz, S. K. (1980). *Behind closed doors: Violence in the American family*. Anchor, NY: Doubleday.

Stuart, R. B. (1969). Operant–interpersonal treatment of marital discord. *Journal of Consulting and Clinical Psychology, 33*, 675–682.

Stuart, R. B. (1976). An operant interpersonal program for couples. In D. H. L. Oson (Ed.), *Treating relationships*. Lake Mills, IA: Graphic Publishing.

Terman, L. M. (1938). *Psychological factors in marital happiness*. New York: McGraw-Hill.

Thibaut, J. W. & Kelley, H. H. (1959). *The social psychology of groups*. New York: Wiley.

Vaughn, C. E. & Leff, J. P. (1976). The influence of family and social factors on the course of psychiatric illness. *British Journal of Psychiatry, 129*, 125–137.

Weiss, R. L. (1980). Strategic behavioral marital therapy: Toward a model for assessment and intervention. In J. P. Vincent (Ed.), *Advances in family intervention, assessment, and theory*. Vol. I. Greenwich, NY: JAI Press.

Weiss, R. L., Hops, H., & Patterson, G. R. (1973). A framework for conceptualizing marital conflict, a technology for altering it, some data for evaluating it. In L. A. Hammerlynck, L. C. Handy, & E. J. Mash (Eds.), *Behavior change: Methodology, concepts, and practice*. Champaign, IL: Research Press.

Weiss, R. L. & Margolin, G. (1977). Assessment of marital conflict and accord. In A. R. Ciminero, K. S. Calhoun, & H. E. Adams (Eds.), *Handbook for behavioral assessment*. New York: Wiley.

18

Behavioral and Systemic Family Therapy: A Comparison

THOMAS C. TODD
Forest Hospital, Illinois School of Professional Psychology, and The Family Institute of Chicago/Center for Family Studies

HISTORICAL INTRODUCTION

Several years ago, I was asked by Alan Gurman to address similarities and differences between structural family therapy and behavior modification (Todd, 1981). The present chapter provides a convenient opportunity to review the state of affairs of several years ago and to see whether there has been convergence or divergence in the intervening time period.

Before reviewing my earlier analysis, it is important to point out that it was based on a comparison between *structural* family therapy and non-family behavioral programs, such as the inpatient behavior modification programs used for anorexia nervosa. As will be further discussed in the next section, these early remarks would have needed considerable modification and elaboration in order to be applicable to systemic family therapy in general or to behavioral family therapy.

At that time I noted several similarities between structural family therapy and behavior modification. Both focus on observable behavior and on the contingencies that maintain symptomatic behavior. Change in present behavior was seen as more critical than insight. Both forms of treatment were characterized by explicit goals and a focus on the presenting problem as a primary criterion of success.

Differences in clinical practice were also noted. Behavior modification approaches were seen as much more likely to attempt to achieve direct control over the contingencies maintaining symptomatic behavior. In the treatment of anorexia, for example, this led to the use of highly structured inpatient behavior modification programs, with a nursing staff implementing reinforcement contingencies for weight gain. Behavioral change in the patient was viewed as a primary goal, while return to the family environment was seen as "merely" a problem in generalization.

By contrast, structural family therapy was seen as placing consistent emphasis on change in the family system and being cautious about change in the identified patient that occurs out of the context of the family. Structural family therapy also places emphasis on the enactment of symptomatic behavior in the session to allow direct observation (and intervention) by the therapist. Because of the importance attributed to complex sequences of behavior involving several family members, simply having family members report (or even chart) behavior is not considered adequate.

Instruction by the therapist within structural family therapy is rare in comparison with behavioral approaches. When utilized in structural family therapy, instruction is seen as a complex intervention by the therapist, rather than as simple transmission of information.

Finally, the two approaches were seen as different in their use of an open systems model of feedback and circular causality, as opposed to a simple cause-and-effect model. While there was nothing in the behavioral model that would preclude the more complex systemic thinking, much of the early progress in the behavioral field seemed to be based on a model of linear causality. A related and perhaps even more distinctive difference is that structural family therapy consistently includes the therapist as part of the system, viewing him or her as influenced by feedback from the family, rather than as a "free agent" who could influence change without in turn being influenced.

My earlier analysis concluded by noting that behavior therapists and structural family therapists potentially have much to learn from each other:

> Behavior therapists need to consider the multiplicity of factors maintaining symptomatic behavior and the consequences throughout the family system of change in target behavior. This means careful consideration in the choice of target behaviors, who should be involved in treatment, and what role the therapist should play. Structural family therapists, in turn, have much to learn from behaviorists in terms of precise treatment goals and highly effective specific techniques. While resistance and family homeostasis are important, structural family therapy may have paid too little attention to the conditions when behavioral change is straightforward, when behavioral education (particularly of parents) is sufficient to produce change, or when only one or two family members need to be included in therapy. Both structural family therapy and behavior therapy can profit considerably from clinical collaboration and careful research addressing these issues. (Todd, 1981, pp. 115–116)

"SYSTEMIC" FAMILY THERAPY: A BRIEF OVERVIEW

My original mandate for this chapter was to compare behavioral family therapy with "systemic" family therapy (SFT), not merely with structural family therapy. In some ways this is an overly ambitious and unworkable task, since the field of "systemic" family therapy includes a wide variety of approaches with much controversy between schools. Before proceeding with a somewhat modified task, it should be useful to take a quick survey of the field and identify some of the factors which distinguish the different approaches that fall under the overall umbrella of "systemic" family therapy.

Madanes and Haley (1977) have identified eight dimensions or distinctions that serve to differentiate schools of therapy, including the various schools of systemic family therapy. Quite a number of similar categorization schemes have been offered within marital and family therapy; the choice of a particular set of dimensions is not critical here, since the main point is to demonstrate the diversity within SFT.

The dimensions offered by Madanes and Haley are:

1. *Past versus Present.* How important does the therapist consider the identification of past determinants of behavior?
2. *Interpretation versus Action.* Is it important to explore and interpret the past? (The reader will note that the first two dimensions and other subsequent dimensions often tend to be related rather than independent.)
3. *Growth versus Presenting Problem.* How seriously does the therapist take the presenting problem, compared to a more general emphasis on personal growth?
4. *Method versus Specific Plan for Each Problem.* Does the therapist tend to utilize the same set of procedures and techniques for all cases, or tend to develop a specific procedure for each case and each problem?
5. *Unit of One, Two, or Three or More People.* What is the size of the basic "unit" which guides the therapist's thinking?
6. *Equality versus Hierarchy.* Are all participants in therapy assumed to be of equal status or are some, particularly parents, considered to have more influence and power?
7. *Analogical versus Digital.* Therapists who stress analogical communication emphasize metaphor and multiple levels of communication rather than explicit content.
8. *Straightforward versus Deliberately Paradoxical Intervention.* How does the therapist assume that change takes place, and what interventions are employed?

Madanes and Haley go on to discuss various major schools of family therapy (including their analysis of behavioral family therapy). For the present purposes, it is sufficient to note that they find one or more major schools that fall on the extremes of each of the 8 dimensions.

DEFINING A MODEL POSITION

This brief review should make it obvious to the reader that it is virtually hopeless to make overall statements about the general field of systemic family therapy. Virtually the only issue which unites the field is a common allegiance to the view that the family is a system and obeys the principles of General Systems Theory. Even this agreement is somewhat illusory, as Frazier (1982) has shown in his examination of the degree to which various family therapy approaches adhere to the tenets of General Systems Theory.

Before proceeding further, therefore, it seems necessary to stake out a model position on the various issues that will be somewhat broader than structural family therapy, yet only will include a small portion of the broad universe of systemic family therapy. The reader should be warned in advance that the position that will ultimately be described will minimize many potential differences from behavioral family therapy. A different model position, taken by another systemic family therapist whose sympathies were not so close to behavioral family therapy, would obviously yield quite a different comparison to behavioral family therapy.

To begin with, my position is within a broader category labeled by Beels and Ferber (1969) as "systems purists." This view places particular emphasis on the present. It tends to be action-oriented rather than interpretive and generally emphasizes a unit which at least includes the nuclear family. Most practitioners within this larger group typically do not use paradoxical interventions (although I do myself). They are relatively equally divided between emphasis on the presenting problem and emphasis on growth of the individual in the family. The former subgroup tends to develop specific interventions for particular presenting problems, while the latter tends to use more generic family interventions.

Since my model of practice falls within the presenting problem/specific intervention camp, my sympathies for BFT should be obvious. At the same time, however, I recognize that my position is not typical of systemic family therapy as a whole, or even of the smaller universe of systems purists. For the remainder of the chapter the abbreviation "SFT" will be taken to refer to the "systems purists" as a whole. Where further distinctions are critical, particularly with respect to the importance of the presenting problem, these issues will be noted.

GENERAL OBSERVATIONS

I will begin by noting some of the most obvious differences between BFT and SFT, each treated as simplified models. Later sections will be reserved for several issues where BFT seems to be evolving or where there is lack of consensus, as well as some of the current evolution of SFT.

Unit of Analysis

Madanes and Haley (1977) categorized behavioral approaches as considering either the individual patient or at most a dyad as the unit of analysis. My sense is that this is less true today than it was in 1977 when they first made their analysis, and there are many examples in the present book which would seem to bear out this contention.

Although BFT has evolved somewhat in this area, it still seems fair to say that SFT tends to use larger units of analysis. Even when BFT uses a larger unit (e.g. two parents plus symptomatic child), this often is little different from a dyadic model and is quite different from SFT. Parental disagreement, for example, is almost a "nuisance variable" in BFT, while in SFT it is not only expected but is one of the areas of major focus in therapy.

I would also like to note, if only in passing, the link between methodology and unit of analysis. As an infrequent reader of the behavioral literature, the present volume surprised me by the almost total lack of charting of symptomatic behavior or other trappings of hard-core behaviorism. Even within this volume, those chapters which tend to look at the whole family or even larger units are also the "softest" and read most like SFT.

Use of Well-Defined Procedures

It is still much more common for BFT to utilize distinct procedures (e.g., desensitization, skill training, *quid pro quo* contracting) than in SFT. In this regard, the reader will note considerable variability in the chapters of the present volume.

Certain schools of SFT, such as the structural approach (Aponte & VanDeusen, 1981; Minuchin, 1974; Minuchin & Fishman, 1981), and the strategic approach of Haley (1973, 1976, 1984) and Madanes (1981, 1984), are more likely to incorporate specific intervention, even those borrowed from behavioral colleagues. The major difference is that these are generally used within marital or family sessions (rather than individually) and with systemic goals in mind.

Involvement of the Family in Treatment

As noted above, SFT tends to assume that the family is almost universally involved in the symptomatology of a family member, and therefore advocates the routine inclusion of the whole family in therapy. Practitioners may differ in the degree to which they will insist on the involvement of the whole family, yet they would almost always see such involvement as ideal.

By contrast, in BFT the routine involvement of the spouse or family is often viewed as unnecessary and inefficient. The family may be brought in only when individually oriented procedures fail, or when behavioral observation suggests that family members are helping to maintain the symptomatic behavior. It is also consistant with BFT to excuse the family from treatment after that phase is complete and continue with individually oriented procedures.

Inclusion of the Extended Family

A similar point can be made about the extended family. While not all practitioners of SFT include the extended family in their analysis or directly in therapy, they do so more commonly than practitioners of BFT. Although it is undoubtedly true that the therapy gets "messier" when more family members are included, particularly if they come from several households or generations, BFT practitioners would do well to be alert to the potential importance of the extended family. It is particularly true that with populations such as single-parent families, discussed in Morris, Alexander, and Waldron's chapter, inclusion of resources beyond the nuclear family can be critical for success.

Forms of Communication

Haley and Madanes are somewhat unusual, even within SFT, in their degree of emphasis on analogical communication and metaphor. In general, BFT appears to be at the opposite extreme, taking messages quite literally. (The work of Morris, Alexander, and Waldron will be considered separately as an exception to this generalization.) In turn, most practitioners of SFT definitely place more emphasis on analogical communication than most behaviorists would find comfortable.

It is definitely not necessary for therapists to sacrifice rigor in order to take a middle-ground position which includes some consideration of analogic communication and multilevel communication. Communication theory offers a rigorous and comprehensive framework for analysis of the literal or message component of a statement as well as the relationship component of that communication.

The Issue of "Normality"

BFT and SFT appear to differ considerably regarding their general assumptions concerning the role of the family in symptomatic behavior. In general, BFT often sees the family as burdened by the patient, as unwittingly giving responses to behavior that perpetuates that behavior, or, at worst, as a "stressor" on the patient. By contrast, SFT has made much of the concept of "family homeostasis" (Jackson, 1957). Here the assumption is that any change in symptomatic behavior will be met by "error-correcting" feedback that tends to perpetuate the behavior. Thus, SFT tends to assume that the family is almost always relevant and plays an active role in symptom maintenance.

This difference in assumptions has several major consequences. Because it does not assume family "pathology", BFT may be more readily adaptable to a non-therapy setting, such as shown in Falloon and Harpin's chapter on primary care. Straightforward procedures such as stress-reduction are readily utilized in these and other health psychology settings.

Since BFT does not assume that families play a causal role in symptomatology, it seems to me that BFT has been more receptive to nonpsychological causes of behavior. This has been particularly notable in the ready acceptance of the psychoeducational approach to schizophrenia within BFT, while the positive impact of this approach within SFT has developed only recently. Similarly, BFT has had greater interest in areas such as senile dementia (see Zarit, Chapter 15, this volume).

I would expect that this difference in attitudes may carry over into the working relationship between therapist and families in the two forms of family therapy. It would seem likely that families are more receptive to the nonblaming assumptions in BFT, which tends not to assume that the family is the "problem". It seems to be easier to engage families in treatment if they are given a rationale for their involvement such as reducing stress, learning specialized management techniques to deal with a family member with special needs, and so on. Within SFT, only a subset of theorists and practitioners have paid explicit attention to reducing the degree of "threat" perceived by family members when entering therapy. (See, for example, Stanton and Todd's emphasis on the "non-blaming message" [Stanton & Todd, 1982, pp. 93–95].) Others move quickly to insist that the problem is a family problem and want each member to acknowledge this.

Skill-Training and Instructions

Radical practitioners of SFT, most notably Haley (1976), rarely believe that skill-training is necessary or helpful, believing that parents typically possess the requisite skills and that the therapist merely needs to unblock them by reorganizing the family. Others, including me (Todd, 1986), take a less extreme stance and find parent training, communication training, and so on helpful on occasion.

On the other hand, as I have argued elsewhere (Todd, 1986), there are hazards of an overemphasis on instruction. This approach, which is common within BFT, presumes that clients are deficient in skills. It also establishes a relationship between therapists and clients which exaggerates the expert orientation of the therapist, establishing him or her as the person with the answers, rather than one who helps identify strengths.

The Role of the Therapist

As noted earlier, SFT tends to emphasize that the therapist is (or at least becomes) part of the system. This has considerable practical significance, since it implies that the actions of a therapist are at risk of not being "objective" or "clean", but instead being orchestrated, in part, by the family.

Such an emphasis is rare within BFT, which tends to portray the therapist as a laboratory scientist. One of the few exceptions in the present volume is the work of Morris, Alexander, and Waldron. They believe that certain "personal characteristics of certain clients may . . . trigger unproductive automatic processes in the therapist" (p. 120). While this may sound like the age-old concept of "countertransference," their remedy is quite different. Rather than recommending personal therapy for the therapist, they advocate the use of relabeling which "feels believable" to the therapist.

Morris, Alexander, and Waldron go further to suggest that even benign educational efforts may elicit "resistance" unless these efforts are seen in a larger context:

> [T]he myriad educational strategies noted earlier cannot be applied in a random manner. The new behaviors, feelings, and cognitions targeted by the therapists must be consistent with the values of all family members. Positive change is more easily produced, and more reliably maintained, if the educational technologies are fitted to the values and functions of family members. On the other hand, resistance is more actively elicited if we try to change peoples' functions to fit our technologies. (p. 125)

Focus on Specific Populations

Several chapters in the present volume reflect the emphasis in BFT upon working with specific clinical populations. This fits well with the history of behavioral approaches that attempt to develop specific procedures to fit particular problems.

While such a focus may seem natural within BFT, it is a controversial issue within SFT. Because of the emphasis on the family as system, it has generally been seen as desirable to have ways of categorizing families rather than individuals. Several such schemes have been proposed, but thus far they have rarely led to distinct therapeutic approaches. In fact, as I have noted elsewhere (Todd & Stanton, 1983), much of the dramatic progress within SFT has occurred with populations defined by the symptomatology of the individual patient.

CURRENT TRENDS IN BFT AND SFT

A number of current trends in BFT and SFT may indicate that the two fields are converging, or at least that they are beginning to overlap more significantly.

Incorporation of Resistance into BFT

It seems noteworthy that a number of chapters in the present volume place increased emphasis on the concept of resistance, particularly the idea that family members may resist symptomatic improvement in the identified patient. As noted above, this thinking has been embodied in SFT in the concept of family homeostasis since the early work of Jackson (1957).

This change in thinking has considerable practical significance for BFT. It has led to the development of specific procedures to counteract or minimize resistance. Perhaps even more basically, it has led to much more universal inclusion of the family in behavioral analysis and in treatment.

Resistance, Homeostasis, and SFT

Somewhat ironically, there has recently been a strong movement within SFT questioning the utility of concepts such as "resistance" and "family homeostasis" (for example, Dell, 1982). These ideas are seen as defining a relationship between therapist and family that is unnecessarily adversarial.

These new views do not mean a return to the simplistic view that the therapist outlines a procedure and the patient or family gratefully follows it. Instead, a new emphasis is placed on tailoring the therapeutic approach to the expectations and world view of each family.

De Shazer (1982, 1985), for example, places considerable emphasis on learning how each family "cooperates" with therapeutic assignments. This "cooperation" may include complying with a task, partially complying, ignoring it, or even doing the opposite. After learning the typical style of the family, the therapist can develop tasks that fit this style and are more likely to lead to change.

The work of Morris, Alexander, and Waldron in the present volume is an excellent example of the more sophisticated approach to resistance. They state that the behavioral literature had not prepared them for the degree of resistance they encountered to behavioral interventions. They identify two potential sources of resistance, the "function" of behavior and the "meaning" of behavior. Rather than view the obstacles originating in these sources as resistance in the sense used by many authors in the present volume, they see "these impediments as natural consequences of the inappropriate application of technology and the failure of clinicians to understand the meaning of behavior" (p.xxx).

They adopt the "meaning-change" technology of other family therapists, more commonly called "reframing" or "relabelling." Within BFT, it may not be particularly uncommon for a therapist to communicate a new meaning for or explanation of symptomatic behavior to a client. What seems unusual within BFT is the willingness of Morris, Alexander, and Waldron to adopt new labels with an emphasis on plausibility, rather than truth, whereas many BFT practitioners seem to imply a scientific or objective basis for their relabeling.

Combining Individual and Family Theory

Within BFT, it does not seem particularly radical to combine individual and family therapy, since each can be thought of as a procedure to address a given problem. Probably most typical is an approach such as that of Liberman, Mueser, and Glynn in the present volume, where individual procedures are utilized first, with conjoint procedures employed later on as needed.

Most practitioners of SFT tend to see the whole family, a notable exception being the work of the Mental Research Institute (Fisch, Weakland, & Segal, 1982; Watzlawick, Weakland, & Fisch, 1974). In the early days of SFT, many therapists were insistent that the whole family be involved in every session, even sending the family home from an appointment if one family member failed to attend.

Increasingly, such insistence seems unnecessarily rigid. Many SFT practitioners will vary session composition to fit the current needs of the case. Concurrent individual and family therapy has become more common, either with the same therapist or different therapists. (See Todd, 1985, for a more detailed discussion of these issues.)

CONCLUSION

The reader should be reminded once again of the sleight of hand performed at the beginning of this chapter in my definition of SFT. By selecting a definition of SFT which includes a heavy emphasis on current behavior, on change rather than insight, and on the importance of the presenting problem, it is possible to see considerable overlap and convergence of SFT and BFT. Obviously, this convergence would be less noteworthy if a different definition of SFT were selected. But when the two approaches are seen thus as sympathetic, one cannot fail to be struck by the degree to which BFT and SFT have developed in comparative isolation from each other. As is shown in this chapter and, more generally, this volume, both fields are developing in exciting and innovative directions, and it would be unfortunate if this degree of isolation were to continue. I hope that efforts such as the present volume can provide impetus toward greater communication and cross-fertilization between the two camps.

REFERENCES

Aponte, H. J. & VanDeusen, J. M. (1981). Structural family therapy. In A. S. Gurman & D. P. Kniskern (Eds.), *Handbook of family therapy*. New York: Brunner/Mazel.

Beels, C. C., & Ferber, A. (1969). Family therapy: A view. *Family Process, 8*, 280–318.

Dell, P. F. (1982). Beyond homeostasis: Toward a concept of coherence. *Family Process, 21*, 21–41.

de Shazer, S. (1982). *Patterns of brief family therapy*. New York: Guilford.

de Shazer, S. (1985). *Keys to solution in brief therapy*. New York: Norton.

Fisch, R., Weakland, J. H., & Segal, L. (1982). *The tactics of change: Doing therapy briefly*. San Francisco: Jossey-Bass.

Frazier, H. S. (1982, October). *A comparison of family therapy theories on degree of adherence to principles of General Systems Theory*. Paper presented at National Council on Family Relations, Washington, DC.

Haley, J. (1973). *Uncommon therapy*. New York: Norton.

Haley, J. (1976). *Problem-solving therapy: New strategies for effective family therapy*. San Francisco: Jossey-Bass.

Haley, J. (1984). *Ordeal therapy*. San Francisco: Jossey-Bass.

Jackson, D. D. (1957). The question of family homeostasis. *Psychiatric Quarterly*, Suppl., *31*, 79–90.

Madanes, C. (1981). *Strategic family therapy*. San Francisco: Jossey-Bass.

Madanes, C. (1984). *Behind the only-way mirror: Advances in the practice of strategic therapy*. San Francisco: Jossey-Bass.

Madanes, C., & Haley, J. (1977). Dimensions of family therapy. *Journal of Nervous and Mental Disease, 165*, 88–98.

Minuchin, S. (1974). *Families and family therapy*. Cambridge, MA: Harvard University Press.

Minuchin, S., & Fishman, H. C. (1981). *Family therapy techniques*. Cambridge, MA: Harvard University Press.

Stanton, M. D., Todd, T. C., & Associates. (1982). *The family therapy of drug abuse and addiction*. New York: Guilford.

Todd, T. C. (1981). Combining behavioral and structural family therapies. In A. S. Gurman (Ed.), *Questions and answers in the practice of family therapy*. New York: Brunner/Mazel.

Todd, T. C. (1985). Anorexia and bulimia: Moving beyond the structural model. In M. D. Mirkin & S. L. Koman (Eds.), *Handbook of adolescents and family therapy*. New York: Gardner Press.

Todd, T. C. (1986). Structural-strategic marital therapy. In N. S. Jacobson and A. S. Gurman (Eds.), *Clinical handbook of marital therapy*. New York: Guilford.

Todd, T. C., & Stanton, M. D. (1983). Research on marital and family therapy: Answers, issues, and recommendations for the future. In B. Wolman & G. Stricker (Eds.), *Handbook of family and marital therapy*. New York: Plenum.

Watzlawick, P., Weakland, J. H., & Fisch, R. (1974). *Change: Priniciples of problem formation and problem resolution*. New York: Norton.

Index

Q

R